The Reader's Digest

Legal Question & Answer Book

The Reader's Digest

Legal Question & Answer Book

The Reader's Digest Association (Canada) Ltd.

The Reader's Digest

Legal Question & Answer Book

Editor: Alice Philomena Rutherford
Designer: Andrée Payette
Senior Editor: Andrew Byers
Art Supervisor: John McGuffie
Research Supervisor: Wadad Bashour
Photo Researcher: Rachel Irwin
Copy Preparation: Joseph Marchetti
Coordinator: Susan Wong
Production: Holger Lorenzen

Contributors:
Editor: George Ronald
Copy Preparation: Gilles Humbert
Indexer: Jane Broderick
Illustrators: Christopher Calle, Olena Kassian

Legal Consultant:
Nelson Brott, B.A., B.C.L. (McGill)

Copyright © 1989 The Reader's Digest Association (Canada) Ltd.
215 Redfern Avenue, Montreal, Que., H3Z 2V9

Canadian Cataloguing in Publication Data
Main entry under title:
The Reader's Digest legal question & answer book

Canadian first ed.
Includes index.
ISBN 0-88850-159-5

1. Law—Canada—Popular works. I. Reader's Digest
Association (Canada). II. Title: The Reader's Digest legal
question and answer book. III. Title: Legal question and
answer book. IV. Title: Legal question & answer book.

KE447.R43   1989   349.71   C88-090366-X

Printed in Canada

89 90 91 92 / 5 4 3 2 1

This book is an adaptation of the 1988 U.S. edition of *The Reader's
Digest Legal Question & Answer Book,* whose content was based on
research by Hyatt Legal Services. All material in this Canadian
edition has been completely revised and Canadianized to reflect
Canadian law.

Contents

Chapter 4

Your Home 157

Chapter 5

Your Personal Property 205

Chapter 6

Your Car 231

About This Book

THE READER'S DIGEST LEGAL QUESTION & ANSWER BOOK takes a practical approach to the law. It tells you what you need to know to deal with hundreds of situations that may arise in everyday life. We hope you will consult it again and again about everything from getting married to writing a will. You can use it to protect your family, your possessions—and your peace of mind.

In clear question-and-answer form, this book dramatizes commonplace legal problems that could involve you, your family, your job, your money, your rights, and your safety. You will see the law in action and learn how to solve and prevent problems. The answers are short and to the point. They do not confound you with technical theory or legal gobbledygook. They tell you, simply, how to deal with the problem.

More than 2,000 questions are answered in these pages. To make sure that we included the most commonly asked questions, Reader's Digest turned to a group of lawyers who collectively serve more than a million clients. This group submitted the questions most frequently asked in every area of the law and provided answers. Then Reader's Digest editors joined forces with the book's legal consultant to tailor this material, deleting, revising, and adding questions—and answers— that would be of particular interest to our readers. Finally everything was put into plain language, free of any trace of legalese, thus creating a solid, informative, up-to-date law book for Canadians.

You don't have to have a subject in mind to use THE READER'S DIGEST LEGAL QUESTION & ANSWER BOOK. You can pick it up at any time and enjoy leafing through its pages, stopping when something catches your eye. Some questions will seem as though they were put there just for you; others will arouse your curiosity. You'll read on to see how the people portrayed in the questions solved their problems. You'll learn what you are entitled to and what actions you can take in circumstances that may confront you. Reading this book may also help you steer clear of legal entanglements.

When you have a specific problem, turn to the Contents and consult the chapter and section titles. The book is arranged by subject for easy reference. If you want information about traffic tickets, for example, look in Chapter 6, *Your Car,* under the section "Tickets and Violations." If you want an even more specific reference, check the Index, which uses ordinary words such as *traffic, parking,* and *speeding.* The cross-references that appear at the beginning of some sections will lead you to related information elsewhere in the book.

Special box features supplement the questions and answers, and give sound advice on legal and practical nonlegal matters. Some offer step-by-step instructions, such as how to take your case to Small Claims Court. Others have checklists of important questions to ask or points to consider—for example, "Questions to Ask When Choosing a Lawyer" and "How to Hire a Contractor." The book's Glossary provides concise, easy-to-understand definitions of more than 400 key legal terms and the Useful Addresses section gives province-by-province listings of law society and legal aid offices, criminal injuries compensation boards, human rights commissions, ombudsmen, and government information centers.

Of course, not even 2,000 questions will cover every situation—although if you don't find a question describing your exact predicament, you will probably be able to find one that is similar enough to be helpful. Nor can any one book discuss all the different provincial and local laws. Such laws vary from province to province and city to city, and they can change rapidly as a result of court decisions and new legislation. To give you the most helpful information, the answers to the questions are based on general rules of law and on what the laws say in most provinces. In many answers, specific provincial laws are cited. But even if your province is mentioned, you should always check to find out what the law currently says where you live.

Sometimes this means consulting a lawyer. At other times you can find out about the law in your locality by contacting (1) your local or provincial bar association; (2) the government agency that oversees the area of law you are interested in—for example, the motor licensing bureau or the Department of Transport; (3) your provincial attorney general's office or the office of another government official, such as the provincial ombudsman, the mayor or the city clerk; (4) a public service group, such as the Civil Liberties Association; or (5) a consumer advocate group, such as the Consumers Association of Canada. But regardless of how much research you do on your own, you should always consider consulting a lawyer before starting any legal action.

The information, guidelines, and advice offered in THE READER'S DIGEST LEGAL QUESTION & ANSWER BOOK can protect you against lawsuits, alert you to fraud, help you to avoid falling into legal traps, and inform you about available remedies. By consulting this book before you talk to a lawyer, you can save both time and money. You may even discover you don't need a lawyer to solve your problem. If it turns out that you do need legal counsel, this book will help you prepare the right questions to ask in order to get the best advice possible.

—The Editors

CHAPTER 1

You and Your Lawyer

What Is a Lawyer?

***Do the terms** lawyer, attorney, counselor, barrister, **and** solicitor mean exactly the same thing?*

Yes. In Canada, the terms are interchangeable. They all refer to someone trained in the law, who is licensed to practice in one or more provinces and who is in the business of giving legal advice. In England, however, a barrister and a solicitor are not the same. There, a barrister is a lawyer who goes to court, usually hired and instructed by a solicitor. And in England, a solicitor usually researches the case and is the lawyer first contacted by the client.

Tony has noticed that his lawyer writes** Esq. **after his name. What does this abbreviation stand for?

Esq. is the abbreviation for *esquire*, or *squire*. In England a squire was a country gentleman who informally settled disputes among the people living on his land. In North America *esquire* is a title commonly used by lawyers, but it does not refer to any legal certification or specialty. (In Quebec, where the legal system derives from the laws of France and from Roman law, lawyers are known as *maîtres*, which is abbreviated to M^e, as in Me Pierre Untel.)

What is a justice of the peace?

A justice of the peace is a provincially appointed judge who has certain legal powers within a certain district. He may, for example, receive written criminal complaints (known as informations), issue warrants for arrest after hearing witnesses, and even try certain minor cases. In noncriminal cases, the powers of a justice of the peace vary from one province to another, but usually include the authority to act as commissioner for oaths or notary public.

Does a judge have to be a lawyer?

Yes. Judges are appointed by either the federal or provincial government, and nominees usually have at least 10 years' experience as attorneys. Since even those cases involving a small amount of money can be complex and important from a legal point of view, experience and training as a lawyer are the best qualifications for the job. Municipal judges in some small towns may be practicing attorneys who judge minor cases—traffic or bylaw violations, for example—on a part time basis, one evening a week, say.

Why do lawyers and judges use such complicated language?

Although legal language is often difficult for the layman to understand, it is more precise than everyday language, and enables lawyers and judges to interpret the law as carefully as possible. If you don't understand the language your lawyer uses, ask him to translate it into plain English.

The Canadian Law Information Council (5th Floor, 161 Laurier Avenue West, Ottawa, Ont., K1P 5J2) has a Plain Language Centre, which will help governments and businesses translate legal documents into clear language. It also offers law students courses on clear, simple writing.

Bill Barrister, a lawyer, has an ad in the Yellow Pages that says he handles consumer cases. Does this mean he is a specialist?

The question of whether or not lawyers may advertise their specialties is not yet settled in Canada. The law society of each province regulates the kind of announcements their members may publish. A lawyer who advertises that his practice is restricted to criminal law would probably be on safe ground anywhere in Canada, but he is likely to contravene law society guidelines in most provinces with an ad saying he is a specialist in a particular field. Ontario lawyers claiming to be specialists in any field of law must be so certified by their bar association.

Walter needs a lawyer to handle a minor legal matter, but the only lawyer he knows specializes in corporate law. Should Walter look for another lawyer?

No. Just because this lawyer concentrates on corporate cases does not mean that he will automatically refuse a more routine case. Many lawyers who specialize in one or more areas of law began as general practitioners and are qualified to handle basic legal matters as well as complex ones.

When should I consult a tax lawyer instead of an accountant?

Consult a lawyer whenever you could be subject to monetary penalties or to charges of fraud or other criminal wrongdoing. If you are simply seeking advice about preparing tax returns, planning your estate, or getting the best tax advantages, either a lawyer or an accountant should be able to help you. Generally, advice from an accountant is less expensive than advice from a tax lawyer. By and large such lawyers work for large law firms and may charge more than $150 an hour for their time. Often tax lawyers are accountants who went on to study for their law degrees.

What Is a Lawyer?

Stuart discovered that one of his cheques had been stolen and cashed. To make a claim, Stuart had to fill out a bank form that required the seal and signature of a notary public. What is that?

A notary public is a person who verifies that signatures on a document are genuine. He also administers oaths to people taking public office and to witnesses at legal proceedings. A notary public does not confirm the truth of the statements made in the documents or in testimony; he only certifies that the person presenting them has sworn to their truth.

Family Lawyer or Specialist?

No matter how experienced your family lawyer may be, there are certain legal problems that he may not be qualified to handle. A general practitioner may be adequate for reviewing a contract or drawing up a will, for example, but if you're contesting a divorce or have been charged with a crime, you'll be better off with a lawyer who commonly handles such cases.

If your legal problem calls for a specialist, ask your family lawyer to recommend one. If he's unable to provide you with any names, contact the law society of your province or consult a legal directory at your local library. The *Canada Legal Directory*, for example, lists lawyers and firms for all branches of law, including the following common specialties:

Bankruptcy Law	Insurance Law
Business Law	Labor Law
Civil Litigation	Maritime Law
Civil Rights Law	Military Law
Conservatorship and Guardianship Law	Patent, Trademark, and Copyright Law
Constitutional Law	Pension and Profit-Sharing Law
Consumer Law	
Contract Law	Personal Injury and Property Damage
Corporation and Partnership Law	Real Estate Law
Criminal Law	Tax Law
Divorce, Adoption, and Family Law	Transportation Law
Environmental Law	Wills, Trusts, and Estate Planning
Health Care and Hospital Law	Workers' Compensation Law
Immigration Law	Young Offenders Law

Provincial law determines who is eligible to become a notary public, but generally a person must be of good character, have passed a test on the rules and duties of a notary public, and have taken an oath of office. Notaries public are often known as commissioners for oaths.

My father told me that he knows a lawyer who accepts pro bono *cases. What is that?*

It means free legal work for charity or for the public good. *Pro bono* is a shortened version of the Latin phrase *pro bono publico*, meaning "for the public good." A lawyer who provides *pro bono* service does legal work for the public good without charging a fee. For example, in addition to taking clients who pay him, a lawyer might take a client who cannot afford his services, or he might do free legal work for a community project he believes in, such as one involving the rights of the homeless. With the establishment of legal aid societies in all provinces, lawyers are now paid by the government for handling cases where the client is unable to pay. As a result, *pro bono* work is rapidly disappearing.

A man in my town confessed to assaulting and robbing a number of elderly women. How can a lawyer agree to defend such a person and still sleep at night?

At the heart of our legal system is the belief that every person charged with a crime is presumed innocent until proven guilty and has the right to be defended by a lawyer. When a lawyer represents a person charged with a crime, it doesn't mean that he condones the crime, but that he believes the accused person is entitled to a fair trial. The lawyer may also help the accused by making representations to the judge concerning sentencing. Perhaps the accused was mentally ill, or had some other problem which should be brought to the judge's attention.

When Do You Need a Lawyer?

How do I decide whether or not I need a lawyer?

Begin by analyzing your problem. If a dry cleaner has ruined your dress, for example, you may be able to resolve the matter yourself by asking the cleaner for a reimbursement. On the other hand, a more complicated problem, such as suing someone, will probably require the services of a lawyer. When you're not sure if your situation calls for a lawyer, it might be worth a small consultation fee to find out. In some cases, a lawyer may even be able to show you how to resolve the problem yourself.

When Do You Need a Lawyer?

Cori wants to buy a new sports car. Should her lawyer review the sales agreement and loan papers before she signs them?

Although a car is a major purchase, Cori does not need to consult a lawyer if she understands the terms and conditions of the sales contract. Even if Cori isn't clear about certain provisions, a bank officer should be able to answer any questions she may have.

Sam and Ruth want to sell their house. Their neighbor George has read a book on real estate and has sold several houses. Can he represent them at the closing even though he is not a lawyer?

In most cases, anyone selling a house does not have to be represented by a lawyer at the closing. However, the sale of their house may be the largest financial transaction Sam and Ruth ever make, and they would be wise to ask a lawyer who knows local real estate law to represent them.

While George may be familiar with the sale process, he may not be well versed enough in the law to solve any legal problems that may arise. In fact, George's ignorance of the fine points of real estate law could lead to unnecessary expenses for Sam and Ruth, and could even invalidate the sale of their house. If George were to go beyond simply representing Sam and Ruth at the closing and offer them legal advice, he could be charged with practicing law without a license—a criminal offense. (A notary, rather than a lawyer, usually handles real estate transactions in Quebec.)

Martha received a traffic ticket for driving over the speed limit. It's her third speeding ticket this year. Should she hire a lawyer?

Yes. Although traffic violations can usually be handled without the assistance of a lawyer, a driver who has received several tickets during a short period of time stands a greater chance of being fined heavily or having driving privileges suspended. If Martha doesn't want to lose her driver's license, she should contact a lawyer. The lawyer may be able to help Martha keep her license or reduce the penalty for the third ticket.

My girlfriend was hit by a car that didn't stop. She and some neighbors got a good look at the car and driver. Can a lawyer help us find the driver and sue him for damages?

Yes. A lawyer can help find the driver, either by investigating on his own or with the assistance of a private detective. But before you see a lawyer, you should go to the police, who have more expertise in dealing with

Situations Requiring Legal Advice

No matter how lucky or careful you may be, chances are that sooner or later you will find yourself with a legal problem. Deciding whether or not the situation requires a lawyer, however, may not be easy. Many problems fall somewhere between a minor dispute that can be settled in Small Claims Court and a criminal charge that calls for a skillful trial lawyer. If you are in doubt, consult a lawyer, especially if the problem is complex or the consequences far-reaching. Generally, you will need a lawyer if:

- You are about to sign a contract you don't understand or agree with.
- You are served with a summons or other legal document.
- You and your fiancée are considering a prenuptial agreement.
- You want to adopt a child.
- Your child gets into trouble with the law.
- You want (or your spouse wants) a separation, divorce, or annulment.
- Your ex-spouse wants to modify or terminate child support or maintenance payments, or alter your custody arrangements.
- You buy or sell your home or any other real estate.
- You are starting your own business or buying a franchise.
- You are threatened with eviction or foreclosure.
- Your personal property is in danger of being repossessed by creditors.
- You have been notified that a creditor plans to garnishee your wages.
- You suffer property damage because of someone's negligence.
- You are injured in an accident.
- You are asked to make an out-of-court settlement.
- You want to draw up a power of attorney.
- You are writing, changing, or contesting a will.
- You want to create a guardianship or conservatorship for a loved one.
- You are charged with any crime, even a summary conviction offense.

such matters. If they locate the hit-and-run driver who injured your girlfriend, the driver would be charged by the Crown prosecutor. A lawyer may advise your girlfriend to apply for help, either under the provincial Crime Victims Indemnity Act or the Automobile Insurance Law, or offer other useful advice.

Peter is scheduled to appear in Small Claims Court next month. Should he ask a lawyer to accompany him?

It depends on his case. Procedures in small claims courts are simplified to enable people to represent themselves. Although most provinces do

When Do You Need a Lawyer?

not prohibit a lawyer from being present, the cost of the lawyer may turn out to be greater than the amount in dispute. Consulting a lawyer *before* going to Small Claims Court may be a good idea, however, as the lawyer may help Peter organize his case and can advise him on the law. If Peter wins his case and lives in a province where lawyers are permitted in Small Claims Court, he might even be awarded legal costs. In Ontario, for example, a successful applicant may get up to $300 in counsel fees if represented by a lawyer in a case involving more than $500.

Is it a good idea to have a family lawyer, even if I don't need one right now?

Yes. Many legal problems arise when you least expect them. By taking the time now to select a family lawyer, you will have someone you trust ready to help you when a crisis occurs.

I have to go to court next month to defend myself against spurious charges concocted by a malicious business competitor. Can I act as my own lawyer?

Yes, but it is not always advisable. Generally, only an expert in the field— that is, a lawyer—is knowledgeable enough to handle legal issues. If you act as your own lawyer in a trial and you are unclear about the laws relating to your case or even about correct courtroom procedure, you might jeopardize your chance of success. You may also be too emotionally involved in your case to remain objective—even lawyers hire other lawyers when they are personally involved in a legal matter.

My cousin Randall is a lawyer in a neighboring province. Can he write my will or file some legal papers in court for me?

Usually before becoming a member of the bar of a particular province, a lawyer must pass an examination that tests his knowledge of that province's laws. Of course some lawyers are licensed to practice in more than one province, and this may be the case with your cousin. If he is not licensed in your province, however, and if the papers must be filed by a lawyer, you would be wise to hire a local attorney. But if it's simply a matter of drawing up a will, your cousin can probably do the job. According to common law principles, a will signed by the testator in the presence of two witnesses is valid in all provinces, even Quebec. (In many respects, Quebec law, which is derived from the *Code Napoléon*, differs significantly from that in the nine common law provinces.)

I will be out of the country during a period when a lot of personal business matters will need to be handled. Do I have to hire a lawyer, or can I authorize my brother-in-law to act in my name?

You can appoint anyone you feel confident will best represent you, but regardless of whether the person is your relative or a lawyer, you must give him your power of attorney. A power of attorney is a document giving someone else the legal authority to act for you in situations involving your property, finances, or personal needs. For example, a power of attorney can authorize the person you name to grant consent in an emergency for medical treatment for your child or to conduct business for you if you are out of town or are too ill to do so.

Oliver wants to set up a power of attorney. Will he need a lawyer?

No. But if Oliver is unfamiliar with the legal requirements of such a document and makes a mistake in drawing it up, the document could be declared invalid. If Oliver wants to give someone the power to sell his real estate, it is particularly important for him to consult a lawyer, since the agreement may have to be filed in the local real estate public records office to make the sale of the property legal.

A power of attorney can be complex. It may be general and include many powers, or it may be for a specific transaction only—to receive and deposit rental payments, say. It may be for a precise term—long or short—or until a certain event occurs. For these reasons, it would be wise to have it drawn up by a lawyer.

In Quebec, a power of attorney is known as a procuration or mandate.

Should I have my power of attorney notarized?

Yes. This will prevent someone from using a forged or fraudulent power of attorney, to sell your property, for example. A notary public or a commissioner for oaths will be able to confirm the authenticity of your signature because he watched you sign the document or because he can identify your signature.

If I consult a lawyer, will he give me advice even if I don't hire him to handle my legal matters?

Yes, but only to a limited extent. When you first contact a lawyer, he will try to determine what kind of legal problem you have, and how you can go about solving it. In most circumstances, the lawyer will provide general legal advice at this initial meeting, but he may also offer some specific recommendations as to what you should do next. Sometimes a lawyer is unable to give legal advice without first making a preliminary investigation or doing some additional research. If you do not want the lawyer to go that far, be sure to say so; otherwise, you will have to pay him for his time and effort.

Finding the Right Lawyer

Is an older lawyer better than a younger one?

Not necessarily. Age should not be the deciding factor in selecting a lawyer. The most important things are that you should be confident the lawyer can handle your legal problem and that you should feel comfortable with him. Although an older lawyer has more experience, this does not automatically make him more competent. The younger lawyer may have special training in the area of law relating to your problem, while the older lawyer may have handled only a few such cases because he has a general practice. On the other hand, a young lawyer who charges a lower hourly rate will not necessarily be less expensive than an older lawyer. A younger lawyer may take longer to research or prepare a case than a more experienced one.

I consulted a prominent lawyer with an impressive reputation, but he turned out to be rude and intimidating. Should I let my personal feelings stop me from hiring him?

Perhaps. Hiring a lawyer is a very personal matter—not only because you will probably be discussing confidential matters with him, but also because your relationship with the lawyer could affect the outcome of your case. If you conceal important information, for example, because you don't feel you can confide in your lawyer, you risk losing your case if this information is discovered by your opponent's lawyer and used against you. If you have several qualified lawyers to choose from, you should hire the one who is competent, and with whom you feel compatible as well.

Our family lawyer won't help me sue a large corporation. He says the case is too complex for him. Doesn't he have to take my case?

No. If your family lawyer did not believe he could adequately represent you, he was obligated to reject the case. The Canadian Bar Association's Code of Professional Conduct requires that a lawyer turn down a legal

Finding a Lawyer

If you have a legal problem but you don't know any lawyers, begin by asking friends and relatives if they can suggest someone. But even when a lawyer comes highly recommended, you should still do some comparison shopping for cost and expertise as well as for compatibility. To find the names of more lawyers, consult the following:

- ☑ Your accountant, insurance salesperson, banker, or other professional whose judgment you respect.
- ☑ Your employer's lawyer or law firm.
- ☑ Law directories, such as the *Canada Legal Directory*, available at most libraries.
- ☑ Court clerks, court reporters, and clerks to judges.
- ☑ Government offices and agencies (listed in a special section of your telephone directory) that deal with the subject of your legal problem.
- ☑ The alumni offices of law schools.
- ☑ Your local or provincial bar association.
- ☑ The Canadian Bar Association.
- ☑ Advertisements in newspapers and magazines.
- ☑ The Yellow Pages.

case if he knows he is not competent to handle it. A lawyer may take a case in an unfamiliar area of the law, however, if he has time to research the law involved—or obtain the assistance of another lawyer familiar with this type of lawsuit—without delaying the case or causing his client additional expense.

Bernie lives 120 miles from the nearest city. He was painting his barn, when a poorly made ladder collapsed, injuring him. He wants to sue the ladder manufacturer and the local hardware dealer. Should he use a local lawyer or one from the big city?

Bernie should not automatically assume that a lawyer from his own community will not be as good as one from the big city. What really matters is whether a particular lawyer is competent to handle Bernie's case. If Bernie is considering a local lawyer, he should first find out whether that lawyer has any business connections with the local dealer that could pose a conflict of interest. If no conflict exists, Bernie may well prefer a local lawyer who is familiar with the local courts and who won't have to charge Bernie for traveling costs. On an hourly basis, that item alone could be quite expensive. For the same reason, it may be cheaper to hire a city lawyer if the case is to be heard in the city.

Finding the Right Lawyer

Irene suggested that Lucy use a lawyer referral service. What kind of service is this?

Lawyer referral is a service offered by each province's bar association for people who don't know any lawyers and don't have access to a lawyers' directory, which is available in many public libraries. Lucy should bear in mind that because most lawyer referral services rotate the names they recommend, she may be assigned a lawyer on the basis of chance rather than expertise or price. Many lawyer referral services offer a half-hour consultation with a lawyer for about $25.

I'm confused about whether I should go to a law firm or a legal clinic. What is the difference?

If your problem is a fairly common one, such as an uncomplicated divorce, a routine real estate transaction (for example, a closing), bankruptcy, or accident case, a legal clinic would be able to give you the help you need. These clinics are usually located in shopping centers, and are staffed by lawyers who are familiar with everyday legal problems. Often these clinics have standard fees for services such as drawing up a simple will. By telephoning, you can find out the exact fee in advance.

If your problem is a complex or unusual one, however, a law firm might be a better choice. Law firms are usually staffed with lawyers who specialize in different areas of the law, and they often have assistants and extensive private law libraries to help them with their research. The fees charged by these firms are generally higher than those of the legal clinics, since law firms generally have higher expenses and pay their lawyers higher salaries.

Two provinces, Alberta and British Columbia, now permit lawyers to incorporate and thus become companies.

Darlene needs a lawyer to defend her in court, but she can't afford one. Will anyone handle her case for free?

Darlene may be eligible for free legal aid. First she will have to show her provincial legal aid office that she cannot afford to hire an attorney without depriving herself of the necessities of life. In some provinces, Quebec for example, eligible applicants can get a legal aid lawyer without charge; in others, such as Manitoba, the applicant may have to pay part of his legal aid expenses. Alberta applicants have to reimburse the Legal Aid Society but, under legal aid, the lawyer's fee will be substantially less than would be charged otherwise. Easy payment terms can also be worked out.

My neighbor's insurance company is suing me because of damage I accidentally caused to his property. Should I hire a lawyer at a big law firm or one who works on his own?

In terms of cost, an individual lawyer may be less expensive because he has a lower overhead, but sometimes a large law firm can be cheaper because its expenses are divided among more clients. As far as service is concerned, an individual lawyer may be able to give your case more personal attention, depending on his caseload at the time; but a firm may have additional resources, such as research assistants, an extensive law library, and a staff with diverse expertise.

Questions to Ask When Choosing a Lawyer

Even if a lawyer comes highly recommended, you should base your decision to hire him on your own opinion rather than someone else's. Since many of the qualities that distinguish a good lawyer from a bad one are intangible and difficult to define, you'll need to ask some specific questions. Listen to the lawyer's answers carefully, but also pay attention to his manner. It is just as important to have a lawyer who is patient, affable, and willing to explain things you don't understand as it is to have one who is skillful and knowledgeable. Here are some key questions you should be sure to ask:

- ☑ Will you charge me for an initial consultation and, if so, how much?
- ☑ How long has your firm been in business?
- ☑ Are your clients primarily individuals or companies?
- ☑ What materials should I bring to our first meeting?
- ☑ Can you start working on my case immediately?
- ☑ What are the strengths and weaknesses of my case?
- ☑ What kind of strategy do you propose to follow?
- ☑ About how long will it take to complete the case?
- ☑ How much of the work required will you do yourself, and how much will you delegate to another lawyer or a legal researcher?
- ☑ How will you keep me informed about the progress of my case?
- ☑ Will you give me copies of all relevant documents and correspondence?
- ☑ What is your fee for my kind of case? Which services are included in that fee, and which are not?
- ☑ Will you provide a written estimate of all costs before you begin work on my case?
- ☑ Will you send me an itemized bill?
- ☑ Will you work on a contingent-fee basis? If so, will you compute the fee before or after expenses are paid?
- ☑ Do you anticipate any additional costs? If you do, will they have to be paid in advance or as they are incurred?

Finding the Right Lawyer

My company has just announced that it will be offering a prepaid legal plan as a new fringe benefit for all full-time employees. How do such plans work?

Typically, legal plans provide a variety of legal services for which your employer has paid in advance, or for which a payroll deduction is made from your salary. Under some plans, you and your family can use these services without any additional payment.

Make sure, however, that you understand any special limitations that are included in your company's plan. For example, some legal plans provide coverage for a divorce only when both husband and wife can agree on the terms, but do not cover divorces where the spouses cannot agree on how to divide their property or who will get custody of the children, issues which must therefore be resolved in a court battle. A detailed description of your plan's benefits should be available from your employer or union.

Legal Expenses

Cynthia was aghast at the estimated legal costs for settling her father's estate. How does a lawyer decide how much to charge?

Attorneys set their fees on the basis of their experience, the nature of the case, the amount of time they expect it will require, and their office expenses. Other considerations are the amount involved in the dispute, the results obtained, and whether special skills or services are required. The fee for settling a simple estate, for example, would be much less than for settling one with an ambiguous will, which would require more time and effort preparing for a hearing in surrogate court.

Are lawyers' fees negotiable?

Experienced lawyers generally know their fees and rarely will settle for a lower rate. But there are exceptions to every rule and some lawyers are willing to negotiate. Your lawyer may also be willing to let you pay his fee over a period of weeks or months. Be wary if a lawyer changes his fee too readily. Make sure that he still intends to provide all the legal services for your case, and will not simply get his original fee by claiming separately for any additional services needed. According to the Code of Professional Conduct of the Canadian Bar Association, "the lawyer should not stipulate for, charge or accept any fee which is not fully disclosed, fair and reasonable."

Which is better—an hourly fee or a flat fee?

It depends on how long or complex a case will be, which is difficult to predict. Most flat-fee arrangements cover standard services, such as drawing up a will; if your case turns out to be more complicated, you will either have to accept an increase in the standard fee or convert to an hourly rate. Don't be misled by an extremely low flat fee; watch out for unreasonable additional charges, such as an extra payment to have your lawyer appear in court on your behalf in a criminal matter if the case requires more than one court appearance.

What services are generally covered by a flat-fee arrangement?

Prenuptial agreements, marital separation agreements, routine divorces, annulments, simple wills, bankruptcies, incorporating businesses, setting up partnerships, and minor criminal matters, such as traffic violations, are all areas generally covered by flat-fee arrangements. Though a lawyer may agree to handle these types of cases for a flat fee, there may be additional costs if a particular case becomes unusually complicated or involves a long court battle. You should always get a fee agreement, in writing, which describes the specific services that will be provided.

My lawyer won't take my case without a retainer. Why?

A retainer is, in effect, the act that authorizes a lawyer to begin work on a case. If your lawyer were to begin work before you actually hired him, his actions would not be considered legally binding. A lawyer generally asks for a retainer so that he will have a fund available from which he can draw his salary and any miscellaneous out-of-pocket expenses. This fund is put into a trust account and can be used only to pay for expenses related to your case. If you change lawyers, or if the fees and expenses do not exceed the advanced amount, the remaining balance will be refunded to you.

My lawyer says that I have to pay the costs for filing my lawsuit. Since he's charging me so much already, why can't he at least pay for this as part of his overhead?

The fee you pay your lawyer is for his knowledge and experience, the time he spends working for you, and any office expenses associated with your case. Legal ethics forbid lawyers to pay for court filing costs, copies of official documents, court stenographers (who take testimony from witnesses at pretrial examinations), and expert witnesses, such as doctors and engineers. If lawyers were permitted to pay for court costs, the person bringing the claim would not have to risk losing any of his own money or property, which might result in much unnecessary litigation.

My lawyer charges me the same hourly rate for work done by his assistant as he does for his own work. Is this legal?

Since your lawyer is ultimately responsible for all the work done on your case, he will be reviewing his assistant's work, and so he may feel the charge is justified. Still, some large law firms do charge different rates for different lawyers, depending on their experience and position. Before your lawyer begins working on your case, check your agreement to see if its terms are clearly spelled out.

A lawyer told Justin that he could give him only an estimate of his fees. Should Justin get the estimate in writing?

Yes. But Justin should keep in mind that a written estimate would not include costs that could arise from unforeseeable legal complications.

Lynn's lawyer has had to make several lengthy long-distance calls while working on her case. Does Lynn have to pay for them?

Yes. Incidental expenses, such as the cost of telephone, photocopying, and express mail, are usually added to a lawyer's final bill. Lynn will probably have to pay for any long-distance calls related to her case.

Am I entitled to an itemized bill from my lawyer?

If your lawyer is billing you by the hour, you have the right to an itemized bill that details how that time was spent. However, if your lawyer is charging a flat fee, he usually will not give you an itemized breakdown of the time spent on your case.

My lawyer says that he will work on a contingent-fee basis. What does this mean?

This means that the lawyer's fee will be a percentage of the money you win. If you do not win any money, your lawyer earns no fee. Traditionally, contingent-fee arrangements are common in accident and debt collec-

How to Save on Legal Costs

Once you've decided to hire a particular lawyer, have him put the details of your agreement in writing, including his fee, his estimate of any additional costs and expenses, and a statement that he will not exceed a specific dollar amount without first getting your permission. Be sure to ask your lawyer what you can do to help save him time, and therefore save you money. Here are some suggestions:

☑ Organize and write down the facts of your situation and any questions you have before talking to your lawyer.

☑ Bring all relevant papers and information (such as names and addresses of people involved in the matter) to your lawyer's office. Have it organized so you can find what you need quickly.

☑ Do not deluge the lawyer with useless information; this will take up more time and cost you more money.

☑ Be as truthful and accurate as possible, even if the facts are unpleasant. Omissions that come to light later may increase costs.

☑ Listen attentively to what your lawyer tells you. Be sure you understand what he wants you to do.

☑ Be punctual for your appointments and court appearances.

☑ Telephone your lawyer only if you have something definite to ask or tell him about.

☑ Offer to obtain necessary documents, such as police or medical reports, to save him the work of doing so himself.

☑ Offer to help locate witnesses.

☑ If the case involves property damage, get a professional estimate of the dollar amount of the damage.

☑ Don't change your mind about what you want your lawyer to do, or ask him to do anything extra unless you are prepared to pay for it.

tion cases. You will be required to pay any court costs and expenses arising out of your lawsuit, and if your lawyer advances the money to pay for these expenses, you are expected to reimburse him, regardless of the outcome of your case. Most contingency fees range from 15 to 20 percent. In a recent case in British Columbia, however, a contingency fee of 25 percent was considered "eminently reasonable," and contingency fees as high as 30 percent are permitted in certain cases in Quebec.

Terence was arrested for drunk driving. Can his lawyer agree to be paid only if Terence is not convicted?

Yes. In most provinces, contingent fees, once considered unethical, are now permitted if the sum is reasonable and there is a written agreement.

But contingent fees in criminal cases are rare, especially when the accused client risks imprisonment.

Can I pay my lawyer with a percentage of the money I hope to get from my divorce case?

Yes. But it is most important that such an agreement be put in writing, and that the amount paid to the lawyer reflect both the complexity of the case and the time he spent on it. If his fee is unreasonable or unfair, it may be reduced by arbitration of the bar association or by a judge.

Is there a maximum percentage of the money a person wins in a lawsuit that a lawyer can receive as a contingent fee?

The percentage of a contingent fee that a lawyer may charge is governed by the law society or the Bar Act of each province. Usually this is 20 percent although some higher amounts have been found reasonable. As much as 30 percent is allowed in some cases in Quebec, and there have been some 50 percent fees in Nova Scotia. The Code of Professional Conduct of the Canadian Bar Association stipulates that the fees charged by an attorney must be fair and reasonable. Disputes about fees can be submitted for arbitration.

Ontario, the only province that disallows contingency fees at the time of writing, is planning to introduce provisions for such fees.

Marjorie was injured in an elevator crash. She paid a lawyer a $500 advance to sue the building's owner. Now the case is coming to court and the lawyer wants another $500 or he'll quit. Marjorie doesn't have the money. What can she do?

First, Marjorie should try to resolve the fee dispute with her lawyer on an informal basis. Most fee agreements in accident cases are put in writing and provide that any payments beyond an initial advance depend on how much, if anything, the client wins. If Marjorie's lawyer still insists on the $500, she should fire him in writing and instruct him to ask for an adjournment of her trial when he notifies the court that he is no longer her lawyer. Then she should find a new lawyer.

Since a lawyer may not withdraw from a case he has undertaken except for "good cause and upon notice appropriate in the circumstances," Marjorie should report her fee dispute to the local bar association, where she can file a formal grievance against her original lawyer. If her chances of winning her lawsuit have been damaged by his behavior, she may consider filing a malpractice suit against him. Marjorie should also try to get a refund for any portion of the $500 advance that the lawyer did not earn.

I gave a lawyer $2,000 as a retainer to take my case, but now I don't want to go through with the lawsuit. Can I get my money back? If so, how long does the lawyer have to return it?

If you decide to discontinue your lawsuit you are not entitled to a full refund, but you may be able to get any unused portion of your money back. You can determine how much money, if any, was not used by checking your lawyer's bills. Since lawyers generally prepare such statements as part of their regular 30-day billing cycle, you might expect to receive any refund within 30 days of the date you told your lawyer to stop working on your case. However, if your lawyer has already invested $2,000 worth of time and services in your case, you will not be entitled to a refund. If, on the other hand, he has spent no time at all on it, you may be able to get the full amount back.

Diane agreed to pay her lawyer a flat fee, but he had to withdraw before completing the case. Does she owe him the entire fee?

No. Diane should pay only for the work her lawyer actually completed. Her agreement with the lawyer may include an itemized fee breakdown. If not, the lawyer will have to estimate the reasonable value of his services. This value will be based on the time and labor he invested, the difficulty of the questions involved, the extent to which Diane's case prevented him from accepting other cases, customary local fees for services, and the amount in dispute between Diane and her opponent. If, after taking all of these factors into consideration, Diane is entitled to a refund, her lawyer must pay it promptly.

Can I get the other side to pay for my lawyer's fees?

Whether or not the other side will pay your lawyer's fees and expenses depends on the nature of your case. In a divorce case, for example, if a husband has earned all the family income and his wife has always remained at home, the husband may be ordered to pay for his wife's lawyer. In other cases, such as those involving accidents, the losing side in a lawsuit may be required to reimburse the other for certain types of costs and lawyer's fees. But whatever the nature of the case, there is no way to make the other side pay unless it is ordered to do so by the court. Furthermore, neither you nor your lawyer can guarantee that the court will order your opponent to pay.

Legal Expenses

Are fee splitting and referral fees among lawyers legal?

Fee splitting is usually legal, but referral fees are legal only when the first lawyer, who receives the referral fee, keeps some control over the case. As the law has become more complex and as more lawyers have chosen to specialize, it has become increasingly common for lawyers to consult other lawyers and to divide their fees accordingly. This happens most often in complicated cases when a lawyer needs the assistance of a lawyer with expertise in another area. In such a case, the lawyer must obtain his client's approval for the arrangement and explain the division of fees in detail.

Working With Your Lawyer

How can I tell if my lawyer is handling my case properly?

At the very least, your lawyer should keep you up-to-date on the status of your case, give you copies of correspondence and court documents, and let you know about court dates and deadlines. Most lawyers will provide this information routinely. If you feel your lawyer has not kept you thoroughly informed, or if you're not satisfied with the progress of your case, you should discuss the matter with him. But remember, the legal process is often slow, with long periods when nothing seems to happen. To a large extent, these delays are beyond the control of your lawyer, who may well feel as frustrated about the situation as you do.

If Dolores questions the wisdom of her lawyer's advice while her case is under way, should she get a second opinion?

Generally speaking, lawyers avoid giving second opinions. Attorneys do not like to second-guess the judgment of other lawyers, for the very good reason that they may be unaware of a particular development or issue relating to the case in progress. Therefore, if Dolores seeks another lawyer's advice, it is probably best that she not mention that she is looking for a second opinion.

What is an opinion letter?

An opinion letter is a written statement by your lawyer in which he sets forth his opinion of your case or of a question you have asked him. If you are considering a product liability lawsuit, for example, your attorney may provide you with an opinion letter that summarizes the facts of your case, describes the outcome of cases similar to yours, explains which laws apply to your case, and assesses your chances of winning.

What should I do if I'm dissatisfied with the way my lawyer is handling my case?

Dissatisfaction frequently stems from a lack of communication between a lawyer and his client. For example, you may not understand the reasons for your lawyer's actions, or you may feel that your lawyer has failed to keep you properly informed of the progress of your case. The best way to clear up any confusion is to discuss your concerns with your lawyer as early as possible.

If you remain dissatisfied, you should contact your local lawyers' association, known as the bar association. These associations often have a committee that will try to resolve a problem to your satisfaction. If you suspect that your lawyer has seriously mishandled your case, you can file a formal grievance against him with your provincial bar association or sue him for malpractice.

Can my lawyer give me a timetable so that I'll have some idea when my case will come to court?

Your lawyer may be able to provide a rough timetable if he's had experience with similar cases, but since no two cases are exactly alike, your case may not follow a predictable schedule. The date when your case goes to trial is determined by many factors, such as the caseload of the court, that are beyond your lawyer's control. In addition, if your opponent is not as eager as you are to see the case resolved, his lawyer may use delaying tactics to slow up the legal process.

Herb's son Gary got into a fight at school and was suspended. Herb called his lawyer in a rage, claiming that the school's principal was just picking on the boy. Herb wants his lawyer to start a lawsuit against the principal "just to shake him up." The lawyer said he couldn't do this. Why not?

It is against the law to waste a court's time with lawsuits that have no legal basis. If Herb were to sue the principal solely for the purpose of harassing him, the principal could turn around and file a countersuit for malicious prosecution—the offense that is committed when a lawsuit is filed without legal justification. A lawyer is obliged to discharge his duties to the court, his clients and to the public with integrity: as an officer of the court, he should not abuse his powers.

Working With Your Lawyer

Will my lawyer automatically provide me with copies of all the correspondence and documents relating to my case?

Usually a lawyer will provide you with copies of all relevant documents and letters but may not include copies of minor correspondence, such as requests for insurance or police reports. If you want to receive copies of all documents, including those of minor importance, you should specifically ask your lawyer for them. Most lawyers will be happy to furnish this material, although they may bill you for duplicating costs.

Lenore was injured when she slipped on a supermarket's wet floor. She hired a lawyer a month ago, but all he has done so far is send a letter to the store. Why hasn't he filed a lawsuit yet?

Generally, a lawsuit is only necessary in an accident case when both sides can't agree on a satisfactory settlement. It's also possible that Lenore's lawyer needs more time to investigate the accident or prepare his case. Lawsuits do not have to be filed immediately after an accident, but there is usually a deadline set by provincial law after which Lenore can no longer sue. If Lenore is worried about missing this deadline or is concerned about the way her lawyer is handling her case, she should discuss these matters candidly with him. Sometimes it is better to wait a few months before suing, as not all the consequences of an injury are apparent immediately. In other cases, such as suing a municipality for a fall on the sidewalk, the delay is limited—often to six months.

What an Arbitrator Can Do for You

If you need to settle a dispute, but want to avoid a long, expensive trial, one of the alternatives you should consider is arbitration. Arbitration is a process by which an impartial person or panel listens to both sides and makes what it considers to be a fair ruling. To use arbitration, both sides must agree to do so. The process can be used to settle any difference of opinion, including disagreements about contracts or liability in actions for damages.

The arbitrator can be anyone whom both sides approve of, such as a teacher, lawyer, accountant, or business executive. However, if your disagreement involves a technical subject, such as home construction, you will probably need an arbitrator who has expertise in that area. If you don't know anyone suitable, contact the Canadian Arbitration, Conciliation and Amicable Composition Centre in Ottawa.

Hal went into partnership with his best friend, Danny. Three months later, Hal discovered that Danny was stealing money from the business. Hal wants to sue Danny but Hal's lawyer wants to settle out of court. Who gets to decide the course of the case?

Hal. It's his lawsuit, and all decisions regarding its settlement are ultimately his. Hal's lawyer should point out to him, however, that refusing to settle will involve additional time and expense. The lawyer should also discuss what the chances are of winning the amount Hal wants. If Hal's lawyer feels that the settlement is fair, Hal should at least consider taking his lawyer's advice.

Will my lawyer report me to the authorities if I tell him I was involved in a crime that nobody else knows about?

No. Everything you tell your lawyer is considered confidential information. Without your permission, a lawyer may not disclose what you tell him to anyone. Should you admit that you committed a crime, for example, your lawyer cannot inform the police. Even a judge cannot order a lawyer to divulge what a client has told him.

The person who is suing me suggested that we submit our dispute to arbitration. If I agree, do I give up my right to a court trial?

Generally arbitration is a substitute for a court hearing and the decision of an arbitrator is as binding upon both parties as a court judgment. You

The cost of arbitration includes (1) expenses incurred by the arbitrator, (2) the fee charged by the association which supplied the arbitrator, (3) the costs incurred by expert witnesses, and (4) fees for any stenographic notes used. Unless agreed otherwise, these costs are usually split between the parties.

An arbitrator must be fair and neutral and have no personal interest in the outcome of the dispute. Rules for the hearing are similar to those for a trial by judge, unless the parties have agreed in writing that other rules of evidence may apply.

Arbitration is usually done before one arbitrator, but the parties may agree to have three—one chosen by each party and the third by the arbitrators themselves.

The decision of the arbitrator is legally binding and may be appealed only if the arbitrator (1) exceeded his authority, (2) failed to make a final and definite award, or (3) was guilty of misconduct, fraud or corruption.

can usually get a case to arbitration in less time than you can get a court hearing. You can always ask the provincial supreme or superior court, as the case may be, to review the arbitrator's decision if he (1) exceeded his authority, (2) failed to render a final and definite award, or (3) was guilty of fraud or bias.

Ivy was arrested on a drug charge, and her parents have hired a lawyer to defend her. Aren't Ivy's parents entitled to know the details of her case, since they are paying for her lawyer?

No. A lawyer cannot reveal confidential information about his client, even to the person who is paying his fee, without the client's consent. The lawyer's duty of secrecy to every client applies even to those he has ceased to represent.

After having a few beers at lunch with several other workers from the building project, Drew returned to his job and cut his hand while using a power saw. Should he let his lawyer know that he had been drinking?

Yes. A client should always reveal the complete details of his case to his lawyer. If Drew's lawyer is to prepare and present Drew's case properly, he must be completely informed of all the circumstances surrounding the accident. By admitting that he had a few beers, Drew will allow his lawyer to prepare for testimony from witnesses who may have seen Drew drinking at lunch.

As a result of a minor accident, Art has been charged with driving while intoxicated. He confided to his lawyer that, while he wasn't drunk, he may have been "a little tipsy" at the time. Will this admission affect how his lawyer handles the case—especially if Art wants to plead not guilty?

Yes. Art's lawyer will use this information to prepare a strategy to defend Art. For example, it may be better if Art does not take the witness stand in his own defense. If Art were to testify, the prosecuting attorney might raise the issue of Art's "tipsiness," even though Art was not legally intoxicated, and turn Art's admission against him. Knowing about Art's physical condition may also lead his lawyer to seek a plea bargain agreement with the prosecutor. Art would then agree to plead guilty to a less serious offense in order to avoid the severe penalties of a conviction for driving while intoxicated.

My lawyer wants to meet with me before my trial to review his questions and my answers to them. Is this legal?

Yes. In fact, most lawyers meet with their clients before a trial for this very purpose. If you have never before testified, your lawyer will prepare you for the experience by helping you organize the facts you are likely to tell the court. If your case involves a robbery, for example, your lawyer will try to refresh your memory of the details of the event. Your lawyer will also want to prepare you for any difficult questions the other side's lawyer may ask during cross-examination. Finally, your lawyer may want to describe the physical layout of the courtroom and explain how the trial will be conducted. The more relaxed you are, the more reliable your testimony will seem to the judge and jury.

Clara wants to take the stand in her own defense, but her lawyer thinks this is a bad idea. Can Clara insist on testifying?

Yes, but she may have to fire her lawyer and hire another one who is willing to let her testify. If Clara's lawyer feels she would not make a good witness, she ought to consider his opinion carefully. If she testifies, anything Clara says can be used to help convict her. Moreover, Clara has the right not to testify, and if she refuses to take the stand, the prosecutor cannot force her to do so. Once Clara has taken the stand, she may be questioned about her past criminal record, if she has one, about past arrests, and about other facts that may damage her reputation in front of the judge and jury.

My lawyer didn't cross-examine all of the other side's witnesses. Was this irresponsible of him?

Not necessarily. Cross-examination helps your case only if your lawyer can show an outstanding weakness in a witness's story. If your lawyer feels he cannot do this, he may prefer to move on without cross-examination. Your lawyer may also decline to cross-examine a witness in order to suggest that what the witness has to say is not very important.

Arlene's lawyer got so carried away with his courtroom histrionics that the judge has charged him with contempt of court. Does this mean he'll be dismissed from Arlene's case?

No. Arlene's lawyer is not required to withdraw from the case just because the judge has charged him with contempt of court. However, if the judge imposes a fine for contempt of court, Arlene's lawyer could be suspended from all cases, including Arlene's, until he pays it. If the lawyer can show that a fair trial will now be difficult because of the strong dislike or enmity between the judge and himself, he might succeed in having Arlene's case transferred before another judge.

Mason would like to fire his lawyer, but his case is well under way. What should he do?

If the case has already come to court, Mason must ask the judge for permission to fire his lawyer. If the judge decides that the interests of justice might be harmed by such an action, he may deny Mason's request. If the judge does permit Mason to dismiss his lawyer, Mason should make sure that his lawyer requests an official postponement so that the case is not dismissed before a new lawyer has had time to familiarize himself with the issues involved.

A judge would not allow Mason to fire his lawyer if he thinks Mason's sole motive is to delay the trial, thus securing a postponement and possible dismissal.

I've had a series of disagreements with my lawyer. If I fire him, do I still have to pay his fee?

It depends on how your lawyer has been charging you for his services. If he has been charging on an hourly basis, you must pay him for any time he has spent on your case. If you paid a flat fee, your lawyer may be allowed to keep a portion of that fee to cover the work he has completed. If your lawyer was hired on a contingent-fee basis, you may not owe him anything if you have not yet won any money in a settlement. However, if you dismiss your lawyer before a settlement is reached just to avoid paying him his share, you may find that you still owe him the fee or agreed share anyway.

Louise dismissed her lawyer because she wasn't pleased with his performance. Can she ask him to return all the documents relating to her case?

Yes. When you dismiss your lawyer, you are entitled to have any documents, reports, and other materials that you provided returned to you. These materials are your property, and your lawyer may not keep them after he has been fired, provided you have paid his fee in full. If you still owe him money for fees or disbursements, he has the right to retain certain documents, unless by doing so he would materially prejudice your case.

*Theodore's lawyer is retiring. What will happen to all of
Theodore's personal documents?*

Since all the personal documents contained in Theodore's file are his
property, he can arrange for their safekeeping however he chooses. If
Theodore's lawyer does not automatically give back all his client's
documents before he retires, Theodore should certainly ask him to do
so. If another lawyer is taking over Theodore's lawyer's practice and
Theodore decides not to use him, Theodore should pick up his file from
the office.

Legal Ethics

Do lawyers have a code of ethics that they must follow?

Yes. Lawyers have a written code of ethics—known as the Rules, or
Code of Professional Conduct—that guides their professional behavior.
While each province has its own code of legal ethics, all the provincial
codes are based on those developed by the largest lawyers' group in the
country, the Canadian Bar Association. The Code of Professional Conduct defines the standards of conduct that lawyers and their associates
must follow. If a lawyer violates any of these standards, he can be
disciplined or even barred from practicing law.

If I report a lawyer to the bar association for unethical conduct or malpractice, will I have to testify and be cross-examined?

Yes. When the malpractice case comes up for a hearing, you will be
required to testify about your lawyer's misconduct, and if he wants to
cross-examine you, he can do so at that time.

What are some examples of legal malpractice?

A lawyer commits malpractice if he damages his client's case by failing to
exercise a proper degree of skill, knowledge, or diligence; if he does not
prepare adequately for the case or neglects it completely; if he delays
working on the case for so long that the case is dismissed; if he takes
money that is not his or deliberately misleads his client about how much
money he could win from a lawsuit; or if he reveals confidential
information. It is also malpractice for a lawyer to accept a case that he
knows, or should know, he is not competent to handle, or where there is a
possible conflict of interest between his client's case and his own
personal interest.

Legal Ethics

My lawyer suggested that I name him as executor of my will, since I have no close relatives. Would this be all right?

Yes. Many people choose their lawyer as the executor or alternate executor of their will. As long as you feel that your lawyer is experienced and trustworthy, there is no reason for not selecting him for this function.

William's lawyer has assigned his associate to take over the case. Is it ethical for a lawyer to do this?

No. A lawyer should always obtain his client's consent when turning over part or all of a case to another lawyer. It is common practice to have associates assist with cases, such as doing research and handling routine court appearances. But a lawyer should explain what aspects of the case will be handled by the associate and assure his client that he will closely supervise and check the associate's work. If a client is not comfortable with this arrangement, he should discuss it with his lawyer.

My husband and I listed our house for sale with a real estate broker. Afterward, we received a letter from a lawyer we don't know, who offered to help us close the deal. Should we hire him?

At one time it was considered improper conduct for a lawyer to send a letter asking for business, but advertising by lawyers has become more acceptable. Even so, all provinces do not yet permit lawyers to solicit business in this way. Before hiring the lawyer, ask your local bar association if his advertising practices are legal in your province. If they are not, you might be better served by finding another lawyer, who abides by the rules of his profession. Ideally you would choose one on the recommendations of friends or relatives whose judgment you trust. In Quebec, a notary rather than a lawyer would represent you in a real estate transaction.

When my son was hospitalized because of a bus accident, a lawyer we didn't know started to pester us about suing. We don't want to get involved in legal matters. What can we do?

Report the lawyer's conduct to the disciplinary committee of your provincial bar association. This lawyer is guilty of ambulance chasing, which is forbidden by every province. A lawyer who engages in such behavior could be suspended or even barred from practicing law.

You should see a lawyer of your choice about the accident, however.

You or your son might be entitled to certain compensation, such as payments from a provincial auto insurance board, which could be lost through inaction. Most law societies, or lawyer referral services, would arrange a short interview with a lawyer for about $25.

When Stella mentioned to an attorney that she needed a lawyer to handle her divorce, he told her that the family court judge was one of his best buddies, and that if she hired him, she wouldn't have any trouble cleaning out her husband. Has Stella found the perfect lawyer?

Probably not. Stella should look for a lawyer who stresses the quality of his work rather than his connections. Even if the lawyer were to try to use his friendship to influence her case, the judge is bound by oath not to let personal relationships interfere with his decisions. In fact, the judge's close friendship with the lawyer might backfire. If the judge rules in Stella's favor, her husband's lawyer might claim that the judge's decision was in fact influenced by his friendship with her lawyer, and might succeed in having the case tried again before a different judge.

Connie's neighbor Neil recently built a fence that crosses a part of her property, so Connie filed a lawsuit against him. Neil's lawyer turns out to be the same one who handled Connie's child custody case 10 years ago. Should Neil find another lawyer?

Nothing in the legal code of ethics specifically prohibits Neil's lawyer from defending him in this lawsuit just because he handled Connie's child custody case, especially since that case was 10 years earlier. But if there is any connection between Neil's lawsuit and Connie's child custody case, then the lawyer should reject the case and Neil should find another lawyer.

Angelo was injured in a two-car accident. He would like his friend Larry to take the case. But Larry is representing the other driver on a reckless driving charge resulting from the same accident. Can Larry handle Angelo's case?

No. A lawyer must serve the best interests of his client. By accepting Angelo's case, Larry would be placing himself in a conflict of interest between Angelo and the other driver. If the other driver gives Larry confidential information about the accident that is damaging to Angelo's case, Larry might have to use this information against Angelo. If Larry represents both drivers, he would be subject to disciplinary action for violating the code of ethics that governs the conduct of lawyers.

Legal Ethics

Troy and Perry were arrested and charged with destroying property. At their first meeting with a lawyer, Troy swore that everything was Perry's fault; Perry claimed to be innocent and pointed an accusing finger at Troy. Can the same lawyer defend both of them?

No. When a lawyer agrees to represent a client, he commits himself to giving that client the best defense possible. In this case, the lawyer is caught in a clear conflict of interest. He can't represent both, since in defending Troy he must argue that Perry is guilty, and in defending Perry, he would have to argue that Troy committed the crime. Troy and Perry should ask to be represented by different lawyers.

My lawyer can't represent me because of a conflict of interest. Can another lawyer in his firm take the case?

No. If your lawyer can't take your case or has to withdraw from it because of a conflict of interest, no other lawyer affiliated with the firm can represent you in this particular matter. To do so would be to violate the rules of professional ethics of the legal profession. You will have to find a lawyer from a different firm.

Several days after Jerry met with his lawyer, he discovered that the lawyer's secretary was gossiping around town about confidential matters she had learned while transcribing her boss's notes. What can Jerry do?

Jerry should file a complaint with the provincial bar's disciplinary committee. All members of a lawyer's staff, including secretaries, are bound by the same confidentiality that a lawyer promises his client. If someone breaches this confidentiality, the lawyer must assume full responsibility since he has the duty to impress upon his employees the importance of confidentiality and secrecy about client affairs. Jerry's lawyer will probably fire his secretary for this type of behavior.

Priscilla asked her lawyer to testify as a witness at her trial, but he told her that he couldn't honor her request. Why not?

A lawyer is ethically bound to keep everything a client has told him confidential. However, if Priscilla waived her right to confidentiality and allowed her lawyer to testify as a witness, he could be forced to disclose information that Priscilla might not want him to reveal. If the lawyer's testimony is crucial to her case, Priscilla should allow him to withdraw and hire another lawyer to represent her. Then, if Priscilla again waived her right to confidentiality, the new lawyer could call the former lawyer to testify as a private citizen at the trial.

I was unemployed when we divorced and my ex-wife got no alimentary pension for supporting our two minor children, who are in her custody. Now that I'm earning a good salary, I would like to help with their upkeep, but my lawyer told me I would be foolish to make payments when I don't have to. Is he right?

The obligation to support one's children is a moral and a legal duty under both civil and criminal law. Your lawyer has acted in an unethical manner when he advised you to neglect your parental responsibilities in order to save a few dollars. Such advice is a disservice to society and to the legal profession.

My lawyer met with me for just a few minutes after I was mistakenly arrested for shoplifting. He hardly asked me any questions. Just before my trial began, he told me that if I pleaded guilty, I would get a suspended sentence. I took his advice, and now I'm facing a jail sentence. What can I do?

You should consult with a new lawyer immediately for a review of your situation. If your new lawyer can prove that the first one did not give you appropriate advice before your trial, he might be able to get the appeal court to reconsider your case, or even reverse the judgment.

I just read a book by a famous lawyer in which he explains how he won a criminal trial. Isn't it a violation of the lawyer-client relationship to publish facts about the case?

Not if he has the client's consent, and any agreement regarding publication rights was made after the case was over. A lawyer is ethically required to avoid situations that would influence how he represents his client. Acquiring publication rights while the case is in progress could tempt the lawyer to place his own interests ahead of those of his client.

Lorna lost her case in court and told her lawyer to file an appeal. He didn't file the appeal within the time limit. What can Lorna do?

She can file a complaint with the provincial bar disciplinary committee for lawyers. Since her lawyer agreed to file her appeal but failed to do so,

Legal Ethics

Legal Ethics

he violated the Code of Professional Conduct. Lorna may also sue her lawyer for any losses she suffered as a result of his inaction. Failure to file an appeal within the legal delays is a clear case of malpractice. Most attorneys are required by law to carry malpractice insurance.

I am suing my neighbor Harry, who broke my nose in a fight he started while drunk. Two weeks ago Harry offered to settle out of court and since then I have been trying to reach my lawyer to discuss it. But my lawyer refuses to return my calls or answer my letters. What can I do?

You should report your lawyer to his local lawyers' association, the bar. His behavior would seem to be a clear infringement of the Canadian Bar Association's Code of Professional Conduct, which requires lawyers to serve their clients in a "conscientious, diligent and efficient manner." Meantime, you might be wise to find another lawyer. Otherwise, you may miss the opportunity of settling out of court and might even lose your case altogether.

Hugh filed a lawsuit against a pharmaceutical company. The company offered a $22,000 settlement, but Hugh's lawyer rejected the claim without telling Hugh, then lost the case. When Hugh found out about the offer, he was furious with his lawyer for not giving him a chance to accept it. Can Hugh sue his lawyer?

Yes. A lawyer must inform his client of all offers and give the client an opportunity to make the final decision. Hugh's lawyer should have notified him of any offer of settlement, since the decision to accept or reject the offer was Hugh's. In addition to suing his lawyer for malpractice, Hugh could report him to the ethics and discipline committee of his local lawyers' association, called the bar association.

Marriage and Family

What are the legal requirements for getting married?

Without your parents' consent you cannot marry anywhere in Canada until you are at least 18 years old. And you need parental consent until you are 19 in British Columbia, Nova Scotia, Newfoundland and both Territories. (The consent rule may be waived in Newfoundland and the Territories for 18-year-olds who are self-supporting and living away from home.) If the parents agree, girls as young as 12 and boys as young as 14 can marry in Quebec. However, legislation pending at the time this book was written will bring these ages in line with the other provinces: With parental consent, 16 is the minimum age everywhere except Yukon and the Northwest Territories, where it is 15. In some provinces the consent of one parent is enough. But even if both parents object, an underage couple may get the court's permission to marry.

The law forbids marriage between persons too closely related by blood (consanguinity) or marriage (affinity). A man, for example, cannot marry his aunt or his stepdaughter. If a couple does marry within the forbidden degrees of kinship, the marriage would be invalid. These degrees, too, vary from province to province.

Couples in all provinces except Quebec must have a license to marry and must observe a waiting period after the license is issued. The marriage must be solemnized by a recognized clergyman or by a public official who has this authority under provincial law—a marriage officer, judge, or justice of the peace, for example. The couple must be able to understand the rights, duties, and obligations created by the marital relationship and must freely consent to the marriage. Certain other requirements must also be fulfilled, such as having two witnesses attend the ceremony and filing a record of the marriage.

Why is a waiting period required before marriage?

This offers the prospective bride and bridegroom a few days' pause to reflect on their decision. Most provinces have a delay before the license is issued; a few require one between the issuance of the license and the ceremony. The waiting period ranges from 1 to 20 days.

My 16-year-old daughter wants to get married. Can I stop her?

Persons under 18 years of age (19 in British Columbia, Nova Scotia and, under certain circumstances, in Newfoundland, Yukon and the North-west Territories) must have parental consent to marry. If your daughter got a marriage license by lying about her age, you can probably prevent the marriage, or have it annulled if it has already taken place, by refusing to consent to the union. In the Northwest Territories, Alberta, Saskatchewan, Nova Scotia and Newfoundland, however, marriage between minors who don't have parental consent cannot be annulled if the marriage was consummated, or the couple lived together after the marriage as husband and wife. In some provinces, Ontario for example, a judge could allow your daughter to get married if you are withholding your consent arbitrarily and without just cause.

Helen and Frank want to get married right away, but their province requires a three-day waiting period between the issuance of the license and the ceremony. Is there some way for them to have this delay eliminated?

Yes. Most provinces will waive the waiting period for an emergency or other extraordinary circumstances, such as a terminal illness, active military duty, or the imminent birth of a child out of wedlock. A judge or other official designated for this purpose signs an authorization permitting the ceremony to take place before the end of the waiting period.

If Helen and Frank do not have a valid reason for setting the waiting period aside, and they marry immediately, they could be penalized for failing to observe all the requirements of provincial law. So, too, could the person performing the ceremony. Failing to observe the formal requirements will not void or invalidate the marriage, however.

Greg and Nancy obtained their marriage license two weeks before their wedding day, but then Nancy was injured in an accident and was hospitalized for two months. Is the license still valid?

Each province sets its own deadline for the validity of a marriage license. In Quebec, where a license is not required, the marriage must take place no later than 20 days after the banns have been published. In Ontario, and indeed in most provinces, a marriage license is valid for three months. But even if the license has expired, Greg and Nancy can always get a new one for a few dollars.

Wally told Janet two days before their wedding that he had changed his mind about marrying her. Can Janet get Wally to pay for the cost of canceling the wedding?

It depends on where Janet lives. In the past, the person left standing at the altar could sue for breach of promise to marry and, if successful, be awarded damages for wedding expenses, lost wages, mental anguish, loss of reputation, and humiliation. Additional money was awarded when the promise to marry had been made with no intention of carrying it out. Ontario no longer recognizes actions for damages based on breach of promise to marry. Such an action might succeed in most other provinces, however, provided expenses were incurred by the party still willing to go through with the ceremony.

What is the reason for requiring a blood test?

The purpose of a blood test is to detect venereal disease, but only Alberta and Prince Edward Island require such tests. In either of these provinces, a marriage license will not be issued if the tests show that one of the parties has syphilis or other venereal diseases.

My son began an ardent courtship of a girl who was engaged to a soldier stationed abroad. Eventually she broke her engagement. Does the soldier have any legal recourse against my son?

No. Courts are reluctant to interfere when a third person causes a breach of promise to marry. This reluctance is, in part, an effort to protect parents who step in and advise their children about the wisdom of marrying a particular person.

The Marriage Contract

When a man and a woman wed, they are generally full of ideas of love and happiness and a lifetime of caring. They rarely realize that they are also making a legal contract, which will bind them with rights and responsibilities that are defined, regulated, and enforced by the state. A husband and wife are not free to devise the rules by which a marriage may be conducted; they must comply with the laws of their province, and these laws are not negotiable.

As soon as a man and a woman are pronounced husband and wife, they acquire certain rights under the law: the right to be free from parental control, the right to sexual relations and marital privacy, the right to share in each other's property, the right to have society regard their children as legitimate, and the right of one spouse to inherit from the other. In return a husband and wife are given certain responsibilities by provincial law: above all, they must support each other and their children and make sure that the children are properly educated.

Traditionally, the law expected a husband to support his wife, paying for her food, clothing, home, and furniture; the wife upheld her part of

Are some kinds of marriages illegal?

Yes. Every province has restrictions on who can marry whom. No lawful marriage can exist between persons of the same sex or if one of the prospective spouses is already married to someone else. Relatives who are prohibited from marrying each other are brother and sister, parent and child, grandparent and grandchild, aunt and nephew, and uncle and niece. Provinces differ on whether first cousins can marry. Any blood relationship more distant than this is generally acceptable.

Many provinces restrict marriages between people who are related by marriage; unions between stepparents and stepchildren are the ones most frequently prohibited. In some provinces, Quebec for example, the rules prohibiting certain relatives from marrying derive from canon or religious law.

If you want to marry someone who is related to you by blood or marriage, check with your lawyer to see if such a marriage is permitted in your province.

Jim gave Betty a sapphire ring a month before they became engaged. If they never marry, is Betty entitled to keep the ring?

Yes. This was a gift, like a birthday or Christmas present. Jim did not give it to her in exchange for her promise to marry him.

the contract by keeping the home clean, preparing the food, and caring for the children. In recent years the law has given married couples greater freedom in dividing their responsibilities, especially in regard to earning wages and supporting family members. Today both spouses in a marriage may work and share family expenses, or a wife may be the sole support of the family while the husband stays home and minds the children. Moreover, the law expects that a wife will help support her husband and family when necessary, and she may be held equally liable with her husband to pay family expenses.

Generally, the law will not interfere with an ongoing marriage. For example, a judge will not order a working man to give his wife an allowance as long as the family is being provided with the bare essentials of life. Nor will a judge meddle in arguments over the family budget. But when a marriage is dissolving, the law will intervene to help settle disputes, preserve the property rights of those involved, and make sure that the children's best interests are protected. Although other contracts can be terminated by mutual consent, a marriage contract is considered to be so special that it can be ended only by the death of a spouse or by an act of the state—the issuance of a divorce decree, or separation.

Getting Married

Ronald, our oldest son, gave his great-grandmother's diamond ring to his girlfriend, Andrea, for their engagement. Can Andrea keep the ring if they break up?

Not in most cases. Engagement gifts are given with the expectation that the marriage will take place. If the wedding falls through and Andrea insists on keeping the ring, your son can go to court to enforce his ownership right. The court could order Andrea either to return the ring or to pay your son an amount equal to the ring's value. Because this ring is an heirloom, the court would probably make Andrea give it back. An exception might occur if the court found that your son broke the engagement without good reason, or did something—such as run off with another woman—that caused the engagement to be broken.

Brian and Jody are first cousins. They were married in one province and then moved to another where it is illegal for first cousins to marry. Are they still legally married?

Yes. The general rule is that the validity of a marriage is determined by the laws of the province in which it was performed. There is an exception, however. If Brian and Jody married in one province in order to avoid the prohibition of first-cousin marriages in another province, their marriage would not be recognized and could be annulled.

I just discovered that my husband's divorce from his first wife was never made final by the court. Are we legally married? Are our children legitimate?

You are not legally married. Until his divorce is final, your husband remains married to his first wife. He could be found guilty of bigamy if he married you with the knowledge that his first marriage was still valid. Nonetheless, most provinces regard children born during this "non-valid" marriage as legitimate.

Jason was adopted by Karen and Mike. Three years later they had a girl, Tammy. When Jason and Tammy grew up, they wanted to marry each other. Is this possible?

Some provinces would not let them marry, because they are brother and sister as far as the law is concerned. Others would permit the marriage, because Jason and Tammy are not related by blood. If blood relatives were to marry and have children, those children stand a greater than normal chance of inheriting genetic weaknesses and disorders. This is the main concern of laws prohibiting intrafamily marriages. Since Jason is adopted, there is no cause for concern. In Alberta recently, a marriage between an uncle and a niece was permitted by the Alberta Court of Appeal on the grounds that the uncle-niece relationship was the product of adoption rather than blood ties.

Who may perform a marriage ceremony?

People authorized by the provinces to perform marriage ceremonies include clergymen, judges, and justices of the peace. If an unauthorized person performs a marriage ceremony, he is breaking the law and may be subject to a penalty. If two people married in good faith before someone with no authority to perform a marriage, their marriage would generally be considered valid if they had lived together for some time afterward. In Quebec, however, such a "marriage" would be invalid.

Can a ship's captain perform a legal marriage ceremony?

The validity of marriages performed on ships is determined by the location of the vessel at the time of the ceremony. If the ceremony takes place in territorial waters, the laws of the state claiming those waters determine the ceremony's validity. Unless those laws specifically prohibit captains from performing marriage ceremonies, couples would be lawfully married. If the wedding takes place while the ship is in international waters, the governing law is generally that of the place where the ship is registered. Some courts have ruled, however, that the controlling laws are those of the province or country in which the couple resides. Two people who were married at sea by a ship's captain would be wise to go through the ceremony again once they came home. A civil marriage ceremony could be held quickly, informally and inexpensively, and would remove all doubts as to the validity of the marriage.

Frank and Myrna met at a vacation resort in the Bahamas and got married there before returning home. Is their marriage valid?

If Frank and Myrna complied with all the requirements for getting married in the Bahamas, they would be legally married when they returned to Canada. However, Frank and Myrna should check their provincial laws. They may stipulate that a foreign marriage is invalid if the spouses are not legally qualified to marry in their home province. For example, if Frank and Myrna were first cousins and they lived in a province that does not allow first-cousin marriages, then that province would not recognize their Bahamian marriage.

Getting Married

I have heard that a marriage must be consummated for it to be recognized as legally valid. Is this true?

No. Once the ceremony is over, a couple is considered to be legally married. The idea that you are not legally married until you have had sexual relations is mistaken.

Văn and Thúy married in Vietnam but all records of the marriage were destroyed during the war in that country. How can they prove they were married?

In most cases where a man and woman live together for some time, there will be a presumption that they are married. This presumption is reinforced if the spouses use the same name, present themselves to the public as husband and wife, and are of the age of consent. In the case of Văn and Thúy, they could get the proof they need from affidavits of friends and relatives who knew they were legally married in Vietnam.

Martha and Henry were "married" by a man who said he was a religious officer who could perform marriages. Four years later, they discover that this person was a fraud who had no right to perform marriages. Are Martha and Henry married?

After a certain amount of time, usually one year, marriages of this sort would be considered valid for all legal purposes everywhere in Canada except in the province of Quebec. Apart from Quebec, nonobservance of a formality would not invalidate a marriage which a couple entered into in good faith and with the belief that they were complying with the laws of their province.

Martin grew up in an African state where men were permitted more than one wife. Two of Martin's three wives still live there and, as a new Canadian citizen, he wishes to sponsor them both and live with them in Canada. Would this be legal?

No. In Canada, a man or a woman may only have one spouse. Marriage to another party while one marriage is still valid is bigamy, a criminal offense. Here the woman Martin married first would be considered his wife, and the other two marriages would not be recognized. But since the multiple marriages were legal in the country where they took place, Martin would not be guilty of bigamy, and the multiple marriages would continue to be valid in those countries that permit polygyny.

Prenuptial Agreements

Both Scott and Mary went through painful property disputes while ending their previous marriages. Neither wants to go through the same ordeal if their new marriage does not work out. What is the best thing for them to do?

All provinces recognize domestic contracts, made before or during marriage, which establish a couple's property and maintenance rights in case of separation and divorce. These are known as prenuptial agreements in the case of a married couple and as cohabitation agreements if made by a man and woman who plan to live together outside of marriage. Scott and Mary should ask a lawyer to draw up a contract stating what each person owned before the marriage, what each person will own if the marriage ends, and what to do with property acquired during the marriage. Everything should be in writing to avoid future misunderstandings. Scott and Mary should have their own attorneys (notaries in Quebec) advise them on the terms and language to include in the contract. They should sign the agreement and have it witnessed and notarized. Some provinces require that the agreement be recorded in the county where it is made, or filed with the court, in which case it would have the same validity as a court judgment.

The Supreme Court of Canada has recently stated that the courts will not lightly interfere with or alter these private agreements in the event of a later divorce.

My spouse's parents forced us to sign a prenuptial agreement. Will this agreement hold up in court?

No. Just as with any other contract, one of the requirements for a valid prenuptial agreement is that no pressure be used to get either person to sign. A court will not enforce a contract that was not entered into freely. In determining validity, the court would also consider: (1) Were both of you fully aware of each other's property and its value? (2) Was the property divided fairly under the terms of the contract? (3) Did the agreement encourage divorce or separation?

Jeff is in love with Susan, but he is afraid that Susan wants to marry him only for his money. So he had her sign a prenuptial contract in which she agreed to make no claims against his estate upon his death. Is this binding?

Yes. One purpose of a prenuptial agreement is to define property rights in the event of death. If Jeff wants to make sure his property is inherited by his relatives and not his wife, a copy of the prenuptial agreement

What to Include in a Prenuptial Agreement

Signing a prenuptial agreement—a marital contract spelling out who gets what if the marriage breaks up—may seem cold and unromantic, but with Canada's ever-increasing divorce rate, more and more couples are finding these agreements a sensible precaution. If a marriage does end in divorce, a properly drawn prenuptial agreement will eliminate bitter settlement battles and minimize court costs and lawyers' fees. When drafting a prenuptial agreement, you should avoid such trivialities as who's going to put out the cat or wash the dishes; inconsequential matters like these cannot be enforced by a court. If you think some of your considerations may be inappropriate or invalid, be sure to discuss them with your lawyer. The following are the basics you should consider including:

☑ A statement of who will contribute what to family expenses.

☑ An agreement on the means of supporting any children or a spouse of a former marriage or other dependent relatives.

☑ A declaration that each of you is being honest about all individually owned property and its value at the time of your marriage.

☑ An agreement on how premarital property, owned singly or jointly, will be divided if there's a divorce.

☑ An agreement on how property that each contributes during the marriage will be divided in the event of a divorce.

☑ An agreement on what happens to the property acquired jointly during the marriage.

☑ An agreement on how any business partnership between husband and wife will be dissolved.

☑ A statement declaring whether the wife intends to use her maiden or married name.

☑ A statement declaring what surname the children of the marriage will have. Will they bear the name of the father, or the mother, or a hyphenated combination of both names?

☑ A statement that the agreement was not drawn up with the intention of ending the marriage by separation or divorce. (Courts will not accept agreements that tend to promote separation or divorce.)

☑ Instructions on how the agreement can be altered or terminated.

☑ A statement on whether an alimentary pension arising from separation or divorce will end with the death of the debtor spouse, or will continue to be paid by the deceased's estate.

☑ A statement on whether or not maintenance payments will be indexed to the cost of living.

☑ A statement on who will carry insurance, how much insurance, who will pay the premiums, and who will be the beneficiary.

should be presented after his death to the court that handles estates. The agreement would be enforceable even though the law in some provinces gives the wife a right to a share of her husband's estate when he dies. An exception may be the matrimonial home: in some provinces, Susan may have special rights to the home that override the prenuptial agreement.

David and Emily signed an agreement prior to their marriage five years ago, outlining how their property would be divided in the event of death or divorce. Can they cancel the agreement?

Yes, if they both agree. The termination of the prenuptial agreement should be in writing, dated, signed, witnessed, and notarized. A written termination agreement is solid evidence that the original agreement has been canceled. The original and all copies of the prenuptial agreement should be destroyed. If a missing copy of the original prenuptial agreement should turn up later and be presented to a court, a written termination agreement would prove that David and Emily had definitely ended their original agreement. In some provinces, changes to the original agreement have to be announced in the province's official *Gazette* and in local newspapers. This advises creditors that there has been a change in the married couple's property rights.

Before we married, Calvin and I agreed that if we ever divorced, neither of us would make a claim to property the other brought into the marriage. But we never put this in writing. Is our oral agreement enforceable if we divorce?

No. All provinces other than Alberta and Manitoba require domestic contracts to be in writing. Such agreements must also be signed, witnessed and, in some cases, registered. Even where an oral contract is valid, it is better to have one in writing. Not only will it serve as evidence that you have a binding agreement; it will also remind you and Calvin of the promises you have made to each other. Keep in mind, too, that an oral domestic contract would not exclude the provisions of the Matrimonial Property Act of either Alberta or Manitoba—one more reason why all domestic contracts should be in writing.

George wants Anne to sign a prenuptial agreement containing a provision that Anne will not contest a divorce. Is such an agreement enforceable?

Probably not. Our society values the family as a source of strength and stability. The courts are therefore interested in preserving the institution of marriage. By including a provision that prevents Anne from contesting

Prenuptial Agreements

a divorce, George has tried to make it easier for himself to divorce her. Contracts that facilitate divorce are not viewed as promoting or supporting the institution of marriage. Such a clause would also counter the Charter of Rights and Freedoms, which guarantees everyone the right to equal protection and benefit of the law. The courts are very suspicious of agreements that would exclude them from intervening where injustice has been done.

Before they were married, Arthur and Lillian agreed to raise their children in a particular religion. But after the children were born, Arthur changed his mind. Can Lillian get a judge to rule in her favor about the children's religious upbringing?

Probably not. When the upbringing of children is involved, a judge will try to decide what is in the child's best interest, regardless of any written or oral agreements between the parents. Problems such as Arthur's and Lillian's are best settled by mediation, rather than a judge's ruling.

Unmarried Couples

My girlfriend and I are planning to move in together next month. Some friends of ours have a "living together agreement." Should we also have one?

It would be wise for the two of you to sit down and discuss how property should be divided if one of you moves out. Topics to discuss include property owned before moving in, property acquired while living together, real estate or leases, pets, income, and joint bank accounts. Once you have come to an agreement, you should put it in writing and have it signed just as you would any other contract. Although such a contract is not mandatory, it would make it easier to prove that an agreement was reached and to have its terms enforced by a court if the time ever came when you had a serious property dispute.

Wendell and Jola have lived together for several years. During this time they have bought a house, furniture, and appliances. What rights does each one have if they split up and cannot agree on how to divide the property?

If Wendell and Jola made no agreement before they began living together, it will be more difficult for a court to divide the property.

Generally, each of them is entitled to keep any property he or she owned before they began their joint living arrangement. The biggest problem lies in distributing property that they acquired while living together. As a general rule, each would get to share those things bought jointly, in proportion to the amount each contributed. In some provinces, British Columbia and Ontario, for example, Wendell or Jola might also have to maintain the other if that party was unable to provide his or her own upkeep. In Quebec, on the other hand, neither would be eligible for support from the other, even if they had lived together for 25 years.

My boyfriend left me with six months to go on our apartment lease, and the rent is too high for me to pay by myself. How can I get money from him to help out?

If both of you signed the lease, you can be held responsible for the balance due. One recourse is to go to Small Claims Court to compel your boyfriend to pay his share of the rent. Since small claims courts have a maximum amount you can seek, check with court personnel to see if your case qualifies. If this route is unsuccessful, and your lease permits it, try to find someone else to complete the terms of your lease. You could then be relieved of any liability for the balance of the rent. A landlord cannot refuse to accept a new tenant without good reason.

If you moved into your boyfriend's apartment and did not add your name to the lease, you would be able to leave without owing anything since there is no contract (lease) between you and the landlord. Your boyfriend would be responsible for all rent owing until the apartment was rented again.

Beatrice and Andrew had lived together for 14 years when Andrew died. Does Beatrice have any claim on Andrew's estate?

If Andrew did not include Beatrice in his will, she may not be able to claim a penny of his estate. Although the laws of each province automatically give the surviving spouse of a marriage a part of the estate when there is no will, they do not protect unmarried couples. To have a valid claim, Beatrice would have to show either that she bought some of the objects that make up Andrew's estate or that she contributed to the estate in some other way. She could also try to claim a share of the estate based on the principle of "unjustified enrichment," charging that the heirs would benefit unfairly if she was denied a share.

Beatrice should see if she is entitled to any benefits under certain federal and provincial laws such as the Workers' Compensation Act and the various pension, auto insurance and Old Age Security acts. Under these laws, Beatrice would be considered the wife of Andrew, since they lived together for a number of years.

Common-law Marriages

Though Anna and Tony have lived together for several years, they never married. They are thinking of moving to another part of the country. Are common-law marriages accepted in every province?

The effects of being in a common-law relationship vary from one province to another. In some provinces, a man and woman who have lived together for a number of years—for example, two years in British Columbia and three in Ontario—are considered to be spouses, and either party may be awarded support from the other in time of need. Neither Alberta nor Quebec recognize common-law marriages for purposes of maintenance, although people living in common-law or consensual relationships in those provinces may be considered spouses for purposes of various federal and provincial laws, such as Workers' Compensation and the various pension acts. In a case in the Northwest Territories, it was held that a couple married according to Inuit custom was legally married under Canadian law, even though no license was obtained for the marriage.

According to the Canada Evidence Act, one common-law spouse cannot be obliged to testify against the other.

How is a common-law marriage different from a legal marriage?

In a legal marriage performed according to the laws of the province where the couple resides, each spouse has certain rights and obligations which are enforceable by law. Each has a duty of fidelity and the right to financial support. They are jointly responsible for bringing up their children. One spouse may inherit the other's property when that spouse dies intestate (without a will). Children born in a valid marriage are automatically legitimate and may inherit from relatives, such as grandparents, even if the relatives die intestate. Which of the above rights apply to common-law marriage partners depends entirely on the province where the couple lives. But no province permits a common-law spouse to inherit property from the other in the absence of a will. And, of course, a couple in a common-law relationship cannot get divorced.

Family Responsibilities

Are both husband and wife obliged to support the family?

In the past the husband carried the full burden of providing financial support. But with the increasing number of families in which both husbands and wives work at jobs outside the home, this is no longer considered a strictly male responsibility. The obligation to be self-supporting and to contribute to the economic and moral upbringing of the family is now shared equally between the spouses.

If both spouses work, who is legally responsible for paying the household bills?

Generally, both the husband and wife are responsible. The practice of imposing financial responsibility on the husband, and letting the wife escape liability, is no longer the rule. The new trend is to hold working spouses jointly responsible for family debts and individually responsible for personal debts. Each spouse is considered to have the power of attorney (domestic mandate) to bind the other party when purchasing household goods. For example, a merchant may claim the cost of a refrigerator from either or both parties, but he would have much more difficulty getting a husband to pay for a mink coat bought on credit by the wife, as the coat is not a household expense.

If I am a homemaker, financially dependent on my husband, and he is close with the money, do I have any legal recourse?

Generally the breadwinner is allowed to determine the standard of living for the family. If your husband is providing you with the basic necessities, a court would not step in and order him to give you additional money. However, if you are not receiving the necessities of life and must seek welfare assistance, a court may require your husband to provide you with more money to help meet your needs.

Charlie was disabled because of an accident. His wife, Mabel, has never worked. Must Mabel go out and get a job now that Charlie can't earn a living?

Yes. Provinces do not want families to become dependent on public support when one spouse has the ability to work. Since Charlie is unable to support himself or his family, Mabel must take over that responsibility. If Charlie is disabled to the point that he requires Mabel's constant attention, or if there are other family circumstances that prohibit her from working outside the home, the province would be more willing to consider providing some form of assistance to them. If the accident happened at work, Charlie would be eligible for income from the Workers' Compensation Board.

In some provinces, if he was injured in an auto accident, Charlie could be entitled to compensation from his provincial auto insurance board. But whatever the source of his injuries, if they have rendered Charlie permanently unemployable, he may be eligible for a disability pension under the Canada (or Quebec) Pension Plan.

We have been married for two years, but my husband refuses to pay me a dime for support. I've had to use an inheritance from my mother for my expenses. My husband says that he is entitled to half the inheritance and that I should get a job. Do I have to work, or does he have to pay my bills?

The law does not require that both spouses work. As long as you are receiving adequate financial support, the courts will not interfere with who provides it or how it is provided.

Your husband does have a legal obligation to provide you with such basic necessities as food, clothing, a place to live, and medical care. If your husband does not provide these things or give you the money to buy them, you have every right to charge them to him. If your husband won't pay the bill, the creditors may take you to court, where a judge may issue an order requiring him to pay.

If a wife has an income that can adequately support her, a court might rule that any debts she incurs are her own. A court might expect you to pay for your necessities out of your inheritance. However, your husband does not have a right to any of this money; the inheritance is yours to dispose of as you please.

Carrie bought some clothing on a layaway plan, expecting that her husband would pay for it. Is he required to do so?

It depends. A husband is not automatically required to cover all of his wife's obligations. If Carrie's husband is adequately providing her with clothing or giving her a sufficient allowance to buy it, he is not liable for completing her layaway purchases. If Carrie's purchase was a normal clothing acquisition for someone in her economic position, however, her husband would be responsible, as his obligation is based on her needs, his ability to pay and other circumstances such as his economic class.

My husband bought a $2,400 stereo system for his den. He made a $200 down payment and signed a contract to make monthly payments over the next two years. If he stops paying, could I be required to take over the payments?

No. If what your husband bought was a family necessity, you might be required to pay for it. But since a stereo is not a necessity, you cannot be held responsible. Generally, one spouse is not responsible for contracts made by the other. If the debt is in your husband's name, he is responsible for paying it. Under the married women's acts, a creditor cannot force you to settle your husband's debts for items that are not family necessities.

My wife used my credit card to buy a brand-new $2,500 fur coat. Am I obligated to pay for it?

Your duty to pay will be based in part on your past history with that particular credit card. If you have routinely given the card to your wife to use, you would be liable. By allowing her to use the card, you have given her your permission to make charges on that credit card in your name.

If your name alone was on the credit card application, but you requested a duplicate card for her use, you are still liable for the coat. However, if both names were on the application, you are both equally responsible for all charges, regardless of who made them.

My son-in-law, Jeremy, just purchased a house in his own name. If for some reason he defaults, will my daughter be liable for the monthly mortgage payments?

No. Since the title of the house is in Jeremy's name and your daughter did not sign any papers relating to the purchase, she would have no legal obligation to pay for the property. The bank, or other holder of the mortgage, cannot force her to make payments on the house.

Under certain provincial laws, however, the nonpaying spouse may have a legal interest in one half of the matrimonial home. If Jeremy ever does default, it would probably be in your daughter's interest to continue making the mortgage payments rather than lose the house to the bank or mortgage holder.

Is a husband responsible for debts incurred by his wife before they were married?

With recent decisions of the Supreme Court of Canada emphasizing the equality of the sexes and the obligation of each party to be self-sufficient, and with the federal Charter of Rights and Freedoms also emphasizing such sexual equality, the husband would not be responsible for debts incurred by his wife before marriage. Neither would the wife be responsible for her husband's prior debts. The husband would be liable, however, if he agreed to pay her debts and included such a promise in a prenuptial agreement, or if the wife transferred her assets to her husband in an attempt to defraud her creditors.

Family Responsibilities

If I run a newspaper notice stating that I am not responsible for my spouse's debts, will this protect me in any way?

A newspaper notice may not be an acceptable way to notify creditors of your limited liability. Actual notice should be sent to the merchants who have given you and your spouse credit in the past. However, some provinces require that you take out an advertisement in a local paper warning merchants who have never extended credit to you that you are no longer responsible for your spouse's debts.

To avoid liability, you would have to prove that, before the debt was incurred, the merchant *received* notice of your intention not to pay spousal debts.

Can I be held responsible for my husband's unpaid taxes?

Whether or not you are responsible for real estate and personal property taxes depends on your legal interest in the property. You do not automatically have a duty to pay taxes that are assessed on your spouse's property. The primary duty falls on the person who holds legal title to the property. If you and your husband held joint title, you would have to pay the taxes. Even if the property is not in your name, you may want to pay the taxes to avoid losing the property. For example, if title to the family home is in your husband's name, you may want to pay the taxes to prevent the sale of the home to meet tax obligations. There is nothing to prevent one person from paying another's taxes.

Bonnie's grandmother gave her a valuable collection of old coins. Does Bonnie's husband have any claim to this property?

No. Gifts and inheritances acquired while someone is married remain the individual property of that spouse even in Quebec, which has community of property (partnership of acquests) legislation.

Noreen earns $20,000 a year as a data processor and puts all that she earns in a savings account. Her husband wants to invest the money in a get-rich-quick scheme. He claims that as her husband he has just as much right to her earnings as she does. Is Noreen's husband correct?

Only if they live in Quebec, where community of property law (called partnership of acquests) exists. In that province, Noreen's husband would have equal rights to her bank account unless they have a marriage contract stating that their matrimonial regime is separation of property. Elsewhere, Noreen's husband would have no right to her bank account. All the other provinces and Territories have Married Women's Property acts, which give married women the right to hold, acquire and dispose of property as if they were single.

Eight months before she married Christopher, Joyce inherited a $5,000 bracelet. Does Christopher automatically obtain a half interest in the bracelet as a result of their marriage?

No. In all provinces, property owned by one party at the time of the marriage remains that person's personal property unless the couple, by prenuptial agreement, agrees to change this rule. Christopher has no right to Joyce's bracelet, since Joyce inherited it before their marriage. Neither would he have any rights if Joyce lost the bracelet and received insurance money for its replacement.

My husband wants us to open a joint bank account. How much of a joint account can a spouse withdraw? Does a large withdrawal require both signatures?

The general rule is that each person named on the joint bank account can withdraw funds without the other person's consent. Nothing prevents one spouse from making a total withdrawal, leaving a zero balance. Joint bank accounts are a bad idea as a general rule. They lead to more problems than individual accounts and provide few, if any, benefits.

Catherine's stepfather refuses to pay any of her bills. Does he have the right to do this?

At one time Catherine's stepfather would have had every right to refuse to support her, even while she is still a minor. The law recognized only the obligation of the natural mother and father to support their children, regardless of their marital status. The decision to have a child was viewed as a contract, with the natural parents agreeing to provide for the child as a term of the contract. Since the stepparent was not a part of that contract, the law imposed no obligation on the stepparent for support.

Today the courts tend to take the view that if someone acts like a parent toward his stepchildren, he is bound to provide for them financially until they reach legal age. In legal terms, Catherine's stepfather stands in *loco parentis* (in the place of a parent). Recent divorce rulings by both the Ontario Supreme Court and the Manitoba Queen's Bench have made stepfathers responsible for continuing to support their stepchildren even after the parent and stepparent divorce.

Family Responsibilities

Anita's father wants her to quit university and get a job. Anita, 20, still has one year to go to complete her university degree. Since she is no longer a minor, can she force her father to pay for her university education?

In some cases, yes. Since parents are obliged to see to the education and well-being of their children and since a university education is often seen as a normal way to properly prepare for the future, the Supreme Court has held that a parent is responsible for paying for his child's university education. The obligation to pay would doubtless take into account the parent's ability to pay and would probably not include studies for a second degree, nor studies at a foreign university or a private institution where a local public institution is available.

Against his parents' wishes, Victor moved in with some friends after graduating from high school. Are his parents still obligated to support him?

No. A parent's duty to provide necessities ends when a child becomes emancipated by reaching adult age, getting married, entering military service, or leaving home and becoming self-supporting. In this case, Victor would be considered emancipated and responsible for his own

The Changing Role of Stepparents

In the past the law did not require stepparents to support their stepchildren; child support was viewed solely as the responsibility of the natural parents. Nowadays, if the stepparent assumes the role of an absent natural parent—by making decisions about the children's education and welfare, supporting them financially, taking part in disciplining them, and holding himself out to be their parent— the courts will say that the stepparent is acting in *loco parentis*. In these circumstances, the stepparent has the rights and obligations of a natural parent.

The Divorce Act of 1986 defines a child of the marriage as "any child for whom one or both of the parents stand in the place of the parents." Therefore the court could order the stepparent to support stepchildren when the marriage ends in divorce. In fact many courts across Canada have done so, even in the case of children old enough to attend university. The distinction between parental obligations to natural children and to stepchildren is now quite blurred.

debts. However, if Victor's parents' conduct forced him to leave home before he reached adulthood—18 in most provinces—they could be required to support him until he becomes an adult or is able to support himself, whichever is earlier.

With six children in the family, Rosaleen is having a difficult time making ends meet. Her oldest daughter has taken a job after school. Is Rosaleen entitled to the money her daughter makes?

Yes. The law gives Rosaleen a right to claim any money earned by her minor children in exchange for her duty to support them. The obligation of support runs in two directions—from parents to children to grandchildren, and from children to their parents and, in some cases, to their grandparents.

Claire and David are engaged. Claire has a daughter from a previous marriage and wants to make certain the child is protected financially. What is Claire's best course of action?

David and Claire should work out a prenuptial agreement that will provide the financial protection Claire wants for her daughter. Provisions can be included requiring David to support Claire's daughter financially or to give up his share of Claire's estate if she dies first. David may agree to adopt Claire's daughter if the natural father consents or has abandoned the child.

Can a child sue his parents for not providing a good education?

No. A child's right to sue his parents has traditionally not been recognized. The courts want to preserve family unity and the right of parents to provide for their children in the ways they deem best. On the other hand, education is considered a necessity, and parents have a duty to provide it for their children. If parents prevented their child from going to school without just cause, provincial social agencies would enforce local attendance laws. And in some divorce cases, parents have been required by the court to pay their child's college tuition.

Is it true that parents can lose custody of their children if they are too poor to support them?

Although courts are reluctant to take children away from their parents, provincial child protection agencies will intervene to protect the children if the parents neglect or abuse them, or are unwilling or unable to support them. However, courts require that clear and convincing evidence be presented about the abuse, neglect, or lack of support before parental rights will be terminated and custody given to someone else. Poverty alone will not be a factor in determining custody.

What rights do natural parents have when their child is taken from them and placed in a foster home?

Unlike adoption, a child's placement in a foster home does not mean that the rights of the natural parents have ended. The state is considered to have physical custody of a child in a foster home, but the parents continue to be responsible for the child's support. Parents may or may not be allowed to visit the child, depending on the reasons for the child's removal from their home. This could be the result of an extended illness, abuse or neglect of the child, or a decision to put the child up for adoption. Foster care is a temporary measure that occurs as the result of a court order. Usually, the parent is unable or unwilling to provide adequate care.

In dealing with native children, the courts now attempt to protect the children's heritage by trying to place them with foster parents who share the same cultural values.

Does a spouse have a right to sexual relations?

Yes. A right to sexual relations is established when a marriage takes place. A spouse cannot deny sex to the other spouse without good cause—illness, for example. If one spouse continually refuses, the only remedy is divorce or annulment. Unjustified refusal to have sexual relations with your spouse could be considered mental cruelty. Forcing a spouse to have sexual relations could result in charges of sexual assault or assault and battery.

My husband is being transferred but I like where we are now. Must a wife move to a new city with her husband?

Traditionally, the husband, as the head of the household, had the right to determine where the family would live. The wife had a duty to follow him; her failure to do so was legal desertion and grounds for a divorce. Today, there is no legal requirement that a couple live together, although a refusal to move may still be used as a ground for divorce. The rule establishing equality of the sexes has abolished the former rule whereby the choice of residence was left to the husband.

Becoming a Foster Parent

To qualify as a foster parent, you must be at least 18 or 19 years old (depending on provincial law), pass a medical examination, and be fully self-supporting. You can be single or married, divorced, widowed, or separated—as long as you are of sound character and reputation. You need not own a home, but your dwelling place should have airy, well-lighted bedrooms that will not be used for any purpose but sleeping, and you must meet strict standards for the health and comfort of the children. By law, the children's natural parents are allowed to visit if it is considered to be in the children's best interests.

As a prospective foster parent you must undergo a series of searching interviews with people from a provincially approved child-assistance agency. These talks will give the agency some idea of your character, interests, and personal outlook, and thus help them to match you with the right children.

If all goes well, you will be given approval to board up to six children under the age of 18—the number of children varies from one province to another. This approval must be renewed yearly. The provinces hope that in addition to providing day-to-day care you will also bring the youngsters into the life of your community—with after-school programs, religious observances, and other activities that will teach them to get along well with others. Your reimbursement will be a monthly fee for the children's household expenses, plus possible further stipends for dental care, entertainment and other special needs. The fees are not intended to pay you for your services, but merely to cover each child's bed, board, and other expenses. In short, nobody gets rich from being a foster parent. It is a labor of love.

My husband has withdrawn thousands of dollars from my personal account to pay off some business losses. Is it legal for him to sign my name without first getting my permission?

No. The marital relationship does not automatically create a right to sign the other spouse's name on cheques, promissory notes, or contracts. But if you know that your spouse frequently signs your name to such things as cheques on your bank account and you have done nothing to stop it, you have ratified these acts and will probably be liable to the bank for your spouse's forgery. Furthermore, if you benefit financially from a loan obtained by your husband's forging your signature, you may also be responsible for repaying it. However, if a creditor cannot prove that a spouse participated in obtaining the loan or received any benefits from it, liability will not be imposed.

Alice and Mark want to adopt a child. Will they need a lawyer even if they are working through an adoption agency?

Yes, because the agency will have an attorney seeing to its interests throughout the adoption process. While Alice and Mark and the agency all share a common goal—a happy, successful adoption—it is always possible that some unexpected conflict of interest will arise. In that event, the agency's attorney will act exclusively on behalf of his client. So Mark and Alice should retain an attorney to act on their behalf and advise them about how to protect their interests.

Recently Ruth and Edward adopted a baby privately—that is, they and their lawyer dealt with the expectant mother directly instead of going through an agency. They had their lawyer pay all of the expectant mother's medical expenses plus a $5,000 bonus as well. Was this adoption legal?

Private adoptions are very rare in Canada and are permitted only in Manitoba, Ontario, New Brunswick and Newfoundland. Even in those provinces, there are restrictions. Ontario, New Brunswick and New-foundland allow private adoptions only where the prospective parents are close relatives to the child, or where it is the spouse of the child's surviving parent who wants to adopt. In Manitoba, the local family service agency must be notified of a private adoption and must investigate the prospective parents. All other adoptions in these provinces, and all adoptions elsewhere in the country, are handled throughout by the provincial family service organization, according to certain rules and formalities which ensure the welfare of the child.

Since Ruth and Edward are not close relatives of the child, and since they dealt directly with the child's mother without the intervention of the provincial adoption agency, their adoption would be illegal. The $5,000 bonus payment is also illegal as it tends to make an adoption a commercial affair.

Ruth and Edward stand to lose custody of the child and the money they paid. They are also likely to suffer a lot of pain and anguish because they tried to circumvent the law. Their lawyer could lose his license to practice law and may well face criminal charges.

Can an unmarried couple adopt a child?

Yes. However the policies of adoption agencies generally make it more difficult for an unmarried couple to adopt. Courts and placement agencies have always given distinct preference to married couples.

Adoption agencies are usually stricter in this regard than provincial laws. Nevertheless, opportunities for unmarried couples to adopt have been increasing, for two reasons: one is the growing need to find homes for older, less easily placed children; the other is society's growing acceptance of unmarried couples who live together.

Can a single person adopt a child?

Yes. Most provinces allow single persons to adopt children, although some courts still take the view that a child's well-being is best served if he is adopted by a married couple. Nonetheless, if a prospective single parent shows that he can provide the child with a stable home environment, financial security, and a supportive family, the courts are likely to approve the adoption.

Joan and Fred have been reading ads that say many foreign children are waiting to be adopted by Canadian couples. What special problems and procedures do overseas adoptions involve?

Adopting a child from abroad is complicated and frequently expensive because there is a great deal of paperwork to process, not only in Canada, but in the child's country, and a trip to that country is often required. However, the entire adoption process may take no longer than similar proceedings in this country. The process is complex because you must meet three sets of adoption requirements: those of your home province, those of Canada, and those of the foreign country. These requirements may include the following: adoption of the child before he is brought to Canada; the presence of at least one adoptive parent at the adoption proceedings; and the obtaining of both exit and entry visas for the child. The process also requires the adoptive parents to produce numerous supporting documents, such as birth and marriage certificates and statements of the couple's financial worth.

Is it a crime to adopt a baby by buying one on the black market?

Yes. It is illegal to buy or sell a child for profit. Violation of adoption laws can lead to criminal charges and stiff penalties.

Larry and Edith adopted a child from Mexico. Does this automatically make the child a Canadian citizen?

No. Not only is the child not a Canadian citizen: he does not even have the right to enter Canada as a resident (landed immigrant). Larry and

Adoption and Surrogate Parenting

Edith must get permission from Immigration Canada to sponsor their adopted son. The necessary visa or certificate of landing will only be given if the adoption laws of their province have been respected and the child passes a medical test. Certain other requirements of Immigration Canada must be met before the child can come to live in Canada. Once he has lived here for three years as a landed immigrant, he would be eligible for Canadian citizenship.

If my wife and I adopt a child and things don't work out, can we return the child to the adoption agency?

Yes, under certain circumstances. At the time of adoption, the court awards temporary custody of the child for a trial period usually lasting about six months. During this period representatives of the adoption agency conduct home studies to evaluate how the adoption is working out. Meanwhile, the adoptive parents themselves are constantly assessing the situation. If the trial period proves a disappointment, the final

Adopting a Child

If you want to adopt a child, don't be deterred by the long conferences with caseworkers, the blizzard of paperwork, and a seemingly endless wait between application and final adoption. The process helps to protect the adopted child's well-being. Of course if the child you wish to adopt has been living with you for a while, or is a blood relative, or the child of a new spouse, the adoption procedure will be simplified. Otherwise, the first step in adopting a child is finding the right agency.

Children's Aid societies, which exist in most cities and regions, sometimes under slightly different names, handle Canadian adoptions. Several other agencies bring abandoned or orphaned Third World children here for adoption. Contact your local department of social services for information about the agencies serving your province. Write or call those that interest you, and ask about the availability of children, age and medical requirements for prospective parents, restrictions about religion or family size, residence requirements, income requirements, and post-placement services or support groups.

The agency you select will ask you to fill out an application. You may also have to produce numerous documents, including birth certificate, financial records, photographs, verification of your employment, your marriage certificate, and divorce decrees, if any. Single people may also adopt children.

adoption papers are not issued. The child is then returned to the agency, which tries to arrange for a new adoption.

When Polly and Don got divorced, Polly won custody of their children. Don then left town and has not been heard from in five years. Can Bill, Polly's present husband, adopt the children without Don's consent?

Yes, but only under special conditions. First, every reasonable effort must be made to find Don and let him know about Bill's adoption petition so that he can, if he wishes, appear at the adoption hearing and argue against the termination of his parental rights. Some courts would approve the adoption if Don could not be found to give his consent, or if he were located but did not respond to the notice of the hearing. Other courts would give importance to Don's failure to communicate with his children for five years in determining whether or not his consent was required. Unless the court dispenses with the process of acquiring the child's consent, children 12 years or older (7 in Ontario, 10 in Quebec) must agree to the adoption.

When your application is approved, a home study period of several weeks or months will begin. During this time caseworkers will visit your home to get a clear picture of your life-style. The questions will be penetrating, and your answers should be frank. Caseworkers also investigate the background and special needs of the child to be adopted to help make a successful match. If you decide to adopt the child the agency offers, you will generally sign a placement agreement stating your willingness to accept financial responsibility for the child and your intent to adopt. The agency continues to be the child's legal guardian until the adoption is final.

To begin formal adoption you must file a petition with the court. The child welfare authority will be notified of your application and the date of the adoption hearing. This will be held in the judge's chambers or in a closed court. A probationary period of about six months will follow. During that time your caseworker will continue to visit your home to see how you and the child are adjusting to each other. After the probation, a second court hearing will be held and a final decree issued. Some provinces, British Columbia and Ontario for example, hold only one hearing, and it is preceded by the probationary period.

When the judge issues a final decree of adoption, an amended birth certificate is generally prepared, showing you as the child's parent. Adoption records are then placed in the court's files and sealed. They can be opened only by a court order.

Adoption and Surrogate Parenting

Beth and David, who are in their late forties, want to adopt her deceased brother's two young orphaned children. The couple, married for 20 years, have two children of their own, ages 18 and 16. Are Beth and David too old?

There is a good chance that the adoption will go through. While courts do take age into account, the likelihood here is that Beth and David will live long enough to care for the children until they reach maturity. Beth and David's situation is further strengthened by the fact that they are relatives of the children, have been married for many years, and have successfully raised their own children.

Harold's wife, Eleanor, has children by her previous marriage. Harold wants to adopt them. Is her consent to this enough?

No, there are several requirements. Harold's petition must be approved by a court that will consider many factors in addition to Eleanor's wishes. These factors include the children's feelings toward Harold and the couple's ability to provide a sound, stable family environment. Eleanor's consent will, of course, count strongly in favor of Harold's adoption petition. In addition, Eleanor's first husband, if still living, must give his consent and any of the children who are 12 years or older (7 in Ontario, 10 in Quebec) must consent in writing before being adopted.

Paul and Gail had known each other for only a few months when Gail became pregnant. Gail wants to put the baby up for adoption, but Paul wants to keep it. What are Paul's rights?

Paul faces an uphill fight, but he has a fair chance of winning custody. As one of the natural parents, he has legal rights superior to those of a prospective adoptive parent. The court would notify Paul of Gail's adoption petition and Paul could then object—showing, for example, that he can give the baby a good home and adequate financial support.

The courts usually respond favorably to a well-grounded request by the father to keep the child. It would also be very difficult for someone to adopt the child without Paul's consent if he can prove that he is the natural father of the child.

How do you put a child up for adoption?

Adoptions are arranged in two main ways: through a licensed adoption agency or through private placement. Both methods are closely monitored by the provincial department responsible for adoptions. Usually, the mother makes preliminary arrangements with a recognized agency while she is pregnant. When the child is born, the mother signs a consent form saying she is freely and willingly agreeing to end her parental rights by giving the baby to the agency for placement with another family.

Except in Manitoba, private adoptions are generally prohibited, although they are permitted in Ontario, New Brunswick and Newfoundland when the adopting parents are close relatives of the child.

In both methods of adoption, the adoptive parents must fulfill certain requirements and the adoption is not final until granted by a judge.

Sally had a baby out of wedlock and gave the child up for adoption. Now, two years later, Sally is married to the baby's father. Can the couple get their baby back?

Probably not. The big obstacle is the couple's two-year delay. Once an adoption is finalized, the court is very reluctant to return a child to his natural parents. The courts usually assume that the child has developed a strong emotional bond with the adoptive parents, and that pulling him out of this setting might be traumatic.

The fact that Sally has since married the natural father adds little weight to her request. Unless there is evidence that fraud or threat was used to get Sally's consent to give her baby up for adoption, her request will in all likelihood be denied.

If an unwed mother marries a man who is not the father of her child, is it necessary for him to go through adoption proceedings to have full rights as a father?

Yes. Until there is an adoption, there is no legal relationship between the child and the husband. Adoption is the procedure used to create the same legal status and rights that are automatically given to natural children. For instance, until a stepchild is adopted, he can inherit from his mother's husband only if he is specifically mentioned in the will.

If my son wants to put my grandson up for adoption, is there any way I can stop him?

No. The fact that you are the child's grandparent gives you no more legal rights in the matter than any stranger would have. So your son can terminate his parental rights if he so wishes. What you can do, however, is petition the court to allow you to adopt your grandson. If you can show that you have played a significant role in your grandson's life, and that there is a strong emotional bond between you, the court will be more likely to treat your petition favorably. Your age will no doubt count against you, but you may be able to get around this objection by showing that you can offer the child a fine home atmosphere.

Another approach would be to ask the court for the right to visit your grandson after his adoption takes place. Many provinces now have laws guaranteeing grandparents the right to ask the court for visitation rights. The decision to grant or withhold visiting rights will be based on the best interests of the child. You should check your local statutes, however, since many of them do not cover cases involving voluntary termination of parental rights.

Mike and Ellen arranged for a surrogate to have a child for them with Mike as the father. In the last month of her pregnancy, the surrogate announced that she planned to keep the baby. Can Mike and Ellen force her to give the child to them?

No province has yet passed legislation on surrogate parenting. As the law now stands, a natural mother would have the right to keep her own child. Furthermore, a child cannot be the object of a legal contract. It is extremely doubtful, therefore, that a court could order the natural mother to give her child to Mike and Ellen.

Steve and Dorothy have arranged for a surrogate mother to bear Steve's child for them. If the baby is born mentally or physically handicapped, must they accept and raise the child?

There is no clear-cut answer to this question. Essentially, everything depends on the agreement or contract Steve and Dorothy made with the surrogate mother. What does the contract say about genetic and birth defects? Does it require the mother to take medical tests to detect certain physical abnormalities in the unborn child? Does the contract guarantee the surrogate mother's right to continue the pregnancy despite the adopting parents' contrary wishes?

Perhaps the most important question of all is whether or not a contract for surrogate parenting is legal in Canada.

Is it legal for a couple to pay a fee to a surrogate mother to bear a child for them?

Until legislation is passed on surrogate parenting, any discussions on the legality of such a contract or its conditions would be mere supposition. But since everything that is not declared unlawful by law is legal, it would seem that surrogate parenting is now legal. However, it might be considered against public order and good morals to pay a surrogate mother a fee over and above the costs of bearing a child, since payments for this purpose could easily lead to the exploitation of poor women by richer people.

Unwed Parents

I had a child out of wedlock when I was 16. I am now 22 and about to marry the child's natural father. What can I do to get my child declared legitimate?

Even if you do nothing, your child will, in most provinces, be considered legitimate the moment you and the natural father marry. Once you are married, you should apply for a new birth certificate for your child, one listing your husband as the natural father. The certificate should be issued to you routinely, since your husband acknowledges the child as his own. (Yukon, British Columbia, Manitoba, Ontario and Quebec no longer distinguish between legitimate and illegitimate children.)

My husband and I got divorced while I was pregnant. Is my son considered legitimate?

Yes. Your child is presumed to be legitimate, since he was conceived while you were married. In fact, wherever possible, the law presumes that children are legitimate. Some provinces set a time limit for establishing legitimacy in situations involving annulment, separation, or divorce.

I was born out of wedlock, but my father later acknowledged me. Can I have my birth certificate changed?

Yes. For a small fee, your provincial bureau of vital statistics will change the name of a parent or a child on the certificate. Write and tell them what corrections you want. The bureau will send you the appropriate forms and instructions for completing them. In Quebec, applications to amend birth certificates must be filed with the Superior Court.

If I am pregnant and I marry a man who is not the child's father, whose name goes on the birth certificate as the father?

If both you and your husband agree to it, your husband's name will appear on the birth certificate, and the law will presume that he is the child's father. When the natural mother marries a man who is not the baby's natural father, according to the laws of each province, this man can have his name put on the child's birth certificate. Some provinces allow both parents' surnames to appear on the birth certificate.

A woman I know has filed a paternity suit against me. Can she force me to submit to a blood test?

It depends on where you live. The Appeal Court in Quebec has ruled that such a blood test contravenes the provincial Charter of Rights: the Quebec charter declares that the human body is inviolable. But an Ontario court has ordered such a test, on grounds that it does not violate the federal Charter of Rights and Freedoms. Nova Scotia courts will also order blood tests in paternity cases. No matter where you live, it may be in your interest to submit to such a test voluntarily, since it can not only verify but also disprove paternity. Thus legal wrangling can be avoided and court hearings shortened considerably.

Jim and Penny have had a stormy 10-year marriage. Now Penny is pregnant and Jim is convinced that the child is not his. What can Jim do about the situation?

If Jim does nothing and the child is born, the law will presume that Jim is the natural father. He can, however, go to court to prove he is not the father. Such proof might include evidence that he and Penny could not have had sexual relations during the time when she became pregnant. Or Jim might produce blood tests that indicate he could not be the father. Jim would also have to begin his legal action within a relatively short period after the child's birth—usually one year from his knowledge of the birth. If Jim could not prove his case, he would have to provide support until the child reached the age of adulthood.

Does an illegitimate child have the right to inherit money from his natural father's estate?

Yes, in some cases. Traditionally, an illegitimate child had no right to inherit from his natural father unless he was named in the father's will. But today illegitimate children are beginning to gain some inheritance rights. In Yukon, British Columbia, Manitoba, Ontario, Quebec, and New Brunswick, none of which distinguishes between legitimate and illegitimate children, natural children may inherit property from their father's estate, even in the absence of a will.

If a woman has a child by artificial insemination, will the child be considered legitimate?

A child's legitimacy depends solely on whether the mother is married or single. The fact of artificial insemination has no bearing on the matter. If the child is born to a married woman, the husband will be considered the father, even if the semen came from another man. This is a new area of law and only Quebec and Yukon have passed legislation on the subject.

Is it a crime for a father not to support his illegitimate child?

Yes. The law says that if a man has admitted being the father, or if a paternity suit has established that he is, he must support his child —whether or not the child is illegitimate.

Linda had a child by her boyfriend, Philip. They are not married, and Philip denies that the child is his. Can Linda force him to contribute to the cost of raising the child?

Yes. Linda's first step would be to go to court and bring a paternity suit against Philip to prove that he is the natural father. If Linda is successful in proving paternity, she can then petition the court for an order compelling Philip to pay child support.

John left me after we had lived together out of wedlock for a year. Six months later I had his baby. Now I want to bring a paternity action against him because I need financial help. What information must be presented to the court?

You will have to prove, first, that John is the father—unless, of course, he freely acknowledges that he is. Usually, you will have to file a formal declaration giving the date or dates on which you and John had sexual intercourse, the date you believe you became pregnant, and your child's date of birth. The declaration will also contain information on John's current employment and financial status, and on your expenses as a result of the pregnancy.

John will be notified of your action and given a chance to contest your paternity charge in court. As the child was conceived while you were living together, there would be a presumption that John is the father once you have proven that you had sexual relations with him during that time. John could contest this suit by trying to show that you had sexual relations with other men during this period and, depending on where you live, he could submit blood tests for himself and the child, to prove that he could not be the father.

Unwed Parents

My teenage daughter has had a child out of wedlock. Are we, the grandparents, responsible for the child's support?

In most cases, yes. If your daughter and her infant live with you, and your daughter is not able to support the child, you would be responsible for providing them with the necessities of life. The child's father and the paternal grandparents are also responsible for the child's maintenance and could be sued if they refuse to contribute.

Jenny had a daughter out of wedlock seven years ago. Is it too late for Jenny to sue the father for aid in supporting the child?

There is no time limit for Jenny to sue her daughter's natural father, whether she wants to prove paternity or to order him to support the child financially. However, most provinces have limits on retroactive payments. In Quebec, for example, the maximum for arrears of support is three years.

My son, who is 21, got his 18-year-old girlfriend pregnant. He does not want to marry her but is willing to help with the child's upbringing. Can we draw up a contract establishing how much support he has to pay?

Yes, but to be enforceable, the contract will have to be filed in court when the child is born. The court, however, is not bound by such an agreement if it considers its provisions unfair or insufficient in the circumstances.

Susan, who is now married to Brad, had a son by Joseph when she was still single. Joseph insists on visiting his son, often without notice. Can Susan keep Joseph from seeing his son?

Susan has only a moderate chance of legally denying Joseph the right to visit. If the case comes to court, and Joseph proves that he is the natural father, the court will first determine how much child support Joseph must pay. Then, unless there is evidence that visits from Joseph will not be in the child's best interest, the court will set up a reasonable visiting schedule.

The court rarely denies a parent reasonable access to his own child just because such visits and outings would be inconvenient for the other parent. In fact, the court's only concern is what benefits the child most, and the contact and affection of both parents have always been considered beneficial.

Children's Rights

Do children have the same legal rights as adults?

No. Children are denied the right to vote and, with some exceptions, to enter into valid contracts. Provincial laws define when they can marry, drive a car, purchase alcoholic beverages, write a will, select a guardian, or consent to adoption. Parents and other responsible persons have also been given the right to decide where children shall live, when they can quit school, and how their earnings should be spent. Some of these rights are granted fully when the child reaches maturity, 18 years of age in most provinces, 19 years in others. Other rights take effect when young people become emancipated by leaving home and living on their own.

However, children do have some rights similar to those enjoyed by adults—among them due process for youth court proceedings; a right to privacy in matters involving birth control and abortion; and a right to the full protection of the law in matters of school discipline.

We are encouraging our children to earn their own spending money. At what age can we let them work outside the home?

Federal and provincial laws strictly limit the age at which children can begin working and the types of jobs they can have. The minimum age limit varies from 14 in Nova Scotia to 16 in Manitoba and New Brunswick. The nature of a job is also a factor. For example, children must be at least 16 years old to work on construction sites in Ontario and Nova Scotia, and only persons 18 years or older may work in a mine or on construction in Quebec.

There is no minimum age for jobs such as lawn mowing, baby-sitting, snow shoveling and delivering papers. But these may not be done by children during school hours if the children should be in school.

Karen and Chuck have a 14-year-old son who works after school and on weekends in the small health food store the couple own and run. Isn't this against the law?

No, in this instance the youngster's activity is legal. Although there are federal and provincial laws prohibiting child labor, an exception is made when the minor is the employer's child. The law allows a minor to be employed by his parents even when he is under 16 years of age.

However, even when employed by a parent, the child cannot engage in mining or manufacturing, or work in any field that would be unhealthy or otherwise detrimental to a child's well-being. Since Karen and Chuck run a small store that seems to pose no danger to their son's health, no laws are being broken.

Children's Rights

When our son Alex, who is 15, applied for a job, the manager told him he would be expected to work four hours on each weeknight and eight hours on weekends. Isn't there a limit on the number of hours schoolchildren are allowed to work?

Yes. The federal and provincial governments regulate the number of hours and the times anyone under 18 years of age may work. To ensure children are not abused or too tired to attend school the next day, the laws usually forbid more than three hours of work on school days (two hours in Alberta), and forbid working between 10 p.m. and 6 a.m. Since the laws vary somewhat from province to province, check with your provincial ministry of labor to see exactly how many hours your son can work and whether he is old enough to work in that type of job.

Choosing a Day-care Center

If you work days and cannot have a person come in and care for your child at home, you'll need to find a day-care center that will give him all the loving care he needs. In checking out possible day-care centers, you should remember that they have legal obligations to the youngsters who attend them. Some of the obligations are spelled out in specific laws. Others derive from more general laws, such as those calling for safe and sanitary facilities in places of public assembly. Here are some of the things you should look for:

☑ Does the center have a valid license to operate?

☑ Is there reliable transportation to and from the center? Are the drivers bonded and properly licensed? Are the vehicles in good condition? Do they have seat belts?

☑ Does the center have an efficient safety system for fires and other emergencies? Are fire drills held regularly?

☑ Is there enough heat, light, and ventilation?

☑ Are there safety caps on the electrical outlets?

☑ Are there toddlerproof screens or bars on upper-floor windows, and protective gates on stairs?

☑ Are the radiators covered or the heaters protected?

☑ Are incandescent lights at least three feet from the ground?

☑ Is the equipment safe and in good repair?

☑ Is there a well-stocked medicine chest and a "sick bay" area?

☑ Are medicines, cleansers, matches, sharp instruments, and other dangerous items stored out of the children's reach?

☑ Are there enough clean bathrooms?

***My 15-year-old daughter does a lot of baby-sitting. Can she be
sued if a child is injured while in her care?***

Yes. A baby-sitter—even a child—has a duty to take reasonable
precautions to ensure the safety of others. Your daughter's youth will not
relieve her of liability if a child in her care is injured because of her
negligence. She is responsible for her actions and can be sued if she
contributes in any way to a child's injury.

***Can a baby-sitter give consent to emergency surgery or medical
treatment for an injured child if the parents cannot be reached?***

No. A baby-sitter has no authority to give consent to any sort of medical
treatment. Unless an emergency exists, medical personnel will delay

☑ Are there cribs, cots, and other napping facilities?

☑ Are there indoor and outdoor play areas that allow each child a
generous amount of personal space?

☑ Are employees thoroughly screened before being hired? How
much does the director know about their credentials and prior
experience in working with children?

☑ Do the employees take yearly physical exams?

☑ Are the employees warm and friendly? Are there enough
employees to give sufficient attention to all the children?

☑ Do the employees respect your cultural values and religious beliefs?

☑ Is the center equipped to keep food from spoiling?

☑ Do the employees encourage healthful habits, such as always
washing hands before meals?

☑ Are the toys and activities appropriate to the age of your child?

☑ Are the children given opportunities to learn about their own
culture and the culture of others through art, music, and games?

☑ Are the premises secure against intruders?

☑ Are parents free to visit unannounced, without appointments?

☑ What is the reputation of the center and how long has it been in
operation?

☑ Are the children's activities structured and well planned?

☑ How many children will be assigned to each day-care worker?

☑ Are there any government subsidies that will reduce my child's fees
there?

☑ What time does the center open and close?

☑ What are the penalties for picking up my child late?

treatment and try to reach the parents, who ordinarily are the only ones who can give such consent. When a parent cannot be reached in an emergency, the provincial director of youth protection may give his consent, or the doctor or hospital staff may decide whether a minor shall be given treatment.

My three-year-old son, Bobby, was injured while playing outside at a day-care center. I've noticed before that the center has poorly maintained playground equipment. Who should be notified about this problem?

You should notify the director of the day-care center immediately so that the faulty equipment can be repaired or thrown out. The center could be held liable for your son's injury. Should the problem continue to go uncorrected, find out what provincial agency is responsible for licensing and regulating day-care centers. Then contact this agency and report your concern about the safety of the playground equipment. The name of this agency varies from province to province, but there is almost always a department of social services that will be able to help you or direct you to the right place.

Andrew's parents were killed in a two-car crash in which the driver of the other car was intoxicated. Can Andrew sue the other driver, and if so, what sort of damages might be awarded?

It depends on where Andrew lives. The laws concerning injuries and deaths from auto accidents vary greatly from one province to another. In Quebec, which has a comprehensive auto insurance law, he would not be able to sue the driver but would receive compensation from the provincial government. In Ontario, he could sue the driver for loss of his parents' advice, guidance and companionship; loss of his parents' financial support; loss of his parents' services at home. Other provinces have limits on the type of damages Andrew could claim.

Andrew might also be eligible for an orphan's pension from the Canada (or Quebec) Pension Plan.

What happens to money that a child inherits?

Money inherited by a child is usually placed in trust for the benefit of that child until he reaches adulthood or some later, specified age. This procedure is followed because a child is not considered capable of managing large sums of money. Unless the court appoints someone else, a parent acts as guardian of the inheritance and is legally responsible for handling it properly.

Edna inherited $5,000 from her grandmother, and the court appointed Edna's father to handle the money until Edna reached 18. Edna is now 18 and finds that her father has spent the money for his own purposes. Can Edna sue her father for these funds?

Yes. As the court-appointed trustee, her father had a legal duty to (1) act in Edna's best interest, (2) use care and skill in managing her money, and (3) not use her funds for his personal enrichment. By spending Edna's money for his own purposes, her father violated his duties as trustee. He is personally liable and accountable to Edna. She may go to court and sue him for the missing money.

Rights of Adopted Children

What rights does a child have regarding his own adoption?

Children today have considerable say about what happens in their own adoptions. Provincial adoption laws now require that children above a certain age freely consent to the adoption. This is 12 years in all provinces except Quebec, where it is 10, and Ontario, where a child of 7 must give his consent. In Ontario, a child must have an opportunity to obtain counseling and independent legal advice concerning his consent.

Do adopted children have the same legal rights as the natural children in the family?

Yes. Once an adoption has been finalized through a judgment of adoption by the appropriate family court, the adopted child has all the rights and obligations of a child born to the adopting couple. On the other hand, the parent or parents who gave up their child for adoption lose all rights and obligations they may have had concerning the child.

Christine was adopted when she was two years old. She is now 35 and has learned that her natural mother has died. Does Christine have a right to share in her mother's estate?

Once an adoption is final, there is no longer any legal connection between a child and its natural parents. These ties are completely severed by the adoption order, which also transfers all the child's rights

Rights of Adopted Children

and obligations to the adopting parents. It is unlikely, therefore, that Christine can inherit from her natural mother if there is no specific bequest in the will, or if there is no valid will.

Patrick's adoptive father died without making a will. Can Patrick claim part of the estate?

Yes. An adopted child has the same legal right to inherit from his adoptive parents as any other child born to his parents. Patrick can make his claim as any other son would. But when there is no will, the laws decide who will inherit what. Since these laws vary from province to province, Patrick should find out what his province's inheritance laws say.

Children in Trouble

Juvenile misdemeanors and crimes are covered in "Young Offenders" in Chapter 17, *Victims and Crimes.*

My six-year-old accidentally broke a vase in a department store. Must I pay for it?

It depends. Parents have a duty to look after their children and to see that they act in a reasonable manner. If your son was known to be very active and had previous "accidents," you may be held responsible for your lack of supervision. If, however, your child has a reputation for being an obedient child and the accident was unforeseeable, you would not be responsible for the broken vase.

Connie and David allow their 17-year-old son to drink beer at home. Are they breaking the law? What if they also let his friends drink beer in their home?

Every province has laws prohibiting the sale, gift, or furnishing of alcoholic beverages to minors. However, the laws do not apply when children drink alcohol in their own home with the consent of their parents. This is because parents stand in a special relationship to their children and are allowed to make decisions about their upbringing. Therefore Connie and David are not breaking the law by serving beer to their 17-year-old son at home.

They would be acting illegally, however, if they served alcoholic drinks to their son's friends or allowed minors to drink beer in their home— unless they had the consent of the young people's parents.

My son hit a home run through someone's $900 front window. Is it true I don't have to pay?

Yes. Your son is responsible for his own actions. The only times a parent is liable for a child's actions are (1) when the parent knew the child was doing something wrong and didn't try to prevent it, (2) when the child was acting on the parent's behalf, (3) when the parent contributed to the damage by giving the child something dangerous to play with, or (4) when the parent did not bring up the child properly. The home-owner with the broken window is not without recourse, though. He can file a claim with his insurance company.

Are parents held responsible if their children are caught using or selling illegal drugs?

No. The special relationship of parent to child does not make a parent liable for a child's criminal act. Some provinces hold parents liable when their children intentionally cause property damage, but these laws do not apply to criminal cases.

If the Police Ask Questions About Your Child

Suppose an officer of the law arrives at your front door and tells you that the police are investigating a recent crime—an outbreak of, say, vandalism in the neighborhood—and he wants to question you about your child. How should you respond? Here are some guidelines:

- Ask for details of the crime and find out precisely how your child is supposed to be involved.
- Provide only general information about your child, such as name, age, and a physical description.
- Don't volunteer information that could be damaging to your child— anything you say might be used against your child in court.
- If you want to talk to your child before answering any questions, request a later meeting with the police.
- Remember that both you and your child have the right to refuse to answer questions even if you have nothing to hide.
- If the police take your child into custody, you have the right to know where he will be taken and held. The police may not place your child in a jail cell with adults; he must be held in an area for juveniles only.
- He must be brought before a judge as soon as possible. The judge will decide if it is necessary for him to remain in detention.
- Try to make sure that your son was informed of his right to speak with a lawyer before he answered any questions. If he was not told of this right, any charges against him may be dismissed.

Children in Trouble

Ralph and Betty's 15-year-old son is completely out of control. He doesn't go to school, stays out all night, drinks, and steals money from his parents. What will the authorities do if Ralph and Betty can't stop this behavior?

All provinces and Territories have laws dealing with child protection, and a child who constantly disobeys his parents, doesn't go to school, steals, and is otherwise unmanageable would be "in need of protection." His security and development are obviously at risk. The agency responsible for child protection in Ralph and Betty's province has several options for dealing with their son. It can recommend counseling or temporary care outside the home. In some cases, the agency may place the child in a group home or youth detention center.

Should I call the police if my child has run away?

Yes. Many police departments have computer networks linked to provincial and federal systems designed to help locate missing children. The police can also supply you with names and telephone numbers of local and national social service organizations that can help you.

MARRIAGE AND FAMILY

What to Do If Your Child Is Missing

You are far from helpless if your child is missing: a nationwide computer network of police departments and several social service agencies stand ready to assist you in locating your youngster. The steps you should take are as follows:

1. Make a quick check of your home and neighborhood, looking into such places as abandoned refrigerators and little-used crawl spaces.

2. Ask your neighbors and the child's closest friends if they have seen him; many children are found surprisingly close to home.

3. Assemble background information the police may ask for: photographs, names of the child's teachers, favorite hangouts, and a full physical description, including height, weight, color of hair and eyes, birth date, and other identifying characteristics.

4. Notify the police. Information about the youngster will then be available to law enforcement officials throughout the nation. If your child shows up far from home, he can be readily identified.

5. Mount a campaign of your own. Distribute posters and leaflets with the child's picture and description, date of disappearance, reward offered, if any, and where you can be reached.

Harvey lives next door with his 14-year-old son, Maurice. My 13-year-old son, Robert, received some bad cuts and bruises when Maurice beat him up recently. How can I make Harvey pay for what happened?

Ordinarily you could not make Harvey pay for the injuries Maurice inflicted on your son, because the law does not hold parents liable for their children's actions. If Harvey did not encourage his son to fight with your son, and the fight was simply one of the boyish rites of growing up, Harvey could not be held liable. You would have to prove that Harvey committed some kind of fault before he could be held responsible for his son's action.

My son used false identification to buy some liquor the other night. Can he be arrested for this?

Yes. Not only could your son face criminal charges, but the person who let him use the false identification could be charged as well. Your son's use of false identification is a summary conviction offense punishable by a jail sentence, a fine, or both. If the identification that he presented when he bought the liquor was a false or altered driver's license, he could also have his driving privileges suspended.

6. Notify your local TV station and Child Find office.

7. Publish information in local newspapers, shopper's guides, and any other publications that will accept it. Post it on shopping center bulletin boards and any other places you can think of.

8. Check with local hospitals, medical centers, and morgues. The police will probably have done this already, but hearing from you directly may encourage these facilities to check more thoroughly.

9. If your child is a teenager, call the nearest armed forces recruiting office to find out if he has tried to sign up.

10. Ask the Passport Office in Ottawa if the youngster has applied for a passport. If so, the application may give an address where he can be located.

11. If the child has a credit card, ask the issuing company if it has a record of any current purchases, which might supply clues to the place where the child may be staying.

Don't give up hope—thousands of runaway, kidnapped, and missing children have been located by parents who have doggedly run down leads furnished by sources such as those listed here.

Children in Trouble

My 19-year-old son is a troublemaker. Am I within my rights in making him leave the house and support himself?

Yes. The law does not impose a legal obligation on parents to support children who have reached the age of adulthood unless a child is physically or mentally disabled. Adulthood is reached at 18 years in most provinces; at 19 in others. You would of course have a legal obligation to support an adult child who is a student. But even then, if he is a troublemaker, your obligation to support him could be canceled and he could be forced to leave your home.

Am I liable if my child has an accident while driving my car?

Yes. In almost all provinces, both the owner and the driver may be held responsible for property damages and bodily injuries. If the vehicle was used without your permission, however, you may be relieved of liability. In Quebec, where there is a comprehensive no-fault plan, neither the driver nor the owner are financially liable for bodily damages. In British Columbia, Saskatchewan and Manitoba, the government no-fault plan pays for most expenses and injuries, and the injured party can sue the other for any loss not covered by the government plan.

Mike's 14-year-old son borrowed a motorcycle from a senior at his high school. He lost control of the bike, hit the maintenance building at school, and set it on fire. Is Mike responsible for the $15,000 damage to the building?

No, not in this case. Parents are not responsible for the negligent acts of their children except in three situations: if they are aware of their child's tendency to act irresponsibly, if the child is acting on the parent's behalf at the time of the accident, or if the parent contributed to the child's negligence in some way. None of these three cases apply to Mike's son.

My son's driver's license has been revoked, and I have forbidden him to drive our car. What is my liability if he disobeys me?

If you have expressly forbidden him to drive your car, you would not be liable. It would be to your benefit to establish that you not only refused to allow your son to drive but also tried to make sure he did not get another set of keys. If you knew that your son was reckless and disobedient, however, and you had taken no action to ensure your orders would be obeyed, you may be held liable because of your lack of supervision.

Going to School

Whose responsibility is it to see that children attend school?

Parents of school-age children, as well as foster parents and guardians, are required to see that their children attend school regularly.

Can parents be held criminally responsible if their child doesn't attend school?

Yes. A parent or guardian who fails to send a child to school commits an offense, and a court may impose a fine or even a prison sentence in unusually blatant cases.

Howard's parents are not pleased with his progress in their public elementary school. Is it legal for them to take Howard out of school and teach him at home?

It may be, if Howard's parents can provide him with an education that is equivalent to what he's receiving in school. Usually, this means (1) one of the parents must be competent to teach the subjects Howard studies in school, or (2) they must provide him with a qualified teacher. In addition, the amount of time Howard spends in home study each day must roughly equal the time he would have spent in school. The school district might also require Howard to use approved textbooks and other materials. And an inspector from the ministry of education might check from time to time to see if all requirements are being met.

I've just discovered that my child has been sneaking out of school. What will happen to him if he continues to be absent?

A child who refuses to attend school as required by law is classified as a truant, and the law provides a variety of disciplinary tools. These range from reducing the child's grades to sending him to a special school or even charging him under the provincial youth protection act.

Pete, our neighbors' 15-year-old son, was picked up for truancy. Does he have to go to court for such a minor incident?

If Pete was truant just this once, the school authorities would expect his parents to deal with the problem themselves. But if he becomes a chronic truant and his parents are unable to remedy the situation, Pete may have to go to youth court.

Going to School

Greg's son, Matthew, was expelled from school for arguing with a teacher. Isn't the school required to readmit him?

If Matthew's only offense was arguing with a teacher, he will probably be allowed to return to school soon. Students who disobey reasonable rules may be punished, but the punishment must also be reasonable. Only those students who are so disruptive that they prevent the school from performing its function may be expelled permanently.

Our school requires children to be vaccinated against certain diseases. Must we comply?

In most instances students must be vaccinated to prevent the spread of communicable diseases. In some cases exceptions may be made for members of certain religious groups that oppose vaccinations. If you are not a member of one of these religions, you may be subject to criminal penalties for failing to have your child vaccinated. It would be best to discuss the matter of compulsory vaccination with your school board, and if you are unhappy with the outcome, you should contact your provincial ombudsman.

John does not want his daughter to participate in the sex education classes in her junior high school. Does he have a right to keep her from going to the classes?

At one time courts gave their consent when parents insisted that their children be excused from sex education classes. Recently courts have been stricter about this issue and have been requiring students to attend a class even when they or their parents object to its contents. But many school authorities recognize that the issue of sex education is a sensitive one, and have established guidelines for excusing students who object. John should contact his local school board to learn its policy regarding sex education classes.

When our family transferred to a new city, we were surprised to learn that our children started their school day with a moment of silence for prayer. Isn't this against the law?

No. Although it may be unlawful for a school board to order all children to participate in a particular prayer or religious activity, a moment of silence would not violate the freedom of religious belief guaranteed by the Charter of Rights and Freedoms.

Can we take our children out of public school during the week to attend religious instruction classes at a church school? Could we have someone from the church come to the public school to conduct religious classes?

You can take your children out of school to attend religious instruction classes, but a church teacher cannot come to a public school to conduct religious instruction. Your children's religious instruction cannot be held in public classrooms. No expenses can be incurred or administrative time allotted by a public school for religious instruction.

The high school principal has decided that boys who wear earrings may not attend school. Is this enforceable?

Schools can make reasonable rules concerning the dress and appearance of students. In the past 20 years, a number of courts have wrestled with what constitutes reasonable rules. It is impossible to generalize, since much depends on the facts of each case as well as current social attitudes and the standards of the community. But a principal is required by law to maintain order and discipline in his school, and the wearing of an earring by a student may disrupt that order and discipline.

Kevin plays on the high school football team. He broke a tooth during a scrimmage. Isn't the school liable for his dental bills?

Not unless the school or its employees were responsible in some way for Kevin's mishap. For example, if Kevin's accident occurred because the football field was improperly maintained, or if the school didn't provide adequate protective equipment, the school would probably be held liable. The school cannot be responsible for Kevin's absolute safety. Most courts would say that since football is known to be dangerous, Kevin had assumed the risk of injury when he played.

Eddy's fourth-grade teacher slapped his face for talking in class. Can his parents have the teacher reprimanded for her actions?

It depends on provincial law and school district policy. Some provinces have an outright ban on corporal punishment; others permit only the principal to administer it; some require the parents to be notified first. No province permits excessive or unreasonable punishment.

Eddy's parents should call this incident to the attention of the principal and the school board. If the slapping was unreasonable or unauthorized, the teacher may be subject to reprimand or dismissal, and the teacher and the school board may be liable for damages.

Going to School

Philomena is a third-grade public schoolteacher. She has noticed that one of her students has arrived at school several times in the last few months with big bruises on his arms and neck. Should she report this to someone?

Yes. Anyone who believes that a child is the victim of child abuse has a duty to report the case. Failure to do so is a criminal offense in most provinces, although a few simply require certain individuals to report suspected cases of abuse. Professionals such as doctors, nurses, teachers, and other school personnel are generally included among those who must report.

In some provinces Philomena would report her observations directly to the appropriate agency; in others she would tell her principal of her suspicions, and he would turn in the report.

Correcting Your Child's Public School Records

Inaccurate public school records may prejudice teachers and school officials against your child as he moves up through the grades and may reduce his chances of getting into the college of his choice. The provincial education acts and regulations allow parents to inspect their child's public school records and to request the correction of inaccurate entries. Once the child is 18 years old or attends a postsecondary school, he too has the right to see these records. Corrections should be limited to matters other than grades: a grade will not be changed unless it was incorrectly recorded.

If you suspect that your child's school record is inaccurate, write to the principal asking to see the file. If you get no reply after 45 days, or if the school refuses to let you see the file, write to the minister of education or get in touch with the provincial ombudsman.

After examining the file, discuss your concerns with the principal and present a written request detailing the changes you want and your reasons for making them. If the school refuses to make the changes, contact the principal or the superintendent of the school district and request a hearing.

At the hearing you will be given an opportunity to present evidence showing why the statements in your child's record should be changed. You may have a lawyer represent you, if you wish. Afterward, the hearing officer will inform the school officials of his decision, and they will decide whether or not to change the records—they have the right to disregard the hearing officer's decision. If you are not satisfied, you may exercise your right to include your side of the case in your child's record.

Can a girl be suspended from school because she is pregnant?

No. A student cannot be excluded from a public school simply because she is pregnant. A pregnant student's presence in school is not considered disruptive enough to warrant suspension.

Does a college assume my parental rights and responsibilities when my child lives on campus?

Although it was once agreed that colleges stood *in loco parentis* (in the place of a parent) in matters of discipline, very few colleges today attempt to regulate their students' behavior the way they used to. Except at some private and religious schools, students are generally held responsible for their actions. Nowadays, many college dormitories make no attempt to segregate residents by sex. Allowing male and female students to live side by side would have been unimaginable 30 years ago.

Guardians for Children

Under what circumstances does a child need a guardian?

A child needs a guardian if his parents are dead, or unfit or unable to protect, discipline, feed, or take care of him. The fact that parents have financial difficulties is not enough to create a need for the appointment of a guardian. If there is severe financial need, provincial or local agencies will help the family obtain food or social welfare assistance before considering the appointment of a guardian.

Can a child ever choose who will be his guardian?

If a child is in his early teens, he may choose his own guardian, subject to the court's approval. If the court rejects the child's nomination, he has a right to make another selection. If the child does not meet the age requirements for selecting his own guardian, the court may still consider the child's wishes when making its decision.

What are the duties of a guardian?

A guardian must provide for his ward's support, education, and religious training, as well as protect the ward's financial assets. Courts will generally allow a guardian to use income—but not the principal— from a ward's property, or estate, to pay for the child's needs and educational expenses. When the child reaches adulthood, the guardian must report on his stewardship. If the guardian used the money for his own purposes, or was otherwise a bad administrator, the court would probably order him to reimburse the estate with interest.

As a guardian, do I have to spend any of my own money to provide proper care for my ward?

Yes, in some situations. If there are insufficient assets in the estate to pay for your ward's care, and government benefits and programs do not provide enough to meet these needs, you may have to use your own money to provide support for your ward. If you fail to provide adequate support, the court may award custody to someone else.

What factors are considered when a judge is deciding whom to appoint as guardian?

The judge will consider age, health, financial condition, moral character, and emotional stability in choosing a guardian. The judge will also try to appoint a guardian who holds the same religious beliefs as the child. The child's own preferences will be taken into account if he is mature enough to understand what is going on. A parent or relative who has the right qualifications would be preferred to a stranger. (In Quebec, guardians are known as tutors.)

The court wants to appoint someone as guardian for Paula's son. What effect will that have on her rights as a mother?

The decision to appoint a guardian for Paula's son is a serious matter involving a court ruling that she is unfit or unable to care for him. Thus her son will be expected to live with the guardian, and the guardian will take on full responsibility for the boy's upbringing and education. However, if the court decides it is in the child's best interest, it may grant Paula the right to visit her son.

I have been asked to serve as guardian for my niece. If I agree, will I be paid for my time?

A guardian is not paid for his services but is entitled to reasonable expenses from the minor's estate. If the minor and the guardian disagree about the amount, the court will decide what the guardian should get.

As my nephew's guardian, I invested some of his funds in stock whose value dropped. Will I have to replace the money thus lost?

You might well have to replace the money. As your nephew's guardian you are expected to protect his estate from losses. If you had invested in securities that are ordinarily safe, you would not be liable, but you would certainly be responsible if you invested in highly speculative stocks. Some provinces restrict the kind of investments a guardian may make. Usually a guardian may not sell or mortgage any real estate belonging to the child without the court's permission.

If my ward gets married, does that end my guardianship?

As a general rule, the marriage would end your authority and control over your ward's personal life. A minor is considered emancipated by marriage and able to look after his own interests.

Family Problems

What are a woman's legal rights to have an abortion?

The Supreme Court has ruled that a woman has a legal right to an abortion. Prior to the court's 1988 decision in the Morgentaler case, an abortion was permitted only when the life or health of the mother was at stake, and then only with the approval of a committee of three doctors. The judges found that these restrictions violated the Charter of Rights and Freedoms, thus overturning Canada's existing abortion legislation. As a result, new laws will have to be passed on this difficult issue. At the time of writing, these had not yet been tabled in Parliament.

Must a woman get her husband's permission for an abortion?

A married woman does not need the permission of her husband or anyone else in order to get an abortion. However, getting an abortion against the wishes of her husband might give him grounds for divorce.

If a test shows that a fetus is brain-damaged, does the father have the right to force his wife to have an abortion?

No. Since a married woman does not need her husband's permission for an abortion, the opposite is also true—she does not need her husband's permission to have the baby.

Family Problems

Roy's 16-year-old daughter plans to have an abortion. Is there anything Roy can do to stop her?

Ordinarily a parent or guardian must give consent for surgery on a minor but, in view of a 1988 decision by the Supreme Court, this may no longer apply to abortions. The requirement may violate Roy's daughter's right to equal protection and benefit of the law without discrimination on the basis of age, or her right to liberty and security of the person. Both rights are guaranteed in the Charter of Rights and Freedoms, which overrides any other law.

Kermit's girlfriend is pregnant and wants to have an abortion. He doesn't want to marry her, but he does want her to go ahead and have his baby. Can he prevent her from having the abortion?

No. A husband cannot prevent his wife from having an abortion, nor can a man who is not married to the pregnant woman prevent her from ending the pregnancy with an abortion.

My husband attacked me, and I injured him while trying to defend myself. Would this be considered self-defense under the law?

Yes, it is self-defense as long as your actions do not continue to the point of retaliation or vengeance. You can take whatever steps are necessary to resist force and avoid harm to yourself. Using a weapon may be considered self-defense if you are smaller and weaker than your husband. However, if you pursue and injure him with a weapon after he has retreated, this would not be considered self-defense, and you could be prosecuted.

My husband physically abuses me. What legal steps can I take to protect myself?

You should call the police and report the abuse. In most provinces you will have to file a formal complaint before the police will conduct an investigation. If necessary, they will arrest your husband as the first step in criminal proceedings against him. The police themselves may charge your husband with assault, even if you would rather forget the incident.

In most provinces, you can protect yourself from further violence by requesting a court to issue an order restraining your husband. If he ignores this order, you can bring criminal charges against him.

If it is impossible for you to remain in the home with your husband, you should find a family shelter where you and your children can reside temporarily. An attempt should be made to have your husband receive counseling to help him come to grips with his problems. If you do not believe your husband will stop abusing you, you should consider a legal separation or a divorce.

You could also sue your husband in civil court for damages or claim compensation from your provincial crime victims' indemnity board.

Anne and Phil have been married for 10 years. Recently Phil has been drinking heavily and physically abusing Anne. Phil says that there is nothing she can do about it, because a wife cannot testify against her husband. Is this true?

No. Husbands and wives may testify against each other in marital disputes. A wife may always testify against her husband when she has accused him of physical abuse. By law, one spouse cannot be *forced* to testify against the other but a spouse may voluntarily testify, especially when he or she is a victim of the other.

Mary called the police and reported that she had been sexually assaulted by her husband, Bill. When the police arrived, Bill just laughed and claimed he was only exercising his "rights as a husband." Can the police arrest Bill?

In the past Bill would have been correct. Legislatures and courts did not define sexual assault to include an act by one spouse against the other. But this is an area in which the law has changed substantially in recent years. Today a husband may be charged with sexual assault against his wife if he forces her to have sex with him against her wishes. Being married is no longer a defense against such a charge.

Sandra left her husband but now she's living in fear that he will hurt her if he finds out where she is staying. Does she have any way of getting legal protection?

Yes. If Sandra's husband has hurt her in the past, she should ask her local prosecuting attorney's office to petition the court to order her husband to keep the peace. Once the court issues such an order, she should carry it with her at all times. If her husband threatens her, she can call the police, show them the order, and have her husband arrested. Even threatening someone with violence is a criminal offense.

Sandra can also apply for a court injunction ordering her husband not to communicate with or bother her. This injunction would be part of legal separation or divorce proceedings.

MARRIAGE AND FAMILY

Family Problems

If we take our child to the doctor for treatment of some serious cuts and bruises, is he required to report this to the authorities if he suspects child abuse?

Yes. A doctor is required by law to report to the appropriate agency whenever he has reasonable cause to believe a child has been abused or neglected. A doctor who fails to report suspected abuse may be subject to criminal penalties. If your doctor concludes that the cuts and bruises on your child are only the normal bangs and scrapes of growing up, he will not report anything.

I believe in spanking my children, but my husband is taking matters too far. Last month my daughter Jill needed six stitches after a "spanking." What can I do?

If you are not able to persuade your husband to seek counseling to help him with his problems, you should file a complaint with the local or

Reporting Child Abuse

If you suspect or are aware of a case of child abuse, you should report the matter immediately to your provincial child protection agency. Under the law, your name must be kept confidential; so you need not worry that the abuser will learn your identity. Nurses, doctors, teachers, and other professionals who deal with children are legally required to report child abuse cases that come to their attention. If you are the parent of a child who is being abused at home and you do nothing to stop the abuse, you may be committing a crime. If you do not take steps to stop your spouse from abusing your child, for example, you as well as your spouse could face criminal charges. It is also likely that your child would be removed from your custody.

The first step in a child abuse investigation is a visit to the child's home by a social worker. If the report of the child's situation proves accurate, the social worker will make recommendations—such as moving the child to a safer environment. The state then draws up a plan to improve the family situation. This plan may include counseling, day-care services, financial assistance, or other forms of court-directed help for the parents. The court may also place the child temporarily in a foster home. If the family cannot iron out its problems despite all efforts to help, the parents' right to bring up the child may be terminated, and the child put up for adoption.

provincial agency dealing with child abuse. After the agency verifies the abuse, they will press charges against your husband and obtain a court order to prevent it from happening again. In extreme situations, the agency may have your husband removed from the home.

If you tolerate your husband's abuse of your daughter, you could face criminal charges, and your daughter could be placed in a foster home or other institution where she would be safe.

I have just discovered that my husband has been sexually abusing our daughter. How can I protect her?

Your first concern is your daughter's physical and mental health. She should be examined by a doctor to assess the extent of injury and abuse. By law, medical personnel are required to report this abuse to the proper authorities in your community.

You could also make the report to your local child protection agency yourself and have them initiate an investigation. A court order could be obtained requiring your husband to move out of your home and not attempt to see your daughter until the investigation has been completed. Sexual molestation of a minor child is one of the most serious crimes and would probably result in your husband going to jail.

What should I do if I suspect that my neighbor down the street is abusing his child?

Report your suspicions immediately to the child and family service agency that monitors child abuse. After a report is made, the agency will investigate and determine whether the allegation is well-founded. Your name will be kept confidential.

Thousands of children are beaten, maimed, emotionally scarred and even killed by their parents every year. Studies show that these child abusers come from every economic group and social class.

Jack and his wife have been taking care of his 70-year-old mother. I've heard arguments from their home, and sounds of someone being hit. I'm afraid Jack's mother is being abused. Would I get in trouble if I called the police? Are they the right people to call?

The police will be able to provide immediate assistance to the family. Many social agencies have social workers who specialize in problems of the elderly, including cases of abuse. Many communities also have hotlines for reporting child, spouse, or adult abuse. You do not have to give your name, and you will not get into trouble if you report an instance of abuse.

Changing Your Name

Must a woman change her surname when she gets married?

No. The use of one's husband's surname or family name is the result of custom, not law. A woman may continue to use her own surname (maiden name) provided that she does so consistently. But she cannot use her maiden name for some purposes, her married name for others. In Quebec, a woman married after 1983 is legally obliged to continue using her maiden name for all official purposes, such as her driver's license and her Medicare, but may use her husband's name for social purposes. Women in British Columbia, Alberta and Ontario choose at the time of the marriage whether they will keep their maiden names or take the names of their husbands.

Jane wants to change her name to Melody Anne. Can she make this change without a lot of bother?

The procedure for changing one's name varies from province to province. In some, she will have to notify the director of Vital Statistics, publish a notice of the name change in the provincial *Gazette* and, possibly, in various newspapers, or she may have to file a formal motion asking the minister of justice to approve the change on certain grounds. In other provinces, she simply uses the new name and notifies all government agencies of the fact.

Is there a waiting period for a name change? How long does the entire process take?

In provinces where you change your name by merely assuming a new name, there is no waiting period. Additional time may be required if there are other formalities. Some provinces require you to reside in the province for a certain period of time before filing the petition. Others may insist that your petition be published in newspapers for a number of consecutive weeks. If all these conditions have to be fulfilled, a legal name change could take several months.

Our 16-year-old son wants to change his name. Does he need our approval before this can be done?

Usually a minor cannot change his name without the consent of his parent or guardian. But since the laws vary from one province to another, you should ask your provincial director of Vital Statistics, or a lawyer, about your case. If you are residents of Ontario for example, and your son has lived there for one year, he can change his name without your consent. In Quebec, parental consent is required up to 18 years; in Nova Scotia, up to 19.

When my husband and I got married, I chose to retain my maiden name for business reasons. What last name should our children have—my husband's or mine?

You and your husband can choose which name your children will use. Traditionally, the father had the right to have his children bear his last name. However, as women began working outside the home and became substantial financial contributors to the household, the courts began to give them more rights and privileges. You now have as much right as your husband to select your children's surname. If both of you agree that your name will be used, the courts will not interfere. Children born in Quebec since 1983 and in Alberta after September 1, 1985, may have surnames of both parents: Timmy Brown-Jones, for example.

Joe and Anne are planning to marry. Each of them has two children from a previous marriage. How can Anne change her children's last name to that of their new stepfather?

The children can have Joe's last name if he legally adopts them or if the children have their names changed by a court. If Anne's ex-husband is still alive, she will have to get his consent. In certain extreme cases, such as where the natural father had abandoned the children, his consent for a change of name would not be necessary.

My son lives with his mother and stepfather and uses his stepfather's last name. Which is considered his legal name—my last name or that of his stepfather?

The name that is on your son's birth certificate is his legal name. If he has used his stepfather's name for some time, however, and if you and his stepfather consent, your son may have his name legally changed.

Rights of Grandparents

For additional information on visitation rights in divorce cases, see "Visitation" in Chapter 3, *Divorce and Child Custody.*

My son died three years ago. My daughter-in-law is remarrying, and her prospective husband wants to adopt my two

MARRIAGE AND FAMILY

grandchildren. My husband and I are afraid we will never get to see the youngsters if the adoption is approved. What can we do?

The courts in recent years have increasingly recognized the visitation rights of grandparents, and most provinces permit visitation when one parent has died, even if the child is later adopted by a stepparent. If your province recognizes grandparent visitation rights in adoption cases, you can petition the court to enforce your rights.

Sheila's daughter and son-in-law were found to be unfit parents by the court, and the judge took custody away from them. Will Sheila be able to see her grandchildren?

Yes, but Sheila may have to go to court. The judge's only consideration in determining custody or visiting rights is the best interests of the child. He would therefore take the affection, love and other emotional ties between Sheila and her grandchildren into consideration in deciding whether she can see her grandchildren and how often.

Can grandparents adopt a grandchild if the parents are not able to support the child adequately?

Grandparents may petition the court for adoption, and if it is in the grandchild's best interest, the adoption will be granted. Although some courts express concern over the wide age difference, this does not mean adoption will be denied. If the grandparents are in good health and the child has lived with them, or if there is a close relationship, the court is more likely to rule in the grandparents' favor. Being unable to provide for a child does not automatically justify a termination of the parents' rights, however. The court must establish that they are unfit or have seriously neglected the child before taking the child from them.

Do grandparents have the same authority as parents when the grandchildren are in their care?

No. Grandparents have no more authority over their grandchildren than any other nonparent who takes care of the children. For example, grandparents do not have the authority to consent to emergency medical treatment for their grandchild. However, a parent can give the grandparents a medical power of attorney, which will authorize them to consent to medical treatment in emergencies. This is a simple, inexpensive method of avoiding unnecessary delays at the hospital.

Ben's 19-year-old granddaughter, Amy, borrowed a large sum of money from him and hasn't made any effort to repay it. Are Amy's parents responsible for repaying the debt?

In all provinces 19-year-old Amy would be considered an adult, responsible for her own debts. Ben would have to go to court to force Amy to repay the loan. If he feels uncomfortable doing this and does not need the money repaid immediately, he could deduct the amount of the loan from any inheritance his granddaughter would receive in his will. Amy's parents would not be liable for the debt, regardless of Amy's age.

Taking Care of the Elderly

My father is 80 years old and still drives his own car. I worry about the possibility of an accident. I don't want to limit his independence, but I do want to ensure his safety. What can I do?

In most provinces drivers over a certain age are required to take eye and driving tests annually to make sure they are still able to drive safely. You might want to make sure your father has been tested recently. Unless your father failed the eye or driving test or has had traffic accidents or tickets, it will not be possible to have his driver's license restricted or revoked. You should also check your father's automobile insurance to make sure he is adequately covered.

Must I pay for medicines and dental work for my elderly parents?

Canadian citizens and landed immigrants who have reached the age of 65 do not have to pay for most medicines; provincial health plans usually cover these expenses. There are some exceptions, such as dental bills and some nonprescription medications, however. Unless you signed an agreement with a dentist or pharmacist to pay for these bills, you would not be responsible.

My mother-in-law lives with us. Do I have to support her?

Aside from your moral duty of supporting someone who lives with you and is in your charge, the criminal law also requires you to provide the necessities of life for someone in your care who, because of illness or age, is unable to provide for himself. If your mother-in-law was not in your charge or did not live with you, you would not be legally bound to support her. The Canada Pension Plan, private pensions and old age pensions usually meet the minimum needs of the elderly.

Taking Care of the Elderly

My 63-year-old mother has a heart condition, and the doctor has advised her not to work. My father died without leaving a pension, life insurance, or any means of financial support for her. My husband and I can't afford to support her. What can we do?

There are a number of possibilities you can explore. Your mother might be eligible for one or more of the following. She would be entitled to a widow's pension, for example, if your father had contributed to the Canada Pension Plan (CPP) or the Quebec Pension Plan (QPP). Even if he had not, but he was 65 years old or more when he died, your mother would be eligible for her old age pension at 60. She may also be entitled to some benefits from the Department of Veterans' Affairs if your father served overseas during the Second World War. If at 65 she had no income other than her old age pension and her CPP or QPP benefits, she might be entitled to the Guaranteed Income Supplement. Right now your mother might also qualify for disability benefits from CPP or QPP. In addition to the above, just about every community has a variety of local programs that provide assistance for older people.

I want my younger brother to handle my bills and other financial matters when I am no longer able to do so. Is there any way I can set this up now?

You could use a durable power of attorney. This document outlines the duties your brother will have and specifies that they will become effective when you are no longer able to manage your affairs. A regular power of attorney comes to an end when you become incompetent, but a durable power of attorney remains in effect during the period of incompetence.

Another option under a durable power of attorney is to give your brother responsibility now for the things you want him to handle and have this responsibility continue after you become incompetent.

Bob gave Gina power of attorney five years ago. At a court hearing last week, the judge declared Bob incompetent and appointed Jay as his guardian. Does Gina continue with her duties under the power of attorney now that Jay has become Bob's guardian?

If Bob gave Gina a general power of attorney, it would end when he was declared incompetent. But if Bob established a durable power of attorney, Gina's authority would continue despite Bob's incompetence. However, she would now be accountable to Jay just as she had been to

Bob. If Jay decides that Gina's powers should be changed or revoked, he has the authority to do so.

Three months ago I gave Scott a power of attorney to handle my business affairs. I don't like the way he is running things. How do I cancel this power of attorney?

Scott should be informed in writing that his authority is canceled as of a specific date, and you must carry out any other provisions in the original power of attorney relating to cancellation. Any person or business that dealt with Scott should get written notification of the cancellation.

I want to give my cousin Jane a power of attorney to handle my financial matters. How specific do I need to be when writing down all her duties?

You should be very specific when you create the power of attorney. If you make Jane's authority too general, you risk having her conduct business you didn't intend her to handle, or having the power of attorney challenged because it is too vague or too broad. A power of attorney of this type should be drawn up by a lawyer since the question of investments, taxes, mortgages, leases and other complicated matters may arise in the course of managing your estate.

Sarah got a power of attorney so that she could handle her mother's financial affairs. Sarah is the sole heir to her mother's estate. Can Sarah use the power of attorney to transfer her mother's bank account to her name after her mother dies?

No. Sarah's power of attorney expires when her mother dies. A power of attorney may not be used as a substitute for the powers of an executor in the administration of an estate.

Corrine knows she needs help with her finances, but she does not want to give anyone total authority to take over all her financial matters. She is mainly interested in making sure her monthly cheques are deposited and rent payments are made. Is there some way for Corrine to do this?

Since Corrine does not want to give someone broad power over all her finances, she would not want to create a power of attorney, conservatorship, or guardianship. She may be able to set up a direct deposit arrangement with her bank, whereby her old age security and other cheques are mailed to the bank and are deposited directly to her account. She could then establish a direct withdrawal arrangement whereby funds are automatically withdrawn to pay the rent and other bills that she specifies, before they become overdue.

My uncle Ralph is in his seventies and suffers from serious health problems, but his mind has always seemed clear. Now we are not so sure. Last week he announced to the family that he was going to adopt his 22-year-old nurse. Will a court let him do this? Can we stop him?

The court will permit Ralph to adopt any person, regardless of age, if he follows the procedure of his province's adoption law.

In order to stop him, you would have to file a petition challenging Uncle Ralph's competence to handle his personal and financial affairs. A judge would then decide if Uncle Ralph needed a guardian to handle his affairs. If a guardian were appointed, Uncle Ralph would not be able to begin adoption proceedings. In Quebec, such a procedure is called interdiction and the guardian is called a curator.

My 84-year-old grandfather has been having some problems recently. He refuses to take his medicine, he won't eat properly, and he insists that the mailman has planted a listening device in his mailbox. I live 700 miles away. What can I do?

Each province has an agency that can investigate and, if necessary, petition the court to provide a guardian when one is needed. Your grandfather may only need someone to look after him and provide companionship. If you prefer to avoid legal proceedings, contact the local office on aging in your grandfather's hometown. It will tell you what services are available and suggest ways you can help your grandfather. Health and Welfare Canada and your provincial health ministry may also have some helpful advice. In some cases, the public trustee or public curator may be able to help your grandfather.

An employee of the welfare department came to my door wanting to discuss a report that I am not eating properly or keeping my house clean. Do I have the right to refuse to answer his questions and to make him leave?

Yes. Any information you give may be used against you in a court or administrative hearing. Get the name of the agency and of the person who came to see you, and of his supervisor. Then contact the agency to find out what's going on and to obtain copies of any papers relating to the investigation about you.

An old woman lives outside town in an old wooden shack, with six dogs and eight cats. She goes through garbage cans to find food. I think she should be taken to a home for proper care. Is there anything I can do?

This woman's behavior may seem unusual to you, but every person has the right to determine his life-style. She could be completely competent and happy with her way of life. However, if you believe this woman is harming herself or receiving inadequate nutrition, contact a local social service agency that provides services for the elderly. There may be local programs that can provide proper nutrition and health care without intruding on her way of life.

Guardians and Conservators

My aunt wants me to be her guardian. I am not sure I want to do this. What would my obligations be?

Your duties and obligations in this case would depend on whether the court appointed you guardian of your aunt's person or conservator of your aunt's estate. As guardian of your aunt's person, you would be responsible for providing her food, housing, health care, and any other necessities. As your aunt's conservator, you would be responsible for administering and managing her financial affairs. In some circumstances, you would be appointed to carry out the duties of both guardian and conservator. The name curator is used in Quebec instead of guardian, but the duties are the same.

Evelyn has received notice of a guardianship hearing. If the court appoints a guardian, will Evelyn still be able to sign cheques, vote, and make other decisions about her life?

It depends on the type of guardianship ordered by the court. Any powers not given to the guardian will be retained by Evelyn. If there is a court order appointing a conservator, the conservator will be responsible for all the financial decisions, but Evelyn will still be entitled to vote and make other personal decisions.

If the court orders a guardianship over Evelyn's person, the guardian will have the power to make all of Evelyn's personal decisions, including where she will live. Evelyn's ability to vote will depend on her mental capacity and any provincial laws that apply to voters who are under guardianship or who are mentally incapacitated.

Will Kathleen need an attorney if she is asking the court to have her daughter appointed as her guardian?

Yes. Even if Kathleen has complete trust in her daughter she should nevertheless have an attorney at the hearing who is on her side. The appointment of a guardian means that Kathleen will lose many of her rights. In order to protect her interests, she needs a legal representative as an advocate on her behalf. If Kathleen cannot afford an attorney, the Legal Aid Society of her province will provide one for her.

When Eddie goes to court about an involuntary guardianship, can he have the court appoint an attorney to represent him?

Since the court will be ruling on Eddie's competence, most provinces would supply an attorney to represent him in this type of hearing. Since rules vary from one province to another, Eddie should check with his local legal aid society to see if (1) he is eligible for a free lawyer or for one who will charge reduced fees, and (2) if legal aid supplies attorneys for this kind of case. An involuntary guardianship can be canceled when the reason for its appointment has been removed—an alcoholic would not need a guardian when sober, for example.

I think my grandmother needs a guardian. If I initiate a court proceeding to have myself appointed as her guardian, will I have to pay all the costs out of my own pocket?

Yes. However, since you are initiating the guardianship action on your grandmother's behalf, you can reimburse yourself from your ward's property upon your appointment.

My sister and mother live in the same town. Won't my sister have to be the guardian, since I live in another province?

Not necessarily. The court has the authority to select the person who will best serve your mother's interest. Unless the province where your mother lives bars nonresidents from serving as guardians, you could be appointed if the court thought you would do a better job than your sister.

When Conservators Can Help

If a person has difficulty dealing with bills, bank statements, and other routine financial matters, the appointment of a conservator can help considerably. A conservator is a guardian whose authority is limited to taking care of an individual's financial affairs.

Conservators are often appointed for people who are unable to keep track of their financial obligations, or for those who are ill, or who squander their assets because they are compulsive gamblers, alcoholics, or drug addicts. A person who needs a conservator can ask the court to appoint one, or a close relative can make the request.

Conservatorship is a much less drastic step than appointing a guardian who takes full charge of a person's life. The person being helped has the right to consult with his conservator, who is generally required to take the conservatee's wishes into account when making any decision about his affairs. The conservatee also avoids the stigma of being declared incompetent by a court, which must be done before a guardian can be appointed.

Conservators are usually a person's spouse or next of kin, although the court may appoint a more distant relative, a lawyer, or a bank official if this is in the individual's best interests. The conservator may have to post a bond—pay a lump sum of money to the court to be used if he fails to carry out his duties. The court will supervise the conservator and will demand regular accountings to make sure he continues to act in the conservatee's best interests. Conservatorships can be permanent or temporary—for example, if a conservator is appointed for a person who is seriously ill for a long time, the conservatorship can be ended when the person recovers and is once again able to assume full responsibility for his affairs. Where there is no spouse or next of kin to help, the Public Trustee, or Public Curator, will manage the person's property.

If you are appointed, you may have to choose someone within the province to accept legal documents.

I just received notice that my children have filed a petition seeking a guardianship over me. I don't think I need anyone to handle my affairs for me. What can I do to stop this?

You have the right to appear at the court hearing and to contest the guardianship petition proceedings. You are not required to have an attorney, but you have the right to be represented by one. In the circumstances, you would be wise to insist on this right. Your lawyer may submit evidence, such as a medical report from a psychiatrist or a psychologist, attesting to your healthy mental state.

Harold, 80, and Ethel, 81, met and fell in love while living in a nursing home. Can Harold marry Ethel without first obtaining his guardian's consent?

Ordinarily when a guardian is appointed for a person (as opposed to a guardian, or conservator, for the property), the person under guardianship is considered to be incapable of entering into a contract. As marriage is a contract setting out certain rights and obligations, Harold would not be able to marry Ethel.

My cousin was appointed by the court to be our grandmother's conservator. I have never trusted my cousin. How can I be sure she is properly handling our grandmother's financial affairs?

The court will require your cousin to file regular accountings of your grandmother's financial affairs. These accountings are a matter of public record and are available for your inspection. The court may also require your cousin to post bond to ensure that she is handling your grandmother's financial affairs properly.

Richard has had a guardian for six years, but now he is sure that he is quite capable of taking care of himself. Can the guardianship be ended?

Yes. When the reasons for appointing a guardian have been removed, the guardianship can be terminated. Each province has its own procedure for doing this. Some require a formal termination by the court. In others it can be done informally with the consent of those involved.

Nursing Homes

Can an elderly parent be forced to go to a nursing home?

No. No individual can be restrained or placed in a residential facility against his will without a court order. To do so would violate rights guaranteed by the Charter of Rights and Freedoms. It takes a court order to give one adult custody of another or control over another adult's residence. Unless a court determines that an elderly person is mentally or physically incompetent and that residential care is in his best interest, the person's own consent is essential to place him in a nursing home.

My father was just admitted to a nursing home. He could not sign the admission agreement because of poor health. The facility had me sign as the "responsible party." Does that mean I may have to pay all his bills?

When an adult member of the immediate family signs admission papers to a nursing home, he usually becomes obligated to pay the bills if the relative doesn't have sufficient assets to cover them. Always read such documents carefully before signing. If you do not understand something, or you cannot agree to the conditions, get a copy of the agreement from the nursing home director and consult a lawyer before you sign.

Since you have already assumed some responsibility for your father and he is in poor health, you should consider becoming his legal guardian. This would make you his legal representative, acting with the authority of the court, and you would be allowed to use your father's assets to pay his bills. A legal guardianship would also place you in a stronger position to help protect your father's rights if a problem arises in the nursing home.

My family has been visiting different nursing homes before selecting one for our mother. One facility has many of the features that appeal to us, but the administrator wants a contribution to assure her of a place. Is this legal?

No. If a nursing home administrator requests or receives money to guarantee admission to the facility, he may be guilty of bribery. As an institution offering a service to the public, a nursing home cannot demand any payment other than the fee stipulated in the contract. If a "special contribution" is requested, the nursing home should be reported to the minister of social affairs or the appropriate agency. An investigation might result in the home's license being revoked.

My wife and I are getting older, and we are thinking about moving into a continuing care facility. Will it be simple enough for us to handle, or should we have a lawyer review the papers before we sign anything?

Moving into a continuing care facility could be the last decision about where to live that you and your wife make. Because it is such an important decision, it would be wise to have an attorney help you throughout the entire admission process. The financial operations of a continuing care community are extremely complicated, and the medical, recreational, and social services vary considerably. Unless you have an attorney on your side, you could end up paying a great deal of money without getting what you're hoping for.

Your attorney should review the contract before you sign it to make sure it complies with all the legal requirements of your province and that it clearly outlines your rights if the facility goes bankrupt or fails to deliver on any of its obligations.

Choosing a Nursing Home

Information on nursing homes is available from your local golden age group, local YM-YWCA, and from most social service agencies. You might also be wise to inquire from a social worker who deals with older people (a geriatric social worker), as she would be knowledgeable about the nursing homes in your area. Once you have a list of possibilities, visit the homes and check these specifics.

☑ Do the home and its administrator have a provincial license?

☑ Is the home in a safe neighborhood? Is it easy for visitors to get to? Are there parks, libraries, and other senior centers nearby?

☑ Are the rooms and halls clean and well lit? Are there no more than four beds to a room? Is there a window in each bedroom?

☑ Are there curtains and a nurse's call bell for each bed?

☑ Are fire doors kept closed, with exits clearly marked? Do the hallways and bathrooms have handrails and grab bars, wheelchair ramps, and skidproof floors?

☑ Is the food appetizing, and nutritious? Are special diets available? Can relatives visit the dining room without an appointment?

☑ Are residents allowed to have refrigerators and air conditioners in their rooms?

☑ What is the ratio of staff to residents?

☑ Are a doctor and registered nurse on call around the clock? Is there adequate dental care provided?

☑ Are there supervised activities for residents, with day trips and other special events?

☑ Do the residents seem satisfied? Are they allowed to have their own clothing and personal possessions? Do they have access to religious services? Is there a residents' council? (If so, be sure to talk with a council officer.)

☑ Are advance payments refunded if the resident decides to leave?

I do volunteer work at a local nursing home. Lately it seems dirty, and some of the residents are not taken care of properly. Is it my duty to report this?

You may not have a legal duty to report the nursing home's unsanitary conditions and lack of care, but you certainly have a moral duty to do so. Exploitation of old people who cannot protect themselves is a stain on society. You should report your concerns to the ministry responsible for licensing nursing homes, or get in touch with your local social services center. You might also notify your municipal health department, or fire department, which may be able to insist on certain improvements at the nursing home.

My 76-year-old mother signed over all her property to a nursing home in exchange for lifetime care. She is very sick, and we don't think she is being properly taken care of. Can we force the home to return her property so that we can move her to a better facility?

You should review the contract for provisions about returning a patient's property. A contract whereby one turns over all one's property, including old age pension payments, in exchange for lifetime care is probably invalid. The contract could probably be canceled also on the grounds of false or misleading advertising if your mother is not getting the kind of care she was promised. The contract could be canceled even if the care is adequate, but your mother might have to pay a reasonable sum to cover expenses while she was at the nursing home.

When we go to the nursing home to visit our uncle, his roommate always takes over the conversation. We have asked about being allowed to meet in a private room, but with no result. Isn't my uncle entitled to some private time with his family?

Yes. Every nursing home patient has a right to talk privately with anyone without someone else being present all the time. You or your uncle should ask the administrator or director of nursing to reserve a room for family meetings. In fact most facilities of this kind have a family conference room for this purpose.

Audrey and Scott have lived in a continuing care retirement community for three years. They are unhappy with the facility. Can they terminate their contract? Can they get a refund?

Their contract should clearly describe what must be done to terminate the agreement and how refunds are calculated. In a typical continuing care contract, residents pay a substantial admission fee plus a monthly charge. But contracts vary considerably from one institution to another. However, the resident always has the right to terminate the contract.

If Audrey and Scott's contract involves a substantial amount of money, they should hire a lawyer who is familiar with consumer law: not all conditions and clauses in contracts such as theirs are legal. The nursing home might be willing to make a generous settlement with one unhappy couple in order to avoid unfavorable publicity.

When Margaret went to visit her aunt at the nursing home, she found that her aunt had been transferred to another room. This is the fourth transfer in six months, and her aunt is very upset about all these moves. Is there something that can be done to keep Margaret's aunt in the same room?

Doctors and lawyers recognize that frequent room reassignments can disorient nursing home patients and cause psychological stress. Frequent moves also increase the potential for physical injuries from such things as falls in an unfamiliar room. Margaret should alert the administrator to these room changes and request that adequate notice be given so that her aunt can prepare for them. Her aunt's social worker should also be notified.

Nathan lived in a private nursing home but was sent to a nearby hospital for a medical emergency. He has now recovered enough to return, but the nursing home refuses to allow him back. Isn't it required to readmit him?

It depends on Nathan's contract with the nursing home. Some nursing homes stipulate that if a person is away from the home for more than a certain period of time, he loses his rights to his room. It would be unfair if a nursing home had to keep several rooms unoccupied for extended periods of time. If Nathan had been paying for his room while he was in the hospital, however, he would probably have the right to get it back.

Alvin is a difficult resident and sometimes slaps aides when they try to help him. Yesterday, a nurse's aide lost her temper and hit Alvin back. Can she be held responsible for her action?

Under no circumstances is a nursing home employee allowed to hit a patient. The facts of the matter should be investigated, and the nurse's aide disciplined or fired. If Alvin or his family or guardian wishes to take

Rights of Nursing Home Patients

If you are a nursing home patient who has not been declared incompetent by a court, and who does not have a guardian appointed for your property or person, you have the same rights as any other person in society. Among those are the rights:

- To be informed of all available services and their cost.
- To be kept advised of your medical condition and have a voice in your treatment.
- To have your personal records kept confidential.
- To keep and use personal possessions, as space permits.
- To have privacy during visits by your spouse or other persons.
- To be free to communicate privately with others.
- To manage your financial affairs or be given a regular accounting by the nursing home.
- To receive mail unopened.
- To refuse to do any work at the facility, such as vacuuming halls.
- To be free from physical and mental abuse.
- To take part in social and religious activities.
- To receive advance notice of any discharge or transfer to another facility and have some say in it.

If these rights are violated or if you have other complaints about a nursing home, write or call your local social service agency and ask that a social worker investigate your complaints. If you are abused, or if your rights to proper medical care, privacy, and personal security are not respected, the nursing home may lose its license. In some cases you could sue for damages, including exemplary damages.

the matter to court, they have a good case for suing the aide for battery, since she intentionally struck him. Unfortunately, nursing home patients are often demanding and difficult to care for. People who work as aides in nursing homes, however, are required to act with more care and patience than ordinary employees elsewhere.

My mother is in a nursing home, but I want to take care of her at our house. How do I get her released?

If your mother is competent to request the release, she should first check with her physician and then write a note informing the facility that she wants to leave. You should reread the admission agreement for any

Nursing Homes

special conditions or requirements concerning release—some facilities, for example, want two weeks' notice. If your mother has a guardian, that person would have to make the request, and a court may also have to approve the move.

When Frances moved into her nursing home last year, she took a favorite chair, a TV set, and other personal items. Some of her possessions are missing, and she believes they have been stolen. Does she have any recourse against the nursing home?

Yes. Frances can take the nursing home to court for violating regulations that guarantee a resident's right to keep and use personal possessions and to have a secure, private place in which to keep them. If the nursing home was negligent in any way, or if it otherwise failed in its duty to protect Frances' property, it can be held liable for the theft.

Divorce and Child Custody

My husband and I have grown apart, and we have begun talking about a divorce. But neither of us wants to hurt the other with a lot of accusations. Does one of us have to pin the blame on the other, or can we just get a divorce because we both want one?

Since the new Divorce Act went into effect on June 1, 1986, the only ground for divorce is marriage breakdown. If you live apart from your husband for at least one year immediately preceding the date that a judgment is rendered in your case, marriage breakdown will be established, without either of you being "blamed" for the divorce.

Must a couple live apart before being granted a divorce?

Not necessarily. Although marriage breakdown is the only ground for divorce, separation for one year immediately prior to the court hearing is only one of the ways of establishing that marriage breakdown has occurred. Mental or physical cruelty or adultery are others. Provided that the "innocent" spouse has not forgiven or condoned the mental or physical cruelty or adultery committed by the other partner, marriage breakdown may be proven, even if the spouses continue to live together in the same house.

If my wife and I live apart from each other for seven years, will we be considered divorced?

No. Living apart does not make you divorced, no matter how long you do so. Divorce requires a judgment from a court legally terminating the marriage. Without a court decree, there is no divorce.

Henry's wife left him without warning, taking most of their possessions. What might a lawyer advise him to do?

Henry's lawyer would advise him to quickly take several steps to protect the rest of his property. If he and his wife have a safe-deposit box, Henry's lawyer, or a neutral third person such as a bank officer, should inventory the box and put the contents in a new box where they will be safe until a property settlement is reached. If they have a joint bank account, Henry should ask the bank to freeze it to prevent his wife from making any further withdrawals. Since Henry and his wife both have rights to the property she took, it is unlikely that Henry will be able to get any of it back until a separation agreement or a divorce decree specifies how their property is to be divided. Henry may obtain what is known as a *seizure before judgment* on the goods taken by his wife, however. This court order notifies his wife not to dispose of the property until the court has ruled on the respective rights of each toward such property.

What should I discuss with my lawyer the first time I see him about a divorce?

You can get the most out of an initial consultation by being prepared to give your attorney as much information as possible. You should expect to discuss the reasons why you want a divorce. You should also decide on what outcome you are seeking. If you want custody of the children, support, or any specific property, you should let your attorney know. The more information you give your attorney, the better advice you will get—and the more accurate the estimate of legal fees will be.

Must we see a marriage counselor before seeking a divorce?

Marriage counseling before a divorce is not obligatory but it is often a good idea, especially for young couples. Often counseling and mediation services are offered by the court at no cost to the applicant. Lawyers consulted by clients seeking divorce are obliged to inform them of the marriage counseling services available.

Does a husband have to pay his wife's living expenses until a final divorce decree is issued?

The court may order temporary, or interim, support if the wife is not able to support herself while the divorce is pending. However, no spouse has an absolute right to temporary support. When it is granted, it may be payable in a lump sum, or in periodic payments, or both. The court does *not* take the good or bad behavior of one of the spouses into consideration when granting support. The amount will be based on the wife's need, the husband's ability to pay, and the wife's cost of living in a style similar to that she enjoyed during the marriage.

Carole and Ted remained married for their children's sake. Now the children are grown-up, and Ted and Carole want a divorce. Carole is not self-supporting. What steps should she take?

There are many things that Carole should do to protect her interests. The first is to make an appointment with an attorney. The earlier she does so, the better prepared she will be when she and Ted actually separate.
  Before meeting with her attorney, Carole should draw up a list of all the

family assets and debts, including any business interests she and Ted may have. If she is not familiar with these matters, she risks not getting a fair property settlement. She should also know the location of deeds, insurance policies, titles to property, prenuptial contracts, and other important documents.

If Carole has been financially dependent on Ted, she will probably need support. To prepare herself for this, she should draw up a budget, estimating all her monthly living expenses—including those expenses,

---

What to Take to Your Lawyer

The more information you can give your lawyer at your first meeting about a possible divorce, the better he will be able to help you. Since decisions will have to be made about money, property, and custody, the better prepared you are to discuss these matters, the less time, expense, and unnecessary complications there will be. The following checklist will help you compile the facts and materials your lawyer will need:

☑ A copy of your marriage certificate.
☑ Children's and spouses' names and dates of birth.
☑ Copies of any written agreements between you and your spouse that deal with finances, such as a prenuptial agreement.
☑ Copies of the deed to your home and to any other real estate you or your spouse may own.
☑ A list of valuable personal property, such as cars, jewelry, appliances, cameras, and electronic equipment.
☑ A list of bank accounts, stocks, bonds, or other investments that you and your spouse have, and whether they are held singly or jointly.
☑ A list of debts, including mortgages, personal loans, credit cards, and charge accounts.
☑ A list of monthly expenses and copies of paid bills for one month.
☑ Stubs from recent pay cheques for each working spouse.
☑ Copies of federal and provincial income tax returns for you and your spouse for the past three years.
☑ If you own a business, copies of the tax returns for the business for the past three years.
☑ Copies of medical insurance and life insurance policies for both you and your spouse.
☑ Copies of pension plans.
☑ If either you or your spouse has been married before, a copy of the divorce papers.
☑ The name of your spouse's attorney.

such as car insurance and Christmas presents, that don't come up every month. It is important that the budget be accurate because the amount of her support will depend upon her needs.

Carole should try to set aside some money before the separation, to be used while the divorce is pending. She should establish credit in her own name and—since there is no guarantee of support or it may not meet her needs—she should also consider getting a job. Recent Supreme Court judgments have emphasized the duty of each spouse to become self-sufficient. In many cases, support is only granted for a short time to enable the dependent spouse to gain autonomy.

Martha's marriage is falling apart. Does it make a difference if she moves out first?

Yes. If Martha moves out, her husband may claim in a divorce proceeding that she abandoned him and may ask for exclusive use of the home they formerly shared. If Martha and her husband have children and Martha does not take them with her, the court may see this behavior as evidence of her disinterest in having custody of them. Martha's move may also affect how much support she may receive, and requests to have her husband pay her attorney's fees may be denied. These problems can be avoided if both Martha and her husband agree that the marriage is not working and sign a separation agreement.

My wife and I never went through any legal proceedings when we decided to separate. How much responsibility do I have for supporting our children while we are separated?

Your legal duty to provide necessities for your minor children continues even when they live apart from you. The extent of your obligation depends upon several factors: your income and capital, the number of your dependents, and the needs of your children. It may not be sufficient to provide just the bare necessities—depending on your income, you may also have to pay for such things as college tuition.

George is fed up with his marriage and wants to empty all the bank accounts and cancel his joint credit cards. What will the consequences be if he does this?

If George takes all the money, he may be asking for a great deal of legal and financial trouble. He could be charged with nonsupport, or forced to return a substantial amount to his wife later, when a property settlement is reached. The court may also view his actions as evidence of bad faith, and compensate his wife accordingly in the property settlement. And as far as the credit cards are concerned, George can cancel only those cards for which he has sole legal responsibility. If they are joint accounts with both able to sign for charges, his wife will still be able to use them until George has formally notified the credit card issuer—preferably by registered mail—that he will no longer be responsible for charges made by his wife.

Joan, married 10 years, has little in common with her husband. She says they stay together only because they haven't enough money for a divorce. Does it cost a lot to get a divorce?

Divorce costs vary with the complexity of the divorce and the experience and the reputation of the lawyer you hire. An uncontested divorce, where the questions of custody, access, alimentary pension and division of property are worked out in advance by an amicable settlement, would be much cheaper than a case where each of these issues must be decided by a judge after a lengthy hearing. By acting in good faith, with common sense and fairness, and by laying aside all desire for revenge and for hurting one another, a divorcing couple can save substantial amounts of money.

We want a civilized divorce. Would it be a good idea for both of us to use the same lawyer?

No. No matter how civilized a divorce may be, it is never a good idea for both people to use the same lawyer. A lawyer's job is to protect his client's interests, and it is difficult, if not impossible, for one attorney to protect the interests of opposing people in a lawsuit. All too often, friendly divorces encounter unexpected areas of disagreement and become unfriendly. Even if your case is simple and uncontested, two lawyers won't cost much more than having one for both spouses, and each of you will have the benefit of having your own attorney's undivided loyalty.

I am unemployed and want to get a divorce. Is there any way to have my wife pay for my lawyer?

The court will consider awarding attorney's fees to you if you request it. Whether or not you are successful will depend on your need and your wife's income and assets. If you are eligible, your legal aid society would provide you with a lawyer, either without charge or at a reduced fee, according to legal aid provisions in your province.

Sally is thinking about getting a divorce. Can she legally make her husband leave their home until the divorce is final?

If Sally's husband agrees to the divorce, she can try to get him to move out as part of a separation agreement. If Sally can prove there is actual danger of physical or mental harm, the judge may grant her temporary exclusive occupancy of their home. She may also have to show that she did not do anything to provoke the danger, and that her husband can afford to live elsewhere.

If Sally believes conditions exist that warrant exclusive occupancy, she should tell her attorney about this during the initial consultation, because she will need help with the legal process. Sally will be required to sign a sworn statement about the dangerous conditions, and she may be required to testify about them in court.

Often the partner who obtains custody of the children also gets exclusive use of the former common home, since the courts try to reduce the trauma of divorce for the children of the divorcing couple. The need to move to a new home and a new school and to abandon old friends would not be in the best interest of the children.

If my husband files for divorce and I can't afford to hire a lawyer, what should I do?

You should ask your local legal aid society for help. Legal aid societies throughout the country provide legal assistance to those who cannot afford it. Your legal aid society will accept or reject your case on the basis of your financial need; so you will have to provide documents—such as income tax returns and titles to property—that show your income and assets. If you are turned down, ask to be referred to a lawyer who might handle your case for a minimal charge, or who would be willing to accept as payment any fees the court might obtain from your husband.

Does it make a difference who files for the divorce?

Filing itself gives neither spouse any legal advantage or disadvantage in a divorce proceeding. But the person who files may have to pay the filing fees, and it will be necessary for that person to appear in court.

Can I file for divorce without my husband's knowing?

Yes, but when you file, you must give the court your husband's last known address. He will then be served with a summons notifying him that you have filed a divorce action. If your husband cannot be located, the court will advise him of the divorce through a notice published in a

123

newspaper. However, you will not be able to obtain an alimentary pension or child support unless your husband is served with a summons.

If you know where he lives, but only serve him notice through a newspaper, your husband could probably have the divorce judgment against him canceled on grounds it was fraudulently obtained.

How soon can I remarry after I am divorced?

You may marry any time after your divorce judgment becomes final. This occurs automatically 31 days after your court appearance where the judgment was rendered. In cases where it is in the interest of the applicant and society, the waiting period can be waived by the court.

Separation

Marie and Richard are having marital problems and have agreed to separate. Should they get a separation agreement?

Yes. Couples who work out separation agreements have a better chance of avoiding misunderstandings over their rights and obligations and preventing long and costly court battles to settle child custody and property disputes.

Each spouse also benefits from the protection a separation agreement provides. For example, if Richard agrees to give Marie $300 a month for support, a separation agreement would make this a legal obligation, enforceable in court if necessary, rather than a matter of good intentions. Richard is likewise protected if Marie decides to demand $400 instead of $300.

A separation agreement is even more important when children are involved, because it can spell out in detail each spouse's continuing rights and obligations.

Do I have to go to court to get a legal separation?

No, not if your spouse agrees to the separation. There are two types of separation, both of which are "legal": separation by agreement and judicial separation. The two types are similar in content and effect.

A separation by agreement requires only that husband and wife agree to separate. Although it is not legally necessary, couples should have their attorneys draw up a written agreement specifying each person's rights, obligations, and property interests during the separation. Such an

What to Include in a Separation Agreement

Separation agreements start out by giving the names, addresses, birth dates, and other facts about the husband, wife, and children. The agreement then describes each person's rights and obligations during the separation. To cover these points, separation agreements are in writing and usually include:

- ☑ A statement in which the husband and wife agree to live apart.
- ☑ A list dividing personal property.
- ☑ An agreement about who will hold title to any real estate.
- ☑ An agreement about who will pay financial support, what amount will be paid, and whether the amount can be changed.
- ☑ An agreement about who will have custody of the children.
- ☑ A schedule of visitation rights for the noncustodial parent.
- ☑ A provision detailing the children's financial support.
- ☑ An agreement on who will pay medical, dental, education, and other special expenses.
- ☑ An explanation of insurance benefits and premium payments, and who is responsible for them.
- ☑ A statement on when the agreement would terminate and how it could be amended.
- ☑ A description of debts owed jointly and individually, including legal fees, and who will pay them.
- ☑ A statement of whether there are limitations on the right of each spouse to inherit from the other.

agreement would also entitle anyone paying an alimentary pension to his spouse to deduct it on his income tax return. To be deductible, spousal support payments must be included in a court order or in a separation agreement drawn up before a lawyer.

If your spouse won't agree to a separation, you will have to get a judicial separation, commonly called a legal separation. This requires court action. One spouse files a petition for separation much as he or she would in applying to the court for a divorce. If the court rules in favor of granting the petition, it will order the separation and issue a decree.

Laura and Dennis plan to draw up a separation agreement on their own. What risks are they taking by not consulting lawyers?

Laura and Dennis are taking a big risk in drawing up their own separation agreement. They may not know that certain provisos are unenforceable. Such would be the case, for example, if one partner agreed to pay an alimentary pension on condition that the recipient did not have sexual

125

relations with anyone else. They might also overlook certain important rights: perhaps the alimentary pension should be indexed to the cost of living. They may not realize the need for a clause permitting alteration of the agreement if circumstances change. The agreement could be invalid because of a defect of form: some provinces, for example, require that these agreements be drawn up before witnesses.

A separation agreement drawn up before a lawyer need not be expensive, and can save a lot of money and anguish later on. In Ontario a separation agreement may be registered in court and thus have the effect of a judgment.

After a separation agreement has been signed, can either spouse date other people?

Yes, but they should be careful to avoid situations that could complicate their divorce proceedings. Seriously courting or having sexual relations with a person other than one's spouse may provide proof of misconduct that brought about the marriage breakdown. An enduring romance and prolonged absences from home could weaken a spouse's ability to get the best property, support, and child custody settlements.

Sheila, who is separated from Steve, wants to buy a new car. Would Steve have any claim to it as marital property?

It depends on where they live and whether Sheila and Steve are legally separated. In most provinces, anything a spouse acquires after a separation is considered separate property, even if the couple has no legal separation agreement. But not all provinces observe this rule. If Steve and Sheila lived in Quebec, for example, were not legally separated and had not signed a separation of property agreement before marriage, Steve could claim a half interest in Sheila's car, even though they do not live together. However, if they had obtained a legal separation from the court, Sheila could buy her car without worry; Steve would have no claim on it. A written separation agreement protects both spouses.

My wife and I are legally separated. Am I responsible for her credit card purchases?

It depends on whose name the account is in. You are not responsible for credit cards in your wife's name only, but you and your wife are responsible for all purchases made on joint accounts. You can avoid misunderstandings over credit cards by working out a separation agreement that clearly states which financial obligations you are each responsible for. You must also notify each credit card issuer that you are no longer responsible for your wife's purchases and that you want all joint credit cards canceled.

My husband moved out when he decided to divorce me. Although he still wants a divorce, he keeps asking me to let him move back. Would it affect the divorce if I did so?

Since divorce is such a serious decision, and since the Divorce Act encourages reconciliation, you could allow your husband to move back with you for one or more periods not exceeding 90 days in total without affecting your divorce proceedings.

My wife agreed in writing to move out of our home. When she left, she took a lot of property that we had agreed was mine. Can I have it returned to me?

A separation agreement is a contract that can be enforced like any other contract, and you can sue her for violating the terms of your agreement. If you file for divorce, you can request the return of the items when the property is divided.

When my husband died, we were legally separated and living apart. Am I entitled to any of his estate?

Most provinces will allow you to inherit from your husband's estate. Under the law, you are considered legally married until a final divorce decree is issued. Therefore, you are entitled to inherit as though you had been living together, unless, of course, you had given up your right of inheritance in a separation agreement.

Annulment

If I get a church annulment, am I legally free to remarry?

No. There are two types of annulment: a legal or civil annulment and a church annulment. A legal annulment is a court order ruling that the marriage never existed. A church annulment is a declaration by a church authority that the marriage never existed. But church annulments are not legally binding; thus you would also have to get a legal annulment from a civil court in order to remarry.

Annulment

How does an annulment differ from a divorce?

An annulment denies that a marriage ever existed. A divorce acknowledges the existence of a marriage and then terminates it. An annulment also differs from a divorce because there are generally no provisions for support of the dependent person who, according to the annulment, was never married.

What legal reasons can Beth use to prevent Dave from having their marriage annulled?

There are several defenses that Beth may use to contest an annulment. One defense is the statute of limitations. If Dave fails to request an annulment within a specified time limit (which varies widely from province to province), the annulment will be denied.

If Dave is seeking an annulment based on fraud—claiming, for example, that Beth did not tell him she had been married before—Beth can prevent the annulment if she can prove that Dave really was aware of this fact before the wedding.

Another defense is ratification. If Dave had been aware earlier in the marriage of grounds for annulment but did nothing about it and

Grounds for Annulment

An annulment declares that a marriage was not legal to begin with. Grounds for annulment vary from province to province, but the most common ones are:

- *Duress*—Forcing one of the parties into the marriage against his or her will (a shotgun marriage).
- *Fraud*—An intentional deception affecting the foundation of the marriage in order to lure a person into marrying. Some examples:
  — Marrying to obtain landed immigrant status (only the defrauded party could initiate proceedings).
  — Concealing homosexuality.
  — Concealing a serious criminal record.
  — Concealing serious health problems.
- *Mental incapacity*—Inability to understand the nature and quality of marriage and therefore inability to give consent.
- *Underage*—Failure of one or both spouses to have reached the age of consent required by their province.

continued with the marriage, he has now lost the opportunity for an annulment on those grounds.

Apart from countering Beth's defenses, Dave must prove his grounds in court. If he fails to do so, the annulment will be denied.

My husband and I want to get an annulment. Does this mean our six-month-old son will be illegitimate?

No. If you get an annulment, your marriage would be void but your son would be legitimate. All provinces have laws that allow children of annulled marriages to be considered legitimate.

Types of Divorce

What is a no-fault divorce?

A divorce is granted when one or both of the spouses are able to prove that the marriage has broken down and that there is no chance of reconciliation. If a couple has been separated and living apart for more than one year immediately prior to the divorce hearing, then marriage breakdown will have been established. When separation for over a year is the reason given for seeking a divorce, this is considered a no-fault divorce: neither spouse is at fault.

Can I choose between a fault and a no-fault divorce?

It depends on your circumstances. If your spouse has committed adultery, or has treated you with mental or physical cruelty, and you have not forgiven or condoned this behavior, you may—by invoking one of these causes of the marriage breakdown—begin divorce proceedings immediately based on "fault." If you have been separated for one year immediately prior to your divorce hearing, you may seek a no-fault divorce. It is not necessary to be separated for one year before *beginning* proceedings for a no-fault divorce. It is only necessary that you be separated for one year prior to your divorce *hearing.*

Are no-fault divorces quicker than traditional divorces?

Yes. Traditional divorces based on fault—even uncontested ones—require proof of the misconduct that caused the marriage breakdown. This proof usually consists of testimony from both spouses and other witnesses. Uncontested no-fault divorces require only one spouse's testimony that the marriage is over. Nevertheless you would be wise to have a witness who can testify from his own knowledge that you and your spouse have been living apart for more than a year. Some judges look for such corroborating evidence before dissolving a marriage. Witnesses can be family members, friends or even acquaintances.

Won't Alison get more in a property settlement if she accuses her husband of wrongdoing instead of getting a no-fault divorce?

No. The good behavior or the misconduct of one of the spouses is *not* considered by the judge in deciding property settlements. Judgment is based only on the couple's needs, the ability of one partner to pay an alimentary pension to the other, how long it may take either partner to become economically self-sufficient, and the advantages and disadvantages arising from the marriage or its breakdown.

Jean wants to get a no-fault divorce. Will her husband's infidelity have an effect on the divorce proceedings?

No. If Jean and her husband have been living apart for more than a year immediately prior to the divorce hearing, her husband's infidelity would not affect the ultimate decision. Jean would not have to prove the adultery; she only has to prove that she and her husband have been separated for a year.

Can I have a jury trial for a divorce?

No. A divorce must be granted by a judge of the Provincial Superior Court (Supreme Court or Court of Queen's Bench) acting without a jury.

What are emergency divorces? How do I go about getting one?

Emergency divorces occur when a waiting or cooling-off period in a pending divorce is waived to resolve an urgent situation—to enable one of the spouses to marry right away, for example, so that a baby will be born legitimate. Requests for such waivers were more common prior to June 1, 1986, when divorce legislation of that time required two judgments. The first, the *decree nisi* or conditional judgment, was followed by a three-month waiting period, after which one of the spouses could ask for the second or final judgment. Provided both spouses guaranteed in writing not to appeal the judgment, the three-month delay was sometimes waived if the judge felt this would best serve the interest of the petitioner and society. Under present divorce laws, the final judgment occurs automatically 31 days after the divorce is granted. As a result, "emergency" divorces are now rare, although the 31-day wait can still be waived in certain circumstances.

Do Mexican mail-order divorces have any legal standing here?

Before Mexico added a residency requirement to its divorce law, mail-order divorces could be obtained through attorneys in Mexico without either spouse being a resident there. Canada never recognized such "quickie divorces." For a foreign divorce to be recognized here, one or both of the parties would have to have a firm connection with the country, or state, where the divorce was granted.

My husband says he can fly to another country and get a divorce by remaining there just 24 hours. Is this true?

A divorce obtained in another country will not be recognized in Canada if neither spouse lives or has lived in that country. A quick visit is not enough to establish residency. Canada would not recognize a Mexican divorce, for example, or even one from the State of Nevada, unless one of the two divorcing people had lived there for at least a year.

A local group helps with pro se divorces. What does pro se mean?

The literal meaning of *pro se* is "for oneself." When a husband or wife acts as his or her own attorney in a divorce, he or she is trying to obtain a divorce *pro se.*

Some legal aid societies conduct *pro se* clinics, providing forms and instructions to help people handle simple, uncontested divorces without a lawyer. But this is risky; going into a divorce case without a lawyer could result in an unsatisfactory settlement of such matters as child custody, visitation, and division of property.

Are do-it-yourself divorce kits a good idea?

Generally do-it-yourself divorce kits are not a good idea, since there is a good chance that some important fact or legal point may be overlooked. The kits are especially risky when the couple has children, or if one of the spouses wishes to obtain a property settlement, or to have a marriage contract or other domestic contract enforced. Besides, few nonlawyers are able to cope with all the technicalities. If you don't comply with the

Types of Divorce

rules of evidence and court procedures, your case might be dismissed. When there is so much to lose, the ultimate price you pay for a poorly handled divorce could greatly exceed the cost of retaining a lawyer to help you right from the beginning.

The Divorce Process

I was just served with divorce papers. What do I do now?

You should consult an attorney at once. There is a time limit in which you must officially respond to the papers you were served. If you don't respond within the time limit, you may forfeit your right to contest the divorce or to claim property that you want to keep.

My husband's lawyer has recommended a divorce attorney for me. Would it be OK to hire him?

You should hire the attorney who is best for you, regardless of what your husband's attorney says. If you have trouble finding a good divorce lawyer, call your local bar association for a list of qualified ones.

My wife and I can't seem to agree on anything. Are there services available to help us reach a settlement that will satisfy both of us?

Yes. Many couples find mediators very helpful in reaching a settlement. Mediators are professionals trained to work with couples who have decided to divorce but cannot agree on property distribution or child custody. Since mediators cannot give legal advice or prepare legal documents, you and your wife should hire attorneys before you begin the mediation process. They can refer you to experienced mediators. In some provinces, Manitoba and Quebec for example, mediators work with the courts, and their services are free. In other provinces, such as Ontario, you must pay for the services of a mediator.

Do I have to appear in court to get a divorce?

If you are the spouse who has filed for the divorce, usually you must appear in court for the hearing or your case will be dismissed. If your spouse has filed for the divorce and you do not wish to contest it, you are not required to appear. But if you don't attend the court hearing, the

Steps in Getting a Divorce

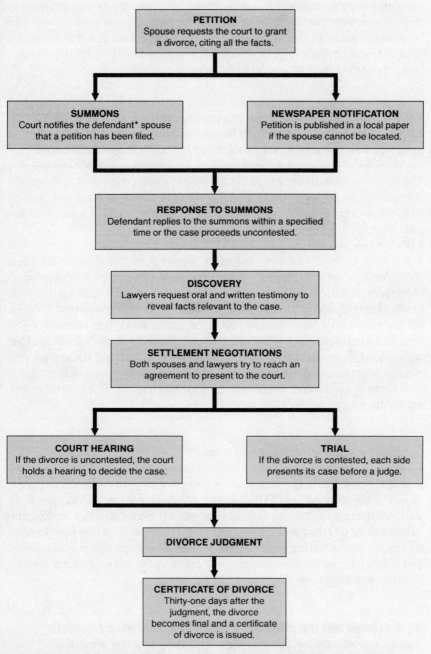

PETITION
Spouse requests the court to grant a divorce, citing all the facts.

SUMMONS
Court notifies the defendant* spouse that a petition has been filed.

NEWSPAPER NOTIFICATION
Petition is published in a local paper if the spouse cannot be located.

RESPONSE TO SUMMONS
Defendant replies to the summons within a specified time or the case proceeds uncontested.

DISCOVERY
Lawyers request oral and written testimony to reveal facts relevant to the case.

SETTLEMENT NEGOTIATIONS
Both spouses and lawyers try to reach an agreement to present to the court.

COURT HEARING
If the divorce is uncontested, the court holds a hearing to decide the case.

TRIAL
If the divorce is contested, each side presents its case before a judge.

DIVORCE JUDGMENT

CERTIFICATE OF DIVORCE
Thirty-one days after the judgment, the divorce becomes final and a certificate of divorce is issued.

* In certain cases, such as where both spouses have lived apart one year before the divorce judgment is rendered and where all issues, such as custody, alimentary pension, and property rights division have been agreed upon, the spouses may file a joint application in divorce, where technically there would not be a defendant.

DIVORCE AND
CHILD CUSTODY

divorce will usually be granted by default. However, you should still consult with an attorney to make sure all your rights are protected. Recent amendments to rules of procedure in Quebec allow a divorce to be granted without the applicant appearing in court. Proof is made by affidavit instead. This type of affidavit is permitted only when the divorce is uncontested, and when no children are involved.

Todd's lawyer explained the general procedure of a divorce to him, but he was so upset that he doesn't remember it. What, in general, are the steps you have to go through to get a divorce?

The first step in a divorce is to file a petition asking the court to grant the divorce. Once the petition is filed, Todd's wife will be served with a copy of it. She will then have a specified period of time in which to answer the petition and state what action she intends to take.

Once her answer has been filed, the attorney for each spouse will put all the facts of the case together. Sometimes this can be handled informally; otherwise it must be done through a formal procedure called discovery, in which written questions and answers are exchanged or oral testimony is given by the two spouses and, if necessary, witnesses. When all the necessary information has been assembled, the attorneys will conduct negotiations to work out any unresolved issues. If Todd and his wife—and their attorneys—are able to work out all the issues, a fairly simple court hearing will be scheduled for a final resolution of the case. If any issue is contested, there will be a formal trial in which a judge will settle the issues in dispute.

If I don't want a divorce, can I stop it?

A judge will grant a divorce if your spouse can prove marriage break-down by showing either (1) that the two of you have been living separate and apart for a certain period of time with the intention of ending the marriage, or (2) that you have been guilty of mental or physical cruelty or adultery. Contesting the divorce or appealing it may gain you a delay, but it could be an expensive one because, if the grounds are proven, the divorce will be granted.

My husband left me about two years ago, and now I want to marry someone else. How long will it take to get a divorce?

The more complex the case, the longer it will take. Contested cases, where the spouses cannot agree on property settlements and child

Grounds for Divorce

Since no-fault divorce was introduced in 1986, marriage breakdown is the only ground for divorce. Proof of such a breakdown would exist if the spouses agreed to live separate and apart for one year. Adultery or such mental or physical cruelty as would make future cohabitation impossible would also serve as proof that the marriage had broken down. Some other points concerning grounds for divorce:

- The spouse asking for the divorce cannot have forgiven or condoned the act complained of. If your husband committed adultery and you have forgiven him because he apologized and promised not to do this again, you cannot later use this adultery as grounds for divorce.
- In some cases, a couple could be considered to be living separate and apart even though they share the same house. If they don't share the same bed, don't eat meals together and don't share a social life, they would be considered to be simply living "parallel" lives and sharing the residence only for economic reasons.
- If mental cruelty is the cited ground, the behavior must affect you adversely. Suppose your spouse acts in a way that would humiliate or hurt the average person, but you simply find this funny and are not affected by it—this would hardly be considered mental cruelty in your case.
- If you have been separated for a few months and then live together for a period or periods of not more than 90 days in all to give your marriage a last chance, such periods would not interrupt the separation begun a few months before. If, for example, you began living apart on May 1, then on September 1 got back together for two months to try to save the marriage, your separation would still date from May 1.

custody, take longer than uncontested ones. A divorce begun in a large metropolitan area such as Vancouver, Toronto or Montreal would take longer than one in a smaller community, simply because the small town court would have fewer cases to hear.

When Clyde left Beverly six months ago, he moved to another province. Where should the divorce be filed?

A divorce is filed in the province where one of the spouses has resided for at least 12 months immediately prior to the proceedings. In this case, the divorce would be filed in Beverly's province, assuming she has lived there for the past year.

The Divorce Process

Brian and June have lived together for 20 years. Does Brian have to divorce June before he can marry Alice?

No. To get a divorce in Canada, a couple must be legally married.

I know of at least one instance when my husband was unfaithful. Is this enough grounds for a divorce?

Yes. Adultery can be proof of marriage breakdown. However, whether a divorce will be granted also depends on your behavior. If you have condoned his actions by failing to raise the issue or by voluntarily resuming or continuing marital relations with him, your husband may be able to prevent the divorce by showing that you have forgiven him.

If my husband wants to move to an area of the country where I will be unlikely to find the work for which I'm trained, will he have grounds for divorce if I refuse to go?

Thanks to the Charter of Rights and Freedoms and various provincial statutes concerning equality between the sexes, a wife is no longer obliged to follow her husband. But if your husband goes through with his plans and you have no intention of following him, you or he may have grounds for divorce: living separately for one year prior to the court hearing would be proof of marriage breakdown.

I don't know where my husband is, and I want to divorce him. How long must he be gone before I can get a divorce? Can I divorce him without his consent?

You don't need your spouse's consent for a divorce. If you don't know where your husband is, you can notify him of the divorce application by placing a notice in your local newspaper. If you have not been living with your husband for one year immediately preceding your divorce hearing, the judge will grant you a divorce.

Bill was an alcoholic when we married, but I didn't understand the seriousness of his drinking problem then. Can I use this as grounds for divorce?

Yes. If Bill's drinking problem is a serious one, it probably changes his personality so that he becomes violent, aggressive, insulting, rude or just

136

plain silly. If his behavior causes you embarrassment, or otherwise adversely affects your lives together, his conduct would probably constitute mental cruelty, one of the grounds for establishing marriage breakdown.

Gary's divorce hearing is several months away. If he dates Barbara while his divorce is pending, will it affect the divorce or his request for custody of his children?

If Gary and Barbara merely go out for dinner and a movie occasionally, there will probably be no effect on his divorce or request for child custody. If Gary and Barbara are involved in a serious relationship, however, the court will certainly consider whether this relationship is harmful or beneficial to Gary's children when it rules on custody, support, and visitation.

We have been separated for three years. I live in Newfoundland and started divorce proceedings here on January 10. Five days later, I got divorce papers from my husband in Manitoba. His were dated January 5. Where will the divorce be heard and does it matter that my husband started his divorce before mine?

When divorces between the same spouses are presented before two courts in different provinces, the court where the first application was made would normally have exclusive jurisdiction over the case. The divorce registrar in Ottawa will write to your lawyer informing him of your husband's application and asking that you or your husband withdraw one of the applications. Since your husband filed his divorce five days before yours, you will have to withdraw yours if he chooses to let his stand, and the divorce will be heard in Manitoba.

Tim and Louise rewrote their wills before they divorced. Does the divorce affect the wills?

If Tim and Louise are included in each other's wills, those portions of their wills are revoked by the divorce. This could change the intent of the entire will of each; thus Tim and Louise should consult their lawyers and rewrite their wills as soon as possible.

Can a divorce decree be set aside?

A final divorce decree cannot be set aside except by an appeal instituted within the legal time limits.

Alvin and Marcia are involved in a very bitter divorce. Who will decide how the property is to be divided?

If Alvin and Marcia and their attorneys are unable to reach an agreement on a fair division of their property, the judge who handles their case will divide the property according to the laws of their province. The methods of dividing property are complex and vary from one province to another. One consideration will be the type of matrimonial regime or regulations that existed during the marriage. Were they married under the regime of *partnership of acquests* or under *community of property*? Was there a prenuptial contract or other domestic contract involved? Another important consideration is the matrimonial home, usually the couple's major asset. Under the Divorce Act, judges have considerable discretion in determining the most equitable distribution of the property. Depending on what he sees as just and fit in the particular circumstance, a judge may also order one spouse to pay a lump sum or periodic payments, or both, toward supporting the other spouse and any children of the marriage. Alvin and Marcia would save many hours of court time and most likely thousands of dollars in legal fees if they could reach some compromise on their own.

I signed a prenuptial agreement prepared by my husband agreeing to take only $10,000 if we ever divorced. Later I found out he owned real estate valued at over $200,000. Can I get more than $10,000 if I go to court?

Since your husband did not reveal all his assets at the time of your marriage, it is likely the judge will rule that the prenuptial agreement was unfair. But this will not necessarily bring you a larger property award. The judge will still divide the property according to the laws of your province and these can vary considerably. Under the Ontario Family Law Act of 1986, for example, the court may set aside such a contract if it feels the terms are unfair or unconscionable. In Quebec, a spouse may get a compensatory allowance or share of property that she or he had helped to acquire. In Nova Scotia, a judge may give both partners equal shares in property that was exclusively owned by one of the spouses.

After 20 years of marriage, Bill decided to divorce his wife. The deed to their house is in his name only. Does this mean his wife will be forced out of her home after the divorce?

No. In most provinces the matrimonial home has special status no matter which spouse has the registered title. Each case is judged on its own merits and according to the circumstances involved. In some cases, the court may order that the home be divided equally; in others, ownership may be transferred from one spouse to the other. Or the judge may give one of the partners the use of the home even though the deed is in the other's name.

My wife and I agreed on how we wish to divide our property. Can a judge change our agreement?

A judge can, but probably won't. Every property division agreement must be approved by a judge. If he believes that the way you want to divide your property is unfair to either of you, or that it is inconsistent with your provincial legislation, he has the right to change it. In practice, however—and in keeping with recent Supreme Court decisions—a judge will rarely change such an agreement. For this reason, this very important part of divorce proceedings should always be discussed with a competent lawyer.

I inherited a substantial amount of money while our divorce was pending. Can my wife get any part of it?

Virtually every province recognizes an inheritance as the sole property of its beneficiary, not subject to division with a spouse. An inheritance is generally considered separate property no matter what the status of your marriage.

When I married, I had a car. We sold it, and I took over the use of my husband's car. Can I get him to give me his car or buy me another one now that we are divorcing?

The value of property brought into a marriage is only one factor that is considered when property is divided. You will not necessarily leave the marriage entitled to an automobile.

When Diane was going through her divorce, she wasn't concerned with the property settlement. Now she believes she should have received more. Can she have the settlement changed?

Probably not. A judge will not revise a property settlement that a spouse agreed to and had approved by a court unless there is a very good reason, such as evidence to prove that a spouse lied to the court about the couple's assets. It is most unlikely that the judge will find Diane's dissatisfaction sufficient reason to change her settlement.

Division of Property

My husband is hiding assets and making a property settlement difficult. How do I find out how much we really have?

First, start your search by examining all the financial records to which you have access, such as bank statements and income tax returns. Second, your attorney can use a formal legal procedure, called discovery, to ask your husband questions under oath and force him to produce such records as personal or business income tax returns, financial statements, loan applications, and pension plans. Third, for a small fee,

DIVORCE AND CHILD CUSTODY

The Search for Hidden Assets

People who are otherwise honest sometimes become deceptive during a divorce and try to hide assets so that the court won't give them to the other spouse. Hidden assets can include such things as bank accounts, investments, valuable personal property, or real estate. When hidden assets are suspected, there is a legal procedure called *discovery* that can be used to bring the assets to light.

In a discovery procedure, the attorney will ask your spouse to produce all relevant financial records. These might include:

- Personal and business tax returns.
- Chequing and savings account statements.
- Dividend and interest statements.
- Real estate records.
- Loan applications.
- Expense accounts submitted to an employer.

By checking and comparing the information in these documents, your attorney can get a better picture of your spouse's financial situation. If your spouse has not provided a full accounting of his assets, your lawyer can then send him *interrogatories,* which are written questions that must be answered in writing under oath.

If hidden assets are still suspected, your lawyer can proceed to *depositions,* in which your spouse is questioned under oath with a court reporter recording the answers. Bank officials, your spouse's employer, business associates, and others who know about his finances may also be asked to provide depositions. Those who do not cooperate can be served with subpoenas, directing them to answer questions and produce papers. The discovery procedure can be expensive and is called for only when valuable assets might otherwise go unnoticed as a settlement is worked out. In some cases, you might be wise to hire a private detective, or an agency that specializes in tracing hidden assets, to help you in your search.

you can hire an agency to make an assessment of your husband's financial condition. Finally, if you suspect that your husband has a substantial amount of hidden wealth, it may be worthwhile to hire a private detective to locate these assets.

We used my inheritance for the down payment on a business, which we operate jointly but which is in my husband's name. How will it be divided if we divorce?

You should get credit for the amount of your inheritance that you invested in the business. The remaining value of the business will be divided in the same manner as your other marital property, and your contributions to the business should be taken into consideration.

My husband and I each want to keep our prize cocker spaniel after the divorce. How will the court decide the matter?

Because this issue is not going to seem as important to the court as it does to you, your attorneys will try to seek some compromise. If they are unsuccessful, the court will review information about the past care of the pet, the original motive for acquiring it, and similar details to determine who should keep it.

Amy received legal notice that her husband had filed for divorce. She discovered on the same day that he had also withdrawn all the money from their joint chequing account, leaving no balance to cover the cheques she had just mailed to pay the household bills. What can Amy do?

Amy can request a court order—a *seizure before judgment*— and an order for interim relief to prevent her husband from spending the money from the account and to make good on the outstanding cheques. Although Amy probably will not be reimbursed immediately for her part of this money, her husband's actions will be taken into account when their property is divided. Obtaining a court order in a situation like this involves many legal technicalities; Amy should retain an attorney to handle the matter for her.

My wife has built up hefty charges on several store credit cards. Will I have to pay these debts if we get divorced?

Maybe. If the credit card accounts are in joint names or if you cosigned the credit agreements, you and your wife are equally liable for the

Division of Property

charges. On the other hand, you could be liable even if you didn't sign the credit agreements. Debts are divided along with assets in a property settlement. The court will divide these credit card charges on the basis of your ability to pay, the nature of the items purchased, your wife's motives in making the charges, who benefited from the charges, and other relevant information.

When I got divorced, my ex-husband's attorney was supposed to have the deed to our house recorded in my name. It has been six months now, and I haven't received the recorded deed. The attorney won't return my phone calls. What should I do?

Ask your attorney to contact your ex-husband's attorney. If he still won't cooperate, you may be able to have the court certify the portion of the final divorce judgment that deals with the real estate and then have it recorded in the same office as the deed. This would have the same effect as a recorded deed. You could also file a complaint against your ex-husband's lawyer with the local bar association.

My doctor's wife quit college to support him while he finished medical school. Now they are getting divorced. Is she entitled to a share of her husband's future earnings?

This is a rapidly changing area of law. Many provinces now have some way of compensating the wife for her efforts. An award to her of a share of his future earnings is only one method that has been developed to accomplish this purpose. Other methods include granting her a higher alimentary pension, a larger share of marital property, and repayment of expenses invested in his professional education.

My husband and I were married for more than 35 years before divorcing. Do I have a right to receive Canada Pension Plan benefits based on his work record?

Yes. If you had lived together for at least 12 consecutive months and were divorced after January 1, 1978, you would be entitled to share in your husband's Canada Pension Plan (CPP) benefits. How much you get depends on how many years you and your husband lived together and how many years he paid into the plan. Since January 1, 1987, CPP credits or entitlement to future pensions are split equally between the partners when marriages break up. This mandatory splitting is automatic and cannot be set aside by a separation agreement signed after June 4, 1986.

DIVORCE AND CHILD CUSTODY

142

To be eligible for pension splitting under the Quebec Pension Plan, you and your spouse would have to have lived together for 36 consecutive months. But pension splitting isn't granted automatically; you must apply for it within 36 months of the divorce.

Scott and I were married for nine years before divorcing last year. He died last month. Am I entitled to a survivor's pension?

No. Since you were no longer Scott's wife at the time of his death, you are not entitled to a survivor's pension.

Support for Spouse (Alimentary Pension)

Under what conditions is a woman usually granted support?

The goal in granting support is to enable a woman to become self-supporting at a standard of living reasonably comparable to the one she enjoyed during the marriage. Support is granted at the discretion of the court; it may continue until a woman becomes self-supporting or remarries, or it may continue indefinitely if it is clear that there is no possibility of self-support.

Linda's lawyer told her that she may be awarded maintenance. Is this the same as an alimentary pension?

Yes. The term alimentary pension is gradually being replaced by the terms *maintenance* and *support*.

Does a wife ever have to pay support to her ex-husband?

The factors that justify support payments to a former spouse apply equally to men and women. If, for example, a wife has been the main source of support in her family, the court may order her to make support payments to her ex-husband.

I heard from some old friends that my ex-husband recently received a big raise. Can I get my support increased?

Possibly. You will need to prove that your ex-husband is now able to pay more. And you will also have to convince the court you need the increased support and that your need is the result of your dissolved marriage. Of course your former husband could ask that his present support payments be canceled. He might, for example, claim that you did not make an honest effort to become self-sufficient.

At her divorce, Lisa didn't ask for support. Can she do so now?

Yes. A court can order support payments after a divorce, even if support was not granted at the time of the judgment. Lisa might not have requested an alimentary pension originally, even if she needed it, if her husband was unemployed, for example. If she was still in need when he started working, she would probably be entitled to support, however.

My ex-husband isn't making his support payments. What can I do?

Your ex-husband is violating a court order (your divorce decree); you can request that the judge enforce the order and make him pay. Divorce judgments are enforceable across Canada, and most provinces have a court officer to carry them out. He can garnishee your husband's salary or seize and sell his property on your behalf. Usually you can claim no more than two or three years of arrears. The federal justice department now has a Family Orders and Agreements Enforcement Assistance Service to trace delinquent debtors and otherwise help in enforcing maintenance and support orders (see box, page 154).

Tim and Cathy have filed for divorce. Cathy did not work outside the home for 12 years while she was raising their children. Will the court make her find a job? Will Tim still have to pay support?

Courts vary widely in awarding support to spouses. Cathy will certainly need to seek employment, and Tim will very likely have to pay her some support. The amount will be determined by comparing Tim's ability to pay with the amount Cathy needs to live on and the time it will take her to become self-supporting. Both Cathy and Tim would be equally obliged to support their children according to their means and abilities until the children are able to take care of themselves.

Larry pays Kay support. Can Larry use this as a deduction on his income tax? Is Kay required to report it as income?

Larry's support payments are taxable as income to Kay, and Larry can deduct the payments on his income tax returns. However, since there are specific tax rules and exceptions relating to support payments, Larry and Kay would be wise to consult with specialists about their situation before filing their tax returns.

When Betty and Joe divorced, Joe agreed to pay support for 10 years. A year after the divorce, he was killed in an accident. Joe's will left his entire estate to his new wife, Marianne. Can Betty seek the rest of her payments from Joe's estate?

She can try to get the payments from Joe's estate, but she probably won't be successful. Unless their divorce decree included a provision instructing Joe's estate to continue Betty's support, Joe's death will terminate any obligation to support his ex-wife.

Child Custody

Robert and Mary want a divorce. If they agree on custody and support issues, will their wishes be followed?

Since Robert and Mary agree on custody, support, and visitation issues, the court will probably accept their wishes if they are reasonable. However, the judge makes the final decision and will not approve what they work out unless it is in the best interest of the children.

What factors does a judge consider when deciding what is in a child's best interest?

The judge takes many factors into account. He will consider the wishes of the child and the parents; the age, health, and sex of the child; the home environment and the character and life-style of each parent; and their financial circumstances. In some cases, the judge may appoint a social worker to investigate these issues and make a recommendation.

Chris and Nancy both want custody of their children. Since the parents can't come up with a workable arrangement, will the judge follow the children's wishes when making his decision?

Whether the judge will follow the children's wishes depends on their age and maturity—he is less likely to follow the wishes of a three-year-old than those of a teenager. The judge will also consider many other factors in designating the custodial parent. He will not grant custody to an unfit parent even if the child requests it.

Child Custody

Do courts still give preference to the mother in awarding custody?

The traditional view has been that the best interests of young children, female children, and children in poor health were served by giving custody to the mother. The trend today, however, is to give mothers and fathers equal preference in custody cases.

If a custody fight becomes especially hostile, can the judge take the children away from both parents?

Yes. Custody decisions by the court are always guided by what is in the best interests of the child. The courts prefer that custody remain with one of the natural parents, but if the court determines that both parents are unfit because of the extreme hostility between them, it has the power to assign the custody of the children to a third person.

Once custody has been awarded, does the court then leave all decisions about the child's welfare to the parent with custody?

It is the custodial parent's responsibility to make decisions regarding the child's care, discipline, education, religion, and health. The court will defer to the decisions of the custodial parent, as long as they are in the child's best interest. However, the noncustodial parent still has the right to inquire into the health and education of the child, and to be informed of these things, and can challenge in court decisions he or she feels are harmful or inappropriate.

When Ray and Melissa were divorced, she got custody of their two young children. Now that she has remarried, can she change the last name of her children to that of her new husband?

No. The children of Melissa's first marriage keep the name of their natural father unless he consents to the name change. Melissa cannot change the children's names on her own.

Roger and Cynthia have asked for joint custody of their children. What is joint custody?

Joint custody is an arrangement in which both parents share legal and physical custody of their children after a separation or divorce. Roger and Cynthia would participate equally in reaching major decisions

Joint Custody Arrangements

Many divorcing couples feel that joint custody is the best way for each parent to have meaningful contact with the children as they grow up. Joint custody also relieves the children of the responsibility for choosing which parent to live with and helps prevent them from feeling that one parent doesn't want them. Since the Divorce Act also favors maximum contact between the divorced parents and the children of the marriage, the court may order joint custody.

There are two parts to joint custody: legal and physical. Legal custody requires the parents to make decisions together about the children's education, health, and overall welfare. Physical custody establishes the amount of time each child spends with a parent. Courts generally require divorcing parents who want joint custody to submit plans detailing aspects of both legal and physical custody. Courts will agree to a wide variety of physical custody arrangements as long as they are fair, workable, and in the best interests of the children. Here are some typical divisions of parental custody time:

- Alternate 3½ days with each parent.
- Alternate workweek with one parent, weekends with the other.
- Alternate one or two weeks with each parent.
- Alternate one month with each parent.
- Alternate two or three months with each parent.
- Spend school year with one parent, summer vacation with the other.
- Child remains at home and parents alternate according to a prearranged schedule.
- Child moves freely between two parental homes, with parents getting approximately equal time.

concerning their children, and the time spent with each parent would be more nearly equal, unlike the time allocated in sole custody.

Jeff and Sarah were recently divorced, and Sarah was given custody of their two children. If Sarah decides that she is going to move out of the province and take the children with her, what can Jeff do to prevent the children from going?

Sarah must notify Jeff or the court of her plan to move the children. If Jeff objects, he can request that the court prevent the move. In making its decision the court will consider the expense of visitation, the children's standard of living in the new province and the closeness of the children's relationship with Jeff. The judge will also determine whether the move is planned for the sole purpose of denying visitation to the father.

Child Custody

Joanna and Tom are in the process of getting a divorce, and Joanna has temporary custody of their children. If Joanna lives with another man, will the court deny her custody?

The court will not deny Joanna custody if it finds that her conduct has no harmful effect on the children. The court will limit its examination of a parent's conduct to its effect on the child's welfare and will weigh other factors, such as the age of the children and Joanna's relationship with them, in making its final determination.

What should I do if my ex-husband disappears and takes the children with him?

If you were granted custody and your ex-husband has taken the children and disappeared, he has committed a serious crime, and you should contact the police. Be prepared to give a detailed description of your children and your ex-husband, and provide the names and addresses of people that he is likely to contact. Recent photographs of your children can also be very helpful to the police.

Parental Kidnapping: What to Do if Your Child Is at Risk

It is unlikely that parental kidnappings can ever be stopped completely. However, there are some steps you can take to reduce the chances of this happening, and to facilitate the return of the kidnapped child if the worst should happen. First and foremost, make sure that your child knows your address and telephone number, and encourage him to go to a policeman if he is abducted by the other parent. Here are some other things you can do:

1. Obtain passports for your children so that they will not be able to board a plane or boat to leave the country with anyone but you. This is especially important if your ex-spouse is a citizen of another country. Send a copy of your custody judgment to the consulate of your ex-spouse's country of origin, along with a letter alerting it to the possibility that your children may be kidnapped.

2. If you suspect that your ex-spouse may kidnap the children, your lawyer should request that your divorce judgment order your ex-spouse to give you *his* or *her* passport during any visitation period. (If your ex-spouse has dual citizenship, you should ask to hold both passports.) This way your ex-spouse will be unable to leave the country.

Most provinces have signed international treaties designed to facilitate the return of children who have been abducted to other countries. But you can take some simple steps to prevent this happening in the first place. If you suspect that your ex-spouse may try to take the children overseas, get passports for them. And, if your husband was not born in Canada, send a copy of your divorce judgment to the consulate of his native country. Because two passports will not be issued for the same person, your husband will then be unable to get this essential travel documentation for the children, and so will be unable to get them on board a plane.

My wife and I don't get along or communicate with each other very well. However, we would both like to be involved in the care of our children. Would joint custody work in our situation?

Joint custody works best when the parents cooperate and work together on the issues concerning their children. If you and your wife can overcome your problems when dealing with the children, joint custody may be a good arrangement for you. If not, you should explore other custody options before making your decision. Discussions with a psychologist or a mediator might be helpful.

3. Inform your child's teacher and the day-care center director or the school principal *never* to allow anyone but you to remove your child from their care. If you have a court judgment awarding you custody of the child, give a copy to the school or day-care center. If your ex-spouse shows up at the school and makes a fuss, they should call the police.
4. Make sure you know your ex-spouse's social insurance number. This would make your ex-spouse easier to trace if he or she disappeared with the children. The number—and an address—would surface when an income tax return or an application for unemployment insurance or welfare is filed.
5. If you are living apart from your ex-spouse, and have reason to fear kidnapping, take action to get legal custody of the children. Most provinces have reciprocal agreements to help locate and return children to the parent with custody. Similar agreements exist between most provinces and other countries.
6. If your child is kidnapped, contact the police immediately and lay charges against your ex-spouse.
7. Contact your local Child-Find agency or other groups that help parents locate missing children.
8. After your child is returned, ask the court to cancel future access rights for your ex-spouse, or at least to severely restrict future rights.

Child Custody

My ex-wife, who has custody of our daughter, has remarried. Her new husband is an alcoholic and my daughter is afraid of him. Will the court let my daughter live with my new wife and me?

The courts are usually reluctant to change custody orders. But since your daughter is afraid of her stepfather, you may be able to get the custody order changed. The court will look at evidence you provide to show that living with your ex-wife's husband may have a harmful effect on your daughter. The judge will consider all the factors and award custody to the parent who can provide the best care for the child.

My ex-husband, who lives in another province, has told me that he and his new wife want sole custody of our son, who lives with me. I haven't remarried and he says the court will give him custody so our son can live in a "real family." Will the court do this?

As a general rule, the fact that your ex-husband has remarried is not reason enough to make a change in custody. He would have to go to court and present convincing evidence that there have been changes in your circumstances which are harmful to your son. If he cannot do this, custody will not be changed.

When Alice and Allen were divorced, Alice was awarded custody of their children. Allen left town five years ago and has not been seen or heard from since. Can Wayne, Alice's new husband, adopt Allen's children without Allen's consent?

Wayne can adopt the children without Allen's consent only if Allen's parental rights are terminated. Termination of parental rights occurs when a parent has abandoned a child or is judged to be unfit to be a parent. Specific grounds for termination are spelled out in each province's laws. The court would very likely find that Allen's five-year absence is sufficient to terminate his parental rights.

My husband adopted my child from a previous marriage. Now I want a divorce. Will my second husband have any rights to the child he adopted?

Yes. By adopting your child, your husband was granted the same parental rights and duties as a biological father. In awarding custody the court will consider him, as well as you, in determining which of you will serve the child's interests best.

If I let my ex-wife's new husband adopt my children, do I still have to pay child support?

No. If your ex-wife's new husband adopts your children, your parental rights would end and you would be relieved of any further financial obligations to the children.

This is a very serious decision, and it should be carefully weighed, because any and all legal relationships to the children will be ended when they are adopted. You will no longer be able to visit the children or have any say in their upbringing.

Sue is divorced and has custody of her daughter. Can she add anything to her will to make sure her ex-husband will not regain custody if something should happen to her?

No. Sue can put a paragraph in her will stating her wish that her ex-husband not be given custody of their daughter, but such a provision will have no legal effect.

Visitation

For further information on grandparents' rights, see "Rights of Grandparents" in Chapter 2, *Marriage and Family*.

My ex-wife has custody of our two children, and I was given visitation rights. Now my children say they don't want to see me. Is there anything I can do?

If your children's refusal to see you is without good reason, the court will enforce your visitation rights. But court action may not be your best approach. Your children may not want to see you because of resentment about the divorce. If the court forces them to visit you, it may increase their hostility. In most cases, patience seems the best remedy. After a while children usually decide on their own to see the noncustodial parent. Sometimes a few visits with a child psychologist for you and your children could straighten out this problem. Some communities offer these services free if the parents are unable to pay.

My ex-wife has remarried and moved to another province. Can I get my visitation rights changed so I can have my child for a whole month during the summer?

You may ask the court to modify your visitation rights. The judge will consider the child's age and what effect a one-month absence from the mother might have on the child. Other considerations are the child's wishes, and any previous restrictions that may have been imposed on your visits. Modifications of visitation rights are common when a child moves to a different location.

Do I have to let my children have overnight visitation with my ex-husband if he is living with his girlfriend?

If the court has ordered overnight visitation, you must abide by the order. If you believe that your children are being harmed by the overnight visits while their father is living with his girlfriend, you may ask the court to change the visitation arrangement. However, you may be required to prove harm to the children when they visit their father, such as physical or verbal abuse by the girlfriend or serious neglect when she is present.

Can a wife refuse to let her husband see their children while their divorce is pending?

No. Parents have a legal right to visit their children, even while a divorce is pending. However, if this visitation turns out to be harmful to the children, the court can limit or end the visitation rights.

Visitation for Grandparents

One of the cruelest blows that grandparents can suffer is the loss, through no fault of their own, of any chance to visit with their grandchildren. Suppose, for example, a former daughter-in-law wins custody of the children and refuses to let her ex-husband's parents see the youngsters. Or she marries a man who adopts the children and then refuses to allow the natural grandparents to visit the children. In the past, grandparents had no legal right to visit their own grandchildren, no matter how close they might be.

Happily, this situation is rapidly changing. Some provinces, Quebec and Ontario for example, have enacted laws enabling the courts to give grandparents permission to visit their grandchildren. Grandparents may also get visitation rights to their grandchildren and sometimes even get custody of them within the provisions of the Divorce Act. Of course the judge's decision to grant such visiting rights, and their duration and frequency, will be based on the child's best interest.

*My son and daughter-in-law are getting divorced. Will I have
visitation rights to see my grandchildren?*

In the past, grandparent visitation was not even an issue considered by
the courts. However, recent changes in the law recognize a grandparent's right to visit if it is in the child's best interest. If you have a close
relationship with your grandchildren, you can be granted the right to
visit them.

*Mike is three months behind in child support payments. Is there
any way that Sandra can prevent him from seeing their children
until the payments are made?*

No. As a general rule, visitation rights may not be withheld to enforce
child support obligations. If Sandra continues to prevent Mike from
seeing their children, Mike can ask the court to enforce his rights or to
change the custody and support order in his favor.

Child Support

*If the husband gets custody of the children, will the wife have to
pay child support?*

Both parents are responsible for supporting and bringing up the children
according to the children's needs and the ability of the parents to pay.
In this regard, the law makes no distinction between a father's and a
mother's obligation.

*Martha has temporary (interim) custody of her 2-year-old son.
Can she get child support payments while her divorce is pending?*

Martha has a good chance of getting some help if she requests it. Most
courts will not force one parent to bear the financial burden alone while
a divorce is pending. If Martha's husband is able to pay, he will be
ordered to contribute to the support of his child.

Can a court force a parent to go into debt to pay child support?

No, but when a court orders support payments, they must be paid, and
the parent may choose to go into debt rather than cut back on other
expenses. In most provinces, the court will base the amount of support
on the parents' income and ability to pay, taking expenses and debts into

consideration. But debts owed for a luxury automobile, for example, would not play much of a part in the court's deliberation about child support payments. In such cases, a free-spending parent would be expected to rearrange his or her finances.

Joan has a child by her boyfriend, Brent. Can Joan get child support from him?

Joan may collect child support if the court finds that Brent is the father. The amount will be based on Joan's need and Brent's ability to pay. It will be computed similarly to child support in a divorce.

What age does a child have to reach before child support payments can stop?

Child support payments usually stop when the child reaches legal adulthood, which is 18 in most provinces, 19 in others. Support payments can be extended beyond the age of adulthood so the child can continue his education. Since this is considered a normal necessity of life, parents must provide it for their children whenever they can afford to do so.

What to Do When Your ex-Spouse Won't Pay Child Support

Having a judge award support doesn't guarantee payments each month. However, most family courts now have collectors. If your spouse owes you support, contact your local court collector and give him a certified copy of your judgment, as well as your ex-spouse's address or the name of the company he or she works for.

Some points about support payments:

• As with any debt, arrears in support payments can be collected by seizure of salary or property that can be sold to pay what is owning.
• Declaring personal bankruptcy will *not* wipe out a debt for support.
• Collection of a support debt can be enforced even if the debtor lives in a province other than the one which ordered the payment.
• Arrears of support payments cannot accumulate indefinitely. Most provinces only allow the collection of arrears for two or three years.
• The Family Orders and Agreements Enforcement Assistance Service, P.O. Box 2730, Postal Station D, Ottawa, Ont., K1P 5W7, will help trace those who have not paid court-ordered support.

What if my ex-husband doesn't pay his child support on time?

It depends on how late your ex-husband is with the payments. If he doesn't actually miss payments and is only a week or two late with them, you may not want to antagonize him with a court action. If the late payments are a hardship for you, your options are the same as if he didn't make payments at all: you will have to take him to court.

Norman's ex-wife has missed several child support payments. Can her wages be garnisheed in order to get payment?

Norman's ex-wife's salary could be garnisheed and her property seized and sold by the sheriff or bailiff to pay for the arrears. Many courts now have collectors whose sole job is to enforce support orders and the federal justice department may also help (see box, page 154).

Can I get a cost-of-living increase with child support?

Yes. Many courts will approve automatic increases in child support to match an increase in the cost of living. If your court order does not do this, you should request it. You may request an increase if other costs of supporting your children also go up. The most common reasons for higher costs as the children grow older are clothing, transportation, and education. A child with special health or education needs may also increase your expenses substantially.

I lost my old job and the one I have now pays less. Can I go to court and get my child support payments reduced?

A reduction in income will be considered as a reason for reduced child support payments. However, the court will also look at a number of other factors. For instance, you may be in a position to make child support payments from resources other than wages, such as income from savings, investments, or real estate. And if the child's needs have increased, the court may feel that this circumstance overrides your reduced ability to pay.

Can I be put in jail if I can't make my child support payments?

A court has the power to jail anyone who willfully fails to abide by its orders. If you are unable to meet your child support obligations because of changes beyond your control, the court may consider modifying the amount of the award rather than putting you in jail.

Child Support

My divorce decree requires me to pay $200 a month for our daughter's care. My ex-wife and I now agree that $150 a month is enough. Can we just write out a new agreement and sign it?

You can, but you may encounter some problems by writing your own agreement. (1) You may unintentionally alter other provisions in the original support order. (2) You may have to obtain a court order to modify a provision of a divorce decree. (3) You may have to file the new agreement in court, which sometimes requires a court hearing. (4) The new agreement may have no legal effect if you don't follow the correct legal procedures. You should have an attorney help you draw up the new agreement in order to avoid these problems.

When Chuck and Debbie divorced, Chuck told their son, Bob, that he would pay for his university tuition. But now Chuck has changed his mind. Can Bob force him to pay?

Probably. Parents must provide their children with food, shelter and educational opportunities. If Chuck is financially able to pay for Bob's university education, he should do so, since this will give Bob a better chance in life. Chuck might not have to pay, however, if Bob is not a serious student or wants to attend an overseas university rather than a local institution. The outcome of such cases depends on the particular facts presented to a judge, but the odds are that Bob would be able to successfully sue both Chuck and Debbie for a university education.

The clerk of the court keeps a computer record of my support payments. It is in error. How do I go about correcting it?

You should notify the clerk of the court immediately of this error. Ask him if the error can be corrected without an order from the court. If it cannot, then it will be necessary to schedule a court hearing to prove that an error was made and to request an order correcting it.

Does Bill have to continue making his child support payments if both he and his ex-wife marry again?

Yes, the payments must continue. However, if Bill feels that his remarriage has added financial obligations that make his child support payments a heavy burden, he may ask the court for a reduction in the amount. Likewise, he may also request a reduction if his ex-wife's remarriage has made it easier for her to help support the children.

Your Home

I am about to rent an apartment. What precautions should I take before signing the lease?

Thoroughly inspect the apartment you will be renting, especially if you have seen only a model apartment—your own unit may not be as well situated or as well maintained as the model. Write into the lease any repairs or improvements the landlord has agreed to make. Initial these notes and have the landlord initial them when he signs the lease. Verbal promises to do certain repairs are almost impossible to enforce; get them in writing.

Make sure that the apartment is vacant or will be vacant by the date you want to move in. Try to get the name and phone number of the present tenant and ask to see his lease. In many provinces a new tenant cannot be charged a rent that is considerably higher than the previous tenant paid. If possible speak to the present tenant about possible problems such as noise or the presence of cockroaches or other insects. Be certain who will pay for electricity, heating, hot water and cable television, and whether a refrigerator and a stove are supplied by the landlord. Before you sign, have a lawyer review the lease if it contains anything you don't fully understand.

Greg has found the perfect apartment, but there is something in the lease he doesn't like. Can he do anything about it?

If he can get the landlord to agree, Greg can cross out the objectionable provision, then initial the margin of the lease next to the deleted clause and have his landlord do the same.

Are there circumstances in which a landlord can rightfully refuse to rent a house or an apartment to someone?

Yes. The law generally permits a landlord to refuse to rent property to someone as long as that refusal is not based on sex, religion, race, or national origin. He might, for example, refuse to rent to someone with insufficient income considering the rent to be paid, or to someone who has a notorious reputation for violence or drunkenness.

We are having a difficult time finding an apartment. Most of the places we like won't accept children. Is this legal?

Probably not. Manitoba, Ontario and Quebec are among provinces that now prohibit discrimination against families with children unless the apartment is clearly too small for them. And challenges under federal and provincial charters of rights and freedoms will probably end this type of discrimination everywhere else in the country eventually. It is doubtful that a couple could be forced out or denied a lease renewal because a child was born to them during the term of the lease.

Ken signed a lease and paid a month's rent on an apartment that was to have been vacated within two weeks. The apartment is still occupied a month later. The landlord refuses to return the rent and says that Ken will forfeit it unless he waits until the apartment is vacated. What legal recourse does Ken have?

He may sue his landlord for return of his deposit and for damages. If a landlord cannot deliver the premises a tenant has rented, the tenant may sue for (1) cancellation of the lease, and (2) damages, such as the increased rent he may have to pay elsewhere, inconvenience, storage costs and any other amount incurred because of the landlord's refusal to honor his obligation. Actions of this kind are usually taken before the Small Claims Court or the Provincial Rental Board.

I want to rent an apartment for six months. Should I request a written lease even though it will be for less than one year?

A written lease is always preferable because it provides reliable proof of the terms of the agreement in the event of a dispute. Although a verbal lease is legal, all provinces have legislation requiring that a copy of the written lease (even if for less than a year) be given to the tenant within a certain time, usually 10 to 21 days after the signing. In New Brunswick and Newfoundland, a copy of the lease must be given to the tenant at the time of signing.

Adam never signed a lease when he rented an apartment near the college he attends. What are his rights?

Even without a written lease, certain basic rights and responsibilities are implied in the agreement between Adam and his landlord. Adam is entitled to the quiet enjoyment of his apartment. This means he should be free from unreasonable interference from his landlord, as well as from other tenants. The landlord has to provide such basic services as hot and cold water, and adequate ventilation, and keep the hallways, stairs, and other public areas in good repair. Who pays for heat and electricity depends on the landlord-tenant agreement. In any case, the landlord must maintain the premises in at least the minimum conditions required by the local municipal building code and bylaws.

Renting a Home

Marge has been years in the same apartment. Her original written one-year lease was never formally renewed. Is it still valid?

It depends on where Marge lives. For example, Quebec law would consider her lease renewed for one year since she continued to live in the same apartment after the expiry of her first lease. In Nova Scotia the lease would be automatically renewed every year after *five* years of occupancy, unless Marge or her landlord gave a notice of termination within the legal deadlines. The need for written renewals, the deadline for giving notice, the term renewal, and the reasons for which a landlord can refuse to renew a lease differ from one province to another. Even so, most provinces would follow Quebec's example on annual renewals, although it could be argued that the lease is renewed only on a month-to-month basis since her rent is payable monthly. A simple *written* agreement to allow for an annual renewal would clear up this problem.

At the end of a one-year lease, without discussing renewal of the lease with his landlord, Joe continued to pay the same rent. Three months later, Joe's landlord increased the rent. Can he do this?

Yes, but the landlord must give Joe adequate notice of the proposed increase so that he has the option of moving out. An advance notice of 90 days is usually required although in some provinces the notice must be given only 30 days before the increase takes effect. In Saskatchewan, Ontario, Quebec, and Nova Scotia, where there is some form of rent control, Joe could contest the increase. Even where there is no rent control, a tenant could contest the increase if he could show that the real motive behind an unreasonable increase was to force him to leave—that it was in fact a disguised eviction.

What should we look into before signing a lease or rental agreement in a mobile home park?

Check the local zoning bylaws for any restrictions on what you plan to do with your mobile home—some municipalities, for example, will not let you build an addition. Look into the requirements for foundations, tie-downs, and connections to electric, gas, water, and telephone lines. Can you hook up to the sewer system or must you provide a septic system? Find out if the fees include utilities, garbage and snow removal, laundry facilities, and entrance and exit fees. Ask if there are limitations on the number of occupants, children, pets, fences, or landscaping. Check your lease as you would if renting an apartment; be particularly wary of provisions that would allow sharp rent increases.

*Craig has found a beautiful apartment at a reasonable rent, but
to get it he has to move out of his old apartment before his lease is
up. Can he sublet his old apartment?*

Yes, but he should choose his subtenant carefully. Craig remains
responsible to the original landlord for making rent payments according
to the terms of his lease. If the subtenant fails to pay the rent, Craig may
have to pay it.

Can Blanche sublet her apartment even if the lease says no?

In British Columbia, Saskatchewan, Manitoba, Ontario, Quebec, Nova
Scotia, Newfoundland, and the Territories an apartment can be sublet,
and a landlord cannot refuse consent without just cause, even if the lease
does not allow for subletting. If, however, Blanche's landlord has a good
reason for refusing this sublet—if, for example, he knows the sublessee
is a notorious alcoholic or drug user—Blanche probably should not sign
a sublease; the landlord, perhaps, could have the lease canceled and sue
for damages.

*Mack is having trouble making ends meet and wants to have a
friend move in to share expenses. Can his landlord prevent him
from taking in a roommate?*

Probably not. The landlord is obliged to give Mack peaceful enjoyment
of the premises and Mack is free to take in anyone he chooses. The only
restriction would be that the dwelling be large enough to accommodate
another person. If this were not the case, Mack would be unable to have
his wife live with him in the apartment if he got married during the term
of his lease.

*My roommate Penny and I agreed to split our bills fifty-fifty,
but Penny hasn't paid her share for several months. If we don't
pay last month's rent, the landlord will throw us out. Is there
some way to make Penny pay?*

You can pay Penny's share and then take her to court to get it back, but it
can be difficult to live with someone who is your opponent in a court
case. If your name and Penny's are both on the lease, a court might order
Penny to pay the landlord what she owes. However, if only your name is
on the lease, the courts will hold you liable for the full amount of the rent
when it is due. In any event, you and Penny would be allowed to remain
in the apartment until the proceedings came to an end. It is best for only
you to sign the lease and for you to sign another agreement with your

Renting a Home

roommate whereby she undertakes to pay half the rent. That way you would have full control over the apartment and if she did not pay her share you could have her evicted and find another roommate.

Erica's landlord slipped a note into her mailbox stating that her rent would go up $10 per month beginning with her next payment, which is due in three weeks. Must Erica pay the increase?

Yes, if her lease states that three weeks is adequate notice for a rent increase. But if it has no provision about the amount of notice, the law in Erica's province will apply. Most provinces require that notice of an increase be given at least one month in advance. Notices of increase or refusal to pay an increase, or *any* notice from one party to the other, should be sent by registered or certified mail.

Must I give my landlord notice before I move out of my apartment?

Not if you leave on the date your lease expires and it is not renewed automatically. If your lease allows you to leave before its expiration date, however, you must give the amount of notice specified. In most provinces, if you are in a month-to-month tenancy following the expiration of your written lease, you must give one month's notice of your intention to move. Deadlines for giving notice are very strict: if you are even one day late, your notice may be declared invalid. For example, if you want to move by April 30, your notice must be sent no later than March 31; if you send your notice April 1, you will have to pay rent until the end of May, unless the landlord agrees to accept your late notice.

After Jill rented a house, a disco opened nearby, causing her many sleepless nights. Can she break the lease?

There is a good chance she can. A lease agreement, like any other contract, is subject to a legal doctrine called frustration of purpose. If Jill's peace and quiet was destroyed by the disco, and its opening was unforeseeable when she signed the lease, she may claim frustration of purpose and break the lease without having to pay the rest of the rent.

Does a job transfer justify Terence breaking a one-year lease?

A lease can always be broken, but Terence should be prepared to pay the price for doing so. He may have to pay the rent during the remainder of the lease or for the period that the apartment remains empty. However, since Terence has a good reason for breaking the lease, he should try to negotiate with his landlord for a release from the remaining term, or find a subtenant. In most cases, the landlord would accept three months' rent as an indemnity to cancel the lease. If Terence anticipates another job transfer, he should seek in his next lease a clause permitting him to terminate it on one month's notice, when his company relocates him.

Greta left her apartment in good condition, but her landlord still has her security deposit. How can she make him return it?

All provinces except Quebec, where security deposits are illegal, have laws dealing with such deposits, detailing how much can be charged, what they can be used for, whether interest is payable, and when and how they are to be returned. Greta should complain to her rental board or sue the landlord in Small Claims Court if she feels he is unlawfully keeping her security deposit.

Are rent strikes legal?

No. These strikes, in which a tenant or a group of tenants decide on their own not to pay rent until certain repairs are made or other conditions are met, are unlawful. Instead, an individual or a group should consult a lawyer, who may ask a court or rent tribunal for permission to withhold rent. Withholding rent without permission could result in the defaulting tenants being evicted.

Stan was mugged in the lobby of his apartment building. Can the landlord be held liable because of poor security?

Probably not. A mugging or robbery is usually considered "an unforeseeable event" and is not the fault or responsibility of the landlord. His obligation is to take reasonable care of the common areas of his building. If, however, he had been warned of previous assaults in the lobby and refused to put on a new lock, he might in some cases be held responsible for damages that probably could have been avoided.

I replaced some of the light fixtures in my apartment with my own chandeliers. Now that I'm ready to move out, the landlord claims that he can keep the chandeliers. Is this legal?

If your lease permits your landlord to keep any equipment or other improvements that you make to his property, he can legally keep your chandeliers. If it contains no such provision, your right to take the chandeliers will be determined by what a reasonable person would believe you and the landlord intended. Courts in most provinces would probably presume that a reasonable person would not expect a tenant's chandeliers to become part of a landlord's real estate. The general rule is that objects that can easily be removed without causing structural damage to the property remain the property of the tenant, but the landlord has the right to keep things incorporated into the building, such as built-in bookcases.

Landlord Difficulties

I've had no heat in my apartment for more than a week even though I've tried repeatedly to get the landlord to do something about it. Can I move out without being obligated under the lease?

Yes. If you can prove that your landlord knew about a furnace malfunction and failed to have it repaired within a reasonable time, you will be considered to have been "constructively evicted." Most provinces have

---

The Rights of Tenants

You've just signed a lease that you believe to be fair, right down to the small print, and you're preparing to move into the place you will call home. There is no better time to make a mental checklist of your rights as a tenant. Even though your landlord seems a reasonable sort of person, it is comforting to know that the law provides solid support for you, the tenant, if you ever need it.

● You have the right to "quiet enjoyment" of your rented home. So long as you respect the terms of your lease, and do not break any laws, you may entertain anybody you choose, or do anything you please, in your home. And if, despite your polite reminders, your neighbors won't stop making too much noise, you have every right to inform your landlord and expect him to talk to the noisemakers.
● You have the right to refuse to let your landlord come into your home without your permission except in extraordinary circumstances: to make emergency repairs, for example, or to demand rent that is overdue.
● You have the right to a livable property, or in legal terms, to a "warrant of habitability" from your landlord. The walls, windows, floors, and ceilings must be safe and in good repair, and the plumbing must work.

laws requiring landlords to maintain all major building systems, including heating. Even in provinces that have no such laws, landlords have a duty to see that their tenants have "quiet enjoyment" of their apartments. So if your landlord's failure to repair the furnace interferes with the reasonable enjoyment of your apartment, especially if his inaction poses a danger to your health or otherwise renders your dwelling unfit for human habitation, you may be relieved of your duty to remain there until the end of the lease.

Approximately how long does it take to evict someone?

A week or several months. It depends on the law of the province, the facts of the case, and the tenant's willingness to fight the eviction.

My landlord keeps promising to fix my toilet, but it still doesn't work. If I hire a plumber to fix it, can he bill the landlord?

No. In most provinces, a tenant is not authorized to obligate the landlord to pay for repairs. Most leases specify who is to make repairs. If your landlord is responsible for fixing your toilet, you should give him written notice of the need for repairs. Send the notice by certified mail and keep

● You have the right, if you live in an apartment building, to be provided with certain services, such as heat, hot and cold running water, garbage collection, pest control, and locks and keys that work—unless the lease says you are responsible for such services. If you rent a single-family house or, in some cases, space in a multiple-family house, your lease usually makes you responsible for at least some of these services.
● You have a right to install temporary fixtures, such as pictures, room dividers, shelves, and light fixtures, unless your lease states otherwise. When you move out, you generally have a right to keep such equipment. If you damage the property while taking out your equipment, however, the landlord probably has the right to deduct the cost of repairs from your security deposit or to collect the cost of repairs from you. To be sure of where you stand, always insist that your landlord give you a receipt for the security deposit and a statement detailing the conditions under which the deposit will be returned to you. (Security deposits are illegal in Quebec; in other provinces, the landlord is obliged to pay interest on your security deposit.)
● You have a right to receive a copy of your lease, signed by the landlord, either at the time of the signing (in New Brunswick and Newfoundland) or no later than 21 days after signing.

YOUR HOME

Landlord Difficulties

a copy of it. If the landlord doesn't have the repairs made within a reasonable time, hire a plumber, pay him, and send a copy of the paid bill to your landlord, requesting reimbursement. If he refuses to pay the bill, sue him in Small Claims Court or go to your provincial rental board or commission. Remember, though, if the problem was your fault—for example, if you threw something in the toilet—you and not your landlord would be responsible for the repairs. If it was not working because of age or normal wear and tear, the landlord would be responsible. Do not unilaterally decide to deduct the plumbing bill from your next month's rent.

If your landlord is consistently irresponsible about keeping essential equipment in good working order, you may report him to the local board of health or building inspector. But first ask yourself whether you want to remain on friendly terms with him!

Grace is two months behind on her rent because she lost her job. Two days ago the landlord went into her apartment and took her TV and stereo equipment. He says he is holding them until Grace pays the back rent. Is this legal?

Except in an emergency, such as fire or broken water pipes, a landlord is not allowed to enter a dwelling without the tenant's permission or without a court order. He cannot remove property even if rent is owed. Having entered Grace's apartment and taken her property, he could be charged with theft. The landlord's proper recourse is to sue Grace for the back rent or to sue to cancel the lease and evict her, or both. If a judgment is rendered against Grace, a bailiff or sheriff may seize and sell some of her property (there are certain exemptions), the proceeds going to pay the back rent.

Violet's landlord keeps coming into her apartment unannounced or while she's at work. Isn't he required to notify Violet of when he plans to come in?

Generally a person who rents an apartment has the right to keep other people from entering. Even the landlord must have permission to enter. Violet should review her lease, however, because it may allow her landlord to enter the apartment to inspect the premises for such purposes as making emergency repairs, or to show the apartment to prospective tenants as the term of the lease draws to an end. If Violet's lease contains such a provision, it may also require the landlord to notify her before coming into her apartment. If he doesn't give her adequate notice, Violet can ask a court to order him to abide by the terms of her lease. She might also be able to recover money damages from her landlord for the intrusions, which constitute a violation of her rights to privacy and peaceful enjoyment of her premises.

My previous landlord said I could keep a cat. She sold the building, and the new owner says the cat has to go. Does it?

If there is a written provision in your lease allowing you to keep a cat in your apartment, that provision is legally enforceable. But if the agreement with your landlord was merely an oral one, your right to keep your cat is more than likely a privilege that your previous landlord allowed you. A new landlord is usually obliged to take over existing leases under the same terms and conditions that existed under the former owner. And some courts tend to allow a person to keep a cat or dog, even if the lease prohibits such an animal, providing the pet is well behaved, has caused no damage, and is not the source of complaints from other tenants.

Eloise wants to have cable TV installed but her landlord won't let the cable company hook it up. What are Eloise's legal rights?

Because of her landlord's obligation to give her "peaceful enjoyment" of her apartment, and because cable TV is probably included as part of that right (much as a telephone is), Eloise would probably be allowed to have a hookup if she took the matter to court or a rental tribunal.

As I was entering the house that I rent, I slipped and fell on the icy front steps and hurt my back. Is my landlord liable?

Probably not. Local law generally places on the tenant the responsibility for clearing the steps. In fact, the landlord may have assigned this duty to you as one of the terms in your lease. However, if your landlord has agreed to keep the steps free of ice, and you can prove that he knew about the icy condition and failed to live up to his agreement, he can be liable for your injuries. You might also have to show, however, that you did not know that the steps were icy and that the landlord had ample time to clear away the ice.

The apartment building where I rent is going condo. I don't want to buy. What are my rights?

Many provinces and cities require that written notice of a developer's plans be given months before a tenant is required to move. You may be

Landlord Difficulties

permitted to break your lease without penalty if you find another apartment.

Some provincial and municipal rules require the condominium developer to compensate tenants of converted buildings for part or all of their relocation expenses or to provide low-income families with monthly rental assistance payments. Because these laws are so local in nature, you should call city hall or your local provincial department of housing for information.

John broke his leg when he tripped over some frayed carpet outside Mike's apartment door. John wants Mike to pay his ambulance bill. Mike thinks the landlord should pay. Who's right?

Mike's landlord has a duty to keep the common areas of the building safe. For Mike's landlord to be liable for John's injury, it would have to be shown that the landlord knew that the carpet was frayed and that it presented a danger.

A fire in Brenda's apartment was caused by faulty wiring. Most of her belongings were destroyed, and her insurance did not cover everything. Can she make the landlord pay for the losses not covered by her insurance?

Landlords in all provinces are obliged to maintain their properties in a safe condition. If the cause of this fire was proven to be faulty wiring, the landlord could probably be held responsible for Brenda's loss; he would also likely be insured against this. The landlord or his insurance company could probably sue the electrician who installed the faulty wiring. If the installation was satisfactory but the wiring was frayed because of age and normal wear and tear, the landlord would still be responsible for the fire damage. Most city bylaws and building codes require that electrical wiring be maintained in a safe condition.

Buying Your Home

I'm buying a house. At what point should I consult a lawyer?

It's a good idea to have a lawyer involved from start to finish. He can be invaluable in helping you negotiate the purchase, draft the purchase agreement, perform the title search, and arrange for an appraisal, and can provide advice on financing and represent you at the closing.

You can, of course, complete the purchase of a home without the services of a lawyer, but it may not be in your best interests to do so. Buying a home is probably the largest investment you will ever make, and you owe it to yourself to obtain expert advice so that you get everything that is due you in the transaction. In Quebec you would seek the services of a notary rather than a lawyer. Notaries are experts in real estate law, and in Quebec they are the only professionals allowed to draw up deeds of sale.

How binding is an offer to purchase?

Once an offer is accepted by the seller, both parties are bound by the contract and neither can withdraw from the deal. Because of the nature and importance of an offer to purchase, great care must be taken in drawing it up, and all the conditions of the sale should be included. Some of the more important are the price, the warranties or exclusion of warranties pertaining to the property, the time limit within which the offer must be accepted, the condition that the offer to purchase will be valid only if the prospective buyer is able to arrange financing within a certain time, and the date on which the property must be transferred if the parties agree to the sale.

In some cases, the parties may stipulate in the offer to purchase that either party may withdraw from the sale by paying a certain amount of money called earnest. This earnest is deposited by the prospective purchaser at the time of his offer to purchase. If he refuses to go along with the sale, he forfeits this earnest. If the seller changes his mind, he must return the earnest to the buyer and also give him an equivalent amount of money. Contracts involving earnest money are rare, and the conditions of earnest and the right to withdraw from such a contract must be expressly stated in the offer to purchase.

If I need an extension of time on my purchase agreement, must I get it in writing?

Yes. Every province requires a contract for the sale of real estate to be in writing; any modifications to such a contract must also be in writing.

Can an offer to purchase make the purchase of a new house contingent on the sale of the old one?

Yes, as long as the seller agrees. Since few people can afford the cost of financing and maintaining two homes at once, most buyers insist on a provision of this type in their offer to purchase. The seller will probably agree rather than risk not selling his house.

Buying Your Home

Irma and Brian are buying a house. If the house burns down after they sign the purchase agreement but before the closing, who takes the loss?

Unless the parties agree otherwise, in writing, the risk would be assumed by Irma and Brian, the purchasers. The vendor, however, has the obligation to maintain the property in good condition during this period.

We are in the market for a new home. How do we make sure that the house we are buying has no outstanding liens or other unpaid surprises hidden somewhere?

Arrange for a title search—a detailed investigation of public records concerning the history of ownership of a piece of real estate. The title search will show whether or not the seller has full title, or rights of ownership, to the property. In effect, it will confirm the seller's right to sell the house and determine the existence of any other claims to it, including liens or mortgages.

At the end of a title search an abstract of title is prepared, summarizing all sales, transfers, judicial proceedings, recorded liens, and similar transactions involving the property. If something threatens to interfere with your full use of the property or requires payment of bills or taxes, have the current owner resolve these problems before the closing. A bank or other lender will probably require you to have a title search done before approving mortgage financing.

Meg and Jerry are newly married and want to buy an old house that they can fix up and move into. They keep seeing ads for houses that have been seized by the municipality for unpaid taxes. Should they buy one?

A property seized for taxes can present a good opportunity to become a property owner for a small purchase price. Lists of such properties are usually advertised by the municipality in the local newspapers. They are sold by public auction, so the price paid often exceeds the amount the city is claiming in unpaid taxes. There are usually conditions. The purchaser must pay about 10 percent of the purchase price immediately by cash or certified cheque, the balance within a short time. The original owner often has the right to buy back the property within one year of the sale by paying the purchaser the amount he paid plus an indemnity of about 10 percent. One should be careful in purchasing a property in bad repairs: the cost of maintaining it in the condition required by municipal bylaws could exceed the real value of the property.

My attorney is concerned about a clear title to the newly renovated home I'm buying. What is he talking about?

In most provinces, if a contractor has not been paid for work he did on a house, he is given a claim against the house in the form of a lien. This mechanic's lien puts a cloud over the title to the house—in other words, the contractor's claim would cast doubts upon your ownership rights because the contractor could have the house sold to get the money to pay him for his material and labor. To make sure you have a clear title (one that is not subject to a mechanic's lien), your lawyer will probably require verification from the current owner that the contractor and his subcontractors have been paid in full. Liens (known as privileges in Quebec) can be registered by contractors, suppliers of materials, subcontractors and others who worked on the house.

Lucille is about to buy a house. Should she get title insurance?

It's advisable. Even when a title search—a thorough investigation of a property's history—is conducted, incidental transactions may not show up in the local land record office. Title insurance will provide Lucille with protection against someone turning up later and claiming to have better title (ownership rights) to the property. For example, suppose Tom, a 17-year-old whose parents had just died, sold his family house to Rick, and Rick sold it to Lucille. The fact that Tom was a minor when he sold the house will not appear in the land records. But because he is a minor, most courts will let him cancel his contract, and so Rick's sale of the house to Lucille would be invalid. This means, in effect, that Tom could demand the house back from Lucille. If Lucille had title insurance the insurance company would refund her money. Otherwise, she would have to sue Rick for a refund and hope he had the money to pay her when she won her case.

Should a husband and wife put their home in both names?

For most married couples, it's a good idea. With joint ownership, called tenancy by the entirety, neither the husband nor the wife can sell the house without the other's permission, and when one spouse dies, the ownership of the property is automatically transferred to the surviving partner. Tenancy by the entirety usually results in fewer problems, especially at the time of bereavement. Without it, if husband or wife died without a will, the property might go to their children, who, if they so chose, could sell the house, forcing the surviving parent out. However, in most provinces, even if one spouse is the sole owner, the surviving spouse may be entitled to at least partial ownership. Under the Ontario Family Law Act 1986, and similar legislation in British Columbia, Alberta,

Buying Your Home

New Brunswick, Nova Scotia and Newfoundland, certain rights to the matrimonial home are given to the spouse in whose name the property is *not* registered. In Quebec, a matrimonial home owned by only one spouse cannot be sold or mortgaged (hypothecated) without the consent of the other.

Two or more persons who are not husband and wife may also share ownership in a house. This is called joint tenancy; it gives the owners all the benefits and restrictions of tenancy by the entirety.

As a purchaser, what should I look for in a deed of sale?

The most important thing is that the seller guarantee in writing that he has a clear title to the property, and that there is no legal claim against it from an ex-spouse, a mortgage creditor, or workmen or others involved in the construction or repair of the building. The buyer should make sure there is no exclusion of guarantee for defects that become apparent later on—such as cracks in the foundation or inadequate heating apparatus. If the building is old, some guarantee should be given concerning the water pipes, the wiring, the roof and the foundation.

The seller told Warren he can give him no more than the existing title, not one that is free and clear. Should he take it?

No. By accepting to buy without a guarantee of a title free and clear, Warren would have only as much right to the house as the seller had. If the seller's title is not valid, Warren could lose the house. If the seller is only half owner, Warren might have to share the house with the co-owner. If the house has liens against it, Warren would have to pay them off or lose the house. He would be taking a great risk and would find it difficult if not impossible to find financing.

What happens at a closing?

A financial accounting is made, detailing all of the costs associated with the sale and specifying who will pay for them. All expenses must be accounted for, from the selling price, through payment of the heating bill up to the day of the closing, to the fee for filing the deed. The documents transferring ownership of the property are signed. These documents include a deed, a mortgage or deed of trust, and any others associated with the financing of the sale. In some places, the buyer and seller and their attorneys meet together; in others, each side meets separately with a settlement officer—an employee of the lender or title company.

What do closing costs cover?

Closing (or settlement) costs are the expenses over and above the price of the property; they must be paid before the property can be turned over to the buyer. They may include appraisal and credit report fees, the seller's lawyer or notary fees, fees for preparation and recording of mortgages and other documents, surveyor's fees, and reserve funds for insurance and property taxes.

Terms of a Real Estate
Sales Contract or Purchase Agreement

The sales contract, or purchase agreement, is the most important document you sign when buying a home. It should include:

- ☑ A detailed description of the land and dwelling, including any restrictions or special rights (such as to water or timber).
- ☑ A list of furnishings the seller has agreed to leave, such as draperies, carpets, stove, and lawn equipment.
- ☑ The purchase price, method of payment, and any special financial arrangements, including taxes, legal fees, and contingencies if the buyer cannot obtain financing within a specified time period.
- ☑ The amount of the deposit, the name and address of the escrow agent, and a statement of who pays the escrow agent and under what circumstances the deposit can be returned.
- ☑ Requests for satisfactory termite and engineering inspections.
- ☑ Who will pay for repairs if the property fails inspection or is damaged before the closing.
- ☑ Whether title is to be free and clear.
- ☑ The kind of deed to be delivered.
- ☑ Provision for a title search and title insurance to show the extent of your ownership rights (title) to the property and to protect you in case someone claims rights to the property at a later time.
- ☑ Who will pay the real estate agent and the lawyer or notary involved in drawing up the deeds, easements and other documents.
- ☑ Whether the property is sold with or without a guarantee against latent defect.
- ☑ A statement, if the vendor has a balance owing to him, outlining what would happen to the property in the event the purchaser defaulted in his payments.
- ☑ A statement, if this is a duplex or apartment building, of the rents received from the property.
- ☑ A declaration as to liens or pending legal actions.
- ☑ Time and place of the closing.
- ☑ Date of occupancy.

Why do I have to prepay interest at my closing?

It covers the time between closing and the date when your first mortgage payment is due.

We're closing on our house next week. Is there anything that could go wrong at this point?

The great majority of closings are conducted without any problems, but various things could go wrong at or before the settlement. See that all papers are prepared correctly, including documents your lender may require, such as policies for title insurance and property insurance.

A few days ahead, call the person handling the closing and ask if all is in order. Have your lawyer or notary review all the documents. On the day of the closing, inspect the premises to make sure that everything is as it should be. Check that the seller has left the furnishings he agreed to leave and that he has completed the repairs he agreed to make.

What can I do if the seller does not turn the property over to me at the closing?

First, determine why. If you have met all of the conditions specified in your purchase agreement, there should be no reason for him to renege on his agreement. If he refuses to complete the sale, you will have to go to court to have him evicted and to obtain a writ of possession. You may be entitled to damages for expenses incurred in connection with the purchase, in addition to the return of your deposit. Situations where the seller changes his mind at the closing are fortunately extremely rare.

Emily and Daniel are thinking of buying a condo. What are the major differences between owning a condo and owning a house?

A condominium is a special form of ownership. Not only do you own your own apartment, or unit, but also—together with the other condominium owners—you own a portion of the land and certain common areas of the building. These generally include lobbies, hallways, laundry rooms, stairways, elevators, the exterior of the building, sidewalks, parking areas, and other open spaces.

While you are solely responsible for the upkeep of your own unit, you are jointly responsible with others for the upkeep of the common elements. All the owners form an association, which elects officers and a board of directors. The association either manages the land and common areas directly or hires managers to do so. Condo owners are assessed a monthly maintenance fee for the running and upkeep of the complex. A condo contract may limit the owner's right to rent his unit or impose a restriction on who may buy it. Some contracts require the association's approval if you wish to paint the exterior of your property. Read the rules of your condominium carefully and have a lawyer check the agreement before you sign.

A condo we like has a monthly assessment fee at least 25 percent less than in comparable units. Is this too good to be true?

It may be. If the assessment is not high enough to cover all the expenses of the condominium complex, you will probably be faced with unanticipated bills after you move in. While the fee varies from complex to complex, it should be enough to cover all the expenses, including taxes, maintenance and upkeep of the common areas, salaries of employees, and insurance. It should also be large enough to include a reserve fund for major repairs and replacement of such things as the roof, central heating, and air conditioning.

Our condo association voted to install a swimming pool. I can't afford to pay my share, which is $2,000. Can they evict me?

You cannot be evicted from your condominium, but the condominium association could get a lien against your property, requiring you to pay the $2,000 pool assessment before you could sell your unit, or it could start foreclosure proceedings against you, which could have the same end result as an eviction. In either case, you could stop the process only by paying the assessment.

Is a cooperative apartment riskier than a condominium?

Yes. Each cooperative owner shares in the payment of the mortgage of the entire complex. If one or more owners default, the rest must make up the difference. A condominium owner is responsible only for the mortgage on his own unit.

Reggie and Myrna want to buy a lot in the country and put a mobile home on it when they retire. Are there special laws or regulations governing mobile home lots?

Yes. Virtually every municipality has zoning regulations and restrictions on mobile home lots. Typically, these regulations provide for minimum lot sizes, adequate sewage treatment and sanitation, minimum health and safety standards, and requirements for tying down the units. In some areas mobile homes are prohibited. Because regulations vary widely from one community to another, Reggie and Myrna should check with their local zoning board to determine exactly what regulations and restrictions apply in that community.

Questions to Ask When Buying a Condo

Before signing a contract to purchase a condominium, read the following documents thoroughly: the prospectus, also called the offering plan; the bylaws; the operating budget; an engineer's report; and the management agreement. Although the following questions will help uncover potential pitfalls, you should have all the documents reviewed by an attorney to make sure you are fully protected.

☑ Who holds the major interest in the building or complex—the developer or the residents?

☑ What is the developer's reputation? Does the Better Business Bureau have any information about him?

☑ Does the developer have sufficient funds to complete the project without your down payment?

☑ Are the residents in other condos built by this developer satisfied?

☑ Who owns the land underneath the buildings? Who owns the parking and recreational facilities?

☑ Can you inspect the unit or location where you'll be living?

☑ Does there seem to be a high turnover of owners?

☑ Has the value of the units increased or decreased? (To check this and the turnover rate, ask local realtors or call the nearest municipal office and ask where you can see title transfer records.)

☑ How is the monthly assessment computed? (A percentage of occupied units is more expensive than a percentage of total units.) Is the assessment reasonable for the services it covers? (If it's too low, you may be faced with a drastic increase after you move in.)

☑ Is the development's reserve fund adequate to cover major repairs?

☑ How is the reserve fund financed?

☑ Can young children in your family visit or stay over?

☑ Will you be allowed to keep pets or to plant flowers or bushes?

☑ Can you rent or sell your unit without special restrictions or the association's approval?

☑ If your condo is in a new development, what plans are there for future development of the area? Will there be schools, churches, shops and public transportation?

☑ Can you see a copy of the condo regulations?

How can I be sure that my new mobile home will be safe?

Provincial sales of goods acts and consumer protection acts require the contract of sale to contain a warranty that the mobile home meets the Canadian Standards Association minimums concerning electricity, plumbing, heating, etc. If you have problems during the warranty period, you can force the seller and the manufacturer to repair or replace faulty parts free of charge.

Where should I keep the deed to my land?

The best place is your safe-deposit box.

Buyer Beware

When buying a house, how can I make sure that the seller will leave me the refrigerator, stove, and drapes as promised?

See to it that the purchase agreement includes a list of the furnishings to be left by the seller. Make the list as specific and thorough as possible. Using a broad term like *furnishings* is not good enough. Sellers have been known to remove built-in dishwashers, ovens, light fixtures, and other items normally considered part of the house. Inspect the premises just before the closing to be sure that the agreed-upon furnishings are there.

The Hurleys bought a house six months ago. Last week they got a notice of a lien on the property from a plumber who is threatening to sue them for his unpaid bill. What can the Hurleys do, since they didn't agree to pay for his work?

Generally, once the purchase is completed, the buyer is responsible for any outstanding bills or taxes. If the Hurleys were given a full covenant and warranty deed, they can sue the seller for the amount of the lien. If they have title insurance, they can file a claim with their insurance company for payment. Otherwise, their only recourse is to pay the bill themselves and sue the former vendor for reimbursement.

The Thompsons have discovered that the roof of their new house leaks. Can they sue the broker who assured them that it didn't?

Yes, but only if they can prove that the real estate broker intentionally misrepresented the condition of the roof. Their best recourse is to sue the broker and the builder of the house in the same action. The builder or construction company is assumed to know of any defects in the property and is therefore responsible for repairing the roof. The builder could also be responsible for damage the leaking did to carpets or furniture. When buying a new or recently built house, you should ask the municipal building permit department whether the property has passed all inspections or whether some problems remain to be fixed. Do this *before* signing the deed of sale. Your best protection is to have guarantees against defects included in writing in the offer to purchase and the deed of sale.

When Nick agreed to buy Colin's property, the purchase agreement they signed included some warranties by Colin about the condition of the house. When the deed was drafted, these warranties were not included. If problems arise later, will Nick be able to force Colin to honor the warranties?

No. Once the buyer and seller sign the deed, the purchase agreement is no longer in effect. The provisions in the deed take over. Nick might, however, have a legal recourse against the lawyer or notary who drew up the deed of sale, because the fact the deed did not contain the warranties may be due to the negligence of the person who did the paperwork.

The seller has assured me that the house I want to buy doesn't have termites. Should I take his word on the subject?

No. He may be mistaken, so insist on a mechanical and structural inspection. Your purchase agreement should specify that if the inspection shows a major flaw, the seller will fix it or the buyer can back out of the deal and have his deposit refunded. A thorough inspection should cover the basement, roof, plumbing, water heater, electrical system, heating and cooling system, and foundation. A buyer usually has no recourse against a seller for defects that could easily be spotted by an engineer or an architect. Many engineers and architects do house inspections for prospective buyers.

My condominium complex has been occupied for a year, and the landscaping still hasn't been finished. What remedy do I have?

In a condominium development, there is usually a condominium association, led by a board of directors. Your first step should be to contact the board to find out when the landscaping work is to be completed. If the work will not be finished in the time period that was promised, and if you can show that the value of your unit has diminished as a result, you can sue the developer. The association itself, however, may be responsible for completing the landscaping, in which case you, as a member of the association, would in effect be suing yourself.

Building a New Home

Gladys bought a treed lot and gave her contractor specific written instructions to save the trees so they would shelter her new house. The contractor leveled the lot. What can Gladys do?

Because she gave him specific instructions in writing, Gladys can sue the contractor. The amount of the damages would not be based on Gladys's feelings about the trees, however, but on the dollar amount by which the value of the property is judged to have decreased because the trees were cut down. If the court decides that the value is significantly decreased, Gladys may be able to cancel her agreement with the contractor. (The contractor would have been equally bound by oral instructions but these might be difficult to prove in court.)

Who is responsible for making sure our house will comply with local zoning restrictions?

The primary responsibility rests with you, your architect, and your building contractor. Zoning restrictions are designed to protect property values in a given area. Before you begin construction, check with your zoning office to make sure that your plans comply with local regulations.

How can I be sure that the contractor is following the plans we agreed on and obeying all the local building codes?

In most communities, the local building department requires contractors to submit plans and specifications for new houses before construction begins. While construction is under way, the building department makes periodic inspections, and when it is completed, the building inspector issues a certificate of occupancy, which states that the house conforms to the local building code.

To be on the safe side, make sure that your agreement with the contractor includes a clause that permits you to withhold some of your payment until a certificate of occupancy is issued. It is easier to get a contractor to cooperate if he has not been paid in full. You should also agree with the contractor to withhold a further sum, usually about

15 percent, to cover part of the cost of subcontractors. This would keep workers and suppliers to whom the contractor owed money from registering a lien against your property.

We are having problems with our newly built house. The windows leak, the floors sag, and there's a crack in the foundation. Isn't the contractor responsible for making the necessary repairs?

Probably. Nearly every contractor who builds new houses provides warranties for materials and workmanship. In most cases, these warranties apply for up to a year after the house is completed. In some areas, you may be able to purchase an extended warranty for an additional cost. Warranties for all new houses are required by law in both Ontario and Quebec. In the other provinces, too, the purchaser of a new property marred by faulty workmanship or materials would have an excellent chance of winning his case. The old rule of *caveat emptor* (buyer beware) has to a large extent been softened by statute law as well as by court judgments.

Buying an Undeveloped Lot

Many of us dream about buying a piece of land where we can build a family home, a vacation house, or a retirement retreat. The sale of undeveloped lots is a multi-billion-dollar business, and some unscrupulous operators may try to sell you practically worthless land at hugely inflated prices. There are federal and provincial laws against such shady practices, but the wheeler-dealers are experts at staying just inside the law. You should be very alert and very cautious when you read or hear about what seems an incredible, once-in-a-lifetime opportunity to buy a dream property.

Jokes abound about people who have bought, sight unseen, a lot described as an earthly paradise and later found it was in a swamp or desert, or on a cliffside or mountaintop. Many of these stories are true, so never buy property you haven't seen. Ideally, you should see it at all seasons of the year, wet and dry, hot and cold. If you don't know about the area's weather extremes, ask the local residents. Once you have seen the place, if you still want it, there are additional questions to consider:

• How does the price compare with that of similar lots in the area?
• What financing arrangements are offered, and how do they rate against others available in the area?
• Is the lot you saw the one you are actually going to get?

The contractor has promised to finish painting the interior of my house after the closing. How can I protect myself?

Have your attorney draft an agreement between you and the contractor that specifies exactly when the painting will be completed. At the closing, sign the agreement and have the contractor sign it. The money for the painting can be placed in escrow until the contractor completes the project. If he doesn't finish the job within the agreed time, you can use the escrow money to have the work done by someone else.

When Justine had her house built, she specified a certain brand of ceiling tile, but the contractor used a cheaper brand that looks similar. Does Justine have to pay him the full price?

No. As long as Justine specified the brand and quality of tile to be used, her contractor is required to refund the difference in price. Depending on the local laws, Justine might also be able to have the tile replaced with the brand that she originally specified. Her contractor might be required to do the work at no additional cost, or he might be required to pay another contractor to complete the work to her satisfaction.

- Will the seller or developer give you a chance to read sample copies of the contract and other legal papers you will be expected to sign *before* you make the decision to buy?
- Will the seller give you a property report, a statement of pertinent information about the lot to study before you sign anything?
- Where are the nearest communities? Are there paved roads?
- Are there mortgages or liens on the property?
- If you make a deposit, will your money be put in escrow until you close on the property?
- If recreational or other common facilities are promised, where are they and when and how can they be used? At what cost?
- Are the water supply and sewer systems operating?
- What are the projected utility services and charges?
- What percentage of the homes planned in the development is currently built? Currently occupied?
- Have you seen a report of the site's soil and foundation conditions?
- What title (ownership rights) will you get to the site, and when will you receive it?
- Is this land zoned for the type of property you wish to build?
- How high are the taxes?

Be sure to get in writing the seller's assurances on these points.

YOUR HOME

Building a New Home

Gene's contractor did not conform to the local building code when he wired the house. What should Gene do?

Contact the office that grants building permits. Once this office finds the wiring unsatisfactory, it will order the contractor to correct the situation. If he does not, Gene can have the work done by another contractor and then seek reimbursement from the first contractor.

Financing a New Home

For homeowner's insurance, see "Insuring Your Home" in Chapter 8, _Insurance._

Jack is about to be married and is buying a house. But he can make a down payment of only 5 percent. The bank told him that he must therefore buy mortgage insurance. What is this?

It is a policy in which, for a monthly fee or premium, an insurance company undertakes to make the monthly mortgage payment if the insured falls ill and has no income, or loses his job through layoff or other reasons not his fault. This protects the lender's money in case of default by the borrower. Where there is no such policy, the lender can take possession of the house and sell it to get his money back, but this procedure is costly and time-consuming. If Jack could make a down payment of 10 percent, he might be eligible to have the mortgage guaranteed by Canada Mortgage and Housing Corporation.

Jon wants to sell his house to Elliot and have him assume the mortgage. When Elliot read over Jon's mortgage, he noticed a due-on-sale clause. Will this have any effect on their agreement?

Yes. A due-on-sale clause requires the homeowner to pay the balance of the mortgage upon selling the house, thus preventing a buyer from assuming the loan. Jon and Elliot can ask the bank to modify the mortgage agreement, but it is not required to do so.

Albert and Cora, who have a mortgage at 9 percent interest, are selling their house, and they want to transfer the mortgage directly to the buyers. Can the bank raise the interest rate?

Usually not. Albert and Cora probably could transfer the mortgage at the same interest, informing the lender in writing. Mortgages guaranteed by Canada Mortgage and Housing Corporation are generally transferable at the same rate. Albert and Cora should check their deed of mortgage, however, as it may prohibit a transfer; in that case the bank would issue a new mortgage to the new buyer at the prevailing rate of interest.

Our buyer would like us to finance part of the purchase price. Should we do this?

While there is nothing wrong with becoming a lender, there are risks involved. The major risk is that the buyer will not be able to make his payments to you. This becomes even more serious when a bank holds a first mortgage on the property. If the buyer defaults, the bank will be paid first. There might not be enough money left to pay you.

There is a further disadvantage. Instead of getting a lump sum of cash at the closing, you will be receiving small portions of this money over a long period. To a certain extent, you can compensate by charging the buyer interest. But if interest rates rise during the course of the loan, you will lose any income you might have earned had you been able to invest the lump sum at a higher rate. Financing part of the purchase price may be worthwhile, however, if it makes the sale more attractive to potential buyers and if you can realize a higher purchase price on your home. The part of the sale price owing to you by the new buyer is called the balance of sale.

Is it more difficult to get a mortgage for a condominium when the majority of the units are occupied by renters?

In some cases. Mortgage lenders are interested in the amount of risk they take when making a loan. They want to be sure that the real estate involved will maintain or increase its value, and prefer to lend money where the borrower occupies the premises rather than rents them.

Two years ago Maurice sold his house to the Morgans, who assumed his mortgage. The Morgans ran into financial problems and couldn't make the payments. Now the bank that holds the mortgage says Maurice is responsible for making the payments. Can this be true?

It depends on what the deed says. If it clearly states that the buyers "assume the seller's mortgage," the Morgans are fully responsible, and there is no liability on Maurice's part. On the other hand, if the deed says that the Morgans bought the home "subject to the mortgage," Maurice will probably be liable for making the payments. If he refuses to make them and the house is sold at foreclosure, he may be liable to the bank for any shortfall that arises from the sale. For example, say that the house was valued at $90,000 at the time of the sale and the Morgans bought it subject to Maurice's mortgage of $70,000. After making only $2,000 in payments against the principal, the Morgans defaulted, and the bank foreclosed. If the house has depreciated in value over the two years the Morgans had it, and it sells for only $62,000, Maurice will have to make up the $6,000 difference. This is an extremely complicated area of real estate law; Maurice should contact a lawyer.

When I bought my house five years ago, I used financing that requires small monthly payments and then a large balloon payment at the end. The balloon payment is coming up early next year, and I won't be able to pay it. What can I do?

Try to arrange new financing for this mortgage right away. Under the terms of a mortgage, if you are unable to refinance the loan or make the

Types of Mortgages

When you buy a new home you will probably pay for most of it with a mortgage loan—money lent to you against the value of your home by a bank or other financial institution. The lender will put up the money to pay for the house (less the down payment you make at the closing), and you will get the deed to the property. In return, you will sign a loan (mortgage) agreement that says you will give up your home to the lender if you default on paying back the loan. This means that the lender can sell the house to get the money you owe him. There are various types of mortgages:

● *Conventional mortgage*—The buyer pays the lender back in equal monthly installments, including interest at a fixed rate.

● *Purchase money mortgage*—A conventional mortgage in which the seller, rather than a bank or other financial institution, is the lender.

● *CMHC mortgage*—Up to 90 percent of the mortgage is insured by the Canada Mortgage and Housing Corporation. Should the buyer default, the lender is protected against losing his money. CMHC-backed mortgages have low interest rates and are available to anyone who has a good credit record and can afford a down payment of at least 10 percent for residential property, 15 percent for commercial.

● *Variable-rate mortgage*—The lender can raise or lower the interest rate in response to changes in money market rates and the demand for mortgage loans. Typically, the adjustment is made annually; but it can be made after a shorter or longer period. In most cases, a variable-rate final payment on time, the lender can foreclose. If you have a good payment record, you may be able to have your lender refinance the loan himself or grant an extension until you can arrange a new mortgage. If you feel you'll be unable to refinance the mortgage, try to sell the property. You may get enough to pay the amount owing on the mortgage and have some money left over.

The Scotts are planning to spend a year in Australia. They have a mortgage on their home. Can they rent the house without permission from the mortgage holder?

Many mortgage contracts require the buyer to obtain the permission of the mortgage holder before renting the property. The Scotts should check the mortgage contract to see if such a provision is included. Other restrictions often found in a mortgage are limitations on the right of the borrower to make major renovations or otherwise change the building on which he is paying the mortgage.

mortgage specifies both the minimum and the maximum rate that can be charged and the amount the mortgage payment can increase in a given year.

● *Graduated-payment mortgage*—The buyer's monthly payment gradually increases over a number of years according to an agreed schedule. Usually, payments rise annually over a period of three to five years, and then level off. This type of loan is often attractive to people who expect to have higher incomes after a few years.

● *Balloon mortgage*—The buyer's monthly payment consists almost entirely of interest, with only a small fraction being repayment (amortization) of the actual amount borrowed (principal). These payments are made over a specified number of years, and then a single large payment, or balloon payment, is made to pay off the loan. Over the life of this kind of loan, interest is higher than on conventional mortgages because the principal remains high. Generally when the balloon payment comes due, the buyer can refinance the loan in order to get the money to pay it.

● *Installment contract*—As in a purchase money mortgage, the buyer makes payments to the seller, but the seller need not deliver the deed until the last payment is made. In theory, missing one payment on an installment contract permits the seller to declare the buyer in default and repossess the house. In practice, however, many courts treat an installment contract in much the same way as a conventional mortgage. The seller must begin foreclosure proceedings, and the buyer can remedy the default at any time during the proceedings.

YOUR HOME

Financing a New Home

I cosigned a loan when my father bought his house. If I declare bankruptcy, will my father lose his house?

No. If you are just a cosigner and not part owner of your father's home, your bankruptcy petition will not affect your father's ownership. As long as your father makes his payments, the lender has no right to foreclose.

Home Improvements and Repairs

What kinds of home improvement usually require a permit?

Those involving major structural work, such as adding a room, require building permits. Many municipalities require permits for projects that involve electrical or plumbing work, such as converting a walk-in closet into a powder room. If a contractor does the work, have him obtain the permits. If you do the work, get permits from the building inspector or city hall.

When I put a new roof on my house, I carefully followed the city building codes. Now some homeowners' association I've never heard of has written to say I must use different, more expensive material. Can they force me to replace my new roof?

Restrictions on building materials and even architectural styles are not necessarily only those of the municipal building code. In some residential subdivisions and especially in planned communities, many deeds require uniformity in order to protect the value of neighboring property. Such restrictions are generally overseen by homeowners' associations. Even if you didn't know about the association or its restrictions, a court might rule that it was your obligation to be diligent in observing any restrictions in your deed when you bought the property.

What responsibility do I have if workers are injured while remodeling my house?

If they are employees of a contractor, the basic responsibility falls on him. All provinces require licensed contractors to have workers' compensation insurance to cover injuries. But if you direct the remodeling yourself, you may be personally liable for any injuries. Before starting a project, check with your insurance agent to determine the amount and type of liability protection you should have.

A contractor told Arthur he is bonded. What does this mean?

It means he has bought surety bonds as a kind of liability insurance. They provide payment for any loss or damage that may result from the contractor's work. For example, if the contractor fails to complete the project according to their contract, Arthur can seek payment from the bonding company for any additional costs he incurs. Always check with your provincial Consumer Protection Office as to whether a contractor is obliged to put up a bond.

I hired a contractor to add an attached garage to my house and gave a $2,000 down payment. He worked for one day and hasn't returned since. It's been three months now. What can I do?

Notify the contractor in writing that unless the garage is completed by a certain date, you will cancel your contract and hire someone else to finish the job. If the original contractor has not completed $2,000 worth of work, you can sue for the amount you overpaid. He may be liable for any damages you have suffered, and you may be able to collect whatever amount you must pay a new contractor over the price you agreed to pay the first one. Your provincial Consumer Protection Act may allow you to claim not only the amount of your loss but also punitive damages to discourage this kind of practice.

Susan hired George to add a family room to her house and he in turn hired several subcontractors. When the job was finished, he gave Susan a bill. Should she pay it in full?

She should first make sure that George has fully paid all his subcontractors. If he has not done so, they may obtain mechanics' liens, forcing Susan to pay them or lose her house. In effect, Susan would be paying twice for the same work. She should ask the subcontractors to sign releases waiving their rights to mechanics' liens. This is a common practice and they should be willing to do so.

Earl had his basement renovated a few months ago and the new concrete floor is already cracking. Can he force the contractor to redo the work?

If he has a written contract, the terms of that agreement apply. Most reputable contractors provide some warranty on their materials and workmanship. If Earl has no written contract, however, the situation is different. Ordinarily a new concrete floor should not crack after a few months, but there may be a number of defenses that the contractor could raise. The variables of weather and the condition of the floor at the time the concrete was poured might have made it impossible to do a better job. Without a written warranty, a court would have to decide whether the contractor had performed in a reasonable manner.

We've heard many stories about contractors' escalating bills. Won't a written agreement prevent this from happening to us?

Generally, a written agreement can do whatever it was intended to do. This could include putting a limit on escalation of costs. However, if you're having a house built, make sure you understand the terms of the contract and that it says what you want it to say. Usually the advice of a lawyer is necessary.

Contractors typically use a cost-plus provision allowing them to pass along to the owner increases in the costs of materials and supplies, wages and salaries, accident and indemnity insurance, and anything else needed, but perhaps unanticipated, for the job. All this is perfectly legal.

How to Hire a Contractor

Getting the right contractor is a matter of asking the right questions. Here are the basic ones:

- ☑ Is he licensed by the city or province?
- ☑ Does the Better Business Bureau have a record of any legitimate complaints against him?
- ☑ Will he give you the names and addresses of satisfied customers you can contact?
- ☑ Does he have a street address or just a post office box number, which may make him hard to reach quickly?
- ☑ How long has he been in business?
- ☑ Will he show you copies of his insurance policies, including workers' compensation and liability insurance? Is the coverage adequate?
- ☑ Has he obtained a surety bond, whereby a bonding company will fulfill his obligations if he fails to do so?
- ☑ Will he obtain necessary permits and give you copies?
- ☑ Will he guarantee materials and workmanship in writing?
- ☑ Will he request your written approval before making changes or substitutions in materials and workmanship?
- ☑ If he is late in completing the work, will he pay a penalty until the job is done?

Contractors also charge for changes you request in the original plans, so it is wise to discuss extra costs before telling the contractor to proceed with any changes. If cost-plus exists in the contract, you are usually bound to pay these charges. On the other hand, courts have not usually allowed contractors to bill their cost-plus customers for increases in office expenses or for redoing work that was not done properly the first time. Generally it is better to have work done by written estimate rather than on a cost-plus basis. In contracts done by estimate, courts rarely allow the estimate to be exceeded by more than 10 percent and it is up to the contractor to justify any increase over the written estimate.

Priscilla's house did not turn out the way the interior decorator said it would. Does she have any legal recourse?

It depends on the contract Priscilla had with the decorator. If he agreed to decorate to Priscilla's satisfaction, and she was not satisfied, she has the right to sue him no matter how much her tastes differ from his. However, if there was no written agreement that he would specifically satisfy her tastes and if he did everything he promised up to a reasonably professional standard, Priscilla has no legal right to complain.

I hired a painter to paint my living room for $400. When he finished, he demanded an additional $200, claiming $400 was for the walls alone: when I told him to paint the doors and windows, that had changed the price. He'd said nothing about a change in price at the time. Do I owe him the $200?

It depends on your original agreement. If you agreed to pay him $400 for painting the walls, that is all he was required to do to satisfy his part of the contract. If you then asked him to do additional work, he is entitled to additional compensation. If, however, your agreement was that he would paint "the living room" for $400, you may not have to pay the extra $200. A court would probably rule that it was reasonable to assume doors and windows would be included, or that the terms of the painting trade would include doors and windows in the phrase "living room."

Connie's house painter accidentally broke her favorite lamp. Can she deduct the cost of the lamp from his fee?

Not unless he agrees or their contract permits this. Otherwise, most courts would require Connie to pay the painter in full and file a separate claim with the painter's insurance company for the damage to her lamp. If the painter has no insurance and refuses to pay for the damage, Connie can sue him in Small Claims Court.

YOUR HOME

Home Improvements and Repairs

Kathleen hired a tree trimmer to trim her shrubs. When she came home, she found all had been destroyed by excessive trimming. Can she make the trimmer pay for new bushes?

Yes. If the tree trimmer disregarded her specific instructions, Kathleen is entitled to collect damages. A court would probably order the trimmer to pay for replacing the bushes.

I want to plant a tree outside the front door of my condominium. Do I need permission?

If where you want to plant the tree is part of a common area, you need permission from the condominium association. Check your condo's regulations and covenants to determine how to request approval.

You and Your Neighbors

For information on neighbors who borrow, see "Borrowing and Lending" in Chapter 5, *Your Personal Property.* For information on intrusive neighbors, see "Your Right to Privacy" in Chapter 12, *Your Individual Rights.*

What can I do if my neighbors blast their stereo at 2 A.M.?

First contact them personally and ask them to turn down the stereo. If this proves unsuccessful, and if they are tenants in an apartment building or house, your next step is to bring the noise to the attention of your landlord. You have a legal right to quiet enjoyment of your home, and your landlord has a legal obligation to see to it that this right is not disturbed by other tenants. Finally, if the noise continues, call the police. Unreasonable noise at an early hour of the morning is a breach of the peace and is against the law. A visit from a uniformed police officer usually puts an end to it.

Larry bought his house because it commanded a clear, sweeping view of the river. Now his next-door neighbor has put up a fence that blocks his view. Can Larry force him to take down the fence?

Probably not. Larry is asking for an easement (in Quebec, servitude)—a right to limit someone's use of his property in some way. In most parts of Canada, easements cannot be granted for light, air, or view without some written agreement. If Larry doesn't have such an agreement, he will have to live with his neighbor's fence.

Since my neighbor had his driveway repaved, rainwater runs into my basement. He says he is not responsible. If he's not, who is?

No matter what your neighbor says, he is probably responsible for the damage to your basement. Legally, any use by your neighbor of his property that interferes with your right to enjoy your property is called a nuisance. If you can prove that the water leaking into your basement is caused by the way your neighbor repaved his driveway, you should be able to recover for the damages you have suffered.

Tom has lived at his present address for 10 years. Jack bought the adjoining lot and began to build a house. After the basement had been dug and construction had begun, Tom's basement walls settled and cracked. Is Jack liable for Tom's repairs?

He may be if Tom can show that the settling and cracking in his basement were caused by construction activity on Jack's property. This may not be easy to prove, since foundation settling can occur for various reasons. An engineering report may be needed to determine the cause. If the construction work is the likely cause, Jack may go to court and seek restitution from his contractor for any damages he must pay to Tom.

Pierce owns a lakeside house. Can the other property owners on the lake keep him from sailing his boat over the entire lake?

Probably. If the lake is owned as a common area by all of the property owners, there is probably an association that regulates access to and use of the lake. When Pierce purchased his lakefront home, he most likely agreed to abide by these regulations. He should check his deed for any restrictions. If the lake is publicly owned, provincial and local laws may restrict his sailing rights. Such laws are often enacted to protect wildlife, provide undisturbed fishing spots, and limit noise and pollution.

What can I do about a neighbor who is gossiping about me?

Not much, unless the gossip has damaged you in some way that a court could measure. For example, if you lost your job or were denied credit because of your neighbor's gossip, you could sue your neighbor for slander. You could bring suit in some provinces if your neighbor accused you of a serious crime or of having a disease that is held in "some special repugnance" by the general public. But slander is hard to prove, and any financial loss may be even harder to connect to your neighbor's gossip. You would probably have to prove also that your neighbor was the original source of the gossip about you.

You and Your Neighbors

My neighbor's tree has grown so much that one branch hangs over my roof. Can I cut the limb off at the property line?

Although technically the tree branch is trespassing on your property, it may not be in your best interest to cut it off. If you cut it improperly, or destroy the tree, or in any way cause damage to your neighbor's property, you could be held liable. If your neighbor will not arrange to have the offending branch removed, you can go to court and sue him for trespassing but you will likely have to prove that the overhang causes you prejudice. If you can show that the branch may likely damage your roof, or is blocking some light, you will probably succeed in your action to have the branch cut. In British Columbia, Ontario and Nova Scotia, if a branch has overhung a property for 20 years, the owner of the tree will have acquired the right for the branch to remain uncut.

Archie has painted his house orange, and his neighbor Elvira thinks this lowers the value of her house. Can she force Archie to repaint his house?

Not unless Archie's deed restricts the colors he may paint his house or grants a right of approval to a homeowners' association. Esthetic values differ from individual to individual, and courts are reluctant to make decisions on the basis of personal tastes. If Elvira can prove that the value of her property has been diminished, she may be able to recover for the lost value of her property. But any damage she suffers must be substantial and beyond speculation. In other words, it is not enough that she thinks her neighbor's orange house has reduced her property's value; she must be able to prove it. Generally, a person may do to his property what he wishes, providing he does not do so with the intention of causing damage to other people's property.

Gary recently bought land alongside a country road. A neighbor drives over the property every day to get to and from the road. She says there is no other way. Can Gary charge her a fee?

No. If the neighbor has no other way to reach her property, she has a right to cross Gary's property—an easement by necessity. Even though there may be no written agreement allowing her to cross, a court would be unlikely to permit him to charge her a fee. The right-of-way must be a route chosen by Gary or a route that causes him the least disturbance. If the neighbor finds another route, the right-of-way ends. If Gary can show that another route is available, he can seek a court order prohibiting his neighbor from driving across his land.

YOUR HOME

Homeowners' Problems

For information on household accidents, see "Accidents Inside Your Home" and "Accidents Outside Your Home" in Chapter 13, *Accidents.*

Does a homeowner need a permit to rent out a spare room?

In many places, yes, and these places may demand that certain health and safety requirements be met before issuing the permit or license. For example, the homeowner may have to provide the roomer with a separate entrance or separate bath.

Even if his area has no licensing requirement, a homeowner should check with his local zoning authority before advertising for a roomer.

Jason is thinking of using part of his home as an office. What steps should he take before doing so?

First, he should decide what percentage of the space in his house he wants to use and check with his local zoning authority to make sure he would not be violating any regulation. For example, is the type of work he plans to do permitted in his neighborhood? Will he be permitted to display signs or advertising? What parking space must he provide for customers or clients? Second, Jason should talk with his accountant. Using part of his home as an office may provide a tax deduction. His accountant can let him know the extent of his tax savings. Finally, he should contact his insurance company to make sure he is covered for liability in the event of an accident or injury to a customer or client.

Am I responsible for shoveling snow off the sidewalk in front of my house and keeping it clean?

It depends on where you live. In some places, even though the sidewalk may belong to the city, you are responsible for keeping it free of ice, snow, and debris. Failing to shovel a snow-covered sidewalk within a reasonable time after snowfall may make you liable for injuries suffered by passersby. Check with your city or town hall.

Does Aunt Sophie have to buy workers' compensation insurance to cover the person who cleans her house once a week?

Probably not. Workers' compensation insurance is governed by provincial laws that limit the numbers and types of employees who are covered. Generally, household and domestic workers are excluded from workers' compensation coverage. Furthermore, if Aunt Sophie employs her cleaner through an agency, the agency will be responsible for providing

YOUR HOME

workers' compensation insurance, if required. However, Aunt Sophie, like anyone else, should have liability insurance in the event that someone is hurt while in her house, whether she owns or rents it and whether she has anyone working for her in the house or not.

Elizabeth loved to sit in the shade of a maple tree in her backyard. One day she discovered her tree being cut down by a power company crew. When she protested, the foreman shrugged and said the tree was getting tangled in the overhead lines. Can Elizabeth sue the power company for cutting down her tree?

Probably not. Most modern deeds give utility companies the use of private property for installing, maintaining, and repairing their lines and equipment. If the tree was planted where it might grow to interfere with the lines, the power company was justified in cutting it down.

When the Garlands bought their house, the developer showed them a map indicating that the whole area was reserved for single-family homes. Now he is planning to build a shopping center across the street from the Garlands' house. Can they prevent the shopping center from being built?

It depends. The municipality must decide whether to change the zoning from residential to commercial. If the Garlands and other residents get together, they could put pressure on the city council to refuse the developer the rezoning he needs. If the shopping center is built, however, and the Garlands' property value declines as a result, they could probably sue the developer for damages.

The city plans to convert an old school in my neighborhood into a halfway house for recovering drug addicts, many of whom have prison records. Can I stop the city from doing so?

Courts will generally permit a property to be used in any lawful and reasonable way until it becomes clear that an actual threat to the safety, health, and welfare of the community exists. Because a halfway house for recovering drug addicts might cause apprehension and fear in a neighborhood, property values might decline. But courts have ruled that fear about declining property values is not enough to justify their interference in the way neighboring property is to be used. Once a halfway house is opened and damages can be proved, however, a court might order it closed.

YOUR HOME

Who has to pay if the city puts sidewalks on Laura's block?

In most cities, the owners of the property adjoining the new sidewalks have to pay, the justification being that they receive a direct benefit from the improvement. Laura's local property tax authority will issue a special assessment requiring her to pay her share. She and her neighbors may be able to challenge the decision to install sidewalks if they can show that the sidewalks are unnecessary.

When the city takes part of my property to widen the street in front of my house, must it replant the hedge and move the fence?

No. When the city uses its power of expropriation to take part of your land, it must compensate you for its fair value, including the cost of fences and hedges, but you bear the responsibility for replacing them.

Theo and Alice's land is part of a former city-supervised landfill project. A high level of carcinogens has been found in the water and soil. What is Theo and Alice's legal recourse?

They should contact the Environmental Protection Service of Environment Canada in their area. If it is determined that the high level of carcinogens is a result of improper disposal of hazardous waste, Environment Canada will move Theo and Alice and their neighbors out of the area and do what it can to detoxify the damaged soil and water.

Environment Canada may also pay for the cost of relocating Theo and Alice and their affected neighbors, besides compensating them for the loss of their property. Help and compensation may also be forthcoming from the provincial environmental authority.

Can I shoot a burglar who is looting my house?

Only if he threatens to kill or seriously injure you or someone else. You cannot shoot an intruder simply because he is trespassing. Even if you discover a burglar stuffing the family silver into a shopping bag, you are not justified in shooting him if he offers no threat of bodily danger. A burglar generally presents a threat to your property only, and deadly force cannot be used solely to protect property, no matter how valuable. However, if you have good reason to believe that you or your family are threatened with serious injury or death, you can use any force, even deadly force, in self-defense. But if you are tempted to use force, be careful. The intruder may be able to sue you for unreasonable injuries you inflict upon him, and if you kill him there is a chance you may even be found guilty of homicide.

Homeowners' Problems

How do I contest an increase in property taxes?

You do so by appearing before a board of review to explain why you think the new rate is unfair or illegal. The most common reason for objecting to a tax increase is that it is disproportionate to the tax assessed on similar homes in your area, or that your home is being assessed at more than its actual value. If the board of review refuses to reduce the tax increase, you can appeal the decision in court.

Challenging Real Estate Tax Assessments

If you think your real estate tax assessment is too high, you may be able to have it lowered. The assessed value of your home should be in proportion to its relative value in the community; the taxes on a $50,000 home should be about half of those on a $100,000 home. As soon as you get your assessment, check the information the assessor's office used to determine your property's value. Some of the figures may have been typed incorrectly, such as the number of square feet of livable area or the year the house was built. Be sure that the assessor did not overestimate the grade of the materials used in constructing your house or the quality of the workmanship or the desirability of the neighborhood. And watch out for the "obvious" mistake: Did the assessor claim you have two bathrooms when you have only one, or report your narrow carport as a two-car garage? Did the assessor take into consideration the fact that you need a new roof, new windows or other major repairs?

The assessment is usually accompanied by a notice about your right to appeal. Read this notice carefully. In some areas you have as little as 10 days from the time you receive your assessment to begin the appeal process.

As soon as you can, contact the assessor's office and set up an appointment. Go to this meeting armed with specifics and figures. Your chance of success depends on how well you can document your claim. If the assessor agrees that you have a valid complaint, he may make an acceptable adjustment then and there; but you may have to take your appeal to an assessment review board—sometimes called a board of appeals or a board of equalization. There, you'll be required to present your case for a lower assessment all over again.

Finally, if the board won't see things your way, you can file suit in the court that hears assessment cases in your province. Those proceedings will be very formal, and you'll almost certainly want an attorney with you. In cases where the tax difference is only a few hundred dollars, the case may be heard in Small Claims Court.

Last fall Ronald moved onto a farm near a small airport. Since summer's arrival, the noise of low-flying aircraft has made outdoor activity unbearable and has frightened the chickens so badly they have stopped laying eggs. What can Ronald do?

When noise causes actual physical discomfort and prevents a property owner from using and enjoying his property, it may legally be considered a nuisance. Ronald should seek a court order prohibiting the airplanes from flying over his property. If he can convince the court that any reasonable person would be harmed by the amount of noise the planes are making, the court will either prohibit further flights over his land or restrict them to certain hours. Ronald might even be entitled to damages from the owner of the airport or the aircraft that disturb his enjoyment of his property. He should contact Transport Canada about the situation. However, the fact that Ronald knew the location of the airport when he bought his property may severely limit his recourse.

When Mark bought his land, the neighborhood was very rural and quiet. Now some of his neighbors are operating a sawmill. The noise is horrible, and Mark's property has become less valuable because of it. What can he do to remedy the situation?

He should check the local zoning bylaws, and if they do not permit this kind of business, he should notify the municipality. If the zoning legislation is not being violated, he should seek a court order prohibiting or limiting the noise at the mill on the grounds that it is unreasonable or excessive. While Mark can proceed alone, he might do better to join with other irritated neighbors in pursuing this matter in court.

Ways You May Lose Your Home

What can I do if I can't make my mortgage payments?

Contact your lender immediately. You may be able to renegotiate the terms of your loan and avoid foreclosure. For example, extending the period of payment would reduce the amount of your monthly payment. But if foreclosure proceedings are begun, you can redeem your property by bringing your mortgage payments up to date at any time before the foreclosure sale. Is your mortgage guaranteed by Canada Mortgage and Housing Corporation (CMHC)? If so, try to have your mortgage transferred to CMHC and make new arrangements for payments. Although the usual mortgage makes the entire amount due when even one payment is missed, most provinces prohibit foreclosure for several months. In Ontario and Manitoba, the debtor must be three months behind in his payments; in Quebec, two months; in some other provinces, six months. In Saskatchewan, the mortgage creditor must seek a court's permission to sue for foreclosure.

If you feel that meeting payments in a reasonable time will be impossible, try to sell your property. You may be offered more than you need to pay off the balance owing on your mortgage.

The city is going to build a school on Anna's block, and is offering Anna $60,000 for her house. She feels it is worth at least $75,000. Must she accept the price the city is offering?

No. Laws in every province require a price based on fair market value. If Anna can prove her property is worth $75,000 on the open real estate market, the city must pay her that amount.

David and Christine bought a house in an adults-only community. They are now expecting a baby. Do they have to move?

Probably not. A clause in a deed of sale prohibiting children would be very difficult to enforce. Most courts would probably consider a no-children condition antisocial and against the public good. Such a clause in a contract would probably also be considered an unlawful interference with one's peaceful enjoyment of his property, and a discrimination based on social condition.

The province plans to build a highway through Jerome's land. His family has lived there for three generations, and he doesn't want to move. Can he be forced out?

Yes. Every level of government has the power to take private property for a public use, such as building highways, creating parks, or clearing slums to construct low-income housing. Expropriation is permitted on the principle that benefits to the public outweigh the rights of individuals. But the power of expropriation is not unlimited. Jerome must be fairly compensated for his land, and he has the right to contest the expropriation in court.

What happens if the bank forecloses on my house?

Most commonly, the lender begins a court proceeding in which he must prove that you have defaulted on the mortgage agreement. If he

YOUR HOME

succeeds, the court will issue an order allowing him to sell the property. At a foreclosure sale, the property is sold to the highest bidder.

The proceeds of a foreclosure sale are applied against the amount owed on the mortgage plus court costs and expenses incurred in the sale; if the lender receives a greater amount from the sale than you owe him, he must turn the excess amount over to you. If the property sells for less than the amount you owe, your lender can return to court and sue you for the difference; most mortgages contain a "personal covenant" which gives the lender not only a right to take back the property, but also a personal right against the borrower for any shortfall.

I have lost my job and can't pay my real estate taxes. Is there any way to keep from losing my house?

In most provinces, the only way to prevent a tax sale is to pay the overdue taxes before the property is sold. Some provinces let you redeem your property even after a tax sale, on condition that you pay not only the back taxes but also any penalties and the expenses of conducting the tax sale.

Most mortgage lenders insist that you pay a portion of your real estate taxes along with the monthly payment of your loan. To protect their interest, lenders may even pay the overdue taxes to avoid a tax sale. Of course, you will ultimately be responsible for reimbursing your lender.

George and Mary are facing a foreclosure on their house. How much time will they have before they have to move out?

Once the foreclosure sale is held, they will no longer have the right to remain in the house. But they should not move out just because they have been threatened with foreclosure. They should contact a lawyer immediately; it may still be possible to save their home before foreclosure or to have the sale delayed for many months.

Doris invited her cousin Rachel and her daughters to live with her in her new condominium. Doris defaulted on the payments, and the condominium association has repossessed the apartment and is threatening to charge Rachel with trespassing. Can it do that?

The association may be able to sue Rachel for trespassing, but it is more likely to begin eviction proceedings. Because Doris defaulted, she no longer owns the apartment, and Rachel and her daughters have no legal right to stay there. Rachel might try to rent the apartment for herself and her daughters, but the condominium association is under no obligation to let her do so.

***I'm going to sell my house, and I don't know whether to hire a
real estate agent, a broker, or a realtor. What's the difference?***

Technically, a real estate agent is one who works for a broker or realtor
and whose job is to sell property on behalf of the broker/realtor. But in
essence there is no difference. With the advent of independent real
estate agents, multiple listings, and real estate companies, the distinction
has been blurred. Realtors, brokers, and real estate agents all have
passed qualifying examinations and are trained, licensed professionals.
They represent the seller and for their services receive a commission or
percentage of the selling price.

What services do real estate brokers generally provide?

The broker's primary responsibility is to find a buyer who is ready,
willing, and able to purchase the property on terms and conditions the
seller finds acceptable. Additional duties and responsibilities are set
forth in the listing agreement, the contract between broker and seller.
Usually, the broker advertises and shows the owner's property. When a
buyer is found, the broker often acts as an intermediary, arranging for
inspections and the like. He may act for the seller in determining the
terms and conditions of the contract for sale. But he is not a lawyer and
should not be relied upon for legal advice.

***When I told my neighbor that I was putting my house up for sale,
he offered to find a buyer. If he does, do I have to pay him a
broker's commission?***

No. Unless you have a contract with your neighbor, you may sell your
house to the prospect he has located without owing a commission—
even if your neighbor is a broker.

***Vern is hesitant about using a broker to sell his house. He feels
that a broker may switch his allegiance to the buyer if doing so
will help him sell the house and get his commission. Is it legal for
a broker to give the prospective buyer a deal that would be to the
detriment of the seller?***

No. Although a real estate broker may seem to represent both the seller
and the buyer, he cannot do so under the law, because seller and buyer
have conflicting interests: the seller wants to charge the highest possible
price, and the buyer wants to pay the lowest. Therefore, since the broker

is hired and paid by the seller, he is considered the seller's representative, and must always look after the best interests of the seller.

The broker must always get the approval or authorization of the seller before making promises or accepting or rejecting an offer to buy real estate. If Vern hires a broker who fails to represent him to the best of his ability, he can fire him and sue him for any damages caused.

What is the most important thing to do when working with a real estate broker?

Establish the terms under which you want the broker to sell your home. Decide whether he will be the exclusive broker or one of several. Set the price of the property and the size of the broker's commission and put a limit on how long the agreement with the broker will last. Be sure the broker knows the condition of your property and its special features so that he will represent it accurately to prospective buyers. Remember, if your home is sold to someone who *saw* it during the period you had an agreement with the broker, you owe the broker a commission even if the *sale* takes place *after* the end of the broker's mandate.

Is a real estate broker's commission firmly fixed, or can it sometimes be negotiated?

Like any terms of a contract, the broker's commission is subject to negotiation. While most brokers will try to persuade you that their commission is firmly fixed, you may be able to negotiate a lower one. For example, if your home is in a very popular area where houses sell quickly, the broker will have little work to do, and it is reasonable to pay him a smaller commission. Similarly, a home that commands a large selling price will bring the broker a large commission; you may be able to negotiate his commission downward. On the other hand, if your home is in an area where houses sell very slowly, your broker may be less willing to negotiate the commission rate.

Must I repair my house before I put it on the market?

You are under no obligation to make repairs to your home before you put it on the market. However, in most provinces, if you don't tell a buyer about repairs that you know need to be done and he later discovers this, he can sue you to cancel the contract or to reduce the selling price. Many homeowners make minor improvements to their property before putting it up for sale, since these may increase the price a buyer is willing to pay. A fresh coat of paint and some fertilizer on the lawn can return many times their cost.

Selling Your Home

A real estate broker found a buyer for our house at the price we wanted. Now we've changed our minds about moving. The broker insists we pay his commission. Must we?

When you signed the listing agreement, you agreed to pay a commission to the broker when he found a ready, willing, and able purchaser. Having done so, he has earned his commission. Despite your change of mind, he has a right to expect you to live up to your end of the agreement.

A real estate broker appraised Lois' home for $95,000 and was able to sell it at that price to the first prospective buyer. Lois later found out that houses in her neighborhood were selling for much more, and that she could easily have found someone to buy her house for $115,000 or more. Does she have any legal recourse against the broker?

If she can prove that the broker knew that $95,000 was significantly less than the actual value of her house, Lois may be able to recover the difference between the amount she received from the sale and the actual value of the house. Brokers have a duty to protect their clients' interests and to use their best efforts to get them the highest possible price. A broker who does not fulfill his duty may be accountable for any loss the client suffers as a result.

In addition, Lois might be able to recover the commission she paid the broker on the grounds that he did not earn it in accordance with the

Types of Real Estate Broker Listings

If you are planning to sell your house, you should be aware of the various listings brokers use, and try to get the one most likely to work for you. Each type of listing has its advantages and disadvantages.

● *Multiple listing* is the most common and successful arrangement. You make an agreement with one broker or agency, who passes the information about your property to other brokers in a cooperating group that shares information about all the properties they have available for sale. The broker who finds a buyer for your home splits his commission with the broker you hired. However, you may have to pay the commission even if you locate a buyer yourself without the help of a broker; check the contract for such a provision.

● In an *open listing* agreement, a broker has the right to sell your property, but you can list your property with other brokers as well or sell accepted practices of other brokers in the community. In any event, if Lois decided to sue the broker, the case would be a difficult and involved one because it would be hard to prove that the agent really knew the true value of the house.

Bea, who is getting married, is selling her house on June 1, but she wants to stay in it until the wedding on June 29, when she will live with her new husband. How can she arrange this?

Bea will have to negotiate an agreement with the buyer in order to remain after June 1, since she has no right to be in the house after the closing. Agreements of this type are not unusual. Generally, Bea would be required to pay rent for the extra month and possibly contribute to the new owner's insurance, taxes, and utility expenses; some buyers might request an adjustment in the purchase price. Any agreement of this sort should be written into the sales contract.

Kurt's real estate broker found a buyer who put down a deposit, then backed out before the closing. The broker claims that he should get his commission anyway. Is he right?

It depends on the terms of the listing agreement. If it states that no commission is earned until the closing of the sale, Kurt's broker is not entitled to a commission. If the terms of the listing agreement do not indicate when a broker is owed a commission, provincial law takes over. In most provinces, the broker earns his commission when the property

it yourself. The broker who actually finds the buyer gets the entire commission. If you sell the property yourself, you don't owe anyone a commission. However, you may find it difficult to convince a broker to agree to an open listing, because he may spend time and energy in advertising and showing your home, only to receive no commission at all.
● If you agree to an *exclusive agency listing* with a broker, you promise not to list your property with any other broker while the agreement is in effect. Because the exclusive listing agreement gives only one broker the right to earn a commission, it theoretically increases his incentive to find a buyer. With only one broker on the job, however, your home may not be shown to as many potential buyers.
● Be wary of contracts that give the broker an *exclusive right to sell*. Although they are similar to exclusive listing arrangements, there is one important difference. If you sell the property, you must still pay the agent a full commission, even if he had nothing to do with the sale.

is sold. In finding a buyer who was unable to fulfill the conditions of the purchasing agreement, the broker has not fulfilled his duty and is not entitled to a commission. The deposit given by the prospective purchaser could be kept by the seller or split between the seller and the broker.

Jessica signed a 90-day agreement with a real estate broker to put her house on the market for $80,000. Her broker found a buyer, but he offered only $72,000. Jessica initially turned down this offer, but four months later agreed to sell. Does she still owe the broker a commission?

Probably, if her listing agreement contained an extender clause, which obligates the seller to pay a commission when the buyer is located by a broker even though the sale is agreed to after the listing agreement expires. The extender clause protects brokers from being deprived of their commissions by buyers and sellers who agree to wait until the listing agreement expires before making a sales contract. Since Jessica's buyer was located by the broker's effort during the listing agreement, the broker is entitled to his commission on the sale.

Dawn wants to sell her condominium, and she has just found out that her condominium association has a right of first refusal. What does this right involve?

It means that the association has the option to purchase Dawn's unit before she can sell it to anyone else. If Dawn puts her condominium up for sale and receives a written offer from a buyer, she must offer the condo to the association before accepting the buyer's offer. The association must at least match the price offered by the prospective buyer. If it agrees to meet this price, Dawn must sell her condo to the association. If it does not match the buyer's offer, Dawn can sell the condominium to the person who made the original offer.

Your Personal Property

Owning Personal Property

I have heard it said that possession is nine tenths of the law. What does this mean?

The saying is an exaggeration, but it illustrates an important point: Anyone who claims to own property that another possesses must have a very good case to take that property away. In most instances, a person who already has property in his possession will be able to defeat the claim of anyone except the true owner. Being in possession of something creates a legal presumption of ownership.

Our lawyer asked us to draw up a list of our real property and personal property. What's the difference?

Real property is the legal term for real estate. It includes land and anything erected or growing on the land, such as houses, garages, storage buildings, and gardens. *Personal property* is everything else that may be owned, such as automobiles, clothing, furniture, appliances, pets, and money, including stocks and bonds.

Are crops considered personal property?

It depends on whether the crops are growing in the field or have already been harvested. If the crops are still growing, they are considered part of the land, and are therefore considered real property. If the crops have already been harvested and are in storage, however, then the law considers them personal property.

Our banker asked us to make a list of our tangible personal property. What is this?

Tangible personal property includes things that are valuable in themselves—furniture, appliances, automobiles, and pets. Intangible personal property consists of things that represent something of value—stocks, bonds, copyrights, and patents. Tangible property is also called corporeal, as contrasted with incorporeal property.

One of my neighbor's children stole my son's brand-new bicycle. What should I do?

Your first step would be to approach your neighbor and ask him to have his child return your son's bike. If this fails, send a registered letter formally requesting the bike's return. If there is still no result, your next step is to contact the police. In addition, you may be able to sue your neighbor in Small Claims Court. There you could show the judge the bill of sale for the bicycle (ask the store for a duplicate if you have lost the original) and a copy of the registered letter you sent.

Susan put Jeff's old hunting coat out with the garbage where Wayne found it. Later Jeff saw Wayne wearing his coat and asked for it back. Who is entitled to keep the coat?

If it came to a court case, Wayne would be allowed to keep the coat. Once property is abandoned, anyone may claim it. The only way in which Jeff would be able to force Wayne to return the coat would be by proving that Susan did not have the authority to dispose of it. But if Susan had regularly disposed of old things this way, a court would probably find that Jeff had granted her the authority to act on his behalf.

Harry leased some farmland from George and built a workshop and shed on it. Who will be the legal owner of these buildings when the lease expires?

Generally an improvement, such as the addition of a physical structure, becomes the property of the landlord. The workshop and shed will belong to George when the lease expires, unless Harry and George have agreed otherwise in writing. Much depends on whether Harry has incorporated the workshop and shed into the ground by building a foundation, or whether it can be removed easily and made portable.

Pets as Property

One of our neighbors goes away for long periods of time and leaves his dog outside, unfed and untended. The dog comes around begging for food during the day, and then it howls and whimpers all night. How can I put a stop to this?

Report the problem to the local police. The dog's owner could be charged with: (1) cruelty to an animal, because he does not feed the dog or provide adequate shelter, and (2) maintaining a nuisance, because the dog's howling and whimpering deprive you of the use and enjoyment of your property. You can also seek a court order requiring the owner of the dog to stop the noise. You would be wise to notify your local humane society as well. It may be able to have the dog taken away and to prevent your neighbor from owning other dogs in future.

Pets as Property

My daughter Cheryl just received a puppy as a birthday gift. Do we have to get a license for it?

Yes. Nearly every municipality requires that a dog be licensed. Dog licenses serve two purposes. They protect the health of the public, since many municipalities require that the pet be immunized against rabies and distemper before issuing a license. Licenses also help in identifying a pet that has strayed from its owner. Courts have consistently upheld the right of cities and towns to require licenses for dogs.

My son wants to keep a turtle he found at a public pond. If he does, will he be breaking the law?

It is against the law for your son to keep the turtle unless your province has a statute that specifically permits him to do so. Your province is considered the legal owner of wild animals located on public property. Courts have held that this ownership is really a trust, whereby the province acts to preserve wild animals for the benefit of all the people. For further information on the status of wild animals, contact your provincial ministry responsible for wildlife management.

My dog dug under the fence and destroyed our neighbor's vegetable garden. Do I have to pay for the damage?

If your dog is normally well-behaved and has never done anything like this before, you probably will not be liable. However, if your dog had previously dug under the fence, and you made no effort to restrain it or prevent it from doing so again, you would probably have to pay for the damage to your neighbor's garden.

Ingrid raises champion Labrador retrievers. Gerald, her neighbor, owns a scraggly mongrel. Gerald's mutt burrowed under the fence and had a brief but passionate relationship with one of Ingrid's female Labradors. The Labrador is now pregnant. Can Ingrid sue Gerald?

She can try, but she probably won't have much luck. Historically, a dog owner has not been held liable for damages unless he knew beforehand that the dog was mischievous or vicious. However, a Prince Edward Island court did hold the owner of an escaped bull responsible for damages, when the bull impregnated someone else's six heifers. The heifers were too young to breed and had to be replaced. The judge felt

The Legal Responsibilities of Your Veterinarian

Veterinarians, like physicians and other professionals, must conduct their practices according to a set of ethical principles. These principles direct veterinarians to prevent and relieve the suffering of animals, to give proper medical attention to their patients and never neglect them, and to render service during emergencies to the best of their ability. Veterinarian ethics include an obligation to treat lost animals that are brought in when sick or injured, although the person who brings such an animal for veterinary care must be prepared to pay the bill just as he would for his own pet.

Veterinarians, like other doctors, cannot guarantee cures for their patients. Many factors beyond their control—such as age, the seriousness of an injury, or a previous illness—can affect the health and well-being of an animal in their care. Although veterinarians are not subject to the same malpractice laws that apply to physicians, they can be held responsible for the suffering, injury, or death of an animal if it results from: (1) a negligent diagnosis, (2) an unskillful operation, (3) poor care in feeding and housing the animal, (4) neglecting or abandoning the case, or (5) the actions of an unskilled or negligent employee. For example, it might be a case of poor care if you left your cat overnight for routine shots and it caught an infectious disease from another cat. A veterinarian might also be held responsible if your dog fell off the examining table and injured its head because the animal wasn't secured properly, or if the vet's assistant forgot to lock the cages at night and your dog was attacked and injured by a larger one.

A veterinarian who is guilty of negligence may be suspended from practice and could be liable for civil penalties. However, an owner who sues a veterinarian can usually recover no more than the actual dollar value of the animal.

that it was "reasonably foreseeable" that if the bull escaped his pasture it would mate with the heifers.

I want a dog to help safeguard my home. If I post a "Beware of Dog" sign, will I be liable if the dog hurts someone?

Posting a "Beware of Dog" sign may actually work to your disadvantage, since it would be an admission that you were aware of your dog's vicious temperament. If you acquire a dog that you know is vicious or dangerous, you must restrain it to prevent it from injuring anyone, including trespassers.

Pets as Property

Is it true that a dog is entitled to one bite before its owner is liable for damages?

Not really. The owner's liability is not based on the number of people that the dog bites, but on the owner's knowledge of the dog's general behavior around people and its tendency to bite. The "one bite" rule is merely a shorthand way of indicating that a dog owner will not be liable for unexpected and unpredictable injuries if he has no prior knowledge of his dog's vicious tendencies and has taken reasonable care to prevent his dog from causing damage to others.

I was riding down a bicycle path when a large dog ran into me, causing me to fall and smash my glasses. The dog owner's insurance company will pay for my glasses but not for the damage to my bicycle. Can I expect to get any additional monetary compensation?

Since the dog owner's insurance company accepted liability for replacing your eyeglasses, it may also be required to accept liability for other losses or damages that you incurred as a result of the accident. You should submit an accounting of your damages and insist on payment.

Max's next-door neighbor refuses to put a leash on his dog even though Max is expecting a visit from his young nephews. Max is afraid that one of his nephews may be harmed. What can he do?

Max could report his neighbor's refusal to leash the dog to the police. Most cities and towns have statutes that make it illegal for dog owners to let their pets run at large. Max should also send a registered letter to his neighbor stating that, in the event his nephews are harmed, the neighbor will be held responsible. That way, should the dog attack the boys, the neighbor could not escape liability by claiming that he could not have foreseen the damage.

Am I liable if my dog runs out into the street and causes an automobile accident?

If you knew that your dog habitually ran into the street to chase cars, yet you made no attempt to restrain it, you would be liable for injuries or damage caused by the dog. You might also be liable if a statute or ordinance made it unlawful for you to allow your dog to roam unrestrained on public streets.

Ellen's dog bit a neighbor's boy who had climbed over the fence to retrieve his ball. Does the fact that the boy climbed over the fence relieve Ellen of liability?

It may. A dog that would not harm someone who entered through the gate might react unexpectedly to a person climbing over the fence. In addition, Ellen may be relieved of liability if she can show there were ways the boy could have avoided the dog, such as going after the ball only when the dog was tied up or in the house.

Our dog was killed by an automobile. Can I sue the driver?

Yes, but you would be required to show that the driver had failed to use reasonable care—such as driving slowly enough to stop in time—to avoid killing the dog. The driver would not be liable if your dog suddenly darted into the street in front of his car.

I hit my neighbor's dog by accident as I was backing my car out of the garage. Am I responsible for paying the veterinarian's bill?

A court will not hold you responsible unless there is evidence that you were negligent in driving your car. You would be guilty of negligence, for example, if you failed to look behind you as you started backing out of the garage, or if you saw the dog but failed to anticipate its behavior.

On her way home from work Peggy ran over a cat. The cat had no identification on it. Does Peggy have to do anything further to try to find the owner, or can she just drive off?

Since the cat had no identification, the law would presume that it was either a lost or an abandoned animal. Peggy is under no obligation to make further efforts to find the owner unless she wants to. However, local laws may require that she report the accident to the police.

Our neighbor Wadad keeps a full-grown ocelot leashed on her property. We consider this a danger to our children. Can we force Wadad to get rid of this creature?

Many provinces and cities have laws that prohibit a person from owning a dangerous animal. If it is against the law in your area, contact the police, and they will arrange to have the creature removed. Ownership of a dangerous animal may also make Wadad fully liable for any injuries it causes, even if someone provokes it or is trespassing on her property.

John took his best suit to the dry cleaner. When he picked it up, he found unsightly streaks on the trousers. What can John do?

John should first return the trousers to the cleaner. This places the cleaner on notice that John is dissatisfied with the quality of the work, and it gives the cleaner the opportunity to rectify his mistake. In most instances, the cleaner will attempt to undo the damage by recleaning the garment. If this second cleaning proves unsatisfactory, the cleaner will be liable for the damage, unless it was caused by a defect or flaw in the garment itself. If the cleaner is at fault, he will be required to reimburse John for the cost of the suit less depreciation over the time John owned it. Often the cleaner's liability limits are spelled out on the bill the customer gets when he hands in his clothes to be cleaned. The liability is often 30 times the price of cleaning. If there are no such limitations printed on the bill, which is the contract between the customer and the cleaner, yet the cleaner is not willing to reimburse John for the depreciated value of his suit, John could sue the cleaner in Small Claims Court.

The cleaner laundered my cotton slacks instead of cleaning them, and now they've shrunk so much that they're unwearable. Am I entitled to a reimbursement?

Yes, since the cleaner failed to exercise ordinary care in handling your slacks. This does not mean, however, that the cleaner must buy you a new pair of slacks. Instead, the cleaner would be required to reimburse you for the amount of value left in them. For example, if you paid $50 for the slacks when you purchased them a year ago, the dry cleaner might pay you only $25, an amount based on the cleaner's estimate that the one-year-old slacks had a life expectancy of two years.

Janet was going through some old clothes when she found a claim check for a suit she had taken to the dry cleaner six months earlier. When she went to claim the suit, the cleaner told her that it had been sold and pointed to a sign on the wall that read: "Not Responsible for Items Left Over 90 Days." Can Janet sue the cleaner for selling her suit?

Yes. Many courts have held that a posted notice disclaiming liability carries no weight unless it is called to the customer's attention before he hands over his property. Unless the cleaner can prove through witnesses or other evidence that he called Janet's attention to the sign when she brought the suit in, she should be able to recover the suit's depreciated value in Small Claims Court.

If the Cleaner Ruins Your Clothes

You go to the dry cleaner to pick up the silk dress you've worn only twice, and you find that the buttons have melted into the fabric. Your dress is ruined. What do you do now?

The dry cleaner may want to try to fix the damaged garment; legally, he has a right to do so. But if the garment is beyond salvation and the damage is clearly the cleaner's fault, you are entitled to be reimbursed. However, you are not entitled to the amount you paid when the item was new. All clothing has an estimated life span. While you may be reimbursed in full for a brand-new dress, you may receive, for example, only one half the original cost of a raincoat that is 1½ years old and still in good condition.

The majority of cleaners provide very reliable service, and since they depend on repeat business and word-of-mouth advertising, your cleaner will prefer to reach a satisfactory agreement with you and keep you as a satisfied customer. But if all else fails, you may still sue in Small Claims Court to recover the current value of the garment.

The laundry promised Matthew his dress shirt would be ready on Tuesday, but it wasn't. What legal recourse does he have?

While the laundry's failure to return Matthew's dress shirt on the date promised may have caused him considerable annoyance and inconvenience, there is not much legal recourse available. A Latin expression sometimes used by lawyers explains why: *de minimus non curat lex* (the law does not concern itself with trifles). Matthew's best course of action would be to file a complaint with the Better Business Bureau and not use this particular laundry anymore.

I can't wear my raincoat because the cleaner lost the matching belt. Shouldn't he give me the money to buy a new one?

Yes. The cleaner should give you a reasonable amount of money to buy a new matching belt, but he does not have to buy you a new raincoat.

Lenny left his coat in an unattended checkroom in an expensive restaurant. When he went to get the coat after dinner, it was gone. Does the restaurant owe Lenny a new coat?

No. Since the checkroom was unattended, Lenny took his chances in leaving his coat there. If the checkroom had an attendant, the restaurant would probably be liable for the loss. However, much would depend on the particular circumstances. If Lenny hung his coat in the checkroom believing that there was an attendant who was merely away for a few minutes, then the restaurant could be liable. If there was no actual cloakroom, but only racks with hangers, then the restaurant would not be liable, since no fee was charged for using the racks, and there was no indication an attendant would be present to watch the coats.

I left my fur coat in the checkroom at a restaurant. On the ticket stub was a statement limiting the restaurant's liability to $500. If my coat had been stolen, could I have recovered only $500?

Yes. As long as the limitation is reasonable and clearly spelled out to the public, there is nothing to prevent the restaurant from setting an upper dollar limit to its liability. The restaurant should also have a conspicuous sign stating the $500 limitation of liability in order to fully carry out its duty to its customers.

Julie left her hand luggage with the bell captain of a hotel while she paid her bill. She did not ask for a receipt, since she was leaving in a few minutes. When she went to pick up her luggage, the bell captain could not find it. Is the hotel responsible for compensating Julie for her luggage?

Yes. The hotel is responsible for the reasonable value of the luggage and its contents. The bell captain is the hotel's authorized recipient of its customers' property, and he should have made certain that Julie's belongings were adequately protected. In all provinces, special laws hold innkeepers and hotelkeepers responsible for the property left in their establishments by their guests.

Is my employer liable if my purse is stolen while I'm at work?

Usually not. As an employee you are expected to be aware of the general level of security at your workplace and to take care of your personal property. However, there are two exceptions to this general rule. (1) If your employer requires you to keep your personal property in a specific place, such as a locker room, he may be liable if it is stolen from that place. (2) If you can show that the theft of your purse was due entirely to your employer's negligence, he may be held responsible for your loss. An example of negligence might be allowing strangers into an office without having them check in with a receptionist.

After putting on a new pair of jeans in the dressing room of a clothing store, Ned went to search for a mirror. When he returned, he discovered that his old jeans were missing, along with his wallet. Is the store liable for Ned's loss?

Since Ned had to take off and set aside his old jeans in order to buy new ones, the store is liable for the loss of the old jeans—but not the wallet. Stores have a general obligation to see that no harm that can reasonably be avoided will occur to their customers while they are on the premises. This obligation extends to a customer's personal property that has to be laid aside while transacting business—even for a few minutes, as in the case of Ned's jeans. But since it was not necessary to set aside the wallet—Ned could have carried it with him as indeed would most customers—the store is not liable.

Henry took a watch to the jeweler for repairs. The jeweler went bankrupt, and all his assets and all the property in his shop were frozen. How can Henry get his watch back?

Henry will have to work through the bankruptcy court in which the case is pending. If he does so, he will be listed as a creditor of the bankrupt jeweler, and he will receive notice of his right to file a proof of claim. This proof of claim, which the bankruptcy court's clerk can assist Henry in completing, is a formal notice to the bankruptcy trustee that Henry claims ownership of the watch. Within 15 days of receiving Henry's proof of claim, the trustee may either return the watch to Henry or inform him that he disputes the claim. In the latter case, Henry would have to wait until the bankruptcy is settled before getting his watch back.

Ellen shipped an antique table to Jim by a trucking company. When the shipment arrived, the crate was smashed and the table severely damaged. Who is responsible for repairing or replacing the table?

The trucking company is liable for the damage, provided that Ellen packed the table properly before it was shipped and marked the package clearly to indicate that it was fragile. A trucking company or common carrier guarantees the safe delivery of goods entrusted to it and assumes most risks involved in handling and delivering such goods. Thus it is responsible for damages even when the damage is not its fault, unless it was caused by a fortuitous event or "act of God." Regardless of whether Ellen's table was damaged because it was dropped by one of the people handling it, or because it shifted inside the truck when the truck hit a pothole, the trucking company would have to reimburse Ellen for the cost of repairing or replacing her table.

Entrusting Property to Others (Bailments)

When we moved cross-country recently, a delicate mirror was smashed so badly that it could not be repaired. Are the movers responsible for what it would cost to replace the mirror today rather than what I paid for it 10 years ago?

It depends on the contract you signed with your mover. Movers are allowed to limit their liability for damage to only 60 cents per pound ($1.32 per kilogram), but this limitation must be spelled out in the contract. Unless you had arranged for additional insurance coverage,

---

The Law of Bailments

When you give another person temporary custody of your personal property, you create a legal relationship called a *bailment*. You are the *bailor;* the person with temporary custody is called the *bailee*. Bailments are involved in numerous day-to-day activities. Leaving a car at a garage, dropping your shoes off at a repair shop, boarding a pet, borrowing a bracelet from a friend—all are examples of bailments. In fact, bailments are so common that a special set of legal principles has evolved to deal with them.

The liability of another person for loss or damage to your property varies according to your reason for turning the property over to him. If the transaction is for the sole benefit of the other person— lending your guitar to a fellow musician for a concert, for example— he will have to care for your property with extra diligence and return it in exactly the same condition as he received it.

If the bailment is for the mutual benefit of both persons—you deliver an original painting to a frame shop for cleaning and remounting—the other person must use ordinary care in handling and safeguarding the property you entrust to him.

Finally, if the bailment is solely for your own benefit —you leave your coat in an unattended checkroom—the bailee is liable to you only if he acts in bad faith or is negligent in caring for your property.

Bailees often try to limit their liability by printing a notice on a claim check or receipt, or by posting a sign in their place of business. For a limitation of this type to be effective, the notice must be conspicuous to a reasonable person or be called to his attention before he leaves his personal belongings.

In Quebec, bailments are called deposits, which are subdivided into two types: (1) *necessary deposit* as is the case when you leave an object for repairs, and (2) *simple deposit*, as is the case when you check your coat in an unattended cloakroom.

you could collect only $12 for a mirror weighing 20 pounds (9 kilograms), even if it is valued at $1,000. Most movers can offer you various levels of insurance protection. Find out what kind your mover offers *before* you sign the contract. If you want to cover the full current replacement value of your belongings, you will have to pay more for the move than if you were willing to take your chances with the limited protection of less costly insurance.

We plan to move out West sometime during the next few months. Is there some way we can get a binding estimate of how much it will cost to move our household goods to another province?

Moving companies are not required to give estimates, but most of them will do so if requested. There are two types of estimates: nonbinding and binding.

Nonbinding estimates should be in writing, and there is no guarantee that the final cost will not be more than the estimate. However, the mover cannot require you to pay more than the amount of the original estimate plus 10 percent at the time of delivery.

When you receive a binding estimate, you cannot be required to pay the mover more than the amount specified in the estimate. Binding estimates must also be in writing, and the mover is permitted to charge a fee for providing this service.

What is a bill of lading? Why is it so important?

A bill of lading is the contract between you and the mover stating the terms and conditions that apply to your move and who is responsible for the goods while they're in transit. It is legal proof that you are the owner of the goods in case they're lost or damaged en route. Don't sign a bill of lading until you're satisfied that it describes the service you want.

I bought a gold watch for $200 at a pawnshop. Today a police officer told me the watch had been stolen by the man who pawned it. Can I get my $200 refunded?

In most provinces you would have to return the watch and sue for the money you paid, proving that the pawnbroker knew or should have known the watch was stolen. In British Columbia, however, a person who buys an object in good faith in a public market, such as a pawnshop, acquires title to that object and may keep it. To be valid, the sale must be made during business hours and in the normal course of business. If the transaction took place in Quebec, you could reclaim your $200, but would have to return the watch.

Entrusting Property to Others (Bailments)

The pawnbroker sold my antique jewelry box before I returned to pay for it. What are my rights?

If you returned to pay your debt before the time limit was up, you can sue the pawnbroker and recover the fair market value of the jewelry box.

When Pat went to the pawnbroker to pay for his saxophone, he learned that it had been lent to someone to play in a band, and he couldn't have it until the next day. What are Pat's legal rights?

Personal property left with a pawnbroker is considered collateral for a loan, and he may not use it for his own benefit or lend it to others. A pawnbroker is required to return pawned property when the loan is paid off. Pat is entitled to sue the pawnbroker for lending out his saxophone; but as a practical matter, a lawsuit may be pointless if the saxophone is returned the next day. Of course, Pat could report this incident to his province's consumer affairs department, which could revoke the pawnbroker's license if it has had previous complaints about him.

If You Buy Stolen Property by Mistake

Sometimes a bargain isn't really a bargain. Consider the case of the $100 videocassette recorder. It came in a factory-sealed carton, and it was bought from a man who parked his car in the company lot. At retail, the recorder sold for nearly five times the $100 price. The purchaser thought he'd made a great deal and had also helped a stranger who "needed to raise cash in a hurry."

A few weeks later, however, the great deal went sour when two police officers arrived at the purchaser's door. Several recorders had been stolen from a warehouse. The serial number on the warranty card the purchaser had mailed back to the manufacturer matched the number of one of the stolen machines. Although no criminal charges were filed against the purchaser, the police took the video recorder and returned it to its rightful owner. The innocent purchaser was out $100, and there was nothing he could do about it.

To avoid buying stolen property, law enforcement agencies suggest that you: (1) purchase goods from reputable outlets only; (2) question bargains that seem "too good to be true"; and (3) never purchase anything without first noting the seller's identification.

If you buy or accept property that you know was stolen, you could be convicted of a crime and subject to a fine or even imprisonment. Going to jail is no bargain either.

YOUR PERSONAL PROPERTY

218

Borrowing and Lending

If a friend borrows my emerald bracelet to attend an out-of-town wedding, is she responsible for replacing the bracelet if it's stolen from her hotel room?

Yes. The privilege of borrowing an item, especially a valuable one such as an emerald bracelet, carries with it the responsibility of replacing the item if it is lost or stolen. Your friend would also be responsible for repairing the bracelet in the event of its being damaged.

My neighbor, who is much heavier than I am, borrowed our best patio chair. While he had the chair, the seat caved in. Who is responsible for getting it fixed?

Your neighbor should pay for having the patio chair fixed. A person who borrows property has a legal responsibility to repair or replace any broken parts and to return the article to its owner in the same condition it was in when he received it. He might not be held liable, however, if you knew that the patio chair was defective, but did not tell your neighbor about it at the time he borrowed it.

Hal's brother-in-law borrowed Hal's old lawn mower without his permission. It wouldn't start, so he had it repaired without telling Hal. Hal had planned to get rid of the mower and had already ordered a new one. Must Hal reimburse his brother-in-law for the cost of the repairs?

No. A person who borrows personal property may not make repairs or improvements to that property without first receiving authorization from the owner. If repairs or improvements are made without the owner's consent, the owner has absolutely no obligation to pay for them.

Mabel lent her skis to Jessie, who damaged them in a fall. Jessie wants to replace them with secondhand skis, but Mabel wants new ones. Who is right?

If the skis Mabel lent Jessie were new, Mabel would be justified in demanding new ones as replacements. But if the skis were old and worn, a court would require Jessie to replace them only at their depreciated value. The intent of the law is to restore the value the property had immediately before it was damaged. Even if Mabel had to buy expensive new skis to replace the lost ones, the court would require Jessie to pay only the price of secondhand skis.

Borrowing and Lending

Fred borrowed Richard's wheelbarrow a little over a year ago. When Richard went to get the wheelbarrow, Fred said that since Richard hadn't claimed it within a year's time, it had become his property. Is this really true?

Absolutely not. When no specific time is stated for the return of loaned property, the law requires the borrower to return it as soon as he has finished using it, or within a reasonable time afterwards. If matters reach the point where Richard has to demand the return of the wheelbarrow, Fred must comply immediately. In Quebec, however, if Fred kept Richard's wheelbarrow for three years, and during those three years "possessed it in a continuous, uninterrupted, peaceable and public manner," and acted as owner of the wheelbarrow without any opposition from Richard, Fred would acquire title to the wheelbarrow.

What steps should I take if a friend borrows an item and then refuses to return it?

If your friend ignores your first request to return the item, you should present him with a second request in writing. If he still refuses to surrender your property, you can sue him in Small Claims Court. Although you may not wish to go so far, you could also file criminal theft charges at your local prosecuting attorney's office.

Morton lent his boat to Gary. One of Gary's friends fell down in the boat and was injured. Is Morton liable?

He may be. The injured friend could sue Morton for negligence (1) if Morton had entrusted the boat to Gary, knowing that Gary was incompetent, inexperienced, or otherwise incapable of using it safely, or (2) if the injuries were caused by defects in the boat that Morton knew about but failed to correct before he lent the boat to Gary.

Gifts

Tom told Kathleen he would give her his old car, when he bought a new one. Later Tom changed his mind, and gave the old vehicle to Peter instead. Isn't Kathleen entitled to the car?

No. There are only two ways a gift can become another person's possession. The first way is to transfer possession of the property to another by actually turning it over to the other person. The second is to have the transfer of ownership legally recorded, such as by signing over the title to the car. Until one of these two steps is accomplished, the gift has not been given and may be revoked by the donor at any time.

If a husband gives his wife an anniversary gift, such as a videocassette recorder, does the item belong to her, or is it considered joint property?

The videocassette recorder belongs to the wife and is considered separate property because it was a gift from her husband.

I gave my neighbor Marlene an antique doll my father had given me when I was a child. I just found out that the doll is worth a lot of money. Can I make Marlene give it back?

No. You have no legal right to force Marlene to return the doll. Under the law a gift between two persons is irrevocable, except in certain circumstances such as ingratitude—for example, if the recipient murdered or deserted the donor.

Roxanne was near death in the hospital. Betty, a childhood companion she hadn't seen for 40 years, visited her on Wednesday night, and Roxanne gave her old friend a sapphire ring as a gift. Roxanne worsened overnight and she died the next morning. Can her family make Betty return the ring?

Probably not. This gift falls into a category that the law defines as a gift *mortis causa*. A *mortis causa* gift occurs when the donor expects to die soon, makes a gift of personal property, and then actually dies.

Mortis causa gifts differ from other gifts in that they can be revoked at any time prior to the donor's death, and they are automatically revoked if the donor does not die as expected. In this instance, it appears that the legal requirements for a gift *mortis causa* have been met, so Roxanne's family cannot force Betty to return the ring. If Roxanne had lived, however, Betty would have had to return the ring had Roxanne asked her to do so.

If Betty was not a close friend or relative of Roxanne, Roxanne's family could try to cancel the gift on the grounds that (1) there was a lack of consideration or reason for giving such a gift, or (2) Roxanne was in such a bad mental state at the time that she was unable to give her free and honest consent to the gift. Gifts are, in effect, contracts and must respect certain formalities to be valid; consideration and consent are necessary for such a contract.

Lost and Found

I found a wallet containing $100 in the street. There was no identification in it, and no one was around when I picked it up. Can I keep the money?

No. You should turn the wallet and money over to the police department in your community. If no one claims the wallet within the waiting period provided by law—usually 90 days—the police will return everything to you, and you may keep the money. The finder of lost goods acquires a right of ownership to the goods that will stand up against the claim of anyone except the true owner.

While driving along the road to our county dump, I spotted a large shopping bag. Inside were 20 brand-new shirts. They were all tagged with the name of the store, but there was no sales receipt. The shirts were all my size. Can I keep them?

Yes. Since you acquired the shirts honestly, have no reason to believe they were stolen, and also have no way of determining to whom they belong, you can assume that they were abandoned and so keep them. You could try to locate the owner by taking the shirts to the store, but you are under no legal obligation to do so. Had you not found the shirts, it is reasonable to assume that they would have been ruined by the elements if left where they were for another few days.

When Doris's old car had engine trouble on a lonely side road near her isolated country home, she decided to leave it where it stopped. If Frank finds the car, can he tow it away and legally claim ownership?

It depends on what Doris's intentions were when she left the car. If she planned to come back for it, Frank has no legal right to tow the car away, since he is not the owner. The law would continue to recognize Doris as the owner as long as she retained the registration or the title certificate. However, if Doris decided to abandon the car and relinquish her ownership, Frank could claim it, because it would then not be owned by anyone else. But even if the license plates had been removed and the car seemed not only valueless but beyond repairs, Frank would still have no proof of Doris's intention.

To confirm that she was indeed abandoning the vehicle, he must locate her and get that information from her before he tows the car away. And even then, he would still not be the new owner. That will happen only when the car has been registered in his name according to the rules of his province.

Joyce liked to cut across Mary Anne's property on her way to work. One day, she noticed under a bush a sack with several pieces of jewelry in it. Who should be allowed to keep the jewelry?

Mary Anne has a better claim than Joyce. The owner of land is considered to have possession of everything on the property even if the owner is unaware of its presence. However, Mary Anne will have to give up the jewelry if the true owner is ever found. In Quebec, one half of a treasure — "any buried or hidden thing which no one can prove himself owner of and which is discovered by chance" — would belong to the owner of the land where it was found and one half to the person who found it.

I bought three rings from a souvenir shop for $5 each, but discovered later that one was 14-karat gold. Must I return it?

You are under no obligation to return the ring. However, if the shopkeeper discovers that a valuable ring has been mistakenly turned over to you instead of a $5 one, he has a legal right to sue you in order to recover the ring or its value. Error is one of the grounds for setting aside a contract and the selling of a 14-karat gold ring for a mere $5 would be evidence that the shopkeeper sold it by mistake.

Norman gave Gladys an old trunk and told her that she could have what was in it. Gladys found a bankbook of Norman's with a $5,000 balance. Can Gladys keep the money in the account?

No. Even though Gladys is in possession of Norman's passbook, the bank will not permit her to make a withdrawal from his account, since her signature does not appear on the bank's records. Gladys would be committing a crime if she attempted to withdraw any money from Norman's account. The passbook is not the same thing as $5,000 but merely a record of Norman's bank balance. If Norman lost his passbook, he would not have lost $5,000; thus giving Gladys the passbook in error is not the same as giving her the balance in his account.

Selling Personal Property

I am planning to sell my television for $150. Should I prepare a written agreement for the buyer and me to sign?

A written agreement is not required. The act of exchanging the television for payment shows that the buyer and the seller made a legally binding

223

contract. However, it is always a good idea to put such transactions in writing; if there is a dispute later, a written document will make it easier to prove your case. Too often, as film producer Samuel Goldwyn once said, "a verbal agreement is not worth the paper it's written on." If your agreement is in writing, you can include—or exclude—any warranty, and put in any other conditions you feel would best protect your interest.

Is it true that some types of contracts for buying and selling must be in writing?

Yes. Each province has a law, called the Statute of Frauds, that describes what kinds of contracts must be in writing to be enforced. A contract for the sale of land, for example, must be in writing. Contracts that cannot be carried out within a year of their signing and those covering the sale of goods whose price exceeds a specified dollar amount—$50 in most cases—also require written contracts. In Quebec, testimony will be accepted as proof of contracts up to $1,000.

June found a Tiffany lamp at a bargain price at a garage sale. She gave the owner a cheque for the lamp and told him she'd pick up the lamp later. In the interim, the owner sold the lamp to someone who offered more money. June got her cheque back but wonders if she has any further recourse in this situation.

June could go to court and sue for breach of contract. But the money damages she would receive would be limited to the difference between the regular price she would pay for the lamp and the bargain price that was agreed to at the garage sale. However, some courts would rule that June is not entitled to receive any damages at all, because she canceled the contract when she accepted the return of her cheque.

Rosemary agreed to sell Judy an original Emily Carr painting. When Judy came to pick up the valuable artwork, Rosemary informed her that she had changed her mind. Can Judy force Rosemary to sell her the painting?

If they had nothing in writing, it would be difficult for Judy to force Rosemary to sell the artwork. Most provinces will not enforce oral contracts involving $50 or more, and original Emily Carr paintings are worth much more than that. If Judy and Rosemary had a written contract, on the other hand, Judy could sue for breach of contract, and she would have a good chance of getting the painting.

I gave Elaine $50 not to sell her video camera until I decided whether to buy it. When I decided against the deal, Elaine refused to return the $50 deposit. Can she keep my money?

Probably. When you gave Elaine the $50, you created what is called an option contract. In other words, you paid Elaine to keep her offer to sell open; in return Elaine promised not to sell the camera to anyone else. Elaine lived up to her part of the bargain, and she is therefore entitled to keep the money.

Mary agreed to buy my stereo for $400. Later she reneged on the deal, and I was forced to sell it to someone else for only $200. Can I sue Mary for the difference?

Yes. You are entitled to take her to Small Claims Court. In most provinces, a contract for the sale of goods valued at $50 or more must be in writing to be enforceable; in some cases, a note or memorandum could be used as proof of the promise to purchase. In Quebec, testimony can be used to prove contracts involving goods worth under $1,000.

Kevin, Leon, and Mike, who live on the same block, pitched in to buy an expensive new power mower for all of them to share. When Kevin's family decided to move, Kevin demanded to be bought out of his share. Do Leon and Mike have to pay Kevin?

Leon and Mike have both a moral and a legal obligation to pay Kevin for his share of the power mower. However, they are only required to reimburse Kevin for one third of the mower's remaining value. This value can best be determined by asking a dealer for an estimate based on the item's age and condition.

Eddie's father bought him a new bicycle for his 10th birthday. Eddie sold the bike for $20 to the boy up the street. Can Eddie's father get the bicycle back?

Yes. Eddie's father can either get Eddie to ask for it back, or he can go and retrieve it himself. In either case, the $20 will have to be returned to the boy who bought the bike from Eddie. While the law does permit children to enter into oral purchase agreements such as this, it also permits children to get out of them without being penalized for breach of contract. The purpose of this is to protect an immature person from being victimized by an unfair agreement. Eddie's father may act on his son's behalf to set this oral contract aside and get the bicycle back. Such setting aside of a contract made by a minor is called lesion.

Selling Personal Property

I inherited some gold jewelry from my grandmother, and I would now like to sell it. Do I need any kind of papers to prove that I own the jewelry in order to sell it legally?

Personal items such as jewelry can usually be sold without written proof of ownership. You may have received a written report of the assets in your grandmother's estate at the time you received the jewelry. This report, or other estate papers that identify the jewelry, would be helpful to a buyer concerned about the legitimacy of your ownership. If at any time you had the jewelry insured, the insurance policy, with an inventory and description of the jewelry, would also prove ownership.

Bill and his brother Brad have shared a stamp collection since they were children. Can Bill sell any of the stamps and keep the proceeds without Brad's permission?

Bill can sell only those stamps that belong to him. An individual cannot sell the property of another without the owner's consent. If Bill did sell any of the stamps that the brothers acquired jointly, Brad would be entitled to half their value from Bill.

Can my creditors ever take my personal property and sell it without my knowledge?

Your creditors cannot take your property and sell it without first contacting you and going through a legal process to enforce whatever rights they possess. However, if you have moved without informing your creditors of your new address, they may not be able to contact you. The legal notice would be sent to your last address or put in a local newspaper. Thus you may never really learn that your property will be seized, and in this case it could be sold without your knowing it.

Can I sell or give away property that has a lien on it?

Yes, but there are conditions relating to liens that may make this undesirable. You should not make such a sale or gift unless you fully understand these conditions. When you sell or give away property that has a lien on it, the recipient also becomes subject to the lien. The person or company holding the lien now has a legal claim against both of you. If you defaulted on a car loan, for example, and you then sold the car, both you and the buyer would be liable for the loan.

There may be specific conditions in the lien itself that restrict or prohibit you from selling or giving away the property. If you transferred the property anyway, the lienholder could demand that the transaction be canceled and either claim the property himself or accelerate the debt, making the balance due immediately. In any case, you should make sure that the purchaser knows there is a lien on the property you are selling or he can cancel the contract on the ground that you did not disclose an important condition.

Patents, Copyrights, Trademarks ▬▬▬▬

While tinkering with some machinery in my basement, I invented a device that could be very profitable. How can I protect my invention from being stolen?

You should apply to the Canadian Patent Office, part of Consumer and Corporate Affairs Canada, for a patent. Before it will issue a patent, the office must be completely satisfied that your invention is actually new, useful and likely to work. It will examine your application and search publications and patent files to make sure your device was (1) not known or used by others before you invented it; (2) not described anywhere more than two years before you applied; or (3) not sold in Canada or used publicly for more than two years before you applied.

Once a patent is granted, you would have the exclusive right to use or sell your invention for 17 years. After that period, anyone may copy your device and use or sell it. The protection granted by a patent is good only in Canada. If you want to protect your rights in other countries, you should apply for patents in those countries.

Applying for a patent can be complicated, so many inventors call on patent attorneys or registered patent agencies to process their applications. Your application must follow a format that includes an *abstract*, a brief outline describing your invention and how it differs from other inventions; a *specification*, a clear and complete description of your invention, of the manner in which it is to be used, and the technology you claim to own; and a *drawing*, done according to the regulations of the Patent Act.

Send your formal application, fee, and a petition requesting a patent to the Commissioner of Patents. Do not send models of the invention unless the commissioner requests them. You can get more information by writing to the Canadian Patent Office, Place du Portage, Tower 1, 50 Victoria Street, Hull, Que., K1A 0C9. This office, a division of the Intellectual Property Directorate of Consumer and Corporate Affairs, deals with private inventors. Inquiries about publicly funded inventions or those financed by universities, research centers or corporations should be directed to: Canadian Patents and Developments Ltd., 275 Slater Street, Ottawa, Ont., K1A 0R3.

Patents, Copyrights, Trademarks

***I have just purchased a new tool that is marked "pat. pending."
What does this mean?***

The term *pat. pending*—short for *patent pending*—indicates that an
application for a patent has been filed with the Canada Patent Office. This
term has no legal effect, since an item is not protected until a patent is
assigned and a patent number issued.

***Can my wife obtain a patent on an artistic design that is for
decorative purposes only?***

Rather than obtaining a patent on her creation, your wife should register
it as an "industrial design." This term covers any original pattern, shape,
or ornamentation used on a manufactured object such as a decoration
on a table. By registering her design, your wife would protect it for five
years and have an option to renew the protection for a further five years.
For more information about artistic or industrial designs, contact the
Copyrights and Industrial Designs Office, Intellectual Properties Directorate, Consumer and Corporate Affairs Canada, Ottawa, Ont., K1A 0C9.

Pam has an idea for a new board game. Can she patent her idea?

No. Ideas alone are not patentable. However, Pam can protect her game
by developing a prototype and having it copyrighted. In fact Pam would
automatically have a Canadian copyright once she makes her first game.
Nevertheless she should register her copyright with the Copyrights
Office, 5th Floor, Place du Portage, Tower 1, 50 Victoria Street, Hull, Que.,
K1A 0C9. The office will send her a certificate she can use to establish
ownership.

***What is the difference between the kinds of things that can be
patented and those that can be copyrighted?***

Patents protect new inventions and improvements to existing mechanical devices; copyrights protect artistic works. Some broad categories of
things that can be copyrighted are: (1) literary works, such as books,
poems, and magazines; (2) musical works, including accompanying
lyrics; (3) plays and their musical scores; (4) audio records and tapes;
(5) motion pictures, videocassettes, and other audiovisual works;
(6) visual art, including lithographs and sculptures; and (7) photographs.
Except for photographs, government publications, mechanical contriv-
ances such as records or cinematographic films, posthumous works and

228

works of joint authorship, a copyright protects the work for the lifetime of its author or creator plus 50 years. A photograph, for example, is protected for 50 years from the date the original negative is made; a government publication for 50 years from the date it was first published.

Does Richard need to copyright the manuscript of his book before sending it to a publisher?

No. The act of setting down his thoughts in tangible form in a manuscript is sufficient to establish and protect his copyright while it is in the hands of a publisher. To protect his work after it is published, Richard should ensure that it carries a copyright notice.

My parent-teacher group is preparing a cookbook as a fund-raising project. We have been told that we can reprint a small number of recipes from other cookbooks without permission from the publishers. Can we?

No. The owner of a copyright has the exclusive right to print, publish, copy, and sell the copyrighted work. He also has the right to prepare derivative works based upon the original material. In order to reprint the recipes in your cookbook, you must receive written permission from the copyright holder.

Leslie designed an emblem to identify her wood carvings. What can she do to make sure no one else uses this design?

Leslie can register her emblem as a trademark at the Canadian Trademark Office. In 1988 it cost about $350 to register a trademark, but this cost can change from year to year. For more information, Leslie can contact the Registrar of Trade Marks, Place du Portage, Tower 1, 50 Victoria Street, Hull, Que., K1A 0C9.

Is it legal to use a copying machine to copy pages from a copyrighted book without obtaining the publisher's permission?

Whether or not you must seek the publisher's permission depends on whether the copying complies with the copyright law. This law permits copying parts of a copyrighted work for such purposes as scholarship, research, criticism, comment, or news reporting. Teachers are also permitted to make multiple copies of a work for classroom use. However, copying for commercial purposes, such as making reprints for resale, is illegal.

Patents, Copyrights, Trademarks

How can I tell if something is in the public domain?

A work that has been published without a copyright notice or one whose copyright has expired is said to be in the public domain. This means that anyone is free to copy, print, publish, sell, or use it without infringing the rights of another. If you are not sure that a work is in the public domain, write to its publisher. If the present copyright owner refuses to republish or to allow others to republish the work of a deceased author, another person may apply to the Copyright Office for permission to republish this work.

I run a videocassette store, and I know that some of my customers copy the rented videocassettes on their VCRs at home. This is illegal, isn't it?

Yes. The systematic reproduction of copyrighted works to obtain permanent copies without purchasing them is prohibited. In fact most videotapes carry warnings about the legal consequences of copying, in addition to the standard copyright notice. If, however, your customers are copying the videos for personal use only, not in a systematic manner for any commercial use, such copying may be permitted under the "fair dealing rule."

Robert has obtained a trademark for the line of office products he manufactures. What kind of protection does this provide?

Robert has the exclusive right to use his trademark for 15 years and can renew this right for a further 15 years. In order to notify the public of his ownership of the trademark, he should display it with the words "Registered Trade Mark," or the letter R enclosed in a circle following the word or phrase he uses for a trade name. If he fails to provide this notice, he will be unable to collect damages from anyone who uses the same trademark unless he can prove that his product has developed a public reputation associated with his unregistered trademark.

Your Car

Tony obtained a car loan from his bank based on a price quoted to him by the salesman. When he returned to pay for the car, the manager of the dealership said he wouldn't sell the car for that price. What can Tony do?

If Tony's agreement with the salesman was in writing, he can sue for breach of contract. If he wins the case, the court will require the dealer to fulfill the contract, and Tony will get his car at the price originally quoted. Even if Tony and the salesman had only an oral agreement, Tony would still have a good chance of winning if someone witnessed the salesman's offer and testifies to that fact. British Columbia's Trade Practices Act, Ontario's Business Practices Act and Quebec's Consumer Protection Act all allow you to use spoken testimony to prove the existence of certain oral consumer contracts, such as those for the purchase of a car. Without a witness, though, it would be Tony's word against that of the salesman, and Tony would probably lose.

What are my rights if I put down a deposit on a car and then the dealer sells it to someone else?

You are entitled to a refund. If you have a written contract with the dealer, and he sells the car to someone else, you can cancel the contract and get back the money you left as a deposit. Depending on the fine print in the contract, however, the dealer may have the right to replace the car with an identical one. If you did not have a contract but left a deposit, you are still entitled to get your money back. In British Columbia, Ontario and Quebec, you could also ask for "specific performance," that is, you may ask that the dealer get back the car you originally chose, failing which you may sue him for exemplary damages—for your inconvenience—as well as for your deposit.

A car dealer wanted me to subtract 20,000 kilometres from the odometer statement on the car I was trading in. I wouldn't do it. Should I report this incident to someone? What might have happened to me if I had signed this statement?

If you had gone ahead and signed the statement, you could have been charged with a crime. In addition, the buyer of your old car could have sued you in a civil court for damages as a result of fraud. You should report the matter to your provincial attorney general's office or to the nearest consumer protection office for possible prosecution. Tampering with an odometer, or issuing a false odometer statement, is an offense that can be prosecuted in both criminal and civil courts.

Jackie's car dealer sold the car she traded in before the loan was approved for her new car. Does a dealer have the right to do this?

Probably not. Most contracts to purchase new cars are contingent upon financing. This means that if the buyer can't get a loan, the contract is canceled. If Jackie's contract was contingent upon financing, the dealer had no right to sell her trade-in because title to the car had not yet passed to him. In essence, he sold a car that still belonged to someone else. If Jackie's contract was not contingent upon financing and she had transferred the car's title to the dealer, he did have the right to sell it.

Edith has taken her new car back for service five times in the past two months, and each time she had to rent a car for several days. Can Edith get the dealer or manufacturer to reimburse her for the cost of the rentals?

Yes. Both the dealer and the manufacturer are responsible for Edith's damages because they sold her a defective automobile. The cost of renting another car while hers is being fixed would be reasonable damages. Most dealers would have supplied Edith with a loaner while her own car was being serviced.

I bought a new car six months ago and haven't had any problems with it. But this model is now being recalled. Should I worry about the safety of the car? Can I force the dealer to take it back?

If you comply with the recall and take your car in for inspection and repair, it should be safe to operate when you get it back. Recalls are initiated when a safety problem shows up in a group of cars of the same make, model, and year. Any defect discovered when you take your car for inspection will be corrected free of charge. If you've had no trouble with your car, and the recall prevents a future problem, you cannot force the dealer to take the car back.

Fred is frantic. His car has been in the repair shop four times since he bought it 10 months ago, and he's written to the manufacturer three times, but the car is still not running right. What can he do?

Since Fred's car is only 10 months old, it is covered by the manufacturer's warranty. If the problem is one not covered by the warranty, Fred may be protected by "implied warranties" contained in the Consumer Protection Law of his province. In almost all cases, Fred would have to give the dealer a reasonable opportunity to make the necessary repairs. If the car

233

has not been adequately repaired after four tries, Fred has fulfilled his obligation as far as giving the dealer a chance to repair the vehicle, and he would stand a good chance in court of having his contract canceled and having his money returned. The Supreme Court of Canada has held that both the dealer and the manufacturer of an automobile with hidden defects are responsible to the consumer. When someone buys a new automobile, he is entitled to expect a product with a certain degree of quality and one that will serve the purpose for which it was bought.

Can I withhold payments on a new-car loan if the car is a lemon?

It depends upon who arranged the loan. If you personally arranged the loan with a bank or other lending institution, you may not withhold payments. The loan is between you and the bank and, whether or not the car works, the bank is entitled to repayment. If the car dealer arranged the financing, however, you may be able to withhold payments. But before doing so, consult an attorney about your rights and responsibilities. He may advise you to withhold future payments and sue for cancellation of the contract. In that case you should also stop driving the car and return it to the dealer from whom you bought it.

What to Do If You Bought a Lemon

Most provinces have laws that protect you from getting stuck with a new car that presents a safety hazard, or one that keeps breaking down no matter how many times it's been back to the shop for repairs. You can also look to private automobile associations whose purpose is to help the motorist get the most out of available warranties. If you have bought a new car that is a constant source of problems, there are several things you can do. You should:

● Bring the car in for repair before the warranty period ends. This will ensure your right to have the defect fixed even after the warranty runs out. It will also guarantee you other legal options if the problem persists.
● Keep accurate, detailed records. Give the dealer a written list of what needs to be fixed every time you take the car in for repair. Always keep a copy for yourself. Save all copies of the dealer's bills and repair orders.
● Notify the dealer in writing that you are dissatisfied with your vehicle, and ask him to refund your money or give you another similar model at no cost to you.
● Write to your local automobile association about your problem and about the dealer's response.

Alexander lives in Ontario. He bought a car in Quebec. In which province does he pay the sales tax?

Alexander will pay the sales tax in Quebec, where he bought the car. However, if he plans to register his car in his home province, Alexander may also have to pay a use tax on the car. Provinces impose use taxes to recover some of the tax revenue they lose when people go to another province, as Alexander did, to make a major purchase.

One morning Jay discovered that his car was missing. He reported it stolen but later learned that the bank had repossessed it. Is it legal for a bank to repossess a car in this manner?

Yes. If Jay missed a few payments, and the car was collateral on the loan, the bank has the right to repossess the car. Once the bank has obtained a judgment on its loan contract, it won't notify the delinquent borrower that it is about to claim the car lest there be any attempt to hide the vehicle. Under some contracts, the creditor has the right to repossess without court authorization. Much depends upon the nature of Jay's contract and the consumer protection law of his province.

In all likelihood, the bank would have sent Jay several notices informing him, politely at first, then more firmly, that he was behind in

● If the problem concerns safety, write to the Federal Government, care of Vehicle Recall Office, Road and Motor Vehicle Traffic Safety Branch, Place de Ville, Tower C, 28th Floor, Ottawa, Ont., K1A 0N5.
● Write to the manufacturer of the automobile; even foreign automakers have Canadian offices. If the defect in your car is one that the manufacturer is aware of, you could probably benefit from an unpublicized "extended" warranty given to consumers who are persistent in pressing their claims.
● If you still have not received satisfaction, see an attorney about suing the dealer and the manufacturer to cancel the sale and to recover the amount you paid for the car, the repairs, and any other expenses you incurred because of the defective auto. If the manufacturer was aware of the defect before you brought it to his attention, he may be liable for punitive damages for false and misleading acts. Failure to disclose a known defect would contravene many consumer laws.

If you bought a used car from a dealer, most of the above recourses would still apply, but much would depend on the price you paid, the model, the year of the auto, the mileage and the warranty, if any, given by the dealer.

his payments. He must have ignored these notices. In most cases the repossession would cancel Jay's debt with the bank.

Even though Loretta's car was repossessed when she couldn't keep up her payments, the bank claims she still owes $1,000. How can she owe anything when the bank has the car?

Once the bank repossessed the car, the contract with Loretta was canceled, unless it clearly stated that Loretta would be responsible for any shortfall. When a car is repossessed and sold under those conditions, the borrower must pay the difference if the resale price is less than the amount outstanding on the loan. So if Loretta owed the bank $6,000 on the car loan when she defaulted, and the bank sold the car for only $5,000, Loretta would still owe the bank $1,000. If the bank had sold the car for more than the amount due, however, Loretta would have received the difference. In some provinces, Ontario and Quebec for example, repossession is not allowed without court permission once two thirds of the sale price has been paid.

I bought a used car from a dealer whose ad said the car was "never wrecked." A mechanic told me later that the car had indeed been in a major accident. What can I do?

Sue the dealer for fraud. Since you based your purchase decision on his fraudulent statement, you can sue him even if you bought the car "as is."

Pete bought a used car from a dealer who said that the car was in fine working condition. What can Pete do if the car keeps stalling?

When the dealer told Pete the used car was in "working condition," he made a warranty, or promise, that the car would operate properly. If the dealer can't repair the car, Pete is entitled to have it fixed elsewhere and obtain reimbursement from the dealer for the repair work.

Rufus bought a used car from Carl, but he has not been able to register the car because the title doesn't match the vehicle's registration number. What should Rufus do?

Rufus has the right to return the car and get a refund. When Carl sold Rufus his car, he made a promise, or warranty, that he was transferring a valid title to Rufus. Carl has breached that warranty.

***Many married couples put their homes in joint ownership.
Should we do the same with our car?***

If you do, you will both have equal rights to it, and neither of you will be able to sell the car without the other's consent. If the vehicle is in an accident, both you and your spouse could be held liable. This would be the case even if one of you lent the car to a third party, who was involved in an accident. Since there are many more risks than benefits in having the car registered in both names, it is better not to do so.

Renting or Leasing a Car

***The car rental people told Audrey that for a little extra, she could
get a "collision damage waiver." Should Audrey have taken it?***

The waiver would protect Audrey from liability for damage to the rental car if she were involved in a collision, regardless of who was at fault. If Audrey rejects the waiver, she will have to pay for any collision damage to the rental car. However, since most automobile insurance policies also cover the use of a rental car, Audrey should check her own policy—if she is already covered, she doesn't need the collision damage waiver.

Some rental companies also offer options that cover personal injury. Again, if Audrey is already covered by her own insurance, she doesn't need extra protection.

What happens if I have an accident while driving a rental car?

Your liability depends on your own automobile insurance and the type of agreement you sign with the car rental agency. Some car rental agreements would make you liable for everything; with others you would be responsible up to a fixed dollar amount. The car rental agency cannot hold you liable if (1) you paid extra for collision and bodily injury coverage, or if (2) your own automobile insurance covers you for an accident with a rental car.

***Harvey leased a car for a five-year period. Two years into the
lease he was given a company car for his own use. Can he get out
of the three remaining years of his lease?***

It depends on the terms of Harvey's contract. If the contract includes conditions and penalties for terminating the lease, Harvey will have to abide by them. If there are no such provisions, the dealer can sue Harvey for any losses he suffers if Harvey breaks the contract.

Renting or Leasing a Car

After signing a lease agreement with John's Auto Leases, Joe and Julie realized they couldn't afford the payments. A friend told them that they had a three-day grace period in which to cancel the contract. Is this true?

No. Unless their lease agreement specifies a three-day grace period, Joe and Julie cannot cancel it. Their friend was probably thinking about consumer protection laws that allow a three-day cooling-off period in which a buyer can change his mind after signing a purchase agreement with a door-to-door salesperson. A lease for a car is very much like a lease for an apartment, in that both parties are bound for the term of the lease, and notice of cancellation must be given within the time limits set out in the contract.

Marlene leased a car that turned out to be a lemon. Is she entitled to turn the car in and get a new one?

Yes. The person or company leasing the vehicle to Marlene is required by law to give her "peaceful enjoyment" of the vehicle. In other words it is required to supply Marlene with a vehicle that works properly.

I leased a vehicle last year, but I can't afford the payments now. The leasing company is demanding payment as usual, regardless of my personal circumstances. What can I do? Can I sell the car?

Do not try to sell the car you're leasing; it does not belong to you. Selling a leased car is as illegal as selling an apartment you rent. Read your lease agreement to see if it includes procedures for terminating the contract. You may be able to cancel the lease by returning the car and paying a penalty. However, not all leases provide for termination. If you break the lease by turning in the car and defaulting on your payments, the leasing company can sue you to recover any monetary losses it incurs.

Selling a Car

What records do I need in order to sell my car?

You must have a certificate of title and a valid registration. You may also be required to give the buyer a bill of sale. Every province has its own regulations regarding the transfer of vehicles; you should contact your local department of motor vehicles to find out the proper procedures.

What steps should Laurie take to sell a car on which she has an outstanding bank loan?

First, she should check her loan agreement. It may not allow her to sell the car without the bank's permission. If it's all right with Laurie's lender to sell the car, she is still obligated to pay the balance due on the loan or keep her monthly payments up to date. Laurie must tell the buyer about the loan because if she defaults on it, the bank may be able to repossess the car from the buyer.

Last week, Lloyd sold his car to his 15-year-old neighbor. The boy came to Lloyd's house today and said he no longer wanted the car. Does Lloyd have to give him back his money?

Yes. Children who have not yet reached the age of adulthood, usually 18 or 19 years of age, are considered legally incompetent to make a valid contract. Selling a car involves a contract, either written or oral, and in this case it is not binding because of Lloyd's neighbor's age. Minors can make valid contracts only for the necessities of life, to rent housing or to purchase food and clothing, for example.

If I sell my car to a friend, do I have to give any warranties? She knows that it barely runs and is paying me only $50.

You are not required to give a warranty when you sell a used car. To avoid any misunderstandings, write on the bill of sale that you are selling the car without any warranty for hidden defects. This lets your friend know that you are making no promises about how the car will perform. By taking the car as is, she is accepting it in whatever condition it is in.

When Albert bought a new car, he sold his old one to Hank, his best friend, for $400. After Hank had the car for two weeks, the transmission gave out. Hank wants his money back. Does Albert have to return Hank's money?

It depends on what Albert said at the time of the sale. If he made any promises about the car's performance to persuade Hank to buy it, Hank may be able to get his money back. For example, if Hank bought the car relying on Albert's assurance that the transmission would be good for another 15,000 kilometres, Hank is entitled to a refund. But if Hank bought Albert's car without any warranty, Albert owes him nothing. When someone buys a car without warranty from a private individual, the seller need not make any promises about the car and is released from responsibility for any defects or problems.

Precautions to Take When You Sell Your Car

Selling your car instead of trading it in often means a higher profit for you and a better bargain for the person who buys the car. But there are precautions you should take, or the sale might end up creating legal problems for you. Here are some of the steps you should take:

● Contact your provincial motor vehicle department before you sell the car and find out how to make sure that the transfer of ownership will conform to all your province's required procedures.

● Check with your town or city government before putting a For Sale sign on your car. Many communities restrict the size of these signs or prohibit them entirely.

● Be accurate in what you say in newspaper advertisements and in any notices you put up on community or office bulletin boards. Buyers have used exaggerated or false statements about a car's condition to have the sale voided later in court.

● Ask for a nonrefundable deposit if the buyer can't pay in full at the time you make the deal. This will eliminate people who are not serious about buying and will help compensate you for taking the car off the market and losing other customers if the original buyer changes his mind or never shows up again.

● Give the buyer a written receipt for the deposit; it should include the buyer's name, a description of the car, the total price to be paid, the amount received, and the date the car will be put up for sale again if

Car Warranties

Henry and Patsy bought a new car last year. About six months after the purchase, they had to take it to the car dealership for repairs. Two days after the one-year warranty was up, the same problem occurred. The dealer refused to honor the warranty. What can Henry and Patsy do?

Henry and Patsy can insist that the dealer correct the problem because it first developed while the warranty was still in effect. Although the one-year period is over, this does not mean the dealership is absolved from all further responsibility. A warranty guarantees that defects arising during the warranty coverage will be fixed by the dealer.

What is the difference between a full warranty and a limited one?

A full warranty, which is unusual, must meet several requirements. It must state its duration clearly and agree that defects will be repaired the buyer does not complete the deal. The receipt should state that the buyer understands the deposit is nonrefundable if the sale isn't completed by the date indicated. Keep a copy for your records.

● Have two copies of a bill of sale completed when the car is turned over to the new owner. (Standard bill of sale forms can be obtained at office supply or stationery stores, or you can prepare your own.) Include the year, make, model, identification number, and engine number of the car, names and addresses of buyer and seller, and total selling price on the bill of sale. Include a statement that the car is being sold "as is" with no guarantees of any kind.

● You must indicate the mileage on the date the car is sold and declare that the odometer has not been turned back nor the car driven while the odometer was disconnected.

● If the car is being purchased by a minor, have his parents sign the bill of sale. Otherwise you have no legal recourse if the young person changes his mind.

● Even if you know the buyer, ask for payment by certified cheque, money order, or cash.

● Hand over the car title or registration only when you have the cash or certified cheque in hand.

● Make sure that the motor vehicle bureau changes the registration from your name to that of the buyer. You will be entitled to a refund of the unused portion of your annual registration fee.

● Cancel your insurance on the car as soon as it's sold.

within this period without charge to the customer and within a reasonable time. If a defect cannot be repaired within a reasonable time, or has not been fixed after a reasonable number of attempts, the manufacturer or dealer offering the full warranty must replace the car or refund the purchase price.

A warranty that does not meet all these standards is a limited warranty, the most common type of coverage for a new car. Typical limitations require that you pay the labor costs when defective parts are replaced, or that you pay for renting a car while yours is in the repair shop. Some items—such as spark plugs, filters, hoses, belts, and other maintenance parts—may not be covered by a limited warranty. Tires and batteries usually have their own separate warranties.

Whenever I pick up my car after warranty work, I always have to pay some charge or other. Is this legal?

If your repairs are covered by a full warranty, you should not have to pay anything. If you have a limited warranty, which is usually the case, it may

Car Warranties

require that you bear part of the cost. Read your warranty carefully to make sure that you are not being charged for costs that should be paid by the dealer or the manufacturer.

Nearly every car salesman I've spoken to has told me about the benefits of purchasing an extended warranty. Are extended warranties as good as they say?

The value of a warranty depends on its terms, its cost, and the solvency of the company offering it. If you want protection for situations not covered by your warranty or if you want repairs guaranteed after your warranty runs out, consider buying an extended warranty. But first compare it to the warranty that comes with the car you are buying. An extended warranty may not be a good investment if it contains too many restrictions, conditions, or limitations, or if it provides little more than the original warranty.

Audrey sent in a claim under her extended service plan for repairs she had done on her station wagon, but she was turned down because they weren't done by an authorized dealer. Shouldn't she be reimbursed for the cost of the work?

No. Audrey's problem illustrates the difference between warranties and service plans. Under a service plan, the manufacturer has the right to limit coverage to its own dealers whether or not one is readily available when needed. A warranty, on the other hand, guarantees performance of the car's parts. A warranty can ask the consumer to use authorized dealers, but only if such a dealer is readily available when and where the car breaks down. If Audrey's car had broken down in an isolated area and she wasn't able to get to an authorized dealer, she could have been reimbursed for the cost of the repair work if her warranty had still been in effect. Such is not the case with service contracts, however; regardless of where the breakdown occurs, Audrey must either take the car to an authorized dealer or bear the repair cost herself.

When Sheldon bought his used car, the dealer gave him a warranty that included free repair or replacement for a limited time. Who makes the final decision to replace or repair the defective part, Sheldon or the dealer?

The dealer has the right to decide whether to repair or replace a defective part, and Sheldon must go along with the decision.

Car Repairs

Andrea's mechanic said he couldn't fix her car until he did a thorough inspection, so he asked Andrea to sign a blank order for repairs. Is this OK?

No. Never give a mechanic a blank authorization for repairs. If he is unscrupulous, you could end up with a bill for thousands of dollars. By signing a blank authorization, Andrea would be agreeing to let the mechanic do anything he wanted and charge her for it.

A mechanic is entitled to charge you only for work that you authorize. You have the right to insist on an explanation of all repairs he thinks are necessary plus a written estimate of the costs of those repairs. Some provinces, Quebec for example, require that repair estimates be in writing and that no repairs be done without the express permission of the car owner. Making extensive repairs without such prior permission could be considered an unfair trade practice in other provinces as well.

In most provinces, a mechanic who has repaired your car may retain the vehicle until he has been fully paid for his work, regardless of how long it takes to satisfy the debt. This right of retention is called a *mechanic's lien.* In Manitoba, when there is a dispute about a mechanic's bill, the mechanic must return your car at once if you deposit in court the amount claimed plus 10 percent. The court will rule later on the amount you must pay the mechanic.

Marvin took his car to have an oil leak repaired. The mechanic went ahead and made other repairs without his permission. Must Marvin pay for all the repair work?

No. Marvin is obligated to pay only for the repairs that he authorized. The mechanic has no legal ground to demand payment for any work that Marvin did not approve.

A garage fixed Dorothy's car for $1,250 without first getting her approval. It took her six months to save enough money to pay the bill, but when she tried to pay it yesterday, the garage demanded an additional $180 for storing her car for six months. Is Dorothy responsible for paying the storage costs?

Dorothy does not have to pay for repairs that she did not authorize, and the service station had no right to keep her car or charge her storage costs. However, if she signed a blanket authorization form, it might have required her to pay storage costs if the repairman had to keep the car in order to collect his bill. By law he has a "right of retention," that is, the right to hold on to a car he has worked on until the bill is paid.

Car Repairs

When Charles took his car for repairs, the mechanic did a poor job. Charles doesn't want to give the mechanic a chance to make things right, and he doesn't want to pay for bad work. Does he have an alternative?

Charles's best strategy is to pay the bill and then consider suing the mechanic for the amount it will cost to have someone else do the work. Otherwise, under the provincial mechanic's lien law, the mechanic is allowed to keep the car and sell it if Charles does not pay him—even if the mechanic's work is unsatisfactory. Once the car was sold, it would be almost impossible to prove that the repairs were not done properly.

Phyllis had her car's carburetor repaired, drove 80 kilometres, stopped for lunch, and couldn't restart her car. It had to be towed to the nearest town, where a mechanic found a part on the carburetor was stuck. Can Phyllis collect from the first mechanic?

Yes. If Phyllis's carburetor failed because the first mechanic was negligent and did not do the job properly, he must reimburse Phyllis for the cost of having her car towed and repaired a second time.

How to Avoid Car Repair Rip-offs

Having your car in the repair shop is always an inconvenience, but even worse is the discovery that you have been charged for unnecessary or incompetent work, or for work that was not done at all. Here are some practical ways to make sure you get your money's worth when you take your car in for repair:

● Understand the procedure your mechanic uses to make estimates. Some provinces require written estimates, which list the costs for parts and labor separately and indicate if parts are used, rebuilt, or reconditioned. If major work is recommended, get a second opinion.
● Check the items on the work or repair order; they should describe exactly what you want done. When you sign a work order it becomes a legal contract between you and the repair shop. Do not sign it if it is incorrect or too vague. Do not sign a blank work order. If you do, you will be authorizing the mechanic to make any repairs he wants to do, and you will have to pay for them whether or not they were necessary.
● Find out about the shop's warranty for parts and labor; it should be in writing somewhere on the work order. If you don't find it, ask someone at the shop to give you a copy of their warranty policy, or have them write it on the work order. If the shop will not give you its warranty in writing,

Gabrielle took her car to a repair shop and was told that the engine needed to be rebuilt and that it would cost $800. The actual bill came to over $2,000. What can she do?

If Gabrielle did not get the estimate in writing, she is legally obligated to pay the bill. However, if the final cost of the work greatly exceeds the estimate, as it does in this case, she may be the victim of a type of fraud called lowballing. This occurs when a mechanic gives you an extremely low estimate in order to persuade you to authorize repairs. He knows the work cannot be done at that price and he has no intention of honoring his estimate. Gabrielle's best course of action is to pay the inflated repair bill and then sue the mechanic for fraud. If she wins her case, she will get her money back and may also be awarded punitive damages—a sum of money the court will order the mechanic to pay her as a punishment for committing the fraud.

If I take my car in for minor repairs and the mechanic causes further damage, can he be held responsible?

Yes. When you leave your car with a repairman, he is required to take proper care of it. The mechanic must repair the additional damage to your car or reimburse you for the expense of having someone else do it.

you should seriously consider taking your business elsewhere. Unless the warranty is in writing, you have no recourse if the work is unsatisfactory.
● Ask about the policy regarding the return of your car's replaced parts. You may want to have another mechanic examine them if you believe unnecessary work was done. You generally have the right to keep these parts unless they are under warranty and have to be returned to the manufacturer or dealer. There is usually a box on the work order that you can check to indicate whether or not you want the replaced parts. If not, have your request written on the work order.
● If the shop calls and recommends additional repairs, go back to the shop and sign another work or repair order. If you don't authorize the new work in writing, you may end up being billed for unnecessary work.
● If, after two or three days of normal driving, it is obvious that the repair work is not satisfactory, return the car to the shop and insist that the shop live up to its warranty and fix the problem.
● If you are out of town, try to find a full-service dealership that sells and services your type of car. If you belong to an automobile club, ask the local office to recommend a repair company.
● Always deal with a company that you know well or that a knowledgeable friend has recommended. It is generally best to deal with one that has existed for a while and has built up a good reputation.

Car Repairs

Melanie's car bumper fell off four months after it was repaired at a body shop. Has too much time passed for Melanie to claim that the repair shop is responsible?

No. If the bumper fell off because it was mounted improperly, Melanie has every right to insist that the body shop correct the problem at no cost to her. She should inform the shop immediately; delaying may weaken her case for having it fixed free. In some provinces, various repairs are guaranteed for a certain period. In Quebec, for example, mechanical repairs are guaranteed for three months.

A tire store rotated and balanced Eugene's tires for $25. Four days later, one of the wheels came off, and the car was ruined in an accident. Is the tire store responsible?

Yes. If the wheel came off because of defective work at the tire store, the store is responsible for all the resulting damages.

While Gilbert's car was in the repair shop, his brand-new golf clubs and fishing tackle were stolen from the trunk. Is the repair shop responsible?

If Gilbert informed the shop manager that his sports equipment was in the trunk, the manager was required to protect it as he would his own property in the shop. If the shop was locked and the thief disconnected a burglar alarm to get in, the shop owner is not responsible for the loss, because he took reasonable steps to protect Gilbert's property. On the other hand, if he left Gilbert's car behind the shop with the keys in it, he did not exercise proper care and is responsible.

Licenses and Registrations ▪▪▪▪▪▪▪▪▪

If I allow my son to drive the family car for practice before he gets his learner's permit or driver's license, will I be given a summons if he is caught?

Yes. In all provinces it is illegal to allow an unlicensed driver to use your car, even if you accompany him. The penalties for doing so range from fines to imprisonment. If an unlicensed driver has an accident with your car and causes damage or injury, you too will be liable. In most provinces a would-be driver may practice only after he receives a learner's permit.

Phil has retired to a rural area bordering another province. Can he drive in the neighboring province with the driver's license from his home province?

Yes. Most provinces have agreements among themselves so that a driver's license issued in one is valid in another. There are some restrictions, however. Usually a nonresident with a valid license from his home province can operate a vehicle in another province provided he does not stay or carry on business in that other province for more than six months. Quebec requires an out-of-province driver of a commercial vehicle, taxi, bus or minibus to pass a new driver's test if he decides to live in Quebec and operate commercially in that province for more than 90 days. Other provinces have similar requirements.

Kim will attend college in another province. Must she get a new driver's license and new license plates there?

Probably. Many provinces require nonresidents to obtain driver's licenses and new registrations if they will be driving their cars extensively in the second province. Since Kim will be in the province nine months each year, she will probably have to obtain a new driver's license, register her car in the new province, and pay the required fees and taxes.

Does Robert need a special license to drive a delivery truck?

Yes. Most provinces require that a person who drives for a living have a chauffeur's license. Truck drivers, deliverymen, bus drivers, and taxi drivers are among those who must have a chauffeur's license. If Robert's job requires him to drive only once in a while, however, he may not need the special license. Nevertheless, if he does occasionally drive a truck, he should check with his insurance company to make sure he would be covered if he had an accident. Failure to disclose such occasional truck driving could invalidate Robert's insurance.

Reggie has been driving with an expired driver's license. What can happen to him if he gets caught.

He can be fined and even sentenced to jail. In some places his license can be suspended, and he wouldn't be eligible to get a new one until the end of the suspension period. If you are caught driving with an expired driver's license, you should renew your license before you appear in court. The judge may be more lenient if you show him that you are now complying with the law. Driving with an expired driving license is equivalent to driving without any license at all.

Licenses and Registrations

YOUR CAR

Can my license be suspended if I'm in an accident?

Yes, if you have violated a law in connection with that accident. If you leave the scene of an accident or have been driving under the influence of alcohol or drugs, it may result in an automatic suspension of your license. Your license may be suspended if you have accumulated several moving violations, or points, on your record, or if you don't carry the insurance your province requires.

James was driving with an expired driver's license when he was in an accident. James was not at fault. Will his expired license prohibit him from collecting damages?

No. The fact that James's driver's license had expired does not make him responsible for the accident. He should be able to collect damages for personal injury and property damage. But he would still be liable for the fine and other penalties imposed for driving with an expired license.

What is the difference between having my license suspended and having it revoked?

When your license is suspended, you are deprived of driving privileges for a certain period of time, usually 30, 60, or 90 days. Afterward, your license can be reinstated. In some cases, you may have to take the written test or the road test again. When your driver's license is revoked, you are permanently banned from driving. However, most provincial laws allow you to appeal a decision to the registrar of vehicles that suspends or revokes your driver's license.

How many tickets must I receive before my license is suspended?

Each province sets its own standards for suspending or revoking a license. Licenses are often suspended when a driver has accumulated a certain number of violations in a stated period of time, usually one or two years. Some provinces, Ontario, Quebec and New Brunswick for example, use a point system to determine when a license should be suspended. Driving through a stop sign might be a one-point offense, and reckless driving might be four points. When a driver exceeds the allowed number of points within the period specified by the laws of his province, his license will be suspended. Offenses such as leaving the scene of an accident and driving under the influence of alcohol or drugs automatically result in a suspension of driving privileges in most provinces.

Ray works in my store. If his license is suspended for one year but he is given a permit that allows him to drive to work, can he drive company vehicles for purposes that are work-related?

No. Ray must comply exactly with the conditions imposed on him when his license was suspended. If he is caught violating any of these conditions, he could be subject to severe penalties, including jail.

Since I was away several months, I was unable to renew my car registration before it expired. Will they give me an extension?

Your province may allow a 30-day grace period in which you can renew your registration after it expires. Call your provincial department of motor vehicles for information. If there is no grace period, it is illegal for you to drive your car once the registration has expired, regardless of the reason why.

Eric has been restoring an old car and had to replace the engine. A friend told him he had to let the motor vehicle department know he was doing this. Is this correct?

No. But even though most provinces do not require that such replacement be reported, Eric would be wise to keep the bill of sale and a record of the serial number of his new engine, especially if he got it from someone other than a reputable manufacturer or dealer. There is a country-wide network of people who steal and dismantle automobiles for parts they then sell. Before Eric bought the replacement, he should have contacted his local police or the RCMP to be sure the serial number was not that of a stolen engine. He should do so now.

Tickets and Violations

Jennifer parked her car at a two-hour meter. When she returned an hour later, one of the car wheels had a "boot" on it—a metal device that locks around the tire to prevent the car from being driven away. It took her several hours and cost her $50 to have the boot removed. Jennifer thinks that she is being punished without the opportunity to defend herself. Isn't this illegal?

No. Most people who find boots on their cars have several unpaid parking tickets. This is one method cities use to catch scofflaws—people who ignore parking tickets. Courts have consistently ruled that using boots and towing away illegally parked cars are not illegal.

Tickets and Violations

Kenneth was arrested and spent the night in jail for 17 unpaid parking tickets. Is this legal?

Yes. Most traffic tickets are also summonses, which require the driver to appear in court. If you don't pay a ticket or appear in court in answer to the ticket summons, a warrant may be issued for your arrest. A very large proportion of prisoners in provincial jails are there because they failed to pay fines. These prisoners could be released once the amount owing is paid.

A police officer ticketed Agnes last night because the taillight on her car had burned out. Shouldn't she have received a warning instead of a summons and a fine?

In all provinces it is illegal to drive with defective equipment: thus the officer was right to issue the ticket. As a practical matter, a judge may not fine Agnes if she brings proof to court that she replaced the light, although she may have to pay court costs.

If I'm stopped by a police officer and my passenger is not wearing a seat belt, as required by law, who must pay the fine?

Most laws requiring the use of seat belts make each individual responsible for himself. However, the driver is often held responsible for making sure that any children in the car are wearing their seat belts.

Will Charlene be fined if she lets her baby ride on her lap instead of in his car seat?

Yes, if she is driving in a province that requires children to ride in car seats. If she cannot afford to buy a car seat for her child, she may be able to borrow one from a local agency that lends car seats to parents who need them.

Oliver's province has a mandatory helmet law for motorcycle riders. If Oliver allows his daughter to ride a motorcycle without a helmet, can he be fined?

No. Oliver's daughter, not Oliver, would receive the citation for driving or riding without a helmet. Not all provinces have helmet laws, and these laws have created considerable controversy over the proper role of government intervention in our daily lives. The Appeal Court of Manitoba recently held that helmet laws do not infringe the Charter of Rights and Freedoms, since the purpose and effect of such laws is to promote safety and to minimize the costs of accidents. In some jurisdictions, charges will not be laid for not wearing a helmet if some other protective headgear is worn. Britain passed a special law exempting Sikhs, who by religious law must wear a turban, from wearing helmets. Whether such an exemption will apply in Canada has not yet been determined by the Canadian Supreme Court.

When I walk downtown, I have difficulty crossing the street because cars come around the corner too fast. Don't pedestrians have the right-of-way?

Yes. Pedestrians do have the right-of-way at crossings. If cars are not yielding the right-of-way at an intersection, inform the police so they can monitor the intersection for traffic violations and unsafe conditions.

Is it against the law to hitchhike or pick up a hitchhiker?

Yes. Most places make it illegal to solicit a ride, and prohibit drivers from picking up hitchhikers. These laws are not enforced in emergency situations such as accidents.

May went through an intersection on a yellow light. A police officer saw this and gave her a ticket for failing to obey a traffic control signal. Should May have been given the ticket?

Yes. May was required to stop before entering the intersection when the light was yellow, unless she could not do so safely.

Dennis came to a stop sign and stopped. He saw another car approaching on the main road and knew that if he moved quickly, he could get across the intersection safely. He did so, but a police officer gave him a ticket for not yielding the right-of-way. Dennis insists that he is not guilty, because he obeyed the stop sign. Is Dennis right?

No. Dennis was required to yield the right-of-way to any approaching traffic at the intersection. This does not mean that he had to wait until every approaching car passed, but that he had to use reasonable care in determining if he could cross the intersection without a collision. If Dennis had to hurry to get across, or if the approaching motorist had to hit his brakes or swerve to avoid a collision, the police officer was correct in ticketing Dennis.

Maurice received a ticket for speeding. The only evidence against him was the radar reading. Is this sufficient for a conviction?

Yes. In most provinces radar readings are considered reliable measurements of actual speed. The prosecutor must establish, by testimony of the police officer who took the reading, that the radar equipment was set up properly, was in good working order, and had been tested for accuracy before and after the reading. Maurice may be able to contest the reading's accuracy if the officer acknowledges that there was other traffic between the radar equipment and Maurice's car.

When Laura was stopped for speeding, the police officer told her that her speed was calculated by timing how long it took her car to travel a measured distance. How does such a method work?

A police team measures a section of highway, marks its boundaries, and times the cars as they enter and leave the measured section. Knowing the distance and the time it takes to cover the distance, they can easily calculate a car's speed. Often motorists are timed by police observing from an aircraft.

Jodi's speedometer shows a speed lower than her actual speed. Is this a good defense if she gets a speeding ticket?

No. The fact that Jodi didn't intend to speed is not an adequate defense. Many judges, however, will excuse offenders like Jodi if they submit proof that the speedometer was faulty and that it has been repaired. However, the Ontario Court of Appeal held that speeding is an offense of "absolute liability, in the sense that reasonable mistake of fact is not a defense." In other words, an inaccurate speedometer is not an excuse.

Seventeen-year-old Brandon was stopped for speeding in a school zone. What penalties is he subject to?

Brandon will probably receive a fine, and the judge may require that he attend a driver education or driver improvement course. The fact that Brandon is 17 will have no impact on the punishment he receives; most traffic courts treat teenagers and adults the same way. In addition to the fine, Brandon's speeding violation will be counted against his driving record; too many violations in a certain time period could cause him to lose his license.

As Mitchell slowed down at a roadblock, a police officer waved him over and asked to see his driver's license and registration. After a few minutes, the officer sent Mitchell on his way. Did the stop violate Mitchell's rights?

Probably not. The police in many provinces use license and registration checks at roadblocks to detect drunk drivers and unsafe vehicles. Most courts have ruled that these roadblocks do not deny the driver his constitutional right to be free from unreasonable searches and seizures, provided they are part of a well-publicized campaign to reduce the number of drunk drivers on the road. The Supreme Court of Canada recently ruled that a person who is asked to take a breathalyzer test does not have a right to consult a lawyer before the test, *if the test is conducted at a roadside stop.* Such a driver could not be charged with impaired driving, however, until the breathalyzer test had been repeated at the police station. Before submitting to the second test, the driver has a right to consult a lawyer, provided he does so within a reasonable time.

When my son pleaded guilty to reckless driving, he was fined $200 and placed on probation, his driver's license was suspended for six months, and he has to go to driver education classes. Isn't this a severe penalty for careless driving when there was no accident?

Traffic code violations are divided into infractions, punishable by fines, and more serious violations, punishable by fines, jail, or such other sentences as driver education or improvement courses, suspending and revoking driving privileges, community service, and one or more weekends in jail—commonly called shock probation. A judge can order any or all of these punishments.

Can I be arrested for not paying traffic tickets in another province?

Yes. Some provinces enforce each other's judgments against traffic violators. If you live in Ontario, for example, and are convicted in Quebec or New Brunswick of speeding or not paying parking tickets, Ontario's courts can exact from you whatever penalties that other province imposes. This reciprocal arrangement makes it very difficult to avoid paying your fines. Some border provinces have similar arrangements with their neighboring American states.

Tickets and Violations

Rita was given a ticket for not yielding the right-of-way, and will have to appear in traffic court. Should she hire a lawyer?

No, unless she has so many moving violations, or points, on her record that her driving privileges could be revoked if she is convicted. In such an event, a lawyer could try to persuade the prosecutor to let Rita plead guilty to a lesser charge so that she wouldn't lose her license.

Do I have a right to a jury trial for a traffic violation?

Not in most cases. Traffic violations are usually petty offenses and carry light penalties. Of course violations such as drunk driving, or causing bodily injury while driving impaired, carry more serious penalties. Defendants involved in these more serious charges would have the right to choose a jury trial.

What will happen if Audrey cannot pay her traffic fine?

If Audrey gives the judge good reasons why she is unable to pay, he may sentence her instead to do community service. Some judges will give her additional time to pay the fine. However, if Audrey does not pay the fine within the specified period, the judge can issue a warrant for her arrest and sentence her to jail.

Drinking and Driving

What can a policeman legally do to determine if a person has been driving while intoxicated?

If from his observation a police officer has reason to suspect that you're driving while intoxicated, he has the right to stop you. Generally, police watch for erratic driving or other signs of impaired judgment, such as driving at night without lights. If you are stopped and you appear intoxicated, or if there is a strong odor of alcohol about you, the officer may ask you to perform a field sobriety test such as walking a straight line, picking something up from the ground, or extending your arms and leaning backward. He may also ask: "Have you been drinking?" "How many drinks have you had?" and "When did you start and stop drinking?" You are not obliged to answer these questions. Finally, the officer may ask you to take a chemical test of your breath, blood, or urine to determine the amount of alcohol in your blood. The breath test—

using a breathalyzer—is given at the time a driver is stopped. Blood and urine tests are administered at the police station or a medical facility. Although you have the right to see a lawyer before the breathalyzer test at the police station, no such right exists at a roadside test.

Beverly's father has great difficulty keeping his balance and flunked the field sobriety test. Does that mean he will be convicted of drunk driving?

No. The court will consider many factors, along with balance, in determining if a driver was intoxicated. The court will take into account the driver's physical condition at the time of the arrest. Were his eyes red or glassy? Was he disheveled? Was there an odor of alcohol about him? If he was given chemical tests, did they show a high blood alcohol content?

The court will also consider his behavior and attitude. Was his speech slurred? Did he admit to drinking too much? Was he able to speak rationally, or was he incoherent? Was he belligerent or cooperative?

If Beverly's father has difficulty keeping his balance because of some health condition, however, he should not drive an automobile. If he continues driving under such circumstances, his driver's permit could be revoked by the motor vehicle authorities on the grounds that his condition poses a public danger when he is at the wheel of a car.

Can I be convicted of impaired driving even though I passed a breathalyzer test?

Yes, if the amount of alcohol you have consumed has affected your ability to drive as demonstrated by the results of a field sobriety test. The Criminal Code prohibits you from driving or even sitting behind the wheel of a motor vehicle if your blood alcohol level is over 0.08 percent, *or* if your driving ability is impaired by alcohol or a drug.

A policeman stopped Bill's car because he suspected that Bill had been drinking. Does Bill have to submit to a breathalyzer test? Can he talk to a lawyer before the test is conducted?

If the policeman has reasonable and probable cause to believe that Bill has been drinking, he can require Bill to submit to a breathalyzer test. According to a recent Supreme Court ruling, the policeman is not obliged to inform Bill of his right to speak to a lawyer before taking the test if that test is being given during a roadside stop. However, before the policeman can charge Bill with impaired driving on the results of the roadside test, he must give him a second test at the police station, and must inform him of his right to consult a lawyer before taking the second test.

Drinking and Driving

How Many Drinks Make You Legally Drunk?

In all provinces, anyone with a blood alcohol concentration (BAC) greater than 80 mg of alcohol per ml of blood (a reading of 0.08 on a breathalyzer) is considered legally drunk. The number of drinks it takes to make you drunk varies from person to person and depends on such factors as the amount of alcohol you've consumed, how much food you've eaten, your individual tolerance for alcohol, your age and weight, whether you're taking medication, and whether you are male or female. (Women have a higher proportion of body fat than men, so equal amounts of alcohol will cause a higher BAC in a woman than in a man of the same weight.) The charts below show approximate BAC levels for men and women who have consumed one to eight drinks in one hour. To see what drinking does to your BAC level, read across from the figure nearest your body weight to the figure in the column under the number of drinks you have had. Since the body eliminates about 15 mg of alcohol per hour, you can subtract 15 for each hour you've been drinking beyond your first hour. For example, a 200-pound man who has had six drinks over three hours would have a BAC level of about 130 minus 30, or about 100 mg of alcohol per ml of blood, well over the legal limit for driving.

WOMEN'S BODY WEIGHT	Number of drinks*							
	1	2	3	4	5	6	7	8
100 lb. (45 kg)	50	101	152	203	253	304	355	406
125 lb. (57 kg)	40	80	120	162	202	244	282	324
150 lb. (68 kg)	34	68	101	135	169	203	237	271
175 lb. (79 kg)	29	58	87	117	146	175	204	233
200 lb. (91 kg)	26	50	76	101	126	152	177	203
225 lb. (102 kg)	22	45	68	91	113	136	159	182

MEN'S BODY WEIGHT	Number of drinks*							
	1	2	3	4	5	6	7	8
125 lb. (57 kg)	34	69	103	139	173	209	242	278
150 lb. (68 kg)	29	58	87	116	145	174	203	232
175 lb. (79 kg)	25	50	75	100	125	150	175	200
200 lb. (91 kg)	22	43	65	87	108	130	152	174
225 lb. (102 kg)	19	39	58	78	97	117	136	156
250 lb. (113 kg)	17	35	52	70	87	105	122	139

*A drink is 12 oz. (340 ml) of beer, 6 oz. (170 ml) of wine, or 1½ oz. (43 ml) of liquor.

Is it legal to have an open beer in my hand while driving?

Since all provinces prohibit open containers of alcohol in motor vehicles, you could be arrested for driving with an open beer in your hand. You could also be arrested for having an open beer—or any other alcoholic drink—on the seat beside you or on the floor. It is illegal to carry even unopened containers of alcohol in your car, except to bring them home from the store or to take them to someone else's house as a gift. Even under those circumstances, you would be better off if you kept the alcohol in your trunk.

After traveling a few blocks, Cliff realized he was in no condition to drive. He parked his car on the street, shut off the engine, and went to sleep. He woke up to discover a policeman at his window. After a brief conversation, Cliff was arrested for drunk driving. Was Cliff's arrest justifiable, since he was not driving when he was arrested?

Yes. If Cliff admitted to the police officer that he had driven a few blocks before pulling over, he could be arrested for driving while intoxicated. It is more likely, however, that he was arrested for having control of a motor vehicle while intoxicated. Cliff was in the car, had the car keys in the ignition, and could have started driving again at any time; therefore, he was considered to be in control of his car. It is illegal for an intoxicated person to have control of a vehicle, even if that person is not operating it at the time.

Does Anne have the right to a lawyer if she is arrested and charged with drunk driving?

Whenever a person is charged with a crime, he has the right to be represented by a lawyer. If Anne cannot afford to pay for a lawyer, the court will appoint one for her.

Doug's son, Allen, was arrested for drunk driving. It was his first offense. Will his license be suspended?

Probably. Under the Criminal Code, a person convicted of impaired driving loses his license for three months for a first offense, for six months for a second offense and for one year for a third offense. The provincial penalties for alcohol-related driving offenses are even stiffer. In Quebec, for example, a first offender loses his driver's license for one year, and in Ontario a person convicted for the third time loses it for three years.

Drinking and Driving

My son-in-law was in a car accident after drinking too much liquor in my home. Can his injured passengers sue me?

It depends. If the passengers saw that your son-in-law was intoxicated, or had reason to believe that he was, you could not be held liable, because they assumed the risk of driving with him. (This defense is expressed by the Latin maxim *violenti non fit injuria*, which means that a person cannot sue for damages when he accepts the risk of damage.) If, however, the passengers had no reason to believe that your son-in-law was impaired by alcohol, the situation might be very different. In recent years, some courts in the United States have held the host responsible when he served liquor to an obviously intoxicated guest and that guest later caused an accident. This could be a trend that Canada may eventually follow.

In Quebec, which has a comprehensive automobile insurance law, the injured passengers could not sue the host, but would be compensated by the Quebec Automobile Insurance Board for loss of revenue, for bodily injuries, and for pain and suffering.

If a tavern serves me several drinks and I have an accident on the way home, can I sue the tavern?

It depends upon the facts of the case. If you were a regular patron of the tavern, known to the bartender, and you were served alcohol while you were obviously intoxicated, the tavern could be held responsible for any damage you cause to yourself or others. The tavern owes "a duty of care" to its patrons—in other words it must make sure that they can get home safely. If the tavern keeper knew you were drunk, and knew you were going to drive home, by serving you more liquor he not only would have breached the common law duty of care, but would also have violated liquor license laws.

In 1973 the Supreme Court of Canada held an operator of a hotel liable for injuries a patron suffered when he was struck by a car while he was walking home from the hotel. The hotel had served him alcohol when he was drunk, then later threw him out without caring how he would make his way home. The court held the hotel responsible because (1) the staff knew this person had a tendency to act irresponsibly when he got drunk, and (2) they ejected him from the hotel without taking any precaution to ensure his safe return home. The court felt the hotel should have called a taxi or the person's employer to ensure that he would get home safely.

If you cause an accident after drinking too much in a tavern, the people you injure, or whose property is damaged, could sue both you and the tavern keeper. This would not apply in Quebec, however, under its no-fault insurance law.

Penalties for Drunk Driving

Drunk driving has aroused so much public concern that the Criminal Code and provincial traffic laws have been amended in order to toughen the penalties for offenders and thus reduce the carnage and medical expenses of traffic accidents. Probation, unconditional discharges and suspended sentences, once the rule for first offenders, no longer prevail. The consequences of being convicted of an alcohol-related auto violation, even a first offense, now include some or all of the following:

- A criminal record.
- Loss of driver's license for at least three months and up to three years.
- A fine ranging from $300 to $2,000.
- The possibility of imprisonment for up to six months.
- Curative treatment.

These penalties apply when no one was injured as a result of the alcohol-related offense. When someone is injured or killed by a drunk driver, the fines are much higher and the penalties much more severe. Causing bodily injury could result in a 10-year prison sentence; killing someone could mean a 14-year prison sentence. In these cases, the judge *must* prohibit the driver from driving for a period ranging from 10 years to life. And the judge no longer has the option of allowing an offender to operate a motor vehicle for purposes of his work: the prohibition against driving is now total and unconditional.

Joanna rode home from a party with her boyfriend. She knew he had been drinking, but she didn't think he was drunk. If he had been arrested for drunk driving, could Joanna too have been arrested for letting him drive?

No. Joanna could not be arrested merely for riding with her intoxicated boyfriend. The law does not prohibit passengers from riding with a drunk driver.

While Victor was traveling through another province, he was arrested and convicted for drunk driving. Can his license be suspended?

Yes. When a nonresident driver commits a traffic violation, it is common practice to send proof of the conviction to the agency that issued the driver's license. So Victor's violations will count against his license just as if they had been committed in his home province.

Drinking and Driving

Gwendolyn was driving home from a party despite the fact that she was drunk. She was involved in an accident that caused an injury, but the accident was not her fault. Will the fact that she was drunk affect her liability?

If Gwendolyn's intoxicated condition did not cause the accident, she will not be liable. For example, if Gwendolyn had been waiting for the traffic light to turn green at an intersection and a station wagon hit her from behind, she is not responsible for the accident, and therefore not liable, regardless of her physical condition. However, Gwendolyn could still be arrested for drunk driving.

Alex was involved in an accident with Bob and is now being sued in two separate lawsuits. One charges him with driving while intoxicated; the other seeks damages for Bob's injuries. What's going on here?

If Alex was driving while intoxicated and the accident was his fault, his actions have both criminal and civil consequences. He will be prosecuted in criminal court for breaking the law against driving while intoxicated. The case will be brought against him by the provincial prosecutor; he can be punished by a fine, jail, or probation with special conditions such as alcohol counseling or community service.

Bob's lawsuit for damages against Alex will be heard in a civil court. In a civil case, it is the person who has been injured who files the lawsuit, not the government. The goal of the civil case is to determine if the injuries or property damages suffered by Bob were Alex's fault, and if so, how much Alex should compensate him. Quebec's no-fault insurance law does not allow such civil suits.

At the Scene of an Accident

On his way to work, Patrick witnessed a car accident. But he was in a hurry and didn't stop. This failure to help shocked his co-workers. Did Patrick have a legal obligation to stop or to notify the police and make a statement?

No. Patrick was not required by law to stop at the scene of an accident in which he was not involved, nor was he required to report the accident to the police. But if he thought his testimony as a witness could be helpful later in court, he should have stopped and identified himself to the people involved in the accident or to the police.

Do all accidents have to be reported to the police—even minor fender benders?

If an accident injures someone or causes damage to someone's property in excess of a certain amount—usually about $400—it must be reported to the police.

A child was hit by a car in the alley behind my house. I wanted to help, so I picked her up, carried her into my yard, and wrapped her in a blanket. Later, I was told that I should not have moved her. Can I be held liable?

If you did cause injury trying to help another person, it is unlikely you would be held liable if you used reasonable care in your attempt. Only Alberta, Quebec, and Nova Scotia, however, have what is called Good Samaritan legislation, which expressly protects people from liability when they accidentally cause damage in attempting to help an injured person. In Quebec everyone is legally obliged to help someone in peril.

While driving, Eleanor accidentally ran off the road and damaged an unoccupied parked car. What should she do?

Eleanor should leave her name, address, and telephone number affixed to the damaged car so the owner will know whom to contact. She must report the accident to the police, and give them the license number of the unoccupied car so they can help her trace the owner.

Keith was driving on a foggy night and killed a deer that was crossing the road. What should he do?

Keith should not move the deer, unless it is blocking the road, and he should absolutely not load it into his car and take it home. That is illegal. Keith should report the accident to the police and then contact the nearest wildlife conservation office.

It was raining as Carole drove along the expressway at the speed limit. Suddenly she saw that cars were stopping up ahead. She hit the brakes, and her car spun around. The cars behind piled into one another to avoid hitting her, but her car was not touched. What should she do?

Although Carole's automobile wasn't struck, she is still part of the accident. She should contact the police, or make sure that someone else

At the Scene of an Accident

does so, then stay at the scene and follow the instructions of the police when they arrive. If Carole drives away, she can be charged with leaving the scene of an accident, a serious criminal offense punishable by fines, jail, or loss of driving privileges.

When Jan's car was hit in a busy intersection, she refused to move it until the police arrived. This created a terrible traffic jam. Would it have been OK for Jan to move the car out of the way?

Yes. If Jan was able to pull her car over to the side of the road or off the road completely, she probably should have done so. By blocking the intersection, she could have caused further accidents and even more damage to her own car. If Jan was concerned about preserving evidence and giving the police an accurate version of what had happened, she should have taken down the names, addresses, and telephone numbers of witnesses to the accident. Their statements, plus an analysis of damage to the cars, marks left on the pavement, and debris from the accident, would help the police reconstruct the event.

Liability for Automobile Accidents

This section deals mainly with the common-law provinces, since Quebec law governing liability for automobile accidents is so different. In Quebec, the Automobile Insurance Act of 1978 drastically changed the laws of liability for bodily injuries, pain and suffering, and loss of revenue caused by auto accidents. Victims of automobile accidents, whether drivers, passengers or pedestrians, can no longer sue the driver who caused them damage, but must file a claim with the Automobile Insurance Board, *la Régie de l'assurance automobile*. This board compensates victims for loss of revenue (up to 90 percent of a maximum $36,500) in the form of payments made every two weeks. Victims can claim an additional indemnity (up to $41,059.61 in 1988) for permanent incapacity, and a further sum for pain and suffering. They can also claim for loss of personal property, such as eyeglasses or clothing, and for transportation costs to medical facilities where they are being treated as a result of the auto accident. The amount of the indemnities payable can vary from one year to another. Payments start one week after a report is filed or one week from the date of the accident. Should a recovered victim have a relapse or aggravation of the condition in the future, his file may be reopened and payment may begin again. To cover property damage, all drivers in Quebec are required by law to have private liability insurance. There is a fund to pay victims of uninsured drivers.

For information on automobile insurance, see Chapter 8, *Insurance.*

In automobile accident claims, what is the difference between negligence and liability?

You are negligent if you do something you should not have done, or you fail to do something that you should have done. If you run a red light, for example, you are negligent. If you fail to use your headlights after sunset, you are negligent. If your negligent act results in an accident, you become liable for any personal injury or damage that you cause. Liability means you are obligated to compensate the person who is injured, or whose property is damaged as a result of your negligence. However, if you live in British Columbia, Saskatchewan, Manitoba or Quebec, which have no-fault auto insurance laws, the answer becomes a bit more complicated. If your negligent driving injures someone, by definition you would be liable, but it's the province, not you, that compensates your victim, through the agency that administers its no-fault insurance program. As the term "no-fault" implies, the question of liability does not affect the compensation.

If I am innocent of negligence in an automobile accident, can I still be liable for damages?

Yes, if someone else causes an accident while driving your car. In most provinces, the owner of the vehicle is usually responsible with the driver for any damage caused by wrongful or negligent use of the vehicle. You might also be liable if you let a member of your family use your car when you knew it had defective brakes, say, and that person caused an accident. If you own a business, you might be liable for damages caused by an employee while he was driving a company vehicle—or his own car—on company business.

If Priscilla lends her car to a friend who is visiting her for the holidays, who will be responsible if her friend has an accident with the car and injures someone or causes property damage?

Generally, provincial laws stipulate that both the owner and the driver of a vehicle causing damage may be held liable. Even if Priscilla's friend was entirely at fault because of her gross negligence or drunkenness, Priscilla, the car owner, could still be held equally responsible. However, Priscilla may later sue her friend to recover the damages she was forced to pay the victim.

If Priscilla lived in a province with a no-fault insurance plan, her liability, and that of her friend, may be limited or (in Quebec) immaterial.

Can the passengers in my car sue me if I have an accident and they are hurt?

You have a duty to take reasonable care to protect all your passengers, including hitchhikers, from injury. If your passengers are injured because of your negligence, or because you didn't use reasonable care, they may sue you. However, if the passengers contributed to the accident by wrongfully interfering with your safe handling of the vehicle,

Liability for Automobile Accidents

or by behaving in a rowdy manner, they may lose their right to collect damages from you. In some cases, they may even be held entirely responsible for the accident. To successfully sue the driver, a passenger must prove that the driver handled the vehicle negligently.

Because my street is very steep, I always set my emergency brake when I park there. Last night my car rolled downhill and struck a parked car. Will I have to pay for the damages?

Everyone is required to use reasonable care when parking a vehicle. When you park on a steep hill, you are expected to angle your front wheels toward the curb and set the emergency brake. If you didn't do these things, you will probably be held responsible for the damages. Provincial laws require you to maintain your vehicle, brakes included, in a safe condition. If your car rolled down the hill because the brakes didn't hold, in this case, too, you will probably be considered responsible, and you—or your insurance—will have to pay.

Edna's car was damaged by a shopping cart in the supermarket parking lot. She wasn't there when it occurred, so she doesn't know how it happened. What can she do?

She should inform her insurance company immediately. If her policy doesn't cover the damages, she could sue the supermarket. It is responsible for the care and control of its property and should have taken care that the shopping carts were not left unattended in the parking lot.

Nell's car was damaged in an automatic car wash. Isn't the car wash liable for the repairs?

Yes, if the damage was caused by defective equipment or a negligent employee, or if the instructions for operating the car wash were wrong, misleading or incomplete. On the other hand, if the damage occurred because Nell disregarded instructions or acted recklessly, the car wash would not be liable.

Adam's car was vandalized while it was parked in a commercial garage. Is the garage owner responsible for the damage?

If the garage is one where Adam parks his own car, locks it, and keeps the keys, the garage owner has no duty to protect Adam's car and is not responsible for the damage done to it. Adam is considered to be renting or leasing space from the garage owner. On the other hand, if Adam gives his car keys to an attendant who parks the car, the law expects the garage owner to care for Adam's car in the same way he would care for his own property. For example, if the owner left the garage unattended and the vandals came in during that time, or if an attendant vandalized Adam's car, the garage owner would be responsible for the damage.

The person who stole Russell's car was involved in an accident. Is Russell liable?

No. Russell is not responsible for damages caused by a thief—or anyone else—who uses his car without permission.

What happens if both drivers involved in an automobile accident are at fault?

Both drivers will be held responsible but only in proportion to how much each one is at fault. For example, if an accident was 90 percent driver A's fault, driver B could sue driver A for 90 percent of his damage, and driver A could sue driver B for 10 percent of his. When two or more drivers are at fault, rules of contributory negligence come into play.

If someone is injured because his car was in my blind spot, can I be held responsible?

Yes. You are responsible for being aware of all blind spots.

I hit a pothole causing $200 worth of damage. Is the city liable?

Yes, if the pothole was wide and deep enough to be dangerous and if the city was aware or should have been aware that this dangerous condition existed. Cities have a duty to be aware of the condition of their streets and to keep them reasonably safe. In suing cities you must act very quickly. Usually you must notify the city within 15 days of the incident and initiate your lawsuit within six months.

Is there something special I should do if I am involved in an accident with a government vehicle?

If the accident was due to the other driver's negligence, and you were injured or your property was damaged, you should consider suing

Liability for Automobile Accidents

whichever government owned the vehicle. Some people may claim that you can't sue the government because it is protected by sovereign immunity. Such concepts came into the Canadian legal system from English common law and date back to the time when the king was the government. The king could do no wrong, so you could not sue the government or any government official or employee. But the law evolved, and the special protection given to federal and provincial governments was taken away by statute. Now both federal and provincial governments (usually called the Crown) can be sued much as any other party that causes damage through fault or negligence. Most actions against the federal Crown must be heard before the Federal Court.

Stephanie was driving at night when she hit a truck that had stopped in front of her. The truck's taillights were not working. Will Stephanie have to pay for damage to the truck?

Stephanie would not be liable if it had been impossible for her to see the truck and avoid hitting it. This would be the case, for example, if the truck had been stopped on the highway right below the crest of a hill, far away from a streetlight. But if the truck was easy to see even without its taillights and Stephanie hit it because she wasn't paying enough attention to the road, she would be responsible or, in some cases, partially responsible for the accident.

I was injured in a four-car accident. How can I tell who is responsible for my injuries if I don't know which car hit me?

In a chain reaction accident, one or several drivers may be responsible for your injuries, regardless of who hit you. If one driver started the events that led to your part in the accident, he is responsible even if his car never touched yours. If several drivers contributed to the accident by their carelessness, they are all responsible. You don't have to find out which of the four cars actually hit you; the important thing is to determine which car caused the accident.

When Ben had his car accident, he was ticketed for running a stop sign. Does this mean he can't collect damages?

If Ben caused the accident by running the stop sign, he will probably not be able to collect damages; in fact, he will probably be liable for the damages suffered by the others involved in the accident. If Ben was not the main cause of the accident, however, he may be able to collect some damages from the person who caused it. If Ben's traffic violation had no bearing on the accident, he would be able to collect from the person who caused the accident.

Following a minor traffic accident in which the other driver was at fault, Harry jumped out of his car and cried, "Oh no, it's all my fault. Look what I've done!" By the time the police arrived, he had regained his composure and denied responsibility. Can his first statement be used against him?

Yes. Such a statement can be used if Harry becomes involved in a court case. However, his statement is not enough, by itself, to shift the blame for the accident to him. The other driver will have to offer evidence, beyond Harry's statement, that the accident was Harry's fault.

After an accident, the other driver offered to pay me $1,000 if I would sign a release from further liability. Is this a good idea?

No. Never sign a release until you know the extent of your injuries and the amount of damage to your property. Signing this type of release usually will prevent you from suing the other driver later if you discover more injuries or greater damage to your car. Get a complete physical examination from your doctor to determine if you have any injuries and how serious they are. Be sure to get estimates for all work necessary to repair your automobile. If your personal injuries and the damage to your vehicle will be covered by $1,000, you may want to consider signing the release. But don't be in too big a hurry; some injuries do not show up until many days after an accident. If you do sign the release, be sure you understand all its legal ramifications.

Gene's car was hit from behind while he was turning left into a parking lot. He estimated the damage at $500. The other driver, who was tipsy, offered Gene a $750 cheque if he didn't report the accident. Should Gene accept the offer?

Definitely not, for several reasons. First, Gene is required by law to report the accident if the damages exceed a certain amount—usually about $400. Second, although his quick assessment at the scene of the accident leads him to believe that $750 will cover his damages, he may have injuries that he has not discovered yet, or the cost to repair his car may be more than he thinks. Finally, he has no guarantee that the other driver's cheque is good. By the time Gene discovers that the cheque is worthless, it will be difficult, if not impossible, to locate anyone who witnessed the accident.

Liability for Automobile Accidents

Angela was seriously injured in a car accident. If she had been wearing her seat belt at the time, she might not have been injured so badly. Could this prevent her from recovering damages from the other driver?

Possibly. If, by wearing a seat belt, Angela could have reduced the extent of the damage she sustained, the court might consider her partly at fault for the *extent* of her injury and thus reduce the amount of her reward.

What to Do If You Are in an Accident

The first few minutes after an accident are critically important in getting medical assistance for the injured and in establishing exactly what happened. The following steps can help you later if there is a dispute about an insurance settlement:

- ☑ Check for injuries among drivers and passengers.
- ☑ Call the police; request an ambulance if necessary.
- ☑ If you can, move your car out of the traffic and turn on its flashing hazard lights to warn other drivers.
- ☑ Get the names, addresses, and telephone numbers of witnesses before they leave the scene.
- ☑ Write down the other driver's name, address, telephone number, make and model of car, license plate number, driver's license number, and the name and address of his insurance company and its local agent.
- ☑ Limit your remarks about the accident; don't discuss who is at fault or the extent of your insurance coverage.
- ☑ Note the time of the accident, the weather, and the road conditions.
- ☑ If possible, take pictures or make sketches of the scene of the accident. Record skid marks, the point where the cars collided, damage to the cars, and the location of any road signs.
- ☑ Take pictures of your car showing all damage in detail.
- ☑ See your doctor immediately, even if you don't seem to be hurt. You may have a serious injury and not know it right away.
- ☑ Keep a diary after the accident, especially if you are injured. It will help you recall specific events if you need to testify later.
- ☑ Don't sign anything hurriedly. Harmless-looking forms may include statements in which you agree not to make any claims against the other person, or in which you accept liability for the accident.
- ☑ Notify your insurance agent of the accident as soon as possible.
- ☑ If there are personal injuries or extensive property damage that might exceed your insurance coverage, consult an attorney.

Christie was involved in a minor fender bender in which no one was cut or bruised. Should she see a doctor anyway?

Yes. Many times people suffer physical injuries in automobile accidents that are not immediately apparent. So she should see her doctor as soon as she can, even if she thinks she is all right. If the doctor discovers an injury that might give her trouble later, this will provide the evidence she needs to make a claim against the other driver. If she waits too long to see a doctor (or if she agrees to a settlement with the other driver before she discovers her injury), she may be unable to make a claim.

Al's teeth were broken when he was injured by a hit-and-run driver. Will he be stuck with the dental bills?

No. Almost all provinces have funds for victims of uninsured, underinsured or unidentified drivers. All provinces and Territories also have crime victims indemnity funds, which pay for certain expenses incurred by crime victims. As the casualty of a hit-and-run driver, Al is a crime victim and should apply to the insurance fund of the province where the accident took place. Al can also sue the driver if he is found. In Quebec, the Automobile Insurance Fund would compensate Al for his injury.

Abigail asked her neighbor for a ride to the grocery store and got hurt when the neighbor ran a stop sign and hit another car. The neighbor says Abigail can't sue a Good Samaritan. Is this true?

No. Abigail's neighbor is confused. Good Samaritan laws protect people who help victims of accidents. They offer no protection to someone simply because she was doing the victim a favor when the accident occurred. Abigail has the same right to sue her neighbor as any other passengers involved in an accident would have to sue their driver.

My wife was driving, and I was asleep in the back seat, when she ran off the road and hit a tree. I was seriously injured. My neighbor said I should sue my wife. What would I gain?

You might get a much higher payment from your insurance company to cover medical expenses and loss of income. If you don't sue, all the insurance company will pay is what is due under the medical payments clause of your policy. But if you sue, you may be awarded damages up to the full amount of your personal liability coverage.

In Yukon, the Northwest Territories, Alberta and Prince Edward Island, the standard insurance policy contains an exclusion concerning such claims by the spouse or children of an insured person.

Liability for Automobile Accidents

While out driving two years ago, Jim hit a child who was riding his bike in the street. The police and an ambulance were called to the scene, but the child appeared to be fine. Now Jim is being sued for injuries to the child. What should he do?

Jim should contact his automobile insurance company, or the one he had at the time of the accident if he has changed companies in the meantime. If his policy covers this type of claim, the insurance company will provide an attorney to defend Jim. If Jim's insurance does not cover this accident, he should consult his own attorney right away. He has a limited amount of time to respond to the lawsuit, and there are complex legal rules that he must comply with or run the risk of damaging his case. On the other hand, time may be on Jim's side. Provincial laws require the person who has a right to sue another to do so within a reasonable time. In personal injury cases, the limit is usually about two years, after which the victim loses his right. It may well be that the suit taken against Jim has been filed too late, and Jim would not have to defend it.

A year ago Robert was held liable for an accident that he felt resulted from a defect in his car. Now his car has been recalled. Shouldn't the manufacturer be responsible for the money Robert had to pay the other driver?

The fact that Robert's car is being recalled is not proof that the accident was due to a possible defect. However, if the recall discovers a defect that could have caused or contributed to his accident, he may have a case against the manufacturer. Robert would have to prove that the accident would not have happened if the defect hadn't existed or that, even if it was not the only factor, the defect contributed to the accident.

Are there agreements or releases that Janet should get from the parents of children she drives to school in her van?

Janet should consider having the parents sign a release agreeing not to sue her if she has an accident that injures the children. However, such a release may not hold up in all courts. Some courts will not recognize agreements protecting someone against suits for injuries that have not yet occurred. Many courts also hold that parents cannot sign away rights that belong to their children. If a child is injured in an accident where Janet is responsible, the child could sue Janet (through a guardian acting on the child's behalf) and the release signed by the injured child's parent would be of no value. However, the parent could not sue Janet for any loss that the parent suffered.

Your Money

Financial Institutions

For as long as I can remember, my family has dealt with a local trust company. Recently my friend Dudley advised me to switch my money from the trust company to a bank because I will get more services and be charged lower fees. Is he right?

Not necessarily. The only way to know for sure is to check the services and fees of your trust company against those of banks. Also compare the minimum balances required, and interest paid for their various kinds of accounts. Nowadays, banks and trust companies offer the same services, such as saving and chequing accounts, term deposits, loans, credit cards, safety deposit boxes, traveler's cheques, and financial advice.

There seem to be so many choices — Canadian banks, foreign banks, trust companies, mortgage loan companies, credit unions. Is my money as safe in one kind of institution as another?

Yes, as a general rule. The safety of your money depends to some extent on the management of the financial institution, but in most instances your account will probably be insured by one or more government agencies. For example, the Canada Deposit Insurance Corporation (CDIC) insures accounts in qualifying financial institutions up to $60,000. To qualify, institutions must meet federal standards and submit to regular examinations of their records. If you are worried about the safety of your deposit, ask a bank officer for proof that your accounts are government-insured. To obtain a list of institutions covered by CDIC, write to: Canada Deposit Insurance Corporation, P.O. Box 2340, Station D, Ottawa, Ont., K1P 5W5.

On a holiday weekend, I deposited $500 in cash in my bank's automatic teller machine. It took the money, but it didn't give me a receipt. What should I do?

You should contact your bank on the next business day. By law customers must receive proper receipts for transactions made at automated teller machines. While failures are rare, they can occur. Deposits from automatic teller machines are balanced daily, and your bank will provide you with a receipt as soon as your deposit is verified. In addition, many automatic teller machines print and retain duplicate receipts; your bank may be able to give you a copy of this duplicate.

The law dealing with automatic teller machines is in its infancy, and many cases boil down to the client's word against the bank's. Unfortunately, if the bank has no record of your deposit, your chances of recovering your money are slim.

Rose's trust company went bankrupt and was closed by the federal government before she could withdraw her lifetime savings. Will she get her money back?

If her trust company was a member of the Canada Deposit Insurance Corporation (CDIC), Rose's account was insured for up to $60,000, and CDIC will let her know about repayment within days of the closing. It may arrange for the trustee in bankruptcy to pay her directly or it may have her account transferred to another institution. If Rose had more than $60,000 deposited, she would become an ordinary creditor of the bankrupt trust company for any amount above the insured $60,000.

What does the Canada Deposit Insurance Corporation insure? How do I apply for this insurance, and what will it cost me?

The Canada Deposit Insurance Corporation (CDIC) insures savings and chequing accounts, bonds and debentures issued by a member institution, money orders, guaranteed investment certificates, and term deposits whose terms do not exceed five years. The CDIC does not insure stocks, mutual funds, mortgages, bonds issued by companies other than member institutions, or the contents of safety deposit boxes. You need neither apply nor pay for this insurance. When you deposit money with a member institution, your deposit is covered automatically. The institution pays the insurance premiums.

Is it legal to have a Swiss bank account?

Yes, provided the account is not being used to hide income from Revenue Canada, or to launder money (that is, hide its original source) obtained from illegal activities. Interest earned in any foreign account, like that from a Canadian bank account, must be reported on your income tax return. At the time of writing, the federal government was preparing legislation to enable it to confiscate laundered money which cannot be attributed to legitimate sources.

Is it legal for Jack's bank to deduct more in service charges than it pays in interest on his account unless he increases the balance to a figure named by the bank?

Yes. Banks can set their own service charges as well as the interest rate they pay on accounts. Since the costs of handling small and large accounts are similar, many banks prefer not to carry accounts below a certain minimum balance. If Jack doesn't like his bank's requirements, he should look for one that will give him a better deal.

Financial Institutions

I was charged a $2 transaction fee when I made a withdrawal from my savings account using an automatic teller machine. How can the bank charge me for access to my own money, especially since the bank makes a profit by lending out my money?

Under the Bank Act of 1980, banks cannot charge a depositor for withdrawing money from an account, unless there is an express agreement to that effect. Check the documents you signed when you opened your account to see if they contain such a clause. Since trust companies, credit unions, and mortage loan companies are not governed by the Bank Act, they are freer to charge for access to your money.

I suspect that the bank has wrongly added some charges to my account. Where can I file a complaint?

You should first discuss these charges with the bank manager, and if you don't get a satisfactory explanation, contact the bank's head office. If you are still not satisfied, file a complaint with Finance Canada, which acts as a watchdog over banks. Write to: Superintendent of Financial Institutions, 255 Albert Street, 13th Floor, Kent Square, Ottawa, Ont., K1A 0H2.

My most recent bank statement shows that I have $1,000 more in my account than my own calculations say. Can I keep this money?

Not if the $1,000 was credited to your account by mistake. If you withdraw the money, knowing that it is not yours, criminal charges could be filed against you. Notify the bank immediately if you think an error has been made.

Edmund deposited his pay cheque on Friday afternoon. That night, he wrote a cheque to a department store for a new suit. The cheque bounced despite his deposit. How could this happen?

Edmund's bank, like most others, requires customers to wait a number of days before drawing on cheques deposited in their accounts from other banks. The banks feel that they must wait to see if a cheque is good before letting a customer draw on it. As a general rule, the more distant the bank on which the cheque is drawn, the longer the wait will be. Some banks offer overdraft protection so that a depositor can write cheques up to a certain amount, even if there are insufficient funds in his account. Interest is charged on the amount of the overdraft, much as it would be on a personal loan. See if your bank offers such a service.

Debbie gave Curtis a cheque. When Curtis tried to cash it eight months later, the bank refused to pay. Is this legal?

Yes. Under the Bills of Exchange Act, a cheque must be cashed within a reasonable time. Custom and usage have determined that this is six months, after which a bank can refuse to honor a cheque. Curtis can ask Debbie to honor the cheque herself or write a new one. If she won't, he can sue her for the amount of the "expired" cheque, which can serve as proof of the debt.

Safeguards for Paperless Banking

While the cashless society isn't here yet, advances in technology bring it closer every day. You can have your payroll or pension cheque deposited at your bank, make loan and credit card payments, pay utility bills, even buy groceries, and never use (or see) a dollar's worth of cash or write a single cheque.

New technologies bring new problems for consumers, however. The electronic machines can malfunction, receipts can be lost, and transaction cards can be misplaced or stolen. Here are some tips to take the glitches out of paperless banking:

☑ Keep a record of each transaction you make. It's easy to forget to subtract a withdrawal or fund transfer unless you enter it in your cheque book immediately.

☑ Check your statement as soon as you get it to see if its balance agrees with your records. If not, contact your bank immediately.

☑ Memorize your personal identification number (PIN) and keep it in a file at home. Never write it on your transaction card or on a slip of paper in your wallet. If you forget or misfile your PIN, ask your bank to locate it in your records.

☑ Give your PIN only to a bank officer in person. Never tell your PIN or lend your card, to anyone. A common scam is for a phone caller to claim he is from your bank and ask for your PIN for "verification." Hang up and notify your bank immediately.

☑ When using an automatic teller machine (ATM), be sure you have your receipt and your transaction card before walking away. Never leave an ATM before your transaction is complete.

☑ Be cautious when using an ATM at night, or in an out-of-the-way location. You could be prey for a robber lurking nearby.

☑ If you lose your transaction card, notify your bank as soon as possible. Up to $500 a day could be charged to your account if you wait; otherwise, your liability is limited to $50.

☑ Keep a record of all your credit card numbers. Give some thought to credit card insurance if you use your cards a lot.

Financial Institutions

Nicole has an arrangement with her bank to have her bills paid automatically. What happens if the bank makes a mistake?

The bank must correct its mistake. Amy should alert a bank officer to the error right away. If her credit rating has suffered because of late payments, the bank may be held liable. Most banks make every effort to rectify their mistakes immediately and to explain the oversight to a creditor if asked to do so.

Harry discovered that the bank had wrongly deducted $500 from his money market account. However, the statement reads: "If you do not object within 30 days, this statement will be presumed correct." The statement is two months old. Does Harry have any recourse against the bank?

Yes. Although Harry's bank limits the time during which he may object to an error, it cannot profit from a mistake in its favor. It must credit the $500, plus the interest it would have earned, to Harry's account.

When I bought my car, the salesman said he would only accept a cheque if it were certified. Why?

In some ways, a certified cheque is as good as cash. When a bank stamps the word *certified* across the face of your cheque, it immediately freezes that amount in your account and holds it until the cheque is presented for payment. A certified cheque means the bank guarantees to cash it for the payee.

What is the difference between a certified cheque and a cashier's cheque or a bank cheque?

A certified cheque is one that is drawn on a depositor's account and upon which the bank stamps the word *certified*. This statement is a guarantee that there are sufficient funds on deposit to allow the cheque to be cashed. A cashier's cheque or a bank cheque, on the other hand, is drawn by the bank on itself and issued by an authorized bank officer. The bank makes sure it has your money behind its cashier's cheque in one of three ways: (1) it transfers the necessary amount from your account to its own, or (2) you give the bank cash (usually plus a fee) to cover the amount of the cheque, or (3) you write a cheque to the order of the bank for the necessary amount. A cashier's cheque is usually considered as good as cash.

Sally received a cheque from her cousin and wants to endorse it over to a co-worker. Can Sally make sure she is not required to pay the co-worker if the cheque bounces?

Yes. Sally should endorse the cheque with her signature followed by the words *without recourse*. By adding these words, Sally disclaims any responsibility to her co-worker if the cheque is not honored by the bank upon which it is drawn. If a cheque endorsed in this way does bounce, Sally's co-worker will have to recover the money from the person who originally wrote the cheque.

How do I get my bank to stop payment on a cheque I have written?

Call the bank immediately and be prepared to give the number, the amount and the date of the cheque, the name of the payee, and your account number. You will be asked to fill out a stop payment request form, usually by the next business day, and you may be charged a fee. If your bank honors a cheque after you have entered a stop payment order, it must make restitution to your account. But if the cheque was paid before the bank received your stop payment order, or if the cheque was certified, the bank is under no obligation to repay you.

My sister added my name to her chequing account so that I could pay her bills if she ever became disabled. She died suddenly. Can I use the money in her account as I wish?

By adding your name to her account, your sister created a joint account, presumably because she wanted you to become owner of the entire account if she died before you. This is a presumption that could, however, be contested by your sister's husband, children or other heirs. Therefore you are not free to use the funds until your sister's estate is settled and you are named heir to these funds. For that matter, upon being notified of your sister's death, the bank probably "froze" the assets in the account pending settlement of the estate.

My father is always telling me not to endorse my pay cheque with just my name. What is the problem with doing it that way?

When you endorse your pay cheque by signing your name on its back, you have created a blank endorsement, which means the cheque can be cashed by anyone. If you intend to deposit your pay cheque into a chequing or savings account, you might add the words *for deposit only* beneath your signature. If the cheque is then lost or stolen, nobody can cash it; it can only be deposited in your bank account.

Financial Institutions

Is it true that I can't stop payment on a certified cheque?

Yes. Unless the person who wrote the cheque dies before it is presented for payment, a certified cheque must be honored by the bank on which it was drawn. Certification makes that bank as well as the person who wrote the cheque liable if the holder presents the cheque for payment.

If a husband dies and the wife wants access to the property in a joint safe-deposit box, does she need a court order?

When a bank is notified of the death of a customer who has rented one of its safe-deposit boxes, it freezes the contents. A spouse, however, is allowed access to make an inventory of the contents and to remove such things as wills and insurance policies, but not securities. The box would be opened jointly with a bank official.

I wrote a cheque for $80. Someone changed the amount to $800, and the bank cashed it. What should I do?

Notify your bank immediately. Most banks will charge you only what you originally intended to pay—$80, in this case. To recover the additional $720, the bank would have to sue the person who altered the cheque. If your bank refuses to credit you with the $720, your only other recourse is to sue the bank. If the alteration was possible because you were negligent in writing the cheque—for example, if you left space that made the alteration possible—you might lose your case.

While Jeannine was on a three-month vacation, someone forged her signature on two cheques. Must she bear the loss?

A bank, which is obliged to know the signature of its customer, should never cash a cheque with a forged signature. Such a cheque is considered a nullity. Jeannine should immediately notify the bank about the forgery. And she must make sure that her personalized cheques are kept in a safe place to which no one has easy access. The bank will bear the loss, if it was at fault, but each case is judged on its own merits.

Can Sylvia use a rubber stamp to endorse her cheques?

Yes. Generally, any symbol that you adopt with the intention of making it an endorsement can be used. This includes using a rubber stamp.

Recordkeeping Tips

Good recordkeeping is simply a matter of putting the right papers in the right place, and disposing of what you no longer need. For example, the original of your will should be kept in a safe-deposit box. And it's a good idea to keep an inventory of your personal property there, too. A home file is probably a safe enough place for canceled cheques and warranties. But there's no point in cluttering your files with 10-year-old cheques and expired warranties. The following chart is a guide to effective recordkeeping.

ITEM	WHERE TO KEEP	HOW LONG TO KEEP
Provincial and federal income tax returns	Home file	Indefinitely (along with canceled cheques of tax payments)
Canceled cheques and bank statements	Home file	Six years
Warranties	Home file	Until after expiration
Deeds, mortgages, titles, agreements	Safe-deposit box	Until property is sold
Stock certificates	Safe-deposit box	Until sold
Insurance (except homeowners), pension, retirement plans	Home file	As long as in force
Inventory of personal property	Safe-deposit box	Indefinitely
Homeowners insurance	Safe-deposit box	As long as the policy is in effect
Pay cheque stubs	Home file	Until you have filed your income tax returns
Annual T-4 forms	Home file	Seven years
Birth and marriage certificates	Safe-deposit box	Indefinitely
Divorce papers	Safe-deposit box	Indefinitely
Military service records	Safe-deposit box	Indefinitely
Adoption and citizenship papers	Safe-deposit box	Indefinitely
Credit card numbers	Home file	Until card canceled
Inventory of personal property	Safe-deposit box	Indefinitely
Burial instructions	Home file	Indefinitely

YOUR MONEY

Financial Institutions

Can someone gain access to my safe-deposit box if I give him a written note?

Probably not. The possibilities of fraud, forgery, or duress in getting you to sign such a note present too great a risk for your bank. However, a notarized statement or power of attorney authorizing access to your safe-deposit box might be sufficient. Check with the manager.

Joe lost the cheque Doris gave him. When he asked for a replacement, she said the cheque had already cleared. Someone must have forged Joe's signature. If Doris refuses to write him a new cheque, what can he do?

Not much. A bank is protected when it pays a cheque even if the cheque has been lost or stolen, as long as it acted in good faith and in accordance with customary and reasonable banking practices. Doris is not required to pay Joe twice to compensate him for his own negligence. In short, Joe can't recover the money from anyone but the forger.

A counterfeit $50 bill turned up in the day's receipts from Jim's store, but it looked so authentic that Jim didn't notice it. When the bank teller saw the bill, he kept it and refused to credit the $50 to Jim's account. Why did he do that?

Because to credit the counterfeit money to Jim's account would be a fraud on the bank. The teller is the bank's agent, and the law requires that he must inform the bank of the counterfeit money. The bank, in turn, is legally required to notify the police.

Establishing Credit

How do I establish credit for the first time?

For a great many people, credit begins with the opening of a charge account at a store in their hometown or at college. By promptly paying the store's monthly bills, you start building a solid credit history. Getting your first loan from a bank can prove much more troublesome than opening your first charge account. Evidence of steady employment, good references, even a chequing account at the same bank, may still not be enough to sway the bank's loan officer. He may ask that someone cosign—in effect, take equal legal responsibility for repaying—your loan. Many first-time borrowers turn to their parents or other relatives and friends to serve as cosigners; but cosigning does carry a financial risk that many people, no matter how much they like and respect you, may not wish to take on.

There is one almost surefire way of making certain that you can get a bank loan in the future—if and when you need it. Borrow a small amount of money from a bank where you have opened a savings account, and let the bank hold your savings account as collateral. Then make all of the monthly payments on time. This will help you establish a credit history. What should you do with the money you borrow? If you have no other use for it, put it in a term deposit at another bank. The interest you earn will help offset the interest you must pay on the loan, and will reduce the cost of establishing credit.

What kinds of things affect my ability to get credit?

A number of factors, including your employment history and income; the amount of time you have lived in the community; whether you have accounts at local banks or other financial institutions; whether you own real estate or other valuable property; and previous credit history. Factors that can adversely affect you are tax liens, records of arrest and conviction, loans and credit accounts that are seriously and repeatedly delinquent, and lawsuits or court judgments filed against you. If a creditor reports that you have been more than 30 days late on an account, that information can stay on your credit report for at least seven years; information on a bankruptcy might remain for 10 years.

When a woman with credit established in her maiden name gets married, what happens to her credit history?

It stays the same. No financial institution can discriminate because of one's marital state. However, a credit rating is related to the ability to repay a loan. If a single woman who had an income marries and gives up her job, she may find that her credit rating has changed, since she no longer has the resources to repay any money she may borrow. In that case, a financial institution or store issuing a credit card may require another person to act as her guarantor. Of course the same would apply if a man decided to quit his job and stay home once he got married.

Arnold is 70 years old and has a full-time job. Can he be denied a credit card simply because of his age?

No. The Charter of Rights and Freedoms, as well as most provincial human rights legislation, protects Arnold against discrimination because

Establishing Credit

of age. If Arnold has reason to believe he was refused a credit card only because of his age, he should file a complaint with the federal Human Rights Commission (if the refusal came from a bank) or with the provincial equivalent (if refusal came from some other issuer, such as a department store).

My friend, who is recently divorced, hopes to get a bank loan to start a small business. Is it difficult for a woman to establish credit in her own name after a divorce?

It should be no harder for her than it is for anybody else. In fact, if a woman's divorce settlement gives her half the family assets or similar compensation, she may find her credit rating has improved because of the divorce.

Betsy receives $1,600 a month from her ex-husband in alimentary pension and child support. She applied for a credit card, but her application was rejected. Is this illegal?

No one has a right to a credit card. If the credit card institution judged Betsy's application fairly and decided that Betsy was too great a risk according to its policies and criteria, it is under no obligation to issue a card to her.

Can a college student get his own credit card if he has no previous credit rating?

Some credit card companies will issue cards to college students because the companies' research indicates that, by and large, a college student is an acceptable credit risk.

Paul and Lois are divorced. Lois has since remarried, and she usually goes by her new husband's last name. But when she wants to obtain credit, she uses Paul's last name because he has a better credit rating than her new husband. Is this illegal?

Yes. Since she is no longer Paul's wife, it is fraud for Lois to use his name without his permission in order to obtain credit. Fraud is a crime, and it is also grounds for a civil suit. Paul has the right to sue Lois if he loses money, if his credit rating is damaged, or if he is sued by someone else because of her actions.

Suzanne just discovered a loan agreement made in 1979 stating that she must repay the loan with interest in a three-year period, which ended in 1982. Suzanne is sure that she never made any payments. Can the bank sue her for the amount of the loan?

Probably not. In most cases, legal proceedings to recoup such commercial debts must be started within six years of the end of the loan period. In this case, the bank would have had to sue Suzanne no later than 1988. Unless she wrote to the bank earlier, acknowledging her indebtedness, it may be too late for the bank to take action. However, if Suzanne had written to the bank in 1987, for example, saying that she realized she owed the money but could not then make any payments, the six-year time limit would restart from that point, and the lender would have until 1993 to institute proceedings. The same rules would apply to loans made by loan companies or other financial institutions. In Quebec, legal action must be taken within five years of the end of the term of the loan.

Andy's company is transferring him to its home office. Will he have trouble establishing credit in a new city?

Probably not, if he already has a good credit history, because credit bureaus around the country can and do exchange information. However, if Andy is worried, he has several options to consider: (1) He can ask his employer for a letter of recommendation describing his work record and salary level. (2) He can request a credit report from the bureau in the city he is leaving. This report will have the most up-to-date information about Andy's credit history. (3) He can apply for a credit card at a major department store in the new city. (4) He can open a chequing or savings account, or both, at a local bank.

Some years ago Nick and Diana fell way behind on their bills because Nick was laid off for four months and Diana was sick. Their financial troubles are now over. How do they go about reestablishing their ability to get credit?

Nick and Diana should write to each of their lenders explaining that the difficulty in meeting their commitments was temporary and their tough times seem to be over. Under most provincial credit reporting laws, they are guaranteed the right to have their explanatory statement made a part of their credit report. At the same time, Nick and Diana should be absolutely sure that they make the required payments on outstanding debts on or before the dates due. If they need more time to pay off past balances and bring payments up to date, they should see if their creditors will accept reduced payments. If the bad credit rating is based on debts owed by only one of them, Nick and Diana might consider

Establishing Credit

applying for credit in the other's name. For example, if the overdue debts were in Nick's name, they could try applying for a loan in Diana's name.

A final point: time eventually improves a person's credit rating. In general, the older credit problems are, the less they will bother potential creditors and lenders.

Do I have the right to see my credit report?

Yes, although in some areas you must make a written request to the credit bureau, rather than just walking in, and there may be a small charge. Since most credit reports are set out in code, it is often better to pick up the report in person so that one of the credit bureau staff can explain it to you.

What Credit Bureaus Do—and Don't Do

If you have established credit with a store or bank (called a *credit grantor*), certain information about you has probably been passed on to a *credit bureau*. A credit bureau collects information about your borrowing and bill-paying record and supplies this information, for a fee, to stores and banks that are considering whether or not to grant you credit. To find out the names of credit bureaus in your area, check the telephone book. Some call themselves credit agencies or credit-reporting bureaus (or agencies, or services).

A credit bureau summarizes the information it has about you into a *credit report*, which may also be called a credit record or credit profile. In addition to basic information about you (name, address, age, social insurance number, employer if known, and so on), the credit report contains your *credit history*, which shows problems you may have had paying your creditors regularly and promptly. Using the credit report, a credit grantor will assign you a *credit rating*, which determines whether or not the bank or store will grant you credit, and if it does, how much—a dollar figure that is often called your *credit line*. Thus, a credit rating is a judgment by one specific store or bank. It is not an absolute or universal grade set by a credit bureau; and if one credit grantor gives you a poor rating, another may not.

You are entitled to see a copy of your credit report, but you may have to pay a small fee for it. Your credit report will include the name of any prospective employer who obtained information about you in the past two years, as well as the name of anyone else who saw your report in the last six months.

Françoise recently learned that the credit bureau in her area disclosed her credit record to an inquiring acquaintance with whom Françoise has no financial dealings. Is there anything she can do to stop the credit bureau from making her private affairs public?

She should sue the credit bureau for breach of confidentiality. Credit bureaus are required to keep their records confidential and are permitted to disclose information only to people or institutions who have a legitimate financial reason for requesting such information. Thus a prospective landlord or lender may be entitled to a copy of Françoise's credit record, but not a nosy neighbor. A credit bureau that uses or discloses a person's credit record improperly would be liable for damages.

Jill believes her credit report contains misleading information. What can she do?

She can ask the credit bureau to reverify the information from the lender or include an explanatory statement in the file. Adding an explanatory statement may be a good idea even if the information in the file is technically correct. If, for example, Jill fell behind on payments last year because of temporary layoff from work, her explanation of why she was late might lead a creditor to overlook her past payment problems. Remember, though, that more than one credit bureau may serve your area, so you may have to add an explanatory statement to reports in two or more offices. If you can't find the names and addresses of local credit bureaus in the telephone book, ask your bank's lending officer for the names of credit reporting agencies that serve the bank.

After I submitted a credit application to buy a new car, the bank told me that a credit report showed I had a slow payment record at Ella's Electronic Bazaar. I believe that information is inaccurate. What can I do to get this statement removed from my credit report?

Ask the bank or the electronics store for the name of the credit bureau that reported you as a slow payer. Write a letter to the bureau explaining why you think the information is not correct. Ask it to investigate. If the information does prove to be inaccurate, the credit bureau will delete it from your file, and it will notify any person you designate that the information has been deleted—if that person has received a copy of the earlier report within the past six months. If you don't already know who has seen the report, you have a legal right to get the names from the credit bureau.

Credit Cards and Charges ▰▰▰▰▰

For disagreements about merchandise and services that you have purchased, see Chapter 9, *Consumer Rights*.

Charlotte wants to apply for a bank card, but she is confused about the difference between a credit card, a debit card, and a travel and entertainment card. Aren't they all the same?

No. Although different kinds of cards are often lumped together in the category of credit cards, there are significant differences. A credit card enables a person to obtain credit from an organization, such as a bank or department store. Most bank cards fall into this category. However, some banks also provide their customers with a debit card, which enables them to withdraw or deposit money in automatic teller machines. In addition, some bank debit cards can be used at stores that have a point of sale terminal, which allows the merchant to deduct the amount of a purchase directly from a customer's account.

Travel and entertainment cards were once used primarily to pay for travel, hotel rooms, and restaurant meals, but are now accepted by a variety of merchants. Some of these cards may not offer extended repayment terms; the amount charged to the card must be paid in full upon receipt of the statement.

Is it wise to shop for credit cards?

Yes. Different credit card issuers charge different fees and interest rates. For example, one bank may charge as much as 10 percent more interest than another bank does. Some banks charge an annual fee for their cards; others don't. And some cards charge interest from the very first day of a purchase, while others give you up to a month of interest-free days (called a grace period) after you make a purchase.

I recently went into a local department store to apply for credit. They handed me a two-page application with lots of personal questions that seemed unrelated to my ability to pay. Isn't there a limit to the kinds of questions a creditor can ask?

Yes. A credit application may ask only for information that directly relates to your credit history and your ability to repay your debts. Most provincial credit reporting legislation prohibits discrimination on the basis of a credit applicant's race, color, religion, national origin, sex, or marital status. If you feel that a question is discriminatory, unnecessary, or improper in some way, ask the credit manager why it is included. If you find his answer unsatisfactory, leave the answer blank. If the store rejects your application for credit, you have the right to know the reason.

If the rejection is discriminatory, you have the right to complain to the Human Rights Commission office in your area. You may also be entitled to sue the department store.

A friend told me that the credit card I received from Graham's Department Store was for a revolving or "open-ended" account. What does this mean?

This kind of account permits a buyer or borrower to purchase goods or obtain loans on a continuing basis. It can be used indefinitely as long as the outstanding balance on the account does not exceed a certain predetermined limit. With a revolving account, loans are repaid and new loans are granted in a continuing cycle.

Mary was in a hurry when she applied for a department store credit card, and roughly estimated the balances due at several other stores. Will this create a problem if the department store discovers that she underestimated the amounts owed?

Probably not. Because many people have a number of credit cards with varying balances, they may be unable to state exactly the amount owed on each card at any given time. If you are not in a position to know the exact balance due on an account, a reasonable estimate is usually acceptable to a creditor.

I applied for a credit card three months ago, but I haven't received it yet. What can I do to find out why it's taking so long?

You should contact the card issuer. Generally, an issuer will notify an applicant within 30 days whether the application has been accepted or rejected. You should also contact the credit card company for another reason: if your application was approved and a card mailed, it may have been lost or stolen in transit. If the issuer is notified that you have not received your card, it can cancel the lost card and issue a replacement.

Are there facts that a credit card holder must be told?

Yes. Under federal and provincial laws, a credit card issuer must tell the credit card holder how much credit costs. In British Columbia, Ontario, and Quebec, credit disclosure rules are part of consumer protection laws; in other provinces, special laws deal with disclosure. Credit disclosure laws usually cover only consumer transactions, not business loans or mortgages.

Credit Cards and Charges

Ada has a well-known credit card and always pays her bills on time. However, she does not make a habit of asking the merchant for the carbon paper from the charge slips. One day, she got a statement showing a number of purchases made in a province she's never been to. What is her legal liability or recourse?

She should notify the card issuer immediately. In her letter, Ada should describe the items in question, give her reasons for knowing they are not her purchases, and decline to pay for them. The credit card issuer must then investigate the problem. If the charges were not incurred by Ada, the company will have to credit the entire sum, plus any interest charged on it, to her account.

A department store has told Barney that the recurring error on his bill is "a computer problem." He's not satisfied with this answer since the bills keep coming. What recourse does he have?

He has the right to withhold payment of the amount in dispute. The department store must correct this error as soon as possible. If the computer problem weakens Barney's credit rating because, for example, the department store mistakenly notifies the credit bureau that Barney is behind in his payments, he could sue the store for any damages he may suffer, and he could have the erroneous information removed from his credit record.

What should I do about my credit cards if I lose my wallet?

You should always keep a list of your credit cards and account numbers in a safe place away from the cards themselves. If your wallet is lost or stolen, call the issuer of your credit card immediately (your credit card statement shows the number to call to report a missing card) and be sure to follow up your phone call with a letter. If you do not alert the card issuer immediately, you may be liable for up to $50 of unauthorized charges per card. You will not be liable for any charges made after you notify the issuer.

I keep getting advertisements in the mail for credit card protection plans. What do these plans do? Are they legitimate?

Credit card protection is a form of insurance. You give a list of all your credit card account numbers to the plan's operator, and if your cards are ever lost or stolen, you call a toll-free telephone number to report the

Protecting Your Credit Cards

Credit card fraud is a multimillion-dollar business. While provincial laws dealing with credit cards usually limit your liability for fraudulent credit card use to $50 per card, the loss of 5 or 10 cards means you could be liable for $250 to $500.

To protect yourself, experts suggest that you:

- ☑ Sign your credit cards immediately upon receipt. An unsigned card can easily be forged and used.
- ☑ Cut old credit cards into pieces before throwing them away.
- ☑ Carry only the cards you need. A wallet or purse bulging with credit cards makes an inviting target for a thief.
- ☑ Cancel cards you don't use. A card from a store in a city you once lived in might disappear without your knowing it—until you receive the monthly statement for goods you haven't purchased.
- ☑ Examine your monthly statement as soon as you get it. Report any suspicious charges immediately.
- ☑ Keep a list of your accounts and the phone numbers for reporting lost or stolen cards. Don't keep this list in your wallet or with your credit cards, where it would disappear if your wallet is lost or stolen; put it in a safe and easily accessible place.
- ☑ Never give your account number over the phone unless you are certain of the person's identity and affiliation or you initiated the call to purchase something. If someone offers to sell you something by telephone and asks for your credit card number, it may be a false sale.

loss. The plan operator then notifies the individual credit card issuers, and reimburses you for any unauthorized charges.

There are many legitimate credit card protection plans. You can check the legitimacy of a particular plan by calling your local Better Business Bureau or consumer protection office.

I tend to use my credit card for everything I buy. Is there any advantage to paying cash for an article?

Yes. Aside from not having to pay interest on any outstanding balance, you'll find many merchants are willing to give a discount to a cash-paying customer. After all, merchants who accept credit cards pay up to 7 percent of the purchase price to the credit card issuer, usually a bank. Whenever you pay cash, ask the merchant if he will give you a 5 percent reduction.

For mortgages, see "Financing a New Home" and "Ways You May Lose Your Home" in Chapter 4, *Your Home.*

Leo wants to borrow enough money to take his wife on a cruise. Should he admit this when he fills out the loan application, or should he say he's borrowing to make home improvements?

He should tell the truth. A false statement will be considered fraud; if it's discovered, the bank may declare the entire loan due at once, and Leo may be subject to civil and criminal penalties as well. The bank may be willing to lend Leo the money for home improvements, since this would increase the value of his home, but it may refuse a loan for a cruise, since this would add to Leo's debt load.

Now that Dora's loan for a new roof has been approved, what should she look for before signing the agreement?

She should pin down the exact amount of credit she is being granted and find out the annual percentage rate she will be charged and the total amount of interest she will pay over the life of the loan. Most provincial laws dealing with consumer credit require a lender to give her all this information in writing before she signs a loan agreement. In addition, Dora should find out if there are penalties for prepaying her loan, what her rights are if she defaults or is late with a payment, and what penalties she may incur if she is late with a payment.

What can I do if I signed a loan agreement, and later realized I misunderstood the terms?

Most courts will presume you understood the terms and agreed to them when you signed the document. However, if the creditor failed to make the disclosures required by the laws dealing with consumer credit (finance charges or dates payments are due, for example), you may have a right to have the loan canceled.

Does payable on demand *mean that the lender can demand complete payment at any time for any reason?*

Yes, unless the agreement restricts when a creditor can do so. However, the lender must act in good faith. If he demands repayment from a borrower who is not in arrears and whose financial situation is not precarious, the lender may be liable for damages caused to the borrower if recalling the loan drives the borrower into bankruptcy.

Mitchell was told that if he missed even one payment on his camper, the company could demand he repay the entire loan immediately. As it turned out, Mitchell missed two payments, and the dealer demanded full payment. Mitchell offered to make three payments to bring his account up to date. Can the dealer reject his offer and insist on full payment?

In some provinces, yes. But if Mitchell refuses to pay in full, the issue will most likely have to be decided in court. A contract provision that permits the lender to demand full payment if a debtor misses one or more payments is called an acceleration clause. In most cases, these clauses are not enforced unless nonpayment has been extensive and continuous. In this case, the dealer can enforce the contract only by taking Mitchell to court. But a court would probably order the dealer either to repossess the camper or to sue for the balance due: it could not grant the dealer both recourses. This choice of recourses, which is often referred to as "seize or sue," is the law in British Columbia, Alberta, Saskatchewan, Manitoba, Quebec, Newfoundland, and the Northwest Territories.

Can a minor use the money in his trust fund as collateral to get a college loan?

It depends to a large extent on the terms of the trust agreement and the duties and powers given to the trustee. However, most student loans are offered on an unsecured basis—no collateral is needed. The federal government usually acts as guarantor and pays the interest while the borrower is studying and for six months after. In Quebec, the provincial government acts as guarantor for student loans. For more information write: Secretary of State, Student Assistance Directorate, Jules Léger Building, 15 Eddy Street, Hull, Que., K1A 0M5.

Mark signed an agreement to repay $4,000 at 10 percent interest. When the loan company typed up the papers, it indicated the finance charge was $510. Mark thought the finance charge was the interest he was going to have to pay—$400. Where did the extra $110 come from?

A finance charge is the total of all the charges that you are asked to pay to obtain credit. While interest is the largest component of this charge, it also includes such items as loan application fees, service charges and "points"—fees for obtaining a credit report, premiums for credit life insurance, and any amount paid as a discount. Mark should ask the loan officer to explain these additional charges in detail. If he feels that the explanation offered is either unclear or unsatisfactory, he may wish to consult an accountant or an attorney before signing the loan agreement.

Personal Loans

Under what conditions can a bank demand full and immediate repayment of a loan or take possession of collateral?

This drastic step is called terminating a loan, and your bank can take this action if you don't make a payment, if you fail to pay off the entire amount when it is due, or if you fail to meet other conditions in the loan agreement. However, most lenders are reluctant to terminate loans, for the simple reason that they derive valuable income from the interest payments.

Michelle was turned down for a personal loan at her bank. Should she try another bank, or will it turn her down as well?

Michelle should try again. While most lenders use similar systems to evaluate applicants, there may be differences that would affect the outcome of a loan request. For example, some lenders give great weight to home ownership, while others consider a stable job history and regular wage increases just as important. Moreover, lenders use different credit reporting agencies. The bank that rejected Michelle's application may have used a credit report containing negative information about her credit history. This mightn't appear in another agency's report.

Two years ago Ben lent me $500 to help pay some unexpected bills. Now Ben says he is willing to forgive his loan to me. Should I get this agreement in writing?

Yes. Forgiving a loan means the lender no longer requires repayment of the loan. In order to avoid future disputes, a forgiveness agreement should always be in writing.

I borrowed $15,000 from a finance company several years ago and haven't missed a monthly payment. But I still owe the company $14,000 because it is charging me 38 percent interest. Is there anything I can do to reduce the interest charge?

Although it is not a crime to charge up to 60 percent interest, civil courts will often intervene when a rate under the 60 percent legal limit is considered excessive or abusive. If you seek relief in court, a judge may agree your 38 percent rate is a bit too much. After taking into account the rates charged by banks and other financial institutions in your area, and the risk the finance company took in lending you the money, the court may lower your interest rate to a more reasonable level.

What exactly is loan-sharking, and is it legal?

Loan-sharking generally refers to the practice of lending money at very high interest rates to borrowers who are unable to obtain credit through the usual outlets. These loans may carry interest charges as high as 100 percent a week, and the borrower soon finds himself unable to make the necessary payments. As a result, the unfortunate borrower is never able to repay the loan. According to the Criminal Code, it is an offense to charge more than 60 percent per annum interest on a loan.

Betty Lou inherited some money from her uncle. She wants to use it to pay off her auto loan ahead of time. Can she expect to have the finance charges refunded?

No. Betty Lou is responsible for repaying the principal remaining on the loan and all interest charges that have accrued until the day that the loan is repaid. However, she is not required to pay any future interest that would have come due if the loan had run its full course.

Sean asked his friend Jonathan for a $300 loan to pay an unforeseen dental bill. Sean said he would give his friend a written IOU, but Jonathan said he'd prefer a promissory note. What's the difference between the two?

An IOU is a document given to the lender by the borrower; written on it are the letters IOU (for "I owe you"), the amount owed, and the signature of the borrower. A promissory note is similar but usually contains the wording "I promise to pay" (the amount borrowed) by a certain date, to a certain person. If Jonathan has to sue Sean to collect the money, some courts would consider a promissory note stronger evidence of Sean's obligation to pay because it sets a specific deadline for repayment. It is always better to have a promissory note than an IOU. Both IOU's and promissory notes should be kept in a safe-deposit box. They should be destroyed when the debt is paid.

What should I do if I can't make a loan payment on time?

Contact your lender as soon as possible. In many cases, the lender will either extend the time for payment or allow you to make a reduced payment. If your past record with this lender has been a good one, he should be willing to work with you to resolve the problem. A late payment can have a negative effect on your credit rating, but the fact that you anticipated trouble and asked for a payment extension or reduction may preserve your good credit history.

The Language of Loans

Your loan application has been approved; the bank's cheque is there on the desk—but before you get it, the loan officer says, there's "just a little paperwork" to do. He hands you a pen and the loan contract, which appears to be in English, but you can't decipher much of it.

Here are translations from legalese into plain English of clauses commonly found in loan agreements. As the comments in parentheses point out, many of the conditions are illegal or unenforceable.

WHAT IT SAYS:	WHAT IT MEANS:
To secure payment hereof, the undersigned jointly and severally irrevocably authorize any attorney of any court of record to appear for any one or more of them in such court in term or vacation, after default in payment hereof and confess a judgment without process in favor of the creditor hereof for such amount as may then appear unpaid.	If you sue us because we haven't paid, we agree to let you win—even if we have a good reason for not paying and your lawyer can represent us. (*You can always raise any valid defense to a court action against you.*)
This note is secured by a security interest in all of the following described personal property and proceeds thereof: If checked at left, consumer goods consisting of all household goods, furniture, appliances, and bric-a-brac, now owned and hereafter acquired, including replacements, and located in or about the premises at the debtor's residence (unless otherwise stated) or at any other location to which the goods may be moved.	If we don't pay, you can take all our household goods. (*Provincial laws protecting certain property from seizure would prevail despite this clause.*)
Each of us hereby both individually and severally waives any or all benefit or relief from all exemptions or moratoriums to which the signers or any of them may be entitled under the laws of this or any other province, now in force or hereafter to be passed, as against this debt.	If we don't pay, you can take even the personal belongings provincial law would allow us to keep. (*It would be illegal to do this.*)
Default in the payment of any installment of the principal balance or charges hereof or any part of either shall, at the option of the holder hereof, render the entire unpaid principal balance hereof, at once due and payable.	If we miss a payment, you can make us repay the whole loan immediately. (*In some provinces, you have the right to pay the over-due amount and be rein-stated as if you never missed a payment.*)

WHAT IT SAYS:	WHAT IT MEANS:
The undersigned, jointly and severally, agree that the lender may at its option communicate with any persons whatsoever in relation to the obligation involved, or its delinquency, or in an effort to obtain cooperation or help relative to the collection or payment thereof.	If we don't pay, you can tell all our friends and relatives. (*A lender could be liable for damages if it uses confidential information improperly.*)
We severally hereby authorize and direct our said employers or any future employers or either of them to pay (a part) of salary, wages, commission or other compensation for services to the said assignee and release such employers or any future employers from all liability to us on account of any and all monies paid in accordance with the terms hereof. We severally give and grant unto the said assignee, full power and authority to demand, receive, and receipt for the same or any part thereof in any of our names.	If we don't pay, just have our bosses deduct the money from our pay cheques. We won't argue about it. (*The amount an employer can deduct under a judgment to pay a creditor is fixed by law and cannot be exceeded.*)
In consideration of the making and acceptance of the within note . . . undersigned cosigner jointly and severally unconditionally guarantees to the said creditor and to any assignee of said creditor, the payment of all monies due or to become due under said note . . . and also the full performance by the said debtor of all the promises and covenants on his or their part therein contained. . . . The undersigned cosigner hereby consents to all extensions of time for the making of any or all payments by the debtor and further guarantees the payment of all said payments due by reason of said extensions. Notice of acceptance of this guaranty, notice of nonpayment and nonperformance, notice of amount of indebtedness outstanding at any time, protest, demand, and prosecution of collection, foreclosure, and possessory remedies are hereby expressly waived.	If we don't pay, you can collect from a cosigner without trying to collect from us first. You don't even have to warn our cosigner we've fallen behind in payments. (*The borrower can contest this in court if he has a good reason for not honoring the terms of the contract.*)
If this agreement is referred to any attorney for collection due to any default or breach of any promise or provision hereunder by debtor, debtor agrees to pay an attorney's fee of 15% of the total of payments then due, plus court costs.	If you sue us, we'll pay for your lawyer.

YOUR MONEY

Personal Loans

Genevieve has agreed to lend Mary Jane $1,200 for six months, and Mary Jane will put up her computer as collateral. What's the best way to formalize this loan agreement between the two longtime friends?

First, Mary Jane should give Genevieve a promissory note for $1,200 that states the repayment date they have agreed upon. At the same time, they should draw up a separate document, called a security agreement, which gives Genevieve the right to sell the collateral if Mary Jane defaults on the debt. Thus, Genevieve would be permitted to recover the balance of the loan plus any unpaid interest and the expenses incurred in selling the computer. Any excess should be refunded to Mary Jane.

Sarah borrowed $250 from Clarence and gave him a promissory note saying she would repay it by January 1. In mid-December, she asked Clarence for another month to repay. He said, "Sure." Should Sarah ask Clarence to sign a statement agreeing to this one-month extension?

Yes. It is always preferable to obtain an extension in writing. This is especially important when the original loan agreement is also in writing. If Clarence changes his mind a week later and demands payment on the original due date, Sarah will need the written extension as evidence of their new agreement.

Two years ago I lent a friend $3,500. I have phoned him several times, but he always says he is too busy to talk, and never calls me back. My patience is exhausted and I need my money. What can I do to get it from him?

Notify your friend in writing that you are demanding payment of the amount he owes you. Your letter should include these specifics: the date you lent him the money; the amount of the debt; the date that repayment was due; and a demand that he make payment to you by a certain date. Send the letter by certified mail, return receipt requested, and keep a copy for your records. If your friend neither responds to your letter nor makes payment by the date you set, he leaves you little choice but to sue him in order to collect the debt. Because $3,500 exceeds the limit for the amount that can be recovered in Small Claims Court, you may want to consult an attorney and find out what he would charge to represent you in a court proceeding. If legal costs for a full scale suit would be too high for you, and the proof of the amount your friend owes you is less than solid, you may be better off reducing your claim to the small claims limit so you can sue in Small Claims Court. It would be nonetheless worthwhile—and affordable—to consult an attorney to help you prepare your small claims case.

Victor would like to lend his daughter Susan $5,000 to help with the down payment on the new house she and her husband want to buy. How should Victor protect his interest?

He should have his daughter sign both a mortgage and a promissory note. If the property will be owned jointly by Susan and her husband, he too should sign the documents. The mortgage and promissory note should then be filed in the land records office of the county in which the house is located. By filing these documents, Victor gives notice to others that the house is being used as collateral to secure the $5,000 he is lending his daughter. Consequently, the house could not be transferred or sold without repaying Victor the $5,000.

Can two or more people shoulder the responsibility of a loan?

Yes. However, each joint applicant may be held solely liable for the entire amount of the debt. If one of the borrowers is unable to pay his share, the other will be required to pay the full amount.

Should Lloyd cosign a loan for his sister?

Only if he is reasonably confident that his sister will pay the loan as agreed, and is willing to pay the debt for her if she doesn't. If a borrower fails to make payments, the lender will look to the cosigner to pay.

I cosigned a loan for my son. He was late with one payment, and now they want the entire balance from me. Do I have to pay?

You may have to if the loan agreement says you must. Most loan agreements allow lenders to do a number of things if a payment is late—they can repossess property pledged as security, accelerate the debt and demand that it be paid in full, or demand payment from cosigners. If the lender opts for the last choice and you end up paying, you would be *subrogated in the lender's rights*, that is, you would then have the same rights to sue your son as the lender had. A borrower could, of course, have good reasons to stop repaying a loan—he may discover, for example, that the lender had misrepresented or failed to disclose the actual rate of interest. In such a case, a cosigner could raise these defenses if the lender sues him for full payment.

Personal Loans

I'm being sued for $3,000 I owe on a car loan, and my car has been repossessed under the terms of the loan agreement. What can I do about this?

In British Columbia, Alberta, Saskatchewan, Quebec; and Newfoundland, the seller can either sue for the amount owing or repossess the car. But he can't do both. If he repossesses the car, the contract is considered canceled, and nothing more is owed. If a buyer in British Columbia, Ontario, or Quebec defaults after he has repaid a substantial part of the loan, the seller can repossess the car only if the buyer agrees or if the court grants permission. In provinces where repossession does not end the contract, the lender must try to get a fair price when he sells the repossessed car. Check the law in your provinces to see if your car loan was canceled by the repossession of your car. You should also find out how much the lender received for your car. In some cases, if it was sold for more than you owed, you may be entitled to a refund of the difference.

Payment Problems

For default on a mortgage, see "Ways You May Lose Your Home" in Chapter 4, *Your Home.*

Sherry is being sued in Small Claims Court because she hasn't paid some bills. Can her creditors demand that she turn over all or part of her family allowance cheque?

No. A family allowance cheque is considered support for children, not for the parent. Veterans' allowances, old age pension cheques, welfare payments, unemployment insurance benefits and workers' compensation cheques are also exempt from seizure or garnishment.

Harvey has some huge debts, and his payments are falling further and further behind. Is a debt consolidation loan the solution to Harvey's problems?

It could be, if Harvey is sure that he can meet the payments. A debt consolidation loan is one large loan for the purpose of paying off many smaller loans and debts. In most cases, this will result in lower monthly payments because the repayment period for a debt consolidation loan is usually longer. However, a longer repayment period usually means more total interest over the life of the loan. Because Harvey's debts are large, he might consider a Chapter X bankruptcy petition, explained in further detail in the final section of this chapter.

Virginia cannot make the monthly minimum payment on several charge accounts. Can she have her payments reduced?

Some stores will agree to a temporary reduction or delay in payments, especially if Virginia takes the initiative in contacting the store. By doing so, she will show that she does not take her indebtedness lightly.

Martha, an elderly neighbor, is behind on her gas bill. Can the gas company legally turn off the heat without notice?

No. The gas company must send at least two (in some provinces, three) notices, giving the last notice 48 hours before it intends to cut off service. If the gas company does not follow the proper procedure, Martha should consult an attorney, who may seek an injunction obliging the gas company to continue or to restore service. If she has no money, Martha should contact the legal aid society. A local golden age group may also be able to help her.

I was a little late paying my phone bill, and now they want a $100 deposit, or they will terminate my service. What can I do?

The Canadian Radio-television and Telecommunications Commission (CRTC) has jurisdiction over federally regulated communications companies such as Bell Canada, BC Telephone, CNCP and Northwestel Inc. Contact the CRTC to see if the $100 deposit is permissible in your case. If $100 is within the allowed limit, you may have to pay it to keep your telephone service. However, you may be able to persuade the telephone company to waive the deposit if a one-time emergency, such as sickness or a death in the family, caused you to be late with your payment.

Gene called in a pledge to Friends of the Sick telethon. The following week, Gene lost his job. Can the charitable organization make Gene fulfill his pledge?

Perhaps. Some courts might order Gene to pay if the charity could show it had initiated some project or activity (such as making a down payment on a new ambulance) as a result of Gene's promise.

My doctor is suing me for cosmetic surgery bills that I owe him. His lawyer said that my property could be seized. Is this possible?

Yes, if your doctor wins his lawsuit. That is why you should try to work out a reasonable solution with the doctor—or with any creditor. For

YOUR MONEY

Payment Problems

example, he may delay his suit if you send small good faith payments toward the full amount. If he does sue, and obtains judgment, the doctor becomes known legally as a judgment creditor; he will ask the court to issue a writ of execution, which the court will deliver to the sheriff or another officer of the court, directing him to seize enough of your property to pay the debt.

The law varies from province to province regarding the kind of property that can be seized and in what order. In some provinces, personal property must be seized before real estate. And many provinces exempt certain property from seizure—up to $4,000 worth of household items, for example.

YOUR MONEY

The only asset Dick owns with any value is a life insurance policy. The cash surrender value is $1,800. Can creditors force Dick to cash in the policy if he defaults on a loan?

No. Creditors cannot force Dick to cash his policy. But if Dick voluntarily cashed in his policy, his creditors could probably seize the money he received.

Duncan bought a carpet on credit, with installation included, but the installers did a bad job. Duncan refused to pay until it was repaired. Two years later, after calling the carpet company many times, he received a summons notifying him that the company was suing for payment. What should Duncan do?

If the poor installation caused Duncan problems or extra expenses, he can countersue the company for breach of contract. When Duncan purchased the carpet, he was entitled to have it installed properly; the carpet company failed to live up to its obligation.

Jenny made a small down payment at a health club and signed a membership contract that said the club had a right to assign her promissory note. Then the club went out of business, and Jenny made no more payments. Now a collection agency demands she pay the full amount of her membership. Must she pay?

Because she signed the contract allowing the club to assign her promissory note—that is, sell it to another company for collection—Jenny is technically liable for the full payment. However, she may be entitled to withhold payment, since the health club breached its contract with her when it went out of business. She should write to the collection agency informing them that the health club has closed down. She should also find out if her province has specific laws regulating the health club and spa industry. These laws may permit her to discontinue payments without penalty, and may even permit her to be reimbursed for the money she has already paid. Jenny should contact the consumer protection office in her province for more information.

Harry bought a freezer on a 12-month installment contract. The appliance store then sold Harry's note to a finance company. Now a mere six months since he made the purchase, the freezer doesn't work. Can Harry refuse to make payments?

Yes. Harry can refuse to pay until the appliance store either repairs or replaces his freezer. At one time, the sale of the installment contract to a finance company would have put Harry in the unenviable position of having to make full payment for his defective freezer; but now provincial consumer laws protect the consumer in such situations.

How to Recognize Debt Trouble

Is there a way to know if your debts are climbing toward the danger level? Financial advisers who study the problems of consumers say to watch for these warning signs:

- You can't ever seem to reduce the balances on your department store credit cards.
- You make smaller down payments on new purchases, and only the minimum payments required on your installment loans.
- You begin to get regular reminders from your creditors that payments are past due.
- Your credit card and installment payments use up a larger and larger percentage of your income.
- You take a debt consolidation loan, and soon find yourself taking on even more credit card debt.
- You use cash advances on your credit card to pay everyday expenses such as food, rent, and utility bills.

If you are receiving some or all of these danger signals, you can do two things that will cost you little or no money. (1) Contact your creditors and ask if they can work out new payment schedules that allow you to make smaller monthly payments over a longer period of time. (2) Contact the nearest consumer debt counseling services office. These are found in British Columbia, Alberta, Manitoba, Ontario, and Quebec. For no charge or a nominal fee, they will advise you on credit problems and how to get out of debt.

Payment Problems

Can my creditors keep selling my installment contracts to other companies for collection?

Yes. The practice is common with every type of installment contract, including mortgages, and is legal as long as the company that buys your contract does not ask you to make higher payments or to put up additional collateral.

My friend Chester is diligently trying to pay off some old debts, but the people at one collection agency keep calling him at all hours. Last night one of them called him after 10:00 P.M. Chester became so incensed that he blew his top. Will this just make it tougher for him?

The law is on Chester's side. Most provinces regulate the behavior and tactics of collection agencies and may suspend the license of one that repeatedly infringes the regulations. A collection agency is not allowed to telephone too frequently or at unreasonable times. If the collection agency uses tactics that are in effect harassment, Chester may be able to sue it for causing him mental stress. Moreover, the collection agency could even be charged in criminal court if, for example, it uses threats against Chester.

Is it possible that I could be sent to prison if I were unable to pay my bank loan?

No. The institution of debtors' prison, which was made famous by English novelist Charles Dickens, has been abolished in the provinces where it once existed. No one has been imprisoned for debts since the mid-19th century.

If I am delinquent in my payments, can a creditor garnishee my wages (arrange with my employer to have automatic repayments taken out of my pay cheque) without going to court?

No. Unless you have given him written permission to do so, a creditor cannot garnishee your wages without a court judgment. Provincial law determines the maximum amount or percentage of your wages that can be garnisheed. Once that maximum has been garnisheed, additional creditors cannot have more taken from your pay cheque. Your maximum garnishment would be shared among all creditors who have judgments against you.

Your Investments

For information about investing for retirement, see "Registered Retirement Savings Plans" in Chapter 15, *Pensions, RRSPs, Social Programs.*

Should married couples put their investments in both names?

As a general rule, it is better for a husband and wife to have separate investments. Thus, one spouse can administer his or her own portfolio without having to get the other's consent to buy or sell property or trade securities. Since spouses don't pay succession duties on anything inherited from one another, they need not pool assets to avoid tax. Besides, when one spouse dies, the other does not always automatically become owner of the joint assets. So there seems little sense in couples putting investments in both names. In fact, the disadvantages of joint ownership outweigh the advantages. Preparing and filing income tax returns, for instance, can be complicated with jointly owned investments. More important, if the investments are in both names, a court judgment against one spouse could be applied to the joint assets of both.

A company Felicia owned stock in went bankrupt. Will she be able to get her money back?

It's possible, but not likely. Stockholders are among the last to be paid when a company goes bankrupt, and the company's assets are usually gone before the stockholders' claims are reached. However, Felicia should still file a claim with the bankruptcy court. If the claims are small enough or if the company is sold or remains in business, she may recoup some of her investment.

I have lost a stock certificate. Can it be replaced?

Yes. Contact a broker and notify him of the missing certificate. He can advise you about the forms you'll need to fill out.

Can I sue a stockbroker for giving me bad advice?

A stockbroker is considered a *fiduciary,* a person who has a legal duty to act in your best interests. If he causes a loss to a client because he acted in bad faith—put your money into risky investments without your approval, for example—or made trades without the client's authorization, the client may be able to win a lawsuit against him. However, it is most unlikely that a client could win in court against a broker simply because the broker was ignorant of certain facts, made an unfortunate error in judgment, or offered poor advice.

Your Investments

Nelson's stockbroker has him buying and selling stocks every week. Despite all this activity, Nelson has become increasingly concerned because his account isn't making money. What should he do to protect his financial interests?

Nelson should put a stop to all the buying and selling and look into the possibility that his broker is "churning"—that is, making numerous stock transactions solely for the purpose of generating commissions. As a fiduciary, a stockbroker must act in his client's best financial interest. Buying and selling securities without a reasonable basis for doing so is a violation of this duty. Under provincial securities laws, a broker found guilty of churning may have his license revoked, and faces other criminal and civil penalties as well.

Can I buy stocks through my bank?

Yes. Federal law permits banks to act as stockbrokers, but they are not required to provide this service.

How to Avoid an Investment Swindle

Investment opportunities that sound too good to be true usually are—but that doesn't keep thousands of people from getting stung by con artists. When called by a salesperson they don't know, most experienced investors answer that they never make such decisions over the phone and hang up. But some people can't resist hearing a little more about a "once in a lifetime deal." If you're that curious sort, here are seven questions designed to expose a fraud. Any one of them might deter a dishonest person—but all of them together won't daunt an honest one. This list is adapted from recommendations by the Chicago-based National Futures Association, a professional self-regulatory organization of firms and individuals that buy and sell commodities (such as metals, foods, and oils) for investors.

● Can I see some literature about your company and the investments you are selling, including the names of stockholders and directors? This won't stop a con artist from giving you false names, but it will serve notice that you are the kind of person who checks details. If there is no written material, or the salesperson explains that the deal is so hot that there hasn't been time to prepare any, you are probably being conned.
● Will you mail me a copy of your proposal? Crooked operators hate to hear this question for four reasons: (1) It takes time, and a crook

A traffic accident left Ron in a coma, but he is expected to recover. What happens to Ron's investments while he is incapacitated?

If prior to his accident Ron had given someone a power of attorney—a document usually drawn up by a lawyer that enables someone to act on another person's behalf—that person could manage Ron's financial affairs. If not, a judge would probably consult with Ron's close relatives and appoint someone to manage his finances. The court-appointed guardian or conservator would be obligated to protect Ron's financial interests. A guardian or conservator may be required to post a bond, although some provinces waive this requirement when the conservator is a bank or other financial institution. The guardian will manage Ron's property until a court determines that Ron can again manage on his own.

After Ed's grandmother died, he found some old Canada Savings Bonds in a box in her attic. Will the government redeem them?

Yes, but not necessarily for Ed. The savings bonds are now part of his grandmother's estate, and only its executor or administrator has the legal authority to redeem them on his grandmother's behalf.

prefers to have your cheque at once. (2) The extra time allows you to think over the details of the proposal and change your mind. (3) A written proposal could be evidence in court. (4) Using the mail means the con man could be charged with breaking federal mail fraud laws.

● Could I meet with you at your office? Most likely, an unscrupulous salesperson won't want you to see the phone-filled "boiler room" from which he calls "mooches" (as the victims of investment scams are called in slang).

● How can I liquidate (sell for cash) my investment? In most honest securities transactions, this can be arranged in a matter of minutes.

● How many dollars or what percentage of my money would go for commissions, management fees, and the like? Don't settle for such glib answers as "These will be negligible compared to your profits."

● What government agency or professional association monitors your firm's dealings? Few things stop a fraudulent salesperson faster than the thought of being visited by an investigator from a regulatory agency or professional association.

● Would you mind describing your investment proposal to my attorney, accountant, banker, or investment adviser? If the salesperson says he would be happy to do so if there were more time, or insinuates that you should make your own investment decisions, your best bet is a quick goodbye.

Your Investments

Since Treasury Bills are guaranteed by the government, does this mean I can't lose money in them?

A Treasury Bill will always pay you its face amount if you cash it in at maturity, which ranges from three months to one year from the date of purchase. Treasury Bills are backed by the full faith and credit of the Canadian government, which means that you could lose all your money in the unlikely event that Canada defaulted on payments to its creditors. And even then, it is extremely unlikely you would lose, since the federal government has the power to print money.

If my stockbroker tells me that he can recommend investing in Nifty Computer Software Company because his friend, who is chairman of the board of Nifty, has given him some reliable information, can I be charged with insider trading?

Yes. It is illegal to buy or sell a stock because you have information that is known only to the corporation. Insider trading is forbidden whether it is done by an officer of the corporation, by a stockbroker who possesses inside information, or by an investor who receives a tip from a corporate insider. Any profit you made from such a transaction would be subject to forfeit, and you might also be subject to other penalties.

I've been seeing a lot of ads by financial planners. Who are they?

Nearly anyone can call himself a financial planner. Because this is a new field, and its standards are not completely formulated, you should be careful in selecting a financial planner. Make sure you understand what fees, charges, and commissions are involved.

Income Taxes

A friend of mine says the federal income tax is unconstitutional, and therefore he doesn't pay it. Is my friend correct?

No. The taxation powers of the federal and provincial governments derive from the British North America Act, Canada's constitutional document. Introduced as a temporary measure during World War I, the Federal Income Tax Act seems a long way from being rescinded. Anyone who does not pay federal income tax when it is due can be fined or imprisoned, or both.

If Ida's accountant makes an error on her income tax form, can Ida be held responsible? What if the person who fills out her form is not an accountant?

The final responsibility for an individual's income tax form lies with the taxpayer. Therefore, no matter who fills out Ida's tax return, she is ultimately responsible for paying the correct tax and will be held liable for interest and penalties if less than the correct amount is paid. However, Ida has the option of suing the accountant for the money she had to pay because of the accountant's mistakes in preparing her return. An accountant is a professional and is held to a high standard of responsibility. In the case of an error made by a friend or relative, who is not held to the same standards as an accountant or an attorney, it would be unlikely that Ida could recover the interest and penalties.

My mother and father are thinking about selling their house but are afraid taxes will take most of the money. Isn't there a special tax rule that helps people in their situation?

Yes. There is no capital gain tax on the sale of the principal residence (the residence occupied by the people in question), provided this is the first sale of the family home by your parents.

Must I report garage sale proceeds on my income tax return?

Generally, you must report income when the sale of an item results in financial gain. But items sold at a garage sale usually bring in less than was originally paid for them, so there is no income to report.

My grandfather gave me $5,000. Should I report it as income on my tax return? Will my grandfather have to pay a gift tax?

Neither you nor your grandfather will have to pay tax on the $5,000 gift. You needn't report the amount on your tax return, either, because gifts are not considered part of your gross income. But you will have to report and pay taxes on any dividends or interest you receive from investing the money.

Joan earned $700 last year by baby-sitting. Must she file an income tax return?

Yes. Anyone who receives income must file an income tax return, even if, as in Joan's case, her income was so low that no taxes are payable.

Income Taxes

Pearl pays her housekeeper in cash and doesn't withhold unemployment insurance money. Is this legal?

It depends. If Julia hired her housekeeper through an agency, the agency usually takes responsibility for withholding and paying unemployment insurance premiums. If not, Pearl must deduct unemployment insurance from the housekeeper's wages, and pay an equal amount as an employer's contribution. Forms and information concerning these payments are available at Employment Canada offices.

What will happen if I don't file my taxes by April 30?

You may be subject to a penalty for late filing, interest on any tax due, and a possible penalty for late payment. If April 30 is upon you, and you have neither the correct figures nor the time to track them down, you can file a return containing rough estimates of your income, deductions, and tax due, and you can enclose payment for what you think you owe. Later, when you have more time, you can file an amended income tax return with the correct information. If you originally underestimated the tax due, you will have to pay the extra you owe plus interest, but at least you will be spared a late filing penalty.

If Nathan owes back income taxes, is it true that Revenue Canada has the power to garnishee his entire pay cheque?

No. The maximum amount of Nathan's wages that can be garnisheed is determined by provincial law. The limit is usually about 25 to 30 percent of gross salary.

Revenue Canada called me in for an audit. Why me?

Usually selection is by computer programs developed by Revenue Canada. In one instance, the computer looks for items that indicate possible error or fraud—deductions that are extremely large in proportion to the reported income, for example. Under this program, a high income earner is more likely to be audited than someone with a lower income. In addition, a sample of returns is selected for audit under a program for research into taxpayers' characteristics. To prevent taxpayers evading audits, Revenue Canada jealously guards the exact criteria its computer uses. Not every return selected by the computer is actually audited—that decision is made by Revenue Canada employees who review the returns selected by the computer.

308

Eric waited until the last minute to figure out his taxes and discovered he owed the government $950, which he doesn't have. What should he do?

He can either take out a loan to make the entire payment by the April 30 deadline or make periodic payments to the government, choosing the least costly route. Eric may find that the interest rate the government charges is lower than the best rate that he can get from a commercial money lender.

What happens at a Revenue Canada audit?

Audits are conducted in several ways. Some are done by letter: these *correspondence audits* require the taxpayer to supply requested information by mail. Usually, however, an audit is conducted at a Revenue Canada office. Most often this *office audit* is limited to one or more issues or items selected by Revenue Canada in advance. The taxpayer is notified by letter which items are in question and will be requested to bring documentation relating to these items. A *field audit* usually takes place at the taxpayer's home or place of business. It is generally very comprehensive, and may require that you give the auditor access to nearly all your financial records. An attorney or certified public accountant, or both, may represent you at an audit, but it is not required. Ontario and Quebec can also audit a taxpayer.

If Revenue Canada audits my federal income tax return, will the authorities at the Quebec tax office find out and audit my provincial returns?

It depends. If the audit indicates that you owe additional federal income taxes, this may affect your provincial liability and Revenue Canada may report this information to the province. However, Revenue Canada does not automatically inform the provincial tax office when it conducts an audit. It could even be argued that it would be unlawful for Revenue Canada to inform the provincial authorities, since tax information is supposed to be confidential.

How long should I keep income tax records?

To be prepared for all eventualities, you should keep your income tax records for about seven years. The minister of finance can call for a reassessment for up to three years from the date of the original assessment. If misrepresentation or fraud was involved, this three-year period may be extended.

Personal Bankruptcy

Barry makes a good salary, but he has overextended himself and owes $10,000. He has been making regular payments on all his bills, but can't get out from under. Should he think about bankruptcy?

For someone faced with debts, that should be the last move to consider. Since Barry makes a good salary and owes only $10,000, bankruptcy may not be the best solution. If he files for bankruptcy, he stands a good chance of losing his home (if he has one) along with his car and other valuable assets such as expensive furnishings or a registered retirement savings plan. And if anyone cosigned a loan for him, that guarantor would have to pay the lender. Barry should first contact each of his creditors and try to renegotiate his debt with them. He could make a *proposal*, an offer to pay part of the debt if his creditors agree. His creditors might also agree to (1) prolong the term of payment; (2) accept a cash settlement for part of the debt if Barry can get a loan; (3) suspend or reduce interest charges; and (4) work out other arrangements to avoid forcing Barry into bankruptcy and thus risk getting much less money. But before Barry makes such a proposal or files for bankruptcy, he should consult a debt counseling service or an attorney.

If Bill declared bankruptcy, would he lose everything?

No. The fresh start concept of the bankruptcy law allows a debtor to keep certain assets and possessions, which are called *exempt* property. The property a debtor must give up to pay off creditors is called *nonexempt* property. What is nonexempt property in one province may be exempt in another, so Bill should consult an attorney or the registrar of the bankruptcy court to find out what property and other possessions his province permits him to keep.

Suppose Fay decides to declare bankruptcy. What happens then?

She begins by filing a voluntary petition of bankruptcy in federal bankruptcy court. The court then sends notices to the creditors listed in her petition, ordering a halt to collection efforts or any court proceedings against her and setting a date for her first meeting with all her creditors, usually held several weeks after the filing. At the meeting, creditors will question Fay about her property, debts, and other facts relating to her bankruptcy; a trustee may be appointed to supervise the sale of any assets that must be sold to pay her debts. The proceeds from this sale are divided among Fay's creditors according to priorities set out in the bankruptcy laws. If Fay is working, she would be required to deposit a certain amount of money every week with the trustee for the benefit of her creditors. Finally, a judge will formally grant Fay a discharge of all the debts listed in her petition. The entire process may take about one year before Fay is liberated from the bankruptcy.

Can a person file for bankruptcy more than once?

Yes. There is no limit to the number of times a person can file for bankruptcy. However, someone who files more than once should not be surprised if the court sets progressively stricter terms for his discharge with subsequent bankruptcies.

Proposed Changes to the Bankruptcy Act

At the time of writing, the federal government was considering amendments to the 1949 Bankruptcy Act that would bring the legislation into line with the economic realities of the late 1980s and beyond. Here are some of the recommended changes:

● The federal government would guarantee up to $2,000 of the unpaid salary of any worker who was employed with a company that went bankrupt.

● The status of the Crown (both federal and provincial) would change from a preferred to an ordinary unsecured creditor. Under this arrangement, other creditors would receive a greater proportion of their claims than they have under the present law.

● A proposal—that is, a compromise offered by a debtor—would be considered accepted if two thirds of the creditors agreed rather than the three quarters now required.

● The rejection of a proposal would no longer automatically make the debtor a bankrupt, which is the effect of the present law.

● A debtor could exclude from assets to be shared by creditors up to $50,000 in his registered retirement savings plan. This amount would be adjusted periodically to the rate of inflation.

● A consumer bankrupt would be discharged nine months after the beginning of his bankruptcy, unless a creditor filed an opposition to discharge or the bankrupt had net earnings in excess of $40,000.

● A bankrupt would be released from any debt or liability incurred for the necessities of life. Under the present law, debts for food, dental or medical care, or certain household necessities, are not discharged through bankruptcy.

● A debt or liability incurred fraudulently would be cleared by a bankruptcy discharge. However, this would not be the case if the debtor was convicted of fraud under the Criminal Code.

Personal Bankruptcy

Is there more than one kind of bankruptcy?

No. Technically speaking there is only one type of bankruptcy. However, Chapter X of the Bankruptcy Act allows for what is called the orderly payment of debts (OPD). Under this scheme, an individual debtor can consolidate most of his debts and pay them off with a monthly payment deposited in bankruptcy court. If an OPD plan is accepted by the creditors and approved by the court, no creditor is permitted to institute or continue legal proceedings against the debtor so long as he makes regular deposits. Not all debts are covered and taxes are excluded. The OPD scheme, sometimes called a Chapter X bankruptcy, is only available in British Columbia, Alberta, Saskatchewan, Manitoba, Nova Scotia, and Prince Edward Island. Quebec operates its own scheme called voluntary deposit or the Lacombe Law. Since a person's credit rating is damaged almost equally by an OPD or a bankruptcy, a debtor may find it preferable to go for the traditional bankruptcy.

Does Perry's employer have to know if he files for bankruptcy?

Not necessarily. But if the court-appointed trustee in bankruptcy needs more information about Perry's salary and benefits, or if the trustee wants the employer to pay part of Perry's wages directly to him, he would of course have to contact the employer. It would be illegal for the employer to discriminate against Perry because he filed for bankruptcy, unless Perry is a lawyer or chartered accountant. While their bankruptcy is being processed, lawyers, chartered accountants and certain other professionals cannot practice without special permission from their regulatory body.

Leroy went bankrupt eight years ago. Can he be refused credit?

It is up to the individual creditor to decide whether he will grant or refuse credit to Leroy. While a recently discharged bankrupt may have a hard time getting credit, there is no law that says he must wait a certain number of years before he can get credit. In fact, if he has a good job and has acquired assets and not taken on debts, a creditor may see him as a good risk and grant him credit. However, an undischarged bankrupt *must* disclose that he is in the process of bankruptcy if he requests credit.

Insurance

Is there a difference between what an insurance agent and an insurance broker can do? Does either one have to be licensed?

An agent is an employee of an insurance company and represents that company in making legally binding contracts. A broker is a self-employed individual who locates suitable coverage for persons seeking insurance. As a general rule, a broker cannot legally bind an insurance company to a contract: the contract is between his client and the insurance company.

Both agents and brokers must meet provincial licensing requirements, which typically include a period of residency in the province, a passing grade on a written exam, references and other evidence attesting to the applicant's good moral character, and in some provinces the posting of a bond that insures clients against default or fraud by the agent or broker.

Roy's mother asked him to look over her insurance policies, but he found he couldn't understand some of them. Don't insurance policies have to be in plain English?

Although they are not yet obliged to do so, more and more insurers are switching from complicated, hard-to-understand policies to ones that are clearly written in plain, simple language.

If Roy is unsure what certain words or phrases mean, he should call the insurance company and ask for a brief, clear outline of what is and is not covered in the policies. If he still isn't satisfied, he should put his specific questions in a letter to the company.

Wendy paid the premium when she filled out an insurance application. Will she be covered if something happens before she receives the actual policy?

Many insurance companies issue a binding receipt, or binder, when the first premium is paid. A binder would protect Wendy for the few days it takes to process her application and payment. If her application is rejected, Wendy would be entitled to a refund of her premium payment.

I gave some incorrect information on my insurance application. Should I correct it now?

Yes. Insurance companies have many ways of verifying the information you give. So if you do not correct any misinformation, and the company discovers the deception in the course of investigating a claim from you,

Questions to Ask When Buying Insurance

Almost everyone needs some insurance but many people are overinsured, are covered for the wrong eventualities, or pay unnecessarily high premiums—usually because they do not shop around. A common misconception is that all companies sell essentially the same coverage at a similar cost. The fact is that you can get more protection for your money by careful inquiry. If you ask the following questions, you will challenge an insurance agent or broker to find you the very best coverage at the lowest cost:

☑ If I need immediate coverage, can I get a binder that protects me while my application is being evaluated?

☑ Is there a waiting period before I can receive benefits?

☑ How does this policy's premium compare with the premiums paid by other policyholders with similar coverage from this company? How do this company's premiums compare with those of other insurers?

☑ How much more do I have to pay for a policy that guarantees replacement value of my loss, rather than the usual depreciated value of my lost or damaged property?

☑ In property insurance, do I have a "floater" clause that covers loss of property which takes place away from my home, such as the theft of my coat in a restaurant?

☑ Is it to my advantage to have term insurance rather than whole life insurance? (Term insurance is usually much cheaper.)

☑ To exactly what date is the policy in effect?

☑ Is there a grace period for late premium payments?

☑ On what grounds can the company cancel my policy?

☑ If I decide to cancel, how much of a refund can I expect?

☑ Can I get a policy the company guarantees is renewable and that cannot be canceled by the company?

☑ How soon must I submit claims and report accidents, damage, injuries, death, or illnesses?

☑ When I make a claim, what documentation and what procedures are required to show proof of loss?

☑ How soon will an adjuster investigate my claim?

☑ How long does it take to settle the average claim?

☑ Can you tell me what percentage of claims by policyholders end up in court and how this percentage compares to the average throughout the insurance industry?

☑ Will rates be raised after a claim is paid, regardless of the amount, or will they be raised after a set number of claims?

☑ Does this policy duplicate coverage I already have?

☑ Should I buy a rider whereby the company will waive the premiums in case I fall ill and cannot pay for them, and how much would such a rider cost?

your claim may be denied and your policy voided. With life insurance, if the insured dies within two years after buying a policy, an untruthful application (one that neglects to mention a family history of heart disease or diabetes, for example) can prevent the payment of proceeds to the beneficiary, because of fraud. If the misinformation on a life insurance application relates to age, the claim won't be denied, but the amount the beneficiary receives will be adjusted to reflect the insured's actual age. Suppose, for example, that Clarence's age on his life insurance policy is 10 years younger than his actual age. If the insurance company discovers the truth after Clarence dies, it will compute the additional premiums that Clarence would have paid as an older person, and subtract that amount from the money his beneficiary is to receive.

For purely practical reasons, then, you would be foolish to wait until you have a claim to see if the erroneous information on your application will be used against you. Write to your company or agent immediately, giving the correct data.

Andrew bought insurance last year and declared he was a non-smoker, because he only smoked occasionally. After he drowned a month ago, the insurance company discovered his smoking habits and now refuses to pay his family. Since Andrew's death had nothing to do with smoking, can the insurer do this?

Even if the false information on an insurance application does not have a direct bearing on the cause of death, the policy could be declared void. In a recent case, a Quebec court held that an insurance company did not have to make any payments to the beneficiaries of a man who died in an auto accident, because his life insurance policy was in effect less than two years and because he told his agent that he was a nonsmoker whereas in reality he was a cigarette smoker. In the field of insurance law, honesty is really the best policy.

If I can't pay the full premium that is coming due, will I still be covered if I pay part of it?

No. Generally, most insurance contracts require premiums to be paid in full to keep a policy in force. For life insurance, there is usually a delay of about 30 days during which you are covered even if the premium has not been paid. But if you do not pay the full premium within the 30-day period, the policy is automatically canceled. For other types, such as accident or sickness insurance, the insurance company must serve notice that if you do not pay within 15 days of their notification, your policy will be canceled.

Two days after Farley filled out an insurance application and paid the first month's premium, he had second thoughts about the cost. If he cancels the policy, is he entitled to a refund?

Yes, but whether it is a full or partial refund depends on where he lives and what kind of insurance is involved. Farley can expect at least a partial refund no matter where he lives and what kind of insurance he invested in. He should read his policy to find out his cancellation and refund rights. If Farley calls the company and is told that his application has not yet been approved, he can withdraw his application and request a full refund. If Farley needs more information concerning his right to a refund, he should contact his provincial superintendent of insurance.

Warren's insurance agent cashed one of his premium cheques but did not send the money to the insurance company. If Warren makes a claim, will the company pay it?

Yes. The company authorizes its agents to act on its behalf. If a broker, and not an agent, were involved, however, Warren's risk of losing his money would be greater, since a broker usually does not legally represent the company. If the insurance company did not honor Warren's claim, his only choice might be to sue the broker and the insurance company together.

I'm having trouble finding a company that will insure me or my property. What can I do?

Except for government insurance programs such as Medicare, certain group insurance plans and, in some provinces, automobile insurance schemes, no one has the *right* to be insured. Thus if the insurance companies that operate in your province refuse to insure you or your property, you cannot force them to do so. Nevertheless, if you look hard enough, you can probably find an insurance company willing to cover you. But the premium you will be obliged to pay may be prohibitive.

Can I buy insurance from the government?

Yes. In addition to the insurance you *must* buy from the government, such as medical, unemployment and (in British Columbia, Saskatchewan, Manitoba and Quebec) no-fault auto insurance, you can also buy provincial crop insurance. And, although strictly speaking you cannot buy it, there are other forms of coverage provided by government. All provinces compensate victims of uninsured drivers. When such natural disasters as catastrophic floods or tornadoes strike, government generally compensates victims who meet the criteria of a program set up to cover the disaster. But government insurance programs do not work the same way as private ones. To find out about government programs in effect in your area, contact your provincial ombudsman or superintendent of insurance.

Joel thought he was buying the same health insurance policy that his friend had; but when he received his policy, it had several riders attached. What should Joel do?

Riders can be used to limit or eliminate coverage offered in a standard policy. In Joel's case, after the company reviewed his medical history, it may have decided not to give him coverage for certain conditions, at least not right away. For example, if Joel had recently recovered from an ulcer, one of the riders might state that he would not be covered for ulcer treatments for three years from the date the policy was issued.

If Joel is not willing to accept the conditions imposed on the policy by the riders, he may demand a refund and look elsewhere for coverage. Or he can negotiate further with the company to try to get one or more riders altered or removed, or his premium reduced.

Is it legal for insurance companies to charge women rates that are different from those that men are charged?

Yes. Generally, because they are expected to live longer, women are charged less for life insurance than men are, but women pay more for health insurance. Insurance rates are based on risk, and if one sex has a greater chance of falling victim to whatever is being insured against, then the rate would differ from that for the opposite sex. The setting of certain types of premiums based on sex has not yet been declared discriminatory by the Supreme Court. Although the Charter of Rights and Freedoms also prohibits discrimination based on age, it is doubtful one can force an insurance company to charge the same premium for car insurance to a 17-year-old boy as it does to a 45-year-old man who has not had an accident in almost 30 years of driving.

When I submit a claim, how fast must my insurance company act?

In most cases, the time limit is written into the insurance policy. Generally, this time limit is whatever the provincial law requires. For fire, theft, automobile, accident and sickness insurance, the company must usually pay within 60 days of receiving proof of the loss. In some provinces, especially where there is some type of no-fault auto insurance, the delay is shorter. In Manitoba, payment must be made within 30 days; in Quebec, payment must begin one week after the accident.

When Constance bought her insurance, the agent said a particular item was covered. Now that she has put in a claim, the company says the item isn't covered. What can she do?

First, Constance should present her case in writing to the insurance company; if necessary, to the company's president. If the company still refuses to pay her claim and she doesn't agree with its explanation, she should send a complaint and copies of her correspondence to her provincial superintendent of insurance, whose address she can get by calling her provincial government information number. Constance also has the option of suing for fraud. Her chances of winning depend on whether she can prove that the insurance company or its agent or the broker deliberately misled her about the policy.

On what grounds can an insurance company cancel a policy?

Grounds for cancellation are spelled out in your policy. The most common ones are (1) not paying your premiums; (2) misrepresenting or concealing important facts on your application; (3) failing to report accidents, claims, or other important information; and (4) not cooperating with your insurance company as specified in your contract.

The insurance company must notify you in writing that it is canceling your policy.

What are my rights if my insurance policy is canceled?

You must be notified in advance that your coverage will be canceled and told the reasons for canceling it. Most provinces define how many days in advance are required, but the exact number of days varies from one province to another and with the kind of insurance. If you believe the company had no right to cancel your policy, you can contest the cancellation. If your policy is canceled during a period for which you have paid the premium, you are entitled to a refund of a portion of the premium you have paid.

Eva's husband canceled their insurance. Can she get it reinstated?

Many policies allow reinstatement within a certain period of time if past premiums, plus interest, are paid. Eva may need to provide evidence that

The Basics of Insurance

she and her husband are still insurable. If their policy does not allow reinstatement, she will probably have to seek new coverage.

What can I do if I have a complaint about either my insurance policy or the company that issued it?

First, send a letter to the person who sold you the policy. If he does not resolve the problem, write a letter to his supervisor and, if necessary, work your way up to the head of the company. You may also get some help from the Insurance Bureau of Canada. If you are still dissatisfied, contact the superintendent of insurance in your province, or the federal Superintendent of Financial Institutions, Kent Square, 255 Albert Street, 13th Floor, Ottawa, Ont., K1A 0H2. A superintendent can impose fines or other sanctions on companies that follow unfair practices. Finally, if you believe the insurance company has acted illegally, you can hire an attorney to help enforce your rights.

Life Insurance

Edwina keeps getting letters urging her to buy credit life insurance. Does she need it?

Credit life insurance is a type of insurance that guarantees the payment of a debt, such as a mortgage or personal loan, after a person's death. Usually this insurance is known as decreasing term because its benefit decreases over the period that the owner is paying off the debt. For example, assume Edwina bought credit life insurance to cover a new car loan that had a four-year schedule of payments. If she dies during the first year, the amount the policy pays will be much greater than the amount it will pay if she dies during the fourth year. Although a lender can legally require that Edwina have some type of insurance to cover a debt, the lender can't require that she buy a particular type or that she buy it from a particular company. Most experts advise having a standard term policy to protect heirs against being saddled with a large debt.

Is it possible to borrow against the cash value of an insurance policy in order to pay the premiums?

Yes. Many life insurance policies have a feature known as the automatic premium loan, or the extended term provision, that allows the insurance company to use the cash value of the policy to pay past due premiums.

This is a loan, however: you will pay interest on it; and if you die before repaying it, the loan amount will be deducted from the proceeds paid to your beneficiary. In some cases, after a number of years, the interest on the cash value of your policy would be sufficient to pay future premiums.

Can I buy insurance that will pay me at a later date, rather than pay a beneficiary after my death?

Yes. This type of insurance is called endowment insurance or retirement income insurance. The face value of the policy is paid to the insured if he is still alive at the date specified in the policy. The beneficiary is paid the face amount if the insured dies before reaching the age specified.

Uncle Harry bought a life insurance policy even though a court had declared him incompetent. Is the insurance policy valid?

No. Contracts signed by persons who have been declared legally incompetent are void. However, contracts with people who are mentally ill, but not legally incompetent, can be voided only by the ill person.

Gerald bought a life insurance policy two years ago. He now has a job that gives him a large amount of life insurance. Will his beneficiary be able to collect on both policies?

Yes. Life insurance contracts do not prohibit double coverage. Gerald may buy as many policies and as much protection as he wishes.

My ex-husband and I had life insurance policies on each other's lives when we were married. Does our divorce automatically cancel this insurance?

Not necessarily. In Quebec, however, divorce or annulment does automatically cancel the designation of the spouse as beneficiary. Elsewhere, if you die while the policy is in effect, your ex-husband will collect the proceeds. As the policy owner, you can cancel the coverage or change the beneficiary unless your divorce decree prohibits you from doing so.

As a nonsmoker, am I eligible for lower premium rates than those charged to smokers?

Yes. Most insurance companies offer reductions of up to 50 percent for people with healthful life-styles. Generally, to qualify for this reduction,

How to Shop for Life Insurance

The life insurance industry is full of fancy-sounding policies with elaborate features. But don't let the complexities intimidate you. Stick to the basics, as suggested by the following three questions, and you'll make life insurance decisions that are right for you.

● *How Much?* When deciding on the amount of coverage you need, total your short-term debts (car loans, credit card balances) and figure how much your dependents will need to settle these accounts and pay your funeral and burial expenses. Then estimate your dependents' costs of continuing to live as they do now. Include their rent or mortgage, food, clothing, and education expenses. Measure this against the financial resources that will remain after your death: your spouse's salary; life insurance you already have; stocks, bonds, savings accounts, and other income-producing investments; real estate or other kinds of property your dependents could sell if they chose. A good rule of thumb is that the head of a family with two young children should be covered by life insurance with a face value five times his annual salary; but financial experts differ about any "right amount." Your best course is to get several opinions (from friends, family, and colleagues, as well as from insurance people), then make up your own mind about how much is enough for you.

you must take a medical examination that shows you have normal weight, blood pressure, and cholesterol levels. You may also be asked to verify that you exercise regularly and use a seat belt when driving.

If you start to smoke during the term of your policy, you must notify your insurance company of the change of risk, or your policy may be considered invalid.

My grandparents bought an accidental death policy believing that it was a standard life insurance policy. My grandfather died recently, and the insurance company won't pay my grandmother anything. Does my family have a case?

Probably not. If your grandparents were simply confused or mistaken about the type of insurance they were purchasing, they have no recourse against the company. The insurance company is obligated to pay only if your grandfather's death was due to an accident. The story would be different, however, if the company's agent misled your grandparents into believing they were buying a standard insurance policy. In that case, your grandmother could sue the company for fraud, and a court could rule that the death benefit be paid.

● *What Kind?* You will need to weigh the pros and cons of two kinds of life policies, permanent and term. Permanent insurance is known by many names, such as *straight life, ordinary life,* and *whole life*, which may add various features to the basic plan. Premiums usually stay the same for the duration of the policy. Unlike term insurance, permanent life accumulates what is called a cash value. Part of each premium goes into a fund that is a type of savings. This amount, or cash value, grows with each premium payment and earns interest at a rate set by the company. The cash value is available to you if you want to borrow all or part of it (for which you are charged interest) or if you cancel the policy.

Term insurance has no cash value and offers protection for a certain period of time, called the term. If you die during the term, your beneficiary receives the proceeds. If not, the policy terminates and you must renew it or buy a new policy. Term insurance is almost always less expensive than permanent insurance. However, the premiums for term go up as you get older. Many people buy renewable term (such as ART, or annual renewable term). This means the insured doesn't have to requalify for insurance when renewing the policy.

● *Which Company?* Premiums and policy provisions vary greatly from company to company, and some comparison shopping is a must to find what's best for you. Various publications that rate insurance companies are available at most public libraries.

Beneficiaries

For information on other kinds of beneficiaries, see "Naming Your Heirs" and "Establishing Trusts" in Chapter 16, *Wills and Estates*.

Can I name anyone I choose to be a beneficiary of an insurance policy on my life?

Yes. However, if you want a child to get the proceeds of your life insurance policy, you may wish to establish a trust as the beneficiary and name a trustee or guardian to manage the money until the child reaches adulthood.

If someone who owns a life insurance policy dies, and the beneficiary is also dead, who gets the proceeds?

The proceeds are paid to the insured person's estate and then distributed, either according to the insured's will or according to provincial laws if the insured died without a will. To prevent your life insurance from going to someone you didn't select, you can add contingent (alternative) beneficiaries to your policy.

Beneficiaries

Richard owes his friend Ellen $10,000. Can Ellen take out a policy on Richard's life naming herself as beneficiary?

Yes. Ellen has what is known legally as an insurable interest in Richard in the amount of $10,000. To have an insurable interest in someone means that, if the person died, you would be harmed in some way or suffer some kind of loss. Ellen could lose $10,000 if Richard died and his estate did not have enough money to pay her and other creditors. The legal concept of insurable interest also applies to a close relative whose death would

If You Are a Life Insurance Beneficiary

In most cases, it is a simple process to collect the benefits to which you are entitled under a deceased person's life insurance policy. Inform the company that issued the policy, or its agent, of the insured person's death. The company will send you the necessary forms and instructions for submitting your claim. Complete the forms and return them by certified mail, along with any documents that the company may request, such as the death certificate and the policy itself. If you cannot find the policy, notify the insurance company, and it will send you a lost-policy receipt.

Before paying, the insurance company will probably ask you to choose between several settlement options. The lump sum option pays in one cheque. Under the interest, or deposit, option, all the money is left with the company until a later time, and only the interest earned on that amount is paid to the beneficiary for the time being. Under the fixed, or installment, option, the money is left with the company, where it earns interest, and is paid out in fixed amounts to the beneficiary until it is all disbursed.

Sometimes—for example, when the insured person died during the contestable period (usually two years after purchasing the policy)— the company may delay paying. If you are notified that your claim is being investigated, you can help yourself by (1) finding out the claim number that the company has assigned to your case and using the number in all contacts with the company; (2) keeping a log of all telephone calls (including the dates and times of the calls), the names of persons to whom you spoke, and the substance of your discussions; (3) sending the company a letter that summarizes each phone conversation; and (4) keeping copies of all correspondence.

Not only will such records help you remember names, dates, and details, but they could also prove useful if you later feel you must take the matter to your federal or provincial superintendent of insurance or decide to challenge the insurance company's decision in court.

deprive the beneficiary of companionship and emotional support. Thus, ties such as a parent-child, brother-sister, and wife-husband are considered insurable interests.

Rhonda's uncle Ned died six months ago, and Rhonda thinks he named her as the beneficiary of his life insurance policy. She has heard nothing. What should she do?

Rhonda should ask to look through her uncle's cheque books and other financial records, contact his previous employers, and talk with family and friends to find out if her uncle had insurance. She may get some help from the Canadian Life and Health Insurance Association Inc., 20 Queen Street West, Suite 2500, Toronto, Ont., M5H 3S2. If there was an executor named for Uncle Ned's estate, she should contact him.

When Jessica and Nathan divorced, the court awarded Jessica the right to the proceeds of a life insurance policy Nathan had bought while they were still married. Jessica is afraid that Nathan will change his beneficiary. Can he do this?

This is one of the few situations in which the owner of a life insurance policy is severely restricted in controlling it. If Nathan tried to name a new beneficiary, and the court found out, he would probably be held in contempt of court, since the divorce decree gave Jessica the right to the proceeds of the policy. Furthermore, if Jessica was named as irrevocable beneficiary, Nathan couldn't name another beneficiary without her consent, nor could he cash in the policy or borrow against it. If he refused to pay the premiums and the policy lapsed, the court could order him to compensate Jessica for her financial loss.

My aunt named me a beneficiary of her life insurance. She died this month. Do I have to report the insurance proceeds on my income tax return?

No. The proceeds of a life insurance policy are not considered taxable income unless you paid the insured to name you as the beneficiary.

How does my last will and testament affect the disposition of my life insurance?

If you have named your estate as beneficiary of your life insurance proceeds, the money will be distributed according to the terms of your will. Otherwise, payment would not be affected by the will and in almost

Beneficiaries

all circumstances would be made directly to the beneficiary. For an exception to this, see the next question and answer.

Can a creditor claim the proceeds of a life insurance policy to cover unpaid debts?

Generally, the beneficiary of a life insurance policy receives the proceeds free of creditors' claims. However, if the insured person pledged the policy as collateral for a loan, the creditor would have a legal claim on the proceeds for the amount of the debt. If the insured person named his estate as the beneficiary, the proceeds would be used, like any other asset, to pay debts.

Paulette's husband disappeared three years ago. Can she have him declared legally dead so she can collect his life insurance?

To have her husband declared legally dead, Paulette must show he has been absent, without explanation, for a certain period of time, ranging from 4 to 10 years; most provinces set the period at 7 years. To check the requirement in her province, Paulette should contact her provincial attorney general's office. She must also show that she has made a diligent search for her husband.

If Paulette's husband disappeared in some disaster, such as an explosion, airplane crash or ship sinking, where it was impossible to find the body, she could ask the court for a declaration of death before the end of the usual 7-year waiting period.

Stella's husband, Trevor, had a terminal illness. He committed suicide to avoid a slow and painful death. The insurance company says that Stella cannot collect the proceeds from his life insurance. Is this true?

Not necessarily. So long as there is no clause in the policy that specifically excludes coverage in the event of suicide, the company is required to pay, with one possible exception. If Trevor died before the end of the policy's contestable period, the company can contest its obligation to pay. During the contestable period, which usually lasts two years after the purchase of the policy, the company can investigate the insured to verify the information on his application. If, in the case of a suicide, the insurance company should discover a history of mental illness that was not reported by the insured, this omission could be legal grounds for refusing to pay on the policy.

Health and Disability Insurance ▬▬▬▬▬

For more on medical charges, see "Paying the Bills" in Chapter 14, *Your Medical Rights*.

My insurance agent suggested that I take out a health insurance policy. Since I'm covered under Medicare, wouldn't a health insurance policy be an unnecessary expense?

No. The government health insurance plan covers most expenses, such as those for surgery, basic hospitalization and many medications, but does not cover all costs of illness or accident. For example, a private health insurance plan might provide you with a private room in hospital and a private nurse, may pay for certain drugs that are not covered by the government plan, and may even provide some income during your period of convalescence. You should discuss the advantages of a private health insurance policy with your agent or broker to find out what benefits are available and at what cost.

Can my private medical insurance be canceled if I get sick?

No. Illness is not a valid reason for an insurance company to cancel your medical insurance. If your policy is guaranteed renewable, the company cannot refuse to renew your policy when its term is over.

Kevin wants to make sure that his health insurance policy won't be canceled. Are such policies available?

Yes. Kevin could buy an individual policy that is noncancelable during its term of coverage and guaranteed renewable at the end of the term. These policies will cover Kevin to a particular age, or for life. If Kevin opts for enrollment in a group health insurance plan through his employer or an organization to which he belongs, he cannot lose his coverage unless the insurance company cancels its policy for the entire group.

Four months ago, Rhoda took out a health insurance policy. When she turned in a claim for treatment of her bad back, the company refused to pay because it was a preexisting condition. How can they do this?

Most individual health insurance policies exclude coverage for preexisting conditions. A preexisting condition is a health problem that began before you bought the insurance policy. If Rhoda previously suffered from a bad back, the company probably has the right to refuse her claim. If Rhoda had a group policy, her preexisting condition would have been covered. If, on the other hand, Rhoda is maintaining that her current back problem does not stem from a preexisting condition, and she cannot settle the matter with her insurance company, she should get in touch with the Insurance Bureau of Canada, which has offices in most provinces. She can also, as her policy probably explains, ask that the question in dispute be settled by arbitration. If the company refuses to put the question to an arbitrator, Rhoda should consult a lawyer to find out if she can do anything else.

Is it legal for an insurance company to reject me for a health policy because I may have had a certain serious disease?

Yes. It is not against the law for an insurance company to decline to sell health insurance to a person who has had a particular disease. However, if you are rejected by one company on the basis of your medical condition or history, another company might very well accept you.

Emma has seen advertisements for policies that cover specific diseases. Should she think about purchasing one?

Most experts on health and medical insurance consider the so-called dread disease policies a poor value because they have high premiums and usually cover a person for just one disease, such as cancer. Before buying such a policy, Emma should carefully weigh its coverage and cost against more traditional policies, such as a comprehensive policy that includes extended health insurance and income replacement insurance.

Tom asked his insurance agent if he should include a one-day hospital stay, three years earlier, on his application for extended health benefits. The agent said, "Don't worry about it." Six months later, Tom required major surgery. The insurance company refused to pay for a private nurse, claiming that Tom had lied on his application. Does the company have legal grounds for not paying?

Tom has been the victim of a practice known as clean-sheeting, in which an agent knowingly leaves out health information that may result in an application's rejection, because it would prevent the agent from earning a commission. Tom's insurance company can claim that he attempted to defraud them, because he signed and verified the application. However, since the company's agent knowingly submitted the incorrect application, a court may rule that the insurance company cannot use the application to deny coverage.

Do I need disability insurance if I have a steady, full-time job?

Most insurance experts recommend it strongly. Disability insurance provides benefits while you are unable to work because of illness or an accident. Workers' compensation and other government programs may not be available to you or adequate for your needs.

My father saw a television commercial stating that anyone over 65 years old can get a health insurance policy without a physical exam, and the policy can't be canceled for any reason. Is there a catch to this?

Yes. The catch to many of these policies is that there is a long period (sometimes as much as two years) before your coverage actually begins. Additionally, this type of policy is usually expensive, and the benefits are sometimes inadequate.

Is it possible to keep my group medical insurance coverage after I quit my job—or even if I'm fired?

As a general rule, no. Group insurance is one of the fringe benefits offered by an employer, or bargained for by a union, and available only to members of a specific group. Once you leave this group, the policy is usually no longer in effect for you or your dependents. Each group plan is different, however, and some will guarantee coverage during a layoff or for a period after one has voluntarily quit the job. In some cases, there is an option of converting a group policy into an individual one. Ask your union leader or personnel manager for more information about your particular group plan, or ask the insurance company for a copy of the master policy to check out the terms yourself.

Jane has dental insurance for her $5,000 dental surgery bill. However, six months have passed, and the insurance company has not paid. The dental surgeon is now suing Jane. Is it legal for him to do this when Jane is clearly not at fault?

Yes. The dental surgeon has the right to sue Jane because it is her bill that remains unpaid, regardless of who is supposed to pay it. Jane should contact an attorney and ask that the insurance company be named as a defendant in the lawsuit. If the insurance company does not have a valid reason for not paying the bill, Jane can request that the company be ordered to pay her legal fees as well as punitive damages as a penalty for acting in bad faith. In most cases, an insurance company must pay within 60 days of receiving a claim and any necessary documentation.

Health and Disability Insurance

Sue was injured in a car accident in which the other driver was at fault. Her insurance paid the medical bills not covered by Medicare. In her settlement with the other driver's automobile insurance company, she was paid for pain and suffering and those additional medical expenses. Does she have to reimburse her own insurance company?

Yes. Sue's insurance policy probably has a subrogation clause, which means that her insurance company, once it has paid Sue's medical expenses, has the right to recover those expenses from the other driver's insurance company. Sue's insurance company does not have a claim on the money she was awarded for pain and suffering. If Sue lived in a

The ABC's of Disability Coverage

The purpose of disability insurance is to provide income if you cannot work for an extended time because you are seriously ill or injured. Insurance companies generally insure you for up to two thirds of your gross salary. Some key points to remember when you are considering disability insurance include:

- The definition of disability can vary considerably from company to company. Most experts say the best policies are those that define disability as being unable to perform in your *usual occupation,* not just inability to perform any job.
- Depending on the policy, benefits can start anywhere from a week to more than a year after you are disabled. The longer the waiting period, the lower your premiums should be.
- The period of time in which benefits are paid varies with the company and the policy. Some policies cover only 13 weeks of disability, while others pay until your 65th birthday, or even for life.
- Many companies offer noncancelable and guaranteed renewable coverage. Ask for it.
- The best policies include coverage for disability from both accidents and sickness; watch out for those that don't.
- You may already have some form of disability insurance, from your employer or union. Furthermore, if you suffer a physical or mental impairment, prolonged and severe enough to prevent you from doing *any* work, you may become eligible for a Canada Pension Plan, or a Quebec Pension Plan, disability pension.
- Some companies offer a rider called a cost of living benefit (for which you pay more), under which the amount you are paid if you become disabled may be increased to offset the effect of inflation.

province that has some form of no-fault automobile insurance, such as Manitoba, Saskatchewan and British Columbia, her insurance company would have no claim on the money she received from that province's insurance plan. In the case of Quebec motorists, bodily injuries that are caused by automobile accidents are entirely paid for by the Quebec Automobile Insurance Board.

I've heard alcoholism referred to as an illness. Does this mean it would normally be covered under a general health policy?

Most health insurance plans include coverage for the treatment of mental health problems and alcohol and drug abuse. However, many policies cover only short hospital stays (or none at all) and limit payments for outpatient treatment.

Marty is now clear of all signs of cancer, but no company will give him insurance for extended health benefits. Is this legal?

Yes, but Marty should not give up trying. If he is no longer in treatment, he may be able to buy insurance coverage at a higher rate, or he may be able to buy a policy that will begin after a six-month to one-year waiting period. Marty should contact a knowledgeable broker or agent who may be able to find coverage for him.

Gus and Trudy's son was treated for dyslexia by a specialist in the United States. Neither Medicare nor their private insurance plan will reimburse the doctor's fee. What can Gus and Trudy do?

Gus and Trudy should have a lawyer review their extended health benefits policy to verify that treatment for dyslexia is excluded. If it is not, the lawyer will demand a review by the insurer's legal department. If the company claims that the treatment is experimental, is an unacceptable medical practice, or is not medically necessary, Gus and Trudy may have to sue to compel the company to pay.

Insuring Your Home

For information on title insurance, see "Buying Your Home" in Chapter 4, *Your Home.*

How much homeowners insurance should I buy?

Many experts advise homeowners to insure their homes for 100 percent of the replacement value, but 80 percent is often considered full

Insuring Your Home

coverage—because even if your home burns to the ground, you will not have to replace the foundation, the basement, and the land on which the house stood. Your replacement cost may be greater than the purchase price you paid for your home, or greater than its current value. You can hire a professional appraiser or work with your insurance company to determine the replacement cost.

If you wish to insure the contents of your home at their replacement value, you will want to think about purchasing a replacement cost endorsement. Without the endorsement, you will probably recover only the actual value (replacement cost less depreciation) of your home's contents in the event of a loss.

In buying homeowners insurance, as in making most purchases, the more you pay, the more you get. For example, a policy that insures you against a greater number of perils costs more than one that covers fewer perils. Most policies are issued for one or three years, with a discount from the full annual premium usually available on the three-year policy. At renewal time, you may change the amount of insurance you carry to reflect the new value of your house.

Hal and Linda's house is worth $100,000. Their agent advised them to insure it for $120,000 with replacement cost insurance. A fire destroyed the house. How much must the company pay?

The insurance company is obligated to pay all the costs necessary to restore the house up to, but not exceeding, $120,000. If the costs are only $110,000, this is all the insurance must pay. Hal and Linda will not get a $10,000 bonus for overinsuring their house. Were that true, the temptation to commit arson would be very great.

If I take out two policies on my house, can I collect from both if something happens?

No. Most homeowners policies exclude double coverage so that you cannot collect twice for one loss.

Carolyn has decided to rent a small house. What type of insurance should she purchase to protect her furniture and other personal property after she moves in?

The standard tenant's policy will protect most of Carolyn's personal property from losses due to fire or lightning and many other common perils. Carolyn may wish to purchase specific coverage for certain items

INSURANCE

of personal property that are only partially covered under the basic standard policy. This kind of coverage, which can be added to a standard policy in the form of attached statements called floaters, is often used for jewelry, furs, cameras, musical instruments, artwork, antiques, deeds, stocks and bonds, and stamp and coin collections.

I am going overseas for six months. If I rent my house to another family, will my homeowners policy cover accidents, theft, or damage during the rental period?

No. Property that you own and rent to another family is usually excluded from coverage under homeowners policies because those policies cover your residence. You may want to consider purchasing a policy designed to protect your property while it is rented.

A spark from the fireplace ignited Karen and Bob's living room carpet, causing a smoky fire, which the fire department had to put out. The smoke and water damage was extensive. Will their losses be covered by their homeowners insurance?

Yes. All standard homeowners policies cover losses due to hostile fires, which are defined as fires that are not where they are supposed to be. Damages due to friendly fires are not covered. Friendly fires are those burning where they are supposed to burn, for example in a fireplace. When the spark left the fireplace, it became a hostile fire. Smoke damage and losses caused by fire fighting, such as water damage, are also covered by the standard homeowners policy.

Our neighbors were burning leaves, and the sparks set our roof on fire. Our neighbors do not have insurance, but we do. Who should pay for the damage?

Your insurance company should pay you for the damage caused by fire. The company may then seek reimbursement from your neighbors, since they were responsible for the damage.

If my house is damaged by fire, and the repairs will not be completed for at least six months, does the insurance company have to pay me for the cost of temporary quarters until my home is made livable again?

Homeowners policies usually cover the additional living expenses that you incur while your home is being repaired (up to 10 or 20 percent of the coverage on your house). If you are living in a motel and must eat all your meals in a restaurant, the company will pay the amount in excess of your usual housing and food costs.

Some insurance companies will advance funds so you don't go into debt for living expenses while waiting for the final settlement cheque. However, some companies will reimburse you for these costs only when the repairs are complete. This can pose a big problem if the repairs take a long time. Some families rent trailers or move in with relatives to keep their expenses down.

Victor's roof was damaged in a hailstorm. His insurance company is rejecting his claim because his premium payment was overdue. What can Victor do?

If Victor's roof was damaged while the payment was overdue, his coverage lapsed, so he'll have to pay for the expenses himself. If the damage occurred after the company accepted his late payment and reinstated his coverage, the insurance company must pay his claim. If, however, Victor was not notified in writing (before the loss) that his premium was late, or if the insurance company had in the past accepted late payments and kept the policy in force, Victor would have a good chance of winning his claim if he sued the company.

If Conrad's home is damaged by a flood, will his homeowners policy cover his losses?

If bursting pipes caused the flood, many home insurance policies would cover the damage. If the flood was from natural forces such as a heavy rainfall, the answer is probably no. Every standard homeowners policy excludes this type of flood damage from its coverage. However, for an extra premium, some insurance companies will cover flood damage from natural causes.

Quite often, when there is major widespread flooding because of a natural event such as heavy rainfall or a river overflowing its banks, the provincial or federal government will provide some financial assistance to victims to help offset their losses.

Our second car was not being driven; so we stopped insuring it. A tree fell on it while it was in our driveway. Will our homeowners insurance pay for the damage?

No. Homeowners policies usually exclude cars from coverage.

Insuring Personal Property

For information about personal property, see Chapter 5, *Your Personal Property.*

I lost a valuable ring. Will my insurance company pay for it?

The company will pay only if the ring is specifically covered by a floater policy. Standard homeowners policies usually do not cover the loss or the unexplained disappearance of a piece of jewelry, although there is limited coverage when valuable jewelry is stolen. With floater insurance, you can protect valuable property such as jewelry and artwork. For each item covered, you must give a specific description and value. A bill of sale or professional appraisal is usually required to prove the item's value. Floater insurance covers mysterious disappearance and loss as well as theft.

George recently inherited his grandfather's stamp collection. Should he have it valued separately on his insurance policy?

Since the standard homeowners policy offers limited protection, George should purchase a floater policy to protect the collection for its full value. He would have to have the stamp collection appraised by a professional stamp dealer, and should have it reappraised—and reinsured—annually, since the value can change dramatically from year to year.

Will floater insurance cover a guest's personal property?

No. Floater insurance covers only the items specifically described and valued by the policyholder. However, if you have standard homeowners insurance, it may cover the loss of a guest's personal property. Check the terms of your policy.

To what extent would my homeowners insurance reimburse me if a thief stole my jewelry or other personal property?

Most homeowners policies will cover losses if your house is burglarized or if property is stolen from a temporary residence, such as a motel or dormitory room or other place you stay outside your home. Many homeowners policies also cover thefts from your automobile if there is evidence, such as a broken window or door, that your car was entered by force. Standard homeowners policies do not cover the theft of credit cards, but you can add this coverage to your policy, usually for a few extra dollars. None of these policies covers the loss of cash. Generally homeowners policies limit coverage for loss or theft of jewelry to a maximum of $1,000. If your jewelry or art is worth more, it should be appraised and insured separately. The premium for such insurance can be expensive.

Most homeowners policies cover the homeowner and members of the household. If you don't have a homeowners policy, some insurers will sell you a policy to cover your losses due to theft. If you have floater coverage for specifically listed items, the theft of these items is covered as well.

No company will give me theft coverage because I live in what is reputed to be a high-crime area. Isn't this discrimination?

No. Insurance companies are in business to make a profit and those you have approached have obviously calculated that the risks against them are too high. Their refusal to cover you would not be discrimination, since it is not turning *you* down, but turning down an unacceptable risk. If, on the other hand, a company refuses to insure you because of your race, national origin, sex, politics or religion, then such practices *would* be discriminatory.

While I was in the dentist's chair, someone took my mink coat from the outer room. Can I recover from my insurance company?

Most likely. Your homeowners policy will cover the theft of your personal property while you are away from home. Unless the coat was brand-new, you will be reimbursed for the replacement cost of the coat, less depreciation. If the coat was several years old, you may not receive very much from your insurance company. Often, however, furs and jewelry must be appraised and insured separately.

Jan left her pocketbook in the car while she ran into the nursery school to pick up her child. Will her insurance cover the loss if her purse is stolen?

Many insurance companies require evidence of forced entry into an automobile before they will cover the loss of property. If the thief broke a window or lock to get to Jan's purse, the company will cover the loss. If the thief opened an unlocked door, the company may refuse to pay. However, even if the insurance company agrees to pay, money and credit cards are usually not covered. And it can be difficult to put a value on personal papers and such items as a driver's license or a Medicare card. Also, there is often a deductible amount in an insurance policy, so that the first $200 of a loss, for instance, might not be covered.

When Clara's home was burglarized, the thieves broke a window and ransacked the house. Will the damage to her home be covered by her homeowners insurance?

Yes. Standard homeowners policies cover vandalism and malicious mischief in addition to theft.

After Jim's house was burglarized, the insurance adjuster valued everything as if it were scrap. Jim wants full value so that he can replace the stolen items with new ones. Who is correct?

Neither Jim nor the adjuster. Unless Jim had a replacement cost endorsement on his homeowners policy, he is not entitled to the full cost of replacing all his stolen items with new ones. Jim is entitled to the actual cash value of the lost property, which is usually defined as the replacement value of each item, less depreciation.

Documenting Your Personal Property

If your home is struck by fire or burglarized, you'll be better off if you have taken the time to prepare a room-by-room, itemized inventory of the contents of your house and, in doing so, marked valuable items with an identifying number. The inventory will help substantiate your claims for personal property losses under your homeowners insurance policy and the identifying numbers will prove your ownership. Here are specific how-to suggestions:

- For each item in your inventory, give all the pertinent information available, including its manufacturer and its serial number, if it has one. A physical description (size, color, etc.) or a photograph could turn out to be extremely useful if the item is destroyed. Keep a copy of this list in a safe-deposit box; update it as necessary, at least every few years.

- Keep all proofs of ownership (warranties, receipts, bills of sale). If you have very valuable items, such as jewelry, works of art, or antiques, get written appraisals of their value, and update them every few years.

- If you have valuable items that you don't need or use at home, keep them in a safe-deposit box.

- Put your social insurance number or driver's license number on your property so you can identify it if it is recovered after a burglary. Many police departments will lend you the marking and etching equipment.

- Shoot a videotape showing the contents of each room. If you don't own a video camera and cannot borrow or rent one, try to find a company or individual offering such a videotaping service.

Insuring Personal Property

A burglar entered our house through a window I left open. Will I be able to collect insurance in spite of my negligence?

It depends on the terms of your homeowners policy. Some policies specify that there must be visible evidence that a burglar had to use force in order to enter your home. If your policy contains such a provision, you may not be able to collect insurance. Such conditions, however, are rare. Insurance companies generally pay, even if you were negligent. Sometimes they pay even when the insured person was responsible for the loss through deliberate carelessness.

If my home is burglarized and I don't have receipts or an appraisal for all the items, how will the insurance company establish what it will pay me?

Most insurance companies have tables to help them arrive at standard depreciation values for personal property. It will be a fairly simple task to determine the replacement cost of each item and then subtract the depreciation value to arrive at the actual cash value.

If you believe that the amount the insurance company comes up with is too low, you may refuse the settlement and negotiate further with the insurance company. Your policy probably allows for any disagreement to be settled by arbitration. In some cases it may be necessary to sue the insurance company for breach of contract, but there is always a waiting period of about 60 days before you are allowed to do so.

Will a homeowners policy cover property that is stolen or missing if I rent out my home?

No. Homeowners policies do not cover dwellings that are being rented to others; neither do they cover the property left in those dwellings. What you need to get is a multiperil policy; with it the house you rent out will be covered for fire and other losses, and you will have medical and liability coverage for persons injured on the premises.

My insurance company refuses to compensate me for property stolen from my house. What can I do?

First find out why the insurance company is not cooperating. If it requires proof of loss, you can use photographs, receipts, warranties, canceled cheques, credit card statements, and witnesses to prove you owned the property you lost. If the insurance company does not believe that the property was stolen, use the police investigation report to substantiate your claim. If, despite all this, the insurance company continues to refuse payment that is clearly due to you under your policy, you may sue for breach of contract.

My home was burglarized. After my insurance company paid my claim, the police recovered my stolen property. Will I have to repay the company?

Yes. You are not allowed to keep both the property and the money that the insurance company paid you for the loss of the property. That would be paying you for something you hadn't lost. Some policies require that you purchase items similar to the ones stolen, and the insurance company pays the store and not you. In any case, if the stolen goods are recovered after your claim has been settled, you could choose to have your property returned to you and pay back the insurance company, or stick with your settlement and let the insurance company keep what was once your property. This is usually referred to as salvage.

Liability for Personal Injury

If a pedestrian trips and falls over the buckled sidewalk in front of my house, and suffers broken teeth and glasses, will my homeowners insurance pay his dental bills and buy new glasses?

Yes, up to the limits stated in your policy. However, because an injured person's claims may exceed the limits of a standard policy, some homeowners purchase additional medical insurance or an umbrella policy that offers up to $1 million or more of protection for situations like the one you describe. If the sidewalk belongs to the municipality where you live and is not your private property, you would not be responsible.

Mildred hired Tommy, the 15-year-old son of a neighbor, to mow her lawn and do other odd jobs around her house and grounds. What kind of insurance should Mildred have in case Tommy is injured on her property?

Mildred's standard homeowners policy will cover a limited amount of expenses if Tommy is injured on her property. If Tommy's injuries are Mildred's fault, she may be personally liable for expenses that exceed her policy limits. Since jury awards for impairment and for pain and suffering frequently amount to tens of thousands of dollars, Mildred should consider purchasing an umbrella policy to supplement her insurance. Umbrella policies usually give up to $1 million or more of liability protection. If Tommy works for Mildred on a regular basis, several days a week, Mildred's homeowners policy will not cover her if Tommy is injured on the job; she should talk with her insurance agent or broker about the possibility of other coverage.

The owner of the house next door was injured while swimming in my pool while I was away for the weekend. Do I have to pay his wheelchair rental bill?

If you invited him, you are not liable for injuries he received while using your swimming pool unless there was an extremely dangerous condition in the pool that was hidden in some way. If your neighbor was using your pool without your permission, you are liable only if you caused his injury by doing something extremely reckless or malicious, like having broken glass all around the pool.

The law is somewhat different if a child sneaks into your pool and injures himself. Legally, your pool is considered an attractive nuisance, and you can be held liable unless you have made an effort to keep children from using it, such as by putting a fence around the pool. It is not a good idea to allow children to use your pool while you are away, since you may be charged with negligence if you are not there to supervise the children and make sure they follow basic safety rules.

Should I report all injuries or property damage at my home to my insurance company?

Yes. Most policies require that you report all losses or possible claims immediately. Check your homeowners policy to find out the time limits for reporting injury or damage. If you wait until someone injured on your property says you are responsible for paying his bills, you may find that your homeowners policy will not cover the claim.

A friend invited me to take the wheel of his high-powered cabin cruiser, and I did. What if I had caused an accident?

If you have an umbrella policy, it would probably cover your liability for personal injuries while skippering the boat. However, umbrella policies have large deductibles, and they don't cover all watercraft. If your friend invites you again, ask him if his insurance policy covers guests who operate the boat at his invitation. If it doesn't, don't play skipper.

Diane just bought a boat. Does she need to buy a special policy?

Diane should buy a policy that covers damage to her boat and liability as well. Some experts advise purchasing $300,000 worth of standard coverage plus an umbrella policy for further protection against catastrophic, high-liability situations.

Insuring Your Car ▰▰▰▰▰▰▰▰

For information on who is liable in an automobile accident, see "Liability for Automobile Accidents" in Chapter 6, *Your Car.*

What kinds of insurance do I need for my car?

Every province and Territory requires that car owners carry liability insurance, which covers damage that you cause while driving your car, whether it is an injury to a person or damage to another's property. Umbrella policies can be purchased to augment your auto liability coverage.

You may buy collision and comprehensive protection as well. Collision covers losses to your car due to your own negligence, such as backing into a telephone pole. Comprehensive is a catchall term that means you have coverage against theft, vandalism, storms, fire, falling or hurtling objects, explosion, earthquake, flood, riot, and collisions with wildlife. Some people choose to forgo collision and comprehensive coverage if they drive an old car with little value. You may also buy uninsured motorist coverage. This covers accidents in which you cannot recover from the driver who is at fault because he is uninsured or underinsured, or because he drove off and cannot be identified.

What is no-fault insurance?

No-fault insurance is a system in which people involved in accidents are paid for their injuries by their own insurance companies. The system is called no-fault to contrast it with the traditional system, in which the person at fault and his insurance company are legally required to compensate all others involved in the accident. Thus the traditional, or fault, system has led to the payment of some huge awards by one driver and his insurance company.

Under the fault system, the victim or victims of a negligent driver can collect for damages, medical expenses, lost wages, and pain and suffering from the negligent driver's insurance company. The major issue in a fault system is establishing negligence, and this can involve many months or years of legal arguments and court proceedings.

Under the no-fault system, the victim of a negligent driver is restricted to recovering his medical expenses and a percentage of his lost earnings from his own insurance company. The victim is not compensated for his pain and suffering, although some no-fault programs allow lawsuits for pain and suffering. Under the no-fault system, the negligent driver also collects from his own insurance company. British Columbia, Saskatchewan, Manitoba and Quebec have some form of no-fault automobile insurance under which the provincial government compensates accident victims. In the three western provinces, such victims may sue the negligent driver, but only for losses exceeding those not covered by the provincial government. In Quebec, where the government pays a twice-monthly pension for bodily injury and loss of income, the victim has no right to sue. The Quebec plan pays the victim 90 percent of his gross salary, but only up to a maximum gross salary of $36,500 (1988). With this ceiling, compensation is often much less than the victim's actual loss.

Ernest says auto insurance is a waste of money for his 11-year-old station wagon, and he's going to stop paying for insurance on the car. Can he do this?

If he intends to drive his car anywhere, Ernest is obliged to carry liability insurance which covers him for damages he may cause to other people. Driving without such insurance is an offense and could result in fines or loss of driving privileges. On the other hand, if Ernest wants to stop insuring his own vehicle, he is free to do so. In fact, this may be a good idea if the value of his 11-year-old car is not much higher than the amount of his deductible ($250 or more) added to the cost of his annual premium for collision and comprehensive coverage.

Are there guidelines that will help me decide how much insurance coverage I need?

All provinces have laws that state the minimum amount of liability insurance you must carry. However, the minimum amount may not afford you adequate protection if you are involved in an accident. Most experts advise that you carry at least 100/300/50 liability coverage. This means up to $100,000 for each injury with a maximum amount of $300,000 per accident, and $50,000 to cover property damage in an accident. If you buy an umbrella policy as well, it will provide $1 million or more of liability protection.

The amount of collision and comprehensive damage you should carry depends on the value of your car. Because of the decline in the car's value, some experts advise car owners to drop their collision and comprehensive coverage if the car is more than five years old.

Finally, you may be offered uninsured motorist or hit-and-run coverage to pay certain medical bills if you are struck by either an uninsured or a hit-and-run driver. Before you decide to purchase this type of coverage, check the health and disability coverage that you already have. Such coverage may be adequate. Most provinces also automatically provide some form of compensation for victims of unidentified or uninsured drivers.

What will happen if someone sues me for a great deal more than I am insured for?

If someone successfully sues you for an amount that exceeds your policy limits, you will be held personally liable for payment of the difference between the amount of money the court awards and your insurance coverage. This means that the person who wins the lawsuit has a claim on your personal assets.

If you check the cost of increasing your coverage, you might be surprised to find that the difference in premium for $200,000 in liability insurance and that for $500,000 is very small. Since most accidents involve less than $200,000, the risk that an insurance company will have to pay $500,000 or $1 million is relatively low, so the cost of this increased coverage is usually affordable. Consider taking out insurance for $300,000 to $500,000, if only for the peace of mind you can have knowing you are well insured.

While Sara was waiting at a stop sign, another driver hit her from the rear, throwing her young son into the dashboard. The insurance company refuses to pay the boy's dental bills because he was not wearing a seat belt. Must the insurance company pay?

Yes. Since the cause of Sara's son's injury was the other driver's negligence, not the fact that her son was not wearing a seat belt, the insurance company must pay Sara.

Denise was involved in a serious accident. Does the fact that she lives in a province that has no-fault insurance mean Denise can't sue the other driver, even though he ran a red light?

Depending on her province's no-fault laws, Denise may be able to sue the other driver. Many no-fault insurance laws allow the victim of a negligent driver to sue for negligence in certain circumstances, such as if death, disfigurement, or a permanent disability resulted from the accident. In British Columbia, Saskatchewan and Manitoba, where there is a form of no-fault insurance administered by the government, a victim can sue for compensation for bodily injury and for the amount of lost income not covered by the government fund. In Quebec, a victim cannot sue the driver at fault.

Is there a limit on no-fault insurance payments?

Under some no-fault plans, payment for expenses and lost wages is limited to a set amount, which can be as low as $2,000. To recover losses above this amount, the injured person must file a lawsuit against the other driver, just as in the fault system. Under other no-fault plans, an injured person may recover up to the limits in his policy. Government-administered no-fault plans also set limits. In Quebec, for example, the maximum compensation for bodily injury in 1988 was $41,059.61 and the maximum annual payment for loss of salary was 90 percent of $36,500. These amounts are adjusted annually according to the cost of living.

When a front wheel fell off Mary's car, it ran off the road. She has collision but not comprehensive coverage. Does her insurance company have to pay for the damage to her car?

It depends. Since Mary's car collided with something (the road, a sidewalk, a tree), her insurance company should pay. It may, however, try to argue that Mary was not involved in a collision in the usual sense, since the cause of her accident was the wheel falling off her car. If Mary cannot settle with her insurance company, she can sue. The judge will probably use a dictionary definition of "collision" in deciding her case.

Can I collect insurance for an accident or damage from poorly maintained roads, such as ones with potholes?

If you have comprehensive coverage, your policy may cover damage to your car from potholes. However, your policy may have a deductible, which would require you to absorb all costs under a specified amount, let's say $250 (it could be much more). If you hit a pothole and the resulting damage to your car cost $400, you could collect only $150 from your insurance company, since you are responsible for the first $250 in damage. In this case, you could probably sue the city or town for the deductible amount: cities and towns are obliged to maintain their roads in good condition. But check with City Hall immediately after the accident, because the rules for suing a municipality are very strict. Usually, for example, you would have to send a written notice within 15 days of your accident, or you would lose all rights to sue.

***My car was stolen and recovered later in another city. Will my
insurance company pay to transport it back and have it repaired?***

Yes, if you have comprehensive coverage that protects you against all
damages related to a car theft. Transportation and repair costs, in this
case, are considered damages caused by theft. However, some policies
specifically exclude the cost of transportation.

Is my insurance in effect if I drive in another country?

Many automobile insurance policies give coverage while you are driving
in another country. Before leaving on your trip, check with your broker
or read your policy carefully to make sure this coverage is not excluded.
If the coverage is excluded, you can purchase travel insurance that will
cover you.

***My son is under 18 years of age. If he has an accident, will my
insurance cover the liability?***

Probably, if your son still lives at home. Most automobile insurance
policies extend liability protection to all relatives who live in the
insured's household. Most provinces require that this coverage be
included in every automobile insurance policy.

***If I have an accident and the other driver is at fault, is his
insurance company obliged to pay for a rental car while mine is
being repaired?***

Yes. Most liability insurance policies will cover some of the extra
expenses resulting from your accident, provided they are reasonable.
The expenses associated with being without your car are called consequential damages.

***Will Griffith's insurance cover him if he has an accident while he
is driving a rental car?***

Probably. Most policies cover a person while driving a rented car under
the "use of other automobiles" clause. However, some policies specifically exclude coverage for property damage by the driver of a rental car.
If Griffith's policy excludes this coverage, he should read his rental
agreement; many rental fees include the cost of insurance coverage. For
an additional fee, Griffith may purchase insurance through the rental
company. This is usually called the collision damage waiver. Most

umbrella policies cover the use of rental cars as well. But Griffith should be sure to check the amount of the deductible, the amount his insurance will not pay in case of an accident. When it comes to use of a rental car, the deductible can sometimes be as much as $2,000, in which case Griffith should take out separate insurance.

If someone destroys my car and the insurance cheque does not completely pay off my car loan at the bank, can the other person be required to pay the balance of my loan?

Probably. If you live in a no-fault province, your insurance company will reimburse you for the value of your car, but it is not required to pay the balance of your car loan. You will probably be obliged to sue the other driver for the amount of loss not covered by the insurance.

In a province without the no-fault system, when you accept a cheque from the negligent driver's insurance company, you are usually required to sign a release forgoing further claims. Once you have settled your claim, you may not later ask for more money to cover your car loan.

James had a 1957 Thunderbird in mint condition. Another driver hit it from the rear, causing damage amounting to an estimated $2,500. The insurance company says the value of the car is only $1,000 and refuses to pay more. How can this be right?

The insurance company is trying to declare James's car a total loss. A car is totaled if the cost of repairs exceeds the value of the car prior to the accident. To arrive at car values, most insurance companies use published guides, which can usually be consulted at public libraries or at car dealers. If James can prove that the actual value of his car is more than $2,500, he has the right to insist on payment sufficient to restore his car to its condition before the accident. If he cannot prove that its actual value is more than the guidebook figure, the insurance company can declare the car a total loss and limit its payment to $1,000.

Owners of similar cars can buy a special type of insurance if their cars are considered "antique" or "classic" autos. For an additional premium James might have had his car insured above the usual book value.

Is it legal for my insurance company to cancel my policy if I am involved in an accident?

Yes, if that's what your policy says—but it must first cover the losses incurred in the accident. If your insurance policy does not say anything about cancellation in the event of an accident, the company cannot cancel your policy. However, it can decline to renew your policy when it expires.

If I don't report an accident and later get sued, will my insurance cover me if I lose the lawsuit?

Many insurance policies require you to report accidents, losses, and possible claims within a specified time. Check your policy. Your insurance company may be able to use your failure to report the accident as grounds for not paying claims arising from the accident.

There is another reason to report accidents immediately. It is easier for your insurance company to investigate the accident, contact witnesses, and prepare a defense for you immediately after the accident.

If I have an accident and am at fault, can I pay the other person directly and not report it to my insurance company?

It is not illegal, but it is extremely risky. If the other driver later discovers more damage to his property or greater personal injury, he may then decide to file a lawsuit against you to get more money. Your insurance company may, at that point, decline to cover you because of your failure to comply with the reporting requirement stated in your policy.

Car Insurance Rates

Beryl's insurance company raised her rates after an accident that was not her fault. Is this legal?

Yes. Insurance companies may base their rates, in part, on the number of claims the insured makes, regardless of who was responsible for the damage or injury. Consequently, victims of hit-and-run drivers, vandals, and thieves often find their rates higher after turning in a claim.

If Jonathan's insurance company finds out that he has been charged with driving under the influence of alcohol, will his premiums go up?

Being charged with driving under the influence of alcohol will not affect Jonathan's auto insurance rates, but a conviction for this offense will cause him to be classified as a high-risk driver. His insurance company may then raise his premiums or refuse to renew his policy.

Car Insurance Rates

If I have an accident with only minor damage, would it be a good idea not to make a claim to avoid a rate increase or cancellation?

Perhaps, if you can be sure there is only minor damage. Insurance companies usually base premium increases on the number of chargeable claims made by a customer, rather than on the amount of any single claim. A chargeable claim is one for losses above a certain amount (usually $200 to $300). If you can afford to pay for the damage and if you

---

How Insurers Set Car Premiums

Automobile insurers commonly consider various factors when setting premium rates. The most important factor is the amount and type of coverage you select. If you carry comprehensive, collision, and uninsured motorist coverage in addition to a high level of liability insurance, your rates will be much higher than someone who carries only the minimum coverage required by law. If your policy has no deductibles or very low ones, your rates will be higher. Many people choose to reduce their premiums by carrying high deductibles. Among the additional criteria used by insurers are these:

- *Your Driving Record.* You'll pay higher premiums if your record shows moving violations, such as speeding. Some offenses, such as drunk driving, may cause your insurer not to renew your policy. If your license is suspended or revoked, your insurance can be canceled.

- *Your Claims.* Many insurance companies raise your rates in proportion to the number, not the dollar amount, of claims you submit. For example, if you have made several claims because of fender benders or vandalism, you may have to pay higher premiums than someone who actually received more money from the insurance company but submitted just one claim following a bad accident.

- *Your Car.* The more expensive your car, the higher the premium tends to be, as a general rule.

- *Your Age and Sex.* In many provinces, males under 25 years of age may be charged more than others for automobile insurance.

- *Your Address.* City dwellers sometimes pay higher rates than residents of rural areas.

- *Members of Your Household.* If you have teenage drivers in your family, your rates will be higher than those who don't.

- *Discounts.* Some companies may have discounts available for senior citizens, nondrinkers, and people who have not had an accident for many years. Most insurers also give two-car families a break by reducing the premium on the second car.

doubt that you'll be sued, it may be a good idea to avoid making a claim. However, if your policy requires you to report all accidents to the insurance company and you fail to comply, the company may use this as a valid reason to avoid paying later claims. You may be best advised to report the accident without making a claim.

While Wilma was shopping, her parked car was hit by another car. Her insurance company paid the damages, but then added a surcharge to her premium. Is this permitted?

Wilma should request an explanation from her insurance company. Usually, a surcharge is a one-time fee imposed on drivers who are at fault. Unless Wilma's manner of parking contributed to the accident, she was not at fault and should not have to pay the surcharge.

Hit-and-run and Uninsured Drivers

Stephanie was crossing the street on foot when she was struck by a hit-and-run driver. Her doctor has prescribed months of physiotherapy treatments. Who should be responsible for paying the physiotherapist's bills?

If Stephanie has insurance for extended health care benefits (which should cover injury from accidents) or hit-and-run and uninsured driver's coverage, these policies may cover physiotherapy treatments. In that case, these policies would pay her physiotherapy bills up to the policy limits. Since virtually all provinces, including British Columbia, Alberta, Saskatchewan, Manitoba, Quebec and Ontario, have a fund to pay the victims of hit-and-run or uninsured drivers, Stephanie should see if she qualifies for reimbursement from her province's fund. Another possibility is the crime victims indemnity fund, operated by all provinces and Territories. Stephanie might be eligible under this program since hit-and-run is a crime.

Shelly bought the maximum insurance coverage for her brand-new sports car. While waiting at a red light, she was struck from behind by Dave, whose old car has the minimum insurance coverage allowed. How can Shelly be properly compensated for her personal injuries and the damage to the car?

If Shelly lives in a no-fault province, she can collect from her own insurance company. If she lives in a province where the traditional fault system is in effect, she can also collect from her own company, depending on her medical and disability coverage and on whether she has uninsured motorist coverage. Although Dave was not actually uninsured, many insurance policies and some provincial laws, such as those in Ontario, provide that an underinsured driver is to be considered the same as an uninsured driver for purposes of collecting from one's own policy or from the provincial uninsured motorist fund. Finally, if Shelly wins a lawsuit and is awarded damages for her injuries in excess of Dave's insurance coverage, she can hold him personally liable for the difference. This means that Dave's assets (real estate, stocks and bonds, car, furniture, bank accounts, wages) can be used to compensate Shelly. Under Quebec's no-fault plan, Shelly would collect money to cover her property damage directly from her insurance company, and would receive compensation for bodily injury and loss of income from the Quebec Automobile Insurance Board. But she could not sue Dave.

I let my automobile insurance lapse because I drive my car so rarely. What happens if I decide to go for a short drive, have an accident and I don't have insurance?

If you caused the accident and have no insurance, you will be personally liable for the damages suffered by the others in the accident. This means that if a court orders you to pay the victims' expenses and damages, you will have to do so out of your own assets and income.

In most provinces, you could be subject to a fine, imprisonment, and the loss of your driving privileges if you operate a motor vehicle without liability insurance. Before getting your license back, you may be required to post a bond covering the other driver's damages and provide proof of insurance.

Jim's car was struck by a van that sped off before Jim could get its license number. His insurance company won't pay the claim. What are Jim's options?

If Jim's insurance policy covers him against uninsured and hit-and-run drivers, and his company doesn't seem to have a valid reason for refusing to pay his claim, he should sue the insurance company. If his province has a fund to cover damages resulting from hit-and-run drivers, he can apply to that fund for payment. He may also apply to the crime victims indemnity fund of his province for payment for loss of income and bodily injury and for part of the cost of his property damage. He should certainly have reported the incident to the police who may be able to trace the van. Once it was found, Jim would be able to sue the owner and driver.

INSURANCE

I was involved in an accident with someone who had no insurance. My insurance company fixed my car, but I had to pay the $250 deductible and rent a car. Can I recover my losses?

Yes. If the accident was the fault of the other driver, you can sue him in Small Claims Court for your deductible and the car rental fees. There is also the possibility that you may qualify for compensation from your province's uninsured motorist fund.

Adjusters and Settlements

Jeff filed a claim with his insurance company after a minor traffic accident. The company said it would send an adjuster to look at the damage. What does an insurance adjuster do?

Insurance adjusters are employed by insurance companies to investigate claims, establish the claims' value, and negotiate settlements. In Jeff's case, the adjuster will examine Jeff's car, give an opinion on how much repairs will cost, and offer Jeff a cheque in payment.

If Your Insurance Company Won't Pay a Claim

If your claim has been denied, and the insurance company has told you its decision is final, your reaction may be to get an attorney—and sue the company. First, however, you should ask yourself these questions: (1) Does the policy state that the claim should be covered? (2) Did you report the loss within the time limit allowed? (3) Did you make accurate and complete statements in your application? (4) If you are being sued, did you keep the company fully informed of all legal actions and notices and follow its instructions?

If you can answer yes to these questions, you are in a strong position to challenge the insurance company's denial of your claim. You should file a complaint with your superintendent of insurance and contact an attorney. Many provinces have laws that prohibit such unethical claims procedures as misrepresenting facts or policy provisions; failing to investigate or pay claims within a reasonable time; settling a claim for much less than a reasonable person would expect; and failing to promptly provide a reasonable explanation for denying a claim.

The Insurance Bureau of Canada, which has offices in all provinces, should also be told how your company has treated your claim. This bureau oversees and regulates about 90 percent of the insurance business of Canada.

INSURANCE

Adjusters and Settlements

After my accident, an insurance adjuster called and asked me to give my version of exactly what happened. Should I discuss the accident with him?

If your accident involved only property damage, and if you were insured, you may discuss the facts of the case with the adjuster to help speed your claim. But it is wiser not to discuss these matters over the phone; talk to the adjuster in person. Do not admit any liability or fault. If you or someone else was injured in the accident, contact an attorney before discussing the matter with anyone. In any case, you should act quickly, for continued refusal to discuss the accident with your insurance company's adjuster could be seen as a refusal to cooperate, which may make it difficult for you to collect. You may, if you wish, hire your own private adjuster at your own expense to verify the amount of property damage.

If Gary accepts the insurance company's cheque to settle his claim for a knee injury suffered in a car accident, can he get more money later if complications arise?

Probably not. Settlement cheques are usually presented after a release is signed. If Gary signs a release that says he is accepting the cheque in payment of all his claims, he gives up the right to pursue claims for injuries that he was not aware of at the time he signed. For this reason, it is best for Gary not to accept a settlement until he has consulted his physician and an attorney. This would not apply in Quebec, where a government fund pays the compensation for physical injury and for relapses and complications arising from an earlier automobile accident.

Should I sign a release or accept a settlement cheque for an automobile accident if I am pregnant?

No. Wait until your child is born to see if he has suffered any injuries from the accident. If you sign a release, you may give up the right to seek compensation for your child's injuries. If you must sign a release, it should be only after you have consulted a lawyer. He could draw up a release that would protect your right to claim for possible damages to your unborn child.

However, even if you do sign the insurance company's release, your child could (with the help of parent, guardian or tutor) sue for compensation should he have any future problems arising from the accident. The law usually does not allow one person to sign away the rights of another without that other party's consent.

Is it legal for insurance investigators to question business associates and friends about my personal habits while trying to settle a claim for an accident I had?

Yes. Insurance adjusters may conduct investigations to verify the information you have given them regarding the accident or your injuries, or even on your application for insurance. In some cases, your personal habits are relevant to your claim or your application. For example, if you made false statements about your drinking habits in your application, the insurance company may have the right to void the policy and deny your claim.

Rupert's car was sideswiped by a truck, and the insurance adjuster has offered him $800 for the damage. Rupert does not think that's enough. How does he go about challenging the offer?

He should contact the adjuster's supervisor, or the insurance company's legal department, or its president. If he can't get these company officials to increase the payment, and Rupert still feels he is right, he should hire his own adjuster to see if in fact his damage toll is greater than the amount offered by his company's adjuster. Most insurance companies provide that matters in dispute be submitted for arbitration. If his own adjuster's estimate of damage is much greater than the insurance company's, and if the company refuses to submit his claim to arbitration, Rupert should hire a lawyer. He should also contact the Better Business Bureau, the Superintendent of Insurance, and the Insurance Bureau of Canada. They may be able to tell him if they had previous complaints of this nature about his company, and suggest other steps Rupert may take.

An adjuster offered Elise $3,000 for the damage to her car, but warned her, "If you get an attorney, I will withdraw all offers." Isn't this against the law?

Although it is not illegal for the adjuster to say this, it is certainly unethical. Everyone has the right to seek legal advice when faced with such a situation. Inform the Superintendent of Insurance and the Insurance Bureau of Canada, as well as the adjuster's supervisor, about this threat.

If my car is damaged in an accident, do I always have to get more than one estimate?

Not all insurance companies require repair estimates. Those that do usually require at least two signed estimates from body shops. If

Adjusters and Settlements

estimates aren't required, getting at least two would be advisable in order to be fully informed about the cost of repairing your car when your claims adjuster offers a settlement. In some provinces, the insurance companies themselves have set up companies whose sole purpose is to supply estimates for car repairs. In settling claims, the insurance companies almost always accept the written estimate from one of these evaluation centers.

Must I use the body shop recommended by the adjuster?

No, but if you don't you may find that your repair bills exceed the cheque the insurance company has issued to you. Insurance adjusters frequently base their estimates on the rates charged by body shops with which they do business. These shops usually charge lower rates in order to get the insurance company's business.

CHAPTER 9

Consumer Rights

Deceptive Advertising

Maryla saw a newspaper advertisement for a product that promised long, beautiful fingernails in 10 days. Can she assume that the product works, because otherwise it would be against the law to advertise it?

No, she cannot make that assumption. Although the federal Competition Act and many provincial laws prohibit false advertising, there is no federal or provincial agency that reviews advertisements before they are published or commercials before they are broadcast. Government agencies investigate the accuracy of an advertisement only after the product has been on the market for a while and if complaints have been lodged against it. Consequently, some ads may contain false promises.

An ad for "Coldchaser Capsules" says they are guaranteed to cure the common cold. Is this false advertising?

Yes. Although laws against deceptive advertising do not keep a manufacturer from expressing an opinion—such as "Bonnie's Bonbons are as sweet as a loved one's kiss"—they do prohibit him from making claims that can't be substantiated. In this case, the manufacturer would have to prove that his capsules cure the common cold—extremely difficult since medical experts claim no cure has yet been developed.

The manufacturer of a certain product claims it kills germs. What will happen to him if the claim proves false?

If it is tested and proved false, the marketing practices branch of Consumer and Corporate Affairs Canada will order the manufacturer to stop making the claim. The company could be fined up to $25,000 and any company directors who knew the claim was false could be sentenced to up to one year in prison. In more serious cases, the punishment would be greater: the amount of the fine would be left to the discretion of the court, and imprisonment could be up to five years upon conviction on indictment.

Connie paid $120 for a six-week computer course, advertised as a "hands-on learning experience." But she was allowed to operate a computer for only 30 minutes of the entire course. Is she entitled to a refund?

Yes. Provincial laws against deceptive sales practices apply to vocational schools as well as to businesses that sell goods and services. In most provinces, Connie would be entitled to a refund, and she could sue the school to enforce her right to it.

How can Fred find out if a product advertised to promote new hair growth is effective?

Before buying the product, Fred should discuss it with his family physician or dermatologist. He might also ask the manufacturer for copies of any scientific studies that back up the company's claim. The marketing practices branch of Consumer and Corporate Affairs Canada can tell him if anyone has complained about the product. And the health

Laws Against False Advertising

The advertising industry is regulated by Consumer and Corporate Affairs Canada and by provincial consumer affairs offices. Among the federal laws protecting the consumer are the Competition Act, the Food and Drugs Act, the Consumer Packaging and Labelling Act, the Textile Labelling Act, and the Broadcasting Act. The following are typical prohibitions:

- A store cannot advertise goods without intending to sell them as advertised. For example, a video shop cannot advertise tapes at low prices when there aren't enough tapes on hand to satisfy a reasonable demand, unless the ad clearly states that the supply is limited.
- When specially advertised items run out, a store must take orders or give rain checks.
- A merchant may not advertise a product at a low price, then tell his customer the model is sold out and try to sell him a more expensive one. This illegal practice is called bait and switch.
- It is illegal to mark up the price of an item, then show a "reduction" to make it appear a bargain.
- A seller may not misrepresent used goods as new.
- A manufacturer may not misrepresent a product's quality, usefulness, reliability, or durability.
- A school may not make false or misleading claims about its job-placement services.
- An advertisement may not falsely claim that a product is sponsored or approved by a professional group. For example, a company cannot legally claim that its stop-smoking program was approved by the Canadian Cancer Society unless the society had specifically approved it. It is not enough to reason that the society would approve because it actively campaigns against smoking.

Deceptive Advertising

protection branch of Health and Welfare Canada can tell him if the product is approved for sale to the public. The government's "Misleading Advertising Bulletin" may help too; he can get it by writing to Information and Public Relations Service, Consumer and Corporate Affairs Canada, Place du Portage, Tower 1, Ottawa/Hull, K1A 0C9.

On the first morning of a three-day sale on humidifiers, Larry was told the advertised models were no longer available. The store refused to give him a rain check. Is there anything he can do?

Yes. He can ask that a similar humidifier be sold to him at an equivalent reduction in place of the rain check. If the store refuses, he can warn the manager that he will advise the marketing practices branch of Consumer and Corporate Affairs Canada that the store is advertising merchandise that is not available.

Gordon saw a newspaper ad for a tool set for $9.95. But the hardware store cashier told him the newspaper had made an error and the price was really $99.95. Can Gordon get the tool set for $9.95 as advertised?

No. There is a difference between an honest error and a deceptive sales practice. Since the price in the paper was the result of a printer's error, and the store had no intention of deceiving its customers, probably no court would force the store to sell the tool sets at the lower price.

If a store displays an item in its window at a sale price, is it required to sell the item at that price?

Yes. It is illegal to deliberately misrepresent the price of an item in order to lure customers into the store. Unless the price in the window is an honest mistake—and it is immediately corrected when employees learn of it—the store cannot charge a higher price.

A shop in town advertises itself as a discount store, but its prices are about the same as, and sometimes higher than, those in other stores. Isn't this illegal?

No. It is not illegal for a store to use "discount" in its name, unless it tries to mislead the public by making specific—and false—claims about its prices. For example, it would be illegal to claim falsely that its prices are

20 percent lower than those of competitors or to misrepresent the prices of its competitors to make its own prices appear lower. It would also be illegal for the store to inflate its price and then pretend that the price has been "slashed," when in fact the selling price is the same as that of its competitors.

Sales Tactics

While shopping, I found a suede coat with a price tag of $19.99. When I went to pay for it, the clerk said it cost $79.99. Doesn't the store have to sell me the coat for the price marked on the tag?

If the coat was mistagged, the store is not required to sell you the coat at that price. However, if the coat was deliberately advertised and tagged at $19.99, the store must honor the price.

Can Deborah demand a refund if a table she bought at an auction turns out to be a reproduction rather than an antique, as was stated in the catalogue?

Yes. Just as it is illegal to label used goods as new, it is illegal to label a reproduction as an antique. Deborah has a right to a refund because her decision to buy the table was based on the seller's misrepresentation.

Reggie purchased a used vacuum cleaner at his neighbor's garage sale. The neighbor said it ran like new, but in fact it didn't run at all. Can Reggie get his money back?

Yes. His neighbor's statement led Reggie to believe that the vacuum cleaner worked. Thus he made a promise or warranty that it would run. Reggie is entitled to a refund, based on the neighbor's breach of warranty. If the neighbor had made no claims for the vacuum cleaner, Reggie would have no recourse after finding it didn't work.

Chuck bought a fishing rod that broke after it was used three times. It was on sale, marked "as is." Can he get his money back?

No. The term "as is" means you buy at your own risk. The manufacturer or dealer does not promise that the product is of good quality or won't break. However, although Chuck is not legally entitled to a refund, he should call the matter to the store manager's attention. The manager may give him a refund to maintain customer goodwill.

Scams, Shams, and Swindles

Uninformed consumers make inviting targets for con artists and swindlers. Knowing something about the way these rogues operate may save you from being fooled.

Some of their most common shady deals follow, along with tips on how to avoid being taken. One precaution that always applies is never to do business with someone you know nothing about—check with the Better Business Bureau or chamber of commerce.

If, despite all precautions, you are bilked, get in touch with your provincial consumer protection office or the local police fraud squad. If the deal involved the mail (even if you only paid by mail), inform the local postmaster. Sometimes the publicity generated by a letter to the consumer reporter of a local radio or television station or newspaper can be most effective in helping you get what you paid for—or a refund.

THE SCAM	HOW TO AVOID BEING TAKEN
Unlucky Winner: Someone phones and says you have won a vacation or some other prize, but to be sure you are the right person, the caller needs your credit card number. If you give it to him, you get nothing and he goes on a shopping spree.	Never give your credit card number over the phone unless you have initiated the call. Ask the names, addresses, and phone numbers of unknown callers, verify the information, and call back. If you inadvertently give out a credit card number, contact the card company immediately.
Work-at-Home Holdup: An ad says you can earn money at home (by stuffing envelopes or doing some other easy job), but first you must buy something and give the names of other people who might be interested.	Make sure you understand all the terms of any agreement you sign. If you suspect the business is a fraud, do not involve others in it, or you might risk investigation by the police.
Unoriginal Art: A reproduction of an artwork is passed off as an original, or a lithograph is falsely said to be signed by the artist.	Check the dealer's credentials with an art museum. Get a certificate of authenticity and a receipt describing the artwork and stating its price. Ask if you can have the work appraised before buying it.
Fake Final Sale: "Going Out of Business" banners announce big sales, but the store is not closing, and its goods are inferior and overpriced.	Comparison-shop before buying. Get details about returns, refunds, warranties, and service *in writing*.

THE SCAM	HOW TO AVOID BEING TAKEN
Mismatched Mates: A dating service promises to introduce you to lots of perfect partners, makes a show of cataloguing your likes and dislikes, and even videotapes you, but in the end the people you meet are few and far between or have little in common with you.	Get a written contract complete with the cost, the dates the service is in effect, the number of introductions guaranteed, and the qualifications you request in a partner (such as age and education).
Franchise Frame-up: The promoter promises that you will earn enormous profits if you buy a franchise or distributorship, and pumps you for the names of others he may be able to sell to. He makes money; you don't.	Ask the promoter for credit references and contact people who have already bought franchises. Find out what the franchise fee covers and doesn't cover and how the agreement can be terminated. Get everything in writing.
Health Club Hazard: Preopening discounts are offered for health club memberships, but the club never opens, or extra charges are added for essential services, or the swimming pool or other facilities can be used only at specified—usually inconvenient—times.	Ask if there is a trial period that can be applied toward your membership. Find out if use is restricted in any way. Ask about cancellations and refunds. Get everything in writing. Don't join the club until it is open for business and you have inspected the premises.
Job Gyp: An ad promises exciting, high-paying jobs, often overseas; you must pay to get information about the jobs, but they are nonexistent. Or an ad offers to sell the names of prospective employers, but the names are simply culled from telephone directories.	Be skeptical of ads where no experience or skills are needed, and of ads guaranteeing jobs, particularly abroad. Never pay in advance for job lists or employment advice.
Miracle Cures: An ad promises that a bracelet cures arthritis, or a diet pill results in instant weight loss, or a face cream keeps complexions young forever, or a lotion puts an end to baldness, but the products don't work, and they may cause some serious health problems.	Ask the manufacturer for supporting evidence and names and addresses of satisfied users. Ask Health and Welfare Canada if the product has been approved for sale to the public.

Continued on page 362

Scams, Shams, and Swindles (continued)

THE SCAM	HOW TO AVOID BEING TAKEN
Unfair Repair: A repairman takes your TV or appliance in for servicing, and because of "lowballing"—giving an artificially low estimate—charges a far higher price than he first quoted, and bills you for work you did not agree to have him do.	Get a written estimate of the repairs and costs and insist on approving any repairs not on the original estimate. If used or rebuilt parts are supplied, make sure the invoice says so—and have the replaced parts returned to you.
Charity Fraud: You are asked to donate to a charity that doesn't exist. The charity's name may resemble that of a well-known one. Your solicitor demands cash, and pockets the money himself.	Get the charity's name, address, and phone number. Check that the solicitor works for the charity. Pay by cheque, made out to the charity, not to an individual. Call the Better Business Bureau. Ask the charity for its tax deduction number and check it with Revenue Canada or Revenue Quebec.
Trade School Trap: Promotions for a trade school promise good jobs to graduates, and the school offers a free aptitude test on which applicants are told they scored very well; but after graduation, there are no jobs.	Ask local employers if they hire graduates of this school. Find out if the school is recognized by the provincial department of education. Ask if you can pay in installments instead of paying in full before starting. Find out if there is an extra charge for placement service and how long after graduation you may use it.
Prize Disguise: A letter informs you that you have won a prize, perhaps a VCR or a stereo. But to claim it, you must either visit a condominium or time-share development or attend a meeting at which great sales pressure will be applied to get you to buy property. Complicated paperwork is required before you get the gift.	Get the exact procedure for claiming the prize in writing before agreeing to anything and ask for the makes and models of merchandise being offered. If you want to buy the real estate, don't pay until you inspect the land or dwelling, check the seller's references, and have a lawyer look over the contract.
Last-Chance Loan: Borrowers rejected by banks and other lending institutions are assured that they can get a loan if they first pay a fee, but after they pay, no loan is forthcoming and the fee is lost.	Never pay fees in advance. Deal only with lenders whose backgrounds and reputations you can verify. Avoid any lender whose only address is a post office box number.

Jack ordered a microwave oven that the appliance salesman assured him would fit into the space he had built for it. It doesn't. The salesman won't exchange the microwave or give Jack a refund, saying he had to place a special order to get this particular one. Is Jack stuck with an appliance he can't use?

No, because he bought the oven relying on the salesman's assurance that it would fit into his space. An implied warranty is created whenever a buyer relies on a seller to supply a product that meets the buyer's requirements. If Jack gave the correct dimensions of the space, the store must replace the oven with one that fits, or give a refund.

When Russell bought his compact disc player, the salesclerk told him he wouldn't find a better model anywhere. Three months later, the player needed extensive service. Does Russell have any claim based on the clerk's statements?

No. The salesclerk was giving a sales pitch, what's known in the trade as "puffing." The law assumes that consumers know sellers will claim their products are of good quality—Russell would not expect to be told that the disc player was mediocre and would give him nothing but trouble. On the other hand, if Russell received a warranty or guarantee that promised to fix any defects or replace the disc player within the first 90 days, he does have a valid claim.

Darren signed an order for a new dishwasher after the salesclerk took $100 off the price. Later, the store manager said the clerk wasn't allowed to offer discounts. Must Darren pay the extra $100?

No. He may cancel the agreement and demand a refund of whatever he has already paid, or he may sue the store for breach of contract. The salesclerk, acting as the store's agent, made a contract with Darren that was legally binding on the business.

When I bought a used motorboat, the salesman told me to look it over carefully. I couldn't see anything wrong with it. After my first ride, the motor conked out completely. Have I any recourse?

You can ask the seller to repair the motor or replace it, pointing out that you have a right to expect your purchase to fulfill the purpose for which it was bought. However, when you purchase a complex machine, such as a boat or a car, a simple inspection may not be enough to find any defects. You should have a mechanic check it out *before* you buy. Such an *expert* check is crucial if you have to cancel a contract involving used goods.

CONSUMER RIGHTS

Buying by Mail

I received some cosmetics in the mail even though I had never ordered them. If I keep them, do I have to pay for them?

No. Under federal law and most provincial laws, you do not have to pay for unordered goods or return them. It is illegal to send consumers unordered merchandise unless it is a free sample, or a gift from a charitable organization to encourage donations. It is also illegal to mail credit cards to persons who have not applied for them.

Are chain letters legal?

Generally, no. Any letter that requires you to send anyone money or anything else of value, or encourages pyramid sales, violates a federal law. If you receive a letter asking you to send copies to potential buyers of an article, and if it stresses that you will be entitled to a percentage of what "your customers" spend, you are involved in "referral selling," which is also prohibited or severely restricted. If you have doubts about some letter of this kind, ask a Better Business Bureau or consumer protection office whether it is legal where you live.

Janet doesn't want the forthcoming selection of the record club she belongs to, but she has missed the time limit for notifying the club. Must she pay for the record?

Legally, if the club mailed the announcement so that she had at least 10 days to accept or reject the record, the company may insist that Janet live up to her part of the bargain. She can write to the company, explaining her situation, and while it is not legally bound to make an exception, it may do so in her case to maintain good customer relations. Clubs like this mail records and books automatically; members should ask that mailings be suspended if they expect to be away on vacation or away for some other reason.

Only after two months did I receive merchandise I ordered from a mail-order catalogue. By then it was too late to give the items as gifts. Do I have a right to return the merchandise?

Yes. If you were not notified that the delivery would take two months, you had the right to expect delivery within 30 days. However, if you were notified in advance that delivery would take two months and, at that time, you did not cancel your order, the company had the right to assume you had no complaint about the delay, and you have no right to a refund. When no delivery time limit is expressed in a contract, it is the seller's obligation to deliver the goods within a "reasonable time," which depends on the circumstances. Goods described as ideal for, say, Christmas would be considered late if delivered after the holiday, and the buyer could refuse to accept them.

A mail-order catalogue stated that its fishing tackle offer would expire July 1. I sent in my order in early June, but got a form letter stating that the offer had been canceled. Can they do this?

No. Canceling the offer after you have accepted it by ordering the tackle is a breach of contract.

Ingrid liked a bedspread she saw in a mail-order catalogue and ordered four, paying by cheque. When the spreads arrived, two were of substitute patterns, which she didn't like. Can she return the substitutes and get her money back?

Yes. If the shipment did not conform to her order, she is entitled to a full refund.

Alexander bought pills by mail to lose weight. They turned out to be vitamin C tablets. A friend suggested that he report the matter to Consumer and Corporate Affairs Canada as well as to Canada Post. What good will that do?

The marketing practices branch of Consumer and Corporate Affairs Canada may decide to prosecute the seller for advertising and selling a product in a way that deceives or misleads the public or creates an erroneous impression about the product's character or composition. Canada Post may prosecute the company for using the mail for fraudulent purposes. Before you buy from a mail order company, you should check its reputation with your Better Business Bureau, chamber of commerce or the Canadian Direct Mail/Marketing Association.

I ordered a set of china figurines by mail, but I'm afraid they may be damaged in shipping. If any pieces are broken when the merchandise arrives, what should I do?

When the figurines arrive, unpack the carton carefully. If you discover a piece that is damaged, unpack no further, but replace everything you have already unpacked, and reseal the carton. Then contact the company and ask for instructions on returning the merchandise.

Buying by Mail

Some companies will guarantee the return postage, others will arrange for pickup. Make sure the company will bear the expense one way or the other. If you are asked to mail back the figurines, return them promptly. Some companies have time limits on money-back guarantees.

The cookware Sylviane bought through the mail was guaranteed to be burn-proof and tough enough to last a lifetime. The first time she used one of the pans, it warped and turned black. She wrote to the distributor, whose only address was a post office box number, but her letter was returned, marked "Addressee Unknown." What can she do?

Sylviane can get the distributor's business address from the postmaster in the city where the post office box is located—information available to the public if the post office box is being used to conduct a business. Once she has the address, Sylviane can write and demand a refund. Many consumer experts advise people not to place orders with a business that does not give a street address.

Door-to-door Sales

People have come to my door selling jewelry, vacuum cleaners, cosmetics, and other products. Are they required to have some type of permit or license?

Door-to-door sales are usually governed by provincial consumer protection or direct sellers legislation. Many provinces have laws requiring door-to-door vendors, or peddlers, to be licensed. Peddling without a license can result in fines, imprisonment, or both.

Jay and Sue bought a $2,000 burial plot from a salesman who came to their home, and wrote him a cheque for $100 as a deposit. On reflection, they decided they didn't want the plot. Can they simply stop payment on the cheque to get out of the deal?

No. Stopping payment will not automatically cancel their order. If the salesman stopped at their home without an invitation, Jay and Sue can cancel the order in writing within the cooling-off period allowed by their province. But if they requested a sales presentation in their home, they do not have the right to cancel the order unless the terms of the sales agreement allow it.

A door-to-door salesman claimed that the ring he sold me was 18-karat gold, but it was only dipped. Can I get my money back?

Yes, because the salesman lied about the gold content of the ring. If your money is not returned, you can sue for fraud.

Guarding Against Door-to-door Sales Schemes

Although underhanded door-to-door sales practices have often been the focus of exposés, legislation, and public outrage, some fast-talkers still make a good living by promising what they can't deliver and trusting the consumer won't complain. Here are some things to look out for:

- Beware of any door-to-door solicitor who claims he doesn't want to sell you anything. The offer of a free inspection of your furnace, roof, or plumbing is often a ploy to sell you repairs that you do not need.
- Don't invite in anyone who says he is taking a survey, or you may find yourself listening to a high-pressure sales pitch and at a loss as to how to get your "guest" to leave.
- If someone appears with a free gift and asks you to sign a receipt for it, read the receipt carefully. It may be a contract to purchase the "gift" at an inflated price.
- If a salesperson is trying to sell you something from a catalogue, look carefully at the picture of the product, noting that the product will be photographed in its best light or made to look even better than it actually is. Remember that the words *simulated, faux,* and *reproduction* in the context of jewelry, art, and antiques mean that the item is not genuine or original.
- Read the disclaimers on the order form or sales contract. They might state that you will have to pay excessive shipping charges or that delivery will take 8 to 12 weeks.
- Pass up offers good for "this day only." This is a ploy used by salespeople to create the false impression that you are being offered a once-in-a-lifetime deal. If the salesperson doesn't want to give you time for reflection, there's probably a good reason.
- Be wary of contractors who are "working in the neighborhood" and have extra materials on hand that they can use to fix your house at a special discount rate. They may do a poor job on work you really don't need—at an inflated price—and you will not be able to locate them afterward to fix the problems they have created.
- If you signed a contract, take advantage of the cooling-off period to reflect on the purchase. This period varies from 2 days in Ontario to 10 in Newfoundland.
- Check the seller's license and note his name, address and license number.

Door-to-door Sales

A door-to-door vendor pressured Francis into buying a lawn-and-garden-care service, but when he got the bill he decided he could not afford the program. Can he cancel the order?

Francis can cancel the service within his province's cooling-off period. All provinces and both Territories have a number of days in which a customer can reconsider a door-to-door purchase and cancel the contract. The period is 10 days in Quebec, Nova Scotia, and Newfoundland; 7 in Yukon, British Columbia and Prince Edward Island; 5 in New Brunswick; 4 in the Northwest Territories, Alberta, Saskatchewan, and Manitoba; and 2 in Ontario.

Telephone and TV Sales

Brenda received a telephone call from someone selling magazines, and she accepted the offer, which sounded terrific. But afterward, she calculated that she had agreed to pay more than the cover price for five years! Can she cancel the order?

A telephone sale is a "direct sale," one in which the seller contacts the buyer and makes the sale elsewhere than at his place of business. In most provinces, Brenda would be allowed a cooling-off period (10 days in Quebec, Nova Scotia, and Newfoundland; 7 in British Columbia, Prince Edward Island, and Yukon; 5 in New Brunswick; 4 in Alberta, Saskatchewan, Manitoba, and the Northwest Territories; 2 in Ontario) in which she could cancel the contract, without giving any reason. If she did not act within this period, the contract would become binding.

If I order merchandise from a TV commercial, do I have less protection than if I order from a printed ad?

No. All televised and printed ads are subject to regulation by Consumer and Corporate Affairs Canada. However, if you dispute the truth of a claim, it is easier to prove what a printed advertisement claimed, unless you have videotaped the commercial.

When I place a telephone order, am I better protected using a credit card or paying by cheque?

It depends. If you use the seller's credit card (a department store's own card, say), you can withhold payment if you have any problem with the order. But if you use a card issued by a bank or other financial institution, you are obliged by contract to pay the amounts the card issuer bills you, regardless of any dispute you may have with a seller. So even if the seller sends you goods that are not exactly what you ordered or charges you more than you agreed to on the phone, you might have to pay your credit card bill in full and sue the seller for the disputed amount. Paying by cheque would make it difficult for the seller to boost the price you agreed to. But the safest way of all to buy something by telephone is to order C.O.D.—and pay after you receive and inspect the goods.

I often get calls from people selling everything from dining-out packages to carpet-cleaning services. Some of the offers sound interesting, but I don't know if the vendors are trustworthy. How can I check on the reliability of a firm selling by telephone?

Check the telephone directory to see if the firm has a street address. If not, you may wish to forgo dealing with it, since you will be unable to locate the firm if there are problems with the product. If the company has an address, ask your Better Business Bureau and your provincial consumer protection office if there have been any complaints about the company. You can also check with the Direct Sellers Association, 4950 Yonge Street, Suite 1400, North York, Ont., M2N 6K1.

Marilyn saw a television commercial for exercise equipment that can be ordered only by telephoning an 800 number. If she orders in this way, will she have any protection if the equipment doesn't arrive or is not as advertised?

Yes. Marilyn is protected against false and deceptive trade practices under the federal Competition Act and provincial consumer protection laws. Before ordering, she should make sure she is dealing with a reputable company, and she should arrange to pay only after she has received the goods, even if C.O.D. charges cost her a few dollars more.

Leo bought a diamond pendant he saw on a television ad, which promised he would get his money back if he were not completely satisfied. The stone turned out to be much smaller than it appeared on the screen. What can Leo do if the company refuses to refund his money?

He can report the company to the marketing practices branch of Consumer and Corporate Affairs Canada. If the ad made a money-back guarantee, the company must give a full refund. If necessary, Leo could sue the company in Small Claims Court.

Prizes, Gifts, and Rebates

Do they really award those big cash prizes that are advertised?

Yes. According to federal law, any company or person trying to promote or sell an article or a service by means of a contest or lottery must (1) disclose the number and value of the prizes, (2) distribute the prizes within a reasonable time limit, and (3) select the prizewinners at random or on the basis of skill.

I find it hard to believe that I don't have to make a purchase to be in the running for a sweepstakes prize. What is the law on this?

The law prohibits any requirement that you purchase anything to be eligible to enter—and to win. If you are required to fill out a special entry form, the sponsor must provide the form free of charge. If entry forms are inserted into a container or printed on its wrapper, the sponsor must give you an alternative way of getting entry forms without buying the product. It is illegal for the contest sponsor to shift the odds of winning to those who have ordered or purchased a product.

Kathy received a letter saying she had won an attractive prize. All she would have to do would be to listen to a 30-minute sales presentation about a vacation time-sharing program. How can Kathy find out if this is a legitimate offer?

She can ask her Better Business Bureau and provincial consumer protection agency whether any complaints have been made about this company. Most promotions of this type are legitimate, but sometimes prize announcements can be misleading. For example, some people have won vacations to Florida, then discovered their food and transportation were not covered and their lodging was in a hotel where they had to listen to another promotional pitch.

Ramona received a notice in the mail that she had won a three-month membership in a fitness club. When she went to claim her prize, she was told she would have to pay equipment rental charges and locker-room fees. Is this legal?

If the health club normally charges separate membership, equipment, and locker-room fees, this promotion would not be viewed as deceptive or misleading by the courts. If, however, these fees are not assessed separately and have been added just for the purpose of the promotion, this may be viewed as a deceptive sales practice.

I was promised a free TV for listening to a sales pitch for lake-front property. I kept my part of the bargain, but the TV never arrived. What can I do?

Contact the land promoters. If they are unwilling to give you your promised gift, inform them that you will report them to the marketing branch of Consumer and Corporate Affairs Canada for conducting a fraudulent promotion. You could also sue the promoter.

How can I check whether a contest promoting a product was fair and that all the prizes were awarded?

In almost all such contests the names of the winners can be obtained by writing to the company that supervises the contest. The name of the supervising company, which is generally different from the company whose product or service is being promoted, is usually printed along with the contest rules. If the contest is fraudulent, contact your local office of Consumer and Corporate Affairs Canada.

Jan sent for a $3 rebate on a hair dryer, but has not received the rebate. What can she do?

She can write to the manufacturer's customer service department, telling them when she made her purchase and when and how she applied for the rebate. She should give the company a reasonable time to reply. If she receives no response, however, she should write again, this time by certified mail, informing the company that she will contact her provincial consumer protection agency and the Better Business Bureau if she does not receive her rebate by a certain date. If the deadline passes without any action by the company, she should get in touch with the consumer organizations mentioned in her letter.

Consumer Contracts

Seventeen-year-old Chip purchased a stereo on the installment plan. After making a few payments, he decided to return the stereo. Does the store have to accept the returned equipment?

Yes. Under the law, minors are considered incapable of making binding contracts, except for the necessities of life. Until he reaches the age of adulthood (18 years in most provinces, 19 in others), Chip will be allowed to back out of his contracts. On the other hand, the store does not have the right to cancel the contract.

Consumer Contracts

What does it mean when an installment payment contract gives the seller the right to assign the contract?

It means that the seller may sell to another company the right to collect payments. Small merchants who require immediate cash often assign their contracts to a finance company, which then collects the payments.

When Jay bought his VCR, he signed a note agreeing to make payments for 18 months. The video store then sold the note to a finance company. The VCR has stopped working. The finance company claims that Jay has to continue making payments or it will repossess the VCR. Is it justified in doing this?

No. Under most provincial consumer protection legislation, the finance company has the same rights and obligations as the store that sold it the contract. If Jay has a reason to withhold payment from the video store, he has the same rights to withhold payment from the finance company.

The sales contract for my new furnace states that if I sue the seller because of defects, I will have to pay the seller's attorney fees. This doesn't sound right to me. What should I do?

Ask the dealer to delete the clause from your contract, initialing and dating the change. In most provinces this type of clause is illegal, and the courts would not enforce it even if it remained in the contract.

According to her sales contract, if Evelyn missed one payment on her mink coat, the furrier could demand the remaining balance on her loan. Evelyn missed two payments, and the furrier wrote to demand full payment. Evelyn offered to make three payments to bring her account up to date, but the furrier refused. Can he legally enforce this clause?

Yes. Many contracts contain acceleration clauses, which state that if a payment is missed, the seller can demand that the buyer make all the remaining payments immediately. The furrier does not have to accept the late payments. If Evelyn can't pay off the balance in a lump sum, the furrier probably has the right, under their contract, to repossess the coat and resell it. If the sale price is not equal to the balance Evelyn owes, the furrier may sue her for the difference. In British Columbia, Ontario and Quebec, the furrier would need the court's permission to repossess the coat if Evelyn had made more than two thirds of the payments.

After signing an order for a living room set, the Morgans discovered that Mrs. Morgan was going to have a baby. Without her income, the couple can't afford the new furniture. Can they cancel their order before the merchandise is delivered?

Not unless their contract lets them cancel. However, they should tell the seller immediately that they cannot pay and will not accept delivery. By refusing to accept delivery, they limit the seller's losses and the amount they may have to pay for breach of contract. The seller may be limited to suing for his lost profit rather than the full price of the set.

When I took my stereo in for repairs, the shop gave me an estimate of $30. But the bill came to $150 and I refused to pay anything. Can the shop keep my stereo if I don't pay?

Yes. The shop has a right to keep your stereo until you pay your bill and under provincial law may even be entitled to sell the stereo to cover its costs. This right to retain goods until payment is made is known as a mechanic's lien. To prevent that, pay the bill, noting on the receipt that you are paying under protest. You can then sue the shop to get back the amount you were overcharged.

Elaine enrolled in dance school and signed a contract to make monthly payments for a year. Next day she changed her mind, called the school, and was told the membership would be canceled. Three months later, she began to receive collection letters from a finance company. Does she have to pay?

Some contracts say that cancellations must be made in writing; so Elaine's attempt to cancel her contract by phone may have been ineffective. However, if the contract Elaine signed did not say a cancellation would have to be in writing, her cancellation was valid, and she does not have to pay the fees.

A salesman offered to reduce the price of a computer by $500 if Eva would give him the names of six friends who might buy one. Is this part of Eva's contract enforceable?

If the salesman alters their contract, in writing, or fills in the price to reflect a $500 reduction, Eva can feel fairly confident that a court will enforce the terms of the contract. She should be wary, however, if the salesman offers to reduce the price only if the contacts she gives him result in sales. He may have no intention of contacting the other people, or if he does, one or more may not buy, leaving Eva to pay $500 more than she expected. A price reduction dependent on another person making a purchase is "referral selling," a practice prohibited by the federal Competition Act.

Cecilia, a dressmaker, agreed orally that she would make Tina's wedding gown for $450. When Tina returned for a fitting, Cecilia said she was too busy to sew the gown. Does Tina have any rights in this situation?

It depends. The law varies from province to province. In Manitoba and Ontario, for example, contracts involving more than $50 must be in writing to be enforceable. In Quebec, verbal contracts for up to $1,000 are enforceable. In this case, if Tina can prove that Cecilia made and broke certain promises, forcing Tina to go elsewhere and pay more to get a gown on time, she can sue Cecilia for the extra cost.

I accepted a health club's offer of a free initial visit, and was pressured into signing a contract for a three-year membership, payable every month. Not only are the payments beyond my means, but I may not be living here a year from now. Can I cancel my membership?

Many health club contracts allow a member to cancel and get a refund for the unused portion of his membership; others allow a member to cancel only if he moves out of town or becomes disabled. Moreover, many provinces have consumer protection laws that allow the consumer to cancel a contract involving "sequential performances," such as yours, by paying about 10 percent of the value of the contract.

Bob and Françoise signed up for time-sharing in a vacation retreat that they were told could be "swapped" with other properties around the country. Then they discovered there were only three other places they could swap for, none in areas they wanted to visit. Can they break their contract?

Only if they were misled by a sales pitch and promotional materials into believing their swapping options would be more extensive than they are. If the promoter sues Bob and Françoise for money due under the contract, they may use his unfair and deceptive advertising as a defense. They should also report the matter to their provincial consumer protection agency, and to the marketing practices branch of Consumer and Corporate Affairs Canada.

Warranties and Service Contracts

For warranties on automobiles, see "Car Warranties" in Chapter 6, *Your Car.*

What is the difference between a warranty and a guarantee?

Both words can be defined as a promise that a manufacturer or dealer makes about a product, although *warranty* tends to be used for goods and *guarantee* for performance of an undertaking. A warranty—or guarantee— can be either *express* or *implied.*

An express warranty is a specific promise—for example, that the product is of a certain quality, is made of a particular material, will do a certain job, or will last for a specified time. A seller or manufacturer obligates himself to repair, replace, or refund the price of a product that does not live up to its warranty. If there is an express warranty, it must be available to the customer to read before buying.

An implied warranty is an unstated promise, assumed by the law in most sales transactions, that the product will be of at least average quality and will do what the average customer would expect it to do. For example, a toaster should toast bread and a vacuum cleaner should pick up dirt. As with an express warranty, the manufacturer or seller must remedy the situation if the product is unusable or defective. A product is covered by an implied warranty unless a disclaimer is specifically made—for example, by using the words "as is."

When Matt bought a color television set, the manufacturer included only a partial warranty for the picture tube, but a full warranty for all the other parts. Shouldn't the full warranty apply to everything?

Not necessarily. The laws dealing with warranties differ from province to province and from one article to another. Some warranties are for the entire article and include the price of replacement parts, labor, and shipping; other warranties are limited. Some automobile manufacturers, for example, offer a warranty for the entire car; others guarantee only the power train.

Two weeks after Tamara bought a new toaster, she discovered that the warranty card should have been returned within 10 days of purchase. If Tamara mails the card now, will she still be protected?

Not necessarily. A dealer or manufacturer may require that a warranty card be returned within a certain time to guarantee coverage. However, to keep customers' goodwill, some dealers honor warranties even when this requirement is not met.

Warranties and Service Contracts

In the warranty booklet that came with my clothes dryer I noticed the words "repair or replace." Do I decide whether the dryer is to be repaired or replaced—or does the manufacturer?

The manufacturer does. However, if after a reasonable number of attempts, the manufacturer has been unable to repair the clothes dryer, you may demand a replacement dryer or a refund.

Eddie bought a lawn mower from a discount store. After numerous engine problems while it was still under warranty, Eddie went to return it but discovered the store was out of business. Is he stuck with paying for the repairs himself?

No. Eddie's warranty was probably provided by the lawn mower's manufacturer. If so, he can contact the manufacturer about repairs.

Understanding Warranty Terms

Not all warranties are printed on tags or in booklets that are packaged with the products you buy. Some are contained in advertisements and promotional materials. Others are never stated, but are implied. All can be enforced by law. To be fully aware of your rights as a consumer, you should understand the terms most commonly applied to warranties:

● *Express warranty*—A specific promise, which may or may not be in writing, that the manufacturer or seller makes about his goods or services. "Rustproof," "14-karat gold," and "parts guaranteed for 90 days" are typical express warranties.
● *Implied warranty of merchantability*—An unstated promise that the product is of average quality, will work, and will do what it's supposed to do: a sewing machine will stitch, a refrigerator will keep food cold.
● *Implied warranty of fitness for a particular purpose*—An unstated promise that a product will fit your needs. This warranty is created in only some situations. If you go to a hardware store and tell the salesman that you need water-resistant paint for an outdoor swing set, you are informing him that you need a product for a particular purpose. If, knowing your purpose, he then sells you some paint, he has created a warranty—even if he makes no spoken promises. He has warranted that the paint won't wash off in the rain. If it does, you are entitled to a refund.
● *Full warranty*—An all-inclusive written warranty. Under provincial consumer laws, defective products or parts covered by a full warranty must be repaired or replaced without charge; the buyer should not have

The warranty on Mark's coffee maker does not apply to damage caused by neglect, abuse, or mishandling. If the coffee maker needs to be repaired, will Mark have to prove that the damage was not caused by his misuse?

No, unless the manufacturer sees signs that Mark has misused the appliance. If there are no such indications, the manufacturer must honor the warranty without dispute.

Even though Darlene has a service contract for her freezer, the repairman won't come to her home to fix it. What can she do?

If the contract specifically does not cover service calls or transportation, Darlene will have to get the freezer to the repair center herself. If the contract is ambiguous or if Darlene was led to believe it included service calls, she can sue, alleging deceptive sales practices. Courts usually interpret ambiguous clauses in favor of the consumer.

---

to pay shipping costs. If the defect cannot be fixed after a reasonable number of attempts, the buyer is entitled to choose between a replacement and a refund.

● *Limited warranty*—A written warranty that covers some defects or problems, but not others. For example, a warranty on a video recorder may include replacement of all defective or worn parts except the recording heads, or may cover the cost of new parts but not labor.

● *As is*—The product carries no warranties, either stated or implied. You have no legal grounds to expect it will be of any particular quality, will last any length of time, or will work at all. Nevertheless, items such as autos or motors must serve the purpose for which they were bought, unless the defect is apparent to an *expert* examiner.

● *Consequential, or incidental, damages*—Losses indirectly caused by a product defect. For example, if a defect caused your new oven to explode, ruining your kitchen walls, and you had to miss work to have the walls redone, the damage to the walls would be direct damages, and covered by the warranty, but your lost wages would be consequential, and not covered.

● *Customer misuse*—A statement that damage that results from a customer's misuse of a product is not covered by a warranty. If you have used a product in a careless manner or have not followed the manufacturer's instructions, the seller is not obligated to repair the product without charge.

● *Unauthorized repairs*—A statement that repairs may be made only at authorized shops or that only a certain brand of parts may be used in repair work. This requirement is valid only if the services or parts in question are provided free under the warranty.

Warranties and Service Contracts

My grandmother bought a dishwasher and, for an extra charge, signed a service contract. When I looked over the fine print I realized that she wasn't going to be getting much service for her money. Isn't there some law that requires limitations and disclaimers in service contracts to be in bold print?

In some provinces, consumer protection laws require that contracts between merchants and consumers be in type of a certain size so as to be easily readable. In Quebec, for example, a contract printed in a type smaller than that required by law can be canceled by the consumer. With the evolution of consumer law in Canada, the days of the contract with

---

Deciding on a Service Contract

If you buy a major appliance, the salesperson usually tries to sell you a service contract as well—an agreement to maintain and repair the appliance for a set period of time. A service contract serves, in some ways, the same purpose as a warranty, but it should not be confused with one. A warranty is a promise that the merchandise you buy will meet certain standards of quality or performance. If those standards are not met, the buyer may demand repairs, replacement, or a refund. A service contract, on the other hand, is a form of insurance. Necessary repairs or maintenance, if covered by the contract, will be performed at no charge or for a reduced fee.

Some service contracts are worth having, others are not. Before investing in a service contract, examine its terms and see if they will really benefit you. Here are some questions to ask:

- Is the coverage far more than what you are given free of charge by the warranty? Will it extend beyond the life of the warranty?
- Are minor defects covered as well as major ones?
- Are repairs for routine wear and tear included?
- Are you offered routine maintenance at no charge?
- Are all parts and labor supplied at no extra charge? (Some service contracts charge a nominal set fee each time the product is serviced.)
- Are there any deductibles involved? (Some service contracts have deductibles like those of insurance policies.)
- Does the contract cover service calls at home or include provisions for moving the product to a service center for repairs?
- Will repairs be made even if the damage resulted from misuse— your not following the manufacturer's directions when using the product, for example?

fine print are numbered. Check with the consumer protection office in your province to find out whether your grandmother's service contract conforms to the law.

If I didn't fully understand a service contract when I signed it, can I get out of it or have it amended?

No. The law presumes that you read and understood the contract before signing it. If there was no fraud or deception, you may not cancel without penalty—unless the contract permits that.

Defective and Unsafe Merchandise

The ice cream maker that Irene bought was defective. Should she complain to the manufacturer or to the store?

She has the right to complain to both because both are responsible for defects in the products they make or sell. As a practical matter, however, it would be more convenient for Irene to seek a refund, repairs, or a replacement at the store.

A canned ham that Penny bought was spoiled. When she took it back for a refund, the supermarket manager told her to return it to the supplier, who in turn told her to return it to the store. What are Penny's rights?

The supermarket should either give Penny a full refund or exchange the ham for one of the same weight. Shoppers have the right to expect that the food they purchase at a supermarket, or any other retail food outlet, will not be spoiled. The store manager must ensure that the food he sells is fresh, and he cannot shift his own responsibility to the supplier, even though the supplier is also responsible. For example, if Penny had eaten the ham before discovering it was spoiled and got sick as a result, she could sue the supermarket, the supplier, and the packer for damages.

If I don't have time to try on a suit but buy it and later discover it is defective, do I have any recourse?

Yes. Generally, you may return the suit for a refund or replacement, especially if the defect is one that could not be easily discovered. However, if you were aware that the store had a no-return policy, you had a duty to inspect the suit closely before purchasing it.

Defective and Unsafe Merchandise

Nicholas bought a digital phone from a department store. When he got home, he discovered the plastic case was badly cracked. What are his rights?

He has the right to return the phone to the store for a replacement or a refund, provided he did not crack the case himself. He may not be entitled to anything, however, if the phone was sold as a factory second or marked "as is"—it would be assumed that he took the chance of getting damaged goods in exchange for paying a low price. Still, if the crack made the phone unusable, Nicholas could get his money back. "As is" usually means there is no guarantee for minor defects, but does not apply to defects that make the article unusable.

Lorraine let Bella, her hairdresser, talk her into lightening her hair. Bella left the solution on too long because she was busy with other clients, and when she removed it, Lorraine's hair was bright orange. Although Bella quickly corrected her mistake, Lorraine's hair was damaged. Can Lorraine sue Bella?

Yes. Hairdressers can be held responsible for any damage they do by carelessly or negligently applying hair bleaches or dyes. They can also be held responsible for damage caused by the careless use of hair waving machines or solutions. The amount Lorraine will be able to sue Bella for will depend on how severely her hair was damaged.

Sarah purchased a home computer, but it is defective, and she wants to return it for a refund. The salesman says she will be charged 20 percent of the purchase price if she does so. Is this legal?

No. The seller cannot charge you for returning defective goods; but in most situations, if an item is defective, the seller or manufacturer has the right to repair or replace it rather than give you a refund.

Jeff bought a tape deck, used it for a week to play prerecorded tapes, then tried to tape a business meeting, and found it didn't record. Can he return the tape deck despite the fact that he used it for a few days?

Yes, because the defect was one that he would not necessarily have discovered upon inspection or on first use. But if Jeff continues to use the deck after discovering the defect, he may lose his right to return it.

Anna bought a silk dress at a designer discount store, but later found a hole in it. She tried to return the dress, but the proprietor of the store pointed out his "No Returns, No Refunds" sign. If Anna sued the store, would she get a refund in spite of what the sign says?

When a store displays a "No Return, No Refund" sign, or when the price of certain items has been greatly reduced, it is assumed that shoppers have been alerted to the possibility of the goods being irregular or damaged. The shopper has the responsibility of carefully inspecting the goods before purchasing. If, however, the "No Refunds" sign was in small letters or in a spot where it was difficult to read, a court might decide that Anna had the right to believe she could return the dress, and might enforce her right to a refund. If the hole made the dress unwearable, here again the court would probably rule in Anna's favor.

John bought a new battery for his expensive 35mm camera and carefully installed it. The battery leaked, and the acid corroded the camera so badly that it cannot be repaired. Can John sue the battery manufacturer for the cost of the camera?

If the battery was new and properly installed, he could sue for the amount the camera was worth at the time. However, if the battery was not used according to the instructions for the camera or the batteries, John does not have a valid claim.

My husband and I are expecting our first baby and we want to be sure the furniture and toys we buy are safe. Where can we get information on product safety?

Contact the product safety branch of Consumer and Corporate Affairs Canada. The Hazardous Products Act, the Textile Labelling Act, and other federal legislation are designed to keep dangerous products off the consumer market. You can also contact the Canadian Toy Testing Council, 881 Lady Ellen Place, Ottawa, Ont., K1Z 5L3.

If a child is injured while playing with a toy, can the parents successfully sue the manufacturer or the retailer?

They may sue both if the injury is due to a defect in the toy or if the toy is inherently unsafe for children. The parents may sue the manufacturer for producing a defective or unsafe toy and the retailer for a breach of the implied warranty of merchantability—a toy that injures a child who plays with it does not work as one would expect a toy to work.

Defective and Unsafe Merchandise

My new air conditioner did not cool properly, so I asked the store for a refund. They offered to replace the machine but won't return my money. Don't I have a right to an immediate refund?

No. The seller of defective merchandise has the right to try to repair it or to replace it with an identical item that works properly. If he can't do this within a reasonable time, you then have the right to a full refund.

A week after I started to use a new brand of makeup, I developed a serious skin condition. Can I sue the manufacturer even though I can't prove that he was negligent in making the product?

If you can show that you suffered injury by normal use of the makeup, the burden of proof would be shifted to the manufacturer. He would have to convince the court that his manufacturing process and testing were reliable, safe, and adequate. Since cosmetics are allowed on the market only after Health and Welfare Canada tests them, it's unlikely an action against a manufacturer would succeed, but it's not impossible. If the makeup was known to pose a possible danger to some groups—for example, people with fair complexions—the manufacturer would be required to have warnings on his product. If you could show some defect in the manufacture, testing, packaging or distribution of the product, or failure to warn of a dangerous substance, you could win your case.

When I lifted my new luggage from a closet shelf, the handle came off, and I fell, injuring my back. Can I sue the manufacturer?

Yes, if you can establish that your injury was the direct result of the defective handle and that the defect was caused by the manufacturer and not by ordinary wear and tear.

Your Rights at a Restaurant

If Shirley doesn't like the chicken in a restaurant that advertises the best fried chicken in town, is she entitled to a refund?

No. The law recognizes that no merchant would claim that his goods are just mediocre or passable. Therefore, the use of "best," "top," or "finest" is not interpreted by the courts as a specific promise or warranty. Shirley may disagree with the restaurateur's opinion that his fried chicken is the best in town, but she is not entitled to a refund.

Beatrice went to a restaurant that advertised "All you can eat for $7.95." When she asked for a third helping of shrimp, the waitress told her she could have chicken, but there was a limit of two servings of shrimp. Would Beatrice be justified in reporting the restaurant for false advertising?

Probably not. The restaurant did not advertise unlimited shrimp; rather, it advertised unlimited food. The restaurant would be guilty of false advertising only if it advertised "All the shrimp you can eat for $7.95."

Is it true that if I'm dissatisfied with the service at a restaurant, I don't have to pay?

No. Dissatisfaction with the service, when the food itself is of adequate quality, does not give you the right to refuse to pay for the meal. Poor service is grounds for leaving a small tip or no tip.

If, however, the poor service results in food that is cold, spoiled, or otherwise unsatisfactory, the customer has the right to request that it be prepared again or to cancel the order.

Arnold was turned away from a restaurant because he wasn't wearing a jacket and tie. Doesn't this violate his rights?

No. Although the manager or owner of a restaurant is generally required to accept anyone as a customer, he is entitled to set a dress code. A restaurant may not refuse to serve customers on the grounds of race, sex, color, religion, or national origin, but these are the only restrictions forbidden by law.

Can I be forced to sit at the counter in a restaurant when I'm dining alone?

Yes. The manager or owner of a restaurant may seat any customer anywhere he wishes, whether alone or not, provided he does not do so because of race, sex, color, religion, or national origin.

A waiter spilled sauce on Amy's dress, and the cleaner can't get the spots out. Must the restaurant pay Amy for the lost dress?

Yes, but not for the full purchase price, unless the dress was brand-new. Amy will be reimbursed for the present value of the dress—for example, one half the purchase price of the dress if it is 1½ years old and still in good condition.

Your Rights at a Restaurant

After buying a soft drink from a store, I discovered a small bug in the bottle and got sick. Can I sue the manufacturer or the store?

If you drank from the bottle before discovering the bug and your illness is due to the bug, you can sue both the manufacturer and the store. The manufacturer can be held liable for the negligence that allowed the creature to get inside the bottle. The store can be held liable for breaching the implied warranty of merchantability—that is, you can sue the store for selling you something that wasn't fit to be sold. Everyone in the chain of distribution, from the manufacturer to the retailer, is responsible for supplying a safe product.

Carole purchased a sandwich at the corner deli, ate part of it, then noticed there were hairs in it. What is Carole entitled to?

She is entitled to a new sandwich or a refund. All provinces and municipalities have laws prohibiting the sale of unwholesome or con-taminated food. Carole should take the sandwich to the deli immediately, show it to the manager, and tell him whether she prefers another sandwich or a refund.

While eating at a restaurant, I found a piece of glass in my food. The food was quickly replaced, but later that night I became very ill. What are my rights?

If you can prove that your illness was caused by the glass in the food, you may hold the restaurant responsible for your out-of-pocket medical bills, lost wages, and pain and suffering. The lapse of several hours before the onset of the illness does not destroy your claim.

Travel Troubles

Harry made airline reservations several days before he was due to leave on a business trip. When he checked in, he was told the flight was overbooked. What are Harry's rights?

Under federal law, if Harry is bumped because of overbooking, the airline must try to get him to his destination on another carrier, buying him a first-class seat if necessary. The company would be responsible for all foreseeable damages Harry incurred as a result of the airline's breach of contract.

***An airline lost my luggage several months ago, and no action has
been taken. What should I do?***

Get a claim form from the airline's passenger service representative and
file a claim. If your flight was a domestic one, you are entitled to an
amount fixed by federal law for lost or damaged luggage and its contents,
excluding cash, jewelry, cameras, or very fragile items. If you were on an
international flight, you are entitled to an indemnity set by the Warsaw
Convention. On future trips, you might consider buying baggage insurance, especially if your luggage and its contents are valuable. Travel
experts advise you never to leave jewelry, cameras, cash, or other
valuables in your checked luggage. Keep them with you on the plane.

***On a flight from Montreal to Vancouver I had to change planes in
Winnipeg. Just after we landed in Winnipeg, the airport was
closed because of heavy snow, and I had to sit in the airport all
night waiting for the weather to clear. Shouldn't the airline have
put me up in a hotel?***

Not necessarily. Although some airlines do provide accommodation and
meals for passengers in such circumstances, they are not required by
law to do so. Most airlines provide telephone service to help stranded
passengers notify those who are expecting them; but this, too, they are
not legally bound to do. The passengers' inconvenience is not their fault,
but due to an "act of God" or a "fortuitous event."

***Nancy bought a ticket for a charter flight to Hawaii and paid for it
three months before the day of departure. Two days before the
flight, she was notified that the price of the ticket had been
increased by $100 and she would have to pay the balance. Can
they make her pay?***

No, unless the contract she made expressly states that she may be liable
for an increased fare charge at a later date.

***Ray and Virginia prepaid a travel agency for a package trip that
proved unsatisfactory. Their rooms were not ready on time, and
they lost three days of sightseeing because of trouble with
their charter flights. Do they have any recourse?***

Yes. They can sue the travel agency for breach of contract. The court
may order the agency to compensate them for the cost of alternative
transportation and meals for the three days, for general inconvenience,
and for the value of the three days of lost sightseeing.

Travel Troubles

Stephanie was bumped from her flight to Europe because it was overbooked. Arriving on a later flight, she found the hotel had canceled her reservation. The only available room was much more expensive. Shouldn't the airline pay the additional expense?

Airlines are allowed to limit their liability for problems indirectly caused by late departures that are not their fault. But since Stephanie was bumped because of overbooking, the airline would probably be held liable for breach of contract. Many travelers guard against this type of inconvenience and extra expense by purchasing traveler's insurance that covers extra expenses caused by delays in travel arrangements.

I planned a vacation near a very popular amusement center and made reservations at a motel two months in advance. When I arrived, the motel had overbooked, and I had to stay some 50 kilometres away. Can I sue?

Yes. By not honoring the terms of your agreement, the motel breached the contract, and you would be entitled to sue for damages, for distress, and disappointment, as well as for any extra expenses you incurred.

When You Have a Complaint

Which government agencies handle what consumer complaints?

Most complaints can be sent to Consumer and Corporate Affairs Canada (CCAC), which has offices across the country. Complaints concerning the accuracy of electricity and gas meters, the accuracy of scales and pumps, the safety of chemicals and toys, and the flammability of textiles can be addressed to this agency. The marketing practices branch of CCAC handles complaints about false or misleading advertising. CCAC also deals with complaints about the packaging and labeling of foods and nonfood products. Health and Welfare Canada looks after complaints concerning cosmetics, over-the-counter medicines and other products that people may eat or apply to their bodies—products regulated by the Food and Drugs Act. Complaints about lawyers, doctors, accountants, dentists and other professionals should be directed to professional governing bodies such as the Bar Association and the College of Physicians and Surgeons. Provincial consumer protection agencies deal with some complaints. If you are not sure where to complain, call a consumer group for information, or call the federal or provincial information center listed in your phone book.

*Vivian bought a sofa bed from a furniture dealer, but the store
has not delivered it. What should Vivian do?*

She should contact the dealer to determine if there's been a mistake or
an unavoidable delay. If the dealer cannot guarantee that she will have
delivery within a reasonable time, Vivian has the right to cancel the sales
contract and demand a full refund.

*Alice paid a repairman $125 to fix her dishwasher, but it flooded
again two hours after he left. She stopped payment on her cheque,
and now the repairman is threatening to take her to Small Claims
Court. Is this the right place to settle their dispute?*

Yes. This court handles simple lawsuits for amounts ranging from $50 to
$3,000, depending on the province. Procedures for filing and presenting
cases are not complicated, and neither the repairman nor Alice will need
a lawyer. See Small Claims Court in Chapter 18, *Going to Court.*

*I asked my hairdresser for a trim, but he lopped off two inches
instead. I'm furious. What can I do?*

A hairdresser or barber can be held responsible for damage done to a
customer's hair through negligence. If your hairdresser behaved negligently, in disregard of your express instructions, you may consider suing
in Small Claims Court. However, if your instructions were vague or
unclear, the court may not hold the hairdresser responsible. You may
also complain to the agency that licenses barbers in your province.

*The butcher shop where Mia dealt for years has changed hands
and she thinks the new butcher is cheating on his weight scales.
What can she do to make sure she is being fairly treated?*

If she complains to the Office of Weights and Measures, a department of
Consumer and Corporate Affairs Canada, an inspector will be sent to
make sure the scale is functioning properly.

Does the Better Business Bureau handle consumer complaints?

You would do better to use the Better Business Bureau *before* you make a
purchase, rather than afterward when you have a complaint. The bureau
collects information on local businesses. By calling the bureau, you can
find out how long a business has operated, what type of complaints have
been made against it, if any, and how the complaints have been settled.

When You Have a Complaint

The Better Business Bureau may not be as helpful to you once you have a complaint. It does not have the power to force settlements between consumers and merchants or to issue orders that are legally binding. But try the bureau anyhow. In some cases it acts as an arbitrator.

Making a Complaint

When faced with a defective product, try these steps:

1. Contact the merchant or manufacturer as soon as possible. If you phone, ask for the name of the person with whom you are speaking and keep a record of the time and date of all calls, as well as the nature of your conversation. If you write, send the letter by registered mail and keep several copies. Give the following information:

—Your name, address, and daytime telephone number.

—An exact description of the product. Include the model name, dimensions, color, and serial number, if any.

—The date and place of purchase and the manner in which you paid (cheque, cash, or credit card).

—An accurate description of the nature of the defect. Be specific. ("This clock radio is garbage" is not a specific complaint. "The alarm on this clock radio does not ring when it should" is.)

—What you expect the merchant or manufacturer to do. Do you want the product repaired or replaced, or do you want a refund? If you simply state, "I demand satisfaction," you are not telling the merchant or manufacturer what you want him to do.

2. If there is no response to your letter within a reasonable time, send a warning by registered mail. In it, refer to your earlier correspondence and list the steps you will take if your complaint is not resolved ("If I do not hear from you by June 1, I will assume you do not intend to rectify this problem, and I will institute legal proceedings" or "I will report you to the Better Business Bureau and the consumer protection office").

3. If this letter of warning produces no result, decide whether you want to sue. If the problem involves a small amount, you can sue in Small Claims Court. If the business was acting fraudulently or a large amount of money was involved, you may consider a lawsuit.

4. Consider instituting a "class action suit" if the facts of your case permit it and if you think that many consumers have been victimized by the company. Provincial governments often help consumers by providing funds for class action suits that are in the public interest.

5. Write a letter to a newspaper "Action Line," describing the treatment you received. Many companies will respond quickly to such a tactic to minimize the effect of bad publicity.

CHAPTER
10

Your Job

Applying for a Job

A help-wanted notice in our local newspaper advertised security guard openings for "men, ages 20–28." Is it legal for an employer to restrict applicants like this?

No. Age restrictions of this kind are illegal unless an employer can show that most people above the specified age cannot adequately perform the tasks required by the job, as might be the case with, say, fire fighters. The advertisement may also be illegal because it prohibits women from applying. Restricting the applicants to men would not be justified, even if the job were in a prison for men, although there might be restrictions on the jobs a female security officer would perform there.

I have heard radio ads for flight attendants for a major airline. The qualifications include height and weight limits. Can an airline rightfully impose such requirements?

Yes. The Canadian Human Rights Act allows an employer to establish height and weight requirements for a job, but only if they are necessary for the safe and efficient operation of the business—as may be the case with flight attendants. In most circumstances, though, height and weight requirements are prohibited because they tend to discriminate against women who are, on average, shorter and lighter than men, and against certain ethnic groups who tend to be slightly built. If a person files a complaint with the Human Rights Commission, he first must make a *prima facie* or self-evident case that he was discriminated against. Once this is done, the burden of proof shifts to the employer, who must show that the alleged discrimination or requirement was reasonable and necessary in the circumstances, was job-related, and was made to eliminate a real risk of damage to the public at large.

After driving a school bus for 12 years, Russell applied for a job with the city bus system. He was rejected because he is 52 years old—two years over the city's maximum age of 50 for a bus driver. Is this maximum legal?

A maximum age of 50 is legal as long as the city bus system can prove that this restriction is reasonably necessary to conduct its business. If challenged, the city would have to show that the physical skills needed to drive a bus decrease as a person gets older, and that there is no practical way to determine the rate at which such skills decrease with age. Courts have recognized that pilots, bus drivers, and police officers require physical skills that are affected by age. Some airline companies oblige their pilots to retire at age 60, and the International Civil Aviation

Organization recommends that no pilot—or co-pilot—60 or over command an aircraft. However, to refuse to hire someone as a bus driver merely because he is 52 years old would be hard to justify. If Russell could show that in his city or elsewhere there were other bus drivers who were 50 and older, there is a good chance the bus system's rule would be declared invalid.

Anne's application for a nursing position was not considered by the local hospital, because she has a hearing disability. Does she have a basis for challenging this decision?

Yes, if her impairment is minor or if it can be corrected with a hearing aid and does not interfere with her job performance. However, if her disability would interfere with her doing the job or endanger the health and safety of her patients or others, the employer would be within his rights in turning her down.

Job Interview Questions You Don't Have to Answer

Federal and provincial antidiscrimination laws limit the types of questions an employer may ask during a job interview or in a job application form. As a general rule, an employer may seek only information that will help him evaluate a person's ability to do the job. If a question is personal or seems irrelevant to the requirements of the job, the prospective employee is not required to answer it. A job applicant should not be questioned about the following:

• Marital status or future marriage plans.
• Spouse's or parents' occupations or job titles.
• Number of children, their ages, or plans for having children.
• Baby-sitting arrangements.
• Whether a spouse would agree to overtime work or business travel.
• Age or date of birth.
• Feelings about working for someone younger.
• Place of birth. (But a foreign-born person seeking employment may be required to prove he is in Canada legally.)
• Race or national origin.
• The origin of a surname.
• Religion or what religious holidays are observed.
• Handicaps, unless they relate to the job.
• Political views or political party preference.
• With whom a person lives.
• Home ownership or rental status.
• Debts and who the creditors are.

Applying for a Job

***While interviewing me for a job, a personnel director asked if I
was married and whether my husband approved of my working.
What should I have said to the interviewer?***

It is illegal to ask these questions during a job interview; all questions
must pertain to your qualifications for the job. You have three options in
such a situation: (1) ask why these questions are relevant; (2) refuse to
answer the questions and remind the interviewer that they should not be
asked; or (3) answer the questions. If you don't get the job and you can
show that your replies—or refusal to reply—were used to disqualify
you, you will have a valid reason to sue the employer.

***On her job application, Amy listed her previous employer as a
reference. The former boss attested to her employment, but
wouldn't comment on her job performance, and Amy wasn't
hired. Does Amy have any recourse against her former employer?***

No. As a general rule, employers need not give references. In fact, many
employers provide only basic information about former employees—
date hired, salary, job title, or position held—lest their comments about
job performance lead to a lawsuit for defamation of character.

***Ned failed to mention a physical impairment on his application
form. Can the firm discharge him if it later discovers he withheld
this information?***

If Ned's impairment affects his job performance, his failure to mention it
could be grounds for discharge. Employment applications often state
that if false information is given, the employee will be dismissed.

***Margaret was turned down for a job because she received poor
references. Does she have a right to find out what was said about
her and by whom? Can she sue her former employer?***

There is no general legal requirement that applicants be given the details
of former employers' comments. And even if Margaret could get a copy
of the employee record her former employer is obliged to keep, it would
probably contain only the bare facts—name, address, date hired, pay,
overtime, job description—not her employer's opinion. Although an
employer is not allowed to slander an employee, neither is he obliged to
praise poor job performance. If Margaret's former employer gave his
opinion in good faith, not maliciously, Margaret has no recourse.

When I applied for a job, the company required a physical examination, which revealed an old back ailment that could lead to future problems. I didn't get the job for this reason. Can the company legally do this?

Yes. Employers are allowed to require medical tests to determine whether an applicant is physically able to carry out a job. These tests must be given to all applicants, and the same criteria must be used to evaluate all applicants' ability to do the work. Discrimination may be indicated if the employer does not consistently require physical examinations or if he uses them to hide the real reason for rejection—such as race, color, religion, sex, age, or national origin. To use the fact of an earlier back ailment to refuse you a job, an employer would have to show that the problem would prevent you from doing the job properly. People who suffer from asthma and from diabetes have been ordered rehired because their afflictions had no direct bearing on their abilities to perform their jobs. The federal government and most provinces bar discrimination based on mental or physical handicaps unless these directly affect the ability to do the job or unless they endanger the public.

Adam's interviewer asked him to sign a waiver allowing the Dynamic Data Processing Company to delve into his medical history. Must he sign this waiver?

No. Adam does not have to grant access to this information unless the interviewer can show a direct connection between the job and Adam's medical history. Medical histories are a legitimate area of investigation only when a job requires definable physical strength or skills.

Can I be denied a job for which I am qualified if I refuse to be photographed and fingerprinted?

It depends on where you live. In British Columbia, Saskatchewan, Quebec, and Newfoundland, which guarantee your right to privacy, you can complain to the Human Rights Commission if you are denied a job because you refuse to be photographed or fingerprinted. Although nothing prevents prospective employers from photographing and fingerprinting you, human rights laws indirectly limit how the photos and fingerprints can be used. These laws prohibit discrimination because of race, national origin, religion, sex, physical or mental handicap, age, political belief, marital status or, in Ontario and Quebec, a criminal record. The federal government, Yukon, and the Northwest Territories forbid discrimination based on a criminal record if a pardon was granted. So if you are denied a job because of something your photo or fingerprints reveal, you can go to the Human Rights Commission.

Applying for a Job

I was promised a job at a specified wage and starting time. When I appeared for work on the agreed date, they told me the job had been filled by someone else. Do I have any legal recourse?

Yes. If you have a written contract, you could sue the employer for breach of contract and for damages. With a verbal contract, it would be more difficult, but not impossible to prove your case. If you were enticed from a secure job to take this new position, you could sue for damages just as a long-term employee who was wrongfully dismissed from the job could sue.

George applied for a job and was told he would be hired if he took a lie detector test. Must he take this test?

Ontario and New Brunswick expressly prohibit employers from using lie detector tests. Where there is no law on the subject, a job applicant could refuse on grounds that such a test intrudes on his privacy, that it is unreliable, and that taking such a test is not a *bona fide* requirement of the job. But George may not get the job if he refuses to take the test, and if he lives outside of Ontario and New Brunswick, there is no guarantee that a complaint to a human rights tribunal would be upheld.

What are my rights if a potential employer wants to give me a psychological test?

You can decline to take the test, but you may not get the job if you do so. Companies can legally give aptitude, personality, or psychological tests to prospective employees as long as the tests are not used to eliminate anyone on the basis of race, color, religion, sex, age, or national origin. Psychological tests and lie detector tests may be challenged for several other reasons as well—that the questions had no relation to the job, that evaluations of the results were incorrect, and that the test was inappropriate for measuring a person's ability to succeed in that job.

When my daughter applied for a job, one question was whether she had ever been arrested or convicted. If so, she was asked to give details. Does a potential employer have the right to ask for this information?

Questions about convictions can be asked if there might be a connection between the job's responsibility and a crime. For example, an employer would be justified in finding out if someone applying for a job as an accountant had ever been convicted of embezzlement; and he would be within his rights in rejecting an applicant with such a conviction. In some provinces and in jobs for the federal government, a person cannot be refused employment because of a criminal conviction *if he has been pardoned.* In Ontario and Quebec, even if no pardon was obtained, a criminal conviction is not reason enough to refuse employment.

The manager who interviewed Wendy said he would hire her only on an at-will basis. What does this mean?

An at-will agreement means that the employer-employee relationship may be terminated at the will of the employer for any reason, at any time; it usually applies when there is no written job contract. Today, however, federal and provincial laws restrict an employer's right to dismiss at-will employees. These laws forbid dismissals because of race, color, religion, sex, or national origin. Nor may an employee be fired in retaliation for reporting safety violations, for being off work for jury duty, or because his salary is garnisheed.

Belinda has always wanted to work for the federal government. Are there special requirements for a civil service position?

Each job in the immense public service network is graded according to the degree of responsibility it carries and the knowledge, skills, and experience it requires. If Belinda applies for a certain civil service job, she will be given points based on the amount of education, training and experience she has, and on the results of certain tests that measure her skills and abilities. Since the government hires applicants on the basis of merit only, Belinda's point total will be compared with those of other applicants, and the one with the best score will get the job.

The federal government, like other employers, is bound by the Charter of Rights and Freedoms, the Canadian Human Rights Act, and the Canada Labour Code. Together, these prohibit discrimination in hiring and employment because of age, sex, religion, race, color, national origin, physical or mental handicap, marital status, political belief, or a criminal record if a pardon was granted.

Victor applied for a job as a mechanic and was told he would hear from the employer within two weeks. Two months later he has had no news, but the job opening is still being advertised in the local paper. What should Victor do?

Victor has no legal recourse to force a prospective employer to answer him, much less to hire him. Since the job probably hasn't been filled yet, he can write to remind the garage owner that he has not heard from him. Better, he can go to see him in person, thus showing he is seriously interested in getting the position.

Michael's interview at the Grand Old Insurance Company was arranged by an employment agency. He didn't get the job at the time, but five months later the insurance company offered him the position. Must Michael pay the agency's fee?

Yes. Michael's agreement with the employment agency probably states that he must pay the agency its fee if he obtains a job within one year. Even if the agreement contains no such provision, an agency is usually entitled to payment if its services directly or indirectly result in a client being hired.

Lester accepted a job through an employment agency, but before he started he was offered a better job at another company. Does he have to pay the agency its fee if he takes the better job?

Yes. Once the agency fulfills its obligation by finding a job that the client accepts, it is entitled to payment.

I found a job through an employment agency but was fired two weeks later. Do I have to pay the rest of the agency fee?

Most agency agreements call for payment of the full fee as soon as you accept a job. However, some contracts may allow the fee to be reduced if it is not your fault you are fired. Reread your contract to see if it contains any such clause, or if the employment agency guaranteed to find you more than one job.

On the Job

Can my job description be changed without my approval?

Yes, unless the change is so drastic that it creates a totally different job or one that pays less than your present salary. Job descriptions often include a general statement that an employee must "perform any other tasks as may be assigned," which allows employers to revise job duties as the needs of the business change.

My supervisor and I disagreed about my job performance, and I'm sure she put negative reports in my personnel file. Do I have a right to see these reports?

If you work for the federal government or a provincial government such as Quebec, access-to-information laws give you the right to consult your file and to obtain copies of its contents. If you work for a unionized company, your collective agreement probably allows you to consult your file. In other cases, reports made by employers may be considered the private property of the employer and therefore confidential. An employer's report or record of an employee's behavior on the job is not to be confused with employees' records, which all employers are bound by law to maintain, and which contain only such basic facts as name, address, date hired, and salary.

By day Sam worked for Harold as a carpenter, at night he worked as a clerk at a convenience store. When Harold learned about the second job, he demanded that Sam quit it. Does Sam have to submit to this demand?

The general rule is that an employee may spend his off-duty hours any way he wishes, including working at a second job. However, if Sam's second job is adversely affecting his first job, he might have a problem. For example, if Sam is making costly mistakes, taking safety risks, or otherwise jeopardizing the quality of his employer's work because he is overtired, Harold has the right to ask Sam to quit the second job.

Can my employer legally forbid me to moonlight for a competitor?

Yes. Every employee has a legal duty to promote his employer's best interests, and helping a competitor is not compatible with this duty. In addition, if you and your employer agreed, when you were hired, that you would work exclusively for him, moonlighting for a competitor could be considered a breach of this agreement.

Dorothy's boss wants her to sign a contract prohibiting her from working for a competitor for three years if she should quit or be fired. What will happen if she signs, then quits a year later to join a competing company at a better salary?

A clause in a contract prohibiting an employee from working for a competing employer or from opening a competing business for a certain period after leaving the job is known as a restrictive covenant. Its conditions must be reasonable. To prevent Dorothy from joining the competitor, the employer would have to prove that Dorothy knew trade secrets or other confidential information that, if imparted to competitors, would cause him substantial harm.

As manager of a local fitness center, Betty developed an aerobic training manual for new employees. She was laid off, but they are still using her manual. Can't she get some remuneration for this?

No. Betty developed the manual as part of her job, and any material prepared as a part of a person's job becomes the employer's property.

Barney, a school custodian, knows that his boss signs for supplies that are never delivered, and suspects his boss is getting a kickback. Can Barney lose his job if he reports this misconduct?

If Barney were fired for reporting the fraudulent behavior of his boss, he could sue the school for wrongful dismissal and for damages as well as reinstatement in his former job. It is against public policy to fire an employee for reporting illegal activities. In fact, if it were found out that Barney knew his boss was stealing from the school but didn't report it, *this* might be grounds for firing Barney.

Can my employer require that I submit to a drug test?

Although a drug test would be an invasion of your privacy, it would be lawful if it related to your ability to do the job or if the safety of co-workers or the public were involved, as with airline pilots and bus drivers. Before conducting a drug test an employer must (1) have a reasonable suspicion of drug use; (2) give notice that testing will be carried out as part of company policy; and (3) keep confidential the information about who is tested and the test results. If you belong to a union, this issue may have been negotiated with your employer as part of the union contract.

When Bruce was passed over for a promotion, he filed a lawsuit against the company for age discrimination, and his attorney has asked Eric, a co-worker, to testify on Bruce's behalf. Is Eric protected if he testifies against the company?

Yes. As a subpoenaed witness Eric is obliged by law to answer all questions, even if an answer would be to the prejudice of his employer. It would be unlawful for the employer to retaliate by firing Eric or demoting him, and if he did so, Eric would have grounds to sue him.

Can Georgette be ordered not to smoke at her desk?

Yes. Because an employer has the duty to provide a safe and healthy environment for his employees, and because scientific studies have established that "secondary smoke" is a hazard to health, it would not be unreasonable for an employer to restrict smoking to designated areas only. More and more companies are restricting smoking, and most provinces and many municipalities have restricted the right of people to smoke in public places.

Because of a series of thefts, my employer hired a security guard to search employees' packages and purses as they leave the building. Can I be fired if I don't let the guard search my purse?

Yes. Your employer has the right to combat the thefts by searching your possessions, and to dismiss you if you refuse. However, the search must be conducted in a reasonable manner. If employees are detained for too long, or the search is conducted in the presence of customers or outsiders, you could refuse to submit to the search and would have a good case against your employer if you were discharged.

Can my boss search my desk looking for stolen property?

Yes. When property has been stolen, an employer has the right to look in desks and other areas if he has reason to suspect an employee might be the thief. The search should involve only those areas where the stolen property might reasonably be found. For example, if a typewriter has been stolen, an employer cannot search a desk drawer. As most provincial charters and codes of human rights protect a person's privacy, or at least his right to dignity and respect, an employer must tread carefully in conducting a search. Unreasonable searches are prohibited by the Charter of Rights and Freedoms. If a court or arbitrator found a search to be unreasonable, abusive and humiliating, an employer could be held liable for damages to the employee.

What if my boss tells me to do something illegal?

This is a difficult situation. If you follow his orders you will be guilty of committing a crime. If you don't follow his orders, you run the risk of being fired. However, if you are fired, you can sue. Since you were dismissed for refusing to break the law, a court would view this as wrongful dismissal and a violation of public policy.

Cori, working at a department store, was asked to take a lie detector test to see if she knew anything about some thefts. Does she have to take the test? What happens if she refuses to take it?

If Cori were fired for refusing to take a lie detector test, she would have a good chance of winning a case for unlawful dismissal. Employment standards acts in Ontario and New Brunswick expressly prohibit employers from using lie detector tests. Such tests are probably unlawful in other provinces, too, because they would infringe upon the right to privacy, which is protected by provincial privacy acts and the Charter of Rights and Freedoms. In 1975, the Supreme Court of Canada declared evidence obtained by a lie detector test inadmissible because of the unreliability of such tests.

Reporting Job-Related Crimes

As you get ready to leave work one night, you notice that a co-worker is putting typewriter ribbons and a package of typing paper into her tote bag. You know she never takes work home, so you suspect that the supplies are for her personal use. Do you say something to her, forget about it, or talk to someone else in your department?

This predicament is not uncommon. Taking office supplies is just one of many unlawful activities that plague businesses throughout the country. Using company property—such as copying machines—for personal purposes, falsifying time sheets or expense accounts, forging signatures, and embezzling company funds cause millions of dollars of losses to Canadian business each year.

Since it is impossible, and undesirable, for employers to monitor each employee's actions, they must rely on co-workers to report thefts and other business crimes. Most companies have established procedures for reporting theft or misconduct. Find out what steps you should take if you know about illegal activities in your company. If your company does not have a reporting procedure, talk to your supervisor or boss. You must let someone in a supervisory or management position know about what you have observed or risk disciplinary measures yourself for not reporting the illegal activity. This is not just a matter of personal choice—Canadian courts have ruled that employees who fail to report a job-related crime may be fired.

YOUR JOB

Judy routinely expresses her political views to other employees and frequently distributes political literature. Her boss has ordered her to stop these activities. Is he permitted to do this?

Her boss can restrict Judy's political activities only if she's neglecting her job, disrupting others' work, or jeopardizing her employer's business.

If my car is vandalized in the company parking lot, is my employer responsible for the repair bill?

No. Vandalism or theft is usually considered an unforeseeable event, and therefore your employer would not be held responsible. If, however, you were obliged to pay for your parking space, and if you had to give your keys to a parking attendant, your employer could be held responsible if he did not take reasonable precautions to avoid theft or vandalism.

Andy wants to start his new job as soon as possible. Does he have to give his current employer a certain number of days' notice?

There is no general rule as to when Andy must tell his employer he is leaving. If Andy signed a contract when hired, it may specify how far in advance he must notify the company. Employees in some provinces, Nova Scotia, Prince Edward Island and Newfoundland for example, and in certain jobs in Quebec, domestic work for example, must give notice—usually one week—to their employers.

Pay and Benefits

For information on employee pensions, see "Pension Plans" in Chapter 15, *Pensions, RRSPs, Social Programs.*

What can I do if my employer doesn't give me my pay?

Seek help from your provincial department of labor or employment or from a similar agency. All provinces require that wages be paid at regular intervals—say, every two weeks—whether calculated by the hour, by piecework, or on an annual basis.

If I am hired as a salaried employee, can the company convert my status to that of an hourly employee without my consent?

If you have a written contract, your employer cannot change your method of compensation without your approval. To do so would be a

YOUR JOB

Pay and Benefits

breach of contract. If you don't have a contract, your employer can change the way you are compensated, but if you lose fringe benefits, such as pension plan eligibility, or if your weekly pay is reduced, you may have legal grounds to challenge this action.

When Monica applied for a job as a manicurist, the manager of the shop said her pay would be the minimum wage less what she would receive in tips. Is her employer allowed to do this?

No; otherwise Monica could end up working for no wage at all if her tips exceed the minimum wage. Moreover, the minimum wage for jobs that earn tips is often lower than for jobs that don't. It would be unlawful for her employer to further reduce her wages.

I thought everyone who worked overtime got overtime pay. My new employer tells me he doesn't pay overtime. Is this legal?

The Canada Labour Code and similar provincial statutes provide for overtime pay—at least 1½ times the regular rate. Domestics, students, people in managerial or supervisory positions, doctors and lawyers are not entitled to overtime pay, however. To find out whether you are entitled to overtime, check with your ministry of labor or, if you work for the federal government, with the federal minister of employment.

Am I obliged to work overtime?

Generally, an employer cannot oblige an employee to work overtime except in cases of emergency or accident. Where workers are unionized, the collective agreement usually defines the rights and duties of employees concerning overtime and the rate of pay for such overtime. Most provinces have laws that limit the amount of overtime that can be demanded. The Canada Labour Code, which governs federal jobs, sets a limit of 48 hours a week including overtime. A permit from the minister of labor is usually required if employees are to work more than 48 hours.

Rosemary works for a company that sells frozen pizza. She makes $2.50 an hour. Doesn't the company have to pay the provincial minimum wage?

Yes. Minimum wage acts apply to all workers in all provinces and Territories. Minimum wages vary from one province to another, and the minimum may vary even within a province. For example, the minimum wage for someone who has an opportunity to earn tips, such as a waiter or waitress, is often lower than the minimum in, say, factory work. Minimum wages were first introduced in Ontario in 1920.

Troy works for a company whose standard workweek is 37½ hours. He worked 45 hours last week but his pay cheque showed only 5 hours of overtime. Shouldn't he be paid for 7½ hours?

No. Each province decides how many hours comprise a workweek— usually 40 to 44; overtime is paid only for hours worked in excess of that. It could be argued, however, that provincial employment standards acts provide for minimum standards of work, and if an employer establishes a workweek of 37½ hours, then any hours in excess of 37½ should be considered overtime. The terms and conditions for unionized employees are usually spelled out in the collective agreement.

Valerie's boss asked her to work late several evenings in a row, and mumbled something about comp time. What is comp time?

If employer and employee agree, an employer can pay an employee any overtime due by giving him 1½ hours off for each overtime hour worked. Thus, if Valerie worked 8 hours overtime, she would be entitled to 12 hours off as compensatory time.

Dora, a seamstress, is paid by the number of garments she sews. For the past month, she has been putting in 45 to 55 hours each week to fulfill an order. The supervisor refuses to pay her overtime; he says it isn't required, since she is paid by the garment. Is he right?

No. Dora is entitled to 1½ times her hourly rate for hours worked in excess of 40 a week (44 in some provinces). Pieceworkers are covered by provincial employment standards acts. A written contract in which a person agreed not to be paid overtime would be invalid; no private agreement can set aside an employment standard set out by law.

The company Ross worked for went out of business without paying him for work he had done. What can he do?

Under the Federal Bankruptcy Act, the salaries due to workers (as opposed to administrators) have a priority over almost all other creditors for up to three months' salary or wages. However, the Canada

Pay and Benefits

Corporations Act holds the directors of a company personally responsible for up to six months' salary or wages if legal proceedings are taken within six months of the company bankruptcy. At the time of writing the federal government had prepared legislation that will guarantee the salaries of workers of bankrupt companies up to $2,000.

When I was hired, the company promised it would give me a raise after six months. Seven months have passed, and the raise hasn't materialized. Doesn't the company have to keep its promise?

Yes, unless the raise depended on your doing satisfactory work. If you received a poor evaluation, the company need not increase your salary.

Free lunches were among benefits of Patricia's job as a waitress until the restaurant was sold and the new owner began deducting $30 a week for meals from her pay cheque. Is this legal?

Yes, provided this complies with her province's labor standards, which specify the type of deductions an employer can make and the amounts that may be deducted for such things as meals and lodging. In some provinces, the employer may also deduct an amount for supply and maintenance of uniforms. In unionized companies, the amount and type of deductions are set out in the collective agreement.

At the end of his shift at a gas station, Stuart's boss told him that $100 was missing from the cash register and that he would dock Stuart's pay $100. Is it legal for the employer to do this?

Yes, provided Stuart is earning more than the minimum wage. Then his pay can be docked as long as this doesn't bring it below the minimum wage rate. But provinces have different laws about docking an employee's pay. In Alberta and Ontario, for example, an employer cannot deduct for missing cash or damaged or broken property if other employees also had access to such cash or property.

Evelyn dropped and broke a computer terminal while moving it from one desk to another. Can her employer dock her pay to cover the cost of repairing or replacing the terminal?

Yes, but the amount deducted cannot reduce Evelyn's pay below the provincial minimum wage.

I'm entitled to two weeks' vacation, but my boss says he can't spare me. It's been a year now, and I badly need a break. Doesn't he have to give me a vacation?

If there is no reason why you can't be spared, your boss should grant the vacation. On the other hand, if he has a good reason, you can't leave without risking dismissal. You may have to make a formal request in writing or invoke seniority to get the vacation dates you want. Although under certain conditions your employer may postpone your vacation, he cannot *refuse* you a vacation; nor may he give you extra money instead of vacation, unless you expressly agree to this.

Does Danielle have a right to her old job when she returns from maternity leave?

Yes. Except in the Northwest Territories, a female who has worked for the same employer for a certain time (20 weeks in Quebec, one year in most other provinces, six months in a federal job) is entitled to maternity leave and to reinstatement in the same or a comparable position at the same wage. During her absence, she remains an employee, though not necessarily a salaried one: a *paid* maternity leave is not always the rule, since such employees are eligible for unemployment insurance.

Part-time Workers' Benefits

Anyone considering part-time work should be aware that wages, fringe benefits, and other employee prerogatives may not be the same as those of a full-time job. Although part-time workers are protected by the same antidiscrimination laws and receive the same workers' compensation coverage as full-time employees, there are a number of areas in which they can be treated differently, including the following:

● *Wages*—Provincial minimum wage laws do not always cover part-time employees. In many provinces, workers who are under 18 and are students can be paid less than the regular minimum wage.

● *Group health insurance*—Part-time workers may be excluded from coverage. Many company policies cover only employees who work a specified minimum number of hours each week.

● *Pensions*—Coverage will depend on the number of hours worked each year as specified in the company's retirement plan and the Canada or Quebec Pension Plan.

● *Unemployment benefits*—If a person does not work the minimum number of hours per week set by the Unemployment Insurance Act, he may not qualify for unemployment benefits.

Pay and Benefits

Pam knew that her 12-week maternity leave would be without pay. Complications developed, and she was absent 13 weeks. Should her company's health plan compensate her for the 13th week?

Yes. Illness caused by childbirth must be treated like any other illness. If the company health plan covers paid sick leave for workers who develop complications from other illnesses, Pam must receive the same benefits.

Doesn't a company have to give the same benefits to everyone?

Some benefits, such as workers' compensation, pension plans, and unemployment insurance must be offered to every employee to comply with labor or employment standards laws. Other benefits, expense accounts for example, do not have to be offered to all employees.

Elmer works as a manager for a department store that has branches across the province. His salary is lower than that of a woman who holds the same position at one of the other branches. Doesn't the store have to pay all its managers the same salary?

Not necessarily. Different salaries may be justified if they are based on seniority, merit, or quantity or quality of production, or because of differences in living costs or in local competition for qualified people.

When Paula resigned from her job, she had accumulated 30 hours of unused sick leave and 40 hours of vacation time. Her employer would not pay her for these days. Is this legal?

Yes. Employers need not pay employees for unused sick leave or vacation hours, unless a written company policy approved such payments, or they were covered in an employment or union contract.

I injured my back while lifting a crate at work, and my doctor advised me to rest in bed. The company has a group disability insurance policy that protects employees' pay while they're out sick, but they said I wasn't eligible. What can I do?

Since your injury occurred while you were doing your job, you should apply for workers' compensation. It is not unusual for an employer's group insurance policy to exclude work-related accidents or illnesses, since these are covered by workers' compensation programs.

Workers' Compensation

Dennis was injured the second day he was on the job. Is he covered by workers' compensation?

Yes. The fact that Dennis was on the job only two days does not affect his right to benefits. This right began when he was hired.

Can I be reimbursed for lost wages if I'm injured on the job?

You should notify your employer at once that you were injured on the job. In some provinces, the notice must be in writing; in others you can simply tell him about the injury. He will then submit a claim to the appropriate provincial agency. The benefits under workers' compensation consist of medical benefits, covering crutches, medication, and necessary treatment, and disability benefits to compensate for lost earnings. The amount is based on the extent of the injury, how long the worker will be disabled (temporarily or permanently), and how much he would be earning if he were not disabled.

Barry was injured on the job and missed several months' work. He was to have been given a light-duty assignment on his return, but wasn't, and was fired because he was unable to do the work. Can Barry still collect workers' compensation?

Yes. In order to persuade the Workers' Compensation Board that Barry was ineligible for compensation, his employer or insurance company would have to prove not only that he was offered a job but also that he was able to do the job in his weakened condition. Since Barry was unable to do the work, he is still entitled to receive workers' compensation benefits. If Barry's disability is permanent, the compensation board may give him some vocational rehabilitation training to enable him to do other work or continue to pay him until he has reached normal retirement age.

Jack was injured while working at an auto repair shop. His employer has made a workers' compensation claim. Can Jack also sue his employer for his injuries?

Probably not. Workers' compensation is generally recognized as the only remedy available to injured workers. If, however, the employer refuses to maintain his workplace in a safe condition after having been advised to do so, or if he fraudulently concealed hazardous or dangerous conditions, he may be liable to Jack.

YOUR JOB

Workers' Compensation

Woody aggravated an old back injury by lifting some heavy cartons and needed three weeks to recover. Will workers' compensation cover him even though he had a previous injury?

Yes. Although Woody's disability is due to a preexisting condition, this will not automatically disqualify him from benefits. But Woody would have to prove through expert medical testimony that lifting the cartons aggravated the previous injury.

Can a worker who suffers a nervous breakdown because of job-related stress collect workers' compensation?

In most provinces a worker is covered only for accidents that happen in the course of his employment, or for certain industrial diseases recognized by the provincial occupational health and safety law or the workers' compensation law. Since a nervous breakdown is not an accident or a recognized industrial disease, a worker would ordinarily not be covered. If, however, he could prove that his breakdown was caused directly by the job and was not brought about by other factors, his claim might in some special cases be accepted.

Because she wanted to pick up a few items to take home, Irene volunteered to go to the bakery shop for her employer's daily order of coffee and rolls. She was injured on the way. Is she covered by workers' compensation?

Probably. An employee's eligibility for workers' compensation is determined, in part, by whether the injury "arises out of and in the course of employment." Since Irene did go to the store on behalf of her employer, as well as for personal reasons, the Workers' Compensation Board would probably give weight to the business reason for her trip and allow her to receive workers' compensation benefits.

Two employees had an argument over an assignment and got into a fistfight. Both landed in hospital. Is either of them covered by workers' compensation?

Compensation would probably be awarded to both employees, regardless of who started the fight. At one time, the aggressor would have been denied benefits, but the trend now is to disregard who threw the first punch. However, if it turned out that the underlying reason for this fight was personal, the benefits would probably be denied.

Hilda was injured as the result of a co-worker's prank. Is she eligible to collect workers' compensation?

Probably. For many years, workers' compensation did not cover injuries caused by pranks or practical jokes, because they were considered unauthorized activities. The trend now is to look at the facts of each case. For example, Hilda may be awarded benefits if she did not participate in the prank, but was attending to her duties at the time she was injured. Or she may receive compensation if her employer knew that his employees were engaging in pranks and took no steps to prevent this activity.

Robert slipped on the ice around a gas pump at work and broke his leg. When his boss heard that Robert had filed a workers' compensation claim, he fired him, stating, "Nobody is going to collect any money from me for getting hurt on my time!" Isn't it against the law for an employer to fire anyone in this way?

Yes. If Robert were fired for exercising his lawful right to report a work accident to the Workers' Compensation Board, this would be unjustified dismissal. Robert could sue his employer for all damages not covered by the Workers' Compensation Act, and might even claim punitive or exemplary damages.

Can an employee receive both disability insurance payments and workers' compensation at the same time?

Yes. Benefits from other sources, such as pensions and disability insurance, usually do not prevent the payment of workers' compensation benefits, nor do they reduce these benefits. However, if an employee receives other government assistance from a source such as the Crime Victims Indemnity Fund or the Canada or Quebec Pension Fund, workers' compensation benefits would be reduced by the amount he receives from the other government agency. For example, a Quebec truck driver injured on the job could not receive benefits from both the Workers' Compensation Board and the Automobile Insurance Board. He would have to opt for payment from one or the other.

I broke a finger at the company softball game and couldn't work for two days. Will workers' compensation pay for the lost wages?

Probably not. As the injury presumably took place after working hours, and as playing the softball game was voluntary and neither during the course of employment nor on company property, such an injury would not be judged a work accident.

Workers' Compensation

How long is a person entitled to receive workers' compensation?

In most provinces there is no limit to the amount that an injured employee may receive or the length of time such benefits are payable. If an employee is permanently disabled and is unable to work even after participating in physical and vocational rehabilitation, he can usually receive benefits until age 65, when his old age pension begins.

Unions and Strikes

If my plant becomes unionized, will I have to become a member?

It depends on the type of agreement the union works out with your employer. Under a *union shop agreement*, employees must join the union and remain as members as long as the agreement is in effect. At the time of writing, the Supreme Court had not yet ruled on an Ontario resident's challenge that having to join a union in order to work infringes the Charter of Rights and Freedoms. If a *modified union shop* is established, you do not have to join the union, but you may be required to pay fees to the union for the benefits you may receive through its efforts. In unionized companies, all workers have the right to be represented by the union, even employees who choose not to join the union.

Can I be fired for petitioning my co-workers to join a union?

No. Your employer cannot fire you or other pro-union employees or use any kind of pressure to discourage you from affiliating with a union. You and your fellow workers have the right to circulate petitions and to meet with co-workers about unionizing. Your right to freedom of association is guaranteed by the Charter of Rights and Freedoms. However, this attempt to form a union should not be done during working hours or on the employer's property without his consent.

Joe was disciplined by his employer for acts done by another employee. He reported the matter to his union within the 20-day delay for filing a grievance, but the union forgot to follow through with the procedure set out in the collective agreement. Now it is too late. Does Joe have any recourse at all?

Joe cannot sue his employer, because his collective agreement states that a grievance must be filed within a period of 20 days, or the right is lost. But if he can prove that his union was grossly negligent or that it discriminated against him, he could sue it for all damages caused to him. In some provinces a labor court judge might even order an employer to reinstate a fired employee whose union did not protect his rights properly.

I'm getting a lot of pressure, including phone calls at home, to join a union I don't want to belong to. What should I do?

You should consider filing a complaint with the Labour Relations Board in your province. The decision to join a union should be made without any force, intimidation, or pressure of any kind. The provincial labor relations acts as well as the various provincial human rights codes and charters prohibit unions from using these tactics.

Our factory is being automated, and many of us will lose our jobs. Will our union be responsible for seeing that we are retrained for other jobs?

Your employer, not the union, will probably be responsible for retraining workers, since it was management's decision to automate that created the loss of jobs. However, the contract your union has with your employer will dictate the terms for retraining workers. Contact your union representative for details.

If I am a union member and I am fired by my company, what does the union have to do for me?

The union must first investigate why you were fired from the company and whether the proper dismissal procedures were followed, and then set in motion a grievance procedure for challenging your dismissal. If the union fails to handle the matter to your satisfaction, you can sue it for violation of its collective bargaining agreement and, in some provinces, the labor code.

Lauren was fined by her union. Must she pay the fine?

Yes, as long as certain procedures were followed. Union members are entitled to a review when they face discipline by the union. Lauren should have been given a written notice of the charges against her, a reasonable time to prepare her defense, and a fair hearing before a panel of union members or officials. She does not have to pay the fine if any of these procedures were not followed.

Unions and Strikes

If the union orders a work slowdown at my place of employment, must I comply?

Yes. In most provinces (and in the federal Canada Labour Code) the definition of a strike includes a work slowdown. Working to rule, in which workers do the minimum amount of work required by their jobs (similar to a slowdown in its effect), would also be considered a legitimate means of union pressure.

What happens if a judge orders strikers back to work, and the union votes not to go?

Defying a court order or an injunction to return to work can result in contempt of court charges and fines against the union. Injunctions are often issued to stop illegal strikes, or those that threaten the health or safety of the public, such as strikes by the police.

During a strike, do I have to observe a picket line if I'm not a member of the labor union?

No. Both nonunion and union members may cross a picket line and continue working if a strike has been called. However, union members

---

If You Go on Strike

The rights of workers who strike are protected under federal and provincial laws, as long as the strike is legal. The labor laws of each province define the rights and obligations of employers and employees during a strike, and regulate rehiring, picketing, notice to be given and so forth. Illegal strikes—such as sit-downs, wildcat strikes (not authorized by a union), or strikes that violate a no-strike clause in a union contract—result in the loss of all labor law protection. The following general principles govern rights during a legal strike:

● *Wages and unemployment insurance*—You are not entitled to wages or unemployment insurance benefits, but you may be paid some money by your union to replace lost income.

● *Picketing*—It is allowed if done by strikers, but it must be peaceful and must not intimidate employees who choose to cross the picket line. If you are a union member, you must honor the picket line during a lawful strike; if you cross the line, you can be fined or disciplined by the union.

can be fined if they go to work during a lawful, union-authorized strike at their place of employment.

After two months in a unionized factory, Moe was disciplined — unjustifiably, he contends. He was suspended from work for three weeks. When he sought help, the union said it couldn't intervene. Is this true?

It depends on the collective agreement. Most collective agreements exclude workers who have been employed for less than 90 days and probationary workers from the benefits of filing grievances or of having their cases put before an arbitrator.

Having obtained new benefits for its membership, does a labor union have the right to withhold them from those members who have retired?

Yes. There is no legal requirement for active members and retirees to receive the same benefits. In negotiations, the union has a duty to represent all members fairly. But this does not mean that equal benefits must be obtained for all members. Labor unions often make concessions that affect a few members in exchange for benefits that apply to a majority. However, the union may not bargain away pension benefits previously vested or guaranteed to its members.

● *Violence*—Strikers are prohibited from blocking the entrance to a plant, destroying property, or threatening employees, the public, or management. If property is damaged or destroyed, the individuals involved, and the union, may be held liable. The union, too, may discipline or expel members who take part in violent activity during the strike.
● *Discrimination*—An employer is prohibited from discriminating against employees while they are lawfully out on strike or after they have returned to work.
● *Reinstatement*—If the strike was called to protest unfair labor practices, such as intimidating workers, the strikers are entitled to be reinstated in their jobs, even if the employer has already hired replacement labor. Those who have been hired to fill the vacancies must be dismissed. In Quebec, employers are forbidden by law to hire workers to replace striking workers; in case of a strike, only management persons are entitled to perform the tasks previously done by workers out on a legal strike.

Job Discrimination

For more information on discrimination, see "Equality Rights" in Chapter 12, *Your Individual Rights*.

Hundreds of people showed up to take the employment test at a local manufacturing plant. Cathy and 10 of her women friends failed the test; all but one of her male friends passed. What would Cathy need to prove bias against women?

She would have to prove that the test was designed to exclude substantially more women than men. Since hundreds took the exam, Cathy would need to find out what the failure rate of all the women was in comparison to that of all the men, rather than just how her friends did on the exam. She would also need to find out why the employer required the test and how the scores were used in selecting employees. She might have to get a court order to make the employer provide this information.

Sarah learned that the new man hired in her department makes as much as she does. Their responsibilities are the same, but Sarah has three years' seniority. Is this discrimination?

Possibly, but the equal pay of the new man does not automatically mean that Sarah is a victim of sex discrimination. Employers consider many factors in deciding how much to pay their employees. The new man may have more experience, training, or education.

Evelyn's allegation of unequal pay for equal jobs is being investigated by the Human Rights Commission in her province. If Evelyn wins, how much back pay can she expect to receive?

It depends on where she lives. In Alberta and Manitoba, she would be entitled to back pay for 12 months prior to filing the complaint. In Quebec, she might be entitled to seek exemplary damages as well. Questions of pay equity are often settled out of court by agreement between the employer and the Human Rights or Pay Equity commissions.

I am the only woman in the packing department of my company, and I am sure my salary is lower than that of my co-workers. Whom should I call? If I report it, will the company know?

The Canadian Human Rights Act, the Charter of Rights and Freedoms, and the provincial human rights charters and codes all prohibit discrimination based on sex. Thus your employer would be obliged to justify the difference in salary between you and your male co-workers. If you work

YOUR JOB

414

for a federal agency or Crown corporation, you complain to the Canadian Human Rights Commission; if you work for a private company, you complain to the Human Rights Commission or tribunal of your province. These commissions have the power to investigate your complaint and to hold hearings at which each party can tell its side of the story. In some provinces, Ontario for example, you can also file a complaint with the minister in charge of the Fair Practices Act, Pay Equity Act, or Employment Standards Act.

I notified the Human Rights Commission of possible discrimination almost two years ago. Should I wait to learn what they determine before filing a lawsuit?

No. You should not wait because there are deadlines you must meet if you want to sue. You should contact the commission for a status report on its investigation, request a right-to-sue letter, and proceed with your lawsuit as soon as possible. Usually, your right to sue is prolonged by the time it takes for the commission to complete its investigation, or for one year, whichever period is shorter. In British Columbia, Alberta, Manitoba, Ontario and Nova Scotia, a decision of the Human Rights Commission has the same force and effect as a court judgment.

My company won't add separate locker rooms for women only. Isn't this illegal?

A company must have appropriate facilities, not necessarily *separate* facilities, for female employees. It could divide the existing facility or establish separate hours for men and women. However, no employer can use the lack of separate facilities as a reason for not hiring women.

Several promotions have opened up in the six years that Jackie has worked in the shipping department, but her boss has refused to recommend her for any of them, saying she would not like supervising 20 men. Jackie disagrees. What are her options?

If Jackie's company has a grievance procedure (either union-run or company-run), she should comply with it to try to resolve her problem. If there is no grievance procedure, she should take her problem to the company's personnel department or to her boss's supervisor. She should prepare a written statement of her complaint, and should follow up her conversations with management with memos about what those conversations covered. She should also keep an accurate record of the key events in the case, the dates, and the names of witnesses. This documentation will be important if a sex-discrimination claim is made. However, if

Job Discrimination

Jackie's efforts within the company fail, she should consider taking her case to the Human Rights Commission or government department in charge of pay equality laws in her province. She should also consider retaining a lawyer who specializes in these matters.

I was passed over for promotion and I'm sure the decision was influenced by my age, but it has taken me two and a half years to assemble the facts. Is it too late to do something about it?

Probably. Most provincial legislation dealing with complaints based on discrimination requires that legal action be taken within one or two years of the event complained of. In British Columbia, the deadline in some cases is only six months from the date of the infraction.

Can an employee be forced to retire at age 62?

In most cases, no. All provinces and the Territories prohibit discrimination based on age, unless the employer can prove that working beyond a certain age would pose a danger to the safety of the employee or the public at large. However, British Columbia, Saskatchewan, Ontario, Nova Scotia and Newfoundland do allow compulsory retirement at age 65.

Francine's religion requires her to observe the Sabbath on Saturday. Can she be fired for refusing to work on Saturday?

No. The law requires Francine's boss to make reasonable accommodations for her religious practices. This includes finding someone to trade shifts with her and letting her work longer hours on other days. However, Francine's employer may successfully defend himself by claiming that it would be an undue hardship on the business to accommodate her religious practices.

Am I being discriminated against if I have to use a vacation day to observe a religious holiday?

No. The law requires an employer to make reasonable accommodations to allow employees to practice their religion. However, if your employer can establish that rearranging schedules, changing payroll records, and finding other employees to perform your job would create an undue hardship on the business, you may have to use vacation time to observe the holiday.

YOUR JOB

Sexual Harassment ▰▰▰▰▰▰▰▰

My supervisor repeatedly makes lewd comments and uses foul language, which I find offensive. What can I do to make him stop?

Tell your supervisor that his comments and language make you uncomfortable and that if he continues you will discuss the matter with his boss. If this fails, you may file a complaint with the Human Rights Commission or sue for sex discrimination. Unwelcome verbal or physical contact that is sexual in nature and creates an offensive, intimidating, or hostile work environment constitutes sexual harassment, which is against the law.

One of Yvonne's male co-workers often makes sexually suggestive remarks when he comes to her desk. She reported this to her employer, but he refuses to do anything. What can Yvonne do?

If the company knows that sexual harassment takes place and does nothing to stop it, Yvonne could sue the company or file a complaint with the Human Rights Commission. If Yvonne is a member of a union, she should report the harassment to her union representative. She could sue for moral damages, on grounds that she suffered mental distress and humiliation, as well as ask for punitive damages.

My supervisor has been pressuring me to go out with her, but I have refused. I want to keep my job but don't want to put up with any more harassment. What should I do?

First write down her every comment and action, to help you later if you file charges against her or your employer. Next, discuss the situation with your personnel manager or follow any established grievance procedures. Although you want to keep your job, you may choose to resign if the situation becomes intolerable. You may then file a complaint with the Human Rights Commission alleging that you have been constructively discharged—that although you quit, your supervisor really forced you out. If the commission upholds your complaint, it may order that you be reinstated in your job and that you be entitled to back pay.

Françoise's boss told her she had to have sexual relations with him if she expected to get ahead in the company. She refused. But now she's worried she'll be fired, because there were no witnesses to what he said. What should she do?

She should immediately write a detailed account of his conduct and statements so she will have some documentation of the incident. She

Sexual Harassment

should also tell a friend or union representative about her boss's conduct. Her friend might be a witness to the fact that Françoise told her about the incident. Her friend's testimony would not necessarily prove that what Françoise said was true, but it would prove that Françoise did complain. Demanding sexual favors in exchange for a promotion, raise, or other type of job benefit is a violation of federal and provincial sex-discrimination laws. If Françoise is fired or denied a promotion or other job benefit, or if her boss continues his demands, she should seek legal advice.

Hazardous Work Conditions

Leo works in a warehouse with 100 other employees. Several fire exits are blocked by boxes. The company has never held a fire drill or distributed written instructions about procedures to follow in the event of a fire. How should Leo report this?

He should report this safety hazard to his personnel manager or the plant safety manager, preferably through his union representative or his supervisor. If he receives no response within a reasonable time, he should inform the local fire department that the fire exits are blocked. This should prompt an inspection that will solve the problem. Most cities have fire codes that require exits to be open and escape plans posted. Alternatively, he could contact the provincial or federal agencies responsible for occupational health and safety. The primary federal agency regulating health and safety in the workplace is Labour Canada, but in certain industries it is Energy, Mines and Resources Canada, Transport Canada, or the Atomic Energy Control Board. These deal with health and safety in Crown corporations such as Canada Post and Canadian National. The law that regulates safety in a federal workplace is the Canada Labour Code. In most other cases, the provincial occupational health and safety commission (in British Columbia, the Workers' Compensation Board) is responsible for work safety.

My husband works in a room with no windows and poor lighting, and he has been getting terrible headaches. Can he sue the company for making him work under hazardous conditions?

No. The occupational health and safety acts do not allow workers to sue employers for safety and health violations. Your husband will have to notify the Occupational Health and Safety Commission office in your area. It will investigate his complaint and impose penalties if it finds violations. Your husband should also file a claim for workers' compensation. If it is determined that his headaches are work-related, he could be reimbursed for loss of income.

Mitchell has noticed several unsafe practices at his factory, but he is afraid to report them because of possible retaliation. Would his employer be told who filed the complaint?

No. Under the occupational health and safety acts and the Canada Labour Code, an employee who makes a complaint about safety violations may automatically be granted confidentiality, or he may request it from an inspector. If, however, the employer suspects or discovers who filed the complaint, and retaliates against that employee, the employee could sue the employer for all damages caused him, and in some jurisdictions he could also sue for punitive damages.

The molding machines on the shop floor have been modified so that the safety gates don't close. The foreman says this increases output. Can I be fired if I call the government safety inspector?

No. The occupational health and safety acts and the Canada Labour Code specifically prohibit an employer from firing, suspending, demoting, or discriminating in any way against a worker who files a complaint with the Occupational Health and Safety Commission (OHSC) office or assists the OHSC in an investigation. If your employer retaliates, contact your nearest OHSC office immediately. If proof of retaliation is found, the commission will see that you are reinstated and that lost wages and benefits are paid to you.

Conditions at the plant where I work have become so unsafe that I have not reported to my work station for the past three days. Can my employer refuse to pay me for those three days when it was his fault that the place was dangerous?

No, not if the plant was really dangerous. You are protected by the regulations of the Occupational Health and Safety Commission (OHSC) of your province if you walk off the job because: (1) the danger to your health or safety was serious and imminent, or (2) you notified your employer of the problem and, if time allowed, notified your nearest OHSC office, and nothing was done. If you refused to cooperate when your employer asked for your help in eliminating the problem, offered to have you work temporarily in another area while the condition was corrected, or asked you to do your job in some other way to reduce the chances of injury, you would not be protected against loss of pay.

If You Lose Your Job

When Ross was informed he'd be out of a job at the end of the week, his boss wouldn't tell him why. Doesn't he have the right to know why he's being fired?

Unless he works for a unionized company and the collective agreement requires that an employee be told why he is fired, Ross has no right to be informed. However, the employer must state the reason when he fills out the separation certificate required by the unemployment insurance law. If the reason is not, say, theft or fighting or being drunk on the job, Ross perhaps can sue for unjustified dismissal if he worked for the same employer for a certain period—for example, 5 years in Quebec, 10 years in Nova Scotia, 1 year in federal jobs. In all provinces, discharged employees must be given reasonable notice, from one week to several months depending on length of time worked and type of job, or they must be paid in lieu of notice.

What are my rights if I am fired for no reason?

Most workers are called at-will employees because they are hired and fired at the will of the employer. At-will employees can be fired for any reason except discrimination—or for no reason at all. However, if you have a written or union-negotiated contract, you may be able to sue your employer for breach of that contract. If you worked for the federal government or a Crown corporation for one year, the Canada Labour Code states that you can be fired only for cause. In Quebec, you can be fired only for cause if you worked continuously for the same employer for 5 years; 10 years in Nova Scotia. In all provinces you are entitled to reasonable notice or pay in lieu of notice; vacation pay; and in some situations a refund of contribution to the company pension plan. You are also entitled to a separation certificate that indicates your firing was not your fault. This is necessary to avoid a penalty from the Unemployment Insurance Commission when applying for benefits. In Ontario and in federal government work, you are also entitled to severance pay.

My company's employee handbook states that people will be fired only for cause. If my supervisor fires me during an argument at a party, can I get my job back?

It depends on many factors. If the argument related to your work or your company, and you made unflattering remarks about your company in front of prospective clients, your action could constitute cause. If the argument were purely personal, it would probably not be cause. If during the argument you were violent and drunk and your behavior put your company in a bad light, there might be cause, especially if you worked in a managerial or fiduciary capacity. A company truck driver might misbehave at a party without serious consequences, but the same might not be true of a bank manager.

One July night Jackie, a waiter, arrived for work wearing a flowered Hawaiian shirt, Bermuda shorts, and fluorescent orange sneakers. The restaurant owner told him that since he was dressed for a vacation he could take a permanent one. Can Jackie be fired for the way he was dressed?

Probably. Employers generally have the right to establish dress codes for their employees as long as these codes are for a reasonable purpose and apply equally to all employees. To challenge his dismissal, Jackie would have to show that the restaurant did not have a dress code that he was aware of, that the owner did not routinely fire others for inappropriate attire, or that he generally warned or suspended employees before firing them for inappropriate attire. If Jackie worked in the kitchen, rather than as a waiter serving customers, he might be able to question the reasonableness of the decision to fire him.

On his job application, Roger said he had a degree from a local college. He got the job and earned excellent evaluations. In a random check by the personnel department, they discovered he was not a college graduate. Can Roger be fired for cause?

If the employer has a policy of terminating all employees who are found to have made false statements on their applications, Roger is probably out of a job. Applications often contain notices indicating that any false statements will result in dismissal. The employer has a strong case if Roger's falsification related directly to job qualifications. This could be interpreted as a deliberate attempt to mislead the employer, whereas an unintentional mistake in dates of previous employment or college attendance would not be so serious.

What are Maryla's rights if she is fired for being habitually late?

Habitual lateness is generally accepted as a valid cause for dismissal. However, Maryla might have a good argument for reinstatement if the company had guidelines for disciplining employees, but did not follow them in her case. For example, if company policy said that being late would result in a warning, a loss of pay, suspension, and finally dismissal, and she had never been reprimanded, she could ask a court to order her company to reinstate her.

If You Lose Your Job

***My employer fired me on payday and stated that since my work
was inferior, he was not going to pay me. What can I do?***

Ask the Employment Standards Commission or your provincial labor
department to help you get the money your employer owes you. All
provinces require that terminated employees receive their wages either
on the day they are dismissed or on the next regular payday.

***I was fired because I accidentally destroyed some of the
company's computer files. What can I do?***

There is not much you can do if the company has a general policy of
discharging employees who damage company property. But if other
employees have had similar accidents and have not been fired, you may
want to pursue legal action against the company for discrimination.

***Reevan had major surgery and missed eight weeks of work. Was it
legal for his boss to fire him?***

The company is justified in firing him if its policy is to dismiss employees
who have been off sick for eight weeks, and if all employees in the same
situation are fired. In a unionized company, the terms of the collective
agreement would determine whether an employee is entitled to sick
leave and for how long. If he worked for the federal government for more
than three months, he would be entitled to 12 weeks' sick leave
according to the Canada Labour Code. In any case, Reevan would be
entitled to notice or pay in lieu of notice.

***I was called for jury duty. When I returned to work, my boss fired
me. What can I do to get my job back?***

You can sue your employer for wrongfully dismissing you. Every
province and Territory protects people from losing their jobs and from
any other reprisal because they took time off for jury duty. Your boss
could be fined or imprisoned for firing you.

***Can an employee be fired if he refuses to accept a transfer to
another city?***

Yes, if that is his employer's general practice. However, if other employees have declined transfers and have not been fired, or if the transfer is

When Can You Be Fired?

In the past, employees who worked without contracts—that is, most workers—had to live with the possibility that the boss could fire them for little or no reason at any time. They had no right to challenge such firings. Today, although employers still have broad discretion in dismissing employees, their right to fire at will is being restricted by laws and court decisions.

Employers should follow the company's disciplinary procedure before dismissing an employee, and they generally must be consistent in disciplining employees for the same violations. If you believe that you have been fired unjustly, you can bring the matter before a court. Here are some guidelines, based on court decisions, to help you decide whether you have a good case. Bear in mind, however, that the law in each province is different, and so too are the circumstances of each case.

You Can Be Fired For:	You Cannot Be Fired For:
Sleeping on the job.	Unsatisfactory work unless your employer warned you that your work was inadequate and gave you guidelines about what was considered acceptable work.
Leaving early without permission unless you have a good reason, such as sudden illness at home.	
Incompetence or failing to learn the job after considerable training has been provided.	Your race, color, religion, age, national origin, sex, or handicaps.
Abusing customers.	Being pregnant.
Permitting personalities to interfere with getting the job done.	Serving on a jury.
Using company property without permission.	Participating in union activities.
Falsifying attendance records or other dishonest acts.	Asserting your rights under wage and hour laws.
Making negative comments about the company's policies or performance evaluations, or otherwise discrediting the company.	Filing for workers' compensation.
	Refusing to do something illegal.
Endangering the health and safety of co-workers.	Reporting unlawful activities, such as payoffs and kickbacks.
Using sick leave to be interviewed for another job.	Reporting unsafe working conditions.
Disobedience.	Testifying against the company in a lawsuit.
Violent or drunken conduct.	Having your wages garnisheed.

being made to retaliate against an employee who has reported a company violation to the authorities, he can sue his employer to get his job back or to be compensated for his loss. If the employee has a union contract or a company employment contract, or if his company's policy permits employees to refuse undesirable transfers, he can sue his employer for breach of contract.

Can a company I've worked for all my life dismiss me if I'm only three years away from my retirement?

Only if there's a good reason. If it is firing you to deprive you of your pension, you could sue the company for damages, perhaps even punitive damages. However, if the company is dismissing you solely on the basis of your age, it is violating federal and provincial age-discrimination laws.

I was fired because customers said they preferred to deal with a white beautician. Do I have grounds to sue?

Yes. All provinces and Territories and the federal Charter of Rights and Freedoms outlaw discrimination that is based on color or race. If your employer fired you because of your color or race, file a complaint with the Human Rights Commission of your province. An employer must respect the law of the land rather than give in to a racist clientele.

Can Mimi be fired if she occasionally needs to stay home with her children?

Whether Mimi can be fired depends on the employer's policy on personal leave. If her employer allows other employees to stay home periodically with their children when needed, the employer would be discriminating against Mimi if he fired her. On the other hand, an employer is not required to grant employees leave for child care. If Mimi is taking too much time off or doing so during times when the work load is heavy, the employer may be justified in dismissing her.

Can I be fired for being a homosexual?

Only Quebec outlaws discrimination based on sexual preference. You should nonetheless complain to the Human Rights Commission if you are fired in any province for this reason. Such action would be discriminatory and, by affecting your ability to work, would affect your right to security of the person.

Can a company dismiss an employee who drinks excessively or uses illegal drugs?

Yes. It is generally recognized that employees have an obligation to report for work sober and free from the influence of drugs. However, an employee fired for this reason could challenge the dismissal if he could prove that the company did not follow established procedures (such as giving him a warning) or that it does not routinely dismiss all employees who drink or use illegal drugs on the job, and that the drinking or drug use was an isolated incident in a long work history.

Can an employee who resigns or is fired continue to receive group medical coverage until he finds another job?

No. Unless there is a provision in a collective agreement or in a contract between an employer and employee, termination of employment ends the employee's rights to receive any benefits such as group medical coverage.

My cousin's employer told her to do something illegal at work. When she refused to carry out his order, she was fired. Can she do anything about it?

Yes, she can sue her employer to get her job back. Although traditionally employees working without a contract could be fired for any or no reason, society does not want to punish citizens for obeying the law. Consequently, as a matter of public policy, an employer cannot fire anyone for refusing to break the law. Your cousin should also check with her provincial attorney general's office. The law in her province might allow her to sue her employer to compensate for her wrongful dismissal and to sue for punitive damages.

Bill saw his supervisor stealing from the company warehouse but did not report it to anyone. When the owner discovered the theft and learned that Bill had known about it, Bill was fired, too. Can his employer do this?

Yes. Many union contracts, company procedure manuals, and employee handbooks contain provisions that require employees to report a co-worker who steals.

Unemployment Insurance

Tim's supervisor was browbeating him for several months. The situation became so tense that Tim finally quit. Is he entitled to unemployment benefits?

Only if he can show that his supervisor's actions created a situation that was so unbearable that he was justified in quitting. The Unemployment Insurance Act distinguishes between employees who leave voluntarily with good cause (such as unsafe working conditions or being asked to do something illegal) and those who leave voluntarily without good cause. An employee who leaves voluntarily without good cause must wait a certain period—usually six weeks more than the usual two-week waiting period—before benefits are paid.

Macka was fired from her job for misconduct. Can she still collect unemployment insurance?

Yes. If Macka worked the minimum number of weeks (usually 20) prior to being fired, she would be eligible for unemployment insurance benefits. But she would have to wait up to six weeks in addition to the normal two-week waiting period. However, she could appeal to a board of referees to have this six-week penalty reduced or eliminated.

When Barry's union was unable to negotiate a new contract, the employer locked the factory gates. Barry and his co-workers continued to show up for work, but the gates remained locked. Are Barry and his co-workers eligible for unemployment benefits?

Employees who are out of a job because of a labor dispute are often ineligible for unemployment benefits. Barry and his colleagues might be eligible, however, if they can show that they are not directly involved in the particular dispute that led to the lockout. For example, if it was the lathe operators union whose actions resulted in the lockout, members of the electricians union, which does not financially or in any other way support the lathe operators, could collect unemployment insurance benefits.

Another employee has been harassing me at work. I brought this to my boss's attention, but he didn't do anything to correct the situation. Can I collect unemployment if I quit?

Only if you can show that you quit for good reasons. The duration, type, and seriousness of the harassment are important considerations. Unpleasant or angry remarks by a co-worker may not be considered good reasons, but sexual harassment or threats of physical harm could justify your leaving. The fact that nothing was done when you reported this harassment will also help your case.

Paul's company is planning to close down several of its branch offices. It has offered to transfer Paul to another branch in a neighboring city, but he would have to commute 60 kilometres each day. Would his refusal to accept a transfer affect his eligibility for unemployment benefits?

It depends. According to the Unemployment Insurance Act, Paul could be denied benefits if, having turned down the transfer, he then refused or neglected to apply for "suitable employment" or rejected an offer of "suitable employment."

Much depends upon the definition of "suitable employment." A student who refused a job at a golf course because he had no car to get there was penalized because it was held that he should have got a bicycle. Another claimant was accepted for benefits because he had no car, and the job was in a place where there was no public transport. In a third case, transportation costs would have taken too much of the applicant's salary for the job to be "suitable employment."

If Paul had to commute 30 kilometres each way, but he had a car or access to public transportation, his refusal to take this job at the branch office would probably be reason enough to penalize him. If, on the other hand, his job was 60 kilometres away, and he therefore had to commute 120 kilometres a day, it would probably be considered "unsuitable employment."

Harry was laid off when the company closed the Ontario plant he worked in. He believes job prospects in his particular line of work are probably better in Manitoba. Can he collect unemployment benefits in one province even though his previous job was in another?

Yes. To be eligible, however, he must be actively engaged in looking for work and be available for work.

Can a person receive unemployment benefits while enrolled in a job-training program?

Yes. While benefits are generally denied if a person is not available for work, the Unemployment Insurance Commission will grant benefits if someone is in an approved job-training program.

Unemployment Insurance

My husband has been out of work for two months. He is depressed and spends his unemployment cheques gambling. Is it possible for me to receive his unemployment benefits?

No. Your husband is the only person who can collect these benefits. The Unemployment Insurance Act prohibits unemployed workers from assigning or pledging their unemployment benefits to anyone else. It also prohibits creditors from seizing or attaching unemployment insurance cheques for any type of debt.

CHAPTER 11

Your Own Business

Starting a Business ▬▬▬▬▬▬▬▬

Can anyone start his own business?

Yes. All you need is something to sell. A business can be built on any kind of service or product. A climbing guide, who sells the service of leading people up and down dangerous mountains, is as much in business as the owner of a company that manufactures jet engine parts. Of course, what you sell and how you sell it must be permitted by federal, provincial, and municipal laws. Your local chamber of commerce is a good place to find out how and where to check on the legality of a new venture.

Does starting my own business mean I will automatically become a corporation, with Incorporated *after my business name?*

No. You have a choice of three basic forms of business, only one of which, a corporation, entitles you to use *Inc.*, *Corp.*, *Co. Ltd.*, or *Ltd.* after your business name. In a *sole proprietorship,* you own and run the business and are personally responsible for its income and expenses, assets and liabilities. The same is true when you form a *partnership,* except that you share responsibility (and liability toward third parties) with one or more partners. The abbreviation *Reg'd.* after the name of an enterprise means that the sole proprietorship or partnership is registered with the provincial authorities rather than incorporated. When you form a *corporation*, you separate the business from your personal assets and create a new legal entity that has its own rights and responsibilities and, in effect, acts like an independent person. The company's liability is limited to its assets only; the shareholders are not personally liable.

Is buying a franchise like starting any other kind of business?

Yes, from a legal standpoint. You can buy and operate a franchise as a sole proprietor, partner, or corporation. However, a franchise often obligates you to a close working relationship with the franchisor.

Do I need special licenses or permits to start a business?

It depends on the kind of business. Provincial and local governments have broad powers to regulate business. For example, restaurants, barbershops, dry cleaners, day-care centers, and nursing homes must pass inspections and obtain licenses before opening their doors to the public. Plumbers, electricians, mechanics, and contractors must meet licensing and bonding requirements and are subject to having their work inspected. Doctors, lawyers, dentists, accountants, pharmacists, and veterinarians must all pass examinations and receive licenses before they can lawfully practice.

If you can't find out what regulations apply to your business by calling your local and provincial government offices, ask the Better Business Bureau, or someone who already runs a similar business.

Some businesses are also regulated by federal laws. To reach the proper agency, call Information Canada. You will find the number in the government section of your phone book.

If Janice operates a small upholstery business in her basement, does she need a special license?

It depends on where Janice lives. Some municipalities prohibit a resident from operating a business in the home. Even if this isn't the case in Janice's community, she may be required to purchase a business license or seller's permit; and since her business is one that often necessitates moving bulky furniture in and out of her house, she may encounter problems with zoning laws that restrict businesses in residential areas. Such laws commonly ban a business that changes the residential character of the house and its grounds, or limit the number of employees or the percentage of square footage that may be devoted to the business. Some bylaws require off-street parking and restrict yard signs. Other provincial or local laws may prohibit objectionable noise, odor, or waste. Since Janice must collect provincial sales tax from her customers, she will have to obtain a tax number from her provincial government.

Do I need to apply to the post office for a permit before I start a mail-order business?

No. Canada Post does not require permits or licenses for mail-order businesses except in cases of bulk mailings.

Does starting a mail-order business pose special legal problems?

Yes. Provincial consumer protection and business practices legislation govern all mail-order transactions. These laws and regulations specify such things as: whether, in a contract between you and a mail-order customer, the laws of your province or those of your customer's would apply; at what point in a transaction a contract has been made; whether the buyer or the seller is responsible for lost or broken merchandise; and what kind of advertising is permitted. Businesses involving chain letters, pyramid sales, or obscene and pornographic material are outlawed. When there is a conflict over a contract, courts generally rule in favor of the consumer. Most complaints about false advertising are addressed to a provincial advertising standards council, provincial consumer protection office or to Consumer and Corporate Affairs Canada. The federal Competition Act is often brought into play, and its penalties for false or misleading advertising can be stiff.

If Victor starts a business that will do frequent large mailings, how can he get a bulk-rate discount?

Victor's local post office should know which branch office will accept bulk mailings; not all stations are equipped to do so. From that branch, he can obtain an application for whichever bulk-rate postal permits he requires. For example, Victor will need one kind of permit for mailings that cost more than $5,000 a year; different permits if he wants to distribute postage-prepaid, business-reply cards or use precanceled postmarks.

Canada Post offers free courses for people making bulk mailings, with tips on how best to profit from using the postal services. For example, Victor can get a free permit that will let him send a number of unaddressed flyers at half the normal postal rate. He can also get a free book and map that will tell him how many residences or how many businesses there are in a certain postal area. Victor should contact Canada Post (Customer Services) for more information.

Is it legal to have a post office box number as a business address?

Yes. However, when you apply for your post office box, you will be required to give your name and a street address. The postmaster will thus have a record of your name and the location of your business.

My wife and I have always dreamed of buying a restaurant, and we have found one we like for sale. The owner is asking $190,000. How can we determine if this is a fair price?

There are many formulas for determining a fair price for a business. One formula says the price should be approximately five times the business's annual profit; another equates a fair price with the amount of gross sales for 100 days; a third suggests the value of the inventory plus one month's gross receipts. None of these formulas guarantees that you will arrive at a perfect price or buy a profitable business. The most you can hope for is to arrive at a reasonable figure, and to do so you should ask for and review the following documents: a prospectus of the business; the current owner's business plan, income tax returns, and balance sheets for the past several years; records of accounts, contracts, and leases; and legal documents in any pending lawsuits. Have an experienced accountant or lawyer review the documents to evaluate the strengths and weaknesses of the business before you commit yourself in any way. If the current owner can't or won't produce several of these documents, your suspicions should be aroused.

Albert saw a magazine ad offering to get him started in a profitable business that he could operate from his home. How can he find out if the company is legitimate?

Albert should call the nearest Better Business Bureau and the consumer affairs ministry in the province where the company is located to see if any complaints have been lodged against the company. If not, Albert should then contact the company for more details. If the answers seem vague or evasive, he would be wise to seek other ways of earning income at home. Albert should be especially careful about companies that offer to sell him equipment and materials and promise to buy articles that he produces. Some of these firms afterward refuse to purchase the completed items—or simply disappear. Extreme caution is also advised when a company claims that it will buy back your unsold inventory, or promises huge profits with minimal risks.

The Laughlins are planning to open a linen shop and hire three employees: one full-time and two part-time. Must the Laughlins provide and contribute to such benefits as life insurance and private pension plans?

Generally, no employer is required to offer these kinds of fringe benefits, although a great many do. However, the law does require employers to contribute to the Workers' Compensation Fund, which covers both full and part-time employees. The Laughlins must also pay the employer's premium for unemployment insurance for any employee who works more than 15 hours a week and match the employee's contribution to the Canada (or Quebec) Pension Plan.

My uncle is willing to put up $10,000 to help me start a plumbing business, but he wants to protect his investment and to be sure that my creditors won't sue him if I can't pay my bills. I have a van and most of the tools I will need. What kind of arrangement can we make that will be fair to us both?

If your uncle is content to be a lender, not your business partner, he can make you a personal loan, and you can put up $10,000 worth of collateral.

With such an arrangement, your uncle would not be liable for any of your business debts.

If your uncle wants part ownership of the business in return for his $10,000, you and he can draw up an agreement that makes him a limited partner. This means that he will have a financial interest in your business but will not participate in any other way. Although your uncle, as a

---

Sole Proprietorship: The Business Is You

The simplest form of business is a sole proprietorship, in which you earn money from selling goods or services on your own. You can become a sole proprietor with no legal formalities whatsoever. You may even be one without knowing it; many self-employed people, such as free-lancers and independent contractors, are sole proprietors.

A person can be a company employee and a sole proprietor at the same time. This would be the case, for example, if you made $20,000 last year as an assistant office manager and $3,000 from your at-home business of making napkin rings.

● *Legal steps*—No legalities are necessary to form a sole proprietorship except obtaining any licenses or permits required by local and provincial laws. If you decide to do business under a name that isn't your own, you will have to register the name with the provincial registry office.

● *Tax treatment*—Income and expenses are reported on your individual federal return. Your business income will be taxed at your federal individual rate. You may also have to pay provincial and local taxes as an unincorporated business, either a percentage of the business's income or on some other basis. And you will have to obtain a tax number from your provincial tax office since you will have to collect provincial sales tax on your sales.

● *Control of the business*—You alone make all the decisions, and negotiate and approve all agreements that concern your business.

● *Your personal liability*—Because a sole proprietorship has no legal identity apart from you, the courts consider your business and personal assets and obligations to be one and the same. If you default on a loan you have taken for business purposes, the creditor may take your personal property to pay the debt; and if you cause a car accident through negligence or carelessness, and an injured person wins a lawsuit against you, he can force you to sell your business assets to pay for damages and losses, if they exceed your insurance coverage. If you use your vehicle for business, even occasionally, be sure to inform your insurance company.

limited partner, could lose his $10,000 investment, he would not be personally liable for any business debts. His home and personal belongings could not be seized by an unpaid creditor of the business.

Vanessa has been a computer programmer for six years. Now she would like to start her own computer programming firm, but she is worried that her current employer will sue and put her out of business. Could this happen?

Yes, but only under certain conditions. If Vanessa signed an agreement that prohibits her from competing with her employer in specific ways for a period of time after she leaves the company, and she breaks this agreement, her employer can sue her for breach of contract. However, most courts require that such no-competition agreements, also known as restrictive covenants, be reasonably limited. For example, an agreement never to operate a competing business anywhere in the province would probably be too broad to hold up in court, while an agreement saying that Vanessa could not open a competing business in the same city for two years after she left the company would quite likely be upheld.

Must an employer contribute to government social security programs for everyone his company employs?

Yes, as a rule. An employer must pay his share for workers' compensation, unemployment insurance and government pension plan for all his regular employees, whether full-time or part-time. This includes domestic help. There are exceptions: people who work for the company but are technically self-employed, such as independent contractors or freelancers; students in particular jobs in schools; and minor children working for their parents. Self-employed persons—housepainters, carpenters, electricians, plumbers—are ineligible for workers' compensation and unemployment insurance and are responsible for making the necessary Canada Pension (or Quebec Pension) Plan contributions themselves.

When he started his investment business, Wendell figured he would save money by not incorporating. Now his accountant tells him he must pay an unincorporated business tax. Do all unincorporated businesses have to pay this tax?

No. Only some provinces and municipalities levy an unincorporated business tax which may be imposed on the value of a business property (such as machinery, equipment, or inventory), or may be a percentage of sales in the province.

Starting a Business

***Kate has just hired three employees to work full-time for her.
What deductions is she required to make from their pay cheques?***

Kate must withhold certain amounts for federal income tax (and for
provincial income tax in Ontario and Quebec); for unemployment
insurance; for the Canada (or Quebec) Pension Plan; and Medicare. The
amounts can be calculated from government tax tables. At regular
intervals, she must send the money withheld to the proper taxing
authority, along with her share of the premiums for unemployment
insurance, workers' compensation, government pension plan, and (in
Manitoba and Quebec) Medicare. If Kate's employees are unionized, she
must also deduct union dues from their pay.

***My wife and I set up an answering service. We were told by
the provincial tax department that we needed a tax number.
What is this for?***

Provinces issue a tax number to all businesses that sell goods or services
to the public. The tax number identifies your business, which is required
to charge and collect a sales tax for the goods or services sold, and to
remit these taxes to the provincial tax department.

***Warren has a degree in landscaping and would like to go into
business for himself. In the past he has fallen behind in making
credit card payments and repaying a personal loan. Will these
credit problems affect his ability to establish a new business?***

Yes, if Warren has to borrow money to get started. If his new business is a
sole proprietorship or a partnership, his personal credit will be very
important to prospective lenders, since his business and personal
finances would be mingled. Even if Warren is considering incorporating
the business, so that his business and personal assets would be treated
separately, creditors may insist that Warren give a personal guarantee
for loans. If his personal credit history shows problems, they may decline
to lend him money for the business.

***Irene and Jerry just started a small business but are running into
problems with marketing and distribution. Where can they get
help without spending a fortune?***

They can turn to the government-run Federal Business Development
Bank, which has offices across Canada. This Crown corporation pro-

motes and assists Canadian businesses at any stage of their development. Its wide range of services includes business seminars and management clinics, and it provides financial planning and loans. Irene and Jerry should ask about its Counseling Assistance to Small Enterprises (CASE) program. Most CASE counselors are successful former business executives.

Forming a Partnership

Stan and Frederick want to set up a business. Are there advantages in forming a partnership instead of a corporation?

The major advantage of a partnership over a corporation is simplicity. Each partner's share of the profits and losses is reported on his individual income tax return. Unlike a corporation, which must pay taxes on its profits and whose shareholders must also pay taxes on the dividends the corporation in turn pays out of profits, partners in a business are taxed only once on the income generated by their business. The main disadvantage of a partnership is that each partner is liable for business debts.

What should be spelled out in a partnership agreement?

It should contain the name of the partnership and the names of its members; a description of the type of business to be conducted; a statement of the financial contribution of each partner; a description of the duties and powers of the partners, along with any restrictions on their power to act for the partnership; the method of dividing profits or losses; procedures for withdrawing from the partnership or admitting new members; steps to be followed in the event of the death of a partner; and procedures and conditions for dissolving the partnership. Some agreements also stipulate the methods to be used for resolving disputes that arise among the partners and even the amount of insurance to be carried for the partnership.

Can a partnership exist legally without a written agreement?

Yes, but an oral agreement could well be a source of trouble in the future. To avoid misunderstandings, and to ensure it will be enforceable, it is best to have such a serious and important agreement in writing and to make sure each of the partners fully understands its terms and how they will apply. The agreement, known as a *partnership agreement*, should be drawn up by a lawyer familiar with commercial matters.

Forming a Partnership

**Becky wants me to be her partner, but I'm not sure we'll get along.
Can we set up a trial period for the partnership?**

Yes. Your agreement can limit the duration of the partnership. For
example, your agreement can state that the partnership will last three

Setting Up a Partnership

In many ways a partnership is like having two or more sole
proprietors running the same business. They are known legally as
general partners, which means they manage the business, share in its
profits, and assume personal responsibility for its loans and
obligations. *Limited* or *silent partners* are restricted to investing
money and sharing in the profits. A limited or silent partner is not
personally liable for partnership debts so long as he stays completely
clear of any management role.

● *Legal steps*—The general partners should check provincial and local
laws for permits or licenses needed for their type of business; and they
must register the partnership name with the provincial registry
office. In addition, they should prepare a document setting out the
purpose of the partnership, its members, the business and accounting
methods to be used, the rights and duties of each partner, and the
method of distributing profits and losses among the partners. A formal
agreement is not legally required; however, when one doesn't exist,
most courts would assume that all partners were meant to share
equally in the profits and losses and to have equal voices in
management.

● *Tax treatment*—Each partner reports his share of the partnership
income on his federal income tax return. Federal tax rates are the
same as for personal income. Some provinces and municipalities also
tax partnership income or assess fees.

● *Control of the business*—Unless there is an agreement that states
otherwise, (1) each general partner may make decisions and negotiate
contracts on behalf of the partnership; (2) the death or resignation of a
general partner dissolves the partnership.

● *Your personal liability*—If the partnership defaults on a loan, the
creditor can hold you (and other general partners) personally
responsible. Thus, if the partnership can't repay a business loan on
time, the lender can sue each of you and you face the risk of losing
personal property. Carelessness or negligence by one partner
may also result in a lawsuit against the partnership, raising the
possibility that you may be held personally liable.

months, with an option to renew at the end of that period. You may also include the right to dissolve the partnership.

Lloyd, Matthew, and Lawrence formed a partnership two years ago. Now Ian would like to join the firm as the fourth partner. Lloyd and Matthew approve; Lawrence does not. Can Ian be made a partner despite Lawrence's objection?

No. As a general rule, new partners must be approved by all current partners. Unless the partnership agreement states otherwise, Ian may not join as a partner over Lawrence's objection.

Veronica and Elaine are experts in the clothing business. Shirley and Heather are investors with no experience in this field. When they draw up their partnership agreement, can they stipulate that Veronica and Elaine will make all management decisions?

Yes. This arrangement is usually known as a limited or silent partnership. A limited or silent partner agrees to contribute financially to the partnership, but to leave the management of the business to the other partner or partners. The advantage to the limited partners is that they are not personally liable for partnership debts. A creditor cannot have their homes or personal belongings seized and sold to pay business debts. The disadvantage is that limited partners cannot participate in running the business. If they do, they become general partners and, as such, become personally liable for partnership debts.

One of my partners was involved in an automobile accident. A lawsuit names him as the defendant. If he loses the case, can the court force him to pay damages out of our firm's assets?

No. If the accident had nothing to do with your firm's business, the court cannot take the partnership's assets. However, the court can require your partner to use his share of partnership earnings to pay damages.

Simon and Joe are going into business as partners. Would Joe's home, which he owns jointly with his wife, be protected from a creditor if the partnership defaults on a loan?

No. Joe's interest in his home could be used to pay a creditor who successfully sued the partnership for an unpaid debt. The court could order that the house be sold, even though it is jointly owned, and that the proceeds be used to discharge the loan. However, the creditor can take

Forming a Partnership

only Joe's interest in the house (one half of the proceeds) and must reimburse Joe's wife for her interest. If Joe's half is greater than the debt, the creditor must give Joe the difference. A lawyer can advise Joe if filing for bankruptcy under Chapter X of the Bankruptcy Act (see page 312) or making similar arrangements for installment payments under provincial law would protect his home from seizure.

Earl is going to retire from his firm at the end of the year. What steps should he take to make sure he isn't liable for business conducted by his partners after he leaves?

Earl should send a letter to all the partnership creditors and clients, informing them that he is leaving the firm and that as of December 31 he is no longer authorized to act for the business, nor is he liable for business debts. If he doesn't do this, he could remain liable for partnership debts. He should also try to have the partnership agreement amended to specify that he will no longer be a partner as of that date.

Incorporating

My son, Ira, wants to set up his own business as an auto mechanic. Is it necessary for him to incorporate?

No. A business need not be incorporated. Ira can operate as a sole proprietor, or he can form a partnership with one or more other persons.

Can I start a corporation of which I am the only shareholder?

Yes. There are no requirements that a corporation have a minimum number of shareholders. You may own all the stock issued.

Sybil has built up a very profitable full-time business word processing on her home computer. Should she incorporate?

Not necessarily. Although by incorporating she would not be held personally responsible for her business liabilities, Sybil could also find herself paying more taxes and putting more time, paperwork, and expense into meeting government requirements for certifying her corporation. She should seek legal and financial advice before making such a decision.

Do I need an attorney to incorporate?

No. There are books on the market that will give you step-by-step instructions. There are also companies that specialize in incorporations, whose fees are generally less than those charged by lawyers. However, by hiring a lawyer to do the job, you can be more certain that everything will be done properly, and you would have a resource to answer the legal questions you might have about incorporation.

If I form a corporation, can my business creditors take my house if they sue me and win?

No. If you have not mixed your personal affairs with corporate business affairs, your personal assets, such as your home, car, or bank account, cannot be seized by business creditors. Corporate creditors may take your personal assets only if you have given a personal guarantee for debts or offered your personal assets as collateral for a business loan. A corporation is considered an entity separate from the people who own it.

I have just incorporated, and I am trying to lease a store in a mall. The owner's agent asked me to sign a personal guarantee. What legal effect does this have? Can they require me to sign it?

Your personal guarantee will make you personally liable for money that the corporation may owe the mall in the future. For example, if the corporation cannot pay the rent, and the mall's owner sues and wins, he may have your personal property seized and sold to pay the overdue rent. The owner may legally require such a guarantee, and creditors of new or struggling corporations quite often demand it. They may even require your spouse to give a personal guarantee if a major asset such as your home is in your spouse's name. However, by signing such a guarantee, you lose a chief advantage of incorporating—protection of your personal assets.

Juliana wants to lend money to her corporation to help it through some financial difficulties. Is this legal?

Yes. However, Juliana should be sure that her roles as owner and creditor do not become confused. This loan should be treated like any other and entered in the corporate records. The corporation should not give preference to Juliana over other creditors, and she should not repay herself out of corporate assets in a way that other creditors cannot. Juliana and her company are distinct entities—she should avoid any conflict of interest with her company.

Incorporating

Mitchel and Della have been running a small bakery for the past two years. Is it too late for them to incorporate?

No. They may change the form of their business at any time—from or to a sole proprietorship, partnership, or corporation.

I'm going to form a corporation. Would it be better for my company to be federally or provincially incorporated?

The main benefit of incorporation—limitation of personal liability—is the same whether you incorporate under provincial laws or under federal laws. Federal incorporation does offer one advantage: it allows you to do business anywhere in Canada without having to register your company in each of the provinces involved. However, if you don't plan to

Incorporation: Business With a Life of Its Own

A corporation has an independent legal existence, distinct from that of its owners. Like a person, it pays taxes; can buy, own, and sell property; can sue and be sued; can commit crimes and be tried and punished for them. To raise money, most corporations issue stock that is bought by the public: you become part owner of a corporation when you buy one or more shares. Creating a corporation requires certain procedures.

● *Methods of incorporation*—To incorporate federally, a would-be company must file *articles of incorporation* with the federal government. To incorporate provincially, the company would follow the same procedure in Alberta, Saskatchewan, Manitoba, Ontario, and New Brunswick. In Quebec and Prince Edward Island, a company-to-be must obtain a document called *letters patent*. British Columbia, Nova Scotia, and Newfoundland require registration, which involves filing two documents: a *memorandum of association* and *articles of association*.

● *Legal steps*—The appropriate documents must be filed with the federal or provincial minister of financial institutions. In most cases, this document must give the names and addresses of the *incorporators*, the name and address of the corporation and its purpose, the number and type of shares of stock to be issued, and the amount of capital the corporation has to work with. On approval, the minister will issue a certificate of incorporation, or charter, at which point *Incorporated*, *Corporation,* or *Limited*, or their abbreviations, must be added to the company name. Once the corporation is chartered, it is responsible for obtaining the licenses, permits, and registrations required for its business operate outside your own province, you might be better off incorporating provincially, since it's often cheaper than incorporating federally.

Art calls his business Art & Sons, Inc., even though it isn't incorporated. Is this legal?

No. Art misrepresents his firm's legal status if he uses *Incorporated, Corporation,* or *Limited,* or their abbreviations. Only the government can grant corporate status.

If we form a nonprofit corporation to publish a consumer newsletter, do we have to file tax returns for it?

Yes. Even nonprofit corporations with tax-exempt status must file information returns with the federal and provincial tax departments.

ctivities. Federally incorporated companies and some provincially incorporated ones can use a number, such as 1234567 Canada, Inc., instead of a name.

Tax treatment—Net profits are subject to corporate income tax rates, which vary greatly from the rates for individuals.

Control of the business—The first job of the incorporators is to call a meeting of the shareholders. The shareholders will vote on the rules (bylaws) by which the company will be run, and elect a board of directors, which has overall responsibility for the major decisions and direction of the corporation. The board then names officers—the president, treasurer, vice presidents, secretary, and so on—to take charge of the day-to-day management of the business. Ultimate control of the corporation rests with the shareholders, who can vote to keep, add, or replace directors; however, there is no law against incorporators, directors, officers, and large shareholders being the same persons. In practice, in large corporations, an individual who owns just a few shares of stock has little direct control over the decisions of the corporation.

Your personal liability—A corporation limits the personal liability of its shareholder-owners, and even of its officers and directors, if the corporation defaults on a loan or is sued for some careless, negligent, or criminal act. For example, creditors of the corporation cannot take the personal assets of a corporate director or officer or those of a shareholder to pay corporate debts. However, if an officer or director participates in a wrongful act—such as signing a cheque knowing that there are no funds in the account—that officer or director could be held personally liable for his actions.

Incorporating

Corporations set up for religious, charitable, scientific, literary, artistic, or educational purposes, or for the prevention of cruelty to children or animals, generally qualify for tax-exempt status. An organization must apply for exemption to Revenue Canada and the appropriate provincial tax department.

The local high school has asked Susan to set up and head a small nonprofit corporation to raise funds for a scholarship program. Is a nonprofit corporation set up differently from a profit-making one? Can Susan get paid for this work?

Generally speaking, a nonprofit corporation is organized in much the same way as a for-profit corporation and is granted a charter by the federal or provincial government to conduct business. There is no law against a nonprofit corporation's hiring salaried employees, and thus Susan can be paid for her services.

Judd has a criminal record for something he did more than 20 years ago. Can he incorporate and run a business?

Yes. But depending on his offense, he may have problems getting a license or permit for certain types of businesses. If he was convicted of illegal gambling, for example, he might be refused a license to sell lottery tickets; if it was a weapons offense, he might not obtain a liquor permit. Judd's conviction, however, is only one factor that the government would consider when granting the license.

Judd could apply to the federal government for a pardon so that his criminal record would no longer adversely affect his career. A pardon is usually granted when a person has been law-abiding for two to five years after the end of his sentence. Judd can get more information from the Clemency and Pardons Section, National Parole Board, 340 Laurier Avenue West, Ottawa, Ont., K1A 0R1.

I own a small business that is incorporated. While driving to work in my own car, I caused an accident. Am I personally liable?

Yes. If you caused the accident through carelessness or negligence, you can be held personally liable for any injuries. Even if corporation business was the sole reason you were driving, you would not be relieved of liability; however, the corporation might share liability with you. In Quebec, the question of liability would be treated differently because you would be covered under that province's comprehensive no-fault insurance program.(See the introduction to Liability for Automobile Accidents on page 262, *Your Car.*)

Elliot operates his catering business as a sole proprietorship, and one of his vans was in an accident. If he files for incorporation immediately, will he be protected from personal liability for injuries resulting from the accident?

No. In determining whether Elliot can be held personally liable for damages, a court would consider the status of his business at the time of the accident, not at the time of the trial.

Can Herbert incorporate his failing business, have it file for bankruptcy, and thus protect his personal assets?

No. Herbert cannot dodge his debts by changing the form of his business. He will still be personally liable for all preincorporation business debts.

Buying a Franchise

Shea is thinking about starting his own fast-food restaurant. He has read about a national group offering franchises. Would Shea own the business if he purchased a franchise?

No. He would own only the right to sell or distribute the franchisor's product or service. Shea would pay a franchise fee that covers many of the costs involved in setting up the business, and then he would have to pay royalties to the franchisor based on the amount of his sales. Many franchise licenses (or contracts) expire after a number of years. At that point, Shea would have to negotiate a new contract to stay in business.

If I buy a franchise, can the franchisor legally tell me what I can and cannot do in operating the business?

It depends primarily on the contract you sign. Many franchisors make it a policy to discourage innovation because they feel that the key to their success is familiarity and predictability. They exert tight control and strictly regulate day-to-day operations. A typical franchisor will select the exact site for a franchise, build the outlet according to standard plans, purchase or lease all the necessary equipment, dictate the quality and appearance of all supplies used at the outlet, and provide training for the employees and managers.

Buying a Franchise

At a Start Your Own Business fair, Sean and Cory found a franchise deal that promised big profits, and the salesman said it was easy to run. How can Sean and Cory check up on the franchisor's claims before they invest the required $120,000?

Sean and Cory can check with the Better Business Bureau to see if there are any complaints against the franchisor. They should obtain a copy of the franchisor's financial statements for the last couple of years and study them with the help of an accountant or lawyer. An officer of the Federal Business Development Bank or a counselor from its CASE (Counseling Assistance to Small Enterprises) program could provide useful advice. They should also talk to current franchisees—in person to those near them, and by telephone to those at a distance. They should ask if the franchisor is supportive of his outlets, if the training and advertising offered are adequate, and if the franchisor is honest and fair in dealing with the franchisees.

Maria would like to invest in a franchise that may open another outlet in her town. What risks does she face?

Most statistical studies show that franchises have a better survival rate than independent single-person small businesses. This better-than-average success rate is attributed, in part, to the already established reputation and goodwill of a franchise and its resources for marketing studies and advertising. For many inexperienced people, franchising is the safest way to start their own business.

However, the franchise formula does not guarantee success. Some franchisors overextend themselves and are unable to continue to offer the advertising and training programs they promised. Sometimes their marketing studies err, and they try to open an outlet in a location already adequately served. And while most franchisors are fair and honest, some sell franchisees used equipment at inflated prices; others divert advertising fees to their own general funds. Maria's best protection is to do a thorough investigation of the history, financial status, and reputation of the franchisor.

What should I do if the company that sold me a franchise tells me it is going out of business?

If your franchisor is unable to fulfill his obligations under your agreement, you may sue for breach of contract. In such a lawsuit, you will need to prove the amount of your loss. If the franchisor has few assets, or if he files for bankruptcy, you may not be able to collect your full loss.

What You Get When You Buy a Franchise

A franchise is a license or permit to operate a business that sells a product or service developed by the franchisor. You, the franchisee, pay a fee and royalties to the franchisor in exchange for the right to sell the product or service. As a franchisee, you are in some ways the owner of your own business, but your autonomy can never be complete because of your relationship with the franchisor. Some franchisors exercise strict control over all aspects of the business, while others give their franchisees great freedom. The terms used for the different types of franchises reveal the amount of control the franchisor wields:

● *Turnkey operation*—The franchisor has full control of the business, and all the new franchisee must do is turn the key in the lock and open his door to begin business. The franchisor chooses the site for an outlet after extensive marketing and traffic-flow studies; builds the outlet and furnishes it according to a standard plan; and trains the manager and employees. Once in business, the franchisee must follow the franchisor's instructions: where to set up displays, when to offer specials, what uniforms the employees must wear, how to enter items in his ledger, what hours he may operate, and from whom he may buy supplies. If the franchisor distributes coupons or runs a promotion or contest, the franchisee may be required to participate. The franchisee may also be required to lease equipment from the franchisor and pay rent on the outlet, thus making his financial obligation to the franchisor more than simply paying royalties.

● *Trade name franchise*—The franchisee sells a product already manufactured by the franchisor. Gas stations, auto parts stores, and specialty clothing stores are examples.The franchisee is granted the exclusive right to distribute the product in a certain area. In return, the franchisee operates his outlet according to the franchisor's guidelines and pays royalties to the franchisor.

● *Business format franchise*—Goods or services are produced by the franchisee at his outlet, such as at a fast-food restaurant. The franchisor provides instructions and equipment to ensure consistent quality.

Running a Business ▬▬▬▬▬▬▬▬

I want to open an appliance store. Are there any guarantees that I'm required by law to offer my customers?

The law does not require you to give, either orally or in writing, any specific guarantees on items you sell. However, there are guarantees that the law considers implied in every sales transaction. Of these implied warranties, the most far-reaching is the *implied warranty of merchantability*. It guarantees that the item is of average quality and will do what it is supposed to do—for example, a new toaster will toast, a can opener won't break on first use, and a new dress won't have a broken zipper.

There is also an *implied warranty of fitness for a particular purpose*. This applies if a customer asks you for a product that will do a particular job or fit a particular space, then purchases the product you recommend. In this case you have, in effect, guaranteed or warranted that the product will work in the way the customer has described. If the customer asks you for a food processor that will knead dough, for example, he can return the machine he buys from you if it does not do the job properly.

In British Columbia, Saskatchewan, Manitoba, Ontario, Quebec, New Brunswick, Yukon, and the Northwest Territories the merchant cannot deny the implied warranties even if he includes a disclaimer on the written contract of sale; such disclaimers can be considered void.

Olivia, age 65, responded to our ad for a new cashier. Will I be guilty of age discrimination if I reject her application?

It depends on why you reject her. The federal Charter of Rights and Freedoms, as well as most human rights codes and charters, prohibits discrimination based on age. You will be breaking the law if you reject or refuse to consider her application solely because she is 65. But you will not be violating the law if you reject Olivia's application because you have found another applicant who has more experience.

Peter would like to run a small consulting business after he retires. He plans to have the firm buy him a car, cover some of his lunch expenses, purchase his life insurance, and even absorb some of his living expenses. Is this possible?

Yes. Peter can establish a corporation, which can hold title to his car, authorize an expense account, purchase life insurance as a benefit, and pay him a salary. Peter must be very careful, however, to keep his personal and corporate assets separate. He should not, for example, charge a birthday gift to his wife on his expense account. If Peter mingles his personal and corporate money, a court may decide that there is really no corporation separate from Peter, and he will be personally liable for corporate debts. Recent changes to income tax laws have virtually done away with most of the tax advantages Peter might have gained once upon a time: cars, lunch expenses and life insurance provided by a company are taxable benefits under the current Income Tax Act.

How can I keep someone else from using my business's name?

Generally, neither the federal nor provincial departments in charge of corporations allow two businesses to register under the same name. A name must be registered with the minister of consumer and corporate affairs if the business is a corporation or if the name does not identify the proprietor or partnership—Up-and-Up Wares, for example. If you are the first to use a name, and another business uses it, you can stop its use through a court injunction. If you feel another company illegally used your name to its gain and your loss, you can sue that company for compensation.

To avoid the headache of inadvertently using another business's name, many firms employ a service that makes name searches. Your corporate affairs ministry can tell you how to locate such services.

Will Glenn be violating any laws if he has his employees work 10 to 12 hours a day to fill unexpected orders?

Glenn should consult his provincial labor department to see if it will grant him a permit allowing him to have his employees work 10 to 12 hours a day. But even with a permit, he cannot force any employee to put in these hours. Provincial laws govern working conditions, including hours of work. Most provinces have a standard eight-hour workday but their workweek standards vary from 40 to 48 hours. Except for certain persons—such as homemakers, watchmen, domestics, fire fighters, supervisors, managers and professionals—the workweek cannot exceed 48 hours, including overtime. Employees of Crown corporations are under federal jurisdiction and have a standard eight-hour day, 40-hour week. But whether federal or provincial law applies, any work in excess of the standard workweek is to be considered overtime and to be paid for by at least one and a half times the regular rate.

I'd like to hire Todd as a clerk in my store, but my partner doesn't trust him. How can I check on Todd's trustworthiness?

You can ask Todd's former employers and his references about his honesty and reliability. Generally, you are not allowed to question Todd himself about his personal finances or whether he has ever been arrested. However, any criminal convictions would usually be in the court records where Todd lives or used to live, unless he committed the offenses elsewhere. Don't count on Todd taking a polygraph (lie detector) test, since most provinces prohibit employers from requiring employees to do so. These tests are seen as an invasion of privacy, which violates a right guaranteed by many provincial charters and codes of human rights.

Running a Business

Sherman has a valuable customer who regularly falls behind in paying his bill. Should Sherman sue the customer for payment?

Sherman should first ask the customer why he hasn't paid and when he expects to be able to pay. Perhaps they can work out a new payment schedule. Sherman can freeze the customer's account, allowing no further credit until the payments are brought up to date. If it still appears that the customer cannot pay his debt, Sherman has the option of suing to make him pay what is owed.

Will Gabrielle need to purchase liability insurance for the business she is about to start?

Most companies need some type of liability insurance. Exactly what type depends upon the nature of the business. Public liability insurance covers accidents to customers on the company's premises. If Gabrielle is going to manufacture merchandise, product liability insurance may be a good idea. This covers injury or damage caused by the manufacturer's negligence in designing, producing, or marketing the product or instructing customers about how it should be used. If Gabrielle will have employees, she will be required to contribute to the Workers' Compensa-

If the Business Fails: Your Choices

Every year in Canada thousands of businesses reach a point where their liabilities exceed their assets, and the only reasonable course is bankruptcy. Sole owners and general partners are personally liable for their business debts and could see personal property such as house and car seized and sold to pay creditors. In the case of corporations however, only the assets belonging to the company can be sold. The shareholders, directors and managers are generally not personally liable for company debts unless they have personally guaranteed certain loans or contracts. However, directors of companies that have declared bankruptcy are personally liable for employees' salaries for up to six months. Some points to remember about bankruptcy:

● A company can be forced into bankruptcy if it can't meet its obligations as they become due and if it owes more than $1,000 to at least one creditor.
● A company may file its own *petition in bankruptcy* (or *assignment*), which stops all legal proceedings against it, even those executing a judgment already rendered by the courts.

tion Fund to cover job-related injuries. Finally, she may wish to buy liability coverage for injuries or damage caused by her employees. Corporations routinely buy liability insurance for their officers and directors, in case they are sued by stockholders or regulatory agencies.

I operate a used clothing business in a suburban shopping plaza. My lease prevents me from placing items on the sidewalk in front of the store. However, the tenant next door displays his items on the sidewalk. How can he do this when I can't?

Your landlord is not required to negotiate identical leases with each tenant. However, if your lease says no other tenants can display goods on the sidewalk, you may sue the landlord to enforce this term of your lease and collect damages for the losses your business incurred.

When I start my business at home, will my existing homeowners and liability insurance be sufficient to protect me, or will I need additional coverage?

Homeowners policies often exclude losses related to the commercial use of your home, and while covering personal property, may not protect business inventory and equipment. They do not cover job-related

● A company may file a *proposal in bankruptcy* whereby it promises to pay its creditors, within a certain period, a percentage of what it owes them. If all agree, and if the court approves, the company may continue operations. A rejected proposal puts the company into bankruptcy.
● If a corporation has public debt, such as outstanding bonds or debentures, it may attempt a *compromise* or *arrangement* with its creditors under the Companies Creditors' Arrangement Act. If creditors representing three quarters of the debt agree, bankruptcy proceedings are stopped and all creditors are bound by the arrangement.
● Creditor claims can be *privileged, secured,* or *ordinary.* A *privileged claim*, one for salaries say, must be paid before all others. A bank holding a failing company's loan collateral, such as a series of Canada Savings Bonds, would have a *secured claim*: the bank may keep the bonds and file a claim for any balance owing. All other creditors, including suppliers of materials, have an *ordinary claim.*
● It is illegal for a company to dispose of its property fraudulently before or after bankruptcy. Thus if a company sells its $100,000 fleet of trucks and cars for $5,000 to the relative of a director, this sale could be canceled and the directors who approved it could be punished.

injuries to your employees. Personal liability or umbrella policies seldom cover business activities, and certainly wouldn't cover product liability. Depending on the nature of your business, you may wish to purchase fire and explosion coverage, public and product liability coverage, burglary coverage, fraud and credit insurance (to cover bounced cheques and bad debts), floater insurance for your inventory and, if you are engaged in medicine or dentistry, malpractice insurance.

Ryan asked his clerk to drive to the stationery store for supplies. The clerk was involved in an auto accident in which he was negligent. Can Ryan be held responsible?

Yes. Since the employee was carrying out his employer's directions when the accident occurred, Ryan can be held responsible.

A mechanic at Vincent's Auto Shop did a tune-up and brake check for a customer, who was involved in an accident the next day. The customer claims the accident was caused by his faulty brakes. Can Vincent's repair shop be held liable for damages?

Yes. If an employee of Vincent's Auto Shop was responsible for the faulty brakes or reported that the brakes were repaired when they were not, the business could be held liable. If Vincent's is incorporated, the corporation would be responsible. If the business is a sole proprietorship or partnership, the owners would be held personally responsible.

As the president of my company, I signed a contract that said I would deliver certain equipment to the Bellwether Grape Company. I have two employees out sick and can't deliver when I promised. Does Bellwether have grounds for a lawsuit?

Yes. You were obliged to honor the contract, even if you had to hire other people to deliver this equipment, and even if these hirings deprived you of any profit from this particular transaction.

Josephine runs a custom-furniture business next to an apartment building, whose tenants object to the noise of her power saw. Can they prevent her from operating a saw on her own premises?

Yes. Josephine's neighbors could obtain a court order, or injunction, against her if the court decides her use of the power saw is a public nuisance or if its operation is prohibited by local zoning laws. In deciding if Josephine's use of the saw is a public nuisance, the court would consider how the surrounding property is used and how much inconvenience, discomfort, or harm Josephine is actually causing her neighbors.

We are hiring an employee who needs a wheelchair to get around. What changes must we make to comply with the laws and regulations about handicapped accessibility?

Most local laws do not order specific facilities for the handicapped. Rather, they require employers to make reasonable changes, which are usually defined as those that do not create undue business hardships for the employer. When making such accommodations, you should consider access to rest rooms, lunchrooms, and parking, as well as to the work site. For someone in a wheelchair, these areas can be made more accessible by installing ramps and nonskid surfaces. For the hearing-impaired, lights can be used to supplement sound signals, such as fire alarms. And for the blind, bells and Braille make elevators less difficult.

Nellie and Penelope incorporated their real estate business last year. Is it important for them to have a stockholders' meeting every year and write up the minutes of these meetings?

Yes. Most laws concerning corporations require them to hold annual stockholder meetings, and to keep minutes of these meetings in their corporate records. If they don't observe the formalities required of corporations, a court may decide their business is conducted more like a partnership or sole proprietorship than a corporation, and Nellie and Penelope will find themselves personally liable for corporate debts.

If Ruth Ann is named a director of a corporation, will she have to put her corporate responsibilities ahead of her personal interest?

Yes, in some respects. As a director, Ruth Ann must act in the best interest of the corporation, even if that conflicts with her personal interest. She cannot use information she has learned as a corporate director for personal gain or against the interests of the corporation. According to the law, Ruth Ann is in a position of trust (she is a fiduciary) and must act with diligence to protect the corporation's interests.

To fulfill this duty, Ruth Ann should attend directors' meetings and keep informed about corporate business by reviewing material provided by the corporation, including past minutes of the meetings, agendas, proposals, financial statements, and stockholder reports. If the other directors propose a course of business that she thinks is wrong, she should make her objections, on the record, at the directors' meetings. If Ruth Ann doesn't act in the corporation's best interest and neglects its affairs, she can be sued by the corporation's shareholders for not fulfilling her fiduciary duty.

As a stockholder, am I liable for the actions of the corporation?

No. Although you are a part owner of the corporation, you cannot be held personally liable for corporate actions. The corporation, not its stockholders, will be sued. However, you would lose this immunity if, for example, you were a stockholder of a family corporation and used corporate assets for personal purposes.

Dan's company has an order to deliver stuffed pandas to a chain of stores in time for Christmas shopping. One of his fabric suppliers closed down because of a strike and can't deliver the necessary material. What are Dan's legal responsibilities?

Dan must still live up to his contractual obligations. If he does not deliver the toys on time, he may be sued for breach of contract. Dan should make every possible effort to get the necessary material from other suppliers. If he must pay higher prices and so suffers a loss, he can sue his original supplier for breach of contract and for the losses he suffered.

Selling or Ending a Business

Van wants to retire from the day-to-day management of his business and his cousins want to buy him out. Van is willing to stretch their payments over a number of years. How can he protect himself if they fail to make the payments?

Van could lend them the purchase price and accept the company's assets as collateral for the loan. His cousins would own and manage the business and he would have the right to take all the business assets if they defaulted on the loan. Or Van might incorporate his business and name his cousins as officers and directors. As officers, they would receive salaries, and they could buy shares of stock in the business from Van according to an agreed-upon schedule. Such an arrangement would allow the cousins to manage the business while gradually acquiring ownership from Van. If they did not buy stock on schedule, the cousins' percentage of ownership would increase at a slower rate.

Julian wants to begin turning over his construction company to his sons. Would forming a partnership be a good way to proceed with the transfer?

A partnership may be best if Julian's sons would gain tax advantages from it. Julian and his sons should consider the corporate form as well, with its limited liability. Whichever form the business takes, Julian and his sons will have to agree on how to share ownership and management and how to resolve disputes if they arise. They should also decide how long Julian will continue to play a role in the business; what that role will be (for example, officer, director, or consultant); and how much he will be paid for his services and for what length of time.

When we formed a corporation, we signed an agreement to keep it always within the family. Now I want to sell my shares to an outsider. Can my relatives prevent me?

Yes, if your corporate bylaws or an agreement with other family members prohibits you from selling your stock to an outsider. However, in many cases, the bylaws or the agreement will let you sell your stock outside the company if you first get the consent of the corporation's board of directors or other shareholders or if you first offer the shares to the corporation or the other stockholders.

I want to sell one-half of my business to my friend Felix for $50,000, but he has only $10,000. How can we both be protected?

If Felix can get a bank loan, be sure that he offers personal collateral, such as his home, car, or personal bank account, rather than his interest in the business. Otherwise, if he defaults, the partnership assets may be seized by the bank to pay the loan. Likewise be certain that Felix does not obtain the loan as a loan to your business. If Felix defaults on a loan made on behalf of the business, the lender could seize your assets, both partnership and personal, to pay the debt. If a bank will not lend Felix $40,000 to buy into your business, you may not want to do so either.

For years Randall single-handedly owned and ran a bookstore, but business is bad and getting worse. Can Randall close the shop and collect unemployment insurance?

No. Randall is not considered an employee under the Unemployment Insurance Act. To be eligible, he would have to be under the direction and control of an employer, and both he and his employer would have had to pay the unemployment insurance premiums for a specified time.

Selling or Ending a Business

Self-employed people do not pay unemployment insurance premiums. Taxi drivers who don't own their own vehicles, clergymen, or people who work in, but don't own, barbershops or hairdressing salons do pay premiums and are eligible for unemployment insurance benefits.

I am running a sole proprietorship. I don't have any children, and my husband does not seem to be interested in the business. What will happen to it when I die?

A sole proprietorship is a personal asset, just like your home or bank account, and would therefore become a part of your estate, to be passed on or divided according to the instructions in your will. In most cases similar to yours, the surviving spouse or executor of the estate sells the business, uses the proceeds to settle claims against the estate, and then passes the remaining funds along to the owner's survivors or the beneficiaries of his will.

Your Individual Rights

Your Rights as a Citizen ▬▬▬▬▬▬

What are one's legal rights?

When we think of rights, we generally think of such things as freedom of speech, freedom of the press, freedom of religion, and the right to a fair trial. These basic rights are protected by the Charter of Rights and Freedoms as well as by the common law. Further rights are protected by other constitutional provisions and by statutes, regulations, and ordinances. They include your right to vote, to marry and raise a family, to work, to own property, to have adequate heat and plumbing when you rent an apartment, to get compensation if you are cheated by others or are hurt because of their negligence, and to leave your assets to whomever you wish when you die.

Does the Charter of Rights and Freedoms apply to the provinces?

Yes. The Charter is described at section 52 (1) as "the supreme law of Canada and any law that is inconsistent with the provisions of the constitution is, to the extent of the inconsistency, of no force and effect." The Charter applies to the Parliament and Government of Canada and to the legislature and government of each province and Territory.

Does the Charter of Rights and Freedoms apply only to citizens?

Certain provisions of the Charter apply only to Canadian citizens: for example, the right to vote in federal and provincial elections. But most of the rights and freedoms are guaranteed to all persons on Canadian soil, citizens or not: freedom of conscience and religion, of thought and expression, of the press and of peaceful assembly and association; the right to a fair trial, to be secure against unreasonable search and seizure, and to reasonable bail, and other legal and social rights.

Why don't all the provinces have the same laws?

The British North America Act of 1867, considered by some to be Canada's most important constitutional document, divided the power to make laws between the new federal government and the governments of the three provinces that formed the new nation: Canada—made up of Upper Canada (Ontario) and Lower Canada (Quebec)—New Brunswick and Nova Scotia. As new provinces joined the confederation, they received the same rights to pass laws about matters deemed provincial. Federal legislation governs such things as national defense, divorce, criminal law, the postal service, and currency and coinage. Provincial laws regulate matters dealing with such things as the solemnization of marriage; property and civil rights in the province; municipal institutions; and the maintenance and organization of provincial courts and jails. Because of the varied nature, customs, and history of the provinces, the laws they pass vary. For example, laws relating to development of oil and gas resources may be more important to Alberta than to Quebec; laws dealing with forest restoration are more relevant to British Columbia than to Saskatchewan.

Can our rights as citizens be taken away without our consent?

Yes, but only temporarily, during an emergency. After a riot or disaster, federal and provincial authorities have the right to declare a state of emergency and impose, for example, a curfew, in which businesses must close early and citizens are ordered to stay off the streets. The most extreme restriction, martial law, may be declared when there is a war or evidence of a real or apprehended insurrection. In October 1970, the then Prime Minister, Pierre Trudeau, declared martial law in Quebec when he invoked the War Measures Act. That act has recently been replaced by the Emergency Act, which forbids the confiscation of property without compensation and the detention of people because of race, religion, or natural origin. This law will do away with abuses such as those inflicted on Canadians of Japanese origin during World War II.

After a disaster such as a bad flood, when a provincial premier declares a state of emergency, can he order the army to help?

No. Only the federal Cabinet can do so, acting on behalf of the Crown, which commands the armed forces through its representative, the Governor-General. A premier can only request the help. Unlike the American states with their National Guards, the provinces maintain no armed forces of their own. Of course federal and all provincial governments are obliged to ensure peace, order, security, and good government, so a request for help would likely be granted.

Does Ray, a sergeant in the armed forces, lose any of his basic rights as a citizen if he's court-martialed?

The sergeant—and everyone else in the armed services—is subject to military law, and his rights closely resemble those of nonmilitary citizens, especially in the area of criminal law. Ray has the right to an attorney, to a fair hearing, and to appeal, but he does not have the right to trial by jury unless he is charged with an offense punishable by five years' imprisonment or more.

What Is the Law?

Perhaps the best definition is the simplest: the law is the set of rules we live by to maintain order in society. Over the centuries, these rules have evolved into an elaborate legal system made up of the following:

● *Constitutional law* is the basic law upon which our government is founded as set forth in the British North America Act and the Constitution Acts of 1982, among others, and in the provincial constitutions. Constitutional law does not provide detailed directives on the subjects it addresses, but states general principles and establishes a foundation of law and government. Our federal and provincial constitutions dictate how laws can be made and enforced, and they name our basic non-violable rights, such as freedom of speech and religion, and the right to vote and to benefit from equal protection of the law.

● *Statutes* are laws passed by Parliament or provincial legislatures, which specify what a person must do (or not do) to keep within the bounds of legality. Statutes cover everything that constitutional law does not declare to be beyond the lawmakers' powers. Among other things, statutes set requirements for marriage, put limits on interest rates, prohibit fraud, establish minimum wages and minimum standards for contracts, protect inventions through patents, and define crimes and give guidelines for punishing criminals.

● *Regulations* are orders enacted by public administrative agencies to

---

A city bylaw prohibits trucks, including pickup trucks used for personal transportation, from traveling on boulevards. Can we get this changed?

Probably. Ask your city council to abolish the bylaw or to amend it to exclude small pickup trucks. A petition signed by a large number of voters would help your case. Appeal directly to the mayor, or if your city has a street department or traffic-planning division, you might want to ask them to study your city's need for truck traffic on boulevards.

Canadian Citizenship

How does a person become a Canadian citizen?

A person becomes a citizen by birth or by naturalization. A person born in any of the provinces or Territories is automatically a Canadian, even if his parents were just visiting Canada. Persons born in Newfoundland supervise or control various matters that affect the public. These agencies—such as the Unemployment Insurance Commission and the Crime Victims Indemnity Board—are set up by Parliament and provincial legislatures, which give them the power to make and enforce regulations. For example, regulations bar discrimination in hiring, set radio and television broadcasting standards, and establish safety standards for food and drugs. Violating a regulation is essentially the same as violating a statute. Violators can be subject to a variety of disciplinary actions, including fines and having their licenses revoked.

● *Ordinances* or *bylaws* are laws enacted by municipal councils. Rules relating to the health, safety, and welfare of residents—such as those involving parking, littering, and snow removal—are examples of ordinances. Since cities and towns derive their powers from the province in which they are situated, they cannot pass ordinances that contradict or violate provincial laws.

● *Uniform codes* are model laws drafted by scholars specializing in such areas as commercial law or family law. Such model laws may be adopted with or without modification by the provinces.

● *Common law (case law)* is a body of principles based on court decisions in similar cases. When no specific statute or regulation applies, the principles of common law are applied by the court. Quebec relies on the Civil Code rather than case law. Civil law in Quebec derives from the laws of France and Rome, rather than from Britain as in the other provinces (known as the common-law provinces).

before 1949, when Newfoundland joined Canada, are citizens of Canada, as are persons born at sea on a Canadian ship. A person born outside Canada is a citizen if one parent is Canadian and the birth is registered in Canada. Landed immigrants may apply for Canadian citizenship after three years in Canada.

Is it possible for a Canadian to have dual citizenship?

If a child is born in Canada of parents who are citizens of another country, or if he is born abroad and one or both of his parents are Canadian citizens, he may have the rights and responsibilities of citizenship in Canada plus those of citizenship in the other country. If, for example, he visited the country of his birth, he may be subject to compulsory military service there, and Canadian authorities would not be able to intervene.

A landed immigrant who becomes a Canadian citizen may retain citizenship of his native country if that country permits its citizens dual citizenship.

Canadian Citizenship

What is a certificate of landing?

It is a document issued to a landed immigrant, identifying that person as someone who is living permanently in Canada in anticipation of becoming a naturalized citizen. A landed immigrant has most of the rights and obligations of a citizen except that he cannot vote or hold public office, and may be deported if found guilty of a serious crime.

I have an opportunity to hire a highly qualified woman from another country as a nanny for my child. What must I do to get her into Canada?

Write a letter to this woman offering her employment for a specific number of months or years, stating the salary, and describing the living arrangements. She then should contact a Canadian visa officer in her home country and apply for a work permit for the period indicated in your letter. After passing a medical examination and a check for any criminal record, she will probably be granted a work permit. The rules applying to a worker other than a domestic are tougher: Immigration Canada grants no work permits until convinced that no Canadian or permanent resident of Canada is available for the position applied for.

Can a Canadian lose his citizenship?

Yes. A Canadian may lose his citizenship if (1) he was born outside Canada but was considered to be Canadian because one of his parents was Canadian, *and* by age 28 he neither lives in Canada nor has applied to retain his citizenship; (2) he becomes a citizen of another country and voluntarily renounces his Canadian citizenship; (3) he obtained Canadian citizenship by false pretenses, by concealing an extensive criminal record, or by some other fraudulent means.

Your Right to Vote

Carla's parents live in one province, but she goes to college in another. In which province should Carla vote?

Carla can choose either province. If she wants to vote in her college town, she may have to establish that she no longer considers her parents' residence her home and that she has made (or intends to make) the college town her legal residence for the time she is a student there.

Who determines a Canadian's eligibility to vote?

Each province establishes the eligibility requirements for voters in provincial and municipal elections. Federal law sets out the requirements for federal elections.

Bernice moved to another province one month before an election. She was told she was ineligible to vote because she had not lived in the province long enough. Was this right?

Yes. A province can establish residency requirements, as long as the requirements are not excessive.

Are persons who have served time in prison allowed to vote?

Yes. And some provinces, Quebec for example, give the vote to prisoners *while* they are in prison.

Can provincial governments require residents to pay their taxes before allowing them to vote?

No. The right of every Canadian citizen to vote in federal and provincial elections is guaranteed by the Charter of Rights and Freedoms. This basic democratic right cannot be set aside by such things as taxes owing to a province.

I will be on a cruise to the Caribbean on election day, and I want to vote before I leave. Can I be denied an opportunity to do so?

Any provincial law intended to keep an absentee from voting would be invalid, a violation of the federal Charter of Rights and Freedoms which guarantees every citizen the right to vote.

Freedom of Religion

I believe that our children should be encouraged to pray. Why can't my province pass a law requiring public school children to join in saying a simple, nondenominational prayer each morning?

The Supreme Court of Canada declared in 1987 that the Canadian Charter of Rights and Freedoms guarantees the individual absolute

Freedom of Religion

freedom of conscience and religion. Thus, the state does not have the power, directly or indirectly, to compel someone to observe a religious duty. A nondenominational prayer would, it seems, infringe upon the rights of nonbelievers and thus violate the freedom of conscience and religion guaranteed by the Charter.

Under provincial law, Arthur must close his shop on Sundays, but he would rather open on Sundays and close on Saturdays, when he celebrates the Sabbath. Would he succeed if he challenged this law as a violation of his right to freedom of religion?

Probably, but much would depend upon the intent and the wording of the provincial statute. Provinces have power to regulate store closing hours, as long as there is neither promotion of nor discrimination against any religion. In a case heard by the Supreme Court of Canada in 1985, Big M Drug Mart of Calgary was found not guilty of violating the federal Lord's Day Act by doing business on Sundays. The act was held to be unconstitutional in enforcing the observance of a Christian day of rest, despite the right of religious freedom guaranteed by the Charter. However, a similar law, whose intent and effect are to establish a uniform day of rest rather than to enforce a religious practice, may be valid. Still, Sunday closing is an issue far from settled in Canada.

Joe had four wives and was convicted of polygamy, which he claims his religion encourages. Hasn't the state thus interfered with his practice of his religion?

No. Although the Charter of Rights and Freedoms includes the freedom to practice one's religion, a person may be prevented from practicing a specific religious practice if it violates the law. Courts have consistently ruled that society is better served by laws that make polygamy illegal than by exceptions that would allow it.

As parents, do we have the right to prevent our children from receiving medical treatment that is contrary to our religion?

No. When a child's health—or the health of the public—is at stake, courts consistently rule against parents who have tried to deny medical treatment for religious reasons. Vaccinations and blood transfusions are examples of medical treatment that courts have ordered against the wishes of the parents. A child's right to life overrides his parents' rights to follow a religious practice that forbids certain medical treatment.

Andrea is an officer of a campus church group at university. When she tried to reserve a room for a church service, the manager at the student union refused to let her do so. Was he justified in this?

No. The manager probably thinks that allowing a church group to use a publicly funded facility violates the constitutional prohibition against the government's promoting one religion over another. This is not the case here. The university can allow church groups to meet on its premises as long as it treats all church groups equally—it cannot allow one group to meet in the school but refuse another.

Freedom of Speech

If my co-workers and I want to protest our employer's hiring practices, do we have the right to carry signs of protest?

Yes. The freedom of speech guaranteed by the Charter of Rights and Freedoms is not limited to oral communication. Opinions expressed in signs and on bumper stickers, buttons, and T-shirts are also protected. However, the messages must not incite people to cause a disturbance or break the law, and of course slanderous, libelous or obscene messages are not protected. Your union may have additional guidelines or restrictions on how your message can be expressed. Your union representative can advise you about the legal requirements.

Can a customer picket a store without getting a permit to do so?

Probably, as long as he doesn't get his friends together to picket in a group. The right of free speech includes the right to picket, as long as the picketing does not intimidate customers or result in violence. Generally, a permit is required only for a group demonstration.

If I get angry and call my boss a crook, can he sue me?

Only if the incident amounted to slander. The circumstances would have to be considered along with the effect, if any, of your statement on your boss's reputation. If you spoke within the hearing of others and in such a way that someone interpreted it to mean that your boss was dishonest, or if the remark resulted in your boss being ridiculed, he may have a legitimate claim for a lawsuit. If he does sue you, he will have to show that someone else heard the remark and that it harmed or was meant to harm his reputation.

Freedom of Speech

Maryla heads an environmental group that the provincial minister of the environment, speaking in the legislature, called "a bunch of crooks living off government grants." No one in the organization has been convicted of any criminal offense and it is supported from private donations. Can Maryla sue the minister?

She can, but she doesn't have a very good case. As a general rule, legislators cannot be sued for statements they make while acting in their official capacities in the House of Commons or the provincial legislatures. The common law has given legislators an absolute protection against lawsuits for slander when they are acting officially, because frank and open discussion is seen as a public good that should not be curtailed. This protection is called a *privilege*. A fair and accurate reporting of what the minister said would also be protected.

In his sermon, Deborah's pastor called her a sinner. Can she sue?

Depending on what precisely he said, Deborah might be able to sue him for defamation of character or for invasion of privacy. Speaking from the pulpit does not give a clergyman any special legal privilege or protect him from being sued. To win her case, Deborah would have to show that the pastor said something about her that would be highly offensive to an average person and did not simply make some general remark about all of us being sinners, "like you and Deborah and me."

Our club would like to propose a new provincial law that would require all schoolchildren to salute the flag or be suspended from school until they agree to do so. Would such a law be valid?

No. The Charter of Rights and Freedoms guarantees everyone freedom of conscience and the right to his beliefs. Schoolchildren must not be coerced if they do not wish to salute the flag.

Freedom of the Press

Can a judge keep news reporters from attending a trial?

Yes, if there is an overriding reason for excluding them. Though reporters have a general right to attend criminal trials, a judge can deny them access if he feels their presence would make it difficult for the defendant to get a fair trial. A judge might keep reporters from covering a civil trial if he felt they might publish testimony that revealed a company's trade secrets or private matters discussed by a couple seeking a divorce.

Chad was interviewed on videotape by a television reporter. The tape that was telecast later had been so edited that it changed the meaning of what he had said. What can Chad do to force the television station to air a more accurate version of the interview?

Chad should contact the reporter or the station manager and ask him to broadcast a statement correcting the false impression given by the edited tape. If Chad believes the station intentionally misrepresented or distorted his comments, he should complain to the Canadian Radio-television and Telecommunications Commission.

A reporter has been given information about a new military weapon, but the government has told him the information must not be published. Isn't this a violation of freedom of the press?

No. Publishing the information might violate the Official Secrets Act, a federal law. The courts have recognized that there is a legitimate interest in keeping some sensitive government information from being published. The government could seek an injunction to halt the publication of this information. However, it would have to prove that national security would be threatened if the material were published.

Our province has set up a motion picture review board. Doesn't this infringe on my right to decide what movies I want to see?

No. Because the state has a legitimate interest in limiting the availability of obscene materials, any province may adopt procedures to review and rate movies. The federal government also can prohibit the importation, manufacture, sale or distribution of obscene materials. There is no general agreement, however, as to what is obscene and what is not.

A newspaper reported that a well known singer and the owner of a local business had been seen in a nightclub with a man "suspected of having organized crime connections." Would the singer and the businessman have a good case for suing for libel?

Possibly. Each would have to prove that his reputation had been damaged. But courts distinguish between public figures and private individuals. The singer would have to establish that the statement was

Freedom of the Press

made with malice—that the newspaper printed the statement knowing it to be false, or that it had reason to believe the statement might be false but made no effort to verify it. The businessman might not have to prove malice; most provinces require a private individual to show only negligence—that the newspaper failed to acquire the facts. Other provinces do require private individuals to show malice or gross irresponsibility—that the standards ordinarily used by journalists to gather and disseminate information were disregarded.

Mobility Rights

Stacey was receiving public welfare assistance in Saskatchewan. When she moved to Quebec she was told she would have to wait one month before she could get welfare. Is this legal?

Yes. The Charter of Rights and Freedoms allows the provinces to enact laws setting out reasonable residency requirements in such cases.

Wendell practiced medicine in Ontario for 10 years, then moved to British Columbia, and was denied the right to practice under the government health plan. Is this legal?

No. Refusing to let a doctor practice in his new province of residence violates the Charter. It guarantees the right to move to any province and to pursue one's livelihood there.

Because of particularly high unemployment in one part of Nova Scotia, the province requires jobs in mining and fish processing to be offered first to residents of Nova Scotia. I was refused a job because I am a resident of Ontario. Isn't this discriminatory?

Perhaps, but this is probably legal. The Charter of Rights and Freedoms allows any province to pass laws to help socially or economically disadvantaged residents if the province's unemployment is higher than the Canadian average.

Can the government limit where a landed immigrant may live?

No. Once a person is admitted as a landed immigrant (permanent resident), he can live and work wherever he pleases.

Equality Rights ▬▬▬▬▬▬▬▬▬▬▬

For information on job discrimination, see "Job Discrimination" in Chapter 10, *Your Job*.

Lawyers in civil rights cases frequently talk about the equal protection clause. What is this, and where is it found?

The equal protection clause in section 15 of the Charter of Rights and Freedoms reads: "Every individual is equal before and under the law and has the right to the equal protection and equal benefit of the law without discrimination and, in particular, without discrimination based on race, national or ethnic origin, colour, religion, sex, age or mental or physical disability." The interpretation of this clause and its full effect will not be known for many years.

Can a province limit professional licenses to Canadian citizens?

Not generally. Any law that automatically excludes foreigners can be challenged in court. Foreigners have won cases against laws that prohibited them from becoming lawyers or engineers. However, courts may uphold citizenship requirements for some government workers if national security may be involved.

People in our neighborhood are concerned about the noise of summer rock concerts at a nearby park and the rowdiness of many of the people attending them. Could we get the city to pass a bylaw allowing the police to deny permits to rock bands?

No. A restriction of this kind would probably be unenforceable. While the courts recognize that limits on the time, place, duration, and manner of noisy performances may be needed, the city would find it difficult to justify a bylaw against all rock bands. Denying one segment of society access to a public forum is denying the equal protection of the laws guaranteed by the Charter. The city would be in a better position to enforce a bylaw that required all park activities to end at a certain time or that restricted the use of loudspeakers.

Angela, president of the parents group at our high school, is upset because one of the new teachers admitted, when asked, that she is a lesbian. If Angela were able to get the teacher fired, would the dismissal stand up in court?

Probably not, unless Angela could show that the teacher was not competent to carry out her school duties. Public schools are publicly funded, and the government may not engage in discrimination.

Equality Rights

Can a fraternal organization exclude people of a certain race?

Not even private clubs are allowed to discriminate on grounds of race or religion and it is doubtful whether a fraternal organization may prohibit women from joining. The refusal of junior hockey teams to allow girls to play has been held to be illegal and in conflict with provincial charters of human rights and freedoms.

Aunt Hazel is confined to a wheelchair. What are her rights of access to public buildings and public transportation?

Discrimination based on physical disability is prohibited by the federal Charter of Rights and Freedoms and by several provincial charters. Public buildings, therefore, should have ramps to provide access for physically disabled people, and publicly funded transit systems should provide a special service for the physically disabled. In fact governments at all levels have begun to make all their services and buildings accessible to the handicapped. Curb ramps at intersections are now commonplace in many towns and cities, and more are being added whenever street improvements are carried out.

Randall, who was just laid off from the electronics firm partly owned by his wife Betty, has now discovered that he won't be able to collect unemployment insurance benefits if Betty owns 40 percent or more of the company. Is this restriction valid?

Probably not. The Supreme Court of Canada has yet to rule on this point of law. A person who works for a friend, lover, roommate or relative who owns 40 percent or more of the company would be eligible for benefits, so excluding a person because of marriage would probably be discriminatory and against the Charter's rights to equal protection and benefit of the law. An Ontario Supreme Court ruling that such an exclusion is valid was overturned by a 1988 decision of the Federal Court of Appeal, which declared such an exclusion illegal and discriminatory.

Marilyn believes she was refused a restaurant job because she is a woman. What can she do?

She can sue the restaurant owner directly on grounds that he discriminated against her on the basis of sex, or she can file a complaint with her provincial human rights organization. In some provinces the human rights body, after investigation, might sue the restaurant on her behalf.

Many road accidents involve 18-to-21-year-old male drivers who have been drinking. Could a law be passed raising the drinking age to, say, 22 for men, but not changing the age for women?

Probably not. Such a law would probably be discriminatory on grounds of sex and age and so would probably violate the Charter's section 15.

Many refugees have moved into our city and a few have applied for positions as teachers. Can the school board refuse to hire them because they are not Canadian citizens?

Not if the applicants are certified to teach in your province, because provinces (and thus school boards) do not have the right to restrict teaching to citizens only. In a British Columbia case, a rule set by the provincial bar association allowing only Canadian citizens to practice law was declared unreasonable and void.

Your Right to Privacy

A reporter interviewed me by telephone and, as I later learned, taped the call without asking my permission. Isn't this illegal?

No. The recording of a conversation between two parties, when the person doing the recording is one of those parties, is not illegal. It does not constitute interception of a private communication—which otherwise is illegal.

My 12-year-old son ran away from home, and I asked the police to help find him. Will records of this incident be kept confidential?

Yes. Police records relating to young people under 18 are confidential and can be consulted only by very few people—judges, the police in certain circumstances, and the child's parents or legal guardians.

Percy lives in a boardinghouse where residents' mail is left on a table in the entrance hall. Someone has been opening Percy's personal mail. What can he do about it?

Percy should report his problem to the local postmaster. It is a crime to tamper with someone else's mail, and it makes no difference whether it is still in the hands of Canada Post or on a hall table. Anyone convicted of tampering can be fined or jailed.

Your Right to Privacy

Can a court force a lawyer to reveal confidential information about a client? What about doctors and priests?

A lawyer cannot be compelled to reveal confidential conversations with a client. The law recognizes that a client must be able to disclose facts about a case to his attorney without fear that they will be divulged to other people.

Most provinces have laws protecting confidential communications between a doctor and his patient and a clergyman and his parishioner. Doctors do not have to release information about a patient unless their silence would threaten the health or safety of others; for example, a doctor may be required by law to report that a patient has a communicable disease. A doctor must also notify the authorities if a child he is treating shows signs of abuse. A clergyman does not have to disclose communications made by a person seeking spiritual comfort—as in confession—or privately discussing religious matters, even if the person admits to committing a serious crime.

Our neighbor Nora sometimes wanders outside our house at night, peering in through our windows. Although we have nothing to hide, we feel uneasy about being watched. Isn't this an invasion of our privacy? How should we handle this matter?

Tell Nora you will call the police the next time you see her looking into your windows. Her behavior might constitute trespass for which she could be sued.

Can a person's photograph be used in an advertisement without his consent?

No. The unauthorized commercial use of a photograph in which a person can be clearly identified can be an invasion of privacy.

Ever since I bought my videocassette recorder I have been receiving ads for X-rated films. I don't want this type of mail coming into my house. Is there anything I can do about it?

Yes. Contact Canada Post and request that your name be placed on its list of persons who do not want to receive sexually oriented advertisements. When you fill out the required form, you can also include the names of your children so that mail is not addressed to them either. It is a federal offense to send obscene or indecent materials by mail.

Several people want to reserve a part of the local beach for nude sunbathing. Can we stop them?

You would have to contact the mayor or city council about enacting a bylaw prohibiting nudity on public beaches and in other public areas. Courts have upheld this type of ordinance as a valid way for residents to ensure the peaceful enjoyment of public property. Your province may also have a law against people exposing themselves in public. If so, the law can be enforced to keep people from sunbathing in the nude.

Brandon wants to know what information the RCMP and other federal agencies have gathered about him. How can he find out?

He should write to each agency and request the information he wants. The Access to Information Act requires federal agencies to release information in their files unless it is confidential for reasons of personal privacy (someone else's medical records, for example) or classified because of national security. Under the Access to Information Act and the Privacy Act, a person may consult his file, correct any mistakes he may find, and add new information. Most large post offices and libraries have directories of federal departments to which Brandon may write. There are fees for consulting one's files. If Brandon does not receive the information he wants, he should contact the office of the Federal Information Commissioner. If a department refuses to let Brandon see his file or to make corrections, Brandon can sue.

Citizens may also use the Access to Information Act and the Privacy Act to dig out useful information such as the results of product or environmental testing. Application forms for requesting information are available in most libraries. The directories published under the two acts cost $10 each.

André was photographed at a gay rights rally, and he has been teased and harassed since the picture appeared in his hometown paper. Can he sue the paper for invasion of privacy?

No. Courts recognize that the right to privacy must be balanced against the guarantee of freedom of the press. When an event is of public interest, a newspaper can publish the names and pictures of participants without getting their permission.

How can I put a stop to obscene phone calls?

Report obscene calls to the police. If possible, tape one. The tape will prove the call took place. If requested by the police, the telephone company will try to trace the number from which the calls are placed. The company is often able to track down the source of obscene calls and can take legal action to put an end to them. The police may also take action. Under the Criminal Code, anyone making obscene phone calls can be punished by a fine, imprisonment, or both.

Dealing With the Police ▬▬▬▬▬▬▬▬▬▬

For information on arrests, see "Rights of the Accused" in Chapter 17, *Victims and Crimes.*

Can a store detective stop me from leaving if I haven't done anything wrong?

Yes. A store detective has the right to stop anyone if he has reason to believe that the person has stolen something, as long as he does not mistreat that person or detain him for an unreasonable time.

When the Police Can Search Without a Warrant

Most searches of a person or his property are considered illegal if conducted without a warrant that describes the person or place to be searched and the things that can be taken. Evidence found during an illegal search usually cannot be used in court. There are several special situations, however, in which the police can legally carry out a search without a warrant:

● *A consent search*—The police may search without a warrant if the person involved gives his consent without being coerced. However, the search must be confined to the area the person authorized. For example, if someone agrees to a search of his living room, the police cannot open a file cabinet in his den without a warrant.

● *A plain-view search*—Police may seize evidence that is out in the open or that comes to light as they search for something else for which they have a warrant. But evidence obtained this way cannot be used in court unless: (1) the police were lawfully at the location where the item was found, (2) it was obvious that the item was evidence of a crime, and (3) the discovery was accidental. For example, if the police are searching a suspect's hotel room for a gun, and unexpectedly uncover a cache of counterfeit money, they may take the money and use it as evidence against the suspect, even though it was not mentioned in the warrant.

● *A stop and frisk*—If a police officer has reasonable grounds to

Ira came to Gordon's home while the police were searching it for evidence of a robbery. Can the police search Ira?

No. The police can search only those areas specified in the search warrant. Unless they have reason to believe that Ira has committed a crime, there is no legal justification for searching him.

The police searched Adrian's car while it was parked in front of his house. Was this legal?

Only if they believed that there was some evidence of a crime hidden in the car, such as stolen goods. Generally, the police must get a search warrant that specifically describes a car before they can open and search it without the owner's permission. However, they may not need a search warrant if there isn't time to get one: Courts make exceptions to the warrant requirement if there is reason to believe that the evidence will be destroyed or the car will be moved before a warrant can be obtained from a justice (a provincial court judge).

believe he is in danger, he may stop and frisk, or pat down, a suspect for a concealed weapon.

● *A search incident to arrest*—When making an arrest, a police officer may search a suspect and the area within the suspect's immediate vicinity for weapons or evidence of the crime that has been committed, in order to protect himself from bodily harm and to keep the evidence from being lost or destroyed.

● *An inventory search*—When the police impound cars or take into their possession other personal property that belongs to a suspect, they may search the property to make a list of everything impounded. This is permitted to protect the suspect's property and to protect the police— not only from possible dangers, such as explosives hidden in a car, but also from claims that they have stolen something.

● *Emergency searches*—The police may search without a warrant if they have a good reason, or probable cause, to believe that they will find evidence that could be moved, hidden, or destroyed—burned or flushed away, for example—before they could return with a warrant. This often occurs when officers are chasing a suspect who enters a building.

● *Vehicle searches*—If the police have probable cause, or good reason, to believe that evidence of a crime will be found in a car, truck, boat, or other vehicle that could easily be moved elsewhere before they could obtain a warrant, they may search the vehicle on the spot. For example, if the police have good reason to believe that a car is carrying illegal drugs, they can stop it and search it on the highway.

Dealing With the Police

I was walking downtown when a man ran toward me.
A policeman across the street shouted to me, "Stop that guy!"
I didn't, and the police officer arrested me. Can he do that?

No. Although you are under a moral obligation to help the police in arresting a criminal, you have no legal obligation to do so. If you did not see the man commit a crime, you would not have enough reason to arrest him, even if a policeman told you to "stop that guy."

In a crackdown on the use of drugs, our high school principal agreed to let the police conduct random drug tests of students. Is this legal?

No. Drug tests are a type of search, and the police cannot conduct searches unless they have what the law calls probable cause to believe there is wrongdoing. Probable cause is defined as a set of circumstances that would give an ordinary person reasonable grounds for believing that the law is being violated. Courts have ruled against random drug tests by government agencies, stating that there must be a reasonable suspicion about a particular person before a drug test can be required.

Can a male police officer search a woman who is suspected of hiding illegal drugs under her clothing?

A body search should be conducted by a female officer. If conducted by a male it would probably be considered an example of unreasonable search, prohibited by the Charter of Rights and Freedoms.

A stranger was walking up and down our street late one night, and two police officers stopped and frisked him because he "looked suspicious." Wasn't this illegal?

Yes, unless there was some reason to suspect the stranger had committed a crime or was about to commit one. For example, if he gave the impression that he was casing a house to rob, the police would have been justified in stopping him.

But the frisk, or pat-down, could legally have been done only to search for weapons if the police officers believed their own safety was at stake.

CHAPTER 13

Accidents

Accidents Inside Your Home ▬▬▬▬▬▬▬

For car accidents, see Chapter 6, *Your Car.* For auto insurance, see Chapter 8, *Insurance.* For information on other types of accidents, see "Liability for Personal Injury" in Chapter 8, *Insurance,* and "Workers' Compensation" in Chapter 10, *Your Job.*

When George came into Joyce's home, he slipped on a throw rug in the hall and injured his back. Joyce helped George up, saying, "I really should move that rug. Everyone falls on it." Could Joyce's statement hurt her case if George decides to sue her?

Yes. Joyce's statement indicates that she knew the rug was a hazard. The court would take this into account when considering whether she had a legal duty either to warn George about the rug or to minimize the risk by using a rug with rubber backing.

If a burglar breaks into my home, slips on my son's roller skate, and fractures his collarbone, can he sue me for damages?

No. When a burglar trespasses on your property, he assumes full responsibility for whatever hazards he may encounter. You are not liable for any accidental injuries a burglar receives while on your property.

Winning an Accident Case

You will not necessarily win a lawsuit just because you were injured or had your property damaged in an accident. Accidents occur even when everyone involved takes the proper precautions. To win an accident case, you must show that the person who caused the accident was negligent—he did something he shouldn't have or he didn't do something he should have. For a court to decide that someone was negligent, three basic conditions must be met:

1. The person did not fulfill his duty to use reasonable care to protect an individual from harm in a particular situation. For example, if someone lights firecrackers to celebrate Canada Day, he should do so in a safe place and not in a crowded area. In some circumstances, a person has a duty to protect an individual because he has a special relationship or responsibility to him. For example, building owners have a duty to keep their buildings safe for tenants and visitors and to warn them of any danger. If the marble floor in the lobby of a building has just been washed and is still wet, the owner of the building has a duty to put up a notice saying Slippery When Wet. But if you see someone drowning in a motel swimming pool, you have no legal duty to rescue him—even if you are an experienced swimmer—unless you are the lifeguard on duty

Olga's bridge club met at her house while it was being remodeled.
Since there were pieces of wood scattered all over the floor,
Olga warned her guests to be careful, but Madge tripped and
fractured her elbow. Is Olga liable for Madge's injury?

Probably not. A homeowner is not automatically liable for every accidental injury in the home. As a hostess, Olga has a duty to tell her guests about any dangerous conditions that are not obvious. Since wood on the floor would be clearly visible, and since Olga warned the bridge players to be careful, she fulfilled her legal responsibility. Even so, she should tell her insurance company about the mishap.

During a party at Greg's house, Cheryl tripped over an extension
cord cracking two ribs. Cheryl is now threatening to sue Greg for
her injury unless he pays her $5,000. Should he pay?

No. The fact that Cheryl was injured in Greg's home does not mean that he is automatically responsible. If the extension cord could be seen, Greg had no responsibility to warn his guests about it. On the other hand, if the danger was not clearly visible, a court would have to decide if Greg should have warned Cheryl.

or the motel owner or manager. In Quebec, however, the law is different. There everyone has the duty to help someone whose life is in danger. In other provinces, the area of law dealing with such duty is rapidly changing.

2. *The person failed to use reasonable care.* To determine what reasonable care is, courts ask the question, Would an ordinary person have acted in the same manner under similar circumstances? For example, in a case in which your neighbor's house accidentally caught fire, the court would consider whether an ordinary person would burn leaves near his neighbor's house on a windy day.

3. *The person's actions or failure to act caused the accident.* For example, if a customer dies in a fire because the owner of the store has blocked the exit with cartons of merchandise, the store owner's action contributed to the customer's death; if you visit your neighbor and fall into a hole he dug in his backyard, you could argue that your neighbor caused the accident because he failed to cover the hole he had dug or warn you about the danger. However, a person is only liable for consequences that can be foreseen, and not for anything unpredictable. For example, a person can foresee that leaving his car keys in the ignition might result in the theft of his car, but not that the thief might then have an accident and injure someone.

Accidents Inside Your Home

The court would also consider whether Cheryl contributed to the accident by drinking too much liquor. It would then allocate a percentage of fault to both Greg and Cheryl. In apportioning fault in this way, the court is using the principle of contributory negligence.

While entering the lobby of my friend's apartment building, I pushed against the glass panel of the door because the push bar was missing. The glass broke, and I cut my arm. Can I sue the apartment building owner?

Yes. A landlord has a duty to keep his building's common areas in good repair. Before you decide to sue, however, make sure that you will be able to prove that the landlord was negligent. For example, if you could show that the landlord knew that the door's push bar was missing but failed to make the necessary repairs, or if you could find evidence that the glass had been cracked or loose for some time, you would have a good chance of winning your lawsuit.

During the summer we rent our vacation home to our friends. Can we have them sign a release waiving any claims against us if they are injured while occupying the house?

You could have your friends sign such an agreement but it would not be valid if you were responsible for what is called gross negligence. Thus, if you knew that the electrical wiring in one of the rooms was dangerous, and someone was injured because you did not tell him of this hazard, even the waiver of claim would not protect you. In any case, even without a written release, you would be responsible only for damages that could be attributed to your fault or negligence—damages from hazards you could have warned about.

Accidents Outside Your Home

Several boards on Anthony's front porch were missing, and others were loose. When a salesperson stepped up to ring the doorbell, he tripped and broke his leg. Is Anthony responsible?

Whether Anthony is responsible or not would depend on several factors. If it were obvious that boards were missing and loose, then Anthony might escape responsibility, as would be the case if he had posted a sign indicating that the porch was dangerous. However, if Anthony knew of

Legal Responsibilities of Homeowners

When you own a home, you have a legal responsibility to keep your property safe for anyone who visits you. In some provinces, however, the amount of responsibility you bear depends on the reason for the person's visit. The law classifies visitors into three categories: invitees, licensees, and trespassers. Homeowners are most responsible for the safety of invitees and least responsible for the safety of trespassers.

● An *invitee* is someone you ask to your home to do some work for you, such as a repairman. A deliveryman, such as a letter carrier or a furniture deliverer, is also included in this category. If an invitee is injured on your property, you will be held liable if you did not take steps to make your home safe or if you did not warn your visitor about the danger. For example, if there is a weak handrail on the stairs, you should have it repaired before the invitee arrives or else warn him about it. Once an invitee is on your property, you have a responsibility to use greater care than usual when performing potentially dangerous tasks, such as backing a car out of the driveway.

● A *licensee* is someone who comes into your home for his own benefit, such as a door-to-door salesperson or a person soliciting for charity. Friends and relatives who come to visit are also considered licensees. You have a legal duty to warn such visitors about any dangers that are not apparent, such as a slippery floor, and to use greater care than usual when performing potentially dangerous tasks.

● A *trespasser* is someone who enters your property without your permission, such as a burglar or a person who is lost. You are not liable if such a person is accidentally injured while on your property. However, a homeowner owes a special duty to children who trespass. He must take extra precautions if an object or condition on his land is both dangerous and likely to attract children. If the seat on a backyard swing is broken, for example, it should be either removed or repaired. If you know that someone repeatedly trespasses—whether the person is a child or an adult—you have a legal duty to make that person aware of any hidden dangers.

The distinction between invitee, licensee, and trespasser is being worn down by case law because the distinction is difficult to maintain in many cases. Take the case of a neighbor who enters your property to pick up a ball thrown into your backyard as an example. Is that neighbor a trespasser or a licensee? In Quebec, the civil law does not make these distinctions. Each case in that province is judged solely on its merits, the rule being that "the owner of a building is responsible for the damage caused by its ruin, whether that damage has happened from want of repairs or from an original defect in its construction." Similarly, the tenant of a dwelling is responsible for damages caused to another, when the damages were the result of the tenant's "fault, imprudence or neglect."

the dangerous situation and did nothing to avert an accident, then he could be held responsible. But such situations are seldom that clear-cut—what may be obvious in daytime could be a hidden danger at night. Generally, the owner or occupier of a dwelling owes a "duty of care" to people who lawfully come onto his property. Thus, some courts could decide that Anthony should have taken reasonable precautions to prevent such a mishap, and might hold him at least partially liable.

Fred borrowed Ryan's chain saw to trim some trees. Fred had an accident with the saw and needed surgery. Can Ryan be held liable for compensating Fred for his injuries?

No, unless Ryan lent the chain saw to his neighbor knowing that it was defective. When you lend property to someone without charge, your only responsibility is to warn the borrower about known defects. However, Ryan could be held liable if he let his neighbor use the chain saw, knowing that Fred did not know how to operate it properly.

I repaired a bicycle that belonged to my neighbor's son Barry. While he was riding down a steep hill, the front wheel loosened, and the bicycle skidded into a wall. Can Barry's parents sue me?

For you to be liable, there must be some evidence that your repairs caused Barry to have the accident. Barry's parents would have to show that your repair work was the most likely cause of their son's injuries. The amount of time that elapsed between your repair work and the accident would be important in establishing this connection.

If there is evidence to attribute the accident to your repair work, Barry's parents must also prove that you did the work negligently. As long as you made the repairs in a reasonably competent manner, you would not be liable for Barry's injuries.

The postman cuts across my lawn even though I have asked him to use the walk. One day he tripped over a garden hose and broke his wrist. Am I liable for his injury?

Possibly. As a homeowner, you are responsible for keeping the premises reasonably safe and must warn guests about any hidden dangers. If the garden hose was clearly visible, you had no obligation to warn the postman that it was in the yard. If the garden hose was hidden under some leaves, however, you were obligated to remove it or to alert guests to the danger, for example, by putting up a temporary sign.

Charlie decided to put a fence around his yard, but only got as far as digging the postholes. That night, Jamie took a shortcut through the yard, fell in one of the holes, and injured his Achilles tendon. Can Jamie sue Charlie?

Unless he had the habit of cutting across Charlie's yard, Jamie would not have a strong case. Charlie could argue that it was not foreseeable that anyone would cross his property that night, and the postholes would have been filled the next day. Jamie would have to persuade the court that Charlie acted irresponsibly nonetheless, because he neither covered the postholes nor indicated somehow that they were there. On the other hand, if Jamie used the shortcut regularly and Charlie knew this, and if Charlie was going to take a few days to put up the fence, he could be held liable for damages.

Had Jamie fallen in the hole during the day rather than at night, he wouldn't have a case at all. Charlie would not be liable, because the hazard would have been obvious in daylight.

Alfred built a swimming pool in his backyard and fenced in the yard. A youngster from next door climbed the fence, fell into the empty pool, and broke his leg. Is Alfred liable?

Under the law, a homeowner is expected to use reasonable care to protect children from serious injury. The primary question in this situation is whether the fence was high enough. Since a young child was able to climb the fence, the fence may not have been adequate, and Alfred could be held responsible for the child's injury.

Kirk has a swimming pool in his yard. Posted near the pool is a large sign that says, "Swim at your own risk." Does this sign relieve him of liability if a young child is injured in the pool?

No. Posting a sign is of little value to children who cannot yet read or understand what the words mean. Kirk should find out from the city clerk what the legal requirements are for residential swimming pools. Local laws may require that a fence be installed, and may even specify its height and the materials to be used.

While adding a garage, the Nelsons had several large rocks dug out and piled in their backyard. Five-year-old Billy fell while climbing the rock pile. Are the Nelsons liable for Billy's injuries?

Perhaps. As homeowners, the Nelsons have a legal duty to protect young children, even if they are trespassing, from potentially dangerous situations that might attract them. The Nelsons should have realized that children would be attracted to the rock pile as a place to play. Swimming pools are the most common objects covered by this legal principle, which is called the attractive nuisance doctrine.

A neighbor's son was injured when he jumped off our diving board backward. We have repeatedly warned him not to try such dangerous stunts. Are we liable?

Possibly. Your best argument for denying responsibility is that the boy contributed to his own injuries by ignoring your warnings. But your liability may depend on the age of the child. Courts have ruled that children under a certain age—some courts say age 7, others 14—cannot be held responsible for their negligent actions. To protect yourself in the future, you should make sure a responsible adult is on guard at the pool when children are using it.

If ice falls off the roof of my mother's house and strikes the meter reader, is my mother liable?

No. In general, your mother has a duty to keep her home and property reasonably safe and to warn invitees, such as the meter reader, about any dangers or defects she is aware of that are not apparent. In this case, however, your mother probably did not know that the ice on the roof was a hazard, and therefore could not have been expected to warn the meter reader about it.

While snowmobiling at night on a farmer's land, Gil and Ross were seriously injured when they hit some barbed wire strung across their path. They had used this path before without incident. Will Gil and Ross be successful if they sue the farmer?

Since Gil and Ross have gone snowmobiling in the same area before, they have a good chance of winning their case. If the farmer knew that his land was used by snowmobilers, he would be required in most provinces either to warn them about hidden dangers or to remove the hazards. A few provinces have statutes that apply specifically to the unauthorized use of private property for recreational purposes. It could be argued that Gil and Ross accepted the risk that one day the owner of the land would put up a barrier on his property, which he has a right to do and which is in no way an irresponsible act. This is the principle of *volenti non fit injuria*, the voluntary assumption of risk.

When Sidney, a door-to-door encyclopedia salesman, was leaving Dawn's home, he slipped on a doll left on the sidewalk by Dawn's two-year-old daughter. Is Dawn liable?

Probably not. Although Dawn has a responsibility to keep the sidewalks clear and to warn invited guests about unsafe conditions that are not apparent, Dawn did not invite the salesman to her house, and the doll could clearly be seen on the sidewalk. Consequently, Dawn had no duty to warn him about its presence.

Julian was helping Pat fix his roof. Pat warned him that one rung on the ladder was weak, but Julian proceeded to climb up the ladder without testing each step first. The weak rung collapsed, and he fell off the ladder. Does Julian have a case against Pat?

No. When Pat warned Julian that the ladder was defective, Julian had the choice of either not using the ladder or climbing it with caution. Because he chose to ignore Pat's warning, Julian assumed the risk involved in climbing the defective ladder.

I hired my son's friend Marty to mow my lawn. Am I liable if Marty is injured while using my mower?

Possibly. Power mowers are considered dangerous tools. For that reason, owners and operators must take special precautions to minimize the chances that someone will be hurt. Several factors would be important in determining your liability, including (1) Marty's age, (2) whether he realized the dangers involved in using a power mower, (3) whether the mower had some defect that you knew about, (4) whether you permitted Marty to use the lawn mower, knowing that he did not know how to operate it, and (5) whether you knew there were dangerous conditions in the yard and failed to warn Marty.

Accidents on Public Transportation

Lena was getting into a taxi when the driver accidentally slammed the door shut on her hand. She wasn't able to work for two days. Is the driver or the taxi company liable for Lena's lost wages?

Both are liable. Under the law, any company that transports people for a fee must exercise the highest degree of care for the safety of its customers. Lena should be able to collect for her lost income. In Quebec, the Automobile Insurance Board would compensate Lena.

Accidents on Public Transportation

Scott told a cab driver, "Get me to the airport in a hurry." As the cab raced away, it hit another cab. Will Scott be able to recover from the cab company for his injuries?

Yes. A cab driver cannot ignore his duty to transport passengers safely and to obey traffic laws simply because he is asked to hurry. Passengers have a right to expect that a cab driver will not exceed the legal speed limit or drive in a manner that is unsuitable for the traffic conditions.

April had just paid her fare on a city bus and was about to take a seat when the bus driver swerved away from the curb. April lost her balance and fell. Is the bus company liable for her injuries?

Probably. A bus driver has a legal duty to drive safely. By pulling away from the curb before April had a chance to take a seat or hang onto a support of some kind, the bus driver was acting inappropriately.

If You Are Injured on Public Transportation

When a vehicle, such as a bus or taxi, transports people for a fee, its operator is required by law to use extreme care to protect the passengers. If you are injured in an accident and you think the driver of the vehicle was at fault, you should seek legal advice to determine whether you should file a lawsuit. It is important to do this at once if you are injured on a vehicle operated by a government agency since, in many provinces, special laws require claims against such agencies to be filed within a few months of the accident. If you're not seriously injured, make some notes about the accident right after it occurs. That way, if you decide to file a claim later, you'll have all the necessary information. Here are the facts you should record:

- ☑ The date, time, and location of the accident.
- ☑ The weather conditions. If you cannot remember what the weather was like, you can ask Environment Canada for a written report of conditions at the time and place of the accident.
- ☑ The vehicle's license number and line (or company) name.
- ☑ The driver's name, his driver's license number, and his identification or badge number.
- ☑ Names, addresses, and phone numbers of other injured passengers.
- ☑ Names, addresses, and phone numbers of witnesses.
- ☑ The condition of the vehicle, road, traffic lights, and warning signs.
- ☑ The physical appearance of the drivers involved.

I was in such a hurry that I twisted my ankle while running down the stairs of the railway station. Is the railway company liable?

Probably not. To prove the railway company liable, you would have to establish that it was negligent in some way. For example, if the steps had not been cleared of debris or if their skid-resistant coating had worn off, you might have a claim against the company. But in this situation, you yourself were the cause of the accident.

Accidents in Public Places

As Marilyn was running to catch the bus, she tripped on a broken area of the sidewalk and hurt herself. Can she sue the city?

Yes. The city is responsible for maintaining its sidewalks and other property in a safe condition, as any individual would be who offers services to the public. But the rules for suing a city or government agency are usually different from those for legal actions against individuals. Before suing, Marilyn must notify the city about her accident, and provide basic information such as her name, address and occupation; the place, date and time of the accident; the details of the injury she suffered. The city must receive her notice within a restricted period, usually 15 days. If no settlement is reached, Marilyn will have another time limit—six months in some municipalities—to bring legal action. To win, she would have to prove that the city was negligent in not repairing its sidewalk.

As Dale was passing a construction site, he saw a woman get struck on the head by a piece of debris. Dale tried to control her bleeding, but when she lost her pulse he panicked and left. The woman died. Does Dale face any consequences for his actions?

Quebec's Charter of Human Rights and Freedoms obliges everyone to come to the aid of a person whose life is in peril. Elsewhere, Dale would not have been legally obligated to help the injured woman, but once he made the decision to come to her aid, he had a legal duty to continue his assistance until a doctor, paramedic, or other medical professional arrived at the scene. The only valid reason for abandoning his rescue attempt would be if it seemed to be doing more harm than good. As long as Dale did not aggravate the victim's condition by acting negligently or imprudently, he will not be liable for damages. In Alberta, the Emergency Medical Aid Act relieves anyone of liability if he voluntarily comes to the aid of an injured person and acts reasonably in trying to help. Such legislation is sometimes known as Good Samaritan Laws.

Accidents in Public Places

Doreen slipped and fell on an icy sidewalk in front of a local shop. Is the store owner liable for her injuries?

Probably not. Although some municipalities pass bylaws requiring the owner of an adjacent property to clear the ice and snow from the public sidewalk in front of his establishment, failure to do so might result in a small fine for the owner, but not in civil liability for damages to someone who slipped on that part of the sidewalk. Keeping public sidewalks clear of ice and snow is a municipal obligation and not one that can easily be transferred to the private landowner. Nevertheless, to be on the safe side, Doreen should sue both the municipality and the store owner together. Then it would be up to the judge to decide who should pay for her damages.

Rosemary accidentally knocked down a department store's pyramid-shaped aisle display of crystal. Must she pay for it?

Probably not. Store owners must display merchandise so that it can be easily removed and returned without injuring customers or breaking. If goods are arranged in a manner that increases the likelihood that they will be knocked over, the store has to absorb the cost of the breakage.

Tammy fell forward and broke her nose, when the brakes on her car malfunctioned at the end of a roller coaster ride. Is the amusement park responsible for her injury?

Court decisions about such situations have not been consistent. In some instances, the amusement park owner has been required only to use reasonable care in maintaining the roller coaster. In other cases, the owner has been held to a higher degree of responsibility because of the serious hazards posed by such a ride. In any case, the owner has a duty to inspect and test the equipment frequently to make sure it's safe.

I was in a bar when an intoxicated customer hit me for no reason. Is the bar liable for my injuries?

There are two ways in which the bar owner might be responsible. First, under provincial liquor laws, the tavern owner may be liable for serving liquor to an intoxicated person. Second, if your province requires tavern owners to oust intoxicated or disorderly customers, you may be able to show that the owner was negligent in not properly supervising the premises. Your case would be strengthened if you could establish that

You Are Injured in a Public Place

If you're injured as a result of an accident in a public place, such as inside a department store or on a sidewalk, and you believe that the property owner was at fault, you may want to sue him for any medical expenses not covered by Medicare and for your pain and suffering and loss of income. Knowing the answers to the following questions will help you with your case:

- If the accident occurred in a building:
  —Who owns the building?
  —Who is the building's manager or superintendent?
  —In which part of the building did the accident occur?
  —Were there any obvious signs of disrepair, such as torn carpeting or loose tiles?
  —How old is the building?

- If the accident occurred on a stairway:
  —Was the lighting inadequate?
  —Which step caused you to slip or trip?
  —Did the stairs have a skidproof coating that was worn?
  —Were the stairs covered with carpeting or linoleum that was ripped or torn?
  —Was the handrail wobbly or loose?

- If the accident occurred on an elevator or escalator:
  —Who is the manufacturer?
  —What is the name and model number of the equipment?
  —When was it manufactured?
  —Who is responsible for maintaining the equipment?
  —When was it last inspected?
  —Was the elevator automatic or run by an employee?

- If the accident occurred on a sidewalk or in a parking lot:
  —Does the sidewalk or parking lot adjoin a home or a business?
  —Who is the owner or who had care and control of the parking lot or the sidewalk where the accident occurred?
  —Was the lighting inadequate?
  —Does the area have a concrete, gravel, or asphalt surface?
  —Was the surface cracked, icy, wet, or muddy?
  —Do tree roots protrude from a broken surface?

ACCIDENTS

the owner (1) knew the customer tended to get into fights; (2) allowed the customer to stay, even though he was disturbing others; (3) let conditions at the bar get out of control; (4) did not have adequate staff to supervise the premises; or (5) ignored warnings that the customer was threatening to hurt someone.

Accidents in Public Places

It was raining and Sarah hurried into a department store. As she stepped onto the tile floor, she slipped and fell, hitting her head. Can she collect damages from the department store?

Sarah's chances of winning a lawsuit would depend, in part, on how carefully the store had tried to keep the entrance dry. On rainy days, a store owner cannot be expected to keep the floors of his property completely dry. However, he should see to it that floor mats are placed at each of the store's entrances to prevent sliding and to absorb some of the moisture. He should also have maintenance workers mop wet floors periodically to prevent water from accumulating.

Another important factor is whether Sarah contributed to the accident by hurrying into the department store. A court might decide that Sarah should have been aware that tile floors are slippery when wet, and that therefore she should have proceeded with caution when entering the store on a rainy day. In such a case, her haste to enter the building may reduce or eliminate the compensation she could receive.

Annette was riding a ski lift when her seat belt unsnapped. She fell out of her seat and broke her leg. Several months later complications set in, and Annette lost the use of her leg. It's been two years since the accident. Can Annette still sue the resort?

Annette may have waited too long to file a claim. Each province has its own deadline, or statute of limitations, for filing negligence lawsuits. The range is one to six years, with one or two years the most common. Annette should consult a lawyer to find out her province's time limit.

Trevor shouted "Fore" before hitting a golf ball, but Janice didn't hear him and was hit by the ball. Is Trevor protected because he has witnesses who heard him call out the warning?

Having given a warning does help Trevor establish that he was not negligent. By checking to make sure that those people who were in the path of the ball's flight knew that he was ready to hit the ball, and then giving an audible warning, Trevor fulfilled his duty.

When my nephew Patrick tried to feed one of the chimpanzees at the zoo, it bit his arm. Shouldn't the zoo pay for Patrick's injury?

Most likely. Because some of the animals housed in a zoo can be dangerous, courts generally require zoo owners to exercise a high degree of care. Since Patrick was able to get close enough for the chimpanzee to grab his arm, the zoo might be considered negligent for not providing a better barrier, such as wire mesh, to keep the chimpanzee from reaching out. Moreover, zoo administrators know that visitors, especially children, often ignore warnings not to feed the animals, which is even more reason for providing better barriers.

When my son enrolled at camp, I had to sign an agreement not to sue the camp if he were injured. Later in the summer he injured his knee when the trampoline he was using collapsed. Am I now prevented from suing the camp?

Not necessarily. The agreement you signed is known as an exculpatory agreement, and the court will very likely scrutinize both the wording of such an agreement and the facts surrounding your decision to sign it. In some situations, a court would uphold the agreement. In this case, however, it appears that you were placed in an unfair position—the camp would not have accepted your son unless you signed the agreement—and a court would probably void the agreement, making the camp liable for your son's injuries. Moreover, such exculpatory agreements are not valid when gross negligence can be proven.

While Sean and his family were staying at a motel, they noticed a sign posted by the swimming pool, stating that it closed at 10:00 P.M. Two of Sean's children, ages 12 and 16, went out to the pool at 10:30 P.M. The 16-year-old slipped on the diving board and suffered a concussion. Is the motel liable?

Probably not. Motel owners are required only to use reasonable care to protect guests from being injured at a swimming pool. This requirement is usually satisfied by warning signs, fences, and lifeguards. At 12 and 16, Sean's children are considered old enough to understand the closing sign and to know the risks involved in diving in a pool at night. Supervising the pair is Sean's responsibility rather than the motel's.

A spectator at a baseball game was hit by a foul ball. Shouldn't the baseball park be held responsible for this?

No. The law assumes that spectators at a baseball game accept the possibility of being injured by a ball that's hit into the stands. Ballpark owners are required to put up protective fencing only in the area immediately behind home plate, which is considered the most dangerous part of the ballpark. If the spectator was hit because the fencing was torn or inadequate, then the ballpark owner might be liable.

Accidents in Public Places

While Ricky was playing second base on his Little League team, a player on the other team ran into him to prevent Ricky from throwing to first base. Is the player liable for Ricky's injuries?

Yes. While a player must accept the risk of being injured during competition, that does not mean that he must assume responsibility for every injury he receives. When playing baseball, a player could anticipate being injured by a bat or a ball, but not by another player deliberately running into him. Since the player on the other team violated the rules of the game, he is fully responsible for Ricky's injuries.

Several youngsters were playing crack-the-whip at a roller skating rink even though there were signs prohibiting this activity. Shannon's arm was broken when she was accidentally pushed against the wall. Can her parents sue the rink owners?

Yes, if they can prove that the owner failed to supervise the skating rink properly. Since the owner had posted signs prohibiting crack-the-whip, he was aware that the game was dangerous for skaters. Therefore, he had a duty to monitor the rink closely and have enough attendants on hand to stop such activity.

My son injured his neck and shoulder on his school's playground equipment during recess period. Should I sue the school or the manufacturer of the equipment?

You might not be able to sue either one. The manufacturer would not be liable unless the equipment was defective. To sue the school, you would have to prove that the playground was not adequately supervised or that the school failed to fix equipment that it knew needed repair.

Betty, shopping for a television set, was walking through a store's video department, looking at the pictures on all the TV screens, when she tripped over a carton in the aisle. Can she sue the store?

Yes. Since shoppers are expected to look at displays as they walk through a store, the store is obligated to keep its aisles clear and properly maintained. The fact that Betty was not watching where she was going should not prevent her from suing the store, even if the carton was left by another customer, rather than an employee. Some courts might hold Betty partly responsible for the accident according to the contributory negligence rule.

Boating Accidents

Whenever I have guests on board my boat, I always provide them with life jackets and ask that they wear them from the time we leave the dock to the time we return. Does this precaution free me from liability if someone refuses to put on his life jacket and then drowns as the result of an accident?

Not entirely. A passenger's refusal to wear a life jacket may be a factor in determining the extent of your liability, but it does not mean that you will be relieved of all responsibility for a passenger's injuries or death. Generally, a court would try to determine whether the person's injuries or death could have been prevented by the use of a life jacket. The court would also want to find out if the accident was caused by your negligence in operating or maintaining the boat. As owner of the boat, you would have an obligation to attempt a rescue if it would not imperil your life.

While swimming one day, I saw a boat that was being steered by a child crash into another boat. Can the child be held responsible?

It depends. Some courts would rule that if a child (other than a very young child) engages in an adult activity, he may be held responsible. If the child was relieved of responsibility, then his parents would probably be responsible because they did not properly supervise their child when he was handling a potentially dangerous object.

When Norman was fishing on the lake one afternoon, another boat rammed into the left side of his boat. Do boat owners have to observe the same rules as automobile drivers when it comes to yielding the right-of-way?

There are several different sets of rules governing boat traffic. The inland rules, which apply in lakes and most other inland waters, state that a boat must yield to another boat that is directly in front of it or to its right. Since Norman's boat was to the right of the other boat, the boat's operator had a responsibility to yield to Norman.

While Gordon was sailing around the lake, he noticed a distress flag on one of the other boats. Was Gordon obligated to help?

If he was in Quebec, yes. Elsewhere, Gordon would not have been obliged to help unless he was a lifeguard, police officer, member of the Coast Guard, or was in some way responsible for the safety of the people on board. However, boat owners frequently offer to assist a boat in distress or notify the Coast Guard about the situation. The Canada Shipping Act levies a fine against a master of a vessel who "fails to render assistance to every person . . . who is found at sea and is in danger of being lost." Whether this obligation applies to someone in distress on a lake rather than at sea is an open question.

Joe had been drinking just before he took the wheel of Leonard's boat so that Leonard could water-ski. Leonard broke three teeth and the boat was damaged when Joe steered onto a rock. Can Leonard be compensated by his own insurance carrier?

It would depend on Leonard's insurance policy. Some policies require the insured person to exercise due care. If Leonard's policy has such a provision, he would not be eligible for coverage if the insurance company determined that Leonard was aware of Joe's drinking and still permitted him to steer the boat.

CHAPTER 14

Your Medical Rights

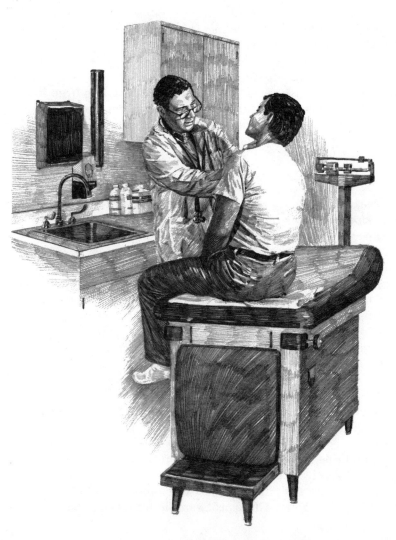

***Howard's doctor has recommended surgery. How can Howard
make sure this surgery is necessary?***

He should have his doctor explain in detail why he feels surgery is the
best medical option, and what the alternatives are. Before a doctor can
proceed with any type of treatment, he must have the patient's consent.
This consent is valid only if all the practical methods of treatment have
been explained, together with the risks involved and the benefits
expected. Telling a patient only about the particular surgery or treatment
that the doctor advocates is not sufficient. It is usually a good idea to get a
second opinion from another doctor when surgery is recommended. In
fact, some health insurance companies require it.

***Does Ruth have the right to refuse laboratory tests even though
her doctor believes they are necessary?***

Yes. She can refuse any treatment, including laboratory tests. However,
Ruth's doctor may ask her to sign a form releasing him from liability,
because her refusal to take the tests may make it impossible for him to
diagnose or treat her illness successfully. Ruth also has the right to refuse
to sign this release. To protect himself, the doctor will note her refusal on
her medical chart.

***Do parents have the right to know if their teenage daughter gets
a prescription for birth control pills from their family doctor?***

No. Although parents are usually required to give their consent for the
medical treatment of minor children, there are legal exceptions to this
general requirement. The Code of Ethics of the Canadian Medical
Association states that the first priority of a physician is to consider the
well-being of the patient, and also to protect the patient's secrets. In one
British Columbia case it was held that, in certain circumstances, fitting a
15-year-old girl with a contraceptive device would be a normal medical
procedure even if the parents refused to give their consent.

***Can a teenager prevent a doctor from letting his parents know
about a drug problem?***

The general rule is that all communication between a patient and his
doctor is confidential, except that the doctor is obliged to inform the
authorities in cases of child abuse or communicable disease. As to
informing parents about a drug problem, the rule of confidentiality may

be subject to various interpretations. The duty of confidentiality may be less strict if the child is 13 than if he is, say, 17 and better able to care for himself. It could be argued that since a child of 13 is dependent on and under the custody of his parents, they have the right to know about the drug problem so they can try to bring it under control. On the other hand, if a child knows his parents may be informed, he may be reluctant to apply for treatment. There is no clear and safe answer to this question other than that the doctor must do his best to help his patient.

A psychiatrist is treating a man who has repeatedly expressed a desire to hurt an ex-girlfriend. Does the psychiatrist have to tell the ex-girlfriend or the police about his patient's intentions?

Yes. If the patient is a genuine danger to his ex-girlfriend, the psychiatrist must notify her or the police or take any other steps necessary to protect her. Although the doctor-patient relationship is confidential, a doctor also owes an obligation to society in general. It is hard to imagine suing a psychiatrist for breach of confidentiality, for example, if he informs the police that his patient, an airline pilot, is suicidal and depressive and intends to crash his plane on the next flight.

When Tracy's doctor explained the purpose of the medication he was prescribing, he didn't tell her that the treatment was experimental. Does Tracy have a right to know this?

Yes. For Tracy to make an informed decision about whether to consent to the treatment, her doctor is legally bound to explain the risks and benefits of the treatment and any alternatives. Telling her that the treatment was experimental should have been part of that explanation. By not telling her, the physician was acting without the informed consent of his patient. If any harm was caused to Tracy, she could sue.

I needed major surgery and asked a top specialist to do it. Later I found that another surgeon had performed the operation. Wasn't it wrong for the specialist to turn me over to someone else?

As a general rule, a physician cannot have another doctor substitute for him without notifying the patient and obtaining his permission, except in an emergency. However, the consent form you signed prior to the operation may have authorized the surgeon "or associates or assistants of his or her choice" to perform the surgery. If so, the substitution was legally acceptable as long as the substitute was fully qualified to do the surgery. If you did not give your permission in any form, you could sue the specialist for abandoning you as a patient unless the substitution was because of an emergency. Patients are often rushed when asked to sign consent forms and do not have time to read thoroughly what they are signing. The signing of a consent under those circumstances would probably not be considered the giving of an informed consent.

A doctor agreed to treat my grandmother, but then withdrew from the case. Is there anything she can do to get him to treat her?

Not if the doctor gave your grandmother sufficient time to find another physician, and did not withdraw so abruptly that her treatment was disrupted. A doctor has the right to withdraw, just as a patient has the right to choose another doctor.

Lorna's children are concerned about her ability to handle any bad news concerning her health. Do they have the right to ask Lorna's doctor to withhold negative information?

They may ask the doctor, but the doctor does not have to comply with their request. As long as Lorna is competent to make medical decisions, the doctor is required to supply her with all the information relating to her case. However, if the doctor believed that disclosing certain information would have a seriously detrimental effect on her, that information could be withheld.

Claude found out he had only six months to live and asked the doctor not to tell his family. Must the doctor honor this request?

Yes. A doctor is generally prohibited from disclosing medical information unless the patient consents to it. However, if Claude had a communicable disease, the doctor would have to inform the family so they could protect themselves, especially if they use the same toilet facilities.

My grandson needs a blood transfusion, but his father will not permit this, as it is against his religion. Can the father succeed, even if it means the child will die?

No. The child's right to life has been held by Canadian courts to be greater than the parents' right to freedom of religion. When parents refuse to consent to necessary and beneficial medical treatment of their children, the local Children's Aid Society can intervene, consider the child "a child in need of protection," and give consent for the treatment.

Can a hospital turn someone away from an emergency room because he doesn't have Medicare?

No. A hospital with an emergency room must attend to anyone seeking medical assistance, regardless of his ability to pay. If a hospital refuses to treat someone in a medical emergency, it could face a civil or a criminal lawsuit.

When I entered hospital, they wrote down some information about me and gave me a form to sign. I was too sick to read all of it. Did I sign away any of my rights?

Probably not. Even if the form contained a blanket consent in which you agreed to any and all services or a statement releasing the hospital and its staff from liability, you still have the right to refuse a medical procedure or course of treatment. When blanket consent forms have been challenged in court, judges have ruled against them on grounds that they don't give the patient enough information to make an informed decision. Courts also do not favor contracts that release a hospital from liability if a patient is harmed as the result of a mistake or accident. Since a patient may not be admitted to hospital unless he signs such a release, courts have ruled that these releases place the patient in an unequal negotiating position, and will not enforce them.

Can a woman insist that she be cared for entirely by a woman doctor throughout her time in hospital?

Up to a point. A patient always has the right to choose a physician. However, she will have to choose one who has admitting privileges or is otherwise affiliated with the hospital she attends. And if she needs an internist or a gynecologist or an orthopedic surgeon, say, she may find that the hospital staff does not include a woman specialist in that field.

Six-year-old Jill was hit by a car. The doctor believed she was all right, but decided to keep her in the hospital overnight for observation. Does Jill's mother have the right to stay with her?

She may stay in the hospital overnight providing she does not disturb or interfere with the doctors, nurses or other patients, but she does not have a right to stay in the same room as Jill. She would probably be required to stay in a waiting room, but it is hard to imagine nurses objecting to her going periodically to comfort Jill.

Your Rights in Hospital

***Arthur's wife may have to have a cesarean section when their
child is born. Can he stay with her throughout the birth?***

He has no legal right to do so. The decision to allow fathers in the
operating room is usually based on hospital policy and the recommendation of the doctor. Even if Arthur is allowed to stay, he may have to sign a
release, agreeing to leave the operating room immediately if asked.

***I'm having major surgery next month. Can I arrange to have an
anesthesiologist, rather than an anesthetist, attend me in the
operating room?***

In Canada, the terms anesthetist and anesthesiologist mean the same — a
medical doctor with training in anesthesia — and anesthetics may be
given only by doctors with this training. An anesthetist is almost always
part of a surgical team. In the United States, however, the anesthesiologist (who is a medical doctor) determines the kind of anesthesia to be
used, but does not necessarily administer it. He may leave orders for an
anesthetist (who is not a doctor but is trained and certified to administer
anesthetics) to follow during the operation.

A Patient's Bill of Rights

Many Canadian hospitals have patient's rights committees, with patients'
representatives and policies often referred to as the Patient's Bill of
Rights. Some hospitals publish manuals outlining policies and practices;
copies of such manuals and bills of rights are in hospital libraries. In
general, a patient's bill of rights entitles you to:

- Considerate and respectful care.
- Complete, up-to-the-minute information from your doctor, in terms you
  can understand, about your condition, treatment, and prognosis.
- Sufficient information from your doctor to allow you to give informed
  consent, including a full description of the procedure or treatment, the
  risks, alternatives, how long you will be hospitalized, and the name
  of the person responsible for carrying out the procedure or treatment
  prescribed for you.
- An explanation of the consequences of refusing treatment and the right
  to refuse treatment to the extent permitted by law (in extreme
  circumstances, a court may order you to undergo treatment to save
  your life).
- Privacy in all aspects of your medical care. Individuals not directly

When Serena's doctor came to examine her following her surgery, he brought six interns and residents, which embarrassed and upset her. Did she have the right to ask these six people to leave?

Yes. Every patient has a right to privacy and confidentiality. If Serena did not agree to the presence of medical personnel not directly involved in her care, her examination should have been conducted in private. Even in teaching hospitals, the attending physician must get the patient's permission before allowing residents and interns to observe a case.

A nurse has awakened Earl from a sound sleep the past two nights in order to give him a sleeping pill. Doesn't he have a legal right not to be disturbed?

In February 1985, the Canadian Nurses Association adopted a Canadian Code of Nursing Ethics. Among its general principles is the following: "Caring, the central and fundamental focus of nursing, is the basis for nursing ethics. It is expressed in compassion, competence, conscience, confidence and commitment." Earl's nurse appears not to have demonstrated compassion in this instance. However, Earl should ask her why it was necessary to disturb him. Perhaps a deep sleep is essential for his recovery, as might be the case with cardiac patients, say, and the sleeping

associated with your care must have your permission to be present during any discussion, examination, consultation, or treatment.
- Confidential treatment of all your records and any communications pertaining to your care.
- A reasonable response by the hospital to your requests for such services as evaluation, treatment, and referral.
- Information about hospital rules and regulations that apply to you.
- An explanation detailing why a transfer to a different facility may be necessary and what, if any, alternatives there are. The new facility must accept you in advance.
- Information about the relationship between the hospital and all other health care institutions or individuals who treat you.
- Information about and a full explanation of any experimental procedure or treatment that will affect you. You have the right to refuse to participate in such experimentation.
- Continuity of care. You have the right to know when and where doctors will be available for appointments, and how continuing care will be provided after you are discharged.
- An opportunity to examine your bill and an explanation of its contents regardless of how it is to be paid.

pill will ensure he is not disturbed by nightmares or wakefulness later on. Toward that end, the doctor's instructions may indicate that Earl must have the nightly sleeping pill.

As a hospital patient, don't I have an unquestionable right to see my medical records?

Not necessarily. Technically, your records are hospital property, and for many years, a patient could not demand to see them. Today, most patients are allowed to see their records unless the doctor in charge feels this might be injurious to the patient's health or chance of recovery. Restriction of access to a patient's medical records is now rarely exercised except in dealing with mental patients.

Todd has been in hospital for two months and needs a further six weeks of hospital care, but he fears he will be transferred to a convalescent home. Can they do that without his consent?

Only if there is an emergency, or if the hospital does not have the proper equipment to treat him. Otherwise, the hospital must explain why a transfer is necessary or desirable, notify Todd of the options available and the risks involved, and then obtain his consent for the transfer.

How much notice must a patient be given before being discharged from hospital?

Generally, a hospital need not give any specific notice. The attending physician may sign the release order on the morning the patient is to leave. A physician's duty is to provide his services until they are no longer necessary. At any point after this, the patient may be discharged.

My doctor says I must stay in hospital for another two weeks, but I don't want to. Can the hospital prevent me from leaving?

No. You cannot be hospitalized against your will. You must be allowed to leave, even if your doctor objects. You will likely be asked to sign a form relieving the hospital of responsibility should your condition deteriorate. The hospital might be justified in trying to stop you only if you have a communicable disease or you present some other danger to yourself or others. In such a situation the hospital would seek a court order; in effect, the court and not the hospital would prevent you from leaving.

Rosemary, who has no family, is dying and wants to go into a hospice. But she has been told that she first must designate someone as "primary care giver." What does this mean?

A primary care giver is the person, usually a relative, responsible for handling the arrangements for a dying patient. With no family, Rosemary could ask a friend to fill this role, or hire a nurse's aide or companion to attend to her needs.

Consent for Medical Treatment

At what age is someone authorized to give consent for surgery or medical treatment?

Most provinces set 18 as the minimum age at which a person can give consent. However, younger people may be allowed to give consent if they are married, pregnant, or living independently of their parents or guardians. Provincial laws permit minors to obtain medical treatment without parental consent for mental health problems, drug or alcohol problems, pregnancy, sexually transmitted diseases, or in emergencies.

Dorothy's doctor recommended she have surgery and carefully explained the proposed procedure and why he felt it was necessary. She agreed to have the operation. Does the doctor now have all the permission he needs to proceed with the surgery?

The doctor must do more than just describe the recommended procedure and its benefits; he must explain the alternatives available, their risks and benefits, and how long Dorothy might be incapacitated after each alternative. The law requires a patient to give his informed consent before any surgery or medical treatment is performed. For Dorothy to be considered informed, she must understand the implications of her surgery, including the pros and cons of all her options.

After Wes was scheduled for outpatient surgery, a nurse gave him a consent form to sign and return the morning of his operation. Can Wes revise the form if he wishes?

Yes. He can make changes or deletions, or make notations in the margins. He may find, however, that his doctor is unwilling to perform the surgery under the conditions he has indicated. If Wes has questions or doubts about anything in the form, he should discuss them with his doctor and try to work out a compromise.

Consent for Medical Treatment

Beverly signed a consent form when she was admitted to hospital. Is it valid for her entire stay?

Yes. The consent form is effective for the duration of a patient's hospital stay. Even so, if Beverly's condition changes significantly or if her treatment is altered substantially, she may be asked to sign a new consent form.

Max signed a consent form for surgery. If he changes his mind, can he revoke his consent?

Yes, but the doctor or the hospital will probably ask Max to sign a form releasing them from liability for the consequences of his refusal.

Can a patient sue a surgeon for malpractice even though the patient signed a consent form before the operation?

Yes. The consent form only authorizes the doctor and his associates, or both, to perform the designated operation. It generally does not include a release from liability. If the doctor didn't follow the established procedures for the operation or if he lacked the necessary surgical skills, he can be sued for malpractice.

When Howard went into hospital for a gallbladder operation, he signed a form consenting to the surgery. After the operation, he learned that his doctor had removed his appendix as well as the gallstones. Did the doctor have the authority to do this?

No. A surgeon is authorized to perform only the surgery listed on the consent form. The only time a surgeon can exceed this authorization is when life-threatening complications develop during an operation. If the surgeon performed any surgery that Howard did not consent to, Howard could sue him for malpractice, battery, and breach of contract.

Karen and Steve took their six-month-old daughter to a hospital emergency room, where a doctor recommended surgery as soon as possible. If the parents refuse to give their consent, can the doctor authorize the operation?

Only if the child's life is in danger, or if not having the surgery would seriously jeopardize her health. While parents generally have the right to make health care decisions for their children, the state will intervene, if needed, to protect the child. However, if the surgery would not prolong the child's life, or if the child would not suffer undue harm by not having the surgery, the doctor would have to accept the parents' decision.

Gloria refused to let her doctor perform the surgery he insists she needs. Her family does not agree with Gloria's decision. As relatives, can they give consent for the operation?

Not unless Gloria has been declared mentally incompetent and one of her relatives has been appointed her guardian. Otherwise, she has the right to refuse medical treatment, even if her decision jeopardizes her life; her family cannot interfere with her decision.

Rocco is divorced, and his ex-wife has legal custody of their son. If the boy is injured while visiting his father, can Rocco sign a consent form to have the boy treated?

Yes. Although Rocco does not have custody, he is the boy's father; as a parent, he can grant consent for medical treatment. However, if the doctors or nurses believe the mother might object to the treatment, they may seek her consent as well.

Malpractice

My doctor gave me a written order for a prescription. The druggist who filled it gave me the wrong dosage. He claims the doctor's poor handwriting is to blame. Who is at fault?

Both the druggist and the doctor may be at fault. The doctor should have taken care to write clearly and the druggist should have called the doctor for clarification if he was unsure about the prescription.

When Sally called her doctor, he prescribed medication over the telephone. Wasn't it malpractice to do so without seeing her?

Probably not. When familiar patients call for prescriptions to alleviate common illnesses such as colds, flu, sunburn, or poison ivy, it is not unusual for a doctor to prescribe a remedy by phone. As long as the doctor was familiar with Sally's sensitivity to various drugs and knew she would suffer no adverse reaction to the medication he prescribed, there is no basis for a malpractice claim. However, the doctor might be guilty of malpractice if he misdiagnosed her illness because he didn't give Sally the examination that a responsible doctor would ordinarily make. For example, if Sally complained about abdominal pains and the doctor said she was constipated and prescribed a laxative, but in fact she had acute appendicitis and her appendix burst, she could sue for malpractice.

If I become addicted to drugs prescribed by my doctor, would he be liable to malpractice charges?

Yes. Prescribing enough narcotic drugs to create addiction may well justify charges. Doctors must use care in selecting drugs for use by their patients and must determine whether a patient is unusually susceptible to a particular drug or likely to become addicted to it or to suffer other adverse effects from using it.

After fathering two children, Paul decided to have a vasectomy. The doctor failed to complete the operation successfully, and Paul's wife, Becky, became pregnant. Can they sue the doctor for the expenses of raising the third child?

They may sue, but it's unlikely they will obtain a monetary award covering all the expenses of their third child. However, they may be able to recover some of the costs. In one New Brunswick case, a woman unsuccessfully sued her doctor because she got pregnant three years after undergoing a tubal ligation. The court held that the doctor had not guaranteed a hundred percent success rate but merely undertook to "faithfully exercise his skill, knowledge and judgment" in carrying out the operation; this he had done.

Carla miscarried because of a medication prescribed by her doctor when she was three months pregnant. She wants to sue the doctor for pain and suffering, loss of wages, and emotional stress. What are her chances of success?

Her chances depend on a number of factors. If Carla told her doctor about the pregnancy, the doctor should have considered the possibility of the medication causing an adverse reaction. If other doctors would not have prescribed the medication, the doctor may be liable for damages. If the doctor was not told about the pregnancy, or current medical knowledge did not indicate any potential risk to pregnant women from that particular medication, the doctor is probably not guilty of malpractice.

After my surgery three years ago, I felt fine. But last week I became ill and visited another doctor. She told me that X rays indicated the surgeon had failed to remove a surgical instrument. Is it too late to sue the surgeon?

Perhaps not. If the deadline for filing malpractice lawsuits in your province has expired, you may still be able to sue. When you are suffering from an injury that you yourself could not discover, and the symptoms develop gradually, a court might rule that the limit under the statute of limitations must be counted from the time you became aware of the problem.

Francine told the doctor not to amputate her foot, but he ignored her wishes. The surgery saved her life. Does she have a right to sue her doctor?

Yes. As long as Francine was mentally competent to make the decision not to amputate, she had the right to expect the doctor to follow her

---

What Constitutes Malpractice?

Because of the many uncertainties in the practice of medicine, the law considers it impossible for a doctor to guarantee that his course of treatment will result in a cure or complete recovery from an illness. Therefore a patient cannot sue a doctor for malpractice if a treatment is unsuccessful. However, if a doctor fails to follow standard medical procedures in treating a patient, he may be guilty of negligence, and a charge of malpractice may be justified if the patient's condition worsens as a result. Doctors and hospitals have been found negligent for:

- Prescribing medication to which a patient was known to be allergic.
- Failing to give a patient medication at the designated time.
- Injecting a drug into the wrong area of the body.
- Wrong diagnosis.
- Improperly setting a broken bone.
- Failing to provide a hospitalized patient with a call button or other device to summon help.
- Failing to put up rails to prevent senile, sedated, young, or unconscious patients from falling out of bed.
- Not checking the identification bracelet of a patient in the operating room before beginning surgery.
- Not warning a patient of the danger that the prolonged use of a prescribed drug might cause.

instructions. Operating without consent, even though the surgery saved her life, is both battery and malpractice.

After having a wisdom tooth pulled, I experienced considerable pain. X rays by another dentist revealed part of the root, which he then extracted. Can I sue my original dentist?

Yes. Dentists, like doctors, can be held responsible for improper treatment. But it may not be necessary to sue. If you explain to your dentist what happened and show him the bill for the second extraction, he may be willing to reimburse you without going to court.

While Matilda was in hospital, she acquired a serious infection that she feels was unrelated to her illness. Does she have to prove the hospital was at fault in order to sue successfully?

Yes. She will have to establish a clear connection between her infection and a lack of adequate care by the hospital staff. Every hospital must have an infection-control program with isolation and sanitation procedures to minimize the possibility of patients acquiring an infection. If the staff was careless and exposed Matilda to a contagious disease or infection, she may have sufficient evidence to sue the hospital and win.

When Caroline took her 2-year-old son to the hospital, she told a nurse that he was very active and asked for extra safeguards, but the nurse took no special precautions. The boy was injured when he climbed over the bed's side railing and fell. Does Caroline have a good case if she sues the hospital and the nurse?

Yes. Since she specifically warned the hospital that her son was very active, the nurse should have taken further steps to prevent injury to the child. If she can show, through expert testimony, that other hospitals would have done more than merely ensure that bed rails were in place, Caroline would have a good chance of being awarded damages for her son's injuries.

A nurse gave Bret an antiflu shot. A day later, an abscess formed on his arm. Is the nurse legally liable for this injury?

Only if Bret can show that the nurse was negligent. If the nurse did not follow standard procedures—such as scrubbing the skin with alcohol before the injection and using a sterilized needle—and if the abscess formed at the point where the injection was made, Bret may have the evidence to support a claim of negligence.

Alice called a nurse to her room and showed her there was water on the bathroom floor. The nurse went to get someone to mop it up, but no one came. Alice had to go into the bathroom, slipped on the wet floor, and fell, injuring her back. Is the hospital liable?

It could be. A hospital is required to maintain a safe environment for its patients, and this would include keeping the bathroom floor dry. In this case, a court would have to decide whether the nurse was negligent in not returning immediately with someone to mop the floor or in not mopping it herself. A court would also consider whether or not Alice was sufficiently careful in walking into the bathroom when she knew the floor was wet. Her own negligence may have contributed to the fall.

Your Medical Records

Are there laws protecting the privacy of medical records?

Yes. Medical records are considered private, subject to the same constitutional protection as other areas of our private lives. Anyone who releases medical information without a patient's consent may be charged with invasion of privacy, breach of contract, or betrayal of confidentiality, depending on the circumstances.

In certain situations, however, the law requires a doctor to release specific information, even if the patient objects. If a patient is suffering from a communicable disease, or if a child shows signs of abuse, the law may require a doctor to notify the appropriate public health or child protection authorities. In certain cases, such as actions alleging personal injury, the defendant may request that the plaintiff's medical records be subpoenaed and examined before the presiding judge.

I asked my internist for a copy of my medical records, but he said I wouldn't understand what was on them and refused to turn them over to me. Did he have the right to do this?

The laws pertaining to confidentiality and access to medical records vary from province to province. What appears clear, however, is that hospital records belong to the hospital and not to the patient—although a patient, in most but not all cases, is entitled to consult his medical file; in some cases, he is entitled to make a copy. If you are refused access to

Your Medical Records

your medical file, the patient representative in your hospital, if there is one, may help you. In Quebec, New Brunswick, Nova Scotia, and Newfoundland access to information laws could be used to obtain permission to consult one's medical file. Alberta courts have held that a patient could have access to his file, since the rule of confidentiality is to protect the patient, and access to the record by the patient himself does not interfere with this protection. Ontario courts have held that a patient's access to his file is better left to the discretion of the hospital.

My 16-year-old daughter went to the doctor for a checkup last week. When I asked the doctor what she and my daughter talked about, she told me it was confidential. Don't I have the right to know what was discussed?

No. Even though your daughter is a minor, the doctor is under a legal obligation to maintain all information about her confidential. Except in cases of child abuse, or communicable venereal disease, a doctor is not free to disclose confidential information to anyone, even a parent. Mind you, all rules seem to have certain exceptions. A parent may have the right to details of a child's medical file if the child is only, say, 13 or 14, but this right seems to diminish with age and it probably does not apply to a mature 16-year-old whose right to confidentiality must be respected.

Does Teresa have a right to ask that confidential records about her illness not be released to a potential employer?

She doesn't even need to ask. A potential employer has no legal right to see Teresa's medical records unless Teresa signs a release. Access to medical records is restricted to the doctor, his or her staff, and those people (if any) whom Teresa might designate.

To be reimbursed for medical expenses, Brad signed a release authorizing his doctor to make his medical records available to the insurance company. Brad now has learned that the insurance company was given his entire medical history, not just the information about his recent stay in hospital. Did the doctor violate Brad's rights?

Maybe. If Brad signed a general release that did not specify which records could be forwarded to the insurance company, the doctor did not violate his rights. On the other hand, if he agreed only to release of the records of his hospital stay, the doctor certainly exceeded his authority, and Brad could sue him for breach of confidentiality. But he may also have difficulty putting a figure on the monetary damages that he suffered.

Paying the Bills

For medical insurance, see "Health and Disability Insurance" in Chapter 8, *Insurance*.

Doris received a bill for lab tests in addition to the ones she had been told were being done. Does she have to pay the bill?

She may have to pay if she signed a form giving general consent to all tests needed to diagnose her illness. But she should check to be sure that the test was actually done for her. Until this is resolved, Doris is within her rights in refusing to pay that portion of the bill. Many lab tests done in hospital are covered by the provincial health insurance plan. Tests done in private labs must be paid for by the person who requests them.

Stephen was visiting Canada when he was taken ill. He will not be able to pay his hospital bills. Can the hospital force him to leave?

No. He cannot be forced to leave until he is well enough to be released. If he were forced to leave and his condition worsened, he could sue the hospital. The hospital will have to bill Stephen after he leaves, then take him to court if he doesn't pay.

Bella had insisted on a private room, but when she was being discharged from hospital, she refused to pay the extra cost. An administrator told her she would not be allowed to leave until she paid her bill. Can the hospital detain Bella against her will?

No. If the hospital did so, she could file charges of false imprisonment— even if the administrator did not use force to keep her but nonetheless gave her reason to fear that force would be used. Moreover, there is no reason for the hospital to detain Bella to bring pressure on her to pay the bill. The hospital can get its money by suing Bella after her release.

After treating Geraldine for a year, her doctor, who had opted out of Medicare, wouldn't do the final surgery because she hadn't paid all his bills. Does he have the right to stop treatment?

No. The doctor must continue to treat Geraldine until she no longer needs medical attention, or he must give her sufficient time to find another doctor. Discontinuing needed treatment before a patient has had time to find a replacement is considered abandonment. Geraldine could sue the doctor if he abandoned her and her condition worsened. The Code of Ethics of the Canadian Medical Association states that an ethical physician "will, when he has accepted professional responsibility for an acutely ill patient, continue to provide his services until they are no longer required or until he has arranged for the services of another suitable physician."

On Jared's first visit to the doctor's office he had to fill out an information sheet. After looking at this form, the doctor—who had opted out of Medicare—refused to treat Jared because he was unable to pay. Is the doctor required to treat patients regardless of their ability to pay?

No. Doctors are not required to treat every person who comes to them for medical care. As long as Jared was not an emergency patient, the doctor could refuse to treat him and not be guilty of breaking the law. But if this had been an emergency, and Jared's condition worsened, the doctor could be held responsible for not treating the emergency. A doctor might also be guilty of professional misconduct if he used someone's inability to pay as an excuse to reject him because of race, color, creed, or national origin.

By and large, doctors who have opted out of Medicare are required to tell you—in advance—that they will be billing you directly.

Living Wills

What is a living will?

A living will instructs doctors to withhold or withdraw life-support systems if a person becomes terminally ill. It is a signed, dated, and witnessed document that states, in advance, a person's wishes about such life-extending measures as mechanical respiration and feeding by tube. It relieves relatives of the need to guess the wishes of someone too ill to communicate his thoughts, and it helps doctors with the difficult decisions they must make. Anyone who has completed a living will should give copies to his family, doctor, lawyer and anyone else who may be consulted about his medical condition.

Canada has no legislation on living wills, but many doctors and patients' rights groups try to give effect to patients' wishes not to be kept alive by heroic measures.

Edith felt strongly about the right to die with dignity and made a living will. Over the objections of the family, the doctors have kept her on a respirator, even though apparently she is certain not to recover. Can Edith's daughter "pull the plug" on the respirator without criminal responsibility?

No. Edith's daughter could be charged with murder if she "pulled the plug" and thereby caused her mother's death. Her best course of action would be to consult with the attending physician; he might consult with the hospital's ethics committee to try to reach a decision that would be in the best interests of Edith and her family. Sometimes a patient and her family may feel there is no chance of recovery, but an experienced doctor, with knowledge of new procedures, medication and new equipment, may feel there is hope.

Susan is terminally ill and has asked her husband, Duane, to help her die peacefully by taking her life. Can Duane be convicted of a crime if he does as she requests?

Yes, Duane could be convicted of murdering Susan. Ending someone's life to prevent further suffering is euthanasia—mercy killing, but murder nonetheless.

No one can legally consent to have his or her life ended.

Ethics Committees

Some hospitals have ethics committees whose purpose is to help doctors decide the best course of action in certain circumstances. Members may include clergymen, social workers, lawyers, doctors and nurses. They do not make decisions—that is the difficult decision of the attending physician—but they raise questions, seek to clarify issues, and give moral support to the doctor. Some of the questions ethics committees handle:

• What should be done with a monstrously deformed newborn child?
• Which of two patients should be chosen when only one life-support system is available?
• How long should an elderly patient be maintained on a life-support system when his chances of regaining consciousness are extremely remote, and there are no relatives or friends with whom to consult?

Answering such questions is never easy. There are no rules or even guidelines; each question must be studied on its own merits and in its own context, with the knowledge, dedication and wisdom of the people who have been given this immense responsibility.

Organ Donations

How do I leave my body for organ donations?

Each province has procedures enabling a person to donate his body or some of his organs for scientific study or for transplantation. The most common methods are to sign a form found on one's driver's license, or to express one's wishes in a letter or will duly witnessed. Ask your provincial ministry of health and welfare for details.

Can I donate my organs to science in my will?

Yes, but you should also tell relatives or others who will be notified of your death. Time is often important in organ donations. If no one is aware of the contents of your will, the organs may be useless by the time your wishes become known. The will does not have to be probated for your organs to be donated.

If I sign an organ donation form, will my family or my estate be responsible for the cost of removing these organs?

No. Hospitals generally pay all costs associated with organ donations. Some private foundations help pay these costs in order to encourage hospitals to take part in organ donation programs.

Can Claire stop the hospital from removing her husband's organs if his driver's license shows he wanted them donated?

Yes. If she gets in touch with appropriate members of the hospital staff, they will probably follow her wishes. Hospitals prefer to have authorization from the next of kin before proceeding with organ donations.

Helen changed her mind after she filled out a declaration for organ donation. How should she revoke this?

It depends on which form Helen used originally to state her wishes. If she used the back of her driver's license, she should write "void" across the back of the card and sign and date it. If her wishes were included in her will, she should have her lawyer prepare a change, or codicil, which should be signed and witnessed. To cover all other possibilities, she should also prepare a statement revoking her previous one, sign it, and have it witnessed. Any other papers stating her wish to be an organ donor, such as letters to relatives, should be located and destroyed.

CHAPTER 15

Pensions, RRSPs, Social Programs

Pension Plans

The company Anton works for has no employee retirement plan. Aren't all companies required by law to offer such plans?

No. However, many companies choose to offer them. And if the plan complies with the requirements of Revenue Canada and provincial pension legislation, the company and the employees can claim tax deductions for their respective contributions.

Gary, 45, has just been hired by a company that does not permit new employees over 40 to join its retirement plan. Should Gary challenge this policy?

Yes. Since the Charter of Rights and Freedoms and some provincial human rights laws forbid discrimination based on age, the company's retirement plan would probably be declared illegal by the courts.

Types of Pension Plans

Here's how pension and retirement plans work:

● *Defined contribution plan*—The amount of contributions, or the formula for determining the amount of contributions, is preset. The amount of your benefit depends on the success of the investments made with the funds (contributions) in your account. Some defined contribution plans allow you to choose how your account is invested.
● *Profit-sharing plan*—A type of defined contribution plan under which your employer's contributions are made according to a formula based on company profits or a percentage of your pay. The employer may contribute a smaller percentage or nothing at all in years when profits fall below a certain level. An *incentive savings* profit-sharing plan lets you make voluntary contributions of a certain percentage of your income.
● *Money-purchase pension plan*—Your employer's annual contributions are based on a percentage of your compensation. The employer must make these contributions every year, regardless of company profits.
● *Target benefit plan*—The company sets a goal for the retirement benefit of an employee, then calculates the schedule of contributions that will be required to meet that goal. The actual benefit at retirement may be greater or less than the goal, depending on the success of the plan investments, as well as on how accurately the company predicted the turnover, retirement, and life expectancy of its employees.
● *Defined benefit plan*—Your future benefit is determined in advance. It may be a set dollar amount (*flat benefit*) per month, or it may be

Will my pension benefits stop accumulating if I work past 65?

It's illegal for a company to stop or slow the accrual of pension benefits just because you work past normal retirement age. However, a plan may specify the number of years during which benefits can accrue.

Is it sex discrimination for a company to pay women lower monthly pensions than it pays men?

Yes. The traditional discrepancy between men's and women's pensions is based on actuarial facts: statistically women live longer than men and thus will collect more payments during their lifetimes. Now, however, paying women lower monthly pensions than men would most likely be interpreted as sex discrimination if challenged under the Charter of Rights and Freedoms. Discrimination on the basis of sex is also expressly prohibited by the Pension Benefits Standards Act and by Manitoba and Quebec legislation.

determined by a formula, such as 75 percent of your annual income at retirement (*fixed benefit*). Contributions are based on the amount necessary to provide a certain benefit amount. You cannot direct the investment; instead, the fund is managed by fiduciaries and trustees. Some defined benefit plans multiply a set amount (called the unit) by the number of years you work to arrive at a *unit benefit* for retirement.

● *Contributory plan*—Both the employer and employee contribute. The *primary contributor* is the employer. *Noncontributory plans* are those to which only the employer contributes.

● *Registered Retirement Savings Plan (RRSP)*—Each year you contribute a specified percentage of your earned income (up to the maximum dollar amount tax rules allow) to a government-approved RRSP and claim a tax deduction. The interest, dividends or capital gains your plan accumulates over the years are tax exempt. When you retire and convert your tax-sheltered nest egg into an income-producing annuity, you will pay income tax on that annual retirement income. If you cash in the RRSP before you retire, to keep you going in a lean year for instance, you will have to include those proceeds in your total income for that year when calculating your income tax. But chances are you will be in a lower tax bracket after you retire or in that lean year than you are at present.

● *Registered Retirement Income Funds (RRIF)*—A plan whereby a certain sum of money is invested for pay out between retirement and age 90. An RRIF holder who so wills can have his fund transferred tax free to his spouse if he dies before reaching 90. Unlike the case with annuities, the RRIF holder also retains ownership and control of his capital.

Pension Plans

**My company's retirement plan is available only to employees who
have worked here for more than three years. Is this legal?**

It depends where you work. Under recent reforms to pension legislation,
employees working for the federal government or for federally regulated
industries such as banks, as well as other employees in Alberta,
Manitoba, Ontario, and Quebec, can participate in a company's pension
plan after working 24 consecutive months with that company. Other
provinces may soon follow suit in their legislation.

**I have worked for the Minnow Company for 15 years. If I quit or
am laid off or fired, will I lose the money that the company
contributed to my retirement plan?**

No. After 10 years of employment, your benefits should be fully vested.
That means that all employer contributions to the plan are yours—even
if you quit or are fired or laid off. Your own contributions to the plan vest
immediately. They were yours to begin with. For employees under
federal jurisdiction, vesting takes place after two years of employment.
In Alberta and Manitoba, contributions are vested after five years.

**After 17 years with one company, where his retirement benefits
are fully vested, Kieran is moving to a new company. Must he
leave his pension funds with his old company until he retires?**

Not necessarily. Many plans now allow an employee to withdraw his
vested benefits when leaving the company, whether or not he has
reached retirement age. Under revised pension plans in many places,
Kieran can now transfer his vested pension funds (both his and his
employer's contributions) to the plan run by his new employer, if that
employer agrees, or he can transfer the funds to a locked-in registered
retirement savings plan. Employees working for the federal government
or for federally regulated companies, as well as workers in Saskatchewan, Quebec, and Nova Scotia, can also purchase a deferred annuity.

**Jean-Pierre's interest in his company's pension plan was vested
before he became disabled as the result of a car accident. Will his
disability reduce his retirement benefits?**

It may. In some cases, company pension plan benefits are reduced by the
amount that the beneficiary receives from other pensions. If, for
example, Jean-Pierre receives a disability pension from the government,

his company may reduce his pension proportionately. Jean-Pierre should discuss this possibility with his personnel manager or union representative. Many private pension plans also reduce benefits by the amount an individual receives from the Canada (or Quebec) Pension Plan. This combining of benefits is called *integration*.

Can my company reduce the amount it contributes to the pension plan during periods when business is poor?

It depends. In both defined benefit and defined contribution plans, the company must make set contributions, regardless of profits, or have a fine imposed by Revenue Canada or a provincial pension benefits board. If, however, a company can show that mandatory contributions would result in a substantial business hardship, the company may be allowed to reduce the contribution without penalty. Under a profit-sharing plan, the company may forgo contributions altogether in a bad year.

If my company goes bankrupt, will I lose all my vested benefits?

No. Pension funds are held in an irrevocable trust for the benefit of employees and do not become assets of the company, so the funds do not have to be divided among the bankrupt company's creditors. However, if there is a pension plan surplus—more pension fund money than would be needed to meet obligations—the trustee may take that part of the surplus containing the company's contributions and distribute it to creditors.

Archie's retirement benefits were fully vested when he left and went to work for another company. Archie is now ready to retire and has learned that his first employer is no longer in business. Can he still get the benefits from his first job?

Yes. Archie shouldn't lose any benefits he earned just because he worked for more than one company. Even if Archie's old employer left no assets, Archie's pension funds are protected either through a provincial or federal pension benefits standards act. Archie will receive his pension up to a specified limit per month, under the plan of the defunct company.

After 28 years of marriage, Kevin and Mimi got divorced. Can Mimi get part of Kevin's pension when he retires?

Yes. Courts have held that private or company pension funds are part of matrimonial property, to be shared when a marriage is dissolved. In most

Pension Plans

provinces Mimi would be entitled to half of that part of the pension Kevin earned or contributed to while they lived together. In British Columbia, Manitoba and Ontario, the pension is expressly described as matrimonial property: Kevin's benefits from the Canada Pension Plan would automatically be split between himself and Mimi in proportion to his contributions while they lived together. If they lived in Quebec, Mimi would have to apply to the Quebec Pension Board within 36 months of the divorce to share in Kevin's Quebec Pension Plan benefits.

Louise retired at 65, but wants to take a part-time job at a supermarket. Will her company pension cheque be reduced?

No. Louise's former employer may not reduce the benefit because she gets another job. There is an exception: if Louise goes back to work for her old employer, her benefit might be suspended during her reemployment. But if Louise is still working for her old employer when she reaches 71, she must be paid her full pension.

Pension Reform

In recent years, the federal government and many of the provinces have introduced pension legislation to reflect changes in the workplace and the effects of these changes on the administration of pension funds. Unlike the past, when the work force consisted largely of men who spent most of their lives with one employer, today's work force is made up more or less equally of men and women, and the average Canadian may work for three or more employers during his or her working life. Pension reform has abolished age and sex discrimination and changed pension regulations in a number of other ways, including the following:

● *Eligibility*—Full-time and part-time employees who have worked continuously for two years for the same employer are now eligible to participate in company pension plans. Part-timers must meet other criteria as well.

● *Vesting*—Under the old pension legislation, an employee's pension fund was not considered vested (it did not belong to the employee) until he or she had worked for the company for 10 years or had reached the age of 40 or 45. The new laws have shortened the period before the fund is vested. Federal employees and those in federally regulated companies now have vested funds after only two years with their employer. Workers in Alberta and Manitoba acquire vesting after five years. Other provinces will probably pass similar legislation.

What happens to my pension if my company merges with another?

The new company would have to respect all the terms and honor all the obligations of your old company's pension plan up to the date of the merger. In other words, you would be entitled to all the pension benefits you accumulated in your company's plan up to the point the two companies became one. And although your new employer would not be legally obliged to offer you a plan as good as the one you now have, or even to offer any plan at all, the chances are you wouldn't be worse off. In most mergers, the company being sold arranges for the acquiring company to provide an equivalent pension plan or, as is sometimes the case, an even better one.

I'm choosing early retirement and may take my retirement benefits either in a lump sum or in monthly payments. Which would be better?

It depends on several factors. If you take all your benefits at once, your income for that year may put you in a higher tax bracket than usual, and

● *Portability*—An employee who moves from one company to another can now transfer his pension funds from the old employer's plan to the new employer's plan, provided the new employer agrees; if not, the employee can purchase a "locked-in" registered retirement savings plan. In some cases, the employee may purchase an insured life annuity, payable at retirement.

● *Optional early retirement*—In some cases, employees may retire up to 10 years before the normal retirement date and still receive pension benefits.

● *Inflation protection*—Some jurisdictions are considering indexation for pension benefits.

● *Equal Employee-Employer Contributions*—Employers will now have to finance at least half the pension. In the past, employee contributions were often the main source of pension funding.

● *Survivor benefits*—If an employee dies before retirement age, the portion of his vested pension fund contributed from the time the new laws were passed will be given to his or her spouse or estate. In the past, an employee who died before reaching retirement age often forfeited these funds.

● *Discrimination*—The practice of paying women monthly pensions relatively lower than those paid to men and the requirement that members of a pension plan be younger than a certain age have been abolished by most new pension legislation and labor relation law.

PENSIONS, RRSPs, SOCIAL PROGRAMS

you could lose a portion of your benefits to income taxes. In the past, income averaging could be used to soften the effects of a lump-sum settlement, but this is no longer permitted. Before choosing a lump sum or monthly payments, figure what each option would cost you in income taxes. You can avoid these taxes when making a lump-sum withdrawal by "rolling over" the funds—that is, transferring the lump sum to a "locked-in" registered retirement savings plan (an RRSP you can't touch until you invest it in an annuity), or converting it into a registered retirement income fund (RRIF). If you are still in your fifties or early sixties, say, have other sources of income, and no immediate need for funds, this may be your best option. The lump sum you put into a rollover RRSP or RRIF can continue to accumulate tax-free earnings until you withdraw the funds.

What Is an Annuity?

An annuity is a contract, purchased with either one lump sum or periodic payments, that assures an individual a certain amount of money, usually paid out at fixed periods for a specified length of time or for life. Annuities that are set up to make payments at some future date, such as when you retire, are called *deferred annuities.* They are typically offered by life insurance companies, because their premium rates and benefit amounts, like those for life insurance policies, are based on actuarial data.

Many people choose to purchase an annuity contract with the benefits that have accumulated in their pension or registered retirement savings plans, thereby guaranteeing them a regular, predictable income. Annuities that provide income for the life of the worker and the worker's spouse are called *joint and survivor* contracts.

A deferred annuity is a type of savings program in which your original investment grows by accumulating interest and, if you choose, by your additional contributions. At the end of this accumulation period, the money is paid out according to the terms of the contract you signed. The major advantage of a deferred annuity is that while the money is accumulating, there is no tax on the earnings. Some deferred annuities earn interest at a set rate—these are called fixed deferred annuities. Other retirement plans such as registered retirement income funds (RRIFs) allow the owner to change the investments in his account—thus the earnings and total value of the account depend on the success of his investment decisions. With an RRIF, unlike an annuity, you maintain control of the capital. However, an RRIF must be entirely paid out by age 90.

Will my wife receive benefits from my retirement plan if I die before she does?

Pension reform laws enacted in the federal jurisdiction and in Alberta, Saskatchewan, and Manitoba require pension plans to pay benefits to surviving spouses. In Saskatchewan and Manitoba only a part of the pension (about 60 percent) is payable to the surviving spouse. Ontario, Quebec, and Nova Scotia are among provinces which have similar reforms in the making.

What is retirement insurance, and how does it work?

It is life insurance that you can convert to an annuity. If you reach the age specified in the policy, usually retirement age (55-70), you can choose to continue the life insurance coverage or receive regular payments.

Registered Retirement Savings Plans (RRSPs)

Nadine and her husband, Paul, who both work, want to open RRSPs. Should they have separate RRSP accounts?

Yes. If both husband and wife work, each can open an RRSP. Tax laws specify how much one can contribute to such plans, normally a set percentage of income up to a maximum dollar amount for a given year. Payments to an RRSP are tax deductible. Taxes are paid when the money is withdrawn, generally at retirement.

Francine plans to open an RRSP. She already contributes to her company pension plan. Will this affect what she puts in her RRSP?

Yes. Because Francine contributes to her company's registered pension plan, what she can contribute to an RRSP will be much lower than it would be if she did not participate in her company's plan. In 1988, for example, a person who did *not* contribute to a company plan could have put 20 percent of income, up to a maximum of $7,500, in an RRSP. (Unless RRSP rules change, the maximum will increase each year until it reaches a limit of $15,000 by 1995.) Francine, too, could have contributed 20 percent of her income in that year, but only up to a maximum of $3,500 *minus* the amount she paid into her company plan. If, for instance, in 1988 she contributed $1,000 to her company pension plan, she would have to deduct that from the standard $3,500 limit to arrive at her $2,500 maximum allowable RRSP contribution.

Registered Retirement Savings Plans

Jan, 70, has no thought of retiring. If he works for several years more, can he continue to make contributions to his RRSP?

No. Jan must stop making contributions to his RRSP and begin withdrawing the money that has accumulated in his account by the time he reaches 71.

Where can I go to open an RRSP?

You can establish one through a bank, a trust company, an insurance company, an investment firm, financial adviser, mutual fund, and similar organizations.

Some years ago, Ophelia began making contributions to an RRSP. She is now 58 and needs money to repair her summer cottage. What are the penalties if she withdraws the money in her RRSP?

If Ophelia withdraws funds from her RRSP, that money must be added to her annual income and she will have to pay income tax on it at her current tax rate.

I would like to invest in some foreign stocks for my RRSP. Does the law restrict where I can put my RRSP money?

Yes. You can invest no more than 10 percent of your RRSP funds in foreign securities. The only other investments that qualify for RRSPs are mortgages secured by real property situated in Canada, and stocks, bonds, debentures, and other such securities issued by Canadian corporations or by corporations listed on a Canadian stock exchange. Guaranteed investment certificates and term deposits must be held in Canada. And you cannot invest in collectibles such as paintings, gems, stamps, rare books, and antiques for your RRSP.

Social Security Programs

Because he has worked for two years, Lonnie says he will receive Canada Pension Plan (CPP) benefits when he retires. Is this true?

Yes. To get CPP benefits one must have contributed to the plan for at least one year, must be at least 60 years old and, if under 65, must have "substantially" ceased working. Of course Lonnie's pension will be very small if he contributed for only two years. He would be entitled to a full pension only after contributing for at least 10 years. The amount he gets will depend not only on the number of years he works and contributes, but also on how old he is at retirement, and on his average "pensionable" earnings over the years he contributes. For someone retiring in 1988, the maximum pension at age 65 was $543.06 a month. (Quebec Pension Plan rules are almost identical to the CPP regulations.)

While her children were young, Bea had to start and stop work several times. Will this affect her Canada Pension Plan benefits?

If Bea has worked for a total of at least 10 years since 1966, when the Canada Pension Plan (and Quebec Pension Plan) went into effect, and has contributed to the plan for 10 years, she would be entitled to full benefits. The plan's child-rearing drop-out provision will work in her favor in determining both her eligibility and the level of pension she receives. In effect, she will not be penalized for periods during which she had low or zero earnings as a result of leaving the labor force to care for young children.

When can I get my Canada Pension Plan and Old Age Security benefits?

You can get Canada Pension Plan (or Quebec Pension Plan) benefits if you retire at age 60. But at 60 you will receive only about 70 percent of what you would get if you waited until you were 65. If you wait until you are 70 to start collecting, your monthly cheque would be about 30 percent higher still.

The Old Age Security (OAS) pension and the Guaranteed Income Supplement (GIS) are paid to Canadian citizens or landed immigrants who are 65 and have lived in Canada for at least 10 years since the age of 18. If you are 60 to 64 years of age, are widowed or married to someone receiving the OAS pension, you may be eligible for a Spouse's Allowance. Only pensioners who have little or no income besides the OAS pension can qualify for the GIS or the Spouse's Allowance.

Will I automatically receive my Canada Pension Plan and Old Age Security benefits when I reach the age of 65?

No. You must apply for these benefits as well as the Guaranteed Income Supplement (GIS) or Spouse's Allowance at least six months before the time you want to start receiving them. If you get the GIS or Spouse's Allowance, you must reapply for it every year.

Social Security Programs

Must a self-employed person pay more of his own money into the Canada Pension Plan than a company employee, even though they have the same annual income and can expect the same benefits?

Yes. A self-employed person in effect pays as both an employer and an employee, whereas a company employee's contribution is matched by that of his employer.

What should I take to the Old Age Security office to prove my eligibility for benefits?

If you were born in Canada, you should bring your birth certificate or baptismal certificate. If you were born elsewhere, bring your birth certificate as well as your certificate of landing (in the case of a landed immigrant) or your certificate of citizenship. If you are ill or otherwise unable to apply in person, someone else may be able to apply for you or you can request that someone from Health and Welfare Canada, which administers Old Age Security, visit you at home to take down the required information.

Aunt Lilly is barely getting by on her Old Age Security pension. She has little other income. Is she eligible for the Guaranteed Income Supplement?

Probably. But her eligibility and the amount of supplement she might get will depend on how much income she has, not counting her old age pension. Since the maximum supplement would be reduced by $1 a month for every $2 of Lilly's monthly income—wages, unemployment insurance, investment income, Canada (or Quebec) Pension Plan benefits, and private pension benefits—the government would have to verify Lilly's income as well as her husband's if she is married. In 1988 the maximum monthly supplement was $369.21 for a single pensioner, $240.47 for each spouse of a married couple. These amounts are adjusted every few months to keep pace with inflation.

Aunt Eleanor, who is 70 years old and very forgetful, never applied for her Old Age Security pension. If she applies now, will she get five years' pension in a lump sum?

Yes. Your aunt will be able to collect retroactively for 59 months. Rules for the Guaranteed Income Supplement are quite different, however. It is retroactive for one year only.

When Anita's aunt applied for Old Age Security benefits, she was asked for a copy of her birth certificate. She was born in Poland, and her town's records were destroyed in World War II. What can she use as proof of age?

Anita's aunt may use school records, her driver's license, voter registration documents, immigration records, her passport, or applications for insurance. If there was a religious record made of her birth or baptism, she will be able to use that. She can also use the testimony or affidavits of friends, relatives, or her physician. A record of military service is another acceptable proof of age.

Felicia has read that she should contact her Old Age Security office six months before her 65th birthday. If she fails to do so, does she lose her right to collect benefits?

No. Felicia would not lose her rights, but her benefits might be delayed because of the paperwork required to establish her eligibility.

Luke, now 65, was born in the United States and lived there until he moved to Canada 10 years ago. Is he eligible for the Old Age Security pension?

Yes. Anyone who has lived in Canada for a minimum of 10 years prior to applying for Old Age Security (OAS) benefits can get at least a partial pension. But Luke would be eligible for the full OAS pension, because Canada has reciprocal social security agreements with several countries including the United States. So even though OAS rules call for a person to have lived in Canada for 40 years after the age of 18 to qualify for the full pension, under the reciprocal agreement Luke can meet the 40-year-residency requirement by adding the time he lived in the United States to his 10 years in Canada.

Uncle Max, who is 75, has not paid his rent for three months. He has no savings and no revenue other than his Old Age Security pension and a small Canada Pension Plan benefit. His landlord has threatened to seize Uncle Max's pensions. Can he do this?

No. Creditors cannot seize Old Age Security or Canada Pension Plan pensions. For that matter, creditors cannot touch social welfare allowances or veterans' pensions either. Neither can your uncle assign these pensions to anyone in a private agreement. Although your uncle must make arrangements to pay the rent he owes, he does not have to worry that the landlord will take his pension.

How is the amount of my Canada Pension Plan retirement benefit calculated?

Your benefit at age 65 is 25 percent of your average "pensionable" earnings over the period you contributed. This period extends either from January 1966, the year the Canada and Quebec pension plans started, or from the time you turned 18, whichever was later. Anything you earned over the pensionable limit set each year—a maximum dollar amount corresponding to that year's average Canadian wage—does not enter into the calculation. To ensure that your overall average is not overly reduced by periods of low earnings—years at home raising young children for instance—some of these periods are excluded when calculating your average. To further boost your average, more weight is given to your pensionable earnings in your final three working years. In 1988, the maximum pension for a 65-year-old was $543.06 a month. If you retire before or after you are 65, your pension will be decreased or increased accordingly. The actual formulas for determining individual benefits are a bit too complex for most people to work out on their own, but you can get an estimate from your nearest Canada (or Quebec) Pension Plan office.

Terence retired when he was 65, but wants to go back to work to help make ends meet. Will the amount he receives in his Old Age Security cheques be reduced?

No. The Old Age Security (OAS) pension is paid to all who qualify, whether or not they are working or need the money. If Terence goes back to work however, he would probably not be eligible for the Guaranteed Income Supplement (GIS), an extra benefit for needy pensioners whose only source of income is the OAS pension. The GIS is reduced by $1 for every $2 of income over and above the OAS pension.

In the past year, my mailbox has been broken open three times. I am retired and my old age pension is my main source of income. How can I make sure I get my cheque every month?

Tell the Income Security Programs office of Health and Welfare Canada that you want your Old Age Security cheques deposited directly into your bank account. Give the government employee handling your request the name and address of your bank as well as your name and social insurance number. And, of course, advise your bank of this new arrangement. Canada (or Quebec) Pension Plan cheques can also be deposited directly to one's account.

Elizabeth has been considering the possibility of early retirement. If she decides to retire early, how will that affect her monthly Canada Pension Plan benefit?

If she retires at 60, her pension would be about 30 percent less than if she waited until she was 65. And if she postpones her retirement until age 70, her pension would be about 30 percent greater than what she would receive at age 65.

Michael, who is 65 years old, will continue to work. He will begin receiving Canada Pension Plan (CPP) and Old Age Security benefits next month. Will CPP contributions continue to be deducted from his pay cheque?

No. Once Michael begins receiving benefits from the Canada Pension Plan (or the Quebec Pension Plan as the case may be), he will not be required to make further contributions.

Thomas will be receiving a company pension when he retires. Will this income affect the amount of his Old Age Security and Canada Pension Plan benefits?

No. Thomas's income from a company or personal retirement plan does not affect either of these pensions. Neither does any salary or wages or income that may derive from savings, investments, annuities, insurance, or inheritances.

Aunt Panagiota who receives Canada Pension Plan and Old Age Security benefits has been thinking of returning to the place where she was born in Greece. Would she be able to receive her pensions there?

Yes. Anyone already getting either of these pensions can continue to receive them, payable in Canadian dollars anywhere in the world and for an indefinite period.

A tax specialist told Isaac that he would have to pay income tax on some of his retirement benefits. Can that be right?

Yes. Since Old Age Security and Canada (or Quebec) Pension Plan benefits must be included in income for income tax purposes, they would be taxed along with any other earnings Isaac has. Only the Guaranteed Income Supplement is not taxable.

Pensions for Dependents

What are Canada Pension Plan survivor benefits?

They are payments to help support the dependents of a wage earner who has died. Among those entitled to dependents' benefits are spouses (both legal and common-law), children, and in some cases, the parents of the deceased wage earner. The Canada Pension Plan (CPP) pays three kinds of survivor benefits. When a CPP (or Quebec Pension Plan) contributor or pensioner dies, the surviving spouse or, if there is none, the estate receives a death benefit. This lump-sum payment equals six times the deceased's monthly pension up to the maximum set each year ($2,650 in 1988). The widow or widower can also apply for a *surviving spouse's pension* which, for a 65-year-old survivor, would be 60 percent of the late contributor's CPP or QPP. Those under 65 at the time of their partners' deaths will receive reduced pensions, the amounts depending on how old they are, whether they are disabled, and whether they are raising dependent children. A surviving spouse younger than 35 with no children and no disability will get no survivor benefits until the age of 65, unless he or she becomes disabled before then.

Dependent children of a deceased CPP or QPP contributor or pensioner are entitled to *orphans' benefits*. Each eligible child would receive a standard monthly payment (in 1988, $98.96 from CPP or $29 from QPP) until the age of 18 or, if attending school or university full-time, until the age of 25. If both parents die and they were CPP contributors, each eligible surviving child would receive a double benefit.

For survivors to be eligible for benefits, the deceased spouse or parent must have contributed to the CPP or QPP in at least three calendar years. If, for example, a person contributed in December 1987, throughout 1988, and in January 1989, he would be considered to have contributed in three calendar years.

Until they separated a year ago, Coreen and Sean lived together unmarried for 12 years. Sean is now 65 and receives a Canada Pension Plan pension. Does Coreen have any rights to part of it?

Yes. Because Coreen and Sean lived together for at least 12 consecutive months and have been separated for at least 12 months, Coreen is entitled to share Sean's CPP pension. Not being a divorced person, who would automatically get part of the ex-spouse's pension, and not having been legally married, in which case she would have no time limit after a separation to apply for a pension split, Coreen would have to apply within four years of the separation for a share of Sean's pension. She would be entitled to share in that portion of the pension he acquired during the time they lived together. Common-law spouses do not have this right in Quebec.

After a 35-year marriage, Rose and Myron both retired at 60.
Since Rose's Canada Pension Plan benefits are less than Myron's,
can she have part of his pension added to hers?

Yes. Provided they are 60 or older, a couple in an "ongoing relationship" can share their Canada Pension Plan (CPP) benefits. Even if only one of them received a pension, it could be split between them. If they make a joint application to have their pensions shared, each will receive a part of the other's pension. How large that part will be depends on whether the couple had been living together for all or just a part of the "contributory period"—the period in which one must contribute to the CPP. If, for instance, a husband had contributed to the CPP for 22 years and been married and living with his wife for the last 11 of those 22 years—half the contributory period—she would get a quarter of his pension. Since Rose and Myron lived together during their entire contributory periods, each could divide his or her pension with the other. The sharing arrangement would end if they separate or one of them dies. The Quebec Pension Plan has no provision for sharing pensions in an ongoing relationship.

Pauline receives a Surviving Spouse's Pension. If she remarries
will she continue to receive this benefit?

Yes. Since the rules changed in January 1987, the remarriage of a person receiving a Surviving Spouse's Pension does not put an end to the pension. In fact, anyone who remarried prior to the rule change and lost his or her Surviving Spouse's Pension as a result may have the pension reinstated retroactively to January 1987.

Donna is 67 years old and receives a monthly cheque based on
her own Canada Pension Plan contributions. Her husband just
died. Can Donna receive both the widow's benefit and her
own retirement benefit?

Yes. Since Donna and her late husband both contributed to the Canada Pension Plan, she is entitled to the Surviving Spouse's Pension and to her own retirement pension.

After Fred died, his widow, Marion, continued to put his Old Age
Security and Canada Pension Plan cheques in their joint bank
account and withdraw the money as she needed it. Is there
anything wrong with this?

Yes. Marion should report Fred's death immediately to the nearest office of Health and Welfare Canada. Not only is she obligated to return all the

Pensions for Dependents

money she receives from Fred's cheques, but she could also face charges of fraud and severe fines if convicted. Marion should request instructions for returning the money and applying for survivor's benefits.

Nat died leaving two children, one adopted child, and three stepchildren, all under 18 years of age. Will they all be eligible to receive survivor benefits?

The adopted child and Nat's two natural children are entitled to survivor benefits. The stepchildren are entitled to these benefits if they had been living with Nat, and if he was contributing to their support.

Medicare and the Senior Citizen

For information on individual and group medical insurance, see "Health and Disability Insurance" in Chapter 8, *Insurance.*

My husband will be in the hospital for the next month and then will be going into a nursing home. Will Medicare cover all his expenses?

There are slight differences in Medicare coverage from one province to another. Generally a stay in hospital, including meals, nursing care, laboratory tests, the use of operating and recovery rooms and their equipment, anesthetics, X rays, and certain devices, pacemakers for example, that are incorporated into the body, is covered by Medicare, but the cost of a nursing home is not. By and large Medicare also pays for most medication for people over 65 and, in some cases, for patients between 60 and 65.

My parents are planning to live in Florida for eight months of the year. Will they still qualify for Medicare?

If your parents live more than 183 days a year in Florida, or anywhere else outside of Canada, they would probably lose their rights to Medicare. If they spend more than 12 months away from their province but still live in Canada, they may lose their right to Medicare from their home province but may be eligible in the province where they took up residence. Those planning to live outside their home province for any length of time should contact their provincial Medicare office to see if there are any exceptions and agreements that would maintain their rights to Medicare, even if they are absent for a long period of time.

Parnell, a war veteran, lives alone and is finding it more and more difficult to take care of himself. Since he has no income other than his Old Age Security pension, he can't afford the cost of a proper nursing home. Will Medicare take care of this cost?

No, but Parnell may be eligible for help from the Veterans Independence Program (VIP). Initiated in 1988, VIP assists veterans who had theater-of-war service and whose Old Age Security pensions prevented them from receiving war veterans allowances. Its services include health counseling, day-care hospitals, and day-care centers that offer recreational activities and certain health services such as physiotherapy and diabetic care. All are designed to enable veterans to maintain or improve the quality of their lives and to remain as independent as possible in their own homes and communities. The program also finances home care, whether for patient needs or housekeeping services, recreational activities, transportation for shopping and, in some cases, subsidized care in adult residential centers or approved nursing homes.

My wife and I are planning a tour of the capitals of Europe. If we need medical or hospital services in a foreign country, will our Medicare coverage pay for those expenses?

Medicare may pay only part of the expenses incurred; so, before departure, you should purchase travel insurance that covers medical costs. For example, Medicare, which varies slightly from one province to another, may pay $700 for emergency hospitalization, plus 50 percent of any amount in excess of this. And it may pay the attending doctor or other health professional what it would pay that health professional in your home province. Unless you have supplementary travel health insurance and documents to prove it, you might have to pay the hospital, pharmacy, doctor, and other medical bills directly, and wait to be reimbursed (or partly reimbursed) by your provincial health plan once you return to Canada.

When Uncle Eric went into a nursing home, I agreed to pay for things he needs. The nursing home buys these items and sends me a bill every other month. Some of the charges are for medications. Doesn't Medicare cover these for anyone 65 and over?

Yes. Medicare pays for most medications for people 65 and older. Each province has an official list of the medications and other articles, such as syringes, disposable needles, and prosthetic devices, that the government plan pays for. Check with your provincial health plan office to see if Medicare pays for the medications and other things the nursing home purchased for your uncle.

Disability Benefits

What is a disability benefit, and who qualifies for it?

This monthly pension is paid to disabled Canada (or Quebec) Pension Plan contributors and to their dependent children up to the age of 18 or, if they are attending school or university full-time, up to the age of 25. To be eligible, the disabled applicant must be under 65, must have contributed to the plan for at least 2 of the last 3 years, or for 5 of the last 10 years, and must meet the plan's criteria for validating disability.

Can I get both a disability pension and a retirement pension?

No. If you are receiving a Canada Pension Plan (CPP) disability pension, it will be converted automatically to a retirement pension once you turn 65. On the other hand, if you retire between the ages of 60 and 64 and become disabled after you have started collecting your CPP pension, you can apply for a disability pension within six months of receiving your first retirement pension cheque and have your retirement pension canceled. When you reach 65, your disability pension would once more become a retirement pension.

Do I have to be completely disabled to receive disability benefits?

To qualify for Canada Pension Plan disability benefits, you must suffer from a mental or physical condition that prevents you from having any kind of substantial gainful employment *and* that is expected to last, or has lasted, at least 12 months, or that is expected to result in death. There is no general agreement on the meaning of the term *substantial gainful employment;* the courts have defined it on a case-by-case basis.

My daughter Karen, a university student, is getting married on her 21st birthday. Because I am disabled, she gets Canada Pension Plan benefits. Will these stop once she is married?

Not necessarily. Marriage will not put an end to your daughter's benefit so long as she is a full-time student under 25 and meets other conditions.

Lionel and his children have qualified for Canada Pension Plan disability benefits. Will his wife be eligible for a pension, too?

Although Lionel's dependent children under 18 years of age are entitled to a Canada Pension Plan disability pension, his wife is not.

Wills and Estates

My insurance agent keeps asking me to get together with him to plan my estate, but I really don't have much—a house, a car, a life insurance policy, and some other personal property. Why should I bother planning my estate?

Estate planning can give you a sense of security by assuring that your assets will be distributed the way you want. And, in many cases, good planning can produce important tax savings. Many people think that estate planning begins and ends with making a will. But it really involves much more than that. For example, property that you and your spouse own separately can be put into joint ownership to keep it from being tied up in court proceedings after one of you dies. Trusts can be created and guardians named to ensure that your children are properly cared for. Money may be put into a registered retirement savings plan to reduce income taxes.

Taking the time now to plan for the future can prevent family arguments and enable an executor to handle your estate smoothly. It can also reduce some of the costs involved in managing and distributing your property so that more is left for your heirs.

What types of property are included in an estate?

An estate consists of all the property a person owns. This includes assets of which the person is sole owner—such as bank accounts, jewelry, life insurance, and pension income—and property in which he or she shares ownership with a spouse, partner, or someone else—such as a home, business, car, or joint bank account. Stocks and bonds, copyrights, patents, and any money owed to the person are also included in the estate, as are any loans, taxes, or other debts owed *by* the person.

What can I do to ensure that my wife will have access to my bank account if she needs immediate cash when I die?

You could set up a joint account, with your wife named as a joint tenant with right of survivorship. But check your provincial law. The entire balance may not be immediately available to her on your death. In some provinces the taxing authorities must be given advance notice before withdrawals are made so that they can compute the true value of your estate and ensure that all provincial taxes have been paid. Or you could set up a payable-on-death account, if such accounts are permitted in your province, and name your wife beneficiary. Money in the account would then be available to your wife immediately after your death. Or you could have a bank account set up as a trust for your wife.

Rosanne wants her husband to inherit her house when she dies, without having the matter go through any court procedures. How can she arrange this?

She can have the house put in both their names. This type of joint ownership by spouses, with the right of survivorship, is called tenancy by the entirety. In this type of joint ownership, the married couple is considered to be one person for legal purposes. However, with the adoption of laws such as the Married Woman's Property Act, and the Ontario Family Law Act 1986, tenancy by the entirety has largely been done away with, and joint ownership only creates a *presumption* that the survivor is owner of the deceased spouse's share of the home. In Newfoundland, however, Rosanne's husband, on her death, would be entitled to receive her share of the house as tenancy by the entirety is still recognized there. In Quebec, if Rosanne made a notarial will giving her husband her interest in the property, court proceedings could also be avoided, as notarial wills do not have to be probated.

Are there advantages if my husband names me as beneficiary of a registered retirement savings plan (RRSP) instead of simply letting the RRSP proceeds become part of his estate when he dies?

Yes. As a spouse, you would have the option of "rolling over" your husband's RRSP into your own RRSP and could therefore avoid paying the income tax that the estate would otherwise be obliged to pay.

Irving and Rozzie are Canadian citizens, but they spend more than six months each year at their retirement home in Florida. Recently, while in Florida, they received a $50,000 gift from a deceased cousin. Will they have to pay inheritance tax?

Yes. Estate and gift taxes exist at the federal level in the United States and also in some states. If Irving and Rozzie are considered U.S. residents, they may have to pay United States inheritance taxes in Florida. Many wills, however, direct that gifts be made free and clear of all taxes—in which case any taxes are paid out of the estate.

What is the difference between estate and inheritance taxes?

Estate taxes are imposed on a person's estate after his death and are based on the value of the estate after all necessary deductions have been made. Inheritance taxes, on the other hand, are imposed on the beneficiaries—those who inherit an estate. The tax is usually based on the value of the property inherited and the relationship of the beneficiary to the person who died. Immediate members of the family are taxed at a lower rate than more distant relatives. Estate and inheritance taxes are no longer imposed in Canada but may be encountered if the person who died left property in a country which does.

Ronnie has $200,000 worth of property in Quebec. In planning his estate, should he keep federal or provincial estate taxes in mind?

No. Federal estate taxes were abolished in 1972, and those provinces that had estate taxes or succession duties have also done away with them. Quebec, the last province to abolish estate taxes, did so in 1986.

Nancy and her husband, Calvin, have built a successful business, but Calvin's health is deteriorating. What can he do to be sure of an income if he becomes incapacitated?

He can give a general or limited power of attorney to Nancy to act for him. He can also set up a "living trust," appointing his wife and another person or persons—perhaps a trust company—or both, to manage the

Planning Your Estate

You don't have to be wealthy to plan an estate. In fact, when you buy life insurance or name a beneficiary on your pension plan, you are planning your estate. Estate planning is organizing your assets for your maximum benefit while you are alive and seeing to it that what is left after your death is passed on to the right people quickly and with a minimum of legal fees. A will is the cornerstone of most estate plans. But a will needs to be approved by a probate court—a process that keeps your heirs from receiving the property immediately and that involves legal fees, which may reduce the amount they receive. (In Quebec wills drawn up by notaries—notarial wills—do not have to be probated.) The most popular ways of leaving assets are these:

● *Last will and testament*—Your will states to whom you wish your estate to go. It also names one or more executors to administer your estate, and a guardian for any minor children.
● *Joint tenancy with right of survivorship*—This type of co-ownership, now used only in Newfoundland, was once widely used by married couples for their homes and bank accounts. On the death of one, the other automatically became sole owner of the property.

property he puts into the trust. The terms should be carefully worked out with a lawyer or agent of the trust company, specifying what kinds of investments the trustees can make, whether their decisions must be unanimous or by majority vote, and so on. A living trust which includes a trust company as a trustee may be more expensive to operate, but it protects Calvin should his wife become incapable of acting on his behalf.

Since there are no succession duties in Canada, can I transfer my property to my heirs without my estate paying any taxes?

Not necessarily. The Income Tax Act deems a person to have disposed of his property at a fair market value at the time of his death. If he bought property for $10,000 in, say, 1975, and died in 1988 when the value was $50,000, his estate would have to pay a capital gains tax on the $40,000 difference.

Sam lives in a house he bought for $40,000, now worth $200,000. When he dies, will his wife have to pay a capital gains tax on the $160,000 increase in value?

No. One's principal residence is not subject to capital gains tax.

● *Payable-on-death accounts*—These bank accounts, also called trustee accounts, can be used to transfer funds automatically to a beneficiary.
● *Life insurance*—Policies are often purchased to provide immediate income to the beneficiaries. Money from an insurance policy which names a specific person as beneficiary is not included in the estate and goes directly to the beneficiary.
● *Gifts*—The problem with gifts is that the value of the gift is determined at the time the gift is made, not at the time the property was acquired by the donor. For example, if shares were bought for $5 in 1980, and were worth $25 at the time of the gift, the person making the gift would have to pay capital gains tax on the $20 difference.
● *Trusts*—Trusts that take effect during a person's lifetime are called *inter vivos,* or living, trusts. Those set up in a will to take effect after death are called testamentary trusts. Only a living trust avoids probate. A typical reason to create a trust is to provide for minor children or others incapable of taking care of themselves. By creating an irrevocable living trust (one that cannot be changed), you remove the property that was placed in the trust and vest it in the hands of the trustee.
● *Pensions and employee benefit plans*—Proceeds from pensions and benefit plans are passed directly to the designated beneficiaries.

Making a Will

Why do I need a will if I am leaving everything to my wife?

You need a will because your wife may not get your entire estate if you die intestate. Each province has its own laws governing the distribution of property when someone dies without a will. Your wife would get only one third or one half of your estate, depending on what relatives outlive you. By not making a will, you give up all right to say how your property will be divided.

Roberto and Dolores are young newlyweds who rent a furnished apartment and own almost nothing but their clothes, a car, and a few household items. Do they need wills?

Yes. Suppose they were killed in an automobile collision. Their heirs might be able to sue the other driver for a large amount. If Roberto and Dolores didn't have wills, the laws of their province would determine who would get the money. Only if they had wills would the money be sure to go to the person or persons of their choice.

Can my 17-year-old son, with $3,000 in a savings account, make a will leaving his assets to me?

A will made by a 17-year-old is valid in Newfoundland, but in most provinces the minimum age for making a will is 18. It is 19 in British Columbia, New Brunswick, Nova Scotia and the Northwest Territories, 21 in Yukon. Generally, if a minor is married, he or she is legally capable of making a will.

Should my husband and I have separate wills?

Yes. Even if a joint will is legal in your province, separate wills are preferable. Any changes that one spouse makes to a joint will may invalidate it for both parties. Since the making of a will is usually neither complicated nor expensive, a couple is well advised to make separate wills. (Joint wills are prohibited in Quebec.)

Must a lawyer write a will if it is to stand up in court?

There is no law that says a will must be drawn up by a lawyer, but so many legalities are involved that it is advisable to go to a lawyer. He can advise you about the latest changes in the laws, various ways to distribute your property, and the best way to word the document to make sure that your wishes are carried out. (In Quebec a notary can draw up a notarial will. Such wills do not require probate.)

I saw a book that has a form in it for drafting your own will. Would this kind of do-it-yourself will be acceptable in court?

A do-it-yourself will is fine if the form complies with the latest laws in your province. However, if you fail to follow the exact legal procedures, or if the language you use is not precise, the will could be declared invalid, and your property would be divided not according to your exact wishes but according to provincial law.

Is a handwritten will valid?

A will that is *entirely* handwritten and signed by the testator is called a holograph will and is valid in all provinces except British Columbia, Nova Scotia, and Prince Edward Island.

Uncle Stanley made a video recording in which he outlined how he wanted his estate distributed, noting the date and naming all the people in the room as witnesses. Is this a valid will?

Probably not. The law accepts only three forms of wills: (1) English form wills (signed by the testator in front of two witnesses); (2) holograph wills (entirely handwritten and signed by the testator), not valid in some provinces; and (3) notarial wills (drawn up by a notary), valid in Quebec only. Another form, the international will, recognized in Alberta, Manitoba, Ontario, and Newfoundland, is more complicated than customary wills and is rarely used.

When Alec became seriously ill, he told some nurses and his doctor how he wanted his property distributed. Did this oral will replace the written will he had prepared five years previously?

No. Because he had a written will, Alec would have had to revoke that will before making a new one. Destroying the old will or writing a new one are the preferred ways of revoking a will.

If Alec had never prepared a will, his oral statements might have constituted a valid will. Some provinces recognize oral wills, but there are many restrictions. In some provinces, the oral declaration is accepted only if the person was in imminent danger of death and the witnesses must have put the oral statements in writing within a certain time limit.

Making a Will

Can Eileen name her childhood friend, Joy, executor of her will, even though Joy lives in another province?

Yes. Eileen may choose whomever she wishes as executor. Joy, however, would find it expensive, difficult and time-consuming to administer the estate from another province. She would have to nominate someone resident in Eileen's province as an agent to receive court documents, and if there were property to be sold, she would have to travel to Eileen's province to make an inventory and to arrange the sale, at which she might have to preside. Eileen should appoint as co-executors both Joy and one or more other persons in her province. Joy could have help in routine matters, thus saving herself time and the estate money.

Pauline asked her neighbors, Moe and Ida, to watch her sign her name to a document and then witness it. Must they know the document is a will in order to be valid witnesses?

No. Moe and Ida are acting only as witnesses of Pauline's signature and do not have to know the contents of the document.

Virginia had Martin witness her signature on her will. After she died, Martin discovered that he was a beneficiary. Does being a witness affect his right to receive the property she left him?

Yes. As a general rule, witnesses and their spouses are not entitled to receive property left to them. In Ontario, however, if it could be shown that Virginia made her gift freely, and that no undue influence was exerted on her, the gift might be declared valid. If there are more than two witnesses, and only Martin was left property, the gift might be valid since only two witnesses are required to prove (probate) the will. (In Quebec, a husband and wife cannot together act as witnesses to a will.)

A terminally ill friend had me witness her signature on her will. When she dies, must I testify in court about the signing of the will?

It depends on the laws in your province. Some provinces require witnesses to go to court to attest that all legal requirements were followed in making and signing the will. In other provinces, the witnesses can sign the will in the presence of a notary public, or file an affidavit declaring that they knew the signature of the testator and that both he and they signed the will. This affidavit could serve as proof, and the presence of the witness in court would not be necessary.

What a Lawyer Needs to Write Your Will

There are many decisions to make when drawing up a will, and a lawyer needs specific information to carry out his client's wishes. You can save time and money by bringing the following information to your first consultation:

☑ Names, addresses, and birth dates of your spouse and children, together with any disabilities or special needs they may have.

☑ The amount and source of your own income, including interest and dividends, and your spouse's income.

☑ All your debts, including mortgages, installment loans, leases, and business obligations, and any legal actions outstanding against you.

☑ A list of your real estate, bank accounts, businesses, stocks, bonds, cars, jewelry, antiques, furniture, property owned jointly with someone else, and any other assets. Note the approximate value of co-owned property and the names of the co-owners.

☑ A list of your life insurance policies, showing ownership, the issuing companies, the policy numbers, face amounts, the beneficiaries, and any loans against the policies.

☑ A list of sources of retirement benefits, including those from company pensions, profit-sharing plans, and registered retirement savings plans.

☑ A list of possible executors and guardians for young children.

☑ A list of specific items that you want to leave to particular relatives or friends, such as family heirlooms or other things of sentimental value.

☑ Documents affecting your estate: premarital agreements, divorce decrees, trust agreements, recent federal income tax returns, real estate deeds, and your current will, if any.

Should there be more than one signed copy of a will?

No. Only the original document should be signed. Having additional signed copies could create problems. For example, if you made a new will but did not destroy all signed copies of the old one, there could be confusion as to which will was the valid one.

How many witnesses are needed for a will?

It depends on the type of will. An English form will must have at least two witnesses. No witness is required for a holograph will (not recognized in British Columbia, Nova Scotia and Prince Edward Island), but the will must be *entirely* in the handwriting of the testator and be signed by him.

Making a Will

Wills made by people on active duty in the armed forces and by merchant sailors at sea do not require witnesses, nor do they have to be in the handwriting of the testator; a printed form will properly signed is valid. In Quebec, a notarial will must be witnessed by two persons.

Where should a will be kept?

A will should be kept in a place where it can be easily located by a member of the family or the executor of the estate. The best place might be in a metal strongbox at home or in your lawyer's office or in a safe-deposit box in a bank. Wherever you keep your will, be sure other people know where it is. Having a will that cannot be found is like having no will at all—perhaps worse. Imagine the problems if a valid will is discovered after the assets have been distributed according to provincial laws dealing with intestate (no will) successions.

Louise has moved to another province. Must she make a new will?

No. Every province recognizes the validity of any will made according to the laws of the province in which the testator lived at the time. Thus a notarial will made in Quebec is valid anywhere in Canada even though only Quebec has this type of will.

I have lost my will. How do I get a new one?

Contact your lawyer (or notary) and have a new will drafted. If you have an unsigned copy of the will you lost, you can use it as a guide in drawing up the new one. But do not just sign a photocopy of the old will; if a court declared it invalid, your estate would be distributed according to provincial law rather than according to your wishes. Since the lost will may someday be found, be sure to state in the new will that all previous wills are revoked.

Naming Your Heirs

Should I leave everything to my wife, or should I divide things among my wife and children?

There is no quick or easy answer to this question. If you feel that your wife could manage your estate and the family without help, you might leave everything to her; if you feel that would put too great a strain on her, you might instead set up trusts for her and your children. Before deciding, find out what tax benefits might be gained or lost if your entire estate went to your wife. Also consider whether you want to make special arrangements in case your wife should remarry or should die before your children were able to provide for their own livelihood.

Alice is afraid that after she dies her husband will remarry and might neglect their children. Can she put a provision in her will stating that if her husband remarries, a portion of what she is leaving him will thereafter go instead to the children?

Yes, but this type of restriction may not be acceptable in every province. Alice could accomplish the same result, with less risk, if she set up a trust. It could let her husband use the interest and any other earnings from the money and property in the trust, or both, but keep him from touching the principal or selling the property. If he remarried, everything in the trust could be transferred automatically to the children, either directly (if the children are no longer minors) or in the form of another trust.

Enid and Phillip both have children from previous marriages. They want all they own to be divided equally among all their children. How do they do this?

The simplest way is to state in their wills that their stepchildren are to be considered the same as their own children. Thus the phrase "to all my children, equally" will include the stepchildren.

If Keith makes a will leaving everything to his mother and stating that he is leaving nothing to his wife, will it be honored?

It depends where Keith lives. In Quebec he can dispose of his share of the family assets and his own property without restriction. In Manitoba, Saskatchewan, Ontario, New Brunswick, Nova Scotia and Newfoundland, the surviving spouse is entitled to an equal share of the family assets, and in some provinces to a share of the business assets as well.

What steps can I take to make sure that my young children will be cared for and educated properly after my death?

Decide who would do the best job of raising your children, then get that person's consent to be named in your will as guardian. Also arrange for a contingent guardian who can take over if the first guardian dies or is otherwise unable to do the job. In addition, you can establish a trust fund in your will for your children's educational expenses. You will need to select a trustee to manage the trust and make sure the money is distributed properly. A good choice is a reputable trust company.

Adele hasn't spoken to her daughter for 10 years, and wants to cut her out of her will. Can she do that?

Probably. In most provinces it is perfectly legal for a parent to disinherit a child, even a young child. But Adele's will must state specifically that she is knowingly and intentionally leaving her daughter nothing. If there is any doubt, a court will probably grant the daughter the portion of the estate she would have received under provincial law if there had been no will. Generally, courts assume that no person wants to disinherit his own child.

Vicki, a well-to-do widow, wants to leave her estate to her only child, Maurice, but she disapproves of his current girlfriend who is of another religious faith. If Vicki's will states that Maurice can't have a penny if he marries this woman, will it be effective?

Probably not. Any restriction based on discrimination—religion, national or ethnic origin, handicap or disability—would be considered contrary to public policy and good morals and would be invalid. If Vicki put such a condition into her will, and Maurice could prove it was based on his spouse's religion, he would be able to inherit his mother's property.

Stan has been Burt's best friend for 30 years. He now lives in Europe. Can Burt leave him something in his will?

Yes. He can leave whatever he wants to Stan, regardless of where Stan lives. However, he should provide specific information as to where Stan can be found so that the executor can track him down when the time comes to settle the estate.

Henrietta wants her jewelry distributed in a certain way after she dies. What is her best way to have her wishes carried out?

She should list these together with any other specific bequests, clearly indicating who is to get what, and ask her lawyer to include this information in her will.

***What happens if a child is born after the parent's will is prepared
and the child is not mentioned in the will?***

Many provinces allow the child to share in the estate as though the
parent had died without a will. After the child's portion is deducted, the
rest of the estate is distributed as much as possible according to the will.
If it reads, "I leave two thirds of my property to my children," the child
born after the parent's death will get a share equal to those of his siblings.

Points to Consider When Making Your Will

Wills follow a traditional format and include many standard terms. But
a will also reflects its maker's wishes and his plans for providing for
the needs of his family. It is difficult to plan for everything that might
happen, but here are points to consider:

☑ Whom do you want to serve as executor of your estate?

☑ Is it likely that additional children will be born or adopted?

☑ Do you want your stepchildren and children born during your marriage to receive a share of your estate?

☑ If you have young children, who should serve as their guardians and contingent guardians?

☑ Do you want to give your spouse complete freedom to sell or give away your property if he or she remarries?

☑ Who should receive the remainder of your estate after all specific bequests have been made?

☑ Would it be a good idea for your estate to pay off real estate mortgages before your property is turned over to your heirs?

☑ Do you want to cancel debts owed to you by any of your heirs, or do you want these debts to be deducted from their inheritances?

☑ In case your assets must be sold to pay your debts, do you want to make a priority list, designating which items are to be sold first and which last?

☑ Are there advantages in paying capital gains taxes out of the assets of your estate?

☑ How should your estate be handled if you and your spouse die at the same time?

☑ Do you want to waive the requirement for your executor to post a bond, and do you want to list the power that your executor shall have in handling your estate? Do you want to create a trust enabling your spouse to live on the interest from your investment and in the former common residence, with this property going to your children after his or her death?

☑ Do you want to extend the executor's power beyond the customary one year?

Naming Your Heirs

To avoid having to change his will if he and his wife have other children, Christopher wants to state that "40 percent of my estate shall be distributed equally among my children." Would this guarantee that his wishes would be carried out?

Not necessarily. A court would want to know whether Christopher meant to include adopted children, stepchildren, illegitimate children, and children born after the will was made. To express his wishes clearly and thus avoid confusion later, Christopher's will should name each child, even if it means making a new will if he has more children.

I am 87 years old and have no relatives. My only companion is my dog, Marmaduke. Can I leave all my property to him?

No. You should make an agreement with someone to take care of Marmaduke after your death, then leave that person enough money or marketable property to carry out your wishes. You should also designate who will receive the balance of your estate after the dog dies. Otherwise it will be distributed according to provincial law as if there were no will.

I want to leave the house I inherited from my first husband to my three children, but I want my new husband to be able to remain if he wishes. What can I do?

One way to protect both your second husband and your children is to create a living trust in your will. It would give your husband the right to live in the house, but he would not own the property. When he died, the property would go to your children. In Quebec such a living trust is called a *usufruct*. It gives the beneficiary the *use* and *fruits* of the property, rentals for example, but does not give him full ownership.

Alfred has $15,000 in a savings account, some stocks, life insurance, and a house with $20,000 left on the mortgage. If he leaves the house to his sister and everything else to his children, would his sister get the house without the mortgage?

She would get it with the mortgage unless Alfred specified in his will that the mortgage should be paid by his estate. While wills usually require all debts to be paid before an estate can be divided among the heirs, mortgages are an exception. Without clear directions to the executor to pay the mortgage from the proceeds of the estate, Alfred's sister would become responsible for paying it.

I am leaving my house to my great-granddaughter, who is attending a local university. Is it sufficient to describe the house in my will by its street address?

Yes, but the more specific the description, the better. Many lawyers include not only the street address but also the number of the lot or tract of land, boundaries, distances, and landmarks.

Ben is divorced and has custody of his child. What provisions, if any, can be made in Ben's will to ensure that his ex-wife will not be named guardian of their child upon Ben's death?

None. Ben could have a paragraph put into his will stating his wish that someone other than his ex-wife be named guardian, but it would probably have no legal effect. In most provinces, a child's natural parent has first priority when a guardian is selected. A court would probably name his ex-wife as guardian.

Although his will cannot guarantee who will have custody of his child after his death, Ben can designate a conservator—a guardian for the money the child inherits. This will ensure that someone Ben approves of will oversee how the child's finances are handled.

Sam wants his will to cancel the unpaid portion of a $10,000 loan he made to his son. What is the best way to handle this?

Sam should state in his will that the balance of the debt is canceled. If he doesn't, the debt will be deducted from the son's share of the estate.

Establishing Trusts

When my wife and I talked to a lawyer about making a will, he suggested that we set up a living trust. What is that?

A living, or *inter vivos,* trust is one that takes effect during your lifetime. If you decided to create a living trust, you would transfer property or money into the fund, and appoint someone (a trustee) to administer it. The trustee, perhaps a lawyer or accountant or a bank or other financial institution, would manage and invest these assets and distribute income from the trust to the beneficiaries—the persons for whom you have set up the trust—according to the terms you have specified.

Since the living trust would already be established when you die, the property placed in it would not have to go through probate court under your will.

Establishing Trusts

Grandfather Johnson has set up testamentary trusts for all his grandchildren. What is a testamentary trust?

A testamentary trust is a fund established by a will and administered by a trustee named in the will. Unlike a living trust, a testamentary trust does not go into effect until the person who made the will dies. Testamentary trusts are frequently set up to provide income or educational funds for young children and grandchildren, and in some cases they can have substantial tax advantages.

If I establish a testamentary trust in my will, can money from it be made available to the beneficiaries without going through probate court?

No. All trusts created in a will must be reviewed by a probate court to ensure they comply with provincial law. A living trust, on the other hand, does not go through probate; it is effective as soon as it has been signed.

Max created a living trust for his sister, Rose. What happens if she dies before he does?

The trust would end and the money or other assets would be returned to Max. However, if Max had named a contingent beneficiary, that person would receive the benefit of the trust after Rose's death.

The Benefits of a Living Trust

A testamentary trust is often included in a will to give the testator some control over how his property is used after his death. But there are some distinct advantages to another type of trust—the *inter vivos,* or living, trust—which goes into effect while you are still alive:

● Giving someone the power to manage your investments or property when you no longer wish to do so. A living trust instructs the trustee to pay you income during your lifetime, and then distribute the trust property to your beneficiaries after your death.

● Protecting your property in case you become incompetent. If you become too ill to handle your affairs, the trustee will continue to manage the property in the trust while guardianship or conservatorship proceedings are held to determine who will manage your other property and your personal affairs.

***Kirk wants his nieces and nephews to inherit his estate, but he is
concerned that Marty, his youngest nephew, will spend his entire
inheritance right away. Can Kirk do something to prevent this?***

Yes. He can establish a "spendthrift trust" that will release a specified
amount of money to Marty at regular intervals—say, once a year. A
spendthrift trust usually conveys precise instructions to the trustee
(administrator of the trust) as to how payments are to be made and the
amount of money the beneficiary is to receive in each payment.

***Must I decide how much money my family should receive each
year from a trust fund, or can I leave it up to the trustee?***

You can let the trustee decide, but you should give the trustee guidelines
for determining your family's needs. Factors to be considered are the
standard of living you want for your family, the provisions another
person might make in similar circumstances, and how much you wish to
contribute toward education and other special expenses. This is known
as a discretionary trust.

***Raymond would like to establish a trust fund five years from now
and have one third of his salary put into the trust each year
thereafter. Can he have the trust agreement drawn up now?***

No. His expectation of future salary cannot be used to create a trust fund.
A trust must contain assets that currently exist. However, he could put a

● Reducing income tax liability. By putting assets into an irrevocable trust
(one that cannot be changed), you give up ownership of the property.
One result of this action is that you may no longer be required to pay
taxes on the income it produces. The trust itself—or perhaps the
beneficiaries of the trust, who may be in a lower tax bracket—will
generally pay those taxes.
● Passing property to others without the delays of probate required by a
will. Following the terms of the agreement, the trustee of a living trust can
distribute its money or property to your heirs after your death without
going to court.
● Keeping the details of how you divided your estate from becoming
public knowledge. Probate proceedings are public records, and anyone
can go to the courthouse and review a probate file to find out how an
estate was distributed. But living trust agreements are private documents
and are not open to public scrutiny.

Establishing Trusts

small sum into a trust fund now and reserve the right to transfer additional assets into it in the future.

Claudia never married and has no close relatives. If she sets up a trust fund, can she name friends as the beneficiaries?

Yes, but she should not designate them simply as "friends." They must be clearly identified by name. If the description of the beneficiaries is too vague, the trust will not be valid.

Daniel has a trust agreement that names Marietta as the beneficiary. Can he amend this to make Clarissa the beneficiary?

Only if a right to amend the trust is included in the trust document. Otherwise, he would have to obtain the written consent of all persons involved, including Marietta—who may be unwilling to give up the income she would receive from the trust. In certain circumstances —if, for example, Marietta showed gross ingratitude or otherwise gave Daniel reason to drop her as a beneficiary—he could apply to the courts to have the beneficiary changed to Clarissa.

Anita did not include in her trust agreement any instructions for its termination. What if she wants to change the trust?

She would have to get the written consent of everyone involved. Without this consent, a trust cannot be terminated, revoked, or amended unless that power is specifically given in the trust agreement. Under certain circumstances a court would allow changes to be made in the trust.

If a trust is set up for Monica's support until she is 18 years old, are there any circumstances in which she can get all the trust money outright before she is 18?

Probably not. Any attempt to defeat the purpose of a trust must be approved by the beneficiary. Because Monica is not of legal age (18 or 19, depending on the province), she could not legally give her approval to terminating the trust. However, if she marries before she reaches the legal age and that marriage makes her an adult in the eyes of the law of her province, she may be able to get an early distribution of funds from the trust. In all provinces except Alberta, Manitoba and Ontario, a trust may be terminated if all the beneficiaries agree.

The Role of the Trustee

What is a trustee, and what are his duties and responsibilities?

A trustee, whether a person, a bank, or other institution, agrees to hold the property of another person in safekeeping for one or more beneficiaries named by the property owner, and must administer the trust in accordance with the trust agreement. In addition to any specific instructions, a trustee must keep the trust property separate from his own property, invest the property, protect it with insurance, keep accurate financial records, pay income to the beneficiaries, deal impartially with all beneficiaries, and seek the advice of experts in investing or managing the trust property. To protect the trust, most provinces permit the trustee to engage in only certain types of investment.

How do I know that the trustee for my children's inheritance will not use some of the money for his own benefit?

Minimize the possibility by choosing a trustee who has earned your confidence. To be doubly sure, require the trustee to purchase a bond that would be forfeited if he didn't carry out his duties properly. You are also protected by the law. If the trustee takes money from the trust for his own use, he can be removed and charged with theft. Any profits he made while misusing trust funds would become part of the trust.

Shay wants to set up a trust for his children. Can he name himself as the trustee?

Yes, if he meets the qualifications in his province. Generally, a trustee need only be competent to carry out the duties specified in the trust.

Does the trustee have to live in the same province as I do?

No. However, some provinces may require the nonresident trustee to appoint a resident agent who can be served with writs, summonses, and other legal documents and who may also have to post a bond.

Can a trustee be fired for doing a poor job?

An incompetent trustee may be fired or removed by the court upon application of the trust's beneficiaries and upon proof of mismanagement. He will also have to forfeit his commissions, and he may have to reimburse the trust for any losses suffered through his mismanagement.

The Role of the Trustee

The trustee named in Nathan's will died four months after his appointment. Does the trust end automatically?

Not unless Nathan specifically indicated that the only person who could serve as trustee was the one he named. Otherwise, the court will appoint someone to fulfill the duties of the trustee who died or the public trustee will take charge.

Isabel set up a trust for her son Floyd, naming Greg as the trustee even though Floyd and Greg never got along. After his mother's death, can Floyd challenge the appointment of Greg as trustee?

Floyd can challenge the appointment, but he may not succeed. Tension or hostility between the trustee and beneficiary is usually not sufficient reason to remove a trustee. However, if it can be shown that Greg would be unable to administer the trust properly because of his hostility to Floyd, the court might consider denying Greg's appointment as trustee.

Robin is the beneficiary of a trust for which Gilbert is the trustee. Gilbert just sold himself some of the trust property at a price below the market value. What if Gilbert continues to do this?

Robin should seek legal advice immediately. Gilbert has violated his duty as trustee by placing his interests above those of the beneficiary. Robin should ask that Gilbert be removed as trustee. She can also ask that the sale be voided and that Gilbert's expenses and commissions be denied. She may even get the court to make Gilbert pay her punitive damages — an amount of money over and above what he cheated her of, as punishment for the wrong he did.

Changing or Revoking Your Will

My wife and I would like to make some changes to wills we made three years ago. Must we write entirely new wills?

Not necessarily. If the changes are minor, you could simply have your lawyer add codicils, or amendments. If major revisions are required, however, it is better to have the wills completely redrafted to eliminate possible confusion. If you want to cut out certain heirs, or change the amount of money an heir will receive, you should revoke the old wills and make entirely new ones.

Are there problems in using a codicil to change a will?

Not if it is prepared, signed, and witnessed according to the same formalities followed in drawing up the basic will. However, the codicil must be worded carefully to make clear the nature of the change—whether some provision of the will is being revoked, a new provision is being added, or an existing provision is being modified.

The will and codicil must be kept together. If they are separated and no one knows about the codicil, the terms of the will could be carried out without the changes designated in the codicil; thus the estate would not be distributed according to the wishes of the person who made the will.

Pierre made a will leaving his estate equally to his son and daughter. Following an argument, he scratched out a paragraph and wrote on it that he wanted his estate to go exclusively to his son. Pierre died two weeks later. Is his change valid?

No. All changes in a will must be made with the same formalities used in making a new will. Whenever a part of a will is crossed out, it makes the validity of the entire will questionable. So by marking through a portion of the will, Pierre risked not only having the revision disregarded, but also having the entire will revoked. Changes should always be made in a codicil, or amendment, or by drawing up a new will.

How can I revoke my will?

Every province has its own law specifying how a person can revoke his will, whether the person wants to revoke the whole will or only part of it. Generally, you can (1) prepare a new will stating that all previous wills are revoked; (2) prepare a codicil, or amendment, that revokes part of the existing will; or (3) destroy the old will by tearing or burning the original document and all copies.

Hildegard's father revoked his will by tearing it up and stating, "I want you to have everything, Hildegard. I don't want to leave anything to your brother." Is this a valid revocation of a will?

The act of tearing up the document was a valid way for Hildegard's father to revoke his will. Furthermore, his statement that he did not wish to leave anything to his son made it clear that destroying the will was not an accident, but was intended. However, for Hildegard to receive the entire estate, her father will have to draft a new will that leaves everything to her and specifically disinherits her brother. Otherwise the brother and sister will share the estate equally.

Changing or Revoking Your Will

When You Should Change Your Will

Because wills do not have expiration dates, one drawn up when a person was 20 would still be valid when he died at 85. But life is full of changes, and a will should be reviewed every two or three years to make certain that it still reflects your wishes. You should also review your will and revise it, if necessary, when any of the following occur:

- Your marital status changes. When you marry, you may want to include your spouse, just as in the case of divorce, you may want his or her name deleted from your will and insurance policies.
- You have a child or adopt one. Provincial laws may allow a child to claim a share of your estate even though he is not mentioned in your will, but it might not grant him as big a share as you would wish.
- An executor, guardian, or trustee dies or can no longer fulfill his duties because of poor health or some other reason.
- The needs of your heirs change. For example, if one of your children marries and has children or your spouse becomes seriously ill, or an heir gets into serious financial difficulties, you may want to leave more to him or her than you originally intended.
- The amount of assets in your estate changes drastically.
- You no longer own something you left to someone in your will.
- Trusts you established for your young children are no longer needed, because the children are now on their own.
- Changes are made in any law affecting your estate.

My will names my sister as executrix, but she died last year. Do I have to write a new will now?

If you don't revise the will, the court will appoint someone else to handle your estate. But you don't have to draw up a whole new will. Instead, you could prepare a codicil, or amendment, that names the new person you want to serve as executor.

Contesting a Will

My sister died six weeks ago and didn't leave me anything, even though I was her only remaining relative. Can I contest her will?

Not unless you have some proof that your sister was incompetent when she made her will or that someone used undue influence to make her write the will in his favor. One's status as sister or brother does not, by itself, give one the right to challenge a will; no law requires a person to provide for his brothers or sisters in his will. In some cases, however, a court may try to ascertain the true intention of the testator. For example, if your sister was very old and often forgot things, if she told you and other people that she would leave you certain property, if you enjoyed a good relationship with your sister, and if she drew up the will herself, you may challenge the document on the grounds of error.

Harvey told his niece, Myrtle, that he would leave her his house if she would move in and nurse him through his final illness. She did. When Harvey died two years later, there was no mention of her in his will. Would it do her any good to challenge the will?

No. An oral statement cannot be used to revoke an existing will. The two years between Harvey's promise and his death allowed him ample opportunity to name Myrtle in his will, if that was indeed his intention. However, Myrtle may be able to sue Harvey's estate for the value of the services she provided him during his final illness.

Clifford's housekeeper turned him against his children and Clifford, a widower, disinherited them and left everything to the housekeeper. Can the children contest the will?

Yes, but they would have to show that the housekeeper used undue influence over Clifford and that there was a connection between her influence and Clifford's decision to cut the children out of his will. For example, if the children could show that their father was so smitten with the housekeeper that he would do anything she asked, and that she deliberately manipulated him into changing his will in her favor, a court might declare the will invalid.

My ex-husband had a child with his new wife. When he died, he left his entire estate to her and their child. Aren't the children from his marriage to me legally entitled to a share of his estate?

Not necessarily. A spouse (but not an ex-spouse) is sometimes legally protected from being cut out of a will, but the law does not provide the same protection for children. If your ex-husband's will explicitly states that he wishes to leave nothing to his children by you, the courts will probably uphold the will. But if he does not mention the children at all, they may challenge the will on the grounds that they were unintentionally left out. If a court rules in their favor, they may be awarded the same amount they would have received if their father had died without a will.

Contesting a Will

Phil's will provides that Shirley is to receive his 1987 Ferrari. But he has now traded in the car for a 1989 Ferrari. If Phil dies, does Shirley get the new car?

Probably not, since it is not the car designated in the will. When a specific item is no longer in the giver's estate when he dies, the bequest is said to have been adeemed by extinction. If Phil's will had simply left Shirley "my Ferrari," without mentioning the model, she would have received the 1989 car.

Tim's will provided that his farm be sold and the proceeds divided among his children, but before he died, he sold the farm for $375,000—$100,000 down, the rest in six months. Do his children have any claim to the $100,000 and the $275,000 balance due?

Yes. The gift Taylor made to his children was not the farm itself, but the proceeds from the sale of the farm. As long as these proceeds are identifiable, the children are entitled to receive them.

While backing his car, Ed accidentally killed his uncle Fred who, it turned out, had willed Ed $5,000. Can Fred's son stop Ed getting the money because he caused his benefactor's death?

Probably not. Although Ed caused his uncle's death, he did not do so intentionally. The death resulted from an accident. Fred's son could prevent Ed from receiving his inheritance only if he could prove that Ed intentionally killed his father.

Hattie had poor eyesight and asked her brother, Gus, to help her draft a will. Gus had the will typed up, substituting himself as the main heir rather than his sister Hester. Hattie signed the will and had it properly witnessed. Can Hester challenge this will?

Yes. Gus has committed a fraud. A will drawn up as a result of fraud can be challenged and declared void.

If the court agrees with Terry's claim that her uncle was not competent to make a will, how will his estate be distributed?

If the court declares the will invalid, Terry's uncle would be considered to have died without a will. Provincial law would then dictate how the property would be distributed. Every province has a descent-and-distribution law that outlines which relatives have priority in inheriting property and what percentage of the estate they will receive.

What steps are necessary to contest a will?

The person or persons contesting a will must go to court and file a petition stating the grounds for their action—for example, fraud, undue influence, or lack of competence by the maker of the will. A hearing is held to determine whether the objections are sufficient to deny the validity of the will. Only the people affected by the will can contest it.

Some of my mother's relatives want to contest a provision in her will. Will this delay my inheritance and my being able to pay for funeral and burial expenses?

Yes. Until the court determines the validity of the will and allows the estate to be settled, no one is authorized to pay the heirs any of their inheritance. The executor of the will is usually limited to collecting debts owed to the estate and preserving property while the will is being contested. If you are the executor of your mother's estate, ask a lawyer or the probate judge what duties you can and cannot perform while the will is being contested. Some provinces allow the executor to administer the estate during litigation, but to administer does not allow for the distribution of the assets. It may include the payment of funeral expenses, however. To be certain, the executor should apply to the court for permission to pay these expenses.

When There Is No Will

Gil died without making a will. He left a wife, one son, and two granddaughters who are the children of a deceased daughter. How will the property be distributed?

The widow will receive one third to one half of the estate, depending on the law in Gil's province. The remainder would usually be divided equally among his children. But since his daughter is dead, the two granddaughters will divide the share that would have gone to their mother. Thus Gil's son will get half what remains after Gil's widow has received her share, and the granddaughters will divide the other half.

When someone dies without a will, he is said to die intestate. Each province has descent-and-distribution laws that specify the percentage of the estate that each heir is to receive when a person dies intestate.

When There Is No Will

Sue and Ron had a son a year before they were married. Ron died without making a will. Can his son inherit part of his estate?

Most provinces have now abolished the distinction between legitimate and illegitimate children, thus giving them equal rights of inheritance. But even if this is not the case in Ron's province, his son became a legitimate offspring, with a right of inheritance, when Ron and Sue married.

What happens to the estate of a person who dies without making a will and has no living relatives?

It goes to the Crown after provincial court proceedings in which any possible claimants have the opportunity to present their cases.

John and Annie never made wills. Both were killed recently in a car accident. Will immediate family members get custody of their four young children or will the youngsters become the responsibility of the state?

The Children's Aid Society and the court will try to find relatives to serve as guardians before turning to someone outside the family. The court may appoint one guardian to provide daily care of the children and another to handle financial matters.

Settling an Estate

What is probate?

Probate is the process by which a special court, often known as surrogate court, establishes that a will is valid and legal, and then oversees the administration of a deceased person's estate. It (1) grants authority to the executor named in the will to administer the estate; (2) supervises and receives reports from the executor; (3) makes sure the executor settles all bills, taxes, and other claims against the estate; (4) sees to it that the executor distributes the remaining assets to the rightful heirs; and (5) closes the estate and releases the executor from further obligations. If there is no will, the probate court appoints an administrator to handle the estate. Any contestation or any demand for removal of an executor or for an accounting of the administration is heard before the probate court.

What an Executor Has to Do

After the person who made the will has died, the executor generally goes to probate court with the lawyer who wrote the will. Once the court has ruled that the will is valid and has authorized the executor to do business for the estate, he then:

1. Opens a chequing account, with printed cheques showing the names of the estate and the executor. All money received by the estate should be deposited in this account, and all expenses paid from it.

2. Conducts an inventory of the contents of any safe-deposit boxes. A representative from the bank or other financial institution may have to be present at the opening of the safe-deposit boxes.

3. Obtains extra copies of the death certificate to use in processing life insurance claims and settling other legal matters.

4. Files a change of address with the post office so that all mail for the deceased person is forwarded to the executor.

5. Publishes notice of his appointment as executor in local newspapers so that creditors will know that they should present their claims against the estate to him. The law in each province determines which publications should carry the notice and how often.

6. Obtains appraisals on real estate and valuable personal property, such as antiques, art, or jewelry, and makes sure they are adequately insured. Rents a safe-deposit box for the jewelry and other small items.

7. Processes claims for life and medical insurance.

8. Applies for any benefits to which the estate is entitled, including Canada (or Quebec) Pension Plan survivor benefits, and company, union, or veterans' benefits.

9. Reregisters stocks, bonds, and other securities in the estate's name.

10. Pursues on behalf of the estate any lawsuits or legal claims that were pending when the person who made the will died.

11. Prepares a list of the estate's assets, including cash on hand or in bank accounts, real estate, personal property, investments, life insurance, business interests, and debts owed to the deceased.

12. Invests funds for maximum return or sells assets to generate additional income, as required by the needs of the estate, paying close attention to the types of investment allowed by provincial law.

13. Pays all the estate's bills, including those for medical care, burial, and administering the estate; settles any leases; takes care of any claims presented by other creditors.

14. Prepares tax returns and pays any amounts due for federal and provincial income taxes.

15. Submits to the probate court an accounting of all the transactions handled for the estate and a schedule for distributing the property.

16. Distributes the property and gets receipts from the heirs.

17. Applies to the court for a discharge, which terminates his authority and releases him from liability to the estate's heirs and creditors.

Settling an Estate

Is it possible to probate a will without a lawyer?

Yes. A lawyer is not legally required to probate a will and settle an estate, and if the estate is a simple one, the executor named in the will should be able to comply with probate court requirements without hiring a lawyer. Many provinces have simplified probate procedures for handling small estates and there are books that give step-by-step instructions on how to probate a will. For large estates a lawyer is almost a necessity.

Before Anthony's father died, he willed everything to Anthony. Since there are no other heirs, can Anthony just take possession of the property without going through probate?

No. All wills, except notarial wills in Quebec, must be probated. Perhaps there *are* other heirs. If the will proves to be invalid because of a defect in form—for example, his signature was witnessed by only one witness—then even distant relatives may have certain rights as heirs.

Can my widowed niece sell her husband's car without going to probate court?

If the car was in her husband's name only, she will have to go through probate. But if she owned the car jointly with her husband with right of survivorship, some provinces would allow the car to become her property without going through probate. The widow would have to present a copy of the will, the death certificate, and proof of insurance to the motor vehicle bureau before transfer would be made.

Can a photostatic copy of a valid will be probated?

A probate court will not accept a photocopy as valid unless evidence is presented to show that the original document was inadvertently lost or destroyed, and that a thorough search for it has been made. Whenever the original will cannot be shown in court, the law presumes that it was intentionally revoked by being destroyed.

Maxine knows that her husband prepared a will, but after his death she could not find it. What can she do?

She must prove that the will was made and what it contained. If she cannot, the court will assume that her husband revoked his will by destroying it and will distribute his estate as though he had died intestate. Evidence of the existence of the will and its contents could include testimony from those who witnessed it and the lawyer who drafted it.

This problem does not arise with notarial wills in Quebec, since the notary always keeps a copy. In other provinces, the lawyer who made the will may have a signed true copy in his files.

My husband and I live in Ontario but spend every winter in Florida. Where will our estates have to be settled?

Since your permanent home is in Ontario, your will should go through an Ontario probate court. However, if you own real estate in Florida, that property must go through the Florida probate court. As a general rule, movable property such as furniture, money, securities, automobiles and jewelry is distributed according to the law of the testator's domicile, in this case Ontario. Immovable property—land and buildings—is governed by the law where it is situated. You should make sure that your will concerning immovable property in Florida fulfills all the requirements of Florida law.

If a husband and wife do not have wills and one dies, are all properties, investments, and bank accounts frozen until the matter goes to probate court?

In all provinces except Quebec, the probate or surrogate court would appoint an administrator and all funds would be frozen until a clearance certificate was issued by Revenue Canada. The administrator could apply to the court for the release of a small amount of money to pay for such things as the funeral and burial costs. In Quebec there would be no probate, since there was no will and the spouse could act as the administrator of the estate. Except for amounts up to $3,000, all the assets are frozen until a certificate is received from Revenue Quebec stating that no income tax is owing.

What happens if a husband and wife are killed in, say, a plane crash and it is impossible to determine who died first?

Every province and Territory has survivorship rules—laws that deal with the presumed order of death. In most provinces, the younger person is presumed to have survived the older. In Quebec the parties are considered to have died at the same time. If one party was observed to have survived the other, if only for a few moments, these presumptions do not apply.

Settling an Estate

How long does an executor have to settle an estate?

In most provinces, one year. This "executor's year" may be prolonged indefinitely by a clause in the will to the effect that the executor is appointed for a period beyond a year and a day.

Must an executor be paid for his services?

Generally, yes. The amount or rate of compensation is either fixed by provincial law or left to the discretion of the probate court. It is usually in the range of 2½ to 5 percent of the gross value of the estate. The maker of the will can even specify the amount of compensation in the will, and if the sum is reasonable, the probate court will probably approve it. However, an executor can waive his right to receive any payment. In Quebec it is presumed that the executor will perform his duties gratuitously, unless the testator has, in his will, provided for payment.

Pearl was named executor of her aunt's estate, but she doesn't think she can handle the responsibility. Can she decline to serve?

Yes. Pearl should file a renunciation with the probate court, stating that she does not want to serve as executor. If her aunt named a contingent executor, he will handle the estate in Pearl's place; otherwise the court will appoint someone. When making a will, you should ensure that the person to be named executor is willing to take on the job. It is also a good idea to name a contingent executor in case the named executor is unable to serve.

Can the executor buy assets from the estate?

Yes, but the law limits his right to do so, to prevent any unfairness to the heirs that might occur when the buyer and seller are the same person. Court approval may be necessary, and the heirs may have to be notified of the executor's intention to buy assets, or the executor may be limited to making purchases at public sales only.

Is the executor of Bella's estate right to refuse Alma the money Bella left her until Revenue Canada has been paid?

Yes. The executor should not give anything to Bella's heirs until he has determined the amount of all the debts and taxes to be paid, and has received a clearance certificate from Revenue Canada (in Quebec, from Revenue Quebec). If the executor gives the heirs what was left them and later discovers that there are insufficient funds remaining in the estate to pay debts and taxes, he could be held personally liable for the payment of these claims.

What happens if there isn't enough money in my estate to pay taxes, burial expenses, and remaining debts?

Creditors have a right to be paid before any money or property is distributed to heirs so when the cash in an estate has been used up, the executor must begin selling other assets to pay the remaining obligations. Each province designates which debts receive priority, and the order in which property will be used or sold to pay these debts. Funeral expenses, the costs of closing the estate, and unpaid income taxes get priority.

Can an executor ever be held liable for the estate's taxes?

Yes. If an executor fails to pay the estate taxes or if he pays other debts that have a lower priority and then doesn't have enough money to pay the taxes, he could become liable for paying them out of his own pocket.

Can children force their surviving parent to sell the family home to finance their share of the inheritance?

No. Most provinces protect the matrimonial home, enabling the surviving spouse to claim it as personal property.

My father's will directs his executor to sell the real estate he owned and distribute the proceeds among his children. My brothers and sisters and I have all agreed that it would be better financially to keep the property. Can we stop the executor from selling the real estate?

You could ask the probate court to approve a family settlement agreement. This is a document signed by all the heirs, agreeing to changes in the provisions of a will. If the judge finds that all persons involved have willingly agreed to keep the property, he may incorporate this agreement into the final settlement. The judge would probably consider it was the intention of the testator to benefit his children as he could, and if keeping the property would best benefit them, the judge would probably allow the change to the will.

Settling an Estate

Herman received a bill for merchandise that his father had ordered and received several weeks before he died. How should Herman handle this?

He should turn the bill over to the executor of his father's estate. The executor will then verify that Herman's father ordered the merchandise and that it was received. Swindlers have been known to deliver or send bills for merchandise that was never ordered.

After her mother died, Trisha received a notice from a life insurance company stating that one final payment was needed in order for Trisha to receive benefits. Is this legal?

Yes, but Trisha should be cautious about this type of notice; it might not be legitimate. Con men sometimes check obituaries and contact a relative about a nonexistent life insurance policy. The unsuspecting relative pays the final premium, but never receives any insurance proceeds. Trisha should make sure that her mother did purchase a policy from this company. If the policy included an automatic premium loan provision, Trisha could request that the outstanding premium payment be deducted from the money she is to receive.

When Frank died, he owed Louis $3,000. What does Louis have to do to collect this debt?

He must submit a claim to the executor of Frank's estate. In settling the estate, the executor must publish a notice in the newspaper informing the public that he has been appointed to administer the estate and advising creditors of the deadline for making their claims. Louis should be sure he meets this deadline.

When Douglas died, a notice was published in the newspaper informing all his creditors of the deadline for filing claims against his estate. Bill was out of town and did not see this notice. Can he make a claim against the estate a year later?

Bill is too late. Failure to file a claim against the estate within the designated time limit prohibits a person from collecting his debt. Without this rule, an executor would never be able to settle an estate, because he could never be sure what outstanding debts remained. Under certain circumstances, however, Bill could apply to the court for an extension of time to file his claim.

If Bridget is named in Vern's will but she can't be located at the time the estate is settled, what happens to her share of the money?

If an heir cannot be found, the property is sold by the executor and the proceeds are deposited with the probate court or an institution authorized by the court to accept these funds. After a period determined by the law of the province, the money would go to the province.

Ruth's estate was closed in August after her house had been sold to Lloyd. When Lloyd remodeled the house in September of the following year, he discovered a tin box containing $10,000 in coins. Is it too late to distribute this money to Ruth's heirs?

No. Estates can be reopened when new assets are discovered. Any interested person could petition the court to reopen Ruth's estate. The same executor or a new one would be appointed to distribute the $10,000 in accordance with Ruth's will.

Funerals and Burials

Jessica wants to make funeral arrangements now to save her family from having to do it when she dies. Can she do this?

Yes, either with the help of a memorial (burial) society or on her own. Memorial societies, which generally charge a modest one-time membership fee, provide information about funeral and burial options and costs. These nonprofit organizations may also be able to get their members reduced rates at funeral homes.

If Jessica wants to contact funeral homes herself, she should inquire about a *pre-need plan*, under which she can prepay funeral costs. Most provinces have laws that safeguard money put into pre-need plans.

What happens if I prepay for my funeral arrangements, and the funeral home later goes out of business?

It depends on what kind of funeral home you deal with. If your funeral home is a cooperative, the money will probably be placed in a trust fund and you would get your money back. It is the law in most provinces that money received for a prearranged funeral plan is placed in a trust account with a recognized financial institution; thus, in case of the bankruptcy of the funeral home, you should get your money back with interest. Contact the association of undertakers in your province to see what arrangements apply in your case.

Funerals and Burials

Uncle Edgar prepaid his funeral costs. He died last week, and the funeral bill is $1,200 more than he had paid. Must his estate or the family pay the difference?

Not if he had a fixed-price contract. If his contract did not guarantee a fixed price, the family or the executor of his estate will have to pay the difference.

Who has the legal authority to arrange for a burial?

The spouse or the next of kin usually takes charge of burial arrangements and is legally permitted to do so. If no one steps forward to accept this responsibility, the body will be buried, or otherwise disposed of, according to provincial and local laws. Later, when the appointment of the executor has been approved by the court, the executor may be required to purchase a tombstone or monument in accordance with the will. When there is no competent relative to take charge of the funeral

Letter of Last Instructions

When a person dies, the family must make a number of decisions fairly quickly about the funeral and burial. Some people include details about these arrangements in their wills. But this is not always advisable, since the will may not be read until some time after the funeral. A better alternative is a letter of last instructions, which is a private, informal statement of what arrangements you prefer. If you write such a letter, give copies to your spouse or anyone else who may be responsible for handling final arrangements. Keep the original in an easily accessible place that the family knows about. Do not put it in a safe-deposit box. The letter should give the following information:

☑ Disposition of the body—whether you prefer to have your body buried, cremated, or donated to medical science, either the whole body or certain specified organs.

☑ Where the funeral service should be held.

☑ Whether you wish your body to be exposed.

☑ A list of speakers and music for the funeral.

☑ The kinds of flowers you prefer.

☑ If contributions are preferred to flowers, the names of the organizations to which the contributions should be sent.

☑ Details about any funeral plan that has been purchased in advance or other funds that have been set aside for final arrangements.

and burial arrangements, the public trustee, sometimes known as the public curator, handles these matters.

To spare her children the expense and bother of arranging her funeral, Gladys is thinking of buying insurance to cover all the costs. Will the funeral home she selects be paid directly by the insurance company when Gladys dies?

No. If Gladys names her estate as the beneficiary of the policy, the funeral home would present its bill to the estate's executor.

I want to be cremated after I die. How can I make sure that my family will carry out my wishes?

You can't. You can clearly state your wishes to the family members or friends who will be responsible for arranging your burial, but oral or written instructions about cremation are not legally binding on your family or the executor of your estate.

Location of the family burial plot—the name and location of the cemetery, the lot, and the grave number—with the names of the cemetery authorities to notify.
Names, addresses, dates of birth, and places of birth for yourself and your spouse, children, parents, brothers and sisters, and, if you are divorced, your ex-spouse.
Name and address of your employer.
Social Insurance number and the location of your card.
Dates of service in the armed forces if you are eligible for veterans' benefits.
Biographical information for use in an obituary.
Policy numbers, insurance company names and addresses, and the location of your life insurance policies.
Information on union benefits, company profit-sharing, and other employment benefits.
Where you keep your will and the name of the person you have named as executor.
Location of your safe-deposit box.
Location of your birth and marriage certificates, prenuptial agreements, divorce papers, trust agreements, other personal documents, deeds, stocks and bonds.
Names and addresses of all banks and other financial institutions you have dealings with.

Funerals and Burials

*My mother is in the last stage of a terminal illness. Can I get the
information I need to compare funeral costs and procedures over
the telephone without actually having to visit funeral homes?*

Yes. Most funeral homes would be glad to describe the range of services
they provide and the cost. Since this is a time of great stress for you,
make sure that you are not intimidated into feeling "cheap" if you do not
select the most elaborate coffin and funeral arrangements.

*If a funeral home offers a package price, can we save money by
excluding some of the services offered in the package?*

Yes. Services can be elaborate or modest, according to your instructions.
If you wish, the funeral home will place a death notice in the local
newspaper, inform distant relatives by telegram, arrange for a casket
and flowers, supply automobiles for the family, and so on. If you
undertake any of these tasks, your bill would be reduced accordingly.
Cremation is usually the least expensive means of disposition as no
embalming or casket is necessary.

Do undertakers and funeral directors have to be licensed?

Yes. Each province has laws and regulations governing the funeral and
burial industry. Also, every undertaker must belong to the provincial
association which monitors the industry's business practices.

*Brandon lives in Quebec but wants to be buried in his family
plot in Manitoba. Are there legal regulations about transporting
a body?*

Yes. Provincial laws govern the transportation of a dead body. Usually
your funeral director can arrange for the necessary permits, probably
including a certificate from the provincial minister of health. Each
province has regulations about the disinterment of bodies to be rebur-
ied elsewhere.

Can a ship's captain conduct a burial at sea?

If the body cannot be safely preserved and transported to shore, the
captain has the legal right to conduct a burial at sea. In most situations,
however, it will be delivered to a port, where relatives can claim it.

Are there time limits within which a body must be buried?

Under provincial laws, burial is usually not permitted within 12 hours of death and must take place "within a reasonable time after death." The burial of an embalmed or refrigerated body may usually be delayed to enable the family to make the necessary arrangements.

Is it true that all bodies have to be embalmed?

No. Each province has laws about embalming, but in general it is not required unless (1) the burial is delayed, (2) the person died from a communicable disease, or (3) the body is being transported any considerable distance. Nor is embalming required if the body is to be cremated.

My father asked to be cremated. Must we provide a casket?

No. Usually the ashes are placed in an urn, mostly made of wood but often of plastic, marble, bronze, copper and increasingly of porcelain, which is then buried or stored in a columbarium, a cemetery vault with recesses for urns. The type of urn and the position in the columbarium (a lower or higher recess) determine the cost.

Katrina requested that she be cremated after death and her ashes scattered on the mountains in another province. Would Katrina's family be within the law if they followed her wishes?

It depends on the laws of the province where the ashes are to be scattered. Some provinces—and cities—restrict to specific areas the scattering of ashes from human remains. Check with the ministry of health of the province where you wish to scatter the ashes.

If I buy a cemetery plot, does the purchase price include maintenance of the gravesite?

Usually not. Maintenance of the plot, which may include the planting of flowers, forms a separate contract or can be done by family or friends.

When is an autopsy mandatory?

A coroner orders an autopsy whenever the cause of death is unknown. Autopsies are usually required to establish the cause of death in violent, unexplained, or suspicious circumstances. An autopsy is usually manda-tory in the death of a prisoner.

Although Jennifer seemed in excellent health, she died quietly in her sleep the other night. The coroner has ordered that an autopsy be performed on her remains. Can this be done without the consent of her next of kin?

Any coroner may proceed with an autopsy without consent if he believes that the death was unusual or suspicious. An autopsy is often ordered when someone who appeared in good health dies suddenly.

Conrad and his family recently purchased a large tract of land and they would like to establish a family cemetery on part of the property. Will they be able to do so?

Very probably not. At one time, owners were free to establish family cemeteries on their land, but this is no longer the case. Zoning and other municipal ordinances usually strictly limit the location of private ceme-teries and put restrictions on who can establish and maintain them.

What to Do When a Loved One Dies

One of the most difficult circumstances a person may ever have to face is the death of a relative or close friend. In addition to the emotional impact of the death, there are many hard decisions that must be made, some of them right away. The following list may be helpful if you are responsible for making these decisions:

- If someone dies at home, you can contact the family doctor or the police or an ambulance service for assistance. If the deceased person had recently been under a doctor's care or had a history of illnesses such as cancer or heart disease, the family doctor will generally sign the death certificate.
- If the death was sudden or occurred under suspicious circumstances, call the police. If an investigation is needed, they will arrange to have the coroner or medical examiner determine the cause of death.
- If death occurs in a hospital, the attending physician will sign the death certificate. An autopsy may be needed if the cause of death is unknown.
- After the immediate formalities have been completed, call a funeral director to arrange for transportation of the body to a funeral home.

Ethan obtained a family plot after his mother had been buried elsewhere. What must he do to have his mother's body moved from one cemetery to another?

He must follow the procedures set by the laws of his province. He will need the permission of authorities at both cemeteries, and possibly the consent of other members of his family. If consent cannot be obtained, he can seek court approval to have his mother's body moved to the family plot. He will also require a certificate from the provincial health minister confirming that his mother did not die of a contagious disease.

Uncle Harold and Aunt Constance have equally eccentric wishes. He wants to be buried at the wheel of his favorite Rolls Royce; she wants her Lhasa apso put to sleep and buried with her. They want me to ensure their wishes are carried out. Will this be possible?

The person in charge of carrying out a deceased's last wishes should keep dignity, legality and good taste in mind. To have your aunt's dog killed and buried with her would contravene all three criteria. Fulfilling your uncle's wishes would violate two, since being buried with his Rolls Royce is probably not illegal but it is certainly wasteful. If Uncle Harold was buried with the steering wheel of his car included in his coffin, the spirit of his wishes would be fulfilled.

- Find out what funeral and burial arrangements should be made. The person who died may have supplied this information in a letter of last instructions or his will. Otherwise, close relatives or the lawyer who drafted the will may know what arrangements were preferred.
- If the person belonged to a memorial or burial society, notify a representative of that society.
- Plan the memorial service and final disposition of the body.
- Notify friends and relatives. The funeral home will help you prepare an obituary for newspaper publication.
- Obtain copies of the death certificate. The executor will need them to administer the estate. The funeral home will probably have copies made if you request it.
- Give the will to the person named executor of the estate so that he can begin to assume his duties in settling the legal aspects of the estate.
- If there is burial insurance, notify the insurance company or its agent. Make a list of any other burial benefits that may be available from the Veterans Affairs office, a labor union, or a fraternal organization. Application for these benefits should be made by the funeral home, executor, or the person responsible for paying these expenses.

Funerals and Burials

***Uncle Jonathan served overseas during the war. My aunt says he
is entitled to a burial payment. How do we apply for this money?***

Your aunt should write to Veterans Affairs Canada for information about
possible burial benefits. Concerning pension benefits, she can write to
Pay Services, Department of National Defence, 101 Colonel By Drive,
Ottawa, Ont., K1A 0K2. If your uncle was receiving a pension, your aunt
and her children are probably eligible for continuing benefits.

***Two of my soldier uncles were killed in France in World War II
and are buried there. Where can I get information about the
cemetery or cemeteries where they are buried?***

The Commonwealth War Graves Commission keeps records and maintains the graves of all Commonwealth soldiers overseas. You can write to
the Commonwealth War Graves Commission at 284 Wellington Street,
Ottawa, Ont., K1A 0P4.

Victims and Crimes

If You Are a Victim

For courtroom procedures, see Chapter 18, *Going to Court.*

If I am the victim of a crime, do I have a legal duty to report the crime to the police?

No. The law does not require a victim to report a crime to the police. However, reporting the crime would (1) make it possible for the victim to receive compensation from the Provincial Crime Victims Indemnity Program (all provinces and both Territories have one); (2) establish details that may be required by his insurance company; and (3) help bring a criminal to justice.

It is a serious offense knowingly to make a false statement accusing an innocent person of having committed a crime, or to report a crime that did not happen. It is also against the law to offer a reward for the return of stolen property or to offer immunity from prosecution (say that no questions will be asked, for example) to the person who returns such stolen property.

Graham parked his car at a shopping mall while he shopped for a new coat. When he returned, the car had been vandalized. What will happen once he notifies the police?

The police will ask Graham to provide important information—such as when he last saw the car, when he discovered the damage, where the car was parked when it was damaged, and whether he or anyone else witnessed the crime—and to sign a sworn statement attesting that the information is true. If a suspect is arrested and prosecuted, Graham will be asked to testify at the trial. Even if the vandal is a minor (under 18 years of age), once he is convicted, the court may order him to reimburse Graham for the damage to his car.

Should Graham receive compensation from his insurance company, he could still sue the vandal in civil court for all damage and loss not covered by the insurance company.

After being robbed in her apartment by a knife-wielding assailant, Nicole reported the crime to the police. How will she be expected to cooperate during the investigation?

Nicole will be asked to give a statement describing what happened. She may also be shown mug shots or be taken to a lineup and asked to identify the robber. If a suspect is charged with the crime, Nicole will probably be interviewed again by both the prosecutor and the defense lawyer. When the suspect comes to trial, Nicole will be asked to testify about the robbery.

Some neighborhood kids slashed the screens on Jake's porch while he was away on vacation. Jake's neighbor, Luke, witnessed the incident and told Jake who did it. Can Jake make the police arrest the children who are responsible?

No. A private citizen has no legal right to force the police to make an arrest—even when he is the victim of a crime or can identify the offenders. Since Jake did not actually see who slashed his porch screens, his testimony is secondary or hearsay evidence, which is not sufficient for legal purposes. Jake's best bet is to persuade Luke, who was an eyewitness, to go to the police and lay charges against those responsible for the deed.

Tara called the police to complain that her husband, Rod, was hitting her. When an officer arrived at their house, Tara asked him to arrest Rod, but he refused and told the couple to sit down and work out their differences. Tara feels that the officer neglected his duty. What can she do?

Tara should seek advice from a lawyer or a citizens' group concerned with preventing family violence. If she decides to sue the police department for not arresting her husband, she may have a good chance of winning the lawsuit. She could claim that her right to security of the person and her right to equal protection under the law, guaranteed by the Canadian Charter of Rights and Freedoms, have been violated.

Attitudes toward domestic violence have changed considerably in recent years—most communities now have crisis centers and other programs to help victims of this crime. Nowadays, too, most policemen would lay charges against Tara's husband and proceed with the case even if Tara decided not to press charges.

Abraham's home has an alarm that is connected to the nearest police station. The alarm sounded during a burglary, but the police didn't respond until long after the thief had fled. Can Abraham successfully sue the police?

Probably not. Although the police have a duty to protect the public, this does not make them liable when an individual suffers as a result of their actions or their failure to act. The judge hearing the case would consider all the circumstances—the number of police available to respond to the crime, the number of minutes the burglar was in Abraham's house, the time needed for the nearest available policemen to reach the house and so on. In order to succeed in his action, Abraham would have to prove that the police either committed a fault (tort) in not acting sooner, or that they were negligent.

If You Are a Victim

Leah was mugged six months ago, but the police still haven't found a suspect. How long can Leah expect the police to search?

There is no minimum or maximum amount of time allowed for a criminal investigation. Generally, the police will continue their investigation as long as there are leads to follow. Since Leah's case may receive less and less priority as time goes by, she should keep in touch with the police to check on the status of their investigation. Once a suspect is found, however, the police will have to put him on trial within a reasonable time.

I haven't heard a word from the police since the day my home was burglarized. Don't they have a duty to keep me informed about the progress of their investigation?

No. The police are under no legal obligation to keep the victim informed about the progress of the investigation. However, many police departments will do so anyway because the success of their investigation frequently depends on the victim's cooperation.

Programs Available to Victims of Violent Crime

Most communities have organizations to help victims of violent crime. Some programs are privately funded; others have been set up with government support. While programs may vary somewhat from one community to another, they generally offer some or all of the following services:

- Free legal counseling.
- Free shelters for battered women and their children.
- Emotional support for people in crisis situations.
- Referral to psychological or psychiatric counseling services to help overcome the trauma of the crime.
- Mediation services if appropriate.
- Courtroom support for victims who must testify or otherwise attend court.
- Group therapy sessions with other victims of crime.

To contact these groups, or to find out what programs are available, call your local YW or YMCA, police department, or social service agency. Every province and Territory also has its own criminal injuries compensation program that provides financial support for victims who suffered financial loss or temporary or permanent impairment or who are not able to work because of a crime.

Hazel's purse was stolen by her sister's 16-year-old son, who is a drug addict. Hazel's father insists that, if she really wanted to help her nephew straighten out his life, she would press charges against him. What does this mean?

When a person presses charges, he agrees to cooperate with the authorities in all phases of their prosecution of an accused person. The process begins with "the laying of an information" (swearing that certain details which compose a crime are true) in writing before a justice of the peace, and may involve many other actions and much time. Attendance at a preliminary inquiry and at a trial and interviews with the police and prosecutors would likely be necessary.

Pressing charges at this stage of her nephew's life might help keep him from committing other and more serious offenses. Because of the boy's age, the judge can rule that Hazel's nephew get treatment for his addiction; the case would be dealt with in a confidential manner.

My neighbor refuses to return the lawn mower he borrowed from me. I want the prosecuting attorney to press charges for me, but he has denied my request. Can I force him to take action?

No. There is no way to force a public prosecutor to bring criminal charges against someone. However, if you think the prosecuting lawyer is abusing the power of his office by refusing to bring charges, you may report him to your provincial attorney general's office. The attorney general has the authority to overrule the prosecuting lawyer's decision not to press charges. In any case, you can still sue your neighbor in civil court, or hire your own lawyer to prosecute the case on your behalf. Private prosecutions, however, are allowed only in minor or summary conviction offenses.

I would certainly like to see the man who robbed me in a bank holdup get put away, but I'm a little nervous about identifying him in a lineup. What will it be like?

To protect your identity, the lineup will be arranged so that its members cannot see you, even though you can see them. The lineup will include the suspect and several other people whose physical appearance is similar to the suspect's. As each individual steps forward, he may be instructed to speak, walk, or turn. You will be asked if you can identify your assailant and, if so, to single him out. To make sure that no one influences your decision, the suspect's lawyer may be present. If he feels that the lineup is unfair to his client in any way, he may later move to prevent your identification of the suspect from being submitted as evidence at the trial.

If You Are a Victim

The police asked Janelle to attend a lineup to identify the man who sexually assaulted her, but Janelle can't bear to look at the man again. Does she have to cooperate?

No. The victim of a crime cannot be forced to attend a lineup, and neither can the suspect be forced to participate in one. However, if Janelle refuses to participate—or if she attends the lineup and is unable to positively identify her assailant—the police may have to drop all charges against the suspect. According to recent changes in the Criminal Code, if Janelle was under 18 at the time of the offense, she would be able to testify out of court, or behind a screen or other device, so that she would not have to face her assailant at the trial.

Jim's home was burglarized while he was on vacation, and his next-door neighbor has been charged with the offense. Jim doesn't want to be responsible for his neighbor being convicted. Can the victim of a crime be required to testify at a suspect's trial?

Yes. If the prosecuting attorney considers it necessary, a victim can be subpoenaed to testify. A victim's testimony is often needed to establish that a crime occurred or to identify the suspect. But even if the victim was not present at the scene of the crime, his testimony may still be necessary. In the case of a burglary, for example, the homeowner may be asked to testify that the defendant did not have permission to be in his home or to take his property.

Although he is a victim of a crime, the victim is often at the same time a witness, and all the obligations of a witness would apply.

Estelle's knitting shop was broken into, and a suspect has been arrested. Will Estelle have to be present at the bail hearing?

No, but since bail hearings are open to the public, Estelle is certainly free to attend if she chooses.

The police recovered Tim's stolen television set, but when he went to pick it up they would not return it to him. Why?

The television is probably needed as evidence at the suspect's trial. At that time, Tim may be asked if he can identify the television as his property, and other witnesses may be called to testify that they saw the television in the suspect's possession after it was taken from Tim's home. Once the trial is over, Tim will have his property returned to him.

Darren was injured during a fight he had with his neighbor, Morris, over the use of their common driveway. Darren wants to press charges against Morris, but the prosecuting attorney suggested that Darren and Morris participate in a dispute resolution program. What is that?

It is a way to avoid the bitterness and conflict that often follow a court trial, and it is especially helpful when the people in a dispute are neighbors, co-workers, or others who must continue to see each other. If Darren and Morris agree to participate in such a program, they will be asked to meet with a mediator, work out their differences, and refrain from violent confrontations in the future.

My sister carries Mace and a knife for self-defense. Is this legal?

Canadians are prohibited from carrying concealed weapons such as revolvers, daggers, blackjacks, brass knuckles, and other dangerous or deadly devices. Under Canadian law, Mace, too, is a prohibited weapon and its possession is an offense. As for the knife, the particular circumstances of the case and the characteristics of the knife would determine whether or not it was a prohibited weapon. A switchblade would be illegal, for example; a bread knife would not.

To defend myself from a mugger, I poked him in the eye with my keys. The mugger lost his sight in the injured eye and is now charging me with assault. Can I argue that I acted in self-defense?

It depends on the circumstances. You have the right to use force, even deadly force, to defend yourself against someone who is trying to injure you. However, once you are no longer in danger, you may not use force against an assailant. If you poked the mugger in the eye while he was trying to strangle you, you could claim self-defense. But if you tried to blind him after he had let go of you, and you were no longer in mortal danger, you could be charged with assault.

Monty was walking down a dark alley when a man pressed what felt like a gun barrel against his back. Monty turned around quickly, and hit the man on the head with the wrench he was carrying; he then realized that the man was holding a piece of pipe, not a revolver. Can Monty plead self-defense?

Yes. When threatened with physical harm, an individual has the right to use enough force to prevent an attack or defend himself from one. Even though Monty's assailant was not actually armed with a deadly weapon,

581

he gave Monty reason to think he was by using an object that simulated a gun barrel. Therefore, Monty was justified in using force to defend himself against his assailant.

After Cecil's sports car was stolen from his garage, he rigged the garage door with a booby trap. When an intruder tried to open the door, he was killed by the device. Can Cecil be held responsible?

Yes. Cecil can be charged with manslaughter. Booby traps and similar devices are capable of deadly force; and deadly force may be used only to defend someone's life or protect a person from serious bodily injury. The law does not permit a person to use such dangerous devices to protect personal property. Although Cecil may not have intended to kill the intruder, the prosecuting attorney may argue that if Cecil only wanted to scare away an intruder, he could have installed a device that would shoot blanks. The prosecution may also try to show that Cecil acted carelessly by installing a deadly device that could not possibly differentiate between an intruder and someone who might need to open the garage door in an emergency, such as a fire fighter or police officer.

Howard got drunk and hit Kelly. If Kelly presses charges, can Howard use his intoxication as a defense?

No. In cases of simple assault, such as this one, drunkenness cannot be used as a defense. The fact that Howard was drunk will not excuse him from responsibility for his actions. Voluntary intoxication to the point where one loses self-control or becomes incapable of resisting an impulse is not a defense.

Noreen was held up at gunpoint. A suspect was arrested but his lawyer is trying to get the armed robbery charge reduced to an assault charge. Can Noreen prevent this plea bargain?

No. Only the prosecuting attorney can stop a plea bargain from being negotiated. Noreen's only course of action is to try to persuade the prosecuting attorney to deny the defendant's request to plea-bargain.

The judge, however, is not bound by the plea bargain struck between the Crown and the defense attorneys, and may sentence the accused to the maximum penalty for assault rather than a minimum sentence for robbery. This could result in a lengthy jail term for the criminal.

A "victim impact statement" has recently been used in some courts. This tells the sentencing judge how the crime affected the victim's life.

**_Does a victim have the right to know when his assailant will be
released on parole?_**

No. The victim does not have the right to know when his assailant will be
released on parole. This may be granted either by the National Parole
Board or by a provincial parole board. There are also different kinds of
parole. After serving one sixth of his sentence, for example, a criminal
may be eligible for day parole; he may work in the community by day but
must return to prison at night. After serving one third of his sentence, he
may be eligible for supervised parole; he may be free during the day but
must spend the nights at a halfway home or similar center outside the
prison. Prisoners who have served two thirds of their sentences are
often freed into the community by a statutory remission of sentence,
commonly known as "time off for good behavior."

**_The man convicted of killing Angela's daughter is coming up for
parole. Will Angela be allowed to address the parole board to
protest his release?_**

Although Angela does not have the right to address the parole board, she
could apply to address it and may be heard. Whether federal or
provincial, the parole board has a duty to act fairly. If Angela's request is
refused without just reason, she can ask the Superior (or Supreme)
Court of her province or the Federal Court, as the case may be, to review
the board's decision.

**_Helen, who has two small children, is often abused by her
husband Bob. Are there any programs that could help Helen and,
if so, what are these programs like?_**

Violence in the home is not rare. According to a 1982 House of Commons
study, some 10 percent of married women are abused. To counter this
crime, most communities now have crisis centers and special programs
for abused and battered women. Helen and her children might seek
shelter in one of these centers, which can also put her in contact with
lawyers who specialize in family matters. They may advise her to initiate
criminal or divorce proceedings against her spouse and will counsel her
on her rights. She and her children will also receive emotional support
and psychological counseling to help them through the crisis. Children
who see violence between their parents are seriously affected and may
grow up believing that violence is a normal and acceptable way of
controlling other people.

Helen can find out what is available in her area by contacting her local
social service agency or police department. Either can direct her to the
nearest crisis center.

If You Are a Victim

A man snatched Marlene's purse and then shoved her in front of a moving car. Because of her injuries, she was off work for months, losing some $10,000 in salary. It is now clear that she also needs thousands of dollars worth of dental work. Can she get financial help from the province?

Yes. All 10 provinces and both Yukon and the Northwest Territories have crime victims compensation programs. As well as filling out a police report, Marlene should contact her province's Criminal Injuries Compensation Board as soon as possible. She could be compensated for loss of salary, her dental treatment costs, and even some property loss, such as ruined clothing, broken glasses and so on. Marlene can qualify for this aid even if her assailant is never arrested. Payments may be made periodically or in one lump sum. Should Marlene suffer a relapse after recovering from her injuries, her file may be reviewed at any time.

Can a criminal be forced to pay restitution to his victim while he is in prison?

Possibly. In many cases a victim cannot be reimbursed because the prisoner has no money, property, or job. However, if a prisoner is enrolled in a work-release program, he may be required by the court to turn over part of his wages to his victim. In addition, if he is employed while on parole, he can be required to pay the victim a portion of his salary. Of course the criminal can also be sued in civil court for reimbursement of all damages and loss that he caused. And if his victim's action is successful, the criminal's goods, such as his car and jewelry, could be seized and sold by the court to reimburse the victim.

What Is a Crime?

Emily's attorney told her that she was lucky to be charged with a summary conviction offense rather than an indictable offense. What's the difference?

Summary offenses are less serious than indictable offenses. For example, the maximum punishment for a summary offense, such as simple assault, is six months in prison with, or without, a fine of up to $2,000. Indictable offenses include crimes such as robbery, sexual assault and perjury. The present maximum penalty for the most serious indictable offenses—first-degree murder, for example—is 25 years in prison before being eligible for parole. Procedures for summary and indictable offenses are also different. There is a preliminary hearing for an indictable offense and, unlike someone charged with a summary conviction offense, the accused is entitled to a trial by jury.

Warren was notified that the extension he built on his house violates his town's zoning law. Does this mean Warren has committed a crime?

No. Violations of municipal zoning laws are not crimes in the strict sense since only the federal Parliament can make criminal law. Provinces and municipalities may pass their own laws but violations of these laws, bylaws, ordinances and regulations are usually less serious and are referred to as infractions, or violations, rather than crimes. However, if a court orders Warren to remove the extension and he refuses, he could be charged with contempt of court, which is a crime.

Lynn moved to a new town with her pit bull terrier, not knowing that the town prohibited such animals. The town confiscated the dog and served Lynn with a summons. Lynn didn't realize that she was breaking the law. Is she liable for penalties?

Yes. Citizens are responsible for knowing what the law is and obeying it. Since pit bulls are banned from some communities because they are dangerous, Lynn should have checked local ordinances, or asked the local humane society branch about pit bulls before she moved.

Maggie tapes movies from a cable television station on her VCR. Is she committing a crime?

It depends on what Maggie does with the tapes. If she records movies only for her own viewing at home, she is within the bounds of the law, which permits the "fair use" of copyrighted material. However, if Maggie rents or sells the tapes, she will be guilty of pirating or bootlegging, which is a criminal offense, as well as being liable to have costly civil actions for injunction and damages taken against her.

While Pierce was away, his friend Alexis borrowed his car, intending to return it before Pierce came home. Pierce returned earlier than expected, and accused Alexis of stealing the car. Can Alexis be arrested?

Yes. Although Alexis did not intend to steal Pierce's car, she violated what is known as the "joyriding" law, which makes it illegal for a person to

What Is a Crime?

borrow a vehicle without the owner's permission. However, Alexis cannot be arrested unless Pierce files charges against her. Her "borrowing," which resembles theft, is a summary conviction offense.

What is a victimless crime?

It is a crime that harms society at large, rather than a particular individual. Drug offenses, gambling, and prostitution are considered to be victimless crimes because their participants are willing—unlike the victims of robbery or murder.

Isn't a crime committed against a person more serious than one committed against property?

Not always. For example, the law considers stealing a car to be more serious than punching someone in a barroom brawl; the auto thief would probably receive a harsher sentence than the person found guilty of assault, even though assault is a crime against a person.

Is the failure to act ever considered a crime?

Yes. It's a crime, for example, if you don't file a federal income tax return annually; if a parent doesn't provide food or shelter for his children; if an employer doesn't provide safe working conditions for his employees; if a citizen doesn't comply with a court order to do, or not to do, something; or if a doctor doesn't report a case of suspected child abuse.

Can a person with AIDS be prosecuted for knowingly infecting another person with the disease?

Yes. A person can be charged with unlawfully causing bodily harm if he knowingly infects another person with AIDS or any other sexually transmitted disease.

If I accidentally pick up the wrong suitcase at the airport and the customs inspector finds illegal drugs inside, can I be found guilty of drug possession?

No, as long as you can prove that the suitcase does not belong to you, and that you therefore did not knowingly or willingly possess the drugs.

Is it true that a person can't be held responsible for a crime he didn't intend to commit?

Yes. A crime has two elements: the criminal act itself and the intent to commit the act. To be found guilty, a person must not only commit a crime but must do so willingly and knowingly. For example, if you were angry at a friend and fired a gun at him and killed him, you could be found guilty of murder. However, if you were cleaning a gun and it went off accidentally, killing your friend, you would not be guilty of murder, because you did not intend to kill him. (But you might be guilty of manslaughter or criminal negligence causing death.) If you were legally insane or mentally incompetent when you killed your friend, you would not be held responsible for his death.

Nannette drove her car past a stop sign without slowing down or stopping, and hit an elderly man. If the man dies, will Nannette be charged with murder?

No, but she may be charged with criminal negligence causing death, a type of homicide in which someone's negligence causes another person to be killed. By ignoring the stop sign, Nannette was guilty of criminal negligence—that is, she showed reckless disregard for the safety of others. If the man dies, Nannette can be held responsible for his death, even though she did not intend to kill him.

If Malcolm buys a handgun with the intention of killing someone but then doesn't carry out his plan, can he be charged with attempted murder?

It depends on what actions he takes. For example, if Malcolm buys a gun but takes no further steps because he has changed his mind, he has not committed a crime. However, if Malcolm purchases a gun, shoots at the intended victim, and misses, he can be charged with attempted murder. Even if Malcolm pointed an empty gun at someone, he would be guilty of an offense.

The prosecuting attorney told the jury he could prove that Curtis had committed a premeditated crime. What kind of crime is that?

A premeditated crime is one that has been planned in advance. To prove that Curtis committed a premeditated crime, the prosecuting attorney must show that some time—even as brief a period as a few seconds—elapsed between Curtis's first thought of committing the crime and his actually carrying out his intentions.

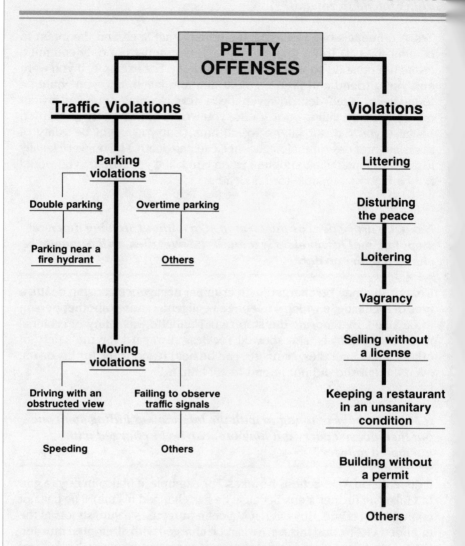

PETTY OFFENSES

Traffic Violations

Parking violations
- Double parking
- Overtime parking
- Parking near a fire hydrant
- Others

Moving violations
- Driving with an obstructed view
- Failing to observe traffic signals
- Speeding
- Others

Violations
- Littering
- Disturbing the peace
- Loitering
- Vagrancy
- Selling without a license
- Keeping a restaurant in an unsanitary condition
- Building without a permit
- Others

VICTIMS AND CRIMES

Crimes are divided into two broad categories—petty and criminal offenses. Petty offenses are usually violations of provincial statutes or municipal bylaws or regulations and are usually punishable by fine or by light jail sentences. They are generally tried before a magistrate or municipal judge and the procedure is usually simple.

Criminal offenses, more serious, fall into two categories—summary conviction offenses and indictable offenses.

Proceedings in summary conviction offenses must begin within six months of the infraction and the maximum punishment is a $2,000 fine or six months in jail, or both.

The most serious crimes are indictable offenses, and their trial is the

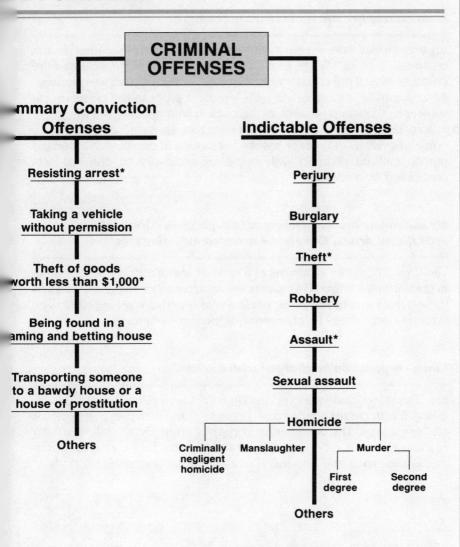

CRIMINAL OFFENSES

Summary Conviction Offenses

- Resisting arrest*
- Taking a vehicle without permission
- Theft of goods worth less than $1,000*
- Being found in a gaming and betting house
- Transporting someone to a bawdy house or a house of prostitution
- Others

Indictable Offenses

- Perjury
- Burglary
- Theft*
- Robbery
- Assault*
- Sexual assault
- Homicide
  - Criminally negligent homicide
  - Manslaughter
  - Murder
    - First degree
    - Second degree
- Others

most formal of all. The accused person has the right to a preliminary inquiry and to a trial by jury. Even at the preliminary inquiry, the Crown must have evidence to prove that the accused should stand trial and that the accusation is founded.

There are also a great number of crimes—theft, assault and resisting arrest, for example—which are called hybrid or mixed crimes. In these cases the prosecutor has a choice of proceeding either by way of summary conviction or by indictment. In making a decision, he will consider the injury caused to the victim, whether it is a first offense and other mitigating or aggravating circumstances.

*May be either a summary conviction offense or an indictable offense.

What Is a Crime?

Is an accomplice the same as an accessory?

An accomplice is one who counsels, incites or helps another in the commission of an offense, even if he is not present at the scene of the crime, or even if the crime is not carried out in the way that was planned. An accomplice is considered by law to be a party to the crime and is subject to the same penalty as the person who actually did the deed.

An accessory is someone who, knowing that a person has committed a crime, receives, comforts or assists that person in escaping. No married person can be charged with being an accessory to criminal acts committed by a spouse.

My son-in-law has been using my daughter as a lookout while he sells illegal drugs. Can she be arrested for doing this?

Yes. If your daughter is serving as a lookout, she is actively participating in committing a crime. This makes her an accomplice to the crime. Even though your son-in-law is the person who is actually selling the drugs, your daughter could be charged with the same offense.

Can a corporation be charged with a crime?

Yes. The law considers a corporation an artificial person, and it can be charged with committing a crime because of the activities of its officers and employees. The penalties for corporate crime usually take the form of a fine. However, officers and employees involved in a corporate crime can also be tried and sentenced to a fine or imprisonment, or both.

Rights of the Accused

For more information, see "Dealing With the Police" in Chapter 12, *Your Individual Rights;* also see Chapter 18, *Going to Court.*

My neighbor complained to the police that I was playing my stereo too loudly. Do I have to let the police into the house when they arrive?

No, unless they have a search warrant. The only times the police may enter your home without your permission or a search warrant are if they have probable and reasonable grounds to believe that someone in your house has committed an indictable offense, or in an emergency, such as if someone inside your home is threatened with injury.

If I refuse to allow a police officer into my home even though he has a search warrant, can I be arrested?

Yes. If a police officer has a search warrant, it is illegal for you to hinder his investigation. If you refuse to allow him into your home, the police officer has the right to arrest you on the spot.

Does a search warrant entitle police to break down a suspect's door, or must they knock first and wait for the door to be opened?

A police officer carrying out an arrest must act in a reasonable manner and use only as much force as is necessary to prevent the escape of a suspect. Thus, police arresting someone who is not dangerous—a person charged with forgery, say—would probably be required to knock on the door and announce their presence. This would not be necessary if they were about to arrest a murder suspect whom they believed to be armed, or if they were attempting to surprise a drug dealer, who might destroy the evidence if warned of their presence.

Several minutes after a jewelry store was held up, Darrell ran down a nearby street to catch a bus. When the police saw him running, they stopped and frisked him. Was this legal?

Yes. The police have the right to stop and frisk anyone if they have reason to suspect that he has committed a crime and that he may be armed and dangerous. Since Darrell was running near the scene of a recent crime, police were justified in thinking that his behavior was suspicious.

Liza was stopped by the police because her car had a broken taillight. The officer offered to check the bulb, and Liza agreed to let him. When he opened the trunk, he found a briefcase full of cocaine. Did the officer have the right to open the briefcase?

No. The police officer had the right to stop Liza's car because the broken taillight was a traffic violation, and to open the trunk because Liza gave her consent. However, to search the trunk or open the briefcase, the officer would have needed (1) Liza's permission, (2) a search warrant, or (3) reason to suspect that Liza was hiding something illegal.

Can a police officer make an arrest without an arrest warrant?

Yes. If a police officer has probable cause to believe that someone has committed a serious crime, then he does not need an arrest warrant—

even if the crime was not committed in his presence. To make an arrest for a less serious crime, such as disturbing the peace, an officer must either witness the crime or obtain an arrest warrant.

If Nicholas feels that the police are totally unjustified in arresting him, should he resist the arrest?

The best strategy would be to accompany the police to the police station where the matter could be resolved. Although it would not be illegal for Nicholas to resist arrest when the police have no reason to arrest him, such conduct might lead to someone getting hurt needlessly.

The police told me that they've issued an arrest warrant for the man who stole my car. What information does a warrant contain?

An arrest warrant is addressed to the peace officers of a particular district and identifies the person to be arrested and his occupation if

Your Legal Rights If You Are Arrested

If you are accused of a crime—whether you are guilty or innocent—our legal system guarantees you certain rights. You have the right to remain silent and not incriminate yourself, the right to be represented by a lawyer, and the right to have one appointed by the court if you cannot afford one. If you are arrested, before questioning begins, you must be advised of these rights, which are guaranteed by the Charter of Rights and Freedoms. You also have the right to:

- Have a hearing before a magistrate or judge, as soon as possible after you are arrested.
- Be notified of the charges against you.
- Have reasonable bail set, if bail is granted.
- Have a fair, impartial trial by jury, if charged with an indictable offense.
- Be present at all stages of the trial.
- Confront your accusers.
- Have your lawyer cross-examine witnesses.
- Have your lawyer call witnesses on your behalf.
- Be tried for a crime only once.
- Receive neither cruel nor unusual punishment if you are convicted of a crime and sentenced.

known. The charge against the accused is described briefly—the nature of the crime and when and where it allegedly took place. The warrant can be issued either by a judge or a justice of the peace and is invalid unless it is issued and signed by such an authorized person.

Is it true that a person who is arrested is allowed to make only one phone call?

No. If you are arrested, you are entitled to make as many phone calls as necessary to arrange for a lawyer to represent you and to arrange for your release as soon as possible.

Celeste received a phone call from her husband, saying that he had been arrested. What should she do?

If her husband hasn't already contacted a lawyer, Celeste should do so as soon as possible. The lawyer can represent and advise her husband during police questioning and at the bail hearing if there is one. Since everyone is presumed innocent, an accused person is usually released on his promise to appear for the trial. If the Crown prosecutor objects, he must convince the court that it is in society's best interest that the accused not be released.

Can someone who is not a police officer make an arrest?

Yes. Anyone can make what is called a "citizen's arrest" given certain circumstances. You have the right to arrest someone you see committing an indictable offense. You can also arrest a person if you have good reason to believe he has committed such an offense and is running away from the police. And you can use as much force as necessary to make your citizen's arrest.

But before you act, be sure of the circumstances and be sure you have the right person. Your mere suspicion that an individual has committed a crime does not empower you to arrest him. Moreover, you have no right to arrest someone committing a summary, or minor, offense. If you miscalculate, you could be sued for false arrest or assault, or both.

When a suspect is told he has the right to remain silent, does this mean he also has the right to refuse to sign any statements?

Yes. A suspect cannot be required to sign a statement or confession after he has claimed his right to remain silent. A statement signed under these circumstances is inadmissible as evidence in court.

Steps of a Criminal Case

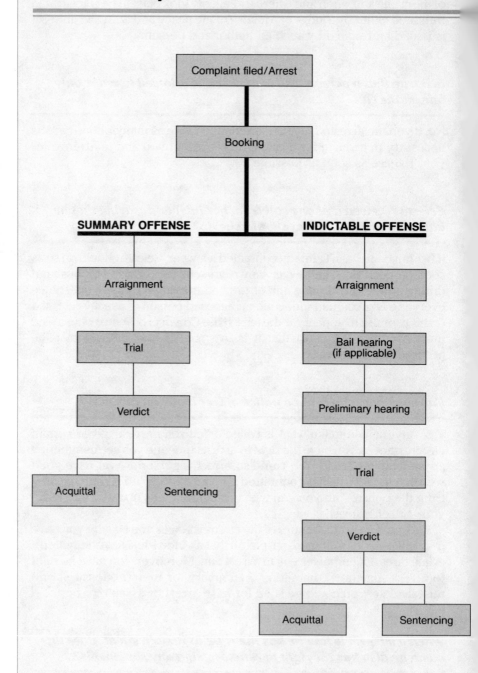

Before a person accused of a crime can be brought to trial, certain steps must be taken to establish that a crime has been committed and that there is reason to believe the accused person committed it. Federal statute has established this sequence of steps in criminal cases.

Complaint and Arrest—After the police investigate a crime, the prosecuting attorney files a written statement (called *an information*) with the court, describing the crime and naming the suspect; if a judge decides there is sufficient evidence, he issues an arrest warrant. Upon arrest, the suspect is informed of his rights. (If a suspect is arrested at the scene of a crime, the charge is filed afterward.)

Booking—At the police station, the suspect is searched, photographed, fingerprinted, allowed to contact a lawyer, and given a receipt for any personal property that is impounded. For a summary offense, the suspect is usually released and assigned a date to appear in court. For an indictable offense, he is often jailed.

Initial Court Appearance—At this hearing, called an *arraignment*, the accused person is informed of the charge against him and pleads guilty or not guilty. In a summary conviction offense, the judge may render a sentence, usually a fine, right away. In an indictable offense, the accused may opt for trial by judge alone or trial by judge and jury. Conditions for release are also set at this time. Generally the accused person is released on his promise to appear for his preliminary hearing, or trial, as the case may be. But if the Crown prosecutor objects and the judge agrees, the accused may be jailed until the trial date.

Preliminary Hearing—The Crown presents its evidence at this hearing, and the judge decides if this evidence is sufficient to warrant a trial. Any doubt at this point weighs against the accused person.

Trial—If the defendant wants a jury trial, jury members are now chosen. If he waives that right, his trial is heard by a judge only. (In a jury trial, the question of guilt or innocence is left to the jury and the sentence is left to the judge.)

Verdict—The judge or jury decides whether the defendant is guilty or not guilty. If the verdict is not guilty, the defendant is released.

Sentencing—The judge decides on the punishment. He may order the defendant to pay a fine or serve a jail term, he may have him released under the supervision of a probation officer, or he may even discharge him. For some crimes, the exact or minimum punishment is laid down in the law enacted by Parliament or the legislatures. For other crimes, only the maximum terms or fines are stated. In some cases, the judge can impose either imprisonment or fines, or both. When the legislation doesn't provide a definite penalty, the judge will likely be guided by *precedent*: what punishment other judges have given for similar violations.

Rights of the Accused

Trisha was arrested and held overnight in jail because the police mistook her for someone else. Can she sue for the emotional trauma and embarrassment this caused her?

Trisha can probably sue the police for false arrest. They are obliged to release an accused person as soon as possible on his promise to appear in court, provided the individual has been identified and is not considered dangerous. If Trisha cooperated with the police, told them who she was and where she lives, it would be hard for them to justify keeping her in jail overnight.

When Ralph approached a scalper and paid him $200 for a ticket to the Stanley Cup playoffs, the man identified himself as a police officer and arrested Ralph. Wasn't this police entrapment?

No. Since Ralph had decided to buy a ticket from a scalper before he approached the police officer, his intent to commit a crime makes him a perpetrator rather than a victim. Ralph would have been the victim of entrapment only if the police officer had tricked Ralph into buying a ticket that he had no intention of buying otherwise.

Willie committed a crime in one province and then fled to another one. Can the police still arrest him?

Possibly. Usually a warrant issued by a provincial court is only valid within the court's territorial jurisdiction. But if the warrant was issued by the Superior Court (also known as Supreme or High Court), and is a "Canada wide" warrant, then police anywhere in Canada can arrest Willie. However, Willie can only be tried in the province where he committed the crime.

My lawyer says he is going to ask for a writ of habeas corpus because I am being held in jail illegally. What is he talking about?

Habeas corpus literally means "you have the body." The writ is a court order directing the officials holding you in custody to bring you to court and justify your being held. The court then determines whether you are being held legally or whether you should be released.

A habeas corpus writ is often used in criminal cases when the prisoner claims that his legal rights have been violated. But this writ can also be used in civil cases—custody cases or cases involving mental patients, for example.

Posting Bail

Is bail the same as bond?

Yes. Both terms refer to the sum of money given to a court to release a person who has been arrested and to help ensure that he appears at his trial. When the accused shows up for the trial, the bail money is returned; if the accused does not, the bond is forfeited.

Can I use my credit card to post bail?

Posting bail is relatively rare in Canada, where most accused persons are released on their promise to appear in court. When bail is required, it must be in cash or other securities.

Nelson wants to post bail, but he doesn't have enough money. What can he do?

Professional bail bondsmen, common in the United States, are illegal in Canada, so Nelson would have to get a friend or relative to post bail for him. Nelson could also appeal the judgment requiring bail in order to have the amount reduced or replaced by conditions such as avoiding certain companions or reporting regularly to the police. If Nelson cannot afford to have an attorney represent him on appeal, one would be provided without charge by the legal aid society of his province.

What factors does a judge consider when setting bail?

Since the law does not specify a fixed amount of bail for any particular crime, a judge must use his own discretion in each case. He must set an amount that is high enough to deter the suspect from fleeing to avoid trial, but not so high that it violates the Charter of Rights prohibition against unreasonable bail. In making his decision, the judge considers several factors, such as the evidence against the suspect, his financial resources, his reputation within the community, his employment record, his health and the nature of the accusation.

The judge told Nat that he would be released on his own recognizance. What does that mean?

Nat will be allowed to go free, without posting bail, if he agrees in writing to appear in court on the date of his trial. A person can also be released on the recognizance of a friend or relative.

Posting Bail

Marshall, who has a long criminal record, was denied bail after his last arrest. Can the judge do that?

Yes. In deciding whether to allow bail, a judge has the right to consider a person's past record as well as the strength of the evidence against him in the case currently before the court. The judge can deny bail if (1) he decides that Marshall is more likely to flee than face trial, (2) Marshall's record indicates that his release might threaten the safety of the members of the community or interfere with the administration of justice (for example, by intimidating witnesses), (3) Marshall is charged with a crime committed while he was at large after being released in relation to another crime, (4) Marshall is charged with murder or another very serious crime such as treason, (5) Marshall is charged with importing or trafficking in narcotics, or (6) Marshall is charged with an indictable offense and is not a resident of Canada.

Young Offenders

For responsibility of parents, see "Children in Trouble" in Chapter 2, *Marriage and Family.*

My 15-year-old daughter has been arrested and charged with shoplifting. What will happen to her?

Anyone 12 to 17 years old who is charged with an offense against a federal statute, such as the Criminal Code, will be dealt with according to the Young Offenders Act. Since shoplifting is a relatively minor crime, but a crime nonetheless, your daughter will be referred to officials of the Youth Court. If she does not have a long criminal record, shows remorse, admits to the crime, and agrees to certain conditions called alternative measures, she could be released without a hearing. Once the conditions of alternative measures have been fulfilled, it will be as if your daughter was never arrested. She will have no criminal record.

Andy, a 16-year-old boy, stole a car and then wrecked it while he was fleeing from the police. What will happen to him?

If he is prosecuted and found guilty, the Youth Court judge could order Andy to do community service or pay a fine, or the judge could put him on probation for up to two years. If Andy has had previous convictions and seems unrepentant, the judge could also sentence him to a youth detention center. If it was a first offense, Andy could receive an absolute discharge. The car owner, or the owner's insurance company, could sue Andy in civil court for all damages caused.

Some of Annabel's older friends were arrested for buying drugs. Even though Annabel wasn't with her friends when they were picked up, she was later apprehended as being "a child in need of protection." What does that mean?

Under provincial law, "a child in need of protection" is someone with serious behavior disturbances whose parents fail to take whatever measures are necessary to remedy the situation, or whose parents or guardian do not exercise stable supervision. The judge of the Youth Court could have Annabel placed in a youth detention center or a foster home, or otherwise deal with her case in a way that ensures she has a better environment for her growing years.

Some neighborhood boys smashed Melinda's mailbox. Can Melinda get them to pay for the damage?

Yes. Melinda should complain to the police so that the matter can be referred to youth court. If the boys are found guilty, the court may order them to pay for repairing or replacing the mailbox. The court may also require the boys to do some form of community service.

Ginger's 14-year-old son is too difficult for her to handle. Can the youth court provide Ginger with any assistance?

Yes. Ginger can file a complaint against her son, stating that he is a troublemaker and beyond parental control. If the youth court agrees, it can provide counseling for Ginger's son or assign a social worker or probation officer to work with the family. If necessary, the court could place Ginger's son in a group home, a foster home, or a youth detention center until his behavior improves.

Carolyn was picked up for truancy. She is 13 years old. Can she be sentenced for not attending school?

It depends. Education is compulsory and all provinces have legislation requiring parents or guardians to make sure that their children attend school until the age of 16 years, unless it can be proven that the child is receiving satisfactory instruction at home or elsewhere. If Carolyn's parents can prove that she is receiving parental home instruction, or schooling at a religious establishment (for example, a school set up by a Mennonite or Hasidic community), the charge would be dropped. If she was simply playing hooky, the judge will take whatever steps he considers necessary to make sure Carolyn attends school. A child may be excused if he or she cannot attend school because of ill health.

Young Offenders

Seymour's parents were notified by the principal of his school that Seymour was being referred to youth court. Is this legal?

Yes. Although most youth court referrals are made by the police, referrals for acts of noncriminal misbehavior, such as truancy and running away from home, are usually made by others. Teachers, principals, and the board of education itself all have the authority to refer a child to youth court.

Most provincial statutes dealing with youth protection also require that cases of child abuse, or cases where the child's welfare seems to be in danger, be reported to the authorities. This requirement applies even to those, such as doctors or clergy, who may learn of these dangers through privileged information.

Does a child have a right to be represented by a lawyer when he appears in youth court?

Yes. According to both the Young Offenders Act and the Charter of Rights and Freedoms, a child has the right to a lawyer from the moment he is arrested and certainly at trial. No written or oral statement by a young person charged under the Young Offenders Act can be admissible against him in court unless he was informed of his right to see a lawyer before he made this statement.

Jackson, who is 17, has been accused of robbery. The police are talking about charging him in adult court. Can they do this?

Yes. Anyone over 14 years of age who is charged with a serious offense may have his case heard in adult rather than youth court. The court would first consider the maturity of the young person, the general interest of society in the case, and other factors it considered important. One such case was that of Stephen Truscott. He was convicted of murder in adult court in 1959—a conviction upheld by the Ontario Court of Appeal. He was only 14 years old at the time of the crime.

Mary Ann was charged with drinking under age. Is there any way for her to avoid a trial before the youth court?

When a child is arrested for a relatively minor offense, such as disturbing the peace, or drinking under age, and has had no previous arrests, court officials may recommend that the child be placed under unofficial supervision instead of having a formal court hearing. Under this arrangement, a social worker will work with the child to try to prevent him from committing any offenses in the future. However, unofficial supervision is voluntary, and the child can refuse to participate.

Brent is scheduled to attend an adjudication hearing next month. Is that the same as a trial?

Yes. The purpose of an adjudication hearing is to determine whether the charges made against a minor are true. At the hearing, Brent's lawyer will present evidence and witnesses on Brent's behalf and cross-examine witnesses who testify against Brent. If the judge rules that the allegations are true, he may order that a youth worker (probation officer) complete a predisposition investigation before he determines Brent's appropriate punishment and rehabilitation.

What is a predisposition investigation?

An examination ordered by a youth court judge of a child's background and of the situation that caused the child to be brought to court is called a predisposition investigation. The investigation is usually conducted by a youth worker (probation officer) to try to understand the causes of the child's delinquent behavior.

The investigator will generally interview not only the young offender himself, but his family and teachers and any other concerned adults, as well as the victim of the young person's offense. The investigator will look still further into the child's background by examining his school and medical records and any previous court records. The investigator will then report his findings to the youth court and make recommendations for the child's placement and treatment.

Chester was arrested for stealing hubcaps from a car. The lawyer his father hired to defend him wants the young man to deny the charge, but the father thinks Chester ought to admit his guilt. Doesn't Chester's father get to decide what's best for his son, since he's paying the lawyer?

No. A lawyer has an ethical duty to serve the best interests of his client regardless of who is paying his fee. If the lawyer does otherwise, he is guilty of malpractice. If Chester's lawyer thinks it is in the boy's best interest to deny his guilt, he cannot allow himself to be swayed by the boy's father. The father's best course would be to follow the advice of his son's lawyer who is experienced in these matters. Perhaps Chester is innocent of the crime, or committed the crime under duress, or perhaps the Crown has no proof that Chester was involved in the hubcap theft.

Young Offenders

Sixteen-year-old Molly stole money from the church poor box. Will reporters be allowed in the courtroom during Molly's hearing?

No. To protect children from harmful publicity, youth court proceedings are held in private, and all facts relating to such cases are confidential. Molly's hearing will be closed to the public, and only those directly involved with the case will be allowed to attend.

How does being charged under the Young Offenders Act differ from being charged under the Criminal Code?

The Young Offenders Act recognizes that although young people should bear responsibility for their actions, their state of development, dependency and maturity should be taken into account. The act also states that young people have all the protections granted by the Charter of Rights and must be informed of all their rights when arrested for an offense. It is only as a last resort that children will be taken from the custody and supervision of their parents. Cases dealing with young offenders, as well as their records, are dealt with in a confidential manner and are usually not open to the public.

After ruling that my brother was guilty of disturbing the peace, the judge ordered him to stay within a two-mile radius of home and be in the house by 8:00 P.M. every night. Does the judge have the authority to do this?

Yes. Once a judge finds a young offender guilty, he has the authority to establish whatever punishment he deems most appropriate. This includes placing curfews and other limitations on the child's activities. If your brother disobeys the judge's ruling, the judge could order that your brother be removed from your parents' custody and placed in a more restrictive setting, such as a group home or youth detention center.

The judge ordered my husband and me to attend counseling sessions with our son. Will we have to pay for these sessions?

Short-term counseling with court personnel, such as social workers, probation officers, and court psychologists, is usually provided free of charge. If your son receives private counseling, however, you will probably have to bear that expense yourself. If you cannot afford the full fee, your son's probation officer can direct you to counseling agencies with adjustable rates.

Do youth court judges always punish children by sending them to detention centers?

No. A judge has many options available to him when dealing with a young offender. He could (1) place the child under the supervision of his parents, (2) place the child with a relative, another family, or a foster home, (3) order the child to devote a certain number of hours to community service, (4) order the child to reimburse his victim for any harm he has done, (5) send the child to a hospital or a group home, or (6) place the child in a detention center or other correctional facility.

Stacy ran away from home for the third time, and was found by the police a week later. Can the youth protection authorities send Stacy to a foster home over her parents' objections?

Yes. By running away from home, Stacy was guilty of an infraction against the Youth Protection Act of her province—misbehavior that is not a crime but is unacceptable to society nonetheless. When a child commits an offense, such as repeatedly refusing to obey his parents or teachers, the authorities have the right to intervene and, if necessary, assume custody of the child. Since Stacy has repeatedly run away from home, the court will be even more likely to remove her from the custody of her parents and send her to a foster home or a youth detention center.

Thornton was picked up for truancy and sent to a detention center with young people who had committed much more serious crimes. Can his parents do anything about this?

Probably not. If Thornton has been placed under the control of the youth court, only a judge has the authority to decide where Thornton will live. Although some youth courts have separate facilities for different types of offenders, most do not. Consequently, children with behavior problems are often placed with those who have committed serious crimes. If Thornton's parents feel they can control him, they may be able to persuade the judge to release him to their custody. The judge might also allow Thornton to move to a private group home for troubled children.

Thornton's parents could always try to appeal the youth court judge's decision. The appeal courts, however, are usually reluctant to interfere with the trial judge's decision in these matters.

What is the function of a youth detention center?

These institutions are staffed by teachers, medical personnel, psychologists and social workers, all of whom try to create an environment where

Young Offenders

young people who have committed certain crimes or who come from troubled homes get an opportunity to grow up in positive surroundings. Detention centers offer educational instruction, balanced meals and professional counseling. Often such a center is the last chance society gives young people to change their attitudes and become useful and valuable citizens.

My son confessed to the judge that he stole a camera. Does this mean that now he'll have a criminal record?

Yes. Convictions under the Young Offenders Act result in criminal records for the young offender, but disclosure of the record is severely restricted. Only the prosecutor, police officials investigating an offense the young person is alleged to have committed, the youth's attorney or parents, and the presiding judge have the right to consult the young offender's record.

Other interested parties must first obtain permission from a judge or

How the Law Protects Young Offenders

Young people accused of breaking the law are granted some special rights intended to protect them because of their age. If a young person is charged with an offense that could interfere with his freedom, he is assured of the following rights:

- To remain silent, and not incriminate himself.
- While in custody, to be placed in quarters separate from adult offenders.
- To be represented by a lawyer, and to have one appointed by the court if he cannot afford to pay.
- That any written or oral statement given by him will be inadmissible as evidence unless he was warned, before making the statement, that he had a right to speak to his lawyer or his parents.
- To be notified of the charge against him.
- To be tried within a reasonable time.
- To confidentiality at his trial.
- To have his records destroyed within five years of the expiry of his sentence.
- When appropriate, to be released to his parents' custody, rather than be sent to a detention center.
- To have his case dealt with other than by trial provided such alternative measures are consistent with the protection of society.

the youth court to consult the records, and permission would only be given for a valid reason. After some time has elapsed, usually five years, these records must be destroyed.

Rachel was arrested for drug possession when she was 14. If she's arrested again, can her youth record be used against her?

It will depend on how old she is when she's arrested for the second time. If Rachel is still under 18, the judge will be allowed to take her past offense into account when determining her sentence. Once Rachel reaches adult age (18), her youth offenses cannot be used against her.

Manny is such a troublemaker at school that the principal wants to expel him. Can the principal check the youth court's records for previous offenses that will help support his case?

No. If Manny's case was tried in youth court, the only people who have access to his record are Manny's parents, the police, the judge, the prosecuting attorney, Manny's attorney, and his social worker. Once Manny's case was closed, his record was sealed and no one can have access to it without an order from a judge.

When Burt was a kid he got into trouble with the law and spent some time in a youth detention center. Does he have to report this when he applies for a job?

No. Burt's young offender record is confidential. He is not required to report his youth offenses to prospective employers, and they will not be allowed access to his records.

Witnessing a Crime

For information on testifying, see "Being a Witness" in Chapter 18, *Going to Court.*

Ordinarily I like to keep my distance from people. Am I required by law to come to the aid of a crime victim?

It depends on where you live. In Quebec, the law specifically requires anyone who witnesses a crime to assist a victim whose life is in peril if it is safe to do so. Generally, however, you would not have to help anyone unless (1) you had caused his predicament, for example, if you injured another driver in a car accident, or (2) you had a special relationship with the victim, for example, if the victim were your spouse or child.

Witnessing a Crime

A friend of mine gets paid "under the table." Am I obligated to report him to Revenue Canada?

No. You have no legal duty to report someone else's tax evasion to Revenue Canada. However, if you deliberately help your friend conceal such a crime, you will be committing an indictable offense.

Mortie told Alfred that he was going to hold up a liquor store on Friday night. Will Alfred be breaking the law if he does not report Mortie's plan?

No. Alfred is not legally required to report this information to the police. However, if he does, he may be able to help prevent the crime.

If Wilson reports a crime, will it be necessary for him to give his name to the police?

No. Wilson can make an anonymous call to the police. However, if Wilson does identify himself, he will make it much easier for the police to apprehend and prosecute the criminal, particularly if Wilson is the only person who witnessed the crime. Once identified by the police, Wilson can be required to testify as a Crown witness even if he would prefer not to go to court.

Bonnie saw a man breaking into her neighbor's house and called the police. Will Bonnie have to get involved any further?

Possibly. The police may visit Bonnie at home to question her about what she saw, and may ask her to go to the police station to look through mug shots of known criminals. If the police arrest a suspect, Bonnie may be asked to identify the criminal in a lineup. If the suspect is tried, Bonnie may be subpoenaed to testify in court.

Marcia saw a knife fight between two neighborhood gangs. After the police broke up the fight, they asked Marcia for her name and address. Can Marcia be required to testify as a witness?

Yes. Either a defense lawyer or a prosecuting attorney can have Marcia served with a subpoena, a court order requiring her to testify. If Marcia ignores the subpoena or refuses to testify, she could be charged with contempt of court.

My neighbor's six-year-old son, Toby, is the only person who saw an intruder leave Pauline's house after it was burglarized. My neighbor is worried that her son may be called as a witness. Can young children such as Toby be forced to testify?

Generally the courts are reluctant to listen to the testimony of children under 14 years of age. Before a child that young can testify, it is the judge's duty to ensure that the child understands the difference between the truth and a lie, and that he understands the nature of an oath to tell the truth. The judge must also conduct an inquiry to determine whether or not Toby could express himself well enough to be understood regarding what he saw. It is unlikely, but not impossible, that Toby would be called as a witness.

If I sign a sworn statement about a crime I witnessed, and some of the information I provided turns out to be incorrect, will I be prosecuted?

No. If you mistakenly give the police inaccurate information, you will not be charged with a crime. However, if you intentionally give false information in a sworn statement, you can be charged with obstructing justice, a crime punishable by up to 10 years in prison.

When Ryan saw an elderly woman being beaten by a man, he ran over and tackled her assailant. The man's head hit the sidewalk. Can Ryan be held responsible for the man's injuries?

Probably not. The law permits a person to use force to protect himself or someone else from death or serious injury. Since the woman Ryan assisted was in danger of being seriously injured, Ryan was justified in using force against her attacker.

Hilary witnessed an assault and reported it. The police arrested a suspect, but he was released on bail. Will the police provide Hilary with protection?

If the police suspect that the person accused of the assault may try to harm Hilary to keep her from testifying at his trial, they will probably offer her protection. But Hilary should not expect to be assigned a personal bodyguard or to be put under 24-hour surveillance. More likely, the police will warn the assailant to stay away from Hilary and will patrol the area around her home more frequently. If the assailant harasses Hilary while he is free on bail, the judge may revoke bail and order him held in custody until the trial.

Witnessing a Crime

A man who identified himself as an RCMP officer called Lizzie and asked her several questions about her nephew. Was Lizzie required to answer?

No. In fact, Lizzie should have refused to answer any questions over the telephone. When the RCMP question someone about a suspect, they are generally required to appear in person and show proper identification. The man who called Lizzie may not have been a Mountie.

My cousin Françoise, 13½, lives with her boyfriend Robert, 17, at Aunt Beatrice's house. Aunt Beatrice knows that Françoise and Robert engage in sexual activity, but she doesn't mind. Could she get into trouble because of this?

Yes. If you knowingly allow a child under 14 years of age to have sex in your home, you could be imprisoned for up to five years. And if you permit young people between the ages of 14 to 18 to have sex in premises you own or control, you could go to prison for up to two years. Beatrice should not only forbid Robert and her niece from having sex in her home, but she should take steps to ensure that it no longer happens.

CHAPTER 18

Going to Court

Is there a difference between the kinds of cases heard in a federal court and those heard in a provincial court?

Yes. The Federal Court, in its trial and appeal divisions, handles only suits brought by or against the federal government. It handles: (1) disputes between provinces and between the provinces and Ottawa; (2) claims against federal agencies, departments and employees; (3) appeals against board, commission or other federal tribunal decisions.

Provincial courts known as Supreme Court or Superior Court, or sometimes High Court, are, strictly speaking, federal courts too: the federal government appoints and pays their judges. These higher provincial courts hear serious criminal and civil cases such as murder, writs of *habeas corpus*, divorce suits or cases involving substantial amounts of money.

Lower provincial courts, with provincially appointed judges, deal with lesser criminal cases and civil matters such as those involving claims under $15,000.

I just lost my case in the provincial supreme court. Can I appeal the decision to the Supreme Court of Canada?

First you must have the Supreme Court of Canada's permission to have your appeal heard. Permission might be granted if the court's decision on your case would have important national significance.

How is it decided which court has jurisdiction over my case?

Where your case is heard depends on a number of factors, including whether it involves a criminal or a civil matter, the amount of money or property in dispute, and the nature of the case. Some cases are first heard before various boards or commissions, a rental board or the Workers' Compensation Board, for example, before being appealed to the courts. Provincial courts have jurisdiction over the majority of civil cases involving individuals. Even lawyers often have trouble determining which court has jurisdiction over a particular problem.

Can a person be charged twice for the same offense?

No. If a person is charged with something that is a crime under both federal and provincial law—offenses against the Criminal Code and the Ontario Highway Traffic Act, for example—he cannot be convicted twice for the same offense. This principle, now contained in the Charter of Rights and Freedoms, derives from a Supreme Court judgment (the Kienapple case) that disallowed multiple convictions. But the principle applies only in cases where multiple charges involving a single incident are supported by the same elements and facts. If, on the other hand, the multiple charges are supported by different elements and facts, there could be separate convictions. Someone could be charged and convicted of both reckless driving (as a provincial offense) and driving with a blood alcohol level above the legal limit (a federal offense), for example.

Jim has been charged with embezzling money. Can Jim's wife, who knew nothing of the crime, be charged with harboring or assisting a criminal?

No. Under Canadian law Jim's wife could not be charged with harboring or assisting a criminal, *even if she did know* that her husband was embezzling money. This is a value judgment that places a greater value on helping a spouse than on helping the state. It is a rare exception to the rule that no one should knowingly receive, comfort or assist a criminal in his attempt to escape justice.

Roger was tried and found guilty of knocking Jaclyn down from behind and stealing her purse and watch. Can Jaclyn also sue him for her injuries and stolen property?

Yes. Two distinct legal matters are involved. First, pushing Jaclyn down and robbing her are criminal offenses, and the state has the duty to prosecute Roger in a criminal trial. Second, Jaclyn has the right to bring a civil lawsuit against Roger for her property and other damages, such as loss of work income, pain and suffering, and any temporary or permanent incapacity. Although the two cases arise from the same incident, they are different under the law and do not put Roger in the position of being tried twice for the same crime, which is forbidden by Canada's Charter of Rights and Freedoms.

Can I be sued for something I did in another province?

Yes. If a person or business in another province wishes to sue you, the court in the other province will determine where the lawsuit should be heard. Generally, the province where the dispute first arose is the proper place for the lawsuit to be filed. Sometimes the court chooses the province in which the greatest number of people involved in the case live. In other cases, the place where a lawsuit is heard may have been agreed upon in advance. For example, a contract may declare which court will hear a lawsuit in the event that the contract is broken. As a general rule, the action is started before the court of the defendant or, if it involves real estate, before the court where the real estate (land or building) is situated.

Monica, charged with driving while intoxicated, is angry because the judge refused to bar the local press from the courtroom. Was she treated unfairly?

No. The right to a public trial and freedom of the press are two of the rights protected by the Charter of Rights and Freedoms. It is only in certain cases of sexual assault and family law cases, or where it is in the interest of public morals or the proper administration of justice that the press or the public would be excluded from attending the trial.

Who decides if evidence is direct or circumstantial?

The evidence itself makes the case. Direct evidence is firsthand evidence, such as an eyewitness's testimony, of a fact. Circumstantial evidence is secondary or indirect evidence that leads to a certain conclusion and is inconsistent with any other conclusion, when certain other facts are proved. Say a man enters a room; there is a gunshot; the man is found shot to death; another man, found later in possession of the gun that fired the fatal shot, is charged with murder; evidence at the trial proves that the deceased and the accused were on very bad terms. If the accused is convicted of murder, he would be convicted on circumstantial evidence—because of the circumstances of the case.

When the court found Henry guilty of shoplifting, Henry's lawyer persuaded the judge to record a discharge rather than a conviction. Does this mean the whole proceedings were a sham?

Not at all. In fact Henry was fortunate that his lawyer was able to convince the court to rule in this manner since the Criminal Code states that, if one is granted a discharge, "the offender shall be deemed not to have been convicted of the offense."

A judge is empowered to record a discharge, rather than a conviction, when he is convinced that such a move is not contrary to the public interest. The discharge may be unconditional or it may be granted with certain conditions, such as attendance at Alcoholics Anonymous meetings, if the facts are appropriate. A discharge is only granted where the accused is charged with one of the less serious crimes and is of otherwise good character.

The Canadian Court System

The Canadian court system consists of trial courts, appeal courts and the court of last resort—the Supreme Court of Canada. But because each province administers justice in its own territory, the names and jurisdictions of trial and appeal courts may vary across the country. Ontario, for example, has district and supreme courts. Courts of similar jurisdiction are known as Court of Queen's Bench in Manitoba and New Brunswick and as Superior Court in Quebec.

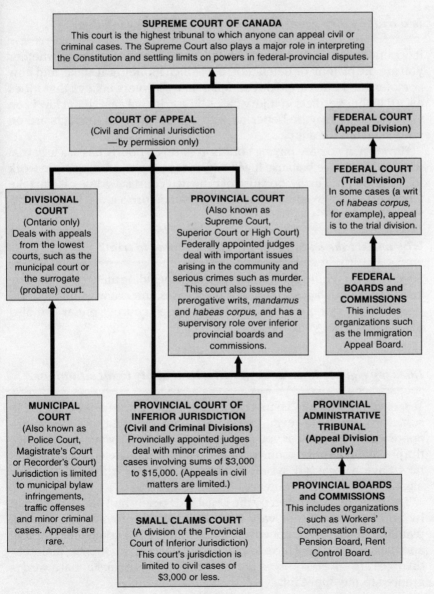

SUPREME COURT OF CANADA
This court is the highest tribunal to which anyone can appeal civil or criminal cases. The Supreme Court also plays a major role in interpreting the Constitution and settling limits on powers in federal-provincial disputes.

COURT OF APPEAL
(Civil and Criminal Jurisdiction —by permission only)

FEDERAL COURT
(Appeal Division)

DIVISIONAL COURT
(Ontario only)
Deals with appeals from the lowest courts, such as the municipal court or the surrogate (probate) court.

PROVINCIAL COURT
(Also known as Supreme Court, Superior Court or High Court)
Federally appointed judges deal with important issues arising in the community and serious crimes such as murder. This court also issues the prerogative writs, *mandamus* and *habeas corpus*, and has a supervisory role over inferior provincial boards and commissions.

FEDERAL COURT
(Trial Division)
In some cases (a writ of *habeas corpus*, for example), appeal is to the trial division.

FEDERAL BOARDS and COMMISSIONS
This includes organizations such as the Immigration Appeal Board.

MUNICIPAL COURT
(Also known as Police Court, Magistrate's Court or Recorder's Court)
Jurisdiction is limited to municipal bylaw infringements, traffic offenses and minor criminal cases. Appeals are rare.

PROVINCIAL COURT OF INFERIOR JURISDICTION
(Civil and Criminal Divisions)
Provincially appointed judges deal with minor crimes and cases involving sums of $3,000 to $15,000. (Appeals in civil matters are limited.)

SMALL CLAIMS COURT
(A division of the Provincial Court of Inferior Jurisdiction)
This court's jurisdiction is limited to civil cases of $3,000 or less.

PROVINCIAL ADMINISTRATIVE TRIBUNAL
(Appeal Division only)

PROVINCIAL BOARDS and COMMISSIONS
This includes organizations such as Workers' Compensation Board, Pension Board, Rent Control Board.

The Judicial System

Doesn't everyone have the right to a trial by jury in all cases?

No. Only in cases that are indictable offenses may the accused choose to be tried by judge and jury. In those provinces which allow jury trials of civil suits, the law of the province sets out when a jury trial is permitted. Usually cases involving $10,000 or more may be tried by a jury which, in civil cases, is made up of six persons.

Is a trial by jury generally better than a trial by a judge?

It depends on many factors: whether the case is civil or criminal, whether you are the plaintiff or defendant, how much money is at stake, and how complex the issues are. For example, many lawyers believe that juries award higher verdicts in injury cases. In a criminal case, if the law is on your side, you may be better off with a judge alone; if the facts are on your side, opt for a jury.

However, if you are paying your lawyer on an hourly basis, a jury trial will cost you more because it will take more time and create more work for your lawyer. Finally, because of crowded court schedules, it can take longer for a case to come before a jury than before a judge sitting alone.

Why will it take so long for my case to come to trial?

Several factors could account for the delay, including the time needed by lawyers for both sides to prepare their cases, interview witnesses, and assemble the evidence they need. A crowded court calendar can also delay the start of your trial.

Does my right to have a lawyer at a trial apply to all situations?

Yes, except for Small Claims Court, where lawyers are not permitted in some provinces. However, you do not have the right to a free court-appointed lawyer unless you cannot afford to hire a lawyer and you face the possibility of imprisonment or fine if you are convicted. All provinces now have a legal aid system which would provide free lawyers for eligible applicants, even in civil matters.

The types of cases taken by the Legal Aid Society and the amount paid by an eligible applicant vary from province to province. In Alberta, plaintiffs' divorces are not covered unless there is a compelling reason, and the applicant may have to pay part of the cost. In Quebec, plaintiffs' divorces are covered and no fee is charged unless a substantial award is granted to the applicant.

The case against Frank was dismissed because the prosecuting lawyer waited too long to bring it to trial. Is there a time limit for bringing a criminal case to court?

The Canadian Charter of Rights and Freedoms requires that "any person charged with an offense has the right to be tried within a reasonable time." Although the time is not strictly defined, the charter allows a court of competent jurisdiction to decide what is "appropriate and just in the circumstances," even to dismissing the action. This rule applies across Canada and includes both federal and provincial criminal law.

Pretrial Procedures

Sydney received a summons, and his wife was served with a subpoena. What is the difference?

A *summons* is a legal notice given to a person that legal action has been started against him. It states that the person is now a defendant and directs him to file an answer with the court by a specified date. Attached to the summons is a complaint, which details the charges against the defendant. A summons may be prepared by the plaintiff's attorney or an officer of the court. A person receiving a summons would not be breaking the law if he did not appear in court, but his absence would most likely result in the plaintiff's winning the lawsuit against him.

A *subpoena* is a court order directing a person either to appear in court to testify or to produce documentary or other evidence that is relevant to a case. A person receiving a subpoena must appear in court or face charges of contempt of court for ignoring the subpoena. Because this testimony of witnesses is so important to our justice system, only the reigning monarch is exempt from the *subpoena*.

I received a summons that said I had to file my answer to the lawsuit by a date that was a week before I received the summons. Does this mean I've lost the case already?

No. You must be given adequate notice of the lawsuit and an opportunity to be heard. If the sheriff or other court official has not delivered the summons to you in time for you to meet the court deadline, the court cannot rule that you've lost the case by default. In fact, your lawyer can ask the court to dismiss the lawsuit, since the summons was served on you after the date you were meant to respond. In such cases, one can also request the court's permission to file an answer after the expiry of legal time limits. Perhaps the most important rule of law is that expressed as *Audi alteram partem* (Let the other party be heard).

Pretrial Procedures

Darren is suing Blaine. Will Darren automatically lose his case if Blaine never receives a summons?

No. It is possible that a summons was legally served upon Blaine without her having personally received it. For example, the summons might have been left with a family member or at Blaine's place of business. If no one knew where Blaine lived, a copy of the summons might have been mailed to her last known address or published in a newspaper. As long as a summons is delivered according to one of the methods described in the provincial laws, a plaintiff can pursue his case—even if the defendant never receives the actual piece of paper on which the official summons is written.

Is a plaintiff the same as a petitioner?

Almost. The terms *plaintiff* and *petitioner* both refer to a person who initiates some type of legal action or proceeding. *Plaintiff* usually refers to the person who sues in a civil lawsuit or to the prosecutor in a criminal case. A *petitioner* is someone who is asking the court, an administrative agency, or a legislative body for a certain action, such as approval to sell property in a deceased person's estate or to have a guardian appointed.

In other words, a *plaintiff* is the initiating party to a suit or action; a *petitioner* is the initiating party to a motion or legal request.

Is a respondent the same as a defendant?

Not necessarily, although both terms are used to describe the person against whom a legal action is brought. If a plaintiff starts a lawsuit or criminal trial, the accused person is called the defendant. If a petitioner initiates some other legal action, his opponent is called the respondent.

Maria has no money for a defense lawyer. How does she ask for a court-appointed attorney?

If Maria is a defendant in a criminal case, she should ask for a court-appointed attorney after being arrested or at her initial court hearing. She will have to fill out a financial statement that proves her inability to pay for an attorney. For civil lawsuits, all provinces have set up their own legal aid societies, which could supply an attorney for Maria free of charge, or for a nominal fee. Some attorneys also do *pro bono* work: they take cases for the "public good" at no cost to the client. Maria's case might make her eligible for such assistance.

Cathy's lawyer told her that her case is now in discovery. What is he talking about?

In its broadest legal sense, the term *discovery* means obtaining information about the case. A case is said to be "in discovery" from the time the case is filed until the trial begins. The purpose of discovery is to learn more precisely which issues are in dispute and to obtain evidence. Methods used in discovery include depositions, interrogatories, requests to produce documents, and requests to submit to physical or mental examinations.

What is a deposition?

It is sworn testimony that is given and recorded outside the courtroom (in a lawyer's office, for example), usually during the pretrial phase of a case. It is the main method that lawyers use to gather evidence about a case before it goes to trial. Any witness—including one who is also a plaintiff or a defendant in the case—may be asked to give a deposition.

If a lawyer wants you to make a deposition, you should arrange to have your own lawyer present, since testimony you give that supports one side of the case may be challenged by the lawyer for the other side. Lawyers for both sides will be present. You will be placed under oath by a qualified officer of the court, usually a court reporter or stenographer, who attends the deposition to record your testimony, which may be used as evidence in the trial. Giving a deposition does not excuse you from testifying at the trial: you may have to do both.

Is an interrogatory the same as a deposition?

No. An interrogatory is a written set of questions requiring written answers from a plaintiff or defendant under oath. A deposition involves asking oral questions of any person who may have information relevant to a legal case. The person answers orally under oath, and an official transcript is made of the questions and answers. In some jurisdictions, failure to answer an interrogatory may be taken as an admission of the fact alleged by the questioner.

I gave a deposition over a year ago. The case is finally coming to trial next week. May I review this deposition before testifying?

Yes. This is an excellent way to refresh your memory about details you may have forgotten. Since the lawyers from both sides will have a copy of your deposition, any discrepancy between the deposition and your testimony will cause them to challenge your memory and truthfulness.

Pretrial Procedures

What if I'm ordered to give a deposition and I ignore the notice?

You could be held in contempt of court, an offense that is punishable by a fine or imprisonment, or both. If you are either the plaintiff or defendant in a civil lawsuit, the court could find that your failure to respond left it no choice but to rule in favor of your opponent on the issues that the deposition dealt with. The court may also order that you be brought before it by the sheriff, police or bailiff: (1) to give the deposition, and (2) to explain why you failed to attend at the place and time indicated on the notice. An unreasonable excuse could result in contempt of court proceedings being filed against you.

Lewis has been asked by a friend to testify at a hearing. Is a hearing the same as a trial?

Not usually. A hearing is less formal than a trial. Hearings are used by courts to obtain evidence needed to decide legal and factual questions

Steps in a Civil Case

If you are involved in a legal dispute that cannot be settled out of court, you will probably end up in a lawsuit. A typical civil case usually follows the steps set out below (for the steps in a criminal case, see "Rights of the Accused" in Chapter 17, *Victims and Crimes*):

1. *A complaint or declaration* is filed with the clerk of the court. In this document, the plaintiff (the one doing the suing) states his version of the situation and demands *damages*—the amount of money he seeks from the defendant (the one being sued) for his loss or injury. Depending on the claim, the plaintiff may have to pay certain court costs at this time for having documents stamped by the court.

2. *A summons or writ* is issued by the clerk of the court and is delivered with a copy of the complaint to the defendant, directing him to respond to the charges. If the defendant doesn't respond by the date shown on the summons, the plaintiff may win his case by default.

3. *An answer or plea* to the summons is filed by the defendant, and a copy of it is sent to the plaintiff. The answer is a document in which the defendant presents his version of the case, admitting or denying the charges made in the complaint. He may also make his own counterclaim against the plaintiff.

4. *Discovery procedures* may be used to uncover evidence that will strengthen the case when it comes to court. Discovery includes

concerning a dispute. Legislative committees such as those of the House of Commons or Senate, or agencies such as provincial housing authorities, also make use of hearings to investigate issues or to resolve disputes. If Lewis is subpoenaed to appear as a witness at his friend's hearing, he will be required to appear or face charges of contempt.

Under what conditions can Pamela's lawyer ask the court to postpone her trial?

A postponement, or continuance, may be requested if it is needed to assure a fair trial. Pamela's lawyer might cite the lack of time to prepare her case or the absence of a witness, defendant, or plaintiff. If important evidence were lost or destroyed or if her lawyer became incapacitated, a continuance could be requested. Another valid reason to ask for a postponement is surprise—for example, if new evidence is presented that is damaging to Pamela's case and her lawyer needs time to analyze it and determine how best to minimize its effect. There is one important proviso, however: that it was impossible for Pamela's attorney to know of this evidence earlier, either by examination on discovery or by personal

depositions (questioning of witnesses and others under oath) and interrogatories (written questions that the defendant or plaintiff must answer in writing under oath).

5. *Pretrial motions,* or requests, may be filed. For example, the defendant may ask that the lawsuit be dismissed, or the plaintiff may amend his complaint, or either side may request a change of venue (ask that the trial be held in a different place).

6. *A trial date* is set by the court.

7. *A pretrial conference* may be called by the judge to discuss the issues in the case with the opposing lawyers. This helps avoid surprises and delays once the trial starts, and sometimes leads to an out-of-court settlement.

8. *The jury is selected* (if one is being used), and the trial begins.

9. *Opening statements* are made by the lawyers for the plaintiff and the defendant, summarizing what each will establish during the trial.

10. *Witnesses* are called by the plaintiff and then by the defendant. The witnesses can be cross-examined by the opposing lawyers.

11. *Closing statements* by the plaintiff's and defendant's lawyers sum up their respective arguments.

12. *The jury deliberates* (if there is a jury) and reaches a verdict.

13. *The final judgment* is handed down by the court in the form of the jury's verdict or the judge's decision. A judge's decision may be rendered immediately at the end of the trial, or it may be sent in writing later.

research. Courts are usually more generous in granting a continuance if the case was never before fixed for hearing on the court roll, or if there is a sincere belief expressed by both parties that the dispute can be settled out of court or, in family cases, a reconciliation can be reached.

My case is scheduled to be tried before a judge with a reputation for being tough in cases like mine. Am I entitled to a different judge if I request one?

No. You cannot expect to be assigned a new judge just because you think the one you have may be too hard on you. However, a judge can be replaced for other reasons, such as if he has a personal interest in the case, a close relationship to either the plaintiff or the defendant, or a personal bias or prejudice against someone involved in the case, or if he might be called as a witness.

The procedure to replace a judge for one of the above reasons is called "recusation," and may be initiated by the judge himself.

Dean is going to be his own lawyer in a civil court case. How can he make sure that his witnesses show up to testify?

Dean should subpoena the witnesses. He can obtain subpoenas from the clerk of the court. The subpoena requires the witness to appear on a certain date or be charged with contempt of court. Dean must issue the subpoena within the legal deadlines and pay the witness's fees and transportation costs. Except in Ontario, Quebec and certain other provinces that have reciprocal agreements, a subpoena can only be sent to a witness residing within the province where the case is to be heard.

Will the judge reschedule my case if all my witnesses cannot appear on the court date?

Possibly. A judge can reschedule, or in legal terms *grant a continuance,* if you can prove that the witnesses' testimonies are important to your case and that no other witnesses can provide the same information. But he will not adjourn a case if he believes you simply want to delay the process of law. Your chances of obtaining a continuance are much greater, therefore, if you had the missing witnesses subpoenaed, rather than simply relying on their willingness to appear. In some instances, your adversary may formally acknowledge that your witness would say what you claim he would say. Such an acknowledgment would do away with the necessity of asking for a continuance.

My attorney tried and failed to reach a settlement with the person whose cats killed my prize parrot. We then took all the steps necessary to prepare for a trial. Now the defendant wants to settle out of court. Is it too late to do so?

No. Because of the crowded court calendars and time needed to complete a trial, the legal system encourages people to resolve their differences outside the courtroom.

I read in the newspaper that a person charged with a notorious crime got a change of venue. What does that mean?

Venue is the county or district in which a trial is held. For example, in a criminal case, the trial is usually held in the county where the crime occurred. Often a change of venue is requested when a plaintiff or defendant believes he cannot receive a fair trial in the county or district where the trial is scheduled. Other reasons to request a change of venue include convenience—for example, if witnesses or evidence are located a great distance from the courthouse—or if the judge turns out to be biased or prejudiced in a particular case.

Courtroom Protocol

Does the general public have the right to sit in the courtroom during a trial?

In criminal cases, the Canadian Charter of Rights and Freedoms guarantees the right to a trial in a "fair and *public* hearing by an independent and impartial tribunal." This guarantee does not apply to civil cases, although it is rare that the public is barred from a civil suit. When a trial is not open to the public (for example, in family law cases in some jurisdictions), the case is said to be held *in camera*, meaning that the hearing is before a judge in his private quarters (chambers), or in a courtroom from which all spectators are excluded.

The purpose of a public trial is to avoid injustice and arbitrary behavior by the judge. The openness is in sharp contrast to the closed, military-style courts favored by many repressive regimes. But even in our open court system, spectators and witnesses may be ordered to leave the courtroom during criminal cases if their presence disturbs the smooth functioning of the trial. In civil cases it is customary to request that witnesses not yet heard be excluded from the courtroom so that they will not be influenced by previous testimony.

It has not been finally decided whether television cameras will be allowed into Canadian courtrooms.

Courtroom Protocol

May I bring a friend to court with me if I'm testifying as a witness or if I'm on trial?

Yes, if the judge says the trial is open to the public, you may ask anyone you want to sit in the courtroom. However, if your friend is going to be a witness, he may be barred as an observer until after he has testified. Witnesses may be excluded by the judge when he or one of the attorneys involved is concerned that the witnesses will be influenced by the testimony of others.

Georgia has to appear in traffic court, but doesn't want to hire a baby-sitter. Can she take her children with her?

Yes, but Georgia will be responsible for their behavior. As a practical matter, Georgia may find it difficult to respond to questions and mind the children at the same time. If she still wants to bring the children to court, Georgia should consider asking a friend to accompany her to the courthouse to help take care of them. As the judge is the master of his court, he may object to the presence of small children in his courtroom.

What will happen to me if I can't go to court on the day I am called to appear?

If you are the plaintiff or the defendant in a civil case and do not show up in court on the day stated in the summons, the court may declare you in default, and you may lose the case. If you know in advance that you will not be able to appear in court, ask for a continuance, or postponement, of the trial to a later date—a delay the court will grant only for a good reason, such as an illness confining you to bed. If you were subpoenaed as a witness in either a civil or a criminal case and cannot appear as scheduled, you should contact the court officer or attorney who issued the subpoena to make other arrangements. Simply failing to appear may result in your being held in contempt of court, a crime that is punishable by a fine or imprisonment, or both. If you have an attorney, inform him as soon as possible of your inability to attend court.

If I plead guilty to an offense for which a fine is levied, do I have to pay my total fine on the day I go to court to make my plea?

It's up to the judge. He may require payment by the end of the day or by some later date. If it is a large fine, the judge may allow you to pay it in affordable installments.

My sister Ursula, who is head of a landmark preservation group, has offered to be an amicus curiae in a rezoning lawsuit. What does this mean?

Amicus curiae is Latin for "friend of the court" and means a person or organization that has a strong interest in a particular case, but is not involved directly as a defendant, plaintiff, or witness. Ursula will ask the court's permission to file a brief (written statement) on the issues as she sees them from a preservationist's viewpoint.

While Suzanne was testifying, she made a nasty remark about the plaintiff, whose attorney objected. The judge ordered what Suzanne said stricken from the record. What does this mean?

Strike from the record means to delete a statement made during a trial from the official transcript. The lawyer for either side may request such a

---

Courtroom Dos and Don'ts

Most of us will never have to be a plaintiff or a defendant in a trial. But if you must go to court, take a few moments to review the following guidelines. They will help you put your best foot forward.

☑ Attend court proceedings as required. If you have been subpoenaed, you could be jailed for not showing up. If you are a plaintiff or defendant, you could lose your case by being absent.

☑ Arrive on time for all scheduled hearings.

☑ Dress in clean, neat, conservative clothes, like those you would wear to religious services.

☑ Don't try to speak to your lawyer while he is questioning witnesses, listening to testimony, or addressing the court.

☑ Never argue with your lawyer in front of the judge or jury.

☑ If you have concerns about your lawyer's performance, discuss them with him during breaks, in private.

☑ Bring pen and paper to write down comments and insights that occur to you during the court proceedings so you can discuss them later with your lawyer.

☑ Be respectful to all the participants in the proceedings: judge, jury, plaintiff and defendant, witnesses, court officials.

☑ Speak in a strong voice so the judge and jury can hear you.

☑ Don't argue with the lawyers questioning you. If they act improperly, the judge will reprimand them.

☑ Answer all questions truthfully; if your lawyer objects to a question, don't answer it until instructed to do so by the court.

deletion when he thinks a witness has given an unthinking or improper answer that may prejudice or mislead the jury and should not appear in the court record. Since the court reporter had already taken down Suzanne's statement, it will be followed by the attorney's objection and the judge's order to sustain the objection and strike the statement in question from the record. Suzanne's remark will not appear in the official transcript of the trial. In cases involving a jury, this striking of the remark is of dubious value, since the jury has heard the statement and may consider it despite the judge's order, but the effect would be different if the case went to appeal, where the remark would not appear.

Trial Procedures

Can I plead guilty or innocent against my lawyer's advice?

Yes, but your lawyer may refuse to continue to represent you. Instead, choose a lawyer in whom you have confidence and follow his advice—the legal system is complex and full of traps. For example, suppose you pleaded guilty to a charge of hit and run when you accidentally backed up into a parked car and failed to report it. Your plea may saddle you with fines, demerit points and a criminal record, when in fact the damage was accidental and you would have had a good chance of being acquitted because you had no *mens rea* or intent to cause this damage.

Ethan's friend, who watches a lot of courtroom dramas on TV, wants Ethan to plead nolo contendere to a charge of drunk driving. How is this different from pleading guilty or innocent?

The plea of *nolo contendere* (I do not wish to contend) does not exist in Canada. When an accused person refuses to plead or does not answer, the court clerk will enter a plea of not guilty. A defendant may only plead guilty, not guilty, *autrefois acquit* (previously acquitted), *autrefois convict* (previously convicted), or pardon (indicating that he has been pardoned by the reigning monarch). In the case of defamatory libel, he may plead that what he published was true and for the public benefit in both the timing and manner of publication—a plea of justification.

Can a defendant be excluded from his own trial?

The Canadian Criminal Code requires an accused party (other than a corporation) to be present in court during the whole trial. Nevertheless, where the court considers it proper, an accused may be allowed to absent himself from his trial. Furthermore, where the accused acts in an unruly manner that disrupts the proceedings, he may be forcibly removed. He may also be temporarily excused from a trial where the question of his sanity is at issue and where his presence during the discussion of this matter may have an adverse effect on his mental health.

Can a defendant choose not to attend his own trial?

It depends on the nature of the crime. If the accused person is charged with a summary conviction offense (one punishable either by a fine of up to $2,000 or up to six months' imprisonment, or both), he does not have to appear personally, but may appear through counsel or an agent. The summary conviction court may, however, require the accused to appear personally. When charged with an indictable offense, the accused person must attend.

If I am on trial, must I testify?

It depends on whether the case is in criminal or civil court. If you are an accused in a criminal case you need never take the stand, because the Charter of Rights and Freedoms expressly excuses the accused from testifying in criminal or penal proceedings taken against him. Not testifying is not always the best strategy, however: the implication is that you have something to hide.

In civil cases, you have no such protection; if you are called to testify, you must take the stand.

Can a defendant who testifies refuse to be cross-examined?

No. An accused person cannot take the stand, present his side of the case, and then sit down. The opposing lawyer has the right to cross-examine. However, the Canada Evidence Act and the Charter of Rights and Freedoms provide that a witness (including the accused) who testifies in any proceeding has the right not to have any evidence he has given used to incriminate him in other proceedings.

Jared is accused of larceny. Does he have the right to make people testify as part of his defense?

Yes. The defendant can compel witnesses to testify in court by asking the court to subpoena them.

How the Court Determines Damages

When the plaintiff in a lawsuit wins his case, the judge or jury decides the amount of money the defendant must pay the plaintiff to compensate him for his loss or injury or for any pain or suffering he has to endure, or to punish the defendant for his negligence, default or unlawful acts. In legal terminology, the money a court awards in a lawsuit is called *damages.* Damages are divided into two categories: actual and punitive.

Actual damages are awarded to restore, as nearly as possible, a person or his property to the condition existing before the problem arose. In setting the amount of actual damages, the judge or jury considers:

- Lost job income.

- Loss of future income (projected on the basis of the person's age, education, job history, life expectancy).

- Hospital and medical expenses, including pharmacy bills and the cost of prosthetic devices and nursing care. (Because Canadians benefit from provincial and federal health plans, awards in Canada under this category are usually much smaller than those in the United States.)

- Pain and suffering, including that caused by fright, grief, shock, humiliation, or indignity.

- Loss of memory or intellectual capacity, temporary or permanent.

- Physical impairment or disfigurement, temporary or permanent. (A six-inch scar on the leg of a 55-year-old man would not be evaluated in the same way as a six-inch scar on the face of an unmarried 15-year-old girl.)

- Increased living costs (for custodial care or remodeling to accommodate a physical handicap, for example).

- Repair or replacement costs for property.

Punitive damages, sometimes called *exemplary* damages, although rare in Canada, are claimed in cases of flagrant abuse by the defendant and can be a fixed amount (statutory) or left to the discretion of the court. In Quebec, the provincial Charter of Rights and the Consumer Protection Act permit the judge to award punitive damages to discourage certain types of abuse. In Newfoundland, a judge ordered the defendant in a case to pay the plaintiff $17,000 for the value of property he unlawfully took from the plaintiff, and a further $20,000 as exemplary damages because of his conduct: he had continued to build on the plaintiff's property, even after the plaintiff had been declared owner of the land.

***A defendant was held in contempt of court for making derogatory
remarks about the judge. What will happen to him?***

If the defendant's offensive behavior occurs right in court, it is called
direct contempt, and the judge usually has the power to impose a penalty
immediately, such as a fine or imprisonment. *Indirect contempt* takes
place outside or away from the courtroom. An example would be
refusing to comply with a subpoena. A hearing (sometimes called a
contempt proceeding) would generally be scheduled, at which the
accused could defend his actions. The hearing would determine whether
or not the individual should be cited and sentenced for contempt of
court. If he is charged with contempt for refusing to testify, he may be
kept in prison until he changes his mind and decides to cooperate. The
question of contempt of court, especially direct contempt, is now the
subject of debate, because the judge in such cases acts as victim as well
as prosecutor and judge.

***Carla is the victim of a crime, but the prosecutor won't let her
testify. Is he allowed to do this?***

Yes. A prosecuting attorney has the power to decide how to prepare his
case and present the evidence. This includes deciding whom he wants to
testify at the trial. Although the victim of a crime generally appears as a
witness for the prosecution, it is not required.

***Does a witness's testimony become part of the public record so
that anyone can read or obtain a copy of it?***

Not always. During the course of a trial, a court reporter, or stenographer, writes down everything that is said. Although this transcript may be
typed up at the end of each day for reference by the judge and attorneys
during the rest of the trial, an official typed copy of the transcript is
generally not made unless the case is being appealed. Then the transcript becomes one of the documents filed with the appeals court.
Access to the transcript may be limited by the court; otherwise, anyone
may ask to see a particular file. In certain cases dealing with national
security, the public may not have access to documents.

***Ken's lawyer wants certain documents to prepare his divorce
case. Ken does not want to part with the originals. Will
photocopies suffice?***

No. Photocopies of documents that are available are not admissible as
proof if the other party's attorney objects. This is based on what is called

"the best evidence rule," which holds that, at trial, only the best type of evidence that could be obtained should be produced. If the originals were lost, then photocopies may be admissible.

If I win my case, can the judge require the other person to pay my court costs?

It's possible, but not automatic. Each province has its own laws about when the judge may order a person to pay his opponent's court costs, such as expenses for filing legal papers, having subpoenas served on witnesses, obtaining expert opinions and stenographers' notes. The awarding of court costs is usually left to the discretion of the judge. Such costs should not be confused with lawyers' fees.

Craig won a court judgment against the Zero Company, but before he could collect, the Zero Company went out of business, and the owners started a business under a new name. What can Craig do?

If the Zero Company was a sole proprietorship or a partnership, Craig can seek payment from the owner's or partners' personal assets. The court would issue a writ of execution, which authorizes the sheriff or other official to seize property and sell it to pay the judgment. If Zero was a corporation, business assets may have to be sold to pay the obligation. If there was fraud by the Zero Company, or if the claim was for up to six months' wages, then the directors would be personally responsible.

How many times can I appeal my case?

Some cases cannot be appealed. Others can be appealed only when granted a "leave to appeal" by the Appeal Court. And some are appealable "by right," which means there is an automatic right to appeal written in the law. For example, a divorce judgment concerning custody or alimentary pension can be appealed by right, since the Divorce Act expressly states that such a judgment is appealable.

A case that is appealed from the trial division would be heard by the Appeal Division of the Provincial Court, variously called the Court of Queen's Bench Appeal Division, or Appeal Court, and only in rare cases could this case be further appealed to the Supreme Court of Canada.

Cases heard before certain provincial boards or tribunals, rental boards or the Workers' Compensation Board for example, are some-times reviewable by the provincial superior or supreme courts by virtue of the latter courts' supervisory power over inferior tribunals.

Appeals are usually quite expensive, since most involve the transcription and printing of the testimony heard by the trial court and involve a lot of time by the lawyer presenting or contesting the appeal. To succeed at the appeal stage, the appellant must convince the appeal court that the trial judge made a mistake in law or in his appreciation of the facts, or that the trial was otherwise irregular.

When I lost my lawsuit, my lawyer advised me to appeal the decision. Does this mean that I will have to testify again?

No. When a higher court reviews the decision of a lower court, there is no trial, no jury, and no new testimony. A judge in the appellate court reviews the case, weighs the arguments of the opposing attorneys, and either affirms the ruling of the lower court or overturns it.

Wesley was being tried for attempted murder. The jury returned a verdict of not guilty. Can the prosecutor appeal this acquittal?

Yes. The Crown has a right to appeal an acquittal involving a serious offense, but the appeal must be restricted to a question of law alone. In the famous case involving Dr. Henry Morgentaler, who was charged with illegally performing an abortion, the Ontario Court of Appeal held that the Crown's right to appeal against an acquittal does not violate the guarantee against double jeopardy (being retried for an offense of which you have been acquitted) in the Charter of Rights and Freedoms.

Small Claims Court

For consumer problems, see "When You Have a Complaint" in Chapter 9, *Consumer Rights*.

What kind of cases do small claims courts handle?

These courts hear uncomplicated civil cases that involve sums of money up to $3,000. The maximum varies from one province to another. If the dollar amount of a case exceeds the limit, it must be heard in a different court. Common cases that are brought to small claims courts include those of tenants who want their security deposits back from their landlords, and consumers seeking refunds for defective merchandise.

Whom and what should I take to Small Claims Court to help me?

Anyone or anything, within reason, that relates to your case. Witnesses to the disputed transactions and events are especially important. Bring

Small Claims Court

all documents that will back up your position, such as warranties, receipts, contracts, leases, correspondence, and canceled cheques. If your dispute is over something you can easily carry, such as a defective radio, bring it with you. If not, bring photographs of the item to court.

I'm going to Small Claims Court to get my money back for a defective dishwasher. Will I need to question my witnesses?

It depends on how the Small Claims Court operates in your area. Talk with someone who has been through it, or go to the court and watch what goes on. In some courts, you might be expected to "examine" your

Taking Your Case to Small Claims Court

If you are involved in a dispute over a fairly small amount of money, you may be able to settle it quickly and easily in Small Claims Court without ever consulting a lawyer. In more complicated cases, however, or where the amount involved is substantial ($2,500 for instance), it may be to your advantage to consult a lawyer before beginning proceedings.

Small claims courts only hear cases where the money in question is under a certain amount—from $50 to $3,000, depending on the province you live in. If there is no Small Claims Court in your area, your case may be heard by a trial court (possibly called circuit, common pleas, county, district, superior, or some other name) or a local court, such as city or municipal, justice's or magistrate's court. You will have a better chance of winning your case if you prepare beforehand, following these steps:

1. Fill out a formal complaint and make a copy for yourself. Many courts have standard forms for complaints. If your court does not, ask the clerk of the court what you should write.

2. Give the complaint to the clerk of the court. He will ask you to pay a filing fee—ranging from $5 to $50, depending on the province. If you win your case, the defendant (your opponent) may be ordered to reimburse you for this fee.

3. Ask the clerk for your court date and the number assigned to your complaint. This number will identify your case; use it in any communication with the court and in any documents, such as subpoenas, that you send.

4. Make sure that your complaint is delivered to the defendant. Usually the clerk will mail it with a *summons* (an order to file an answer to the complaint by a certain day) or have the sheriff's office deliver it. But if witnesses, just as a lawyer does. In other places, you might be expected only to introduce your witnesses (ask them to state their names), and ask them to tell what they saw. A third possibility is that the judge may ask most of the questions. You may also have the opportunity to question any witnesses the store owner brings to court.

Lester got a summons from the Small Claims Court directing him to file an answer to an attached complaint. What should he do?

Lester should ask the court clerk if there's an official form for his answer. If so, he should fill it out, file it with the court, and send a copy by registered mail to the complainant. If there is no official form, he should type or neatly print his own answer. He should use the name of the case

the summons cannot be delivered, you may have to help locate the defendant. The court will not proceed until the defendant receives the summons.

5. If the defendant offers to settle out of court, you may choose to accept the settlement and drop the case. If he files a written answer to your complaint, request a copy so that you will be prepared for the counterclaims he will make in court.

6. If you cannot appear in court on the appointed day, ask the clerk of the court for a continuance (postponement). The defendant can do the same.

7. Appear in court promptly (or you risk losing your case by default). Bring any witnesses with you and whatever documents you think will help prove your claim, such as canceled checks, receipts, letters, and contracts. Have this material organized and neatly arranged in a folder. If damaged property or defective merchandise is involved, and it is portable, bring it with you; otherwise, photograph the property or the item and bring the photographs to court.

8. When the judge (or arbitrator) asks you to present your case, explain the facts simply and clearly, without exaggerating or becoming excited. Be brief but thorough. Try to show that your demands are reasonable and that you have tried other means to persuade the defendant to settle with you. Let the judge know if you have brought witnesses, documents, or other evidence.

9. Answer the judge's questions as best you can and allow the defendant to tell his side of the story. If you are allowed, question your own witnesses and cross-examine the defendant's witnesses. After hearing both sides of the case, the judge will announce his decision. If you win, the court will order the defendant to pay you a specified amount of money.

Small Claims Court

as it appears on the complaint, such as *John Doe* v. *Lester Smith;* use the case number listed on the summons; respond to each point in the complaint; sign his name; and return it by the date specified.

Reginald expected to have his dispute settled by a judge. Instead, a court officer suggested that the case go to arbitration. Why?

So that people can have their disputes resolved quickly, many small claims courts offer the alternative of arbitration. Reginald and his opponent would present their arguments to an objective third person, such as an attorney, who would act as the judge.

Gisela lost her case in Small Claims Court. Can she appeal?

It depends on where she lives. In some places, the decisions of the Small Claims Court may be appealed to the High Court; in others, only a defendant may appeal; and in still others, no appeal is allowed. Gisela should check with the clerk of her court about the law in her area.

How can Mathilda collect the judgment she won in court?

Mathilda should ask the clerk of the court to prepare a writ of execution, which the clerk will then issue to the sheriff. The writ authorizes the sheriff to seize and sell enough of the defendant's property to pay Mathilda what she is owed. (Certain types of property, such as a percentage of the value of the family home, tools of a trade, livestock, or other assets may be exempt from seizure under provincial law.)

Selecting Jurors

Why do some juries have 12 persons and some only 6?

Juries in criminal cases must have 12 jurors: this derives from the common law and is part of our cultural heritage. A section of the Criminal Code permitting a jury of only six persons in criminal cases heard in Yukon and the Northwest Territories was declared invalid, because it violated the Canadian Charter's guarantee of equality before the law.

Where juries are still allowed in civil cases, as in British Columbia, Alberta and Ontario, for example, a jury has six members. (The number of jurors in a civil case is determined by the law of the province involved, but is usually six for reasons of economy.) Jury trials in civil cases are becoming rare because they are costly and more time-consuming than trial by judge alone. In civil cases unanimity is not required; five out of six jurors may decide the case.

Maggie received a legal notice requiring her to appear for jury duty. How did her name get on the list?

Every court system must select its jurors, by a fair and impartial method, from among the citizens in its area, or jurisdiction. This means drawing up a list from a wide cross section of people in the community—using names from tax rolls, city telephone directories, utility records, or electoral lists, for example—then having a public official randomly select names taken from these sources. The individuals whose names are selected, like Maggie, are then notified to appear for jury duty.

Collette, a single mother, received a notice to report for jury duty, but she doesn't have anyone who can take care of the children in her absence. Will the court excuse her?

Perhaps. Collette should call the number given on the notice and ask what she must do to be excused. If she ignores the notice and does not appear on the date requested, she may be arrested and jailed.

Recent service on a jury, illness or disability, lack of child care for small children, and the demands of running a small business are all reasons that might result in a person's being excused from jury duty. Some judges may also excuse members of certain professions, such as police officers, doctors, and lawyers.

Will I be paid for the time I spend on jury duty?

Yes, but probably not very much. Serving on a jury is considered a civic obligation. Jurors are paid about $30 a day, plus the cost of traveling to and from the courthouse. Generally, jurors are not reimbursed for other expenses, such as child care and meals. However, if the jury must deliberate during mealtimes, the court will provide food, and if the jury is sequestered, the court will provide for lodging.

Hope has received a notice to appear for jury duty for two weeks. Will she be deliberating on a jury during that whole time?

Probably not. In fact, Hope may never sit on a jury. When she reports to the courthouse, she becomes one of a pool of prospective jurors waiting to be chosen to sit on an actual jury. Those in the pool are selected at random for questioning by the prosecuting and defense attorneys, who must then agree on the final composition of the jury for the trial. (This process is called *voir dire*.) After being questioned, Hope will either be asked to stay as a member of the jury or be excused from that jury. If excused, she returns to the jury pool to await another call.

The last time I was on jury duty, a defense lawyer sent me back to the jury pool without asking me any questions whatsoever. Why would he do this?

Both prosecuting and defense attorneys have a certain number of what are called *peremptory challenges*, which they can use to dismiss jurors for no reason whatsoever. This allows a lawyer to remove a juror if he has a feeling that the person may have a prejudice about the case. The number of peremptory challenges varies with the gravity of the crime to be tried; from 20 for treason to four for the possession of an unregistered weapon, or any other offense punishable by less than five years' imprisonment.

What kind of questions will the lawyers ask me when they're selecting the jury?

They may ask questions about your occupation and education; whether you have any connection or relationship to the plaintiff or defendant; and how much you know about the case, either from personal experience or from the news media. In addition, the lawyers will try to find out if there is anything in your background that will make it difficult for you to be impartial in deciding on a verdict. If, for example, you had once been robbed, the lawyer for an accused burglar might suspect that it would be difficult for you to be impartial about his client. In some courts, prospective jurors are asked to fill out written questionnaires. Lawyers use this information to reject jurors who may be biased.

When being questioned as a prospective juror, Nelson suddenly realized that the defendant was a former business partner of his father's. Should Nelson tell the lawyers?

Yes. If Nelson is selected to serve on the jury and this connection is revealed after the trial begins, the judge could halt the proceedings and order a new trial before a new jury. If this connection is found out after the trial, it would be grounds for appeal.

Am I likely to be disqualified from a jury if I admit I've read a newspaper account of the case?

No. That alone would not disqualify you, since in highly publicized cases it may be difficult to find jurors who have not heard something about the case. But if you feel you cannot be impartial, and no evidence can change your mind, you should say so during the selection process.

Thomas was selected as an alternate juror at a murder trial. What does this mean?

As an alternate juror, Thomas will sit with the jury in the courtroom and hear all the evidence that the jury hears at the trial. If a juror becomes ill during the trial or is unable to continue for some other reason, Thomas will take his place and the trial will continue as scheduled. Many courts choose alternate jurors to make sure that the case will not have to be retried if a juror is dismissed in mid-trial.

Are jurors ever selected by judges?

No. But once the jury has been selected, a judge may excuse jurors who appear to be unfit to serve. If a juror is ill, disorderly, intoxicated, under the influence of drugs, or is otherwise incapable of fulfilling his duties, the judge may remove that person from the jury and may even charge him with contempt of court.

Ida will be a juror in a trial that is expected to last several weeks. Must her employer pay her for the days she misses work?

Some provinces do require employers to pay employees for time spent on jury duty. Even in provinces where these payments are not required, many employers still pay in recognition of the fact that jurors are fulfilling an important civic duty. Firing or demoting an employee for sitting on a jury is punishable by fine or imprisonment, or both.

I was selected as a juror for a murder trial. If I say that I could not vote for the death penalty, will I be removed from the jury?

Since the death penalty has been abolished in Canada, the question will not arise. The greatest penalty under Canadian law is 25 years in prison before being eligible for parole. If you tell the prosecutor or judge that you could not ever agree to such a severe sentence, you probably would be excused from sitting on the jury.

How is the foreman of a jury chosen, and what are his duties?

The manner of choosing a jury foreman varies from court to court. The foreman may be simply the first juror chosen for the trial. Or he can be elected by the jury members or named by the judge. As foreman, he presides over the jury's deliberations and makes sure all the jurors have a chance to express their views. The foreman also acts as the spokesman for the jury in communications with the court; in some courtrooms, he announces the jury's verdict.

Rory fears that he may forget some of the facts being brought out during the trial. What should he do?

Rory may find that when the jury's deliberations begin and he can discuss the case with the other jurors, he will remember more than he thinks he will. But if he absolutely cannot recall important testimony, he or any other juror can ask the judge to allow portions of the record of the trial to be read aloud by the court reporter. In most situations, the judge will permit this rehearing of testimony, or allow Rory to reexamine any of the exhibits.

When Doug was on a jury that was hearing a complicated case, he started to take notes, but the judge told him to stop. What is wrong with taking notes at a public trial?

Most courts do not allow note-taking, on the grounds that a juror may put too much emphasis on notes that may be incomplete or perhaps inaccurate. Not all courts take this view, however. Doug should check with the judge or a court officer for permission if he feels that taking notes will help him keep the facts of the case straight.

While serving as a juror, Natalie heard a news item that could influence her decision. Should she report this to the court?

Yes. The judge or a court officer and perhaps the prosecution and defense lawyers may wish to question her further about what she heard and its influence on her. If Natalie was shocked, moved to sympathy, outraged, or otherwise strongly affected by what she heard, she might be disqualified from sitting as a juror on this case. If, on the other hand, the news item was not closely related to the major issues in the case, Natalie might be allowed to continue as a juror. The final decision rests with the judge, who must weigh the news item's effect on Natalie.

Deliberating as a Juror

There is no set procedure that jurors must follow when deliberating. Each jury decides its own way of conducting discussions, settling differences of opinion, and polling its members for a vote. It is important to know, however, that if a juror cannot remember exactly what a witness said while testifying or if there is a dispute among the jurors about certain facts, the jurors may ask that the testimony be read to them or that exhibits be shown to them again.

Before the jurors leave the courtroom to begin their deliberations, the judge will tell them how the law applies to the case and ask them to follow his instructions to the best of their ability. Many judges stress the following points in their instructions:

- Jurors must discuss the evidence presented on all important issues before taking a vote on the verdict.
- Each juror should be allowed and encouraged to express his opinion during the deliberations.
- No juror should be pressured into changing his vote simply to arrive at a verdict more quickly.
- Each juror should weigh opposing views carefully and examine his own viewpoint in the light of those other opinions.
- No juror should hesitate to change his vote if the discussion has changed his point of view.

If a news reporter wants to talk to Bud while he's serving as a juror on a trial, should Bud automatically refuse to discuss the case, or is it OK to answer some questions?

Bud should refuse. A judge usually instructs jury members not to discuss the trial with *anyone* until it is over—and not even with fellow jurors until all the evidence has been heard and the jury's deliberations begin.

Discussing the trial before all the evidence is presented may lead a juror to form an opinion before hearing both sides of the case. Even if the reporter was not trying to influence Bud, just answering his questions may lead Bud to form an opinion before learning all the facts. If Bud does talk with a reporter, he could be removed from the jury or charged with contempt of court—an offense punishable by a fine or jail, or both.

While serving on a jury, Dora saw a fellow juror talking to the plaintiff during a court recess. Should Dora report this?

Yes. Dora should tell a court officer, such as the bailiff or judge, who can discharge the juror from service. All jurors should avoid speaking with anyone involved in the case during the trial—even about topics unrelated to the case, such as the weather or who won the Stanley Cup. In some important cases juries are sequestered.

If a juror wants to know more about the people, places, and events involved in the trial, can he investigate on his own?

No. Jurors are not allowed to visit places connected with the case without court approval and supervision. Nor are they permitted to question any of the witnesses or read articles about the case. If a juror is caught pursuing his own investigation, he will be dismissed from the jury, and he could also be charged with contempt of court, an offense that is punishable by a fine or jail, or both. The judge may, however, direct that the jury view a place, thing, or person involved in a case, where he thinks that the purpose of justice may be served. Jurors would, of course, be supervised while doing this.

Does a jury have to reach a unanimous decision?

In criminal cases, the verdict of the jury must be unanimous. In civil cases where juries are still used, as in Alberta, Manitoba and Ontario, five out of six jurors may render a valid verdict. Some provinces, Quebec for example, have abolished jury trials in civil cases.

The jury Thea is on is going to be sequestered. Thea doesn't want to leave her family during the trial. Can she be excused?

Probably not. Separation from your family is not reason enough to be excused from jury duty unless there are some special circumstances, such as the serious illness of a child. If the trial is a long one, the judge may permit Thea's family to visit her even though the jury is sequestered. The visit would probably be in the presence of a court official.

The jury I am on may be sequestered. What does that mean?

It means that you and the other jurors will be kept isolated until the trial is over to keep people from influencing your thinking about the case and to prevent you from being exposed to improper information. You and the other jurors will be lodged in a hotel or motel at the court's expense, and any contact or communication with other people will be severely restricted. In addition, your reading material may be screened to make sure you don't read news accounts of the trial; and the judge may forbid you to listen to radio or watch television news broadcasts. You will be permitted to leave your rooms only in the company of bailiffs and to travel only to and from the jury room.

Naomi is on a jury that has been deliberating for almost a week, and the jurors are still not close to the unanimous vote required in the case. What happens if they can't reach a verdict?

If the judge feels that all the jurors have done their best to reach a verdict but remain hopelessly at odds, he will declare a hung jury (meaning the jurors are unable to reach a verdict) and dismiss the jurors. The person who brought the case to court (the plaintiff in a civil case, the prosecutor in a criminal case) must then decide whether or not to retry the matter before a new jury. Because of the time and expense involved, judges hesitate to declare hung juries and will do so only when they are convinced that further deliberations are useless.

After a jury returned a verdict in favor of the plaintiff, the defense lawyer went up to the jurors and asked them why they decided against his client. Is he allowed to do this?

Yes. Although neither the defense nor the prosecuting attorney may discuss the case with members of the jury during the trial, once the case is decided, the jurors are free to discuss it with anyone they choose. Many lawyers, whether they win or lose, like to discuss the trial with jurors after it is over. Some even ask for comments about their court-room performance in order to improve their skills.

However, no attorney should badger or berate the jurors about the verdict they have given, even though his client lost. Conduct of this sort should be reported to both the judge who presided over the trial and the provincial bar association.

I have been called for regular jury duty several times in the last 15 years, but I have never once been called to serve on a grand jury. What is a grand jury ?

Grand juries, once common in most provinces, have been abolished across the country, most recently in Nova Scotia (1985). A grand jury was a group of citizens (12 to 23), without prior knowledge of an event, to whom a Crown prosecutor presented evidence against an accused person. The grand jury then decided whether or not the facts presented were sufficient to issue an indictment. Grand juries are still used extensively in the United States.

Being a Witness

For more information, see "Witnessing a Crime" in Chapter 17, *Victims and Crimes.*

Lori will be a witness for the first time. Is it proper for her lawyer to help her phrase her answers before the trial?

Yes. Lori's lawyer can discuss her testimony with her, rehearse with her, and advise her on courtroom procedure. But it is improper for him to supply answers for her. When Lori testifies, she must tell the truth on the basis of her own knowledge and observations, not her attorney's.

Kendall is nervous about testifying under cross-examination tomorrow. Should he steel himself for a real ordeal on the witness stand?

Cross-examination can have its tough moments, because it is how lawyers challenge the accuracy and relevance of a witness's previous testimony. The cross-examining lawyer will try to show that his client is less damaged by Kendall's testimony than it might first appear. Kendall might be asked to give more details about an event or observation; he might be confronted with earlier statements he made that seem to be inconsistent with his present testimony. The cross-examining lawyer also might ask Kendall about his relationship with the accused person, in order to try to show that Kendall's testimony is biased.

Kendall's best strategy would be to try to remain calm and not be drawn into an argument with the attorney cross-examining him. Neither should he answer in a flippant or rude manner, no matter how great the temptation. Some attorneys try to throw the witness off balance by using tricks such as standing very close to the witness, grimacing or using sarcasm.

I have been called as a witness in a child custody case and I have no idea what to expect. Who will be questioning me, and how long can I expect the process to go on?

When you take the witness stand, you will take an oath to tell the truth. Then the lawyer who called you will begin the questioning with what is called the *direct examination.* After that, the lawyer for the other side will question, or *cross-examine,* you. If the cross-examination brings up new issues, the first lawyer has another chance to ask questions, or *redirect;* then the other lawyer, too, can ask additional questions, or *recross.*

Redirect and recross-examination can go on for more turns if necessary. Once the lawyers have completed their examinations, the judge may ask you some questions as well, especially if he did not understand your answers or felt important issues were overlooked by the lawyers.

Fast-talkers always confuse me. What should I do if I am a witness and the opposing lawyer tricks me into a misstatement during cross-examination?

Tell the lawyer or judge that you made a mistake in your testimony when you answered the question and that you would like to correct or clarify your answer. The judge will allow you to do so. You have the right to explain any of your answers. If you realize your misstatement after you've left the witness stand, let the lawyer who called you know, and he may ask you to take the stand again to correct your mistake.

What happens if I'm on the witness stand and I simply don't know the answer to a question?

If you don't know the answer, say so. If you don't understand the question, ask the judge or lawyer to repeat or rephrase it. Your duty on the witness stand is to answer all questions put to you as completely and truthfully as you can, and that includes admitting to the court that you don't know the answer.

Mary, a pharmacist, claims she was an expert witness at a murder trial. How could this be?

If Mary was called as a witness by the Crown, or by the defense attorney, to testify to certain facts that she would know about only because of her specialized study of pharmacy, she would be an expert witness. As an expert witness she could give her opinion on matters concerning her area of expertise.

Maureen is not sure she saw the defendant hit the shopkeeper, but that is the only possibility that makes sense to her. Should she testify that she witnessed the attack?

No. A witness should never present a logical deduction or a guess as a fact. Maureen should restrict her testimony to her own observations and knowledge. In some situations, a lawyer might ask a witness to make an educated guess based on his knowledge. If Maureen is asked to do this, and the opposite attorney does not object to the question, then she should make it quite clear that her answer is nothing more than a guess or estimate.

Usually, only expert witnesses can offer opinions as evidence. This type of evidence is often countered by other opinion-evidence from an expert witness for the opposing side, which argues for an opposite conclusion.

Being a Witness

Does a witness have the right to refuse to answer questions?

No. If, however, the opposing attorney objects to a question on the grounds of law, and that objection is sustained by the judge, that question does not have to be answered. An attorney could object because a question is irrelevant or is a leading question (one that contains the answer or assumes a fact not proven, such as "When did you stop beating your wife?"), or because of some other legal principle (the exclusion of hearsay evidence, say). If a lawyer does not challenge a question, or if his objection is not sustained, the witness must truthfully answer the question. The Charter of Rights and Freedoms assures the witness that any testimony given by him at trial cannot be used against him in any other trial, except in the case of perjury.

If I am called as a witness, can I use notes while I'm testifying?

It is in the court's discretion to forbid you to use notes on the witness stand. However, some judges allow you to consult notes to refresh your memory of the facts of the case. Police often refer to notes when testifying, because they are involved in many trials, deal with many people and facts, and much time may have passed between the alleged crime and the trial. Notes made at the scene and time of the event involved are, of course, the most useful.

The defendant's lawyer had the court declare John a hostile witness. Why did he do such a thing?

Ordinarily a lawyer cannot impeach the credibility of a witness that he has called to testify, neither can he ask him leading questions or questions that do not have a direct bearing on the facts at issue. If, however, the witness seems to be eluding the questions asked, or seems to favor the other party, or appears to be lying, the lawyer may request that the witness be declared hostile. If the court declares that witness to be hostile, the lawyer may then treat him in the same manner as a witness produced by the adverse party and thus impeach his credibility and otherwise cross-examine him.

Jonathan feels he lost his case because the evidence of one of his witnesses was ruled inadmissible. How could this happen?

The rules of evidence are vast and complex and their purpose is to ensure that a trial is conducted in the best way possible for the truth to emerge. Thus the adverse party has many legal grounds for objecting to certain evidence, or from allowing a witness to answer a specific question. If the judge agrees with the objections, he can rule that the proposed evidence or testimony is inadmissible. Grounds for inadmissibility include irrelevancy, hearsay, the evidence provided is not the best evidence, or the testimony is privileged communication, as would be the case if a clergyman is asked to testify to something he has knowledge of through his professional relationship.

These are just some of the reasons why the evidence of Jonathan's witness could have been inadmissible.

Martin, who is an avowed atheist, is scheduled to be a witness, but he does not want to take the oath by placing his hand on the Bible. Can he be a witness?

Yes. At one time, his objection to swearing on the Bible would have disqualified Martin from being a witness. Now, those who object to taking an oath may make a solemn affirmation to tell the truth. People of the Jewish faith may swear on the Old Testament of the Bible and Moslems may take their oath on the Koran.

What is a material witness?

A material witness is one who has knowledge about the case that no one else has. The only eyewitness to a shooting would be a material witness because he can give firsthand evidence about a criminal act.

In some cases, a witness who is likely to give material evidence may be imprisoned if the judge feels that he would not attend the trial if a subpoena were issued, or that he is evading a subpoena.

Harold was a witness to an accident in which a motorcycle hit a pedestrian. The lawyers for both sides have sent him a list of questions to which they want his written answers. Are they allowed to do this?

Yes, but Harold does not have to respond. Written questions that are to be answered in writing and under oath are called interrogatories, and only the defendant and the plaintiff in a lawsuit are required to answer them. However, the lawyers may compel Harold to give a deposition, in which he orally answers questions that are put to him verbally, but which may also be written (and read aloud to him). To do this, the lawyers would serve Harold with a subpoena to appear at a certain time and place, such as at one of their offices, and they would have a court reporter record his testimony given under oath.

Being a Witness

Nicole is a witness in an accident case. Can she send in a written statement instead of going to court in person?

No. Witnesses are required to give their testimony in person, so that lawyers for both sides can question them. However, in exceptional circumstances, such as if Nicole were seriously ill or lived far away, her deposition could be used instead of live testimony, provided the other attorney agreed. In some cases a commission may be appointed by the court to visit Nicole at her place of residence (even in another country) and take her deposition there.

Rick was told to wait outside the courtroom until he was called to the witness stand to testify. Why?

Lawyers want to make certain that each witness testifies from his own memory, based on his personal observation and knowledge. Lawyers fear that if a witness hears the testimony of others, he could be influenced, consciously or unconsciously, to reshape his testimony. If Rick is asked to wait outside the courtroom, he must comply. Once Rick has testified he would be allowed to stay in the courtroom for the rest of the trial, unless the trial was being held *in camera*.

Teresa is going to be a witness in a criminal trial. She will have an hour's drive to the courthouse and will have to sit there every day until she is called. Can she get paid for doing this?

Yes, every province provides a tariff for witnesses who are summoned by subpoena to testify at a trial. These tariffs vary from one province to another and cover transportation costs (usually by the least expensive means, such as bus or subway) and compensation for a half-day, full day or several days, depending on the length of the case. In order to be paid, Teresa should present her subpoena to a special officer of the court who will determine the amount she is entitled to receive.

Someone Bill is scheduled to testify against keeps phoning him at home. What can he do to stop this?

Bill should inform the police or the prosecuting attorney. Harassing or trying to intimidate a witness is a crime. The person calling Bill could be both fined and jailed.

Bill should also try to make a tape recording of the phone call from the other person, which would help in the case against that party. It is legal to tape a phone conversation when the person who is doing the taping is one of the participants in the conversation, but not if he is a third party.

Daisy did not tell the truth while under oath as a witness. What could happen to her?

Lying under oath in court is a crime known as perjury, and is punishable by a fine, imprisonment, or both. The party that lost the case could also sue Daisy for damages incurred, if he can prove that his case was lost or damaged because of Daisy's perjured testimony.

What types of protection are available to witnesses who may be in danger because of their testimony in criminal cases?

Generally, a witness who is in danger will be kept under police surveillance or even given a personal bodyguard for the duration of the trial. In some cases he may be detained in prison prior to testifying. After the trial, if the witness is in danger, the federal government's witness protection program would help him establish a new identity, residence and source of revenue, and provide other assistance. The Solicitor General's office in Ottawa can give you more details about this program.

Glossary

abandonment The voluntary surrender of property or rights with no intention of reclaiming them. Putting your old bicycle out to be picked up with the garbage is abandonment; if a neighbor takes the bike and repairs it, you have no right to take it back.

abet To encourage someone to commit a crime.

abrogate To repeal or abolish; for example, to cancel a law by repealing it or declaring it unconstitutional.

abstract Summary or recap; a short history of who has owned a particular piece of real estate.

abuttals Boundary lines around a plot of land.

accessory Person who helps another to commit a crime, but who is not personally at the scene when the crime is committed. An accessory after the fact helps the criminal hide or get away.

accomplice Person who helps or encourages another to commit a crime.

accord and satisfaction Agreement by a creditor to accept something different from what is called for under the contract he entered. For example, if a mason agrees to pave your driveway and does it badly, he may be willing to accept a lower fee for the job than the one you originally agreed to pay him.

acquit To find a defendant in a criminal trial not guilty; to release someone from an obligation.

act of God An unforeseeable event, such as a tornado or an earthquake, which is due to natural causes and which could not be prevented by normal foresight. If a person is unable to fulfill the terms of a contract because of "an act of God," he will usually be relieved of his obligation under the contract.

action Legal proceeding, such as a criminal trial or a civil lawsuit, undertaken to (1) determine whether or not someone has committed a crime, (2) obtain monetary compensation for a wrong or injury, (3) enforce someone's right, or (4) prevent a wrong from being done.

ad hoc Latin phrase meaning "for this," or "for a specific purpose." For example, an ad hoc committee is a group that is formed to study or address a particular problem.

ad litem Latin phrase meaning "for the lawsuit." A guardian *ad litem* is a guardian appointed by the court during a lawsuit, hearing, or other legal proceeding, to represent someone who is considered incompetent because of age or mental condition.

ademption Selling, giving away, or using up of property that a person has left to someone in his will, so that when he dies the property is no longer part of his estate and cannot be given to the heir as the will provides.

adjournment Temporary or indefinite postponement.

adjudication Act or process by which a court reaches a decision; judgment handed down by the court.

admissible Acceptable for use in a court hearing; relevant to the case.

adultery Voluntary sexual relations by a married person with someone other than his or her spouse; for purposes of divorce, adultery is one of the ways of establishing that a marriage has broken down.

advocate To plead someone else's position or case. A person, such as a lawyer, who argues for a specific position or proposal.

affidavit Written statement made under oath and witnessed by a notary public or other authorized person.

age of majority Age of adulthood; age at which a person can legally act on his own behalf—typically, age 18 or 19, depending on the province.

agent Person authorized to act on behalf of another, as in transacting business or managing property.

aggravated Severe or intensified; for example, aggravated assault involves the maiming or disfiguring of the victim and the breaking of the skin, as opposed to simple assault which could be a simple slap or push.

aggravated sexual assault Crime of forcing a person to have sexual intercourse against his or her will. See *rape.*

alimentary pension Money paid to one's ex-spouse by order of a judge. The term *alimentary pension* is gradually being replaced by the terms *maintenance* and *support.*

allegation Accusation made by someone in a lawsuit; it indicates what he hopes to prove.

amicus curiae Latin phrase meaning "friend of the court." A person or organization that is not involved in a lawsuit, but that may be affected by the court's decision, may with the court's permission prepare arguments or point out information that the court ought to take into consideration when making a decision.

amnesty General pardon granted by a government for a crime, often before a trial or conviction.

amortization Payment of a debt,

such as a mortgage, in installments over a specified time period.

annulment Declaration that something is, always was, and will continue to be void. A court or church order stating that a marriage never existed.

answer Written response prepared by the defendant in a lawsuit, which admits or denies accusations made against him; also known as a plea.

appeal Act of asking a higher court to review a case when one disagrees with the judgment of the lower court.

appellate Pertaining to appeals. Each province has its own Court of Appeal, which hears appeals from lower courts. The Supreme Court of Canada is the ultimate appellate court for all Canada.

appropriate To designate money or property for a particular use.

arbitrate To try to help disputants to reach a settlement. Arbitration can be used to settle disputes that might otherwise end in a lawsuit.

arraignment Court hearing in which the charges against an accused person are read to him in order to allow him to plead guilty, not guilty, pardon, *autrefois acquit* (previously acquitted), or *autrefois convict* (previously convicted).

arrears Overdue payments, debts.

arson Crime of maliciously setting fire to a house or other property.

artificial persons Persons created by law, corporations for example, as opposed to natural persons.

assault and battery Acts of violence toward another person. The unlawful, intentional touching of someone else. Assault involves a threat or attempt to do physical harm; battery involves the actual touching or striking of the other person. An assault is more serious if it results in serious bodily injury or if it is committed with a deadly weapon.

assignment Transfer of property rights from one person to another.

attachment Court order, or writ, authorizing the sheriff or other official to seize something a person owns as security for payment of a court judgment; often the property is sold to get money to satisfy the debt.

attest To affirm something, such as a signature, is genuine or true.

attorney-in-fact Person who is authorized to act on behalf of someone else in business dealings or for other purposes. The authority to function in this way is given by a letter of attorney, or power of attorney.

attractive nuisance Something on a person's property that attracts children and that is potentially dangerous to them, such as a swimming pool without a fence around it.

bail Release of a person under arrest in exchange for the posting of a sum of money or a deed to a property, which money or property would be forfeited if the accused did not show up for trial.

bail bond Surety bond, or written guarantee by one person, called the surety, to pay a certain amount of money to the court if an accused person fails to appear for trial.

bailiff Official who maintains order in a courtroom and who in certain jurisdictions serves court papers and helps to execute court judgments.

bailment Entrusting of property to

another for a special purpose, such as repair or safekeeping. Bringing clothes to a laundry or putting a car in a garage for repairs are examples of bailment.

bait and switch This marketing practice, forbidden by the Competitions Act, occurs when a merchant offers at bargain prices an item of which he has only a few to sell. The idea is to draw customers to his store. Once in his place of business, the merchant offers the customer a similar item at a higher price, claiming that the sales item has been sold out.

balloon loan Loan requiring the borrower to make a number of small regular payments and one very large final payment. Often the borrower must refinance the loan in order to make the final balloon payment.

beneficiary Person named to receive property or money, as in a will or insurance policy.

bequest Gift, given through a will, of money or other property that is not real estate.

beyond a reasonable doubt Level of proof required in criminal trials; a jury must be convinced that the defendant committed the crime, not that he probably did so.

bigamy Crime of having two spouses at the same time.

bill of lading Receipt issued by a railway, trucker, or other transport company, showing which goods have been received for shipment; terms of the contract may also be included.

bill of particulars Document that gives the details of the charges being brought against the defendant in a lawsuit; also known as plaintiff's declaration or statement of claim.

bill of sale Documented proof that ownership of property has been transferred from seller to buyer.

binder In insurance, a document providing temporary protection to an insured person, usually setting out in a brief form the terms and conditions of the policy.

binding Enforceable; imposing a duty. A binding contract is one in which the people involved are required to carry out its terms.

blackmail Crime of forcing someone to give something of value to keep from having something revealed that would incriminate him or ruin his reputation; extortion.

BNA Act The British North America Act. One of the principal documents in Canadian constitutional law, this 1867 act sets out the respective powers of the federal and provincial governments as well as other matters.

bona fide Latin phrase meaning "in good faith." Sincere, with good intentions, without fraud or deceit.

bond Written promise to pay a fixed sum of money at a future date and at a specific interest rate—for example, a Canada savings bond; a type of insurance in which a company or individual will reimburse another person for any loss suffered because of the actions of a third person.

boycott Refusal to conduct business with a person or company until certain practices cease.

breach Failure to uphold one's part of a contract; violation of the law.

breach of the peace Disturbing the peace and quiet of a community with disorderly behavior.

bribery Crime of giving or offering a

public official something of value in order to influence his actions.

brief Attorney's written summary of a law case, containing the facts, the law, and the authorities relied on; also known as a factum.

broker Dealer or agent who is paid to buy or sell property, such as real estate or stocks.

burden of proof Responsibility of establishing that a disputed fact is true; presenting evidence in court to prove that the facts are as you allege them to be. In a criminal case, the burden of proof is always on the prosecutor, who must prove that the defendant is guilty; the defendant need not prove that he is innocent. In civil cases, the burden of proof is upon the party who brings the action in law.

burglary Breaking into and entering a house or other building with the intention of committing a crime.

bylaws Set of regulations adopted by a corporation or other organization that governs the way the company will do business. Laws passed by cities and towns are also known as bylaws.

canon Principle, standard, or rule; a law of a religious denomination.

capital offense Any crime that is punishable by death. Capital punishment no longer exists in Canada.

carrying a concealed weapon Illegal possession of a hidden weapon — such as a gun, knife, or explosive device — on a person's body or within easy reach inside his car.

case law Legal principles established by judges in individual cases and used in deciding similar cases; part of the common law.

casualty Disaster or accident; a person who has been injured or property that has been lost or damaged.

caveat emptor Latin phrase meaning "let the buyer beware." In the past this phrase was used to warn consumers that they had no legal remedy if they bought defective merchandise that was not covered by a written warranty. Today consumer protection laws reduce the risks of buying defective goods.

cease and desist Order issued by a government agency requiring an individual or a business to stop a particular practice; similar to an injunction, which is issued by a court.

certiorari Order from a higher court to a lower one to prepare a certified copy of a case for review and to cease proceedings until the higher court has ruled on the issue.

champerty Illegal agreement in which a person who is not a party in the suit agrees to pay someone else's lawsuit expenses in exchange for part of the settlement.

change of venue Moving of a trial from one district to another, or from one court to another, in order to assure a fair and impartial trial.

chattel Item of property other than real estate.

chattel mortgage Loan obtained by putting up property other than real estate as collateral.

circuit court Local court, also called county, superior, or district court, which has jurisdiction (legal authority) over a particular area.

circumstantial evidence Indirect evidence; testimony or facts from which other facts, which are important to the case, can be inferred.

citation Written order to appear in court; legal reference to a statute, court case, or other legal authority.

civil action Lawsuit between individuals or companies to get money, stop a particular activity, or enforce a civil right (as opposed to criminal action, in which the state prosecutes someone for violating a law).

clerk of the court Employee who files court documents (pleadings, motions, or judgments), has access to court records, and issues summonses and subpoenas.

closing Final step in buying a house, in which the deed is given to the owner, money is given to the seller, and the mortgage is secured.

codicil Amendment to a will that changes or explains a part of it.

collateral Property or money pledged as security to ensure repayment of a loan.

collective bargaining Process by which an employer and a representative of his employees (generally a labor union leader) make agreements about the workers' hours, wages, rights, and benefits.

collusion Secret agreement made by two or more people to cheat someone or to defraud him of a legal right or possession.

comaker Cosigner; someone who signs a contract or promissory note and guarantees payment in the event that the borrower defaults.

common carrier Person or business that transports people or property for a fee, such as a bus company.

common law System of law derived from England and based on traditions and customs and on decisions rendered in previous cases (case law) rather than on statutes, as is the case with civil law. Common law is the rule in all provinces except Quebec, which has a civil code derived from French law.

common-law marriage Marriage that is not solemnized by a wedding ceremony. It is created when a couple agree to marry, present themselves as married, and live together as man and wife. Not all provinces recognize common-law marriages.

community property Property acquired by a husband and wife during their marriage, with each spouse holding a half-interest. Generally excludes property acquired through inheritance or as a gift.

commutation Change; reduction in a convicted criminal's sentence.

competent Possessing all the legal requirements to do something. For example, since the law requires a person to have reached a certain age (usually 18 or 19) in order to make a contract, children are not considered competent to do so, and if a child tries to enter a contract it can be declared void.

complainant Plaintiff; one who initiates a lawsuit.

complaint Document initiating a civil lawsuit, typically containing a brief description of the facts and what the plaintiff believes he is entitled to; a charge seeking prosecution for a criminal offense.

conciliation Meeting to resolve a dispute in a friendly manner; pretrial technique used to settle differences and avoid a trial.

condominium Complex of apartments or buildings in which different persons own the individual units but in which all owners have an interest in the common areas, such as stairways, hallways, elevators, and lawns.

condonation Forgiving or pardoning of an offense by acting as if it had not been committed.

confiscate To legally seize property without payment, usually because the owner was using it illegally or did not legally own it. For example, the police may confiscate stolen property from a convicted thief.

consanguinity Blood relationship; kinship. The connection between persons with the same ancestor.

consequential damages Losses, damage, or injuries that are not directly caused by an act, but are a result of that act. For example, in a lawsuit for breach of contract, the profits lost because goods were not delivered on time are considered consequential damages.

conservator Person appointed to handle someone's financial affairs — generally because the person is unable to handle them himself; also known as a guardian or curator.

consideration Something of value offered in a contract in exchange for something else of value. It is an inducement, such as a money payment, to get a person to perform his part of the agreement. For example, in a contract to buy a car, the consideration given the dealer is the price of the car, and the consideration given the buyer is the car itself. For a contract to be valid, however, each side must offer consideration to the other party.

consignment Delivery of property to someone for resale.

conspiracy Illegal or harmful plot between two or more people.

constitutional law Principles of law established in the British North America Act and other documents that determine the legal and political structure of the state.

contempt of court Intentional disregard or disrespect for the authority or dignity of the court, such as by disobeying its orders or disrupting its proceedings.

contested divorce Case in which only one spouse wants a divorce or in which there is no agreement on division of property or child custody.

contingent Dependent on an event, the outcome of which is unknown.

contingent fee Attorney's fee that is dependent upon the outcome of the case or upon factors other than the attorney's time. Contingent fees are often used in personal injury cases, where the attorney receives a percentage of the money awarded to his client if he wins.

continuance Delay or postponement of a court proceeding.

contract Binding agreement between persons or businesses to do or not to do something.

contribution Right to collect from others who are equally responsible for an amount one has paid in excess of one's fair share. For example, if Bob and Jane jointly owe Dan $200 and Bob pays the entire amount, he has a right of contribution from Jane for $100.

conversion Unlawful taking or use of someone else's property.

convey To transfer ownership.

conviction Final judgment in a criminal trial, finding the defendant guilty as charged.

cooling-off period Period of inaction; a time to reconsider. In door-to-door sales transactions, the time given to cancel an order or purchase.

cooperative Multidwelling complex where the tenants lease their apartments, but own shares in the complex, forming a corporation.

copyright Legal protection given to the author or artist for the exclusive right to reprint, publish, or sell additional copies of his work for a specified period of time.

corporation Business or organization formed by a group of people, with rights and liabilities separate from those of the individuals involved.

corpus delicti Latin phrase meaning "body of the crime"; something that shows a crime has been committed, such as a dead body with a stab wound or a safe that has been broken into.

cosign To sign a contract as a backup in case the primary signer does not fulfill his part of the contract. Cosigners are often used to back up persons making loan agreements.

counselor-at-law Attorney, lawyer, advocate, or barrister and solicitor.

counterclaim Claim brought by the defendant against the plaintiff in a lawsuit. If the defendant is successful, the counterclaim may reduce the plaintiff's claim or result in the plaintiff's paying the defendant; also known as a cross-demand.

counterfeiting Making a false copy or imitation of something—especially currency—with the intention of passing it off as genuine.

court-martial Court that tries members of the armed forces for viola-

tions of military law; civilians and members of the armed forces who commit nonmilitary crimes cannot be brought before this court.

covenant Any written agreement, or contract; clause or specific stipulation within a contract.

creditor Person or company to whom someone owes money.

crime of passion Crime committed impulsively under the influence of a sudden outburst of rage, terror, hatred, or some other overpowering emotion. For example, if a man discovers his wife in the act of adultery and kills her in a fit of rage, he has committed a crime of passion. Passion can be a defense against a charge of premeditated murder and may reduce the charge to manslaughter, which carries a less severe penalty.

cross-demand See *counterclaim.*

cross-examination Questioning of a witness by the opposing attorney in a legal case.

Crown The reigning sovereign. In Canadian law, the Crown usually means the government; there is a federal and a provincial Crown. A prosecuting attorney in a criminal case is referred to as a Crown attorney or Crown prosecutor.

Crown attorney See *prosecuting attorney.*

curator See *conservator.*

custody Responsibility for keeping and caring for a person or property. Also, the legal confinement of a person, as in protective custody or arrest and imprisonment.

damages Amount of money that a court may order the defendant in a lawsuit to pay the person who brought the suit to compensate him for any loss or harm the defendant caused.

de facto Latin phrase meaning "in fact"; actually. Used to describe a government, corporation, officer, or state of affairs that has to be accepted, but is illegal or illegitimate.

de jure Latin phrase meaning "by right"; legal or legitimate.

de novo An appeal by way of a trial. In a *de novo* appeal, the case is heard again with witnesses. Usually in cases of appeal, only legal arguments are heard by the appeal court.

debenture Document indicating a debt is owed and will be paid, usually without putting up any collateral.

debt consolidation loan Arrangement for combining and repaying several debts; the debtor makes installment payments to a single creditor who pays the original debts.

decedent Person who has died.

decree Judgment of a court.

defamation Attack on someone's reputation; slander, libel.

default To fail to fulfill a legal or contractual duty.

default decree Court judgment entered against a defendant who failed to appear in court and defend himself; also called a default judgment.

default docket Group of uncontested cases on a court's calendar.

defendant Person who is being sued or prosecuted.

delinquent Late in fulfilling an obligation, such as repaying a loan.

demurrer Response by the defendant alleging that, even if the plaintiff's accusations were true, there would be no need to go further; there is nothing for which the defendant should be made to answer.

deport To send someone back to the country from which he came.

deposition Sworn testimony taken out of court to gather information before trial; a part of the legal procedure called discovery.

descent and distribution Laws governing the distribution of a person's property to his heirs when he dies without leaving a will.

detainer Keeping someone against his will; holding property unlawfully, such as borrowing tools and failing to return them.

devise To transfer ownership of real estate by means of a will.

devisee An heir by will to real property, as opposed to a legatee, who receives movable property.

disbar To revoke an attorney's license to practice law.

disclaimer Rejection of a claim, property, or right; document that rejects such a claim.

discovery Pretrial procedure in which investigations are made to uncover evidence about a case.

dismissal Court order ending a trial before it begins, or while it is in progress but before a verdict is reached.

disorderly house House or building where something illegal is going on that creates a nuisance or threatens the public welfare. Drug houses, gambling houses, and houses of prostitution are examples.

dissolution The act of bringing to an end. Termination of a marriage by divorce; cancellation of a contract; termination of a corporation.

dividend Payment of a share of the profits, given to stockholders in a corporation; payment by an insurance company to policyholders with participatory policies.

docket Calendar, or record, of the cases scheduled to be heard in a court.

double jeopardy Retrying someone for an offense of which he has already been acquitted.

dower Formerly, what a widow was entitled to receive from her deceased husband's estate. Today, the concept of dower has been either abolished or drastically changed by provincial inheritance laws.

due process Legal requirements that must be met, under the Constitution, before a person can be deprived of life, liberty, or property.

dura lex, sed lex Latin for "it's a hard law, but it's the law." It demonstrates the imperative nature of the law, whereby a judge must rule according to the law even if a great hardship would result.

durable power of attorney Authority of one person (the attorney-in-fact) to act on behalf of another (the principal) in business or personal matters even after the principal is determined to be legally incompetent to manage his affairs. Also the document bestowing this authority.

duress Undue pressure or force to persuade someone to do something, such as to include someone in a will or get married.

earnest money Money paid to a seller to show the buyer's intention to carry out his part of the contract.

easement Right to use another's property for a particular purpose, such as the right of the city to run a sewer line across your land; known as a servitude in Quebec.

emancipation Freeing of someone from another's authority or control. A child is emancipated from his parents when he reaches adulthood (usually age 18 or 19, depending on provincial law) or gets married.

embezzlement Crime of misappropriating money or goods by a person to whom they have been entrusted.

eminent domain Authority of the government to take private property for public use for a fair price; also known as expropriation.

en banc Full bench; a court session for which the number of judges hearing a case is at its greatest. For example, three of the five judges may hear a routine case, but for important cases, all five may be present.

encroach To trespass; to illegally intrude on someone else's land.

encumbrance Anything that lessens the value of real estate or hinders its sale; any claim that someone other than the owner has on real estate. For example, a mortgage is an encumbrance on a piece of land.

entrapment Deception perpetrated by an official to trick a person into committing a crime he would not otherwise commit.

equal protection of the law Treating a person the same as others and not denying him the protection afforded by the law. The Charter of Rights and Freedoms guarantees this, to prevent the government from favoring one group of people over another.

equitable distribution Fair division of property, as in a divorce, even if only one spouse's name appears on the title or deed as the owner.

equity Decision based on fairness; value of property after deducting the mortgage and other liabilities.

escheat Right of the government to take property when there is no owner, as when a property owner dies without a will or any natural heirs.

escrow Deed, title, or money held by a third person until all conditions of a contract have been met.

estate Everything a person owns or has a financial interest in; the property of a deceased person.

estoppel Condition by which a person cannot change an earlier statement or action if it will cause loss or injury to another person.

evict To force a tenant to move out.

evidentiary Having the quality of evidence or proof.

ex post facto Latin phrase meaning "after the fact"; routinely applied to a law that makes an act a crime after it has already been committed.

exclusive occupancy Right of only one person to use real estate.

exculpatory agreement An agreement releasing someone from liability for the consequences of his acts, except for harm or damage resulting from willful misconduct or gross negligence.

execute To complete; a document is executed when it is signed or when

its terms have been carried out. In criminal law, to carry out the death penalty, a punishment no longer allowed in Canada.

executor Person designated to carry out the terms of a will.

exemplary damages Award in a lawsuit in excess of the actual loss; punitive damages; an amount assessed against the defendant to punish him for his actions.

expert witness Someone with special knowledge of a trade, science, or activity, who testifies in court to interpret or explain a fact or other evidence.

express Specifically stated or written; a printed warranty with its terms spelled out is an express warranty.

expropriation See *eminent domain*.

expunge To totally erase or destroy something, such as a charge from a criminal record.

extortion Crime of taking money by force, threat, or misuse of authority.

extradition Surrender by one government of a person accused of a crime to another government.

factum See *brief*.

fee simple Full rights of ownership in a piece of real estate.

fiduciary Person, such as an executor, or institution, such as a bank, that has a duty to act for the benefit of another person because he or it is in a position of trust or confidence.

filing Giving a legal document to the clerk of the court so that it can be placed in the appropriate court records or stamped "received" and routed to other court personnel for further action or review.

fixture Anything that has been attached to a house or other type of real estate and is considered part of the property. A built-in closet is a fixture.

foreclose To terminate rights, as in a mortgage, by taking and selling the property to pay the debt.

forfeit To give up or lose something as a penalty for a crime, for neglect of a duty, or for breach of contract.

forgery Crime of making a false document or altering a genuine one with the intention of defrauding someone.

franchise License to sell a specific brand of product or own and operate a branch of a particular business, such as a fast-food restaurant chain.

fraud Crime of intentionally misrepresenting something for personal gain or to harm someone.

fraudulent Misleading or false.

full covenant and warranty Type of deed that transfers ownership of real estate with a guarantee that no one else has a claim to the property.

garnishment Court order allowing a creditor who has won a lawsuit to have access to the defendant's money or property to collect the debt. For example, if the court allows a loan company to garnishee your wages, your employer must deduct money from your wages to pay the loan company the amount ordered.

guardian Someone charged with legal custody of a person who has been declared unable to care for himself.

habeas corpus Latin phrase meaning "you have the body"; a court order directing a person who is detaining someone to bring that person to court and explain why he is being held. Used to obtain the release of a person who is being unlawfully imprisoned.

hearing Proceeding in which evidence is presented or witnesses are heard. Usually less formal than a trial. Hearings may be held before legislative committees or government agencies.

hearsay Testimony by a witness about matters he heard of from someone else, but about which the witness has no personal knowledge. Usually not considered admissible in a trial.

holograph will Last will and testament that is entirely handwritten by the person making it.

homicide Killing of one human being by another, whether justified (as in war or self-defense) or not (as in manslaughter or murder).

hung jury Jury that cannot come to an agreement and therefore cannot reach a verdict.

hypothec A term used in Quebec for mortgage.

illegitimate Contrary to the law; in reference to children, those born out of wedlock.

immunity Exemption from duties or penalties normally required.

impanel To list possible jurors.

in forma pauperis Latin phrase meaning "in the character or manner of a pauper"; being unable to afford court costs or other legal fees; being allowed to file a lawsuit without paying costs.

in loco parentis Latin phrase meaning "in place of the parent"; having parental rights of supervising a child without being the child's actual parent.

incest Sexual relations between two people who are related too closely to be legally married. Incest is a crime.

incriminate To accuse someone of a crime or otherwise imply that he is guilty of wrongdoing.

indemnity Security against injury, loss, or damages. An insurance policy is an indemnity contract under which the insurance company will reimburse you for losses you incur because of injury, loss, or damage.

indict To charge a person with committing a crime.

indictable offense A serious crime for which the accused person has the right to a preliminary hearing and a trial by jury. See *summary conviction offense.*

information A statement sworn before a judge so that a summons or an arrest warrant may be issued.

informed consent Agreement to submit to something, such as surgery, made with full knowledge of all the risks and alternatives involved.

infraction Violation of an ordinance, statute, or law.

infringement Violation of a right. For example, the unauthorized copying of a book protected by copyright is an infringement of the copyright.

injunction Court order to do or stop doing something specific.

inquest Legal investigation by a jury or coroner into the cause of a death.

insolvency Inability to pay debts.

instrument Written legal document, such as a deed, contract, or cheque.

inter vivos Latin phrase meaning "between living persons." An *inter vivos* trust is set up during the lifetime of the person creating the trust to provide income to someone.

interlocutory judgment Temporary court decision during the course of a lawsuit. Often used during a divorce before the final judgment is issued.

interrogatories Series of written questions, given to the plaintiff and defendant in a lawsuit before a trial, which must be answered in writing under oath; a form of the legal procedure called discovery.

intestate Having died without leaving a valid will.

joint property Property owned by two or more persons.

joint tenancy Ownership of the same property by two or more persons at the same time, generally with the right of survivorship. Under the right of survivorship, when one of the owners dies, the property goes to the other owner or owners, and the deceased owner's heirs have no claim to it.

judgment Court decision that resolves a dispute and determines each person's rights and responsibilities in the matter.

jurisdiction Power of the court to rule upon certain issues.

jurisprudence Science or philosophy of law; a system of laws; also the state of the law as determined by a series of judicial decisions.

kidnapping Crime of seizing a person, usually to obtain ransom.

laches Defense raised when the plaintiff in a case has delayed bringing a lawsuit for so long that the defendant has lost the opportunity to defend himself.

larceny Crime of theft; taking someone else's personal goods for one's own personal use.

lease Formal agreement between a landlord and his tenant about the rental of property.

legacy Something other than real estate that is left to someone in a will; a bequest or inheritance

legal duty Something required by law, such as an obligation to act in a reasonable manner in making a contract. A legal duty may be created by a private contract or by operation of the law.

legatee See *devisee*.

legislation Act of passing laws; laws made by a legislative body.

legitimize To make lawful; to make legitimate the status of a child who was illegitimate—that is, his parents were not married at the time of his birth.

letter of credit Document issued by a bank, promising to back up or pay a businessman's or company's financial obligations in another place, usually a foreign country.

liability Duty or responsibility, such as a duty to pay a debt or responsibility for injuries suffered in an accident.

libel Form of defamation involving a written statement that damages a person's or a company's reputation.

lien Legal claim against property to ensure payment of a debt; it allows the property to be taken and sold if the debt is not paid. In Quebec law, a lien is known as a privilege.

life estate Right to use real estate during the lifetime of an individual who is not necessarily the person who will occupy the land. For example, you might grant the use of your house to your brother until his death, at which time your daughter will be given the house to live in. A person with a life estate cannot pass the property on to his heirs.

liquidate To pay and settle a debt.

liquidated damages Set amount of money a person agrees to pay if he breaks a contract.

litigate To sue.

loitering Crime of lingering idly or prowling about in a public place, especially for the purpose of begging, dealing drugs, or soliciting for prostitution.

magistrate Judge who has limited authority. A provincial court judge. The term magistrate was deleted from the Criminal Code in 1985.

maintenance Means of spousal support; synonym for alimentary pension.

malice Intent to cause injury, death, or severe harm.

malpractice Professional misconduct; failure to follow the accepted standards set by a profession in providing service to one's clients.

mandamus An order by a superior court commanding someone to do some official act or duty. A writ of *mandamus* can force a judge to hear evidence he may be refusing to hear, or permit you to have an interpreter, or it can force a municipality to hold elections when its council's term has expired.

manslaughter Killing of a human being without malice. It is *voluntary* if it is committed intentionally, as in a fit of sudden passion; it is *involuntary* if it is committed unintentionally—for example, through carelessness.

marital property Things acquired by a couple while they are married.

mechanic's lien Claim on property for work done or materials furnished. Failure to pay the money owing for goods or services could result in the sale of the property.

mediate To act as a go-between to help settle a dispute.

mens rea Latin for "guilty mind"; the intention to commit an act that one knows is illegal. *Mens rea* is one of the elements of a crime: coupled with *actus reus* (wrongful act), it constitutes a crime.

misdemeanor Category of crime that is not as serious as an indictable offense; generally punishable by a fine or imprisonment of no more than two years.

misfeasance Doing something legal, but in an improper or injurious manner. For example, building a 10-meter-high fence on your property to block your neighbor's light could be misfeasance.

misrepresentation Incorrect or false statement, whether made deliberately in order to mislead someone or made innocently in ignorance of its falsity.

mistrial Trial that is terminated because of legal errors or the failure of the jury to reach a verdict.

mitigating circumstances Facts or events that, although they do not excuse a person's conduct, reduce the blame for it.

mortgage Document that puts up property as collateral to pay a loan—often a loan made to finance the purchase of the property; in Quebec law, a hypothec.

mortgagee The lender in a mortgage agreement, generally a bank or other financial institution.

mortgagor The borrower in a mortgage agreement; the person buying a home who puts it up as collateral for the loan.

mortis causa Latin phrase meaning "on account of death"; in expectation of death. Gifts *mortis causa* are given because the donor expects to die soon.

murder The crime of intentionally and maliciously killing someone.

naturalization Process a foreigner goes through to become a citizen.

naturalized citizen A foreigner who has met the requirements for becoming a citizen and has taken an oath of allegiance to his new country.

negligence Failure to use the standard of care a reasonable person would use in a given situation.

negotiable Transferable from one person to another. A negotiable instrument is any signed, written agreement to transfer money to another person. Cheques, bank drafts, and promissory notes are all examples of negotiable instruments.

negotiate To bargain with someone over something, such as a purchase or terms of a contract; to transfer funds to another person by endorsing something such as a cheque or negotiable stock or bond.

nominal damages Small sum of money awarded by a court to compensate the plaintiff for a violation of his rights or a breach of duty by the defendant, even though the plaintiff has suffered no substantial loss or injury.

non compos mentis Latin phrase meaning "not having mastery of one's mind"; an insane state; not of sound mind.

nonfeasance Failure to perform a required duty.

notary Public officer who administers oaths and witnesses' signatures on documents; in Quebec, a legal officer who has the authority to draw up certain documents such as deeds of sale, wills, and marriage contracts.

note Written promise to pay.

nuisance Anything that interferes with a person's quiet enjoyment of his property or that disturbs, inconveniences, or harms the public at large. Noisy neighbors and the storage of explosives in a residential neighborhood are two examples of nuisances.

oath Formal declaration or promise to do something.

obscenity Offensive material designed to stimulate an obsessive interest in nudity or sex, and lacking any redeeming social value.

obstruction of justice Interference with the operation of a court.

OHSC Acronym for Occupational Health and Safety Commission; in some provinces this agency is known as the Workers' Compensation Commission.

order in council Assent by the governor general (federal) or the lieutenant governor (provincial), which has the effect of law. Usually orders in council are cabinet decisions which are ratified by the governor general, or lieutenant governor, as the case may be.

ordinance Law enacted by a city government or some other municipal body.

parens patriae Latin phrase meaning "parent of the country"; the role of the government to protect and be guardian of those people who are legally unable to act for themselves, usually children.

parole Release of a prisoner from part of his sentence provided he meets certain conditions, including reporting to a parole officer at regular intervals. If the released man does not abide by these conditions, he must return to prison to serve out the rest of his term.

partnership Agreement of two or more people to operate a business with the expectation of sharing the profits and dividing the losses.

party Person, group, or business involved in a contract or lawsuit. For example, the buyer and seller who sign a sales agreement are parties to a contract; the plaintiff and defendant are parties to a lawsuit.

patent Legal protection given to an inventor against the unauthorized manufacture, use, and sale of his invention.

paternity Fatherhood.

paternity suit A legal action taken to prove that a certain man is a child's natural father and to have the courts order the man to support the child.

penal Relating to punishment.

peremptory challenge Right of the plaintiff's and defendant's lawyers in a jury trial to object to a specified number of prospective jurors without having to give a reason.

perjury Crime of knowingly making a false statement while under oath.

permit License, or written permission, to take specific action. For example, a builder may need a permit to remodel a home.

personal property Anything that can be owned, except real estate.

petition Written request to the court for a particular remedy, stating the facts on which the request is based.

plaintiff Person who initiates a court proceeding, such as a lawsuit.

plea Criminal defendant's answer to the charges brought against him. The plea may be guilty, not guilty, pardon, *autrefois acquit* (previously acquitted), or *autrefois convict* (previously convicted).

plea bargaining Negotiation, between the prosecutor and the defense attorney in a criminal case, to reduce the number or type of charges brought against the defendant in exchange for a guilty plea.

pleadings Formal written statements made by the plaintiff and the defendant (the complaint and the answer or declaration and plea) in which they state their versions of the facts of the dispute.

power of attorney Authority granted to one person to represent someone else (act as his agent) and do business in his name. It generally expires when the business in ques-

tion has been completed or when the person being represented is declared incompetent—unless it is a durable power of attorney.

precedent Court decision or legal case that is used as a guide to help decide a similar case.

preliminary hearing Hearing held to decide if a crime has been committed and if there is enough evidence so that the accused should stand trial for that crime. Any doubt at this stage is in favor of the Crown and against the accused.

prenuptial agreement Document prepared by a couple, prior to their marriage, which outlines how property is to be divided in the event of separation, divorce, or death of a spouse.

preponderance of evidence In a civil lawsuit, the need to produce evidence that is more convincing than that presented by the other side in order to win the case.

prerogative writ A citizen's first defense against arbitrary or unfair action by the authorities. The four most common prerogative writs are *habeas corpus, prohibition, certiorari,* and *mandamus.*

prima facie Latin phrase meaning "at first sight"; something assumed to be true or factual in the absence of evidence to the contrary. Prima facie evidence is evidence presented by one side that is so strong that a judge or jury would decide in favor of that side unless the opposing side presented contradictory evidence.

principal Amount of a debt, not including interest; person primarily liable for a debt; person who authorizes someone to act on his behalf.

privilege See *lien.*

pro se Latin phrase meaning "for oneself"; representing oneself without the help of a lawyer.

probable cause Strong reason to suspect something is well founded—for example, that a law has been or is being violated.

probate Court procedure that determines the validity of a will.

probation Permission for a person convicted of a crime to remain free from imprisonment as long as he stays out of trouble and periodically reports to a probation officer.

prohibition writ This writ commands someone not to proceed further with a particular matter—perhaps a trial.

promissory note Signed document promising to pay a specified amount of money either on demand or on or after a designated date.

prosecuting attorney The attorney for the government in criminal cases, who files charges against a person suspected of committing a crime and presents the case in court. Also referred to as the Crown attorney.

proxy Someone authorized to act or decide for another person; also, the authorizing paper.

public nuisance Activity that is offensive, dangerous, or obstructive to a number of people.

public policy Legal principle saying that no one may violate the public good; the people's conscience.

publication Public notification of an impending court action—generally by an announcement placed in a newspaper. Also, making a defamatory statement about someone to one or more others.

punitive damages Money awarded to the plaintiff in a lawsuit in order to punish the defendant for his malicious, negligent, or reckless conduct. It is in addition to any actual losses suffered by the plaintiff and can be used as a warning to others that such conduct will not be tolerated.

purchase agreement A contract for the sale of real estate, goods, or services.

pyramid sales A scheme of selling whereby one person receives a commission or other benefit on sales made by another person he has recruited into the scene. Forbidden by the Competition Act, unless expressly allowed by provincial law.

quitclaim deed Document that transfers ownership of real estate, but contains no guarantees that the seller has a valid right to do so, or that others do not have rights to the land.

rape Forcing someone to have sexual intercourse. Rape has been dropped from the Criminal Code in favor of aggravated sexual assault.

real property Real estate; land and anything that is growing on it or is attached to it, such as trees, fences, and buildings.

rebut To disprove or counter arguments or evidence presented by the opposing side in a trial.

receiving stolen goods Crime of accepting property that one knows has been illegally obtained.

reciprocity Mutual exchange of privileges between provinces or countries for their respective citizens. For example, provinces have reciprocal laws governing drivers' licenses, which allow someone with a license from one province to drive in another.

reckless disregard Action that is taken without regard for the safety and welfare of others.

recognizance Promise to a court to do something, such as pay an overdue debt. Before a trial, a court may choose to release a person suspected of a crime from custody on his own recognizance: instead of posting bail, the suspect gives the court a written statement that he will appear for trial.

recourse Rights and remedies under the law. In banking, right of someone who holds a cheque—or other paper containing a promise to pay—to receive payment from anyone who endorses it, even when the person who originally wrote the cheque cannot pay.

remainder Ownership rights in real estate that take effect only after the rights of another end. For example, if Stephen is given the family house to use during his lifetime, and upon his death the property goes to his brother Nathan, Nathan has a remainder. In Quebec law, such an arrangement is called a substitution.

remand To send back. An appellate, or higher, court may remand a case to a lower court for further action. In criminal law, an accused may be remanded or returned to custody.

remedy Relief available to the person bringing the lawsuit after it has been proved that his rights were violated. Damages (money) are one type of remedy. A court order compelling a defendant to do something, such as honor a contract, is another type.

replevin Lawsuit to recover property that was taken illegally or borrowed and not returned. See *trover.*

representative payee A person or an institution designated to receive money on behalf of another person who is unable to handle his personal affairs.

res ipsa loquitor Latin for "the thing speaks for itself." In a claim for damages, for example, if the plaintiff could show that one of the stairs he slipped on was broken, he could point to the broken stair and claim *res ipsa loquitor,* creating a presumption of fault against the owner of the stairs.

residuary estate In a will, all the property in the estate that is not specifically mentioned elsewhere in the will. A residuary clause in the will names the person or entity that is to receive this remaining property—for example, "I leave all the rest of my property to my beloved wife, Helen."

respondeat superior Latin phrase meaning "let the master answer"; the legal principle making an employer liable for what his employee does in the course of performing his job.

restitution Restoration of something to its rightful owner; restoration of a person to the position he would have been in if a contract had not been broken.

restraining order Court mandate stopping someone from doing something, but valid only until a hearing can be held to determine whether or not the order should continue in force; similar to an interim or interlocutory injunction.

retainer Money a client pays an attorney; the hiring of an attorney.

reversion Legal interest in property that a person keeps after transferring ownership to someone else. For example, if Carl transferred ownership of his property to Ned for life, with no one specified to receive the land at

Ned's death, the property would revert to Carl or his heirs upon Ned's death.

robbery Crime of taking goods or money by force or intimidation.

rogatory commission A person or group authorized by a court to take evidence from witnesses living in a foreign jurisdiction. The evidence would be used by the authorizing court in legal proceedings.

sadism Sexual perversion in which pleasure comes from inflicting pain.

scienter Prior knowledge that something was going to happen and the deliberate failure to prevent it.

search warrant A legal document authorizing police officers to search a premises.

secured transaction Type of loan that gives the lender power to seize the property offered by the borrower as collateral if the borrower defaults on the loan.

security deposit Money a tenant pays a landlord to cover any damages the tenant causes or to cover unpaid rent if the tenant breaks the lease. Security deposits are illegal in some provinces.

self-defense A justifiable violent act in the face of danger, such as using force to defend oneself or one's family from assault or threat.

sentence Penalty given to a defendant at the end of a criminal trial.

sequester To separate or isolate. A judge might order that jurors be sequestered for the duration of a trial.

sequestration A court order placing something in dispute in the hands of a third party, such as a sheriff. The third party must restore the property to the person to whom it is subsequently awarded.

servitude In Quebec real estate law, a servitude is the equivalent of an easement in the common-law provinces; the right of an owner of one piece of land to benefit from the property of another, by a right-of-way, for example.

sheriff A representative of the court charged with certain duties in the court and with the execution of court orders. See *bailiff*.

shoplifting Stealing items of minor value from a store during business hours.

sine die Latin for "without a day"; an expression used when a trial is postponed indefinitely.

slander Talking maliciously about a person, or making false statements that injure the person's reputation.

solicit In criminal law, to encourage or ask someone to commit a crime.

specific performance Carrying out a contract exactly as the terms are written—a remedy sometimes ordered by a court when a contract has been broken, especially when monetary damages would be inadequate, as in the case of agreements to sell one-of-a-kind antiques.

statute Law passed by Parliament or a provincial legislature that declares, commands, or prohibits something.

statute of frauds Law that requires certain contracts to be in writing to be enforceable, such as contracts for the sale of real estate or of goods valued at over $50.

statute of limitations Law requiring a lawsuit or a criminal prosecution to be filed within a certain period of time for it to be heard in court.

statutory Pertaining to a statute, or law. Required by a law.

sub judice Latin for "under judicial consideration." Usually one is forbidden to comment publicly on *sub judice* matters.

sublease Agreement by a tenant to rent premises to a third person during a part of the time the original tenant's lease is in effect.

subpoena Court order to appear and testify at a given time and place.

subrogate To transfer rights to another person.

substitution See *remainder.*

sue To begin legal proceedings against a person or company or against the government because of an alleged wrongdoing.

summary conviction offense A lesser offense, punishable by a fine or a prison term of not more than two years. Similar to a misdemeanor.

summons Court order, or writ, notifying a person that a lawsuit has been started against him and giving the date by which he must go to court to file an answer to the charges against him or risk having a court judgment made against him by default.

surety bond Written guarantee to pay a second person a debt that the bonded person did not meet or to pay for a job he failed to do. For example, a builder might buy a surety bond to cover his work on a house; if something prevented him from completing the job, the surety company would pay to have the work completed by someone else.

surrogate Substitute, such as a surrogate parent; in some provinces, the title of a probate judge.

suspended sentence A sentence that need not be served if the convicted person fulfills certain other conditions.

sustain To uphold or support. A judge may sustain an attorney's objection during a trial, which means the judge agrees with the objection.

tenancy The holding or occupancy of any land or buildings, especially the temporary possession of a house or building that belongs to another person to whom one pays rent.

tenancy in common Arrangement in which two or more people co-own the same property, but with no right of survivorship—that is, when one of the owners dies, his share of the property goes to his heirs, and not to his co-owners, as it would in a joint tenancy with the right of survivorship.

tenancy by the entirety Type of joint tenancy; an arrangement in which a husband and wife co-own property. Neither spouse can sell his or her share of the property without the other's consent, and when one spouse dies, the other automatically takes over full ownership of the entire property without having it go through probate. Largely obsolete today, except in Newfoundland.

term life insurance Type of protection that will pay the beneficiary only if the insured person dies within the time specified in the policy.

testamentary Relating to a will; based on, derived from, or established in someone's will, such as a testamentary trust.

testator Person making a will.

testify To give evidence under oath.

title Rights of ownership of property; paper that indicates ownership.

title search Examination of deeds registered locally to make sure that a piece of real estate can be sold without anyone else's claiming rights to it.

tort Any wrong for which a person can be sued for damages or compensation, except breach of contract.

trafficking Illegally manufacturing, selling, giving, administering, transporting, sending, delivering, distributing or offering narcotics or other illegal substances.

treason Crime of attempting to overthrow the legally elected government to which one owes allegiance or of actively helping the enemies of one's country.

trespass Illegal entry onto or interference with another person's land.

trial Hearing in a court of law, before a judge or jury, to determine certain relevant facts and decide the outcome of a case.

tribunal Any court of law or any body examining or adjudicating a matter of public interest.

trover Lawsuit to seek compensation from someone who has taken property from another without permission and converted it to his own use. See *replevin*.

truant Child who deliberately and consistently misses school.

trust Arrangement by which one person (the trustee) holds property for the benefit of someone else (the beneficiary). The person setting up the trust is called the grantor, settlor, or trustor.

trustee The person or corporation administering a trust and acting in a fiduciary capacity.

turpitude A base act; behavior contrary to justice, honesty, or morality.

ultra vires Latin for "beyond the powers"; used in reference to acts or contracts that are beyond the legal power or authority of a corporation, court, or government.

umbrella policy Type of insurance that increases the amount of protection in return for a relatively small increase in the premium.

unconscionable In contract law, a contract with terms so unfair and oppressive that a court may declare them invalid, or may alter the conditions to make them more reasonable.

uncontested divorce Divorce proceeding in which a couple agrees on such basic issues as child custody, support, and division of property.

under protest A term used to indicate a certain action was taken under duress or under conditions deemed to be illegal or improper.

undue influence Improper use of power or persuasion to the point where consent was not voluntary.

usufruct The right of temporary use and enjoyment of property and things, or both, belonging to another as well as the fruits or profits of such property and things.

usury Crime of charging an illegally high interest rate on a loan. At the time of writing, charging more than 60 percent interest per annum is a criminal offense.

utter To put something into circulation; to pass counterfeit money or forged securities.

vandalism Crime of damaging or destroying someone else's property.

variance Discrepancy between statements or legal documents that should be in agreement.

venue Geographical area in which a court may hear a case; place where a crime was committed or the events leading to a lawsuit occurred.

verdict Final decision made by a judge or jury.

vest To take effect; to confer ownership or the right to future enjoyment. For example, when your rights in your employer's retirement fund are vested, you are entitled to this money if you leave your job.

voidable Can be declared void or invalid. Certain contracts by minors are voidable if legal proceedings are taken in time. If a contract made by a minor is not voided and is left standing until the minor reaches the age of majority, the contract may be considered ratified and therefore valid.

voir dire Old French phrase meaning "to speak the truth"; preliminary questioning of prospective jurors to determine if they are qualified and competent to serve on the jury.

volenti non fit injuria Latin for "damages cannot be claimed by one who has voluntarily assumed the risk." Thus a hockey player who was injured in the normal course of a game by being checked into the boards, for example, could not sue for damages.

waiver Written statement voluntarily relinquishing a right or claim.

ward Someone who has been legally declared unable to take care of himself and has had a guardian appointed; also, a division within a city.

warrant Written authorization or order to do a specific act—for example, an arrest warrant.

warranty Written or implied statement that a product is of a certain quality or has certain characteristics.

warranty of merchantability Statement or promise that a product will function for the purpose for which it was designed and will conform to industry standards.

whole life insurance Type of protection that is in force as long as premiums are paid, rather than for a predetermined period of time (term insurance). The policy premiums remain the same, with a cash value and dividends accumulating while the policy is in effect.

will Document setting out how a person wishes his property or estate disposed of after his death; also known as a testament.

without recourse An endorsement of a negotiable instrument, such as a cheque, by which the endorser merely passes it on, accepting no personal liability for its payment to subsequent holders.

writ Court order requiring a person to do or not to do a specified act.

wrongdoer Anyone who commits any injury, injustice, or crime.

wrongful death Death caused by the willful act or negligence of another person. Dependent heirs of the victim may be able to sue the person responsible for the death for loss of the support they had expected to receive from the deceased person.

zoning laws Legislation dividing a municipality into districts for the purpose of limiting certain types of building or activity.

Useful Addresses

WHERE TO APPLY FOR LEGAL AID

ALBERTA

Suite 401, Melton Building
1600—10123 99th Street
Edmonton, Alta., T5J 3H1

BRITISH COLUMBIA

Legal Services Society of British
    Columbia
Box 3, Suite 300
1140 West Pender St.
Vancouver, B.C., V6E 4G1

MANITOBA

Legal Aid Society of Manitoba
294 Portage Ave., Room 402
Winnipeg, Man., R3C 0B9

NEW BRUNSWICK

Legal Aid New Brunswick
461 King St.
Fredericton, N.B., E3B 1E5

NEWFOUNDLAND

Newfoundland Legal Aid
    Commission
21 Church Hill
St. John's, Nfld., A1C 3Z8

NOVA SCOTIA

Nova Scotia Legal Aid Commission
5212 Sackville St.
Suite 300
Halifax, N.S., B3J 1K6

ONTARIO

Ontario Legal Aid Plan
481 University Ave., Suite 200
Toronto, Ont., M5G 2G1

PRINCE EDWARD ISLAND

Public Defender
Law Courts Building
Box 2200
Charlottetown, P.E.I., C1A 8B9

Commission des services juridiques
(Legal Services Commission)
2 Complexe Desjardins
Tour de l'Est, Bureau 1404
Montreal, Que., H5B 1B3

Saskatchewan Legal Aid
  Commission
820—410 22nd Street East
Saskatoon, Sask., S7K 2H6

Legal Services Board of the
  Northwest Territories
Box 1320
Yellowknife, N.W.T., X1A 2L9

Yukon Legal Services Society
2134 Second Ave.
Whitehorse, Yukon, Y1A 5H6

LAW SOCIETIES

Canadian Bar Association
130 Albert St., Suite 1700
Ottawa, Ont., K1P 5G4

Law Society of Alberta
344—12th Avenue South-West
Calgary, Alta., T2R 0H2

Law Society of British Columbia
1148 Hornby St., Suite 300
Vancouver, B.C., V6Z 2C4

Society of Notaries Public of British
  Columbia
736 Granville St., Suite 1401
Vancouver, B.C., V6Z 1G3

Law Society of Manitoba
219 Kennedy St., Suite 201
Winnipeg, Man., R3C 1F8

Barristers' Society of New
  Brunswick
1133 Regent St., Suite 305
Fredericton, N.B., E3B 3Z2

Saint John Law Society
110 Charlotte St.
Saint John, N.B., E2L 2J3

Law Society of Newfoundland
93 Water St., Box 1028
St. John's, Nfld., A1C 5M3

Nova Scotia Barristers' Society
Keith Hall
1475 Hollis Ave.
Halifax, N.S., B3J 3M4

Law Society of Upper Canada
Osgoode Hall
Toronto, Ont., M5H 2N6

Law Society of Prince Edward Island
42 Water St.
Charlottetown, P.E.I., C1A 1A4

Le Barreau du Québec
(The Quebec Bar Association)
445, boul. Saint-Laurent
Montreal, Que., H2Y 3T8

La Chambre des notaires de
  Québec
(Chamber of Notaries of Quebec)
630, boul. René-Lévesque ouest
Bureau 1700
Montreal, Que., H3B 1T6

Law Society of Saskatchewan
201—2208 Scarth St.
Regina, Sask., S4P 2J6

CRIMINAL INJURIES COMPENSATION BOARDS

Crimes Compensation Board
J.E. Brownlee Building, 7th Floor
10365—97th Street
Edmonton, Alta., T5J 3W7

BRITISH COLUMBIA

Criminal Injury Section
Criminal Injury Compensation Act
6951 Westminster Hwy.
Richmond, B.C., V7C 1C6

MANITOBA

Criminal Injuries Compensation
  Board
696 Portage Ave., Suite 101
Winnipeg, Man., R3G 0M6

NEW BRUNSWICK

Criminal Injuries Compensation
  Board
Department of Justice
Centennial Building, Box 6000
Fredericton, N.B., E3B 5H1

NEWFOUNDLAND

Newfoundland Department of
  Justice
Confederation Building
St. John's, Nfld., A1C 5T7

NOVA SCOTIA

Criminal Injuries Compensation
  Board
Centennial Building, 10th Floor
1660 Hollis St., Box 985
Halifax, N.S., B3J 2V9

ONTARIO

Criminal Injuries Compensation
  Board
439 University Ave., 17th Floor
Toronto, Ont., M5G 1Y8

PRINCE EDWARD ISLAND

Department of Justice
Shaw Building
73 Rochford St., Box 2000
Charlottetown, P.E.I., C1A 7N8

QUEBEC

Service d'indemnisation des
  victimes d'actes criminels (IVAC)
(Crime Victim Compensation
  Service)
525, rue Bourdages, C.P. 1200
Quebec, Que., G1K 7E2

1199, rue Bleury
C.P. 6065, succ. A
Montreal, Que., H3C 4E1

SASKATCHEWAN

Saskatchewan Criminal Injuries
  Compensation Board
Provincial Building, 10th Floor
122—3rd Avenue North
Saskatoon, Sask., S7K 2H6

YUKON

Workers' Compensation Board
4110—4th Avenue, 3rd Floor
Whitehorse, Yukon, Y1A 2C6

NORTHWEST TERRITORIES

Workers' Compensation Board
Box 8888
Yellowknife, N.W.T., X1A 2R3

HUMAN RIGHTS COMMISSIONS

The Canadian Human Rights
  Commission
P.O. Box 2052, Station D
Ottawa, Ont., K1A 5W3

ALBERTA

Human Rights Commission
801 Kensington Place
10011—109th Street
Edmonton, Alta., T5J 3S8

Human Rights Commission
Parliament Buildings
Victoria, B.C., V8V 1X4

MANITOBA

Human Rights Commission
330 Portage Ave., Suite 207
Winnipeg, Man., R3C 0C4

NEW BRUNSWICK

Human Rights Commission
Department of Labour and
  Employment
Box 6000
Fredericton, N.B., E3B 5H1

NEWFOUNDLAND

Human Rights Commission
4th Floor, Viking Building
St. John's, Nfld., A1C 5T7

NOVA SCOTIA

Nova Scotia Human Rights
  Commission
Lord Nelson Arcade
Box 2221
Halifax, N.S., B3J 3C4

ONTARIO

Human Rights Commission
400 University Ave., 12th Floor
Toronto, Ont., M5G 1S5

PRINCE EDWARD ISLAND

Human Rights Commission
Box 2000
Charlottetown, P.E.I., C1A 7N8

QUEBEC

Commission des droits de la
  personne
360, rue Saint-Jacques ouest
9e étage
Montreal, Que., H2Y 1P5

SASKATCHEWAN

Human Rights Commission
8th Floor, Canterbury Towers
224 Fourth Avenue South
Saskatoon, Sask., S7K 2H6

OMBUDSMEN

ALBERTA

Office of the Ombudsman
1630—10020 101 Avenue
Edmonton, Alta., T5J 3G2

BRITISH COLUMBIA

Office of the Ombudsman
9 Bastion Sq.
Victoria, B.C., H1T 1X4

MANITOBA

Office of the Ombudsman
500 Portage Ave.
Winnipeg, Man., R3C 3X1

NEW BRUNSWICK

Office of the Ombudsman
P.O. Box 6000
Fredericton, N.B., E3B 5H1

NEWFOUNDLAND

Parliamentary Commissioner
  (Ombudsman)
Prudential Building
49—55 Elizabeth Ave.
St. John's, Nfld., A1C 5T7

NOVA SCOTIA

Office of the Ombudsman
Box 2152
Halifax, N.S., B3J 3B7

ONTARIO

Office of the Ombudsman
125 Queen's Park
Toronto, Ont., M5S 2C7

PRINCE EDWARD ISLAND

There is no provincial ombudsman
  in Prince Edward Island.

QUEBEC

Le Protecteur du citoyen
2875, boul. Laurier
4e étage
Sainte-Foy, Que., G1V 2M2

Le Protecteur du citoyen
5199, rue Sherbrooke est
Bureau 2931
Montreal, Que., H1T 3X1

Office of the Ombudsman
2310 Scarth St.
Regina, Sask., S4P 3V7

GOVERNMENT ACCESS

Governments, federal and provincial, have "access points" for disseminating information on their services. Write or phone the nearest one to find out which department or agency is responsible for a particular matter. Government Access operators usually accept collect long-distance phone calls. So, too, do offices of Members of Parliament and Senators,.

FEDERAL

OTTAWA
(613) 995-7151
(800) 267-0340

MONTREAL
(514) 283-5454
(514) 873-2111

TORONTO
(416) 973-1993
(800) 387-0700

ALBERTA
(403) 420-2021 (Edmonton)
(403) 292-4998 (Calgary)

BRITISH COLUMBIA
(604) 666-5555
(800) 663-1381

NEWFOUNDLAND
(709) 772-4365
(800) 563-2432

NOVA SCOTIA
(902) 426-8092
(800) 426-8092

SASKATCHEWAN
(306) 780-6683
(800) 667-7160

PROVINCIAL

ALBERTA
Public Affairs Bureau
2nd Floor
10044—108th Street
Edmonton, Alta., T5J 3S7
(403) 427-2711

BRITISH COLUMBIA
Communications Branch
Tour Guide Office
Parliament Buildings
Victoria, B.C., V8V 1X4
(604) 387-3046

MANITOBA
Citizen's Inquiry Service
401 York Ave., Room 511
Winnipeg, Man., R3C 0P8
(204) 945-3744
(800) 282-8060

NEW BRUNSWICK
Information Service
Box 6000
Fredericton, N.B., E3B 5H1
(506) 453-2525
(800) 442-4400

NEWFOUNDLAND
Newfoundland Information Service
Confederation Building, Main Floor
St. John's, Nfld., A1C 5T7
(709) 737-3612

NOVA SCOTIA
Communications and Information
  Centre
Box 54, Halifax, N.S., B3J 3C4
(902) 424-5200

USEFUL ADDRESSES

Ministry of Culture and Recreation
Citizens' Inquiry Branch
McDonald Building, 900 Bay St.
Toronto, Ont., M7A 1N3
(416) 965-3535

PRINCE EDWARD ISLAND

Island Information Service
Box 2000
Charlottetown, P.E.I., C1A 7N8
(902) 368-4000

QUEBEC

Communications-Québec
870, boul. Charest est
Quebec, Que., G1K 8S5
(418) 643-1344

Communications-Québec
3, Complexe Desjardins
Galerie du Nord
Montreal, Que., H5B 1B8
(514) 873-2111

SASKATCHEWAN

Provincial Inquiry Service
3475 Albert St.
Regina, Sask., S4S 6X6
(306) 787-6291
(800) 667-7570

YUKON

Public Affairs Bureau
Executive Council Office
Government of Yukon, Box 2703
Whitehorse, Yukon, Y1A 2C6
(403) 667-5811

NORTHWEST TERRITORIES

Department of Information
Government of the Northwest
   Territories
Box 1320
Yellowknife, N.W.T., X1A 2L9
(403) 873-7110

Index to Box Features

INDEX

Index

C

F

P

Q

R

S

U

XYZ

Typesetting: Alphatext/Quebecor PubliTech Inc.
Printing: Pierre DesMarais Inc.
Binding: Harpell's Press Co-operative
Paper: Rolland Inc.

INDEX